# MENTAL
# RETARDATION

THIRD EDITION

# MENTAL RETARDATION

James R. Patton
*University of Hawaii*

Mary Beirne-Smith
*University of Alabama*

James S. Payne
*University of Mississippi*

Merrill, an imprint of
Macmillan Publishing Company
New York

Collier Macmillan Canada, Inc.
Toronto

Maxwell Macmillan International Publishing Group
New York   Oxford   Singapore   Sydney

Cover Photo: Muriel Orans

This book was set in Garamond Lite.

Administrative Editor: Amy Macionis
Production Coordinator: Victoria M. Althoff
Art Coordinator: Jim Hubbard
Cover Designer: Brian Deep
Photo Editor: Gail Meese

Photo Credits: p. 1 by Gale Zucker; p. 13 by Andrew T. Scull, from *Museums of Madness,* New York: St. Martin's Press, 1979; p. 27 by Donn Brolin; p. 34 by Jim Shaffer; p. 69 by Michael Davis/Franklin County (Ohio) Board of Mental Retardation; p. 78 by Jean Greenwald; p. 82 by the Institute of Human Learning; p. 89 by the Archives of the History of American Psychology; pp. 104, 155, 214, 234, 306, 327, 345, 408, 457 by Lloyd Lemmerman/Merrill; p. 107 by Eugene E. Doll; p. 112 by Rich Bucurel; pp. 131, 171 by Jeremy Rowe; p. 182 by U.S. Department of Housing and Urban Development; p. 195 by Andrew Rakoczy; p. 200 by Tom Myers; p. 238 by Blair Seitz/Robert Maust Photography; pp. 261, 289 by Randy Williams; p. 271 by Tom Hutchinson/Merrill; p. 364 by Celia Drake/Merrill; pp. 392, 485 by Andy Brunk/Merrill; p. 427 by Ben Asen/Envision; p. 495 by the Ohio Historical Society; p. 499 by B. Blatt and F. Kaplan from *Christmas in Purgatory: A Photographic Essay on Mental Retardation* (3rd ed.), Syracuse, NY: Human Policy Press; p. 468 by Randall Williams © Sheryl Ewing: p. 541 by v/DIA-Editorial Photo Archives; p. 551 by Mike Davis.

Library of Congress Catalog Card Number: 89-61335
International Standard Book Number: 0-675-21210-3
Printed in the United States of America
 3  4  5  6  7  8  9—92  91

In memory of
Smitty, Catie, and Mark

# PREFACE

F or the last 200 years, a considerable body of knowledge has been compiled about people with mental retardation: how they learn, how and what to teach them, and how society treats those labeled mentally retarded. Developments of recent years in working with the mentally retarded, such as community-based instruction and residential living arrangements, the regular education initiative transitional planning, and supported employment, have had a significant impact on the field of mental retardation and made critical the need for informed, educated professionals in this area.

The third edition of *Mental Retardation* is intended to provide professionals with up-to-date information on the many facets of mental retardation from a life-cycle perspective. We've tried to digest the literature and add what we've learned through our own experiences. We present the results in a way that we hope is engaging, meaningful, and scholarly without being too technical. The field of mental retardation is exciting to be involved in, and we hope that our interest in and enthusiasm about those with retardation, their families, others with whom they come into contact, and the society in which they live comes through in this book.

Students are sometimes unenthusiastic about taking an introductory course in mental retardation. To combat this attitude, we've designed this book to be useful for all professionals who work with individuals who are mentally retarded. For example, whenever possible, we try to show how understanding a given topic relates to intervention. We are quick to point out the many other valuable resources in the field, directing the reader to them when appropriate. We've also "decoded" much of the terminology found in the literature, particularly that associated with the causes of retardation, and have related these terms to the reality of the classroom, job setting, or community.

Revising a textbook is always a challenge, as one must try to retain what is valuable from earlier editions, highlight what has changed, and add what is now current. Revision starts out as a seemingly manageable task, but it always develops into a formidable endeavor as the process of integrating the new with the old occurs. We have made the following changes.

☐ Every chapter has been updated substantially.
☐ The book has been restructured.
☐ Many chapters have been reorganized.
☐ The chapters on educational assessment, intelligence and intelligence testing, and adaptive behavior have been combined.
☐ Two new chapters have been added: one on severe and profound mental retardation, the other on infancy and early childhood.

In addition, we've continued to use short features in each chapter to broaden the coverage of certain topics in different ways. We used these in the last edition and feel that they are appealing to those who are studying retardation for the first time as well as to those who have more experience. We've retained some of the boxed features from the last edition and have added new ones.

In revising *Mental Retardation* we were inspired by many different individuals. Various people whom we know, love, and spend time with have had a profound effect on us. For this reason, we dedicate this book to three very important persons—Smitty, Catie, and Mark—whose memories spur us on. We also owe appreciation to the people who helped with the development, research, and production of this book. Revision takes a lot of time, and many people contribute to it, so if we have overlooked some individuals in these acknowledgements, we apologize. Those to whom we are deeply indebted include the people who gave their time, energies, and skills to earlier editions of this book: Frances E. Butera, Laurence J. Coleman, Jill C. Dardig, Robert M. Davis, Keith Hume, Allen K. Miller, Janis Spiers, and Thomas J. Zirpoli.

We would also like to acknowledge the efforts of colleagues who have contributed to this revision: Diane M. Browder, Richard F. Ittenbach, Eric D. Jones, John A. Nietupski, Ruth Ann Payne, Greg A. Robinson, and Carol Thomas. Their willingness to participate, their expertise, and their excellent work have been much appreciated.

We want to thank Ed Polloway, one of the contributors to this revision, particularly. His professionalism, wisdom, support, and friendship over the years have affected not only us but also the field of mental retardation. We feel privileged to know him well and to have the opportunity to work with him.

We were very fortunate to have had ten excellent field reviewers. Their guidance and constructive criticism helped this project greatly. We want to thank them for their assistance in providing direction for this revision and for their tireless reading and reviewing of the revised manuscript. These reviewers were: Walter J. Cegelka, University of Missouri at St. Louis; Kent Gerlach, Pacific Lutheran University; John Langone, University of Georgia; Joel E. Mittler, Long Island University; Cindy A. Nixon, East Carolina University; John J. O'Kane, State University of New York at Brockport; Helmi Owens, Pacific Lutheran University; James Van Tassel, Ball State University; Glenn A. Vergason, Georgia State University; and James Yanok, Ohio University.

We are especially grateful to people who have contributed to the production of this book. They include the Hawaiian contingent—Gayle Tsukada and Joy Kataoka—and the Alabama group—Carol Poole, Betsy Bross, and Cynthia Smith. There are a number of people at Merrill Publishing who deserve our thanks as well for their contributions. We would like to thank Vicki Althoff for her gracious style in coordinating this manuscript through the production process. Vicki's understanding way and assistance made this effort more palatable and is much appreciated. We are also indebted to the editorial expertise of Nancy Woodington who was able to take our final drafts and make them more enjoyable to the reader. The value of a copyeditor is realized by very few of those who read a final product. We are among those who do recognize that value.

Lastly, we would like to express our sincere appreciation to Vicki Knight, who has supported us throughout this rigorous journey. She has become a friend as well as a colleague. Without her unending encouragement, understanding, and patience, neither this revision nor the preceding edition could have happened.

J.R.P.
M.B.S.
J.S.P.

# CONTENTS

## PART THREE    PROGRAMMING AND ISSUES ACROSS THE LIFESPAN


## 8    Infancy & Early Childhood                                    263

*Mary Beirne-Smith and Richard F. Ittenbach*

# BASIC

# CONCEPTS

# CHAPTER 1

# Historical

# Perspective

M any events and people have influenced the development of the field of mental retardation, and a look at some of them is an appropriate place to start. From a survey of the history of the field we can gain a better understanding of our present state of affairs and a knowledge of the way to plan for the future (Mesibov, 1976).

While much of the progress made in the field of mental retardation has been due to the unending and dedicated efforts of individuals, strong sociopolitical forces have also been at work to influence the development of the field. When studying history, we must appreciate the social climate of a given time, and in the past, much of what happened to people with mental retardation was determined largely by sociopolitical forces. This is no different today. Rappaport, while referring to social sciences in general, captures the essence of this principle.

> All of man's quest for understanding . . . can be shown to be influenced by social forces, mediated through personal values and beliefs . . . it is difficult for people to recognize the social forces influencing their behavior and beliefs because these forces are often diffused and are mixed with the commonsense beliefs of the time. We cannot easily become "unstuck" in time, and we pay little attention to the importance of when we live or how we think. (Rappaport, 1977, pp. 26–27)

Rappaport's idea that social forces are mediated through personal values and beliefs can be extended one step further: social variables affect the *actions* of people. Rappaport admonishes us to "recognize that applied social science and the human service professions are inherently *political*" (p. 26). For example, social workers are constantly dealing with a system that is political in nature.

Such scholars as Blatt and Sarason have paid much attention to the sociological implications of mental retardation. The conclusion that these professionals reach is that mental retardation is very much a social phenomenon. Blatt (1987) states that "Mental retardation is a concept that developed *with* history. It has changed through time in its nature and in its significance" (p. 9). Sarason (1985) suggests that mental retardation cannot be understood fully unless one examines the society, culture, and history within which it occurs. He further asserts:

> Mental retardation is never a thing or a characteristic of an individual but rather a social invention stemming from time-bound societal values and ideology that make diagnosis and management seem both necessary and socially desirable. (p. 233)

The purpose of this chapter is to give you an appreciation of how social and political forces have affected our interactions with people who are mentally retarded both in the past and today. In addition, we attempt to establish a case for what we call a "recycling phenomenon." Issues that have received our attention in recent years may not be so new as they seem.

> Many people also think that the issues facing special education today are new. But if you read the historical literature of special education, you will see that today's issues and problems are remarkably similar to those of long ago. Issues, problems, and ideas arise, flower, go to seed, and reappear when the conditions are again right for their growth. (Payne, Patton, Kauffman, Brown, & Payne, 1987, p. 244)

Throughout this chapter, we mention issues that were discussed and debated long ago. You may feel dismayed by the fact that so much time has elapsed and these issues still remain just that—issues, with no final "solutions" in sight. Consequently, this chapter has three objectives. First we focus on the historical context of "mental retardation," giving you a glimpse of the sociopolitical influences that have determined where we are today and of some recurrent themes expressed throughout the short documented history of the field. Second we present the "content" of that history; that is, the names, dates, places, and events typically associated with it. Third we hope to introduce you to the complexities of human services as they relate to programming for people with mental retardation.

Chapter 15 explores many of these issues in a future context.

## A HISTORICAL OVERVIEW

While attitudes toward and treatment of persons who are mentally retarded can actually be traced back to ancient civilizations (including Egypt, Sparta, Rome, China, and the early Christian world), for all practical purposes the documented history relating to mental retardation is rather brief, spanning only about the last 200 years. Accordingly, we have divided history arbitrarily into nine periods. These nine eras are:

1. Antiquity                    prior to 1700
2. Emergence of a field         1700–1860
3. Disillusionment              1860–1890
4. Backlash                     1890–1925
5. Gradual movement             1925–1950
6. Reawakening                  1950–1960
7. Limelight                    1960–1970
8. Litigious times              1970–1980
9. Action and reaction          1980–present

Before we proceed through the various periods, we must address the problem of terminology. Throughout this chapter, those who are called *mentally retarded* will be described in accordance with current systems of classification. While this usage will help us maintain a consistent standard, we would be remiss if we did not mention that, historically, other terms have been used officially to describe individuals with mental retardation. Today, however, many professionals find such terms as *fool, moron, imbecile, idiot, feebleminded, mental defective,* and *retardate* (among others) to be historically significant but offensive when used in daily conversation.

## ANTIQUITY: PRIOR TO 1700

Before the 18th century, the concept of *mental retardation,* regardless of the term used to describe it, was enigmatic to a world that did not have a sophisticated knowledge base with which to understand it. As a result, people around the world held a wide variety of attitudes and perceptions toward people who are mentally retarded.

Basically, there was no consensus among Western societies as to who these deviant people were, why they acted the way they did, and how they should be treated. Different societies' responses to these questions ranged from treating these individuals as buffoons and court jesters to perceiving them as demons or as capable of receiving divine revelations. Evidently, throughout ancient history, different patterns of treatment developed, reflecting an overall confusion.

Throughout this early history and continuing until the early 1900s, when we refer to persons with mental limitations, we are specifically speaking of individuals with more severe involvement. "Mild" retardation as we perceive it today had not been defined and was not recognized. As Hewett and Forness (1977) mention, "The borderline retarded individual was not noticeably backward in a day when few could read and write" (p. 30). Most individuals with mild retardation blended into society without too much difficulty; it was not until the 20th century that mild retardation became a describable condition.

*The Renaissance.*   Before 1700, certain developments resulting from the Renaissance of the 14th, 15th, and 16th centuries created a new social climate that would eventually have direct implications for persons who were mentally retarded. Although the Renaissance was important to the world in many ways, the fact that it "increased man's willingness to look at himself and his environment more openly, naturally, and empirically (i.e., scientifically)" (Maloney & Ward, 1978, pp. 21–22) is particularly noteworthy. The prevailing social forces tended to refocus man's concept of himself and of the world. The ultimate effects of these changes were reflected in the development of a climate conducive to the philosophy of humanism and to the revolutionary fervor of the 18th century.

Before 1700, if any service (using the word loosely) was provided to individuals with special needs, it involved merely housing and sustenance and was usually provided in monasteries. We do not have any evidence of systematic programs of training or service delivery. Although obvious changes were occurring in the world, not much was changing for the 17th-century person with mental retardation.

In America at this time, the family unit was of primary importance, and much responsibility was placed on it to take care of any exceptional member. Following European precedents, the colonies enacted laws that "provided" for many of those who could not provide for themselves by creating almshouses and workhouses. Although looked upon as financial burdens, these individuals were at least taken care of by colonial society.

## EMERGENCE OF A FIELD: 1700–1860

Perhaps the two most significant features of the 18th century were the advent of "sensationalism" and the revolutionary changes in both Europe and America. Through the efforts of various philosophers, most notably Locke and Rousseau, new ideas that stressed the importance of the senses for development began to take hold. Their ideas provided new ways of perceiving the nature of the human mind and ultimately influenced educational reform.

As mentioned earlier, Renaissance thinking encouraged a philosophy of humanism, principally concerned with people's worth as human beings and with their freedom to develop to a maximum level. The ideas that all were created equal and had inalienable rights to life, liberty, and the pursuit of happiness were popular. Eventually these ideas came into conflict with the existing philosophies and policies of some established nations, and both Europeans and Americans reacted to these needs for freedom through revolution.

We might wonder what effect these historical events had on people who were mentally retarded. We believe that they had two major implications. First, a new social attitude was established. It held that all "men," even those who were disabled, had rights. This attitude helped lead to a climate that would support efforts to assist these individuals. Second, the times were right for idealistic young people to put the philosophy of humanism and the ideas of Locke and Rousseau into practice.

The first part of the 19th century is best described as a time of enthusiasm for working with people with various disabilities, an enthusiasm displayed by a number of devoted young people. Nurtured by the events of the previous century, these pioneers were willing to try to do something that had never been tried before; they attempted to help less fortunate people through bona fide intervention. The recognized birth of special education and systematic services for disabled individuals occurred in Europe in the early 1800s.

Without question, the field of special education was dramatically influenced by *Jean Marc Itard* (1774–1838). Early in his career, Itard, a medical doctor who initially was concerned with diseases of the ear and the needs of the deaf, became quite interested in a feral child who was found in a wooded area near Aveyron, France, in 1799. Intrigued by this boy, whom he named Victor, Itard thought that he could transform this *homme sauvage* from a state of wildness to a state of civilized behavior (Humphrey & Humphrey, 1962).

Believing that Victor's skill deficiencies were due to environmental limitations, Itard thought he could develop the skills that were lacking by implementing a systematic training program. His program included five major objectives.

1. To render social life more congenial to the boy by making it more like the wild life he had recently kept.
2. To excite his nervous sensibility with varied and energetic stimuli and supply his mind with the raw impression of ideas.
3. To extend the range of his ideas by creating new wants and expanding his relations with the world around him.
4. To lead him to the use of speech by making it necessary that he should imitate.
5. To apply himself to the satisfaction of his growing physical wants, and from this lead to the application of his intelligence to the objects of instruction. (Kanner, 1964, p. 14)

Although Itard worked with Victor for five years, he did not think that Victor progressed as much as he had first envisioned, particularly in the area of oral expressive language, and subsequently terminated the program. From then until Victor died in 1828, he lived under the care of Madame Guérin, the housekeeper hired to take care of him. Itard felt he was a nearly total failure with Victor, but he received many accolades from the French Academy of

# FERAL CHILDREN

The topic of feral children is both fascinating and educational. *Feral* refers to those who have been reared in a nondomestic environment. The most celebrated feral child was Victor, the Wild Boy of Aveyron, whose contact with Jean-Marc Itard led to international attention. There have been other children who have been reared in isolated settings; many of these are described by McNeil, Polloway, and Smith (1984). Some examples are presented below.

The Girl of Cranenburg was found at the age of 18 living alone in the woods of the Netherlands in 1718. She had to be captured by villagers using ropes and nets. She had been kidnapped at the age of 16 months from her parents although no one, including the girl, knew at what age she was abandoned by her abductors. She was mute when found but quickly learned social skills. The last report mentioned that she was beginning to speak, had been reclaimed by her mother, and had been taken home (Zingg, 1966; Ogburn, 1959).

The Songi Girl of Champagne (Zingg, 1966; Obgurn, 1959) was believed to be nine or ten years old when she was found. She walked into a town wearing rags and animal skins and a gourd for a hat. She carried a large stick which she used to kill dogs that bothered her. She swam well, and caught and ate fish and frogs raw. After capture she cried out if strangers came near her. She eventually was taught social skills, learned to speak and write French, did embroidery, and became a nun. "The Girl of Songi is the only case of this sort [prolonged isolation] . . . who recovered speech . . ." to any significant extent (Zingg, 1940, p. 494).

Tarzancito was captured at five years of age in San Salvador. Immediately after capture, he cried out if anyone came near him. He had lived in the treetops, eaten fruit and fish, and was an excellent swimmer. He was mute when captured but it was noted early that he had good imitative abilities. He learned three words within the first three months. Seven years after his capture, Tarzancito was in third grade, making good progress and considered to be completely normal (Zingg, 1966).

Readjustment for these children was easier than for animal-reared children because there was not a competing repertoire of previously imprinted social behavior. While the latter may be considered "antisocial" because they have learned competing animal behaviors, the children reared in wilderness isolation can be thought of as "asocial" because they had no opportunity to learn any system of social behaviors.

Science in recognition of his work. Itard's importance rests not so much in his success or failure with Victor but rather in the precedent that he set by systematically working and achieving gains with a child who was considered severely impaired. The influence he had on others clearly distinguishes him as one of the most significant pioneers in the field of special education. As Blatt (1987) remarks, "It [Itard's work] was the first of its kind, and all 'firsts' of important movements are especially important" (p. 34).

One person who was profoundly affected by Itard's work was *Edouard Seguin* (1812–1880). Encouraged by Itard to get involved in the treatment of "idiocy," Seguin was also motivated by a strong religious influence to help the less fortunate. Like Itard, Seguin also chose to undertake the *éducation de son enfant idiot.* After 18 months of intensive work with this boy, Seguin was able to demonstrate that the boy had learned a number of skills. Seguin extended his methods to other children, and in 1837 he established a program for "educating the feebleminded" at the Salpetrière in Paris.

Seguin's methods and educational programs, which were even more systematic than Itard's, stressed physiological and moral education. This methodology, as Seguin developed it, incorporated a general training program that integrated muscular, imitative, nervous, and reflective physiological functions (Seguin, 1846). Many educational techniques Seguin used in his programs, such as individualized instruction and behavior management, can be found in today's methodology.

Seguin emigrated to the United States in 1848, principally because of the political unrest in Paris at that time. While he lived in the United States, he often served as a consultant to those who sought his advice and expertise on programming in institutional settings. In 1866 he published a book entitled *Idiocy and Its Treatment by Physiological Methods,* which became a major reference work for educating individuals with retardation in the latter part of the 19th century. Seguin also served as the first president of the Association of Medical Officers of American Institutions for Idiotic and Feebleminded Persons. Hervey Wilbur, in his eulogy to Seguin, perhaps best summarized the impact this man had on the field.

> He entered upon the work with enthusiasm. There he toiled, till there he grew, little by little, a system—principles and methods—which has been the guide of all later labors in the same direction, the world over. (Wilbur, 1880)

Another individual who figured significantly in providing services to those who were mentally retarded was *Johann Guggenbühl* (1816–1863). Guggenbühl has been credited with establishing the first residential facility designed to provide comprehensive treatment for individuals who were mentally retarded. This facility, called the Abendberg, which he founded in 1841, was located in the mountains of Switzerland.

Well publicized, through the efforts of Guggenbühl himself, the Abendberg drew the attention of many prominent people. The real significance of Guggenbühl's facility rests in its impact on the visitors it attracted, many of whom were interested in establishing similar facilities. As Kanner notes, "The Abendberg became the destination of pilgrimages made by physicians, philanthropists, and writers from many lands, who promptly published glowing reports when they went back home" (1964, p. 25).

Unfortunately, the glowing reviews and accolades accorded the Abendberg were short-lived, and eventually the facility came under severe criticism. Although forced to close due to mismanagement and the resulting intolerable conditions, in its heyday the Abendberg nevertheless served as the model for many other institutions. It can also serve as an example of a program that achieved recognition but was unable to maintain it. Notwithstanding the problems, Guggenbühl created a prototype for institutional care, the effects of which can still be felt today.

Although special education was conceived and born in Europe, the field also prospered from the work of important people and from events that occurred in the United States during the mid-1800s. Three individuals who had much to do with promoting the welfare of and developing services for persons with mental retardation in this country were Dorothea Dix, Samuel Howe, and Hervey Wilbur.

During the early 1840s, *Dorothea Dix* zealously campaigned for better treatment of the less fortunate who were housed in asylums, almshouses, poorhouses, and country homes (Cegelka & Prehm, 1982). At this time there were no other options for such people. Her efforts are reflected in her own words, directed toward the Massachusetts legislature in 1843.

> I come to present the strong claims of suffering humanity. I come to place before the Legislature of Massachusetts the condition of the miserable, the desolate, the outcast. I come as the advocate of helpless, forgotten, insane, and idiotic men and women; of beings sunk to a condition from which the most unconcerned would start with real horror; of beings wretched in our prisons, and more wretched in our almshouses. And I cannot suppose it needful to employ earnest persuasion, or stubborn argument, in order to arrest and fix attention upon a subject only the more strongly pressing in its claims because it is revolting and disgusting in its details. (Dix, 1843)

Obviously, Dorothea Dix dramatized what advocacy is all about, and through her efforts she was able to focus much attention on those whom she called "suffering humanity." This same plea could be made today in this country for the large number of homeless people who wander the streets.

*Samuel Howe* (1801–1876) contributed greatly to providing services for people who were mentally retarded through his efforts to establish the public's obligation to train them. In 1848, after visiting Guggenbühl's Abendberg and convincing the Massachusetts legislature to appropriate $2500 per year, Howe established the first *public* setting for training mentally retarded individuals. This new setting was a wing of Boston's Perkins Institution for the Blind, of which Howe was the director. A few months earlier in this same year, *Hervey Wilbur* (1820–1883) had founded the first *private* setting for treating individuals with mental retardation at his home in Barre, Massachusetts.

What then was the result of the work of pioneers like Itard, Seguin, Guggenbühl, Howe, Dix, and Wilbur? First, an atmosphere of optimism developed. Many of those persons who were mentally retarded, it was thought, could be trained, "cured," and reintegrated into the community as productive citizens. Second, based upon this very same hope and enthusiasm, many promises were made, reflected in the lofty goals that were set. Ironically, it was precisely the uncontrolled enthusiasm prevalent at the time that would be partially responsible for the pessimism of the next period.

## DISILLUSIONMENT: 1860–1890     *Sept. 24.*

As any student of United States history knows quite well, the 1860s were a time of national disharmony, inflamed by years of growing sectional conflict. Prior to the Civil War, America was basically an agrarian society characterized by small farms and small towns. After the war, the country began to experience a dramatic change in the form of urbanization and industrialization. These changes and others had a strong effect on the treatment of persons who were mentally retarded.

This national metamorphosis precipitated many problems, some of which accompanied the increased growth of cities. Correlates of urban life such as crime, poverty, and disease were later to be associated with retardation. In addition, while industrialization provided vocational opportunities for many people, the skills required were often too demanding for many persons with severe limitations.

Specifically, what happened to the enthusiasm of the mid-1800s? There was a critical change in attitude toward the possibility of reintegrating those with retardation into the community. After initially accepting the grandiose claims of many enthusiastic individuals, who stated that these less fortunate could be "cured," critics began to realize that these goals—while laudable— were unrealistic. A pronounced climate of pessimism developed. We know today that those individuals who were said to be capable of being cured in the 1800s (i.e., severely handicapped people) were indeed capable of skill acquisition, but for most of them, attainment of "normalcy" was not possible. That individuals who were more severely involved had not "changed" enough to be able successfully to move back into community settings resulted in a negative perception of this group.

Many problems contributed to the disillusionment of this era. Four factors, however, seem to be most salient. First, as already mentioned, the population being addressed was not capable of being "cured" or "transformed into totally normal functioning members of society." Second, community reintegration demands more than merely providing training. If successful reintegration requires community preparation and development, as we think it does, then we should not be surprised to discover that this was a neglected issue in the 1800s. Sadly, even today, the provision of community services and support is glaringly inadequate in many locations. Third, after an atmosphere of hope and excitement had been created, many individuals who were retarded were pitied, resulting in two important developments: *(a)* services to individuals who needed systematic, intensive programming were diluted, and *(b)* more institutions were formed (Maloney & Ward, 1978). These developments would have a tragic effect in the late 1800s. Fourth, the previously mentioned demands of the increasingly more complex society created by postwar urbanization and industrialization worked against those suffering from retardation.

Obviously these were formidable obstacles to reaching the goals championed by the idealistic pioneers of the early and mid-1800s. While it is easy now to reproach those enthusiasts for creating a no-win situation that ultimately resulted in many regressive developments for those whom they wanted to help, we need to understand that these early advocates (however naive in not understanding their limitations) were most sincere in their zeal, hopes, and efforts. Unfortunately, those individuals on whom the great expectations were based were now being perceived as "incurable." It was bad enough that the early enthusiasm had waned, but even more discouraging was the fact that the worst was yet to come.

## BACKLASH: 1890–1925

As the 19th century came to a close, disillusionment began to take on a more reactionary tone. A change from a concern for caring about individuals who had special needs to one for protecting society from them was evident. Institutions originally designed to serve as training facilities from which individuals would leave to return to community settings now began to assume a new, *custodial* role.

During this period of alarm, a number of events caused a dramatic change in social attitudes, weakening any movement favorable to the needs of the mentally retarded population. Many citizens were now afraid that these people were dangerous to society. Kanner describes the prevailing perceptions during this time.

> The mental defectives were viewed as a menace to civilization, incorrigible at home, burdens to the school, sexually promiscuous, breeders of feebleminded offspring, victims and spreaders of poverty, degeneracy, crime, and disease. Consequently, there was a cry for the segregation of all mental defectives, with the aim of purifying society, of erecting a solid wall between it and its contaminators. (1964, p. 85)

It did not take long for society to develop ways to control people who were mentally defective; the principal means for doing this included segregation

*This artist sketch of an institutional resident in England around 1815 was mass-produced and used by early reformers in a campaign to improve conditions.*

and sterilization. A committee of the American Breeders' Association, which had been formed in 1911, concluded that "segregation for life or at least during the reproductive years must, in the opinion of the committee, be the principal agent used by society in cutting off its supply of defectives" (cited in Kanner, 1964, p. 136). As an added measure of control, institutions strictly segregated men and women to eliminate their chances of producing offspring who would possibly be feebleminded.

Many contributing factors precipitated repressive events in the late 1800s and early 1900s. Three factors seemed to have a pronounced effect on the creation of this backlash: the eugenics scare, the influx of immigrants to the United States, and the mental test movement. It will be helpful to explore each of these trends.

***The eugenics scare.***    Although the thrust of the eugenics movement was not felt until the late 1800s and early 1900s, its antecedents can be traced to earlier times. This movement was interested in controlling the number of "feebleminded" through selective breeding.

Influenced by the ideas of Charles Darwin, Sir Francis Galton extended Darwin's concept of evolution to humans. In 1869, Galton published *Hereditary Genius,* which espoused the idea that individual traits, most notably genius, were inherited. Galton's work seemed to catalyze the eugenics movement that advocated the genetic control of mental defectives.

What Galton established was a theoretical basis for the inheritance of mental defectiveness. Gregor Mendel's discovery of the laws of inheritance at the turn of the 20th century lent much support to Galton's ideas.

Two publications reinforced society's attitude that mental retardation had genetic implications. *The Jukes, a Study in Crime, Pauperism, Disease and Heredity* (Dugdale, 1877) and *The Kallikak Family* (Goddard, 1912, as reprinted by Macmillan Publishing Co., 1972). Each of these works traced the genetic relationships of the families under study. Dugdale's original work actually focused on criminality and its correlates, and only later was the added correlate of mental retardation inferred. Goddard's work, however, had as its central theme the notion that feeblemindedness was inherited; elaborate pedigree studies (through five generations) were presented as evidence. Goddard's work was very powerful and, along with other related events, fueled the movement to control the menace of feeblemindedness genetically. But many years later Goddard's research on Martin Kallikak's two distinct family lines was called into question. The details of the social myth perpetuated by Goddard are described in Smith's (1985) book entitled *Minds Made Feeble* (see feature).

Strong evidence that eugenics was being taken seriously can be found in the enactment of sterilization laws during the early 1900s. Indiana holds the dubious distinction of enacting the first such law in 1907. Within 20 years similar laws were on the books in 23 states. The constitutionality of these laws was challenged in several states and ultimately upheld by the Supreme Court in the famous case *Buck v. Bell* (1927). As Smith (1987) highlights, this case "became the precedent for the right of state governments to intervene in the reproductive practices of those citizens deemed defective in some way" (p. 148). The case is noteworthy not only for the precedent it set, but also for two other reasons: *(a)* Carrie Buck, the woman used to test Virginia's compulsory sterilization law, probably was not mentally retarded; and *(b)* the prevailing attitude of the time was clearly expressed in the majority opinion given by Justice Oliver Wendell Holmes.

> We have seen more than once that the public welfare may call upon the best citizens for their lives. It would be strange if it could not call upon those who already sap the strength of the State for these lesser sacrifices, often felt to be much by those concerned, in order to prevent our being swamped with incompetence. It is better for all the world, if instead of waiting to execute degenerate offspring for crime, or to let them starve for their imbecility, society can prevent those who are manifestly unfit from continuing their kind. The principle that sustains compulsory vaccination is broad enough to cover cutting the Fallopian tubes. . . . Three generations of imbeciles are enough. (*Buck v. Bell* 1927, p. 50)

*Immigration.*   During the second half of the 19th century, the United States experienced a great increase in the number of immigrants, mostly from southern and eastern Europe. As most of these immigrants flocked to the

# MINDS MADE FEEBLE

In 1912 Henry Goddard reported the results of his study of the inheritance of feeblemindedness. His book, *The Kallikak Family: A Study in the Heredity of Feeble-Mindedness,* was very influential because it underscored the perceived threat of feeblemindedness to society and helped fuel the eugenics movement. The book was very popular, and to this day the Kallikak story is regularly retold in discussions of mental retardation.

The effects of the study are described well by J. David Smith in *Minds Made Feeble.*

> Goddard's book on the Kallikak family was received with acclaim by the public and by much of the scientific community. . . . Only gradually was criticism forthcoming which questioned the methods used in the study and the implications and conclusions drawn from the data collected. Even in the light of substantive and knowledgeable criticism, however, the essential message of the Kallikak study persisted for years. Even today its influence, in convoluted forms, continues to have a social and political impact. That message is simple, yet powerful. Ignorance, poverty, and social pathology are in the blood—in the seed. It is not the environment in which people are born and develop that makes the critical difference in human lives. People are born either favored or beyond help.

It was this message and the social myth that accompanied it that compelled Smith to investigate and report the complete story of the Kallikak family and of Goddard's study. A few highlights of Smith's findings are presented below.

☐ Serious questions as to whether Deborah Kallikak was actually feebleminded arise.

(Deborah Kallikak was the woman with whom Goddard came into contact and whose ancestors he studied.)

☐ Goddard's professional acquaintance with influential eugenic leaders seem to have had a great influence on his work.

☐ The methodology used to study the Kallikak family and the skills of those who collected the information are once again questioned.

☐ The "real" Kallikaks were not as abhorrent as they were described by Goddard. Smith commented, "The truth of their lives was sacrificed to the effort to prove a point. The Kallikak study is fiction draped in the social science of its time."

☐ The implications of the study proved to be a very potent indictment against the poor, the uneducated, racial minorities, the foreign born, and those classified as mentally retarded or mentally ill, resulting in such social policies as compulsory sterilization, restricted immigration, and institutionalization, which adversely and unfairly affected these groups.

☐ Through painstaking investigation, Smith determined the real name of the family Goddard studied (Kallikak was a pseudonym). However, he does not reveal the name.

One of Smith's major contributions is his admonition to be aware of the significance and power of social myths: "Social myths are constantly in the making, compelling in their simplicity, and alluring because we want to believe them. Perhaps understanding the Kallikak story will help in recognizing and resisting them."

growing urban centers, many problems emerged. Americans of northern and western European origin looked upon these immigrants as inferior; this stance was supported by a study performed by Goddard, which concluded that many of these foreigners were feebleminded. One outcome of this generalized concern was enactment of the Immigration Restriction Act in 1924. This legislation restricted the flow of people of Italian, Russian, Hungarian, and Jewish background into this country until 1965.

*The testing movement.* A third major trend contributing to the alarmist climate of the early 1900s was the introduction of the mental test. In 1905, Alfred Binet and Theodore Simon developed an instrument designed to be used in the French schools to screen those students who were not benefiting from the regular classroom experience and who might need special education. It is interesting to realize that Binet was concerned that this instrument might be misused. As Gould (1981) notes, Binet "greatly feared that his practical device . . . could be perverted and used as an indelible label, rather than as a guide for identifying children who needed help" (p. 151). The mental test has had a lasting effect on the field of special education. In essence, in the mental scale of intelligence, Binet and Simon created a new, definable category of retardation, known to us today as *mild retardation;* however, Goddard labeled this group "morons" in 1910. Before this, those recognizable as mentally retarded were more severely involved, but now new alarms were being sounded about the magnitude of the problem, alarms created by the identification of this new group.

Although Binet and Simon introduced their test in France, before long it came to the United States. In 1911 Henry Goddard translated the Binet-Simon scales into English, and in 1916 Lewis Terman of Stanford University refined the mental scales into the instrument known as the Stanford-Binet. (It was W. Stern, a German psychologist, who is given credit for developing the conceptual basis for determining *IQ [intelligence quotient].*)

Since many more individuals could now be empirically identified as mentally retarded, special classes for mentally retarded students developed and grew in number. In 1896, the first special class in the United States for students who were retarded was established in Providence, Rhode Island. Another event of significance was New Jersey's enactment in 1911 of legislation mandating education for this type of student. With the beginning of World War I, the military services needed a way to obtain information relatively quickly about large groups of people for use in assigning personnel. Thus the first group intelligence scales (the alpha and beta tests) were developed. The results of this testing fed alarmist tendencies by suggesting that mild mental retardation was more widespread than anyone had previously believed. Yerkes' 1921 work on the intellectual capacities of World War I soldiers supported this assumption, further exacerbating negative feelings about retardation.

The alarm had indeed been sounded! Society was frightened by the "menace" of retardation. With the recognition of mental retardation's greater prevalence, with its seeming inheritability, and with its correlation with crime, poverty, incorrigibility, and disease, it is not difficult to understand how alarmist attitudes could develop and dominate. Quite strong by the end of the second decade of the 20th century, this aura of fear would begin to fade in the ensuing years. But its impact would be long-lasting.

## GRADUAL MOVEMENT: 1925–1950

Although World War I was hardly a blessing, it did have some positive effects on social attitudes toward individuals with disabilities. As in all wars, many veterans returned to their homes with war-caused handicaps. In 1920, the Vocational Rehabilitation Act (P.L. 66-236) was enacted to allow civilians to benefit from vocational rehabilitation. With the end of the war, the need for providing services to veterans had been acknowledged. Now these services were being extended to others who needed them.

The 1920s were a time of experimentation. Lifestyles changed quickly with the stock market crash of 1929 and the Great Depression that followed. Like war, the Great Depression was not a pleasant experience; however, there were some positive outcomes. The Depression caused the average person, who had been unaware of or uninterested in the problems of human need, to appreciate them, for everyone was needy.

Special education as a bona fide professional field took a tremendous step in 1922, when Elizabeth Farrell established the International Council for the Education of Exceptional Children. Prior to this time, the field had had no unifying organizational structure on a national level. This new organization, which Farrell served as the first president, is now known as the Council for Exceptional Children (CEC) and is certainly a key institutional force in special education.

Following a period of great concern about the social menace of mental retardation in the early part of the 20th century, some movement toward greater enlightenment was evident, as Maloney and Ward (1978) state:

1. The view of mental retardation as a unitary, recessive, inherited trait began to fade as the science of genetics grew in scope and precision.
2. New clinical studies demonstrated the significance of other, nonhereditary, sources of mental retardation, such as trauma, infection, and endocrine disturbance.
3. The methodological flaws and biased interpretations of the pedigree studies were becoming more and more apparent.
4. Other surveys of institutional populations indicated that over one-half of them had intellectually normal parents, further weakening the singular heredity view and associated calls for eugenic solutions.
5. The older research studies that had linked mental retardation with every conceivable social ill were critically reanalyzed and found wanting.

6. Newer, better controlled, and more objective studies failed to reveal the dramatic links of the previous era. (p. 57)

Although alarm was fading, the years between 1930 and 1950 saw few advances directly affecting the mentally retarded. Nevertheless, these 20 years did witness certain events that had either an immediate, indirect effect or a more latent, direct effect on persons with mental retardation.

*Sociopolitical influences.* During the early 1930s, the United States was trying to regain stability both economically and socially. One notable event occurred when President Herbert Hoover convened the first White House Conference on Child Health and Protection in 1930. This conference drew national attention, however briefly, to the needs of exceptional individuals. An important trend was the number of classes for special students, which kept increasing.

After the presidential elections of 1932, the United States went through many changes. The new president, Franklin D. Roosevelt, influenced this country's attitudes toward the welfare of all citizens. Roosevelt's New Deal philosophy was responsible for much social change through legislation and the formulation of new programs. One such piece of legislation that affected exceptional individuals was the Social Security Act of 1935. In a nutshell, during the 1930s two major trends emerged in the treatment of exceptional individuals: *(a)* the generation of a new attitude supportive of a public welfare system and *(b)* the affirmation of responsibility to those in need.

With the direct involvement of the United States in World War II, the attention and behavior of the nation were refocused once again. We can see certain similarities between World War I and World War II vis-à-vis the field of mental retardation. As in World War I, screening of soldiers in the 1940s readjusted the perceived extent of mild retardation. One source of information was a study conducted by Ginzberg and Bray, as described in their book *The Uneducated* (1953). They studied two groups of men being considered for military service. Their primary group consisted of men who were rejected on the basis of mental deficiency; the other group included men who were accepted for service but who experienced major problems in academic skill areas (i.e., literacy). When the war was over, many families, and the nation as a whole, felt the realities of disability. A heightened sensitivity to the needs of disabled veterans developed. World War II also created increased employment opportunities in war-related industries for individuals who were retarded.

*Research and programmatic influences.* During this period many relevant developments took place in both the social and physical sciences. In 1934, Fölling, a Norwegian physician, explained the biochemical mechanics related to the metabolic disturbance referred to as **PKU (phenylketonuria)**. The importance of this discovery goes beyond this single event:

A new era dawned in 1934 when Fölling in Norway discovered phenylpyruvic acid oliophrenia (phenylketonuria) as a metabolic disturbance which could eventually become reversible by means of proper dietary regulation. This contribution, termed "'one of the great discoveries in medical history" by Clemens E. Bonda, at long last made the issue of mental deficiency appear respectable as a legitimate field of research in the biological sciences. Slowly and at first reluctantly, the medical profession began to take an interest. (Kanner, 1964, p. 141)

Two assessment instruments of major importance were developed during this period. In 1935, Edgar Doll published his Vineland Social Maturity Scale (VSMS). Use of this scale allowed professionals to gain additional information about a person's behavior and level of functioning. In 1949, David Wechsler published another intelligence scale, the Wechsler Intelligence Scale for Children (WISC). Like the VSMS, this device became very popular. These instruments have had a pronounced effect on the identification and classification of many individuals suspected of being retarded ever since their publication.

Another influence on the public perception of mental retardation was a number of studies that seemed to stress the importance of environment as a cause of mental retardation. As the nature-nurture controversy was debated, certain studies, most notably those performed by Skeels and his colleagues, questioned the notion that IQ was fixed or constant. Skeels and Dye (1939) inferred that environmental factors have a critical effect on IQ; or, if you will, on one's being classified as mentally retarded.

## REAWAKENING: 1950–1960

As the 1950s began, the field of special education went through changes that would have notable effects in following years. Foremost among these changes was a new national policy concerned with the problems of special people.

After the Second World War, the United States experienced a period of renewed prosperity. This created a climate in which "the demands of parents, the enthusiasm of professionals, and federal, state and private funding gave new impetus to progress in the area of mental retardation" (Hewett & Forness, 1977). These three forces, augmented by other variables, highlighted this turning point in the history of special education. Although institutional changes were beginning to occur, at best these events could be classified only as a "quiet revolution." Individuals were still being institutionalized at an alarming rate; tragically, many persons who should not have been placed in these settings found themselves there. Furthermore, too many had already suffered sterilization, a personal indignity and a violation of their civil rights. By 1938, compulsory sterilizations had been performed on more than 27,000 people in the United States (Marks, cited in Smith, 1987).

*Parent groups.* Certainly one of the most important events in this period was the formation in 1950 of the National Association for Retarded Children (NARC). This organization, composed mostly of parents of children who were retarded, became an important advocate for these children. Functioning as lobbyist, service provider, and promoter of research, NARC has had a profound impact on exceptional people. Most important, NARC was a coordinated effort of its members to express their attitudes, beliefs, concerns, and desires in politically effective ways.

*Sociopolitical developments.*   By the early 1950s, the United States was beginning to adopt a national policy committed to the needs of those who were mentally retarded and a policy willing to give financial support to endeavors that addressed these needs. Over the years, social attitudes toward people with retardation had changed from fear and revulsion to tolerance and compassion. Whether sparked by the troubled times of the 1930s and 1940s that the nation as a whole endured or influenced by purely economic motives, during the 1950s the financial backing required to develop more and better programs was provided. If only for economic reasons, the importance of maximizing the potential of persons who were disabled was acknowledged during this time, as was echoed by President Eisenhower in a 1954 message to Congress.

> We are spending three times as much in public assistance to care for nonproductive disabled people as it would cost to make them self-sufficient and taxpaying members of their communities. Rehabilitated people as a group pay back in federal income taxes many times the cost of their rehabilitation.

By 1952, 46 of 48 states had enacted legislation for educating students who were labeled mentally retarded. This legislation, however, did not provide programming for *all* students with mental retardation. Many children in the moderate range and most children in the severe range were still excluded from receiving needed educational services.

Not until 1975 and the passage of P.L. 94-142, the Education for All Handicapped Children Act, was the issue of educating *all* students with mental retardation formally addressed on a national level. But 1954 is also notable because in that year Congress passed the Cooperative Research Act (P.L. 83-531), which provided money for research that would focus on mental retardation. In 1958, P.L. 85-926 was passed, offering incentives to various organizations (i.e., state educational agencies and institutions of higher education) in the form of grants to encourage the preparation of teachers of this group of students. Thus, if we look at federal legislation as an index of national commitment to a cause, then we can see that policy supportive of the needs of special people was developing in the 1950s.

As the decade came to a close, three forces were beginning to shape future events. First, the publication of *Mental Subnormality,* published by Masland, Sarason, and Gladwin in 1958, reflected the emergence of a new philosophical orientation. This school of thought stressed that certain social and cultural variables have a strong correlation with mental retardation. The influence of this point of view on the field can be observed in the 1959 definition of mental retardation proposed by the American Association on Mental Deficiency (Heber, 1959). This definition associated intellectual deficits with "impairment is one or more of the following: (1) maturation, (2) learning, and (3) social adjustment" (Heber, 1959, p. 3).

Second, educators and advocates began to be concerned about the segregation of students who were mentally retarded in special classes. Existing research tended to support the special class setting. Nevertheless, this issue would continue to be debated, resulting in some major changes in the 1970s. In addition, the Supreme Court decision in the *Brown v. Board of Education* (1954) desegregation case also affected thinking and policy-making for individuals with mental retardation.

Third, when the Soviet Union launched Sputnik in 1957, the United States responded dramatically—at first with shock and then with a commitment to technological development unparalleled in history. The nation's uncontrollable desire to grow technologically would focus very sharply on the institution of education. Changes were evidently needed, and many did come about. Both regular and special education were affected by the vigor of the times. The nation was primed for the tumultuous sixties.

## LIMELIGHT: 1960–1970

If asked to reflect on the decade of the 1960s, one would probably think of the many tragic episodes in a time of rather extreme social change. The violent deaths of national leaders and the widespread opposition and reaction to the Vietnam War are vivid recollections of the 1960s. The early part of this decade was characterized by a generalized enthusiasm, and this enthusiasm was quite evident in the area of special education. For many reasons special education was on center stage during the sixties.

*Sociopolitical variables.* When President Kennedy assumed office in 1961, he symbolized the energy of our country at that time. Kennedy, who had a sister who was retarded, once again brought national attention to the needs of those who were mentally retarded. In 1961, he established the President's Panel on Mental Retardation (PPMR), which was to serve as a guide and source for national policy formation. Under the direction of Leonard Mayo, this panel published *A Proposed Program for National Action to Combat Mental Retardation* (1962), which set the tone for policy decisions for the next decade. The principal recommendations found in the report were

1. Research in the causes of retardation and in methods of care, rehabilitation, and learning.
2. Preventive health measures, including *(a)* a greatly strengthened program of maternal and infant care directed first at the centers of population where prematurity and the rate of "damaged" children are high; *(b)* protection against such known hazards to pregnancy as radiation and harmful drugs, and *(c)* extended diagnostic and screening services.

3. Strengthened educational programs generally and extended and enriched programs of special education in public and private schools closely coordinated with vocational guidance, vocational rehabilitation, and specific training and preparation for employment; education for the adult mentally retarded, and workshops geared to their needs.
4. More comprehensive and improved clinical and social services.
5. Improved methods and facilities for care, with emphasis on the development of a wide range of local community facilities.
6. A new legal, as well as social, concept of the retarded, including protection of their civil rights; life guardianship provisions when needed; and enlightened attitude on the part of the law and the courts; and clarification of the theory of responsibility in criminal acts.
7. Helping overcome the serious problems of manpower as they affect the entire field of science and every type of service through extended programs of recruiting with fellowships; and increased opportunities for graduate students, and those preparing for the professions to observe and learn at first hand about the phenomenon of retardation. Because there will never be a fully adequate supply of personnel in this field and for other cogent reasons, the panel has emphasized the need for more volunteers in health, recreation, and welfare activities, and for a domestic Peace Corps to stimulate voluntary service.
8. Programs of education and information to increase public awareness of the problem of mental retardation. (Mayo, 1962, pp. 14–15)

Other recommendations with a very contemporary flavor were also proposed.

1. That programs for the retarded, including modern day care, recreation, residential services, and ample educational and vocational opportunities, be comprehensive.
2. That they operate in or close to the communities where the retarded live—that is, that they be community centered.
3. That services be so organized as to provide a central or fixed point for the guidance, assistance, and protection of retarded persons if and when needed, and to assure a sufficient array or continuum of services to meet different types of need.
4. That private agencies as well as public agencies at the local, state, and federal levels continue to provide resources and to increase them for this worthy purpose. While the federal government can assist, the principal responsibility for financing and improving services for the mentally retarded must continue to be borne by states and local communities. (Mayo, 1962, pp. 14–15)

Federal legislation relevant to the field of mental retardation continued to be enacted during the sixties. In 1963, Congress passed the Mental Retardation Facilities and Mental Health Centers Construction Act, which provided monies for the construction of Mental Retardation Research Centers (MRRC). These centers conducted organized multidisciplinary research on various complex facets of mental retardation. In 1965, the Elementary and Secondary Education Act (ESEA) (P.L. 89-10) was passed. Part of this legislation focused attention on the needs of disadvantaged students. In 1966, ESEA was amended, and as a result the Bureau of Education for the Handicapped (BEH), a subcomponent of the Office of Education (OE), was created.

National policy directed to the needs of the disadvantaged reached its pinnacle with President Johnson's War on Poverty. With the growing interest in social and cultural determinants of behavior, it is not surprising that much attention was given to environmental causes of retardation. Project Head Start did just that. The concept that early intervention could ameliorate some of the negative effects of unfavorable social or cultural situations was fashionable and encouraged during the mid-sixties.

If nothing else can be said of the 1960s, certainly we can state that it was a time responsive to personal and civil rights. The civil rights movement was consummated by passage into law of the Civil Rights Act of 1964; however, this law did not deal directly with exceptional people per se. Nevertheless, the achievements and impetus provided by the civil rights movement and the resulting legislation would be realized and extended to people with disabilities in the 1970s.

*Trends in service delivery.*   With continuing support from state and federal governments, the proliferation of programs and services for individuals who were retarded grew almost exponentially. But the spotlight was soon to flicker, if not dim. Lloyd Dunn's 1968 challenge of the efficacy of placing students with mild retardation in special classes symbolized some of the reexamination occurring in the late sixties and early seventies.

A new philosophical theme was beginning to become popular. The principle of **normalization**, which originated during the 1950s in Scandinavia, was finding much support in the United States. N. E. Bank-Mikkelsen and Bengt Nirje were eminently responsible for the development and dissemination of this principle in Scandinavia, while Wolf Wolfensberger was instrumental in championing it in the United States. To a great extent this was due to a single publication that had a great impact on professionals in the United States. Entitled *Changing Patterns in Residential Services for the Mentally Retarded,* this publication included a discussion of the principle of normalization by Nirje (1969), sparking a movement in this country that epitomized the next decade. Nirje defined *normalization* as "making available to the mentally retarded patterns and conditions of everyday life which are as close as possible to the norms and patterns of the mainstream of society" (p. 181).

As more professionals recognized the needs of people with retardation, there was a new emphasis on community-based services. This trend has continued. To some degree this emphasis was catalyzed by the fact that many young children had become adolescents and young adults, and their parents continued to be concerned.

During the 1960s, the nature-nuture issue, which had been brewing for many years, seemed to be best answered by those arguing the importance of interaction between heredity and environment. Although supporters of this orientation acknowledged both hereditary and environmental determinants of mild mental retardation, they felt that environmental factors were most influential. In 1969, much attention was drawn to this issue by Arthur Jensen. Jensen (1969) published an article in the *Harvard Educational Review* entitled "How Much Can We Boost IQ and Scholastic Achievement?" He argued that genetic factors are more important than environmental factors in determining IQ (i.e., the high inheritability of intelligence.) Where Jensen's article received the most criticism was in his inference that social class and racial variations in intelligence are attributable to genetic differences.

In the changing social climate of the late 1960s, characterized by many forms of reactionary behavior, services to and concepts of those with retardation were being challenged. The revolutionary fervor of the sixties would wane as the seventies progressed. For exceptional individuals and those working with them, however, the early seventies were reminiscent of the turbulent sixties in many ways.

## LITIGIOUS TIMES: 1970–1980

In the entire history of services to persons who are mentally retarded, there had been no period with more visible gains than the early 1970s. Without a doubt, the pioneers of the early 19th century had made great steps in initiating intervention; however, events of the 1970s were of similar significance. At long last, it was established that Americans who were mentally retarded had certain personal and civil rights guaranteeing services and protection. As can be seen from Figure 1.1, the number of students receiving special education greatly increased during the 1960s and 1970s. (That this number began decreasing toward the end of the 1970s is discussed later.)

Most notably, the early 1970s were litigious times. A new tactic for ensuring services was beginning to emerge. Courts had been used as a last resort previously, but now they were used frequently and strategically. Rights afforded the regular citizenry had been denied to many individuals who were mentally retarded, and the courtroom became the forum in which these rights were secured. This policy was supported by parent groups and at least tolerated by a society responsive to human rights, and many issues were brought to the courtroom. Chief among them were rights to education and proper treatment.

See chapter 13 for more detailed explanations.

The right to education issue was sparked in 1971 by a celebrated class action suit, *Pennsylvania Association for Retarded Children* [PARC] *v. Commonwealth of Pennsylvania*. This litigation resulted in an agreement that established the right to free, appropriate public school education for all children who were mentally retarded within the jurisdiction of this federal court district. The impact of the court-ordered agreement extended beyond Pennsylvania as similar suits dealing with the same issue were filed in many other states in the months following this decision.

Although *PARC v. Pennsylvania* was specifically concerned with the exclusion of children whose primary descriptor was retardation from public education, other exceptional individuals were soon to enjoy the same right. In that same year, a suit on behalf of all exceptional individuals, regardless of type and severity, was filed in federal district court in Washington, D.C. This case, *Mills v. Board of Education of the District of Columbia,* which was decided in favor of the plaintiffs, extended the right to education to all children with disabilities.

During this same period, many individuals living in institutions were receiving very little in the way of services beyond custodial care. During 1971, in the case *Wyatt v. Stickney,* the lack of appropriate treatment provided residents at a state institution for the mentally retarded was contested. Although aspects of this case are still being reviewed, the original decision declared that the residents of Partlow State School and Hospital were entitled to receive treatment, not just custodial care. The judge enumerated the steps to be taken to comply with this decision.

Other important right to treatment cases are discussed in chapter 13.

As can be seen, the courts began to shape the events of the seventies. What may seem strange to the casual observer—and eminently significant to the special education professional—is the critical and influential roles that judges, lawyers, and expert witnesses played during the litigious early seventies. To professionals who were often the main service providers to those who were retarded, it seemed that much of the policy was formed by professionals in other fields. Although to a certain extent this is true, knowledgeable parents and special educators at that time were the ones who had realized that rights had not been secured or guaranteed through committee or panel action and that as a result, legal procedures had become necessary.

The judicial activity of the early 1970s culminated in the enactment of federal legislation that affected individuals with disabilities. Two pieces of legislation stand unparalleled in history for what they mandated. In 1973, amendments to the Vocational Rehabilitation Act (P.L. 93-112) were passed. Serving as a bill of rights for exceptional people, Section 504 of this act ensured that "the handicapped of America *should* have access to education and jobs, and *should not* be denied anything that any other citizen is entitled to or already receives" (LaVor, 1977, p. 249). Two years later, the landmark Education for All Handicapped Children Act (P.L. 94-142) was signed into law. The major provisions of this legislation are:

☐ Every handicapped child between the ages of 3 and 21 is entitled to a free, appropriate public education in the least restrictive environment.

☐ Due process is ensured to protect the rights of students and their parents.

☐ Students are entitled to special and related services which are determined as necessary.

☐ Every student will have a written individualized educational program (IEP) that parents and school personnel agree upon.

☐ First priority is given to students previously excluded from educational services and second priority to those whose programs were inappropriate.

☐ No eligible child is to be rejected from receiving services.

Another federal law that has had an impact on mentally retarded persons was the Developmental Disabilities Assistance and Bill of Rights Act of 1978 (P.L. 95-602). This legislation provided a functional definition of developmental disabilities as well as funding to assist persons who demonstrate problems in major life function areas.

Ironically, after the passage of P.L. 94-142 the field of special education became philosophically cautious. Perhaps relieved by the fact that there were now statutory provisions for educating exceptional people, professionals in the field seemed to be more concerned with reexamining what was happening. To be sure, many exciting developments occurred in the late 1970s. The emergence of a definable group of professionals devoted to working with persons who were severely or profoundly handicapped, emphasis on the development of community services, institutional reform, and deinstitutionalization are but a few of the more recent trends. If we examine these laudable efforts, however, we realize that they have not been undertaken with the blind optimism of the early to mid-19th century nor the runaway enthusiasm of the early 1960s. Perhaps we have learned from history to be a bit more cautious and not to promise more than we can provide or achieve.

## ACTION AND REACTION 1980–PRESENT

Through the 1970s, both special education and the provision of services to persons who were mentally retarded made remarkable progress. But as the 1980s began, two features emerged: *(a)* an eagerness to increase services and to maximize the quality of them; *(b)* an understanding that it is necessary to reevaluate all actions constantly.

*Sociopolitical factors.* We live in more conservative times these days, and the impact of conservatism can be felt in the field of mental retardation. Blatt (1987) states that social services and related programming have suffered severe cuts on the federal level. Witness the effects of the Gramm-Rudman Federal Deficit Reduction Amendment of 1985, which demands both a balanced budget by 1991 and automatic budget reductions. As Brantley (1988) has pointed out, certain programs—Medicaid, Social Security, and Supplemental Security Income—will be protected. But others, including

*Employment in competitive settings is the goal for most adults with mental retardation.*

special education, vocational rehabilitation, and developmental disabilities, may not.

Blatt (1987) comments on the social changes of the last few years:

> The balance of sentiment has shifted during the past few years—ever so slightly, but noticeably. More and more, the courts are (again) deciding on behalf of defendants rather than plaintiffs. More and more, the legislatures of our country are reluctant to either pass progressive legislation or to fully implement current legislation that would cost the taxpayers money. (p. 231)

Notable legislative activity has occurred in the 1980s. In 1982 action was initiated to revise the rules and regulations of the Education for All Handicapped Children Act (P.L. 94-142). The original changes proposed by the Office of Special Education and Rehabilitative Services (OSERS) met with overwhelming public and professional opposition, so that no major changes took place. This law was amended in 1983 as P.L. 98-199, resulting in *(a)* reinforcement of the original act's provisions; *(b)* establishment of several new or expanded programs—transition being one of them; and *(c)* modest increases in the authorization levels for various programs. The Education for All Handicapped Children Act was amended again in 1986 as P.L. 99-457. These amendments contain a number of innovations. They have *(a)* established a new federal preschool program by extending all the rights and protections of P.L. 94-142 to children aged three through five years; *(b)* created a new state grant program for infants and toddlers (birth through two years) who are developmentally delayed; and *(c)* addressed other areas such as agency participation, development of various centers, and personnel development.

Other legislative actions of the 1980s are important as well. The following federal laws have had or will have an impact on persons with mental retardation.

☐ Omnibus Budget Reconciliation Act (1981) (P.L. 97-35)
☐ Developmentally Disabled Assistance and Bill of Rights Act (1984) (P.L. 98-527)
☐ Rehabilitation Amendments (1984) (P.L. 98-221)
☐ Civil Rights Restoration Act (1988) (P.L. 100-259)

Two other important pieces of legislation that have been introduced into Congress are the Medicaid Home and Community Quality Services Act of 1987 and the Americans with Disabilities Act of 1988. The second is comparable in many ways to the Civil Rights Act of 1964.

Three important court cases took place in the early 1980s. The case *Larry P. v. Riles* (1972) was heard in the Ninth Circuit Court of Appeals. This court upheld a lower court ruling prohibiting California schools from using intelligence tests to place black students in classes for students who were mentally retarded. In *Pennhurst v. Halderman* (1981), the Supreme Court reversed the Third Circuit Court of Appeals decision that affirmed the residents of Pennhurst State School and Hospital's right to adequate habilitation under the Developmentally Disabled Assistance and Bill of Rights Act. The Supreme Court made it clear that this act does not create any substantive rights to adequate treatment. The third litigative action was the first case relating to P.L. 94-142 to be heard by the Supreme Court. At issue in this third case, *Board of Education v. Rowley* (1982), was whether a hearing-impaired girl was entitled to interpreter service to provide her with an appropriate education. Although acknowledging the procedural safeguards and need for individual education programs, the Supreme Court determined that states did not have to provide more than a minimal level of the services designated appropriate. As a result of this decision, schools do not have to be concerned with providing optimal educational programs for students with special needs. This has significant implications in terms of programs for students who are retarded.

During the latter part of the 1980s, a dominant theme in general and special education is the growing number of people who are "at risk" in different ways. At the school level this includes students who are at risk of school failure (potential dropouts, substance abusers, pregnant teenagers). At the adult level it includes people who are homeless, those who are unemployed or underemployed, and those who are not able to deal successfully with the demands of daily living. Individuals with mental retardation can be found in all of these groups.

In 1983, the American Association on Mental Retardation* issued its latest definition of mental retardation, one which is more comparable to definitions put forth by the American Psychiatric Association and the World Health Organization. This definition introduced greater flexibility by moving away from strict cutoff points (see chapter 2).

The 1980s have seen further developments in the field of mental retardation. The population is continuing to change, with the number of students identified as mentally retarded decreasing (see Figure 1.1). Polloway and Smith (1983) have suggested several factors to account for this decrease: *(a)* definitional changes and changes in professional thinking, which have encouraged caution and conservatism about identification and misdiagnosis, and *(b)* the effects of early intervention efforts in preventing some cases of mild retardation.

*Trends in service delivery.*   The 1980s have witnessed the advent of new directions in educating and training students with mental retardation. For instance, there is a definite trend toward providing community-based instruction and programming for these students. Great strides have been made in teaching more severely involved students. Transitional programming is in evidence in many areas of the country where just a few years ago there was none. New models for making these individuals employable have been introduced. The supported employment concept is replacing the former sheltered employment model on a widespread basis.

Different models of employment are covered more fully in chapter 11.

A debate is raging currently within the field of special education concerning the regular education initiative (REI). The focus of this federal initiative is to educate all students with mild handicaps (including mild mental retardation) in the regular classroom setting. Although philosophically this concept is acceptable, in fact it must be examined closely before it can be achieved. For students with mild retardation, particularly the "new" group that displays lower levels of skill development, it is necessary to consider whether they are indeed "mainstreamable," as MacMillan and Borthwick (1980) questioned at the beginning of the eighties.

---

*The American Association on Mental Deficiency (AAMD) changed its name in 1987 to the American Association on Mental Retardation (AAMR).

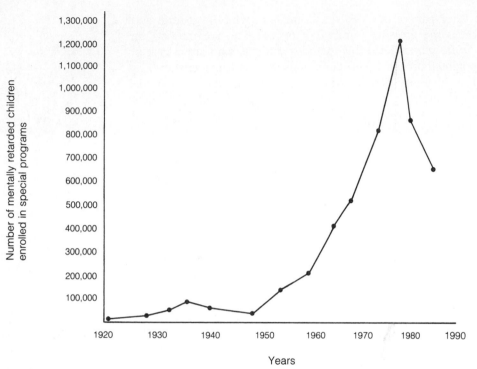

FIGURE 1.1   Enrollment of Mentally Retarded Children in Special Programs, ·
1922–1984

Data are from U.S. Department of the Census and U.S. Department of Education, Office of Special Education.

Other issues have emerged which are still being debated. Some of these include the educability of children who are severely or profoundly retarded, the bioethical issues of withholding treatment, and the continuing effects of poverty. These and other issues must still be resolved. We must be careful that social and public attitudes toward exceptional people do not change drastically in a negative direction. Cutbacks and restrictions may be the result of economic problems or policy shifts. If a positive national policy supportive of people with special needs is not carefully maintained, our society will be guilty of social neglect, and people who need help will not receive it. Blatt (1987) has poignantly captured the gravity of the situation: "If the business of government isn't service to the needy and the business of business isn't charity, and we aren't our brothers' keepers, then some needy people will die before their time, and many needy people will suffer" (p. 83). We must move through the 1990s with guarded optimism, because much of what can be done for people needing assistance has been, and will continue to be, grounded in the sociopolitical and economic context.

Throughout the development of the field of mental retardation, identifiable trends have strongly influenced where we are today. This chapter reviews many of the events, people, and sociopolitical factors that have been particularly noteworthy.

From the optimism of the early 1800s, exemplified in the efforts of Itard, Seguin, and others, to its current state, hedged about by economic and political constraints, the field has undergone many changes. It is important to be alert to what history has to say to us, for we do not want to see history repeat itself. Unquestionably we must resist a reemergence of the pejorative attitudes and dehumanizing treatment that prevailed toward the end of the 1800s. Most disturbing is the fact that some features of the field today are not so different from those of many years ago.

# CHAPTER 2

# Definition, Classification, and Prevalence

M ental retardation is not a simple phenomenon, and the lives of individuals who are retarded can be complex. As Edgerton (1984) notes about adults with mild retardation: "In general, their lives are complex, partly concealed from investigation and highly changeable" (p. 32). There are many different perspectives from which to view this complexity. This chapter provides *(a)* a general introduction to the phenomenon of retardation; and *(b)* a detailed overview of definitional perspectives of mental retardation; as well as *(c)* an explanation of why the number of people classified as mentally retarded has varied over time. Upon completing this chapter, the reader should have a beginning understanding of what is meant by the term *mental retardation*. Later chapters elaborate on many of the critical issues and concepts presented here.

Mental retardation has been defined and will continue to be defined in various and differing ways. On the day-to-day level, "For the individual and the family, mental retardation presents very practical concerns. For the community, state, and nation, it presents educational, social, economic, and political challenges" (Grossman & Tarjan, 1987, p. v). Defining mental retardation is explored in depth in this chapter; dealing with it individually is addressed throughout this book; its challenge to society was underscored in the previous chapter.

*Mental retardation* generally refers to delayed intellectual growth and is manifested in inappropriate or immature reactions to one's environment and below average performance in the academic, psychological, physical, linguistic, and social domains. Such limitations make it very difficult for

---

This chapter was contributed by James R. Patton and Eric D. Jones.

*Although by definition individuals who are retarded are different, they have the same needs as the rest of us.*

individuals to cope with the demands they encounter each day, those with which other people of comparable age and social or cultural background would be expected to deal successfully. For example, in school settings these individuals display patterns of academic and social performance that are below their chronological peers' performance. Unlike other students who are performing below grade level, the principal reason that students with mental retardation do so is their subaverage intellectual abilities, not such factors as excessive absences from school.

Mental retardation encompasses a heterogeneous group of people and is changeable. Individuals may be asymptomatic at various times of their lives (before formal schooling and later as adults). The extent of the condition ranges from mild difficulties to such profound limitations that there is nearly total dependence upon others for basic needs.

Two major types of retardation exist: clinical and psychosocial (see chapters 4 and 5). Clinical retardation is any condition that has a known biological explanation. Psychosocial retardation refers to the large number of individuals who show no clinical manifestations, are more often mildly retarded, and tend to come from lower socioeconomic levels (Grossman, 1983).

People who are in the upper levels or at the border of retardation create problems for most professionals in the field in terms of identification and eligibility. Reschly (1988) has stated that so long as the system is a dichotomy—one is or is not retarded—rather than a continuum, there will always be a problem classifying individuals at the margins. This is in great part because of *(a)* the way we understand and measure intellectual abilities and *(b)* society's definition of acceptable behavior and toleration of behavior that is different.

A challenging way to conceive of mental retardation is to consider it solely a social invention, as some professionals have claimed (Blatt, 1987; Sarason, 1985). They claim that it is really a reaction to how society perceives people who are different. Granted, there are biological manifestations in some individuals who are retarded, but we all have physical differences (e.g., freckles, musculature). Bogdan (1986) describes this orientation:

> The generic term *disabled* and specific disability categories are ways of thinking about and categorizing others. Whether people are thought of as disabled and the criteria used to determine whether someone is disabled has to do with how the definers think about these things. (p. 347)

## TERMINOLOGY

People who are mentally retarded have been called *dumb, stupid, immature, defective, deficient, subnormal, feebleminded, incompetent,* and *dull,* as well as *idiot* and *fool* in earlier times. Although the word *fool* generally referred to the mentally ill, and the word *idiot* was directed toward individuals who were severely mentally retarded, the terms were frequently used interchangeably (Hilliard & Kirman, 1965). Even today many nonprofessionals confuse the conditions. Mental illness, broadly speaking, is a confused state of thinking involving distorted perceptions of people or one's environment. It may be accompanied by radical changes of mood.

Those with cerebral
palsy are also per-
ceived as "childlike"
by many.

The history of mental retardation is further complicated when we consider that retardation has been confused with physical deformity, cerebral palsy, dwarfism, epilepsy, and deafness. The situation is made even more complex because a combination of these handicapping conditions does sometimes appear.

One of the first steps in understanding a phenomenon is understanding the terms used to describe it, no matter how crude or limited they may be.

This term is still used
in everyday
language.

In the past, *idiot* was used to refer to people of all levels of mental retardation, from mild to profound. It is derived from the Greek word *idiotos,* meaning a person who does not take part in public life. The word used to apply to untrained or ignorant people, and it was used in this sense until the 17th century (Penrose, 1966).

According to Kolstoe (1972), the *de praerogative regis* (prerogative of the king [of England]) issued between 1255 and 1290 A.D. defined an idiot as one who "hath no understanding from his nativity" (p. 2). About 200 years later Sir Anthony Fitzherbert stated that an idiot was "such a person who cannot account or number, nor can tell who his father or mother, nor how old he is, etc., so as it may appear he has not understanding of reason what shall be his profit or his loss" (Guttmacher & Weihofen, 1952). The key factor in identification as an idiot appears to be lack of understanding.

Idiocy was believed to be inborn and incurable. As mentioned in chapter 1, one of the first accounts of attempts to cure or at least ameliorate mental retardation was reported by Itard (1801/1962), who worked with a wild boy captured in a forest in 1799. The boy, whom Itard named Victor, did not speak or respond to the sound of gunfire, yet he startled at the sound of a cracking nut. He did not seem to feel differences between hot and cold or smell differences between foul and pleasant odors. Pinel, a well-known physician of the time, diagnosed Victor as an incurable idiot. Itard believed that with proper education Victor could be cured. Seguin, a student of Itard, followed in his footsteps by attempting to cure individuals with severe limitations; Penrose (1966) reports that "Esquirol referred to Seguin's mission as the removal of the mark of the beast from the forehead of the idiot" (pp. 4–5).

The concept "idiot" was elusive, confusing and had no common meaning; its primary use was to signify severe mental retardation. Although new terms like *feeblemindedness* and *mental deficiency* came into vogue, the confusion remained. Only in the 20th century have professionals attempted to systematize the terminology and definitions, although negative repercussions of all labels associated with the concept of mental retardation remain.

## HANDICAPISM AND MENTAL RETARDATION

See Goffman (1963)

Many groups of people in our society are not perceived favorably by the community at large. As Wolfensberger (1985) points out, "How a person is perceived affects how that person will be treated." If a certain group of people is perceived negatively, then its members will be treated less than favorably. Wolfensberger has identified groups of people that are devalued in our society and listed the major negative social roles into which these groups are typically cast. His analysis of this devaluation is presented in Table 2.1.

According to Wolfensberger, only mental disorder evokes more kinds of negative responses than mental retardation. It might be proper to mark the "dread" column as well for mental retardation, as there are sufficient examples of this perception (e.g., parents shielding their children from the group of adults with retardation who are seated near them on the bus). Wolfensberger's analysis has three major implications: *(a)* persons who are considered retarded will be badly treated; *(b)* this treatment reflects the way society conceptualizes deviancy roles; *(c)* the perceptions and resultant treatment by others will greatly influence how people who are retarded behave.

TABLE 2.1  Socially Devalued Groups and the Common Historical Deviancy Roles into Which They Are Most Apt to Be Cast

| People who are devalued due to: | Common Deviancy Roles | | | | | | | | |
|---|---|---|---|---|---|---|---|---|---|
| | Pity | Charity | Men-ace | Sick | Sub-human | Ridi-cule | Dread | Child-like | Holy inno-cent |
| Mental disorder | X | X | X | X | X | X | X | X | X |
| Mental retardation | X | X | X | X | X | X | | X | X |
| Old age | X | X | | X | X | X | | X | |
| Alcohol habituation | X | X | X | X | | X | | | |
| Poverty | X | X | X | | X | | X | | |
| Racial minority membership | | | X | | X | X | X | X | |
| Epilepsy | X | X | | X | | | X | | |
| Drug addiction | X | X | X | X | | | | | |
| Criminal offenses | | | X | X | X | | X | | |
| Physical handicap | X | X | | | | X | | | |
| Deafness/hearing impairment | X | X | | | | | | | |
| Blindness/visual impairment | X | X | | | | | | | |
| Illiteracy | X | X | | | | | | | |
| Political dissidence | | | X | | | | | | |

From "An Overview of Social Role Valorization and Some Reflections on Elderly Mentally Retarded Persons" by W. Wolfensberger, 1985. In M. P. Janicki & H. M. Wisniewski (Eds.), *Aging and Developmental Disabilities: Issues and Approaches* (pp. 61–76), Baltimore: Paul H. Brookes.

It is in light of the fact that many individuals with retardation are treated differently that the concept of **handicapism** is relevant. Handicapism is a phenomenon similar to racism, sexism, and ageism, in its resulting mistaken beliefs, prejudices, and pejorative actions on the part of individuals or society. Bogdan and Biklen (1977), two professionals who have been interested in this theme, define *handicapism* as: "A set of assumptions and practices that promote the differential and unequal treatment of people because of apparent or assumed physical, mental, or behavioral differences" (p. 59). Clearly handicapism affects people who are mentally retarded.

Handicapism can be manifested in various ways, most notably through *stereotyping, prejudice,* and *discrimination.* The following example illustrates this point. Many people view adults with retardation as childlike *(stereotyping),* which leads to the belief that they are incapable of making decisions for themselves *(prejudice),* which in turn results in having others make decisions for them without their input or knowledge *(discrimination).*

There are many other examples of handicapism, some of which will be discussed below. A very offensive example is the popular "moron" joke ("Why did the moron. . .?"). These jokes are heard in everyday conversation and can be found now in books of "tasteless jokes." Although people with mental retardation are not the only group to suffer from malicious jokes, they certainly are one of the prime targets. Handicapism is also evident in media representations of this group. For instance, the character Zero in the comic strip *Beetle Bailey* has features typical of those who are retarded, and he is always portrayed in uncomplimentary ways. Bogdan and Biklen also note another common occurrence: newspaper reports associating criminal activity with a specific disability (mental retardation), implying that the disability is responsible for the crime. It is important to be aware of instances of handicapism and to strive to eliminate them. Far too often, blatant examples of handicapism go unchallenged.

Note that not all media portrayals of individuals with mental retardation are handicapist. Some media images are laudable: the documentary *Best Boy;* the character Benny on the television show *LA Law;* and the television movie *Bill.*

## DEFINING MENTAL RETARDATION

There have been many definitions of mental retardation, all reflecting the different perspectives and perceptions of retardation at a certain time. Blatt (1987) articulates this notion well:

> Because mental retardation is in the most fundamental and important ways a metaphor (people make of it what they want to, people interpret it in light of their own understandings and prejudices), the definition "mental retardation" and the terms used to denote the condition represent a hodgepodge of (sometimes irreconcilable) values, words, and ideas. (p. 69)

Whether or not one agrees with this, we must deal with the reality that definitions exist and are used to make decisions about persons with retardation.

This section covers two major topics: *(a)* a brief examination of traditional definitions; and *(b)* a discussion of the most widely accepted definition of mental retardation—the series of definitions developed by the American Association on Mental Retardation (AAMR).

## TRADITIONAL DEFINITIONS

During the first half of the 20th century, two definitions, one developed by Tredgold and the other by Doll, were referred to repeatedly. Tredgold (1937) defined "mental deficiency" as

> A state of incomplete mental development of such a kind and degree that the individual is incapable of adapting himself to the normal environment of his fellows in such a way to maintain existence independently of supervision, control, or external support. (p. 4)

Doll (1941) defined "mental retardation" when he stated,

> We observe that six criteria by statement or implication have been generally considered essential to an adequate definition and concept. These are (1) social incompetence, (2) due to mental subnormality, (3) which has been developmentally arrested, (4) which obtains at maturity, (5) is of constitutional origin, and (6) is essentially incurable. (p. 215)

Both definitions incorporated several criteria characteristic of the times (intellectual inadequacy, developmental immaturity, deficits in adaptive behavior, and incurability). The importance of each criterion in the Tredgold and Doll definitions was significantly altered in subsequent definitions. The most notable alterations were made in the definitions developed by the American Association on Mental Deficiency (AAMD).

## THE AAMR (AAMD) DEFINITIONS

In 1919, the American Association for the Study of the Feebleminded, which would later become the American Association on Mental Deficiency, and now is known as the American Association on Mental Retardation, appointed a committee on Classification and Uniform Statistics. In 1921 this committee, in collaboration with the National Committee for Mental Hygiene, published the first manual defining the conditions of mental retardation. Subsequent revisions of the manual were printed in 1933, 1941, and 1957.

In 1959, a committee of professionals chaired by Rick Heber developed the fifth AAMR definition of mental retardation. That definition was reprinted and revised in 1961. The sixth revision was developed by a committee chaired by Herbert Grossman in 1973. Although the definition was similar to that developed by Heber's committee some years earlier, the interpretation was significantly more conservative. Fewer individuals could be identified as

# A PERSONAL VIEW OF RETARDATION

Very seldom do we attempt to consider retardation from the eyes and minds of those whom we so label. This approach, referred to as a phenomenological perspective (Taylor & Bogdan, 1977), provides another vantage point from which to understand retardation.

Katie Tager, 29, resides at a semi-independent living apartment building. She is mildly retarded, but that doesn't stop her from keeping her own apartment, contributing to the community, and being actively involved with other people.

She is putting together two books: *Accepting Me,* a collection of her poems and writings, and *Let Special People Be Free,* a collection of essays, poems, personal stories, and artwork by adults and children with disabilities.

The following poem of Katie's was recently published in *Arts Access,* a newsletter of Very Special Arts Hawaii.

**Accepting Me**

accepting me for who
I am some people find
it hard to do
They don't see my disability
I tell them I am mildly
retarded but they don't
believe me
I tell them some disabilities
you can't see but its
in my head where it
happen to me
I think and do things
slower then you and
sometimes its hard for
me to understand what
you find easy to know
I try and learn the
best I can and accept
what I am not able to
do
Try accepting me you
will see how much it
means to me
Its not hard to under
stand and be my friend
then you'll accept me
for who I am

From an item written by
John Oh for *Arts Access.*

mentally retarded under the Grossman definition than under the Heber definition. It is important to mention that the 1973 AAMR definition was incorporated into the Education for All Handicapped Children Act of 1975 (P.L. 94-142) as the federal definition of mental retardation. Grossman's definition was reaffirmed, with minor revisions, in 1977; the most recent revision was published in 1983. The 1983 definition, which corresponds with definitions developed by the American Psychiatric Association (1980, 1987) and the World Health Organization (1978), described important considerations related to interpretation and clinical judgment used to classify an individual as mentally retarded. This AAMR definition, like its predecessors, is from a clinically oriented perspective, relying on measurements and comparisons. Although the definition has been discussed regularly and often criticized within the field, it remains the most widely accepted one and the one used by the federal government.

The APA revised the manual in 1987.

It is worthwhile to review the development of the AAMR definitions. The Heber (1959) definition of mental retardation and the subsequent revisions represent major sociopolitical changes and reflect ways the field has evolved and thinking about those identified as mentally retarded has changed. The Heber (1959, revised 1961) definition stated:

> Mental retardation refers to subaverage general intellectual functioning which originates during the development period and is associated with impairment in adaptive behavior.

**Subaverage general intellectual functioning** refers to performance on a standardized intelligence test which is at least one standard deviation below the mean. The **standard deviation** is a statistic used to describe the degree to which an individual's score varies from the average or mean score for the population. Figure 2.1 illustrates the concepts of the normal curve, standard deviation, and population mean.

In the 1961 AAMR *Manual,* the **developmental period** was recognized to be variable, but for purposes of definition, it was judged to range from birth through 16 years of age. **Adaptive behavior** referred to the individual's adaptation to the demands of his environment. Impaired adaptive behavior could be reflected in maturation, learning, or social adjustment (terms used in the 1959 definition). Impaired adaptive behavior was considered in terms of standards and norms of appropriate behavior for the individual's chronological age group. Although deficient adaptive behavior was only loosely defined, its use in the Heber definition represented a major departure from the earlier definitions of Tredgold and Doll, for it recognized that an individual might be deficient in one or more aspects of adaptive behavior at one time in life, but not at another. Favorable changes in social demands and conditions, or in the individual's increased ability to meet natural and social demands, could mean that a person would no longer be called mentally retarded. According to Heber (1959, 1961), the definition refers to an

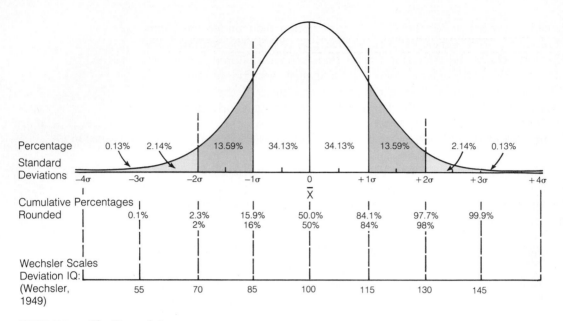

FIGURE 2.1    The Normal Curve
σ = standard deviation
X̄ = population mean—the average score.
The Wechsler Intelligence Scales use a deviation IQ score with a mean of 100 and
a standard deviation of 15. In a normal distribution, a person who scores 1σ above
the mean receives a Wechsler score of 115. One who scores below 70 on a
Wechsler scale (>2σ below the mean) may be classified as mentally retarded if
impairments in adaptive behavior are also present.

From "Methods of Expressing Test Scores," 1955, *Test Service Bulletin, 48,* p. 8. Reprinted with permission.

individual's *current* functioning, not to an ultimate or permanent status.
Unlike earlier definitions, the Heber definitions did not consider mental
retardation incurable.

***Events leading to further revisions.***    The 1961 AAMR definition of mental
retardation was viewed by many professionals as an improvement over
previous definitions, but it was not received without criticism. Perhaps the
only aspect of the definition accepted without controversy was the concept of
mental retardation as an alterable or changeable status based on the
individual's present level of functioning. The concept of adaptive behavior
caused considerable debate. Clausen (1972a) argued that the procedures for
evaluating adaptive behavior were not adequate for diagnosis. He contended
that diagnoses of mental retardation should be based solely upon the data
from **psychometric** evaluations. From an earlier investigation, he revealed
that, in spite of the AAMR's inclusion of the concept of adaptive behavior in
the definition, diagnoses of mental retardation were frequently made solely

on the basis of intelligence test data (Clausen, 1967). Clausen's proposed psychometric definition was highly controversial and apparently unpopular. Two basic grounds existed for opposition to a definition based solely on psychometric criteria. First, such a definition could threaten the concept of mental retardation as an alterable or changeable condition. Intelligence test results are quite stable over time; hence, it was possible that important changes in observable behavior would not show on intelligence tests. The second criticism of the psychometric definition was that, on the basis of tests standardized on members of the majority culture, too many children from minority cultures had been misdiagnosed as mentally retarded.

It was generally recognized that the 1961 Heber definition was overinclusive. With that definition as a guide for diagnosis, it was possible to identify statistically almost 16% of the general population and perhaps greater proportions of the bilingual/multicultural populations as mentally retarded. Clausen (1972b) suggested that the definition be made more conservative by requiring that an individual IQ score be two or more (instead of one) standard deviations below the mean on an intelligence test. Other professionals suggested that the loose connection between adaptive behavior and intelligence be strengthened. Both positions have been consistently reflected in later revisions of the AAMR definition.

*The 1973 definition.*   In 1973, the AAMR committee headed by Grossman was assigned to review the *Manual on Terminology and Classification in Mental Retardation.* The revised definition stated:

> Mental retardation refers to significantly subaverage general intellectual functioning existing concurrently with deficits in adaptive behavior, and manifested during the development period.

In this version, *significantly subaverage intellectual functioning* meant performance at least two standard deviations below the mean on an intelligence test (that is, performance comparable to the lowest 2.28% of the norm statistically). *Adaptive behavior* was defined in terms of the degree and efficiency with which the individual meets "the standards of personal independence and social responsibility expected of his age and cultural group" (p. 11). Adaptive behavior was thus considered to be relative to the individual's age and sociocultural group. An expanded set of criteria was provided for the assessment of adaptive behavior.

The 1961 Heber definition included both subaverage intellectual functioning and deficits in adaptive behavior as necessary qualifying conditions for diagnosis. The relationship between adaptive behavior and intellectual functioning, however, was not clarified sufficiently. Children were consistently labeled mentally retarded on the basis of IQ alone. The two most important distinctions between the 1961 and the 1973 definitions were that *(a)* subaverage intelligence was defined as *two* standard deviations below the mean, and *(b)* the relationship between adaptive behavior and intelligence was emphasized. Instead of simply requiring intellectual functioning and adaptive behavior to be *associated,* the committee stated that adaptive behavior deficits and subaverage intellectual functioning had to *exist concurrently.* In addition, the developmental period was extended from birth to 18 years of age, matching the age when many finish public education.

In spite of the extension of the developmental period, the 1973 revision was a much more conservative definition than those that preceded it. Table 2.2 illustrates this point. According to the 1961 AAMR definition, almost 16% of the general population could have been identified as mentally retarded from a purely psychometric perspective. According to the 1973 definition, less than 3% of the population could be considered mentally retarded from the same perspective. The 1973 revision of the definition resulted in a reduction by more than eighty-five per cent of the number of individuals who could be identified as mentally retarded. This comparison does not indicate the impact of the required connection between adaptive behavior and intelligence, but the two are imperfectly correlated at all levels of performance. Presumably, a number of individuals who might score two or more standard deviations below the mean on an intelligence test would not be referred for evaluation if they demonstrated appropriate adaptive skills.

Two of the most significant documents supporting a more conservative, cautious definition of the mentally retarded were "Special Education for the Mildly Retarded—Is Much of It Justifiable?" by Dunn (1968) and the Report of the President's Committee on Mental Retardation (PCMR) (1970) entitled *The Six-Hour Retarded Child.* Dunn, a respected authority in the field of mental retardation and former president of the Council for Exceptional Children, reported that many culturally disadvantaged children were being incorrectly classified as mildly retarded and placed in special classes. The lack of adequate adaptive behavior scales, coupled with the convenient practice of identifying students as mentally retarded on the basis of IQ score alone, probably fostered the mislabeling of nonretarded children as retarded. Dunn stated:

> I have loyally supported and promoted special classes for the educable mentally retarded for most of the last 20 years, but with growing disaffection. In my view, much of our past and present practices are morally and educationally wrong. We have been living at the mercy of general educators who have referred our problem children to us. And we have been generally ill prepared and ineffective in educating these children. Let us stop being pressured into continuing and expanding a special education program that we know now to be undesirable for many of the children we are dedicated to serve.
>
> A better education than special class placement is needed for socioculturally deprived children with mild learning problems who have been labeled educable

mentally retarded. Over the years, the status of these pupils who come from poverty, broken and inadequate homes, and low status ethnic groups has been a checkered one. (1968, p. 5)

*The Six-Hour Retarded Child* (PCMR, 1970) agreed with Dunn's charge; that is, a significant number of culturally disadvantaged children, especially in urban areas, had been misclassified as mildly retarded and inappropriately placed in special education classes. The "six-hour retarded children" are those who are classified as mentally retarded during the six hours they spend in an academic setting, but who function normally outside school. The reports by Dunn and the PCMR were emotional; although not based on rigorous empirical data, they did grow from systematic observation and a strong philosophical commitment.

Figure 2.2 illustrates how the 1973 AAMR definition attempted to accentuate the dual criteria—intellectual functioning and adaptive behavior. Note that individuals were to be labeled mentally retarded only if they exhibited *concurrent* deficits in both areas. Persons who fit into any other position in the matrix were not to be considered mentally retarded.

*AAMR 1977 definition.* In 1977, the AAMR published its seventh manual on classification and terminology. The wording of the 1977 definition is identical to the 1973 version, but the 1977 manual made a few modifications in its interpretation. To begin with, *significantly subaverage* remained two standard deviations below the mean, and *adaptive behavior* was essentially unchanged. The major change focused on the issue of **clinical judgment**. The manual explains in detail the problems of measuring adaptive behavior. Yet its importance was highlighted in the sentence, "For a person to be diagnosed as being mentally retarded, impairments in intellectual functioning must co-exist with deficits in adaptive behavior" (p. 12). The manual goes on to state,

> Individuals with (intelligence) scores slightly above these ceilings (two standard deviations below the mean) may be diagnosed as mildly retarded during a period when they manifest serious impairments of adaptive behavior. In such cases, the burden is on the examiner to avoid misdiagnosis with its potential stigmatizing effects. (p. 12)

Later the committee elaborated, stating,

> A small minority of persons with IQ's up to 10 points above the guideline ceilings are so impaired in their adaptive behavior that they may be classified as having mild mental retardation. (pp. 19–20)

The 1977 definition, although worded identically to the 1973 definition, allowed a diagnosis of mental retardation to be applied to individuals who, according to the previous definition, would not have been so classified.

TABLE 2.2  Comparison of Heber and Grossman AAMR Definitions of Mental Retardation

| Term | Heber (1959, 1961) | Grossman (1973) | Grossman (1983) | Differences |
|---|---|---|---|---|
| General Definition | Subaverage general intellectual functioning which originates during the developmental period and is associated with impairment in adaptive behavior. | Significantly subaverage general intellectual functioning existing concurrently with deficits in adaptive behavior and manifested during the developmental period. | Significantly subaverage general intellectual functioning resulting in or associated with concurrent impairments in adaptive behavior and manifested during the developmental period. | Adaptive behavior is associated with low IQ (Heber). It exists concurrently with low IQ (Grossman, 1973) and can result from low IQ (Grossman, 1983). |
| Subaverage | Greater than one standard deviation below the mean. | Significantly subaverage: two or more standard deviations below the mean. | Significantly subaverage: defined as an IQ of 70 or below on standardized measures of intelligence; could be extended upward through IQ 75 or more, depending on the reliability of the intelligence test used. | Heber includes one standard deviation more than Grossman. Hypothetically Heber's definition includes approximately 16% of the general population, while Grossman includes 2.3% from a psychometric perspective. |
| Assessment Procedure | General intellectual functioning; may be assessed by one or more of the standardized tests developed for that purpose. | Same as Heber. | Same as Heber for intellectual functioning. Adaptive behavior assessed by clinical assessment and standardized scales. | No difference. |
| Developmental Period | Approximately 16 years. | Upper age limit of 18 years. | Period of time between conception and the 18th birthday. | Grossman extended the developmental period upward from 16 to 18 years of age (1973) and downward to conception (1983). |
| Adaptive Behavior | Impairment in adaptive behavior: refers to the effectiveness of the individual to adapt to the natural and social demands of his environment. May be reflected in: 1. Maturation 2. Learning 3. Social adjustment | Defined as effectiveness or degree with which the individual meets the standards of personal independence and social responsibility expected of his age and cultural group. May be reflected in the following areas: | Defined as significant limitations in an individual's effectiveness in meeting the standards of maturation, learning, personal independence, or social responsibility that are expected for his or her age level and cultural group. | Grossman's definitions specify more areas of adaptive behavior and emphasize that adaptive behavior is relative to the individual's cultural group. |

| Levels of Severity | | | |
|---|---|---|---|
| Borderline retardation IQ 68–84 | *During infancy and early childhood:* 1. Sensory-motor skills development 2. Communication skills 3. Self-help skills 4. Socialization *During childhood and early adolescence:* 5. Application of basic academics in daily life activities 6. Application of appropriate reasoning and judgment in mastery of the environment 7. Social skills *During late adolescence and adult life:* 8. Vocational and social responsibilities and performances | — | Grossman's definitions do not include borderline retardation. |
| Mild retardation IQ 52–67 | Mild retardation IQ 52–67 | Mild retardation IQ 50–55 to approx. 70 | More flexibility; movement away from strict standard deviation cutoffs. |
| Moderate retardation IQ 36–51 | Moderate retardation IQ 36–51 | Moderate retardation IQ 35–40 to 50–55 | Same |
| Severe retardation IQ 20–35 | Severe retardation IQ 20–35 | Severe retardation IQ 20–25 to 35–40 | Same |
| Profound retardation IQ < 20 | Profound retardation IQ < 20 | Profound retardation IQ below 20 or 25 Cannot be determined | Same |

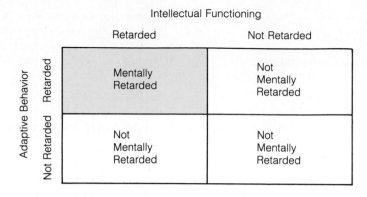

FIGURE 2.2   Twofold Specification in the AAMR Definition of Mental Retardation

From *Manual on Terminology and Classification in Mental Retardation* by H. J. Grossman, 1983, Washington DC: American Association of Mental Deficiency. Reprinted by permission.

**AAMR 1983 definition.**   In 1983, the AAMR published its eighth manual on classification and terminology. Unfortunately, the out-of-date 1977 definition was reprinted mistakenly on page 1 as well as in the glossary of the manual; however, the correct definition was accurately stated on page 11:

> Mental retardation refers to significantly subaverage general intellectual functioning resulting in or associated with concurrent impairments in adaptive behavior and manifested during the developmental period.

Clinical judgment remained an important issue—so important that the appendix cited several short case studies followed by descriptions of the way decisions were reached from the information presented in the cases.

The tone of the manual emphasized that the content was carefully researched and contemplated before publication and the decisions derived were logical, practical, and consistent with a need to explore a worldwide system of mental retardation. The authors collaborated with representatives of two other major classification systems so that the different systems would be as compatible as possible. The two systems are the World Health Organization's (1978) system of *International Classification of Diseases, Clinical Modification* (9th ed.) (ICD-9) and the American Psychiatric Association's (1980) *Diagnostic and Statistical Manual of Mental Disorders* (3rd ed.) (DSM-III).

The AAMR manual defines *significantly subaverage* as an IQ of 70 or below on a standardized measure of intelligence. Yet this upper limit is intended as a guideline and could be extended to an IQ of 75 or more providing behavior is impaired and *clinically determined* to be due to deficits in reasoning and judgment. In this definition, the strict use of standard deviations is discouraged, and the concept of the standard error of measurement inherent in all tests is emphasized.

Clinicians using the system should be well aware that in determining whether a person is retarded and at what level of intellectual functioning the individual is operating, it is important to understand the concept of standard error of measurement and use it when making a clinical determination of retardation and level of functioning. (p. 7)

No tests are perfectly reliable, and some degree of random fluctuation in obtained scores is always expected. The standard error of measurement is an estimate of the degree to which the test scores would be expected to vary because of random error alone. For example, we know that the standard error of measurement on the Wechsler Intelligence Scale for Children— Revised is 3 IQ points. If a child received a score of 72 on that test, the examiner should report that the student's true IQ would probably be within the range 69 to 75. The clinician would then decide whether other conditions, such as concurrent deficits in adaptive behavior or cultural difference, were present and associated with the level of performance on the IQ test. According to the 1983 AAMR manual, an individual with an IQ of 75 or higher could be classified as mentally retarded if deficits in adaptive behavior were also present. On the other hand, an IQ of 70 to 67 or perhaps lower would not alone provide a *sufficient basis* for classifying a child from a minority culture as mentally retarded. The clinician would have to determine to what extent bias affected performance and whether deficits in adaptive behavior were present and associated with the attained level of performance. You cannot measure something precisely unless you can define it precisely. Intelligence, achievement, and adaptive behavior are ready examples of rather imprecisely defined concepts as Blatt (1987) emphasized. Therefore, it is naive arbitrarily to treat scores obtained by those measures as precise; the standard error of measurement is a concept that allows flexibility in interpretation, yet at the same time provides reasonable structure.

The *adaptive behavior* component in the 1983 definition remained unchanged, but again, the need for clinical judgment in borderline cases was emphasized. The measurement of adaptive behavior may involve observation, informal interview, or the use of a standardized scale. Adaptive behavior must be compared to norms for the individual's age and cultural group. The manual emphasized throughout that, because of the present state of affairs with adaptive behavior, clinical judgment must be used.

Although the conceptual basis of *developmental period* did not change, the range did. The new definition stresses that the developmental period *begins at conception* and extends through age 18.

Although the 1983 manual was as up-to-date and definitive as possible, and was supported by other prestigious organizations, the committee recognized that as more data are collected and times change, the definition of mental retardation will also inevitably change:

The 1983 definition, slightly modified for clarity, was introduced in the 1959 manual; it is intended to represent the current status of scientific knowledge in

Issues related to assessment are discussed in chapter 3.

the field and the current thinking about social issues associated with mental retardation. One may anticipate that as both knowledge and philosophy change, there will be modifications reflecting such changes in future manuals. (p. 10)

As this book goes to press, the Committee on Terminology and Classification of the AAMR, chaired by Ruth Luckasson, is being reactivated. Its membership has changed, and new definitional perspectives will most likely be forthcoming.

## CLASSIFICATION OF MENTAL RETARDATION

This section addresses the practice of organizing those individuals who are identified as retarded into established categories. Three systems can be used for this task: *(a)* etiological conditions; *(b)* intellectual dimensions; and *(c)* behavioral descriptors. The first of these has been accomplished by the AAMR and appears in the their most recent manual (Grossman, 1983). (This system is covered in chapter 4.) The second system, usually grounded in test performance, distinguishes individuals on the basis of IQ scores. The third system classifies according to typically observed behaviors. Although it suffers from the criticism of being less sophisticated psychometrically, as Zucker and Polloway (1987) mention, this could be an attractive feature. These last two systems are discussed below.

Although the need for services to people who are mentally retarded continues, authorities are in a state of flux, quandary, confusion, ambivalence, turmoil. . . . They're damned if they use the term *mental retardation,* and damned if they don't. Without any common terminology, the concept of mental retardation would become more hazy, and parents as well as professionals would have difficulties without a generic term to use. In addition, funds would be more difficult to obtain. As Grossman and Tarjan (1987) note, the existing classification system serves two primary functions: *(a)* it is used in various policy-making activities, *(b)* it is clinically useful for communication and research.

As we have seen, periodic changes have occurred in the terminology used to identify those who are mentally retarded. Dunn (1973b) listed three reasons that we continually search for new and more appropriate terms for persons with "intellectual inadequacies."

1. Sooner or later negative values are attached to any term used to describe retarded persons. Thus, the new terms, at least when they are first introduced, are socially acceptable; however, before long they, too, acquire negative connotations.

2. The condition of mental retardation is so complex and broad, with so many causes and levels, it may be virtually impossible to include its entire scope under one rubric.

3. Many different disciplines are involved and interested in the field of mental retardation, including education, psychology, sociology, medicine, speech pathology, and social science; and each develops a definition suited to its particular orientation.

The continual search for different definitions and terms yields diminishing returns. Any word can come to have a negative connotation. For example, one school district, aware of the detrimental effects of labeling children *mentally retarded,* began placing these children in an educational program designed to teach language, arithmetic, and reading directly. A series of commercial programs produced by Science Research Associates, DISTAR (Direct Instructional Systems for Teaching Arithmetic and Reading), was used. Before half the year was over, a group of concerned citizens asked that the program be abandoned because DISTAR was for "dumb" kids, and children not enrolled in DISTAR classes were making fun of the DISTAR children by yelling "DISTAR, DISTAR" at them at recess. It may be impossible to find acceptable terms and useful definitions without proper education and increased understanding of persons who are intellectually handicapped.

Several systems of terminology used to refer to individuals with mental retardation and the corresponding levels of severity based on IQ are presented in Table 2.3. Note that many of the same names represent different levels or even different concepts. For instance, *feeblemindedness* has been used as the generic name of mental retardation as well as for a specific level of severity of mental retardation.

Another way to appreciate the different levels of retardation is by examining "general" behavioral indices. Table 2.4 shows one such attempt. This table represents only generalizations at each level within each domain; many exceptions can be found. A second caveat is that behavioral performance is a function of age, therefore influencing how one interprets this matrix. A sense of expected skill attainment for the different levels can nevertheless be obtained from referring to such a source. For more thorough discussion of the characteristics of all these levels, see chapters 6 and 7.

There is a constant clamor for changing the classification system. One suggestion is to move away from classifying individuals toward classifying which services are needed. Others have advocated different types of reform in the identification and classification system currently in use. Reschly (1984, 1987, 1988) feels that there needs to be a clearer distinction between people who are mildly retarded and those who are more significantly retarded, for three reasons: *(a)* mild retardation is not permanent; *(b)* it is typically restricted to certain situations (school); and *(c)* most instances are not attributable to biological or organic etiologies. He champions the idea of

TABLE 2.3    Terminology and Levels of Severity of Retardation

| Proponents | Generic Term | 95 | 90 | 85 | 80 | 75 | 70 | 65 | 60 | 55 | 50 | 45 | 40 | 35 | 30 | 25 | 20 | 15 | 10 | 5 | 0 |
|---|---|---|---|---|---|---|---|---|---|---|---|---|---|---|---|---|---|---|---|---|---|
| American Association for the Study of the Feebleminded | Feebleminded | | | | | | | Moron | | | | | Imbecile | | | | Idiot | | | | |
| Tredgold & Soddy (Great Britain) | Mental deficiency | | | | | | | High grade; feeble-minded | | | | | Middle grade; imbecile | | | | Low grade; idiot | | | | |
| AAMR (Heber, 1961) | Mental retardation | | | | | Borderline mentally retarded | | Mild | | | | Moderate | | | Severe | | Profound | | | | |
| AAMR Grossman, 1973) | Mental retardation | | | | | | | Mild | | | | Moderate | | | Severe | | Profound | | | | |
| AAMR Grossman, 1983) | Mental retardation | | | | | | | Mild | | | Moderate | | | Severe | | Profound | | | | | |
| American Psychiatric Association (1987) DSM III-R | Mental deficiency | | | | | | | Mild | | | Moderate | | | Severe | | Profound | | | | | |
| World Health Organization (1978) | Mental subnormality | | | | | | | Mild | | | Moderate | | | Severe | | Profound | | | | | |

Note: Dashed rules indicate approximate cutoff points.

renaming this level of retardation and using terms like *educational handicap* or *academic aptitude handicap* (Reschly, 1984). Reschly's suggestions have merit if students displaying characteristics similar to the high functioning group of students with mild retardation of 10 to 15 years ago continue to be identified.

After navigating the maze of actual definitions and issues and philosophies regarding definitions and definitional practices, one may be left with solving the task of determining who is "really" mentally retarded. However, the lesson is not that the emerging definitions are better or more accurate, but that the definition of mental retardation is totally a social and political one that rests with the powers that be, and not in the minds of the people who experience intellectual deficits.

TABLE 2.4  Behavioral Descriptions by Level of Severity

| Level of Retarda-tion | Communication Skills | Physical Dimensions | Social Adjustment | Independent Functioning | Occupational/Vocational Level | Academic Performance |
|---|---|---|---|---|---|---|
| Mild | Ability to listen & speak effectively<br>Can carry on an involved conversation<br>May have difficulty understanding some concepts & vocabulary<br>Restricted expressive vocabulary | No major problems | Interactions with others are reasonably acceptable<br>Some social skill deficiencies | Self-supporting | Good potential for competitive employment | Can achieve academic competence and literacy |
| Moderate | Can carry on simple conversations<br>Problems in listening and speaking are likely | Some motor and health problems | Can interact with others but may be awkward<br>Friendships possible | Can master self-help skills<br>Typically live in supported settings<br>May require financial support | Can gain employment in competitive or supported settings | Survival and functional skills can be learned |
| Severe | Can understand very simple communication<br>Limited verbal skills<br>May use nonverbal techniques (e.g, gestures, sign language) | Typically have significant motor and health problems | Social interactions may be limited | Need certain amount of assistance with daily activities | Employment possible for some<br>Typically found in sheltered settings but can perform in supported settings | Focus on functional needs<br>Can acquire requisite self-help skills |
| Profound | Communication skills are very limited, if they exist at all<br>Often communication is through nonverbal sounds<br>No effective speech | Few useful motor skills<br>May be medically fragile | May be nonexistent | Totally dependent | Employment or training not likely | Focus on basic skills such as attending, positioning |

Some information in this table was taken from Grossman, 1983.

## ALTERNATIVE CONCEPTUALIZATIONS OF MENTAL RETARDATION

*(out)*

The 1983 AAMR definition bears the distinction of being the legal definition of *mental retardation*. It is also the most frequently cited definition of mental retardation in the professional literature. But, in spite of the endorsement and popularity of the Grossman (1973, 1977, 1983) definitions, they have not met with universal approval among professionals. The AAMR definitions have been criticized because of their clear clinical overtones.

But other definitions and conceptualizations do exist, and selected ones are presented below. Except for the developmental disabilities definition, none of the following points of view enjoys widespread recognition. Yet each presents an orientation important to the field of mental retardation.

*de-emphasis on 1 a*

*Developmental disabilities perspective.* During the last few years the concept of **developmental disabilities** has been used more frequently, particularly with adult populations. The meaning of this term overlaps with that of mental retardation. As defined in the Developmental Disabilities Assistance and Bill of Rights Act of 1984 (P. L. 98-527), the term refers to "a severe, chronic disability of a person which—"

> (A) is attributable to a mental or physical impairment or combination of mental and physical impairments;
> (B) is manifested before the person attains age twenty-two;
> (C) is likely to continue indefinitely;
> (D) results in substantial functional limitations in three or more of the following areas of major life activity: (i) self-care, (ii) receptive and expressive language, (iii) learning, (iv) mobility, (v) self-direction, (vi) capacity for independent living, and (vii) economic self-sufficiency;
> (E) reflects the person's need for a combination and sequence of special, interdisciplinary, or generic care, treatment, or other services which are lifelong or of extended duration and are individually planned and coordinated.

The definition accentuates functional limitations in major life activities, suggesting problems associated more with a moderately or severely retarded population. Notwithstanding, it may apply to some persons with mild retardation during some part or all of their lives. The implication of chronicity, however, may not apply very well to this group, and for this reason it differs from the AAMR definition. Nevertheless, for most individuals who are considered moderately, severely, or profoundly retarded the concept of developmental disabilities is appropriate, useful, and frequently invoked.

*Sociological perspective.* Mercer (1973a, 1973b) rejects the traditional approaches to defining mental retardation. Traditional approaches (Heber, 1959, 1961; Grossman, 1973, 1983) to identifying abnormal behavior have taken a clinical perspective, which tends to define mental retardation on the basis of either a pathological model or a statistical model. The pathological (or medical) model regards mental retardation as a disease, recognized and defined by the presence of its symptoms, although it is also possible for the pathology to exist without a complete manifestation of its symptoms. The statistical model will always identify a certain portion of the population as abnormal. The distinction is made by comparing an individual's performance with the performance of a standardized norm group. Whether or not the individual is regarded as abnormal depends upon the degree to which he or she deviates from the average of the population in the performance of a particular task. Mercer (1973a, 1973b) argues that neither the pathological nor the statistical approach is adequate for identifying cases of mild mental retardation. In her estimation, the AAMR definition is unsatisfactory because it contains aspects of both approaches. As an alternative, she offers a social-system perspective, which defines mental retardation as "an achieved social status in a social system."

> · The status of mental retardate is associated with a role which persons occupying that status are expected to play. A person's career in acquiring the status of playing the role of mental retardate can be described in the same fashion as the career of a person who acquires any other status such as lawyer, bank president or teacher. (Mercer, 1973b)

Mercer's research findings (1973a, 1973b) suggests that individuals are labeled *mentally retarded* as a function of their performance in social situations. She asserts that the social-system approach is able to account for the disproportionate numbers of school age children from lower socioeconomic groups and minority cultures who have been labeled mildly mentally retarded. She advocates a more conservative definition of mental retardation, one that would operationalize the measurement of adaptive behavior. While the AAMR definitions have become more conservative and have encouraged operationalization of the adaptive behavior measure, Mercer (1973a, 1973b) contends that they are still inadequate. According to her view, multiple norm frameworks must be developed to describe children from different sociocultural settings adequately. That is, children must be described (and labeled if necessary) in relation to their own social and cultural background, without prejudging that background "deviant" or "deficient." Mercer also recommends that the identification and diagnosis of mental retardation be based upon data that include the children's competencies as well as their deficits. Children whose problems are school-specific should not be labeled mentally retarded. Because neither the AAMR definitions nor other traditional approaches incorporate her recommendations, Mercer considers them inadequate for identifying mild or borderline cases of mental retardation, especially among members of minority cultures.

Gold (1980) has developed a different sociological conceptualization of mental retardation. His perspective focuses on the ability or failure of society to provide adequate training and education as the measure of retardation rather than on the failure of the individual. Gold's ideas are reflected in the following statement: "The height of a retarded person's level of functioning is determined by the availability of training technology and the amount of resources society is willing to allocate and not by significant limitations in biological potential" (1980, p. 148).

*Psychometric perspective.* The earliest definitions of mental retardation defined it in descriptive terms involving social incompetence (deficits in adaptive behavior). This approach has several serious shortcomings. First of all, cumbersome, imprecise descriptions of mental retardation made the definitions subjective in their application; moreover, they permitted only the most gross comparisons of individuals who were identified as retarded. These definitions did not admit the possibility of objective diagnoses and bases for comparison. However, with the advent of psychometric techniques (intelligence testing) during the early part of this century, the problem of subjectivity was partially solved. IQ tests were presumed to offer three advantages when used to diagnose mental retardation: *(a)* they were fairly objective; *(b)* they were relatively simple to administer and score; and *(c)* because of standardization, they indicated the relative status of an individual within a group. Yet despite these advantages, the use of conventional intelligence tests in the definition and diagnosis of mental retardation has been widely criticized. Opponents of IQ testing note that anxiety, poor health, and lack of motivation, for example, can detract from a person's performance on any test. When IQ test performance is so affected, children can be permanently labeled because of an inaccurately derived low score. Furthermore, scant attention is given to the error inherent in any derived score. In addition, most standardized IQ tests are heavily verbal; children whose linguistic background is not standard, edited American English (e.g., children who are Black, Asian, Hispanic) are at a serious disadvantage. Critics also contend that traditional mental measures do not consider the demands of the individual's environment. Court cases (e.g., *Larry P. v Riles,* 1972) have articulated one of the most serious criticisms: IQ tests give a biased assessment of intelligence when administered to children from cultural minorities or lower socioeconomic groups. As a result, children from these groups are overrepresented among those labeled mentally retarded.

*Educational perspective.* Kidd (1977) has criticized the 1973 Grossman definition, contending that it did not adequately present the educational perspective. First of all, the 1973 definition implied that subaverage intellectual functioning and deficits in adaptive behavior are separable; Kidd objected to this concept of separation. Second, Kidd objected to the requirement that mental retardation be "manifested during the developmental period." He asserted that, since brain damage manifested during the developmental period is often indistinguishable from brain damage manifested after the developmental period, it is logically indefensible to preclude the later cases.

Robinson and Robinson (1976) have similarly noted that

> the specification that retardation be evident by age eighteen serves the conventional but *perhaps dubious purpose* of differentiating mental retardation from traumatic or deteriorative disorders originating in adulthood. (p. 31)

The 1983 AAMR revision has affirmed that the developmental period be defined as the time between conception and the 18th birthday. Interestingly, only since the passage of the 1986 amendments to the Education for All Handicapped Children Act (P.L. 99–457) has the delivery of services to individuals with special needs begun to approximate the time span included in the developmental period.

Kidd (1979), representing the Council for Exceptional Children—Mental Retardation (CEC-MR) on the Committee on Terminology and Classification, proposed the following working definition:

> Mental retardation refers to subaverage general human cognitive functioning irrespective of etiology(ies), typically manifested during the developmental period, which is of such severity as to markedly limit one's ability to (a) learn and consequently to (b) make logical decisions, choices, and judgments, and (c) cope with one's self and one's environment. (p. 76)

Kidd's educationally oriented definition differed from Grossman's (1973, 1977) earlier definitions in that he proposed that the standard error of measurement be considered at each level of classification of mental retardation. Kidd (1979) also argued that a ceiling IQ of 70 was too low for use in educational settings. He proposed that the ceiling IQ be raised to 75 plus or minus the standard error of measurement. Thus, it would be possible, for example, to identify some individuals with measured Wechsler IQs as high as 78 as mentally retarded.

Many changes in the 1983 AAMR manual resembled Kidd's suggestions and were acknowledged as such:

> While not adopting the CEC-MR recommendations verbatim, the 1983 manual does incorporate the essence of these four points:
> 1. the new "ceiling" IQ for mental retardation is "70 to 75 or more."
> 2. the standard deviation as formerly used was abandoned.
> 3. the deficits in adaptive behavior now must "result from or be associated with" subaverage intellectual functioning.
> 4. flexibility in IQ scores as classification units is provided, e.g., moderate mental retardation—IQ 35 to 40 to 50 to 55. (Kidd, 1983, p. 243)

Kidd (1983) also drew attention to the unequal representation of disciplines among members of the AAMR Committee on Terminology and Classification. Kidd challenged the organization to follow its bylaws, which stipulate that not more than two members from any one discipline are to be represented, more closely.

*Behavioral analysis perspective.*    Bijou (1966) has taken the position that mental retardation should be dealt with from a behavioral perspective. He suggests that

> Developmental retardation be treated as observable, objectively defined stimulus-response relationships without recourse to hypothetical mental concepts such as "defective intelligence" and hypothetical biological abnormalities such as "clinically inferred brain injury." *From this point of view a retarded individual is one who has a limited repertory of behavior shaped by events that constitute his history.* (p. 2)

According to Bijou, research that concentrates upon "the processes that prevent, reduce, or delay the formation of stimulus-response functions will produce more adequate principles and techniques for dealing with retardatoin" (p. 2). He regards the development of retarded behavior as a function of the individual's observable interactions with the social, physical, and biological environment.

Repp (1983) has argued that Bijou's approach to mental retardation is the only approach that addresses the problem with a solution. Bijou's behavioral definition is based upon two important assumptions. First, all behaviors (adaptive and maladaptive) are acquired and maintained according to the same principles of learning. Persons who are retarded are capable of learning; they may learn more slowly than persons who are not retarded, but they do not learn by a different set of rules. The second basic assumption is that all behavior depends on environmental conditions. In support of that assumption are thousands of demonstrations that systematic manipulations of environmental conditions will produce predictable improvements in the behaviors of persons with retardation.

Like Mercer (1973a, 1973b), but for different reasons, Bijou rejects the notion that retardation is a symptom of an underlying condition or pathology. He claims that approaches that have conceptualized retardation as a symptom of more fundamental problems (e.g., subnormal mentality) have contributed relatively little knowledge to the field.

It is difficult to determine whether or not Bijou's behavioral analysis approach to describing mental retardation has had a direct effect upon the AAMR or other formal definitions of mental retardation. Both the behavioral and the AAMR definitions of mental retardation apply only to current levels of functioning, and the condition of mental retardation is regarded as modifiable. Bijou, however, has articulated the most logical basis for considering mental retardation a changeable condition. His definition has had an important impact on the development of educational and therapeutic interventions. Ullman and Krasner (1969) considered Bijou's behavioral analysis approach to have been largely responsible for a productive trend in the development of principles and techniques used to teach students who are retarded.

The relationship between theory and practice in mental retardation is a tenuous one. As the previous sections have focused mainly on conceptual issues of definition, it is useful to look at how definition is put into practice. This section reviews the research that has examined state guidelines in the area of mental retardation, presents some of the current issues concerning the roles of intelligence and adaptive behavior in identification practices, and suggests some possible directions.

A number of studies (Frankenberger, 1984; Huberty, Koller, & Ten Brink, 1980; Patrick & Reschly, 1982; Utley, Lowitzer, & Baumeister, 1987) have analyzed various aspects of state departments of education's guidelines for defining, identifying, and classifying students with mental retardation. These studies have regularly found a great deal of interstate variability. Inconsistency is common in the use of terminology, in the adoption of the federal definition of mental retardation (1983 AAMR definition), and (when adopted) in the implementation of the definition as originally intended.

Utley et al. (1987) surveyed all 50 states and the District of Columbia in the area of definition, identification criteria, and classification. Table 2.5 presents a summary of the data they obtained. Their findings are suggestive of what is currently occurring in this country. Major findings are highlighted below:

☐ only 56% of the states used the term *mental retardation*
☐ 61% of the states cited the AAMR definition
☐ 84% of the states provided intelligence criteria
☐ only 61% of the states emphasized adaptive behavior
☐ only 10% of the states identified instruments, cutoff points, or deficit areas in adaptive behavior
☐ 74% used a classification system of some type (only 14% used the AAMR's four-level system)

These data make one more cautious about claiming dominance for the AAMR definition.

This information represents state-level reports and does not necessarily tell us what happens on a daily basis. Simply stated, IQ has played and continues to play the superordinate role in the decision-making process (Furlong & LeDrew, 1985; Polloway & Smith, 1987; Prout & Sheldon, 1984). Adaptive behavior is not being used in the ways that have been suggested. Brady, Manni, and Winikur (1983), in their three-year study of identification practices, state: "There was no trend over the 3 years of this analysis to lead one to believe that evaluation-team members are becoming more aware of the need to consider adaptive behavior as part of their assessment" (p. 298). Prout and Sheldon (1984), in their examination of vocational rehabilitation

TABLE 2.5   Summary of States and Their Definitions, Eligibility Criteria, and Classification Schemes

| State | Terminology | | Definition | | Intelligence Criteria | | | | Adaptive Behavior | | Classification Schemes | | |
|---|---|---|---|---|---|---|---|---|---|---|---|---|---|
| | AAMD | Other | AAMD PL94-142 | Other | Test Score Ranges | Standard Deviation | Other | NS | Criteria | NS | AAMD | Other | NS |
| AL | yes | no | yes | no | yes | no | no | no | yes | no | no | yes (3-level) | no |
| AK | yes | no | no | yes* | no | yes | no | no | no | yes | yes | no | yes |
| AZ | no | MH | no | yes | no | no | no | yes | no | yes | no | yes (2-level) | no |
| AR | yes | no | yes | no | no | no | no | yes | no | yes | no | yes (3-level) | no |
| CA | no | IEN | yes | no | no | no | no | yes | no | yes | no | no | yes |
| CO | no | IC | no | yes* | no | yes | no | no | no | no | no | no | yes |
| CT | yes | no | no | yes | no | no | yes | no | no | yes | no | yes (3-level) | no |
| DE | no | MH | yes | no | yes | no | no | no | no | yes | no | yes (3-level) | no |
| DC | yes | no | no | yes | yes | no | no | yes | no | yes | no | no | yes |
| FL | yes | no | yes | no | no | yes | no | no | no | yes | no | yes (3-level) | no |
| GA | no | MH | yes | no | yes | no | no | no | no | yes | yes | no | no |
| HI | yes | no | yes | no | yes | no | no | no | yes | no | yes | no | no |
| ID | yes | no | yes | no | yes | no | no | no | no | yes | yes | no | no |
| IL | no | MI | no | yes* | no | no | no | yes | no | yes | no | yes (3-level) | no |
| IN | no | MH | yes | no | yes | no | no | no | no | yes | no | yes (3-level) | no |
| IA | no | MD | yes | no | no | yes | no | no | no | yes | no | yes (2-level) | no |
| KS | yes | no | yes | no | no | no | no | yes | no | yes | no | yes (2-level) | no |
| KY | yes | no | yes | no | yes | no | yes | no | no | yes | yes | no | no |
| LA | yes | no | yes | no | no | yes | no | no | yes | no | yes | no | no |
| ME | no | MD | no | yes* | no | no | no | yes | no | yes | no | yes | no |
| MD | yes | no | yes | no | no | no | yes | no | no | yes | no | no | yes |
| MA | | NS | no | no | no | no | no | yes | no | yes | no | no | yes |
| MI | no | MI | no | yes | no | yes | no | no | no | yes | no | yes (2-level) | no |
| MN | no | MH | yes | no | yes | no | no | no | yes | no | no | yes (3-level) | no |
| MS | no | EH | yes | no | no | yes | no | no | yes | no | no | yes (3-level) | no |

| | | | | | | | | | | | | | |
|---|---|---|---|---|---|---|---|---|---|---|---|---|---|
| MO | yes | no | yes | no | no | no | yes | yes | no | no | no | yes (2-level) | no |
| MT | yes | no | yes | no | no | yes | no | no | no | yes | no | yes (1-level) | no |
| NE | yes | no | no | yes* | no | no | yes | no | no | yes | no | yes (1-level) | no |
| NV | yes | no | yes | no | no | yes | no | no | no | yes | yes | no | yes |
| NH | yes | no | yes | no | no | yes | yes | yes | no | no | no | no | yes |
| NJ | yes | no | no | yes* | no | yes | no | no | no | yes | no | yes (3-level) | no |
| NM | no | MH | yes | no | no | yes | no | no | no | yes | no | yes (3-level) | no |
| NY | yes | no | no | yes* | no | yes | no | no | no | yes | no | no | yes |
| NC | no | MH | no | yes* | no | no | yes | no | no | yes | no | yes (3-level) | no |
| ND | no | MH | no | yes* | yes | no | no | no | no | yes | no | yes (2-level) | no |
| OH | no | DD | yes | no | yes | no | no | no | no | yes | no | no | yes |
| OK | yes | no | yes | no | yes | no | no | no | no | yes | no | yes (2-level) | no |
| OR | yes | no | no | yes* | no | yes | no | no | no | yes | no | no | yes |
| PA | yes | no | no | yes* | yes | no | no | no | no | yes | yes | yes (3-level) | no |
| RI | yes | no | yes | no | yes | no | no | no | no | yes | yes | no | no |
| SC | yes | no | yes | no | yes | no | yes | no | no | yes | no | yes (3-level) | no |
| SD | no | MH | no | yes* | no | no | no | no | yes | yes | no | yes (1-level) | no |
| TN | yes | no | no | yes* | no | yes | no | yes | no | no | yes | no | no |
| TX | yes | no | no | yes* | no | yes | no | yes | no | yes | no | no | yes |
| UT | no | IH | yes | no | yes | no | no | no | no | yes | no | yes (2-level) | no |
| VT | no | LH | no | yes | no | yes | no | no | no | yes | no | no | yes |
| VA | no | EH | yes | no | yes | yes | no | no | no | yes | no | yes (3-level) | no |
| WA | yes | no | yes | no | no | no | no | yes | no | no | no | yes (3-level) | no |
| WV | no | MI | yes | no | yes | yes | no | yes | no | no | no | yes (3-level) | no |
| WI | yes | no | yes | no | no | yes | no | yes | no | no | no | yes (5-level) | no |
| WY | yes | no | yes | no | no | yes | no | no | no | yes | no | no | yes |

aMH = mentally handicapped, MI = mental impairment, MD = mental development/disability, IEN = individuals with exceptional needs.

bEH = educationally handicapped, IH = intellectually handicapped, LI = learning impairment, DD = developmentally disabled, IC = intellectual capacity

c* = includes adaptive behavior concept

dNS = not specified

From "A Comparison of the AAMD's Definition, Eligibility Criteria, and Classification Schemes with State Departments of Education Guidelines" by C. A. Utley, A. C. Lowitzer, and A. A. Baumeister, 1987, *Education and Training in Mental Retardation, 22*, pp. 35–43.

evaluations of clients with mental retardation, found that only 4% of these individuals had any record of formal adaptive behavior assessment in their files.

For a number of plausible reasons, less importance is given to assessment of adaptive behavior than to IQ. Zigler, Balla, and Hodapp (1984) contend that the concept is "too elusive and ill-defined to be a criterion of mental retardation" (p. 218). Zucker and Polloway (1987) offer another explanation:

> The concept of adaptive behavior has neither the psychometric history of IQ nor the stability across settings expected by diagnosticians for other scores. Although these concerns may actually represent strengths of adaptive behavior measures, their effect has been to prevent full utility of the measures. (p. 71)

Whatever the reason, adaptive behavior takes a back seat to intellectual functioning in the decision-making process. This undermines the value of determining typical behavioral regimens and may be a disservice to many students at the margin of eligibility.

It is becoming increasingly obvious that the assessment of adaptive behavior has two dimensions: in school and out of school. To date, when adaptive behavior has been measured, less attention has been given to the in-school dimension. But too heavy a reliance on out-of-school behavior could lead to the virtual elimination of identified mild forms of retardation (Reschly, 1981). Although on one level this sounds appealing, it may fail to address students' needs and best interests.

What options does this situation leave us? We offer four different ideas. The first is to abandon the use of adaptive behavior, as Zigler et al. (1984) suggest. They argue that mental retardation should be defined and assessed solely in terms of intellectual functioning. Problems with this approach arise when we are confronted with students whose linguistic, cultural, and economic backgrounds are significantly different from the norm. A second suggestion is that differential assessment systems be developed. Some of these would incorporate behaviorally or functionally based measures (Zucker & Polloway, 1987). This idea is attractive but improbable at the present time. The third view is grounded in the reality that adaptive behavior will continue to be a second-class citizen in the identification process. Instead of being a criterion, it should play a supporting role in *(a)* justifying eligibility for individuals with IQs above 70; *(b)* questioning the certification of an individual with an IQ below 70 but with acceptable adaptive behavior skills; and *(c)* influencing placement and curricular decisions. This may not be the most desirable solution, but it may be the best compromise now available. The fourth and last perspective is more stouthearted. It argues that we should continue to strive to develop a system in which the two major facets of adaptive behavior play a key role. One conceptualization of such an idea has been developed by Reschly (1988) and is presented in Figure 2.3. The

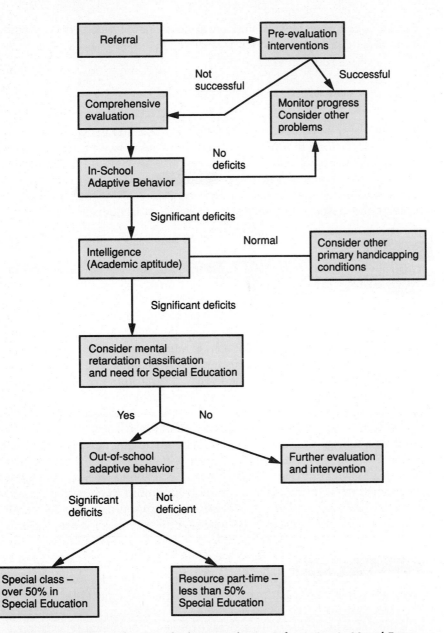

FIGURE 2.3   A Scheme for Use of Adaptive Behavior Information in Mental Retardation Classification

Adapted from Reschly, D. J. (1988). Incorporating adaptive behavior deficits into instructional programs. In G. A. Robinson, J. R. Patton, E. A. Polloway, & L. R. Sargent (Eds.), *Best Practices in Mental Disabilities* (Vol. 2). Des Moines, IA: Department of Education.

overriding goal is to identify students in need and provide services to them in the most appropriate manner.

## INCIDENCE AND PREVALENCE

Prevention and treatment are two of the most pressing issues in the field of mental retardation. In order to determine causal factors and to deliver services and treatment efficiently, professionals have used two estimates of the frequency of mental retardation: **incidence** and **prevalence**. Although the words *incidence* and *prevalence* are considered synonymous in some contexts, they refer to different types of statistical frequencies.

### INCIDENCE

*Incidence* refers to the number of *new* cases identified within a population over a specific period of time. The data for most estimates of incidence are obtained from cases that were clinically identified when an individual entered a type of treatment (Stein & Susser, 1975). Incidence figures are valuable for investigating the causes of a handicap and developing prevention programs. For example, researchers have found that maternal age at a child's birth and the incidence of the chromosomal aberration that results in Down syndrome in the child are related. That relationship was determined by comparing the incidence rates of Down syndrome births with populations of mothers from different age ranges. For instance, a child born to a mother between the ages of 20 and 30 has a 1 in 1500 chance of having Down syndrome; to a mother between 35 and 40, a 1 in 300 chance; to a mother between 40 and 45, a 1 in 70 chance; and to a mother over 45, a 1 in 40 chance of having Down syndrome (Bunker et al., 1972). While researchers have not determined *why* chromosomal aberrations are more frequent among older mothers than younger ones, the relationship between maternal age and the incidence of Down syndrome has suggested possibilities for prevention.

### PREVALENCE

*Prevalence* refers to the total number of cases of a disorder *existing* within a population at a particular place or at a particular time (Dorland, 1957). Prevalence rates are frequently represented as percentages. MacMillan (1982) uses the following equation to express prevalence of mental retardation as a percentage.

$$\text{Prevalence} = \frac{\text{The number of persons who are identified as mentally retarded within a given period of time}}{\text{The total number of persons within that population}} \times 100$$

Unlike incidence, prevalence is not concerned with the number of new cases. Therefore, it is not as useful in determining causal relationships. Prevalence statistics are, however, better than incidence statistics for determining need for services. Need is more accurately determined by directly surveying the population than by relying upon service use (Stein & Susser, 1975).

There are two ways of conceptualizing prevalence: identifiable and true (Grossman, 1983). *Identifiable prevalence* refers to the cases that have come in contact with some system. *True prevalence,* which is a larger figure, indicates that a number of people who may meet the definitional criteria of mental retardation exist unrecognized by our systems. True prevalence would not include those who once met criteria but no longer do so.

For several reasons, variations in estimates of the incidence and prevalence of mental retardation have been found across studies and populations. Among factors influencing the incidence and prevalence of mental retardation are differences in criteria, methodologies, gender, age, community, race, and sociopolitical factors. We look at each of these below.

## VARIATIONS DUE TO DEFINITIONAL PERSPECTIVE

The difficulty of defining retardation is reflected by the number of reviews on the prevalence of mental retardation that mention the imprecision in definition and the general haziness of the concept (e.g., Blatt, 1987; Dunn, 1963; Jastak, MacPhee, & Whiteman, 1963; Kirk, 1962; Masland, Sarason, & Gladwin, 1958; O'Connor, 1966; Osgood, Gorsuch, & McGrew, 1966; Penrose, 1966; Williams, 1963; Zigler et al., 1984). The problem of defining this population was emphasized when Johnson (1959) criticized one of the most widely quoted surveys (Census of Referred Suspected Mental Retardation, conducted in Onondaga County, New York, in 1953). Johnson criticized the Onondaga study because it used an all-inclusive definition of mental retardation and, therefore, possibly reported more cases of mental retardation than actually existed according to generally accepted definitions.

It is not unusual for prevalence figures to be estimated without a survey's ever being conducted. Hypothetical prevalence statistics can be projected from formal definitions of mental retardation that rely entirely upon psychometric data (e.g., Wechsler, 1949) or depend substantially upon such data (e.g., Heber, 1961; Grossman, 1973).

If IQ were the only criterion for defining mental retardation, approximately 2.3% of the population could be considered mentally retarded. In fact, the United States Office of Education reported in 1971–1972 that 2.3% of the school age population was mentally retarded (0.8%, moderate and severe; 1.5%, mild retardation). The President's Committee on Mental Retardation estimated that approximately 3% of the population is mentally retarded. However, the validity of the often-cited figure of 3% prevalence has been seriously challenged. Mercer (1973a) conducted a prevalence survey in a

California community that supported a 1% prevalence. Tarjan, Wright, Eyman, and Keeran (1973) had hypothesized a figure of 1%, feeling that the 3% model assumes that

> *(a)* The diagnosis of mental retardation is based essentially on an IQ below 70; *(b)* mental retardation is identified in infancy; *(c)* the diagnosis does not change; and *(d)* the mortality of retarded individuals is similar to that of the general population. (p. 370)

Tarjan et al. (1973) claimed that these assumptions are not supported by clinical evidence. For example, they report:

> First, the commonly accepted criteria for the clinical diagnosis of mental retardation require that concurrently with a significant impairment in intelligence, as measured by psychometric tests, a similar impairment in adaptive behavior also be present, and that both of these symptoms manifest themselves during the developmental years (Heber, 1961). Many preschool children and adults, however, do not show major impairment in general adaptation even with relatively low IQs. As a consequence, the clinical diagnosis of mental retardation, particularly when it is of mild degree, is age-dependent. It is usually not established before school age and often disappears during late adolescence or young adulthood.
>
> Second, mortality in retarded individuals is inversely related to IQ, with only the mildly retarded having life expectancies which approximate those of the general population. . . . Though 3% of the newborn population will be suspected and even diagnosed as mentally retarded some time during their life, probably during their school years, it is incorrect to assume that at any given time 3% of the population is so identified or is apt to be so diagnosed. Generally, most professionals regard a prevalence figure of 1% or less as the best indicator of reality. (p. 370)

## METHODOLOGICAL VARIATIONS

Farber (1968) has listed four commonly used techniques for estimating the number of individuals who are retarded in a population: genealogical random-test, birth register, period, and census methods.

> The genealogical random-test method involves random sampling of a number of normal individuals to test relatives (usually siblings and parents) for possible mental retardation. The error usually made with this technique is using convenient, easily obtained samples. . . .
>
> The birth register technique involves random sampling from the birth register of a political unit. While it provides a complete sampling list, this method depends upon accuracy of the vital statistics and the residential stability of the persons born in the area. . . .
>
> The period method of estimating the number of mentally retarded individuals involves everyone born or living in a specific area during a certain period of time. This type of investigation is generally feasible in rural areas with low migration rates. . . .

The census method is the most widely used means for estimating the prevalence of mental deficiency. It is independent of rates of migration, fertility, and mortality, but it usually results in underestimation of the rates of mental deficiency in the community. The usual procedure is to contact persons in institutions where the probability of finding mentally retarded individuals is high. For example, Akesson canvassed institutions, hospitals, and clinics who might have contact with the retarded; he consulted with local informants, including ministers, teachers, district nurses, representatives for social organizations, superintendents in homes for the aged and for children, and persons knowledgeable of local conditions. Akesson then examined referred individuals by *(a)* an interview, *(b)* a short screening test, *(c)* the revised Stanford-Binet test (Swedish version), *(d)* objective data concerning the individual's accomplishments and social environment, and finally *(e)* a medical examination. (pp. 56–57)

Most prevalence surveys are conducted by reviewing case files, analyzing agency referral data, or counting tabulated census data. A few studies actually locate the subjects for testing or interviewing. As can be expected, prevalence figures differ markedly based on the method used to calculate them.

## GENDER VARIATIONS

In general, more males than females are identified as mentally retarded at all age levels. Three generally accepted explanations account for these sex differences in prevalence. First, biological defects associated with the X chromosome have a greater probability of being manifested by males than females. Second, it appears that different child-rearing practices and different social demands are associated with sex differences in prevalence. For example, aggressive behavior for males is typically reinforced during child-rearing. An aggressive boy who is mildly retarded may not perceive the differences between appropriate and inappropriate situations for being aggressive. And individuals who exhibit behavior problems have greater chances of being identified as retarded than those who do not (Masland et al., 1958). Finally, society's demands for self-sufficiency traditionally have been higher for males than females (Robinson & Robinson, 1976).

## AGE VARIATIONS

Prevalence figures vary considerably as a function of the age of the individuals identified as mentally retarded (Lewis, 1929; Penrose, 1966). As indicated in Table 2.6, more cases of mental retardation are identified during school years than during pre- and postschool years. The personal and social demands a person must meet change with age. Failure to cope efficiently with social demands may lead to the individual's being labeled mentally retarded. On the other hand, individuals who have been labeled as mentally retarded during their school years are able to shed that label by successfully meeting the demands of adult life. Individuals who are identified during early childhood and whose difficulties continue through adulthood are more apt to be the

TABLE 2.6 Identification and Visibility of Mental Retardation

| MR Classification | Approximate Percentage of Total MR Population | | Age(s) When Identification Typically Occurs | Individual(s) Typically First Recognizing Problems | Individual(s) Typically Confirming Diagnosis of MR | Visibility of Person as MR |
|---|---|---|---|---|---|---|
| | Traditional | New | | | | |
| Mild | 70–75% | 60% | 6 years + | teacher parent | school psychologist diagnostic team | Change with chronological age; tend to be identified upon entry to school and to lose label upon exit from school setting. |
| Moderate | 20% | 32% | 1–5 years | parents physician | physician diagnostic team | For most part, tend to be recognized as MR throughout their lifetimes. |
| Severe/ Profound | 5% | 8% | 0–1 years | physician | physician | Maintain MR distinction throughout their lifetimes. |

more severely affected (Gottlieb, 1975; Mercer, 1973b). Note that the percentages in column 2 ("Approximate Percentage of Total MR Population") differ depending upon the time frame considered. The "traditional" group refers to conditions of 10 to 15 years ago; the "new" group relates more closely to the situation today, accounting for changes that have occurred within this population.

This phenomenon is discussed later in this chapter.

*It is important that children with mental retardation remain in integrated settings whenever possible.*

## VARIATIONS DUE TO COMMUNITY DIFFERENCES

Communities vary in their ability to absorb individuals with limited talents. For example, individuals are more apt to be identified as retarded in urban communities than in rural ones (MacMillan, 1982). That variation has been subject to different interpretations. First, urban communities are generally described as more complex than rural communities. It is commonly believed that the social demands of urban communities are, therefore, more difficult to meet. MacMillan has suggested that individuals with borderline retardation from urban districts are more likely to be identified as mentally retarded because urban districts tend to have better developed referral and diagnostic services. Some marginal cases may never be formally diagnosed in rural districts.

Socioeconomic conditions within communities are also related to differences in prevalence rates. Children who are born and reared in deprived, lower socioeconomic groups are 15 times more likely to be labeled mentally retarded than children from the suburbs (Tarjan et al., 1973). Many attempts have been made to account for the much higher rates of mental retardation among children from lower socioeconomic groups and deprived environments. Prevalence figures indicate that, as the severity of retardation increases, cultural and socioeconomic factors become less pronounced. Just as many wealthy families as poor families have children with severe retardation.

Prevalence figures also vary according to a country's level of development. In less developed countries, the situation is paradoxical, the Committee on Terminology and Classification of the AAMR noted (Grossman, 1983):

In underdeveloped countries lacking mass immunization programs, proper nutrition, hygiene and sanitation, prenatal care for pregnant women, and other public health services, the incidence of mental retardation and other disorders is high. Under these conditions, whereas *incidence* may be high, prevalence may be comparatively lower because of excessive infant mortality. (p. 75)

*This relationship is examined more fully in chapter 5.*

Another relevant fact is that such characteristics as literacy and cognitive ability, which are highly valued in more developed societies, may not be so important in social settings that are largely subsistence oriented.

## VARIATIONS DUE TO SOCIOPOLITICAL FACTORS

Evidence suggests that the number of retarded individuals identified at a given time is influenced significantly by prevailing attitudes, policy, and practices. For instance, since the implementation of P.L. 94-142, the number of students classified as mentally retarded by school systems throughout the United States has dropped substantially. Polloway and Smith (1983) have analyzed federal data in light of these changes for the period 1976–1981. They found that the number of students between the ages of 3 and 21 served under P.L. 94-142 and P.L. 89-313 dropped approximately 13%. An update of

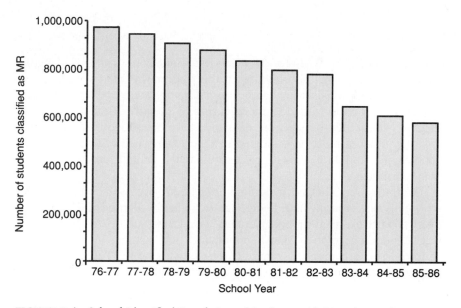

FIGURE 2.4    School-Identified Population of Students with Mental Retardation
(1976–1986)

these changes through 1986 indicates an even more dramatic reduction: a 39% decrease since 1976. (Figure 2.4 graphs these changes.) It is important to note that not all states and, for that matter, local education agencies have experienced decreases; but some areas have seen greater decreases. In the aggregate, however, fewer students are identified as mentally retarded. Furthermore, the mild group has been most affected. The moderate, severe, and profound groups have remained stable.

Why this dramatic change? In large part it is because of sociopolitical factors that have influenced how we identify and serve students who are decidedly below the norm. One of the most important reasons for this change is a more conservative posture on identifying students as mildly retarded, especially if they are from culturally diverse backgrounds. The field is noticeably wary of the misdiagnosis and misplacement of minority group students. Another reason is that a number of higher functioning mildly retarded children are now being served in classes for learning-disabled students. These settings are less stigmatizing than classes for students who are labeled educably mentally retarded. Other factors are also playing a critical role in the changing numbers of retarded students, such as the positive effects of early intervention efforts. Nevertheless, it is important to remember that much of what happens to people who are retarded, including how many of them are so identified, is a function of prevailing opinion.

## FINAL CONSIDERATIONS

The enactment of P.L. 94-142 and its expanded provisions as amended in 1983 and 1986 gave official recognition to the importance of developing case registers of individuals with handicaps. That law required local education agencies to conduct and document efforts to identify all children at risk residing within their jurisdiction. After they have been identified as being at risk, the children must be evaluated to determine whether or not they are handicapped and thus qualify for educational and related services. This task was enormous.

While some child-find programs have been successful, it appears that school districts typically have been unable to identify all the children in their districts who are handicapped. Kennedy and Danielson (1978) pointed out that, depending upon a state's population, the number of unidentified children who are mentally retarded may be significant. The newsletter *A Report on Education of the Handicapped* (1979) suggested that school districts have tended to identify children according to already existing services, not according to the individual needs of the children. The report quoted a high school principal as saying, "It doesn't do any good to identify them [handicapped children] if we can't do a thing about their problem" (p. 5). Another school official acknowledged that the identification of handicapped children "had everything to do with what the evaluator knows the school will be able to do for the child" (p. 5). It appears that, while an increased number and variety of services have recently become available, the numbers and types of new cases identified depend in part upon existing service levels in the community. There are probably many children who are believed to have handicaps but who are not identified by the schools. Parents may not refer their children for several reasons. They may fear stigma. They may be aware of the problem and prepared to deal with the possible stigmatization of their child, but may not realize that, by law, the school is obligated to provide their child with an education and necessary related services. Some parents have also been intimidated by school officials who were not willing to provide services to children with special needs. In many cases, teachers have become discouraged by the apparent inaction (or inappropriate action) taken on referrals. The teachers' discouragement possibly results in their making fewer referrals or making referrals only when they are fairly sure service will be provided. The National Association of State Directors of Special Education (1977) also suggested that, although the numbers of children identified for special education have increased, those numbers depend in part upon services already available.

Most policy decisions result either directly or indirectly in allocations of resources to meet goals. Public policymakers include the president, members of federal and state legislatures, county commissioners, school administra-

# CHILD-FIND PROCEDURES

Because extensive child-find procedures are required by the Education for All Handicapped Children Act, many enterprising efforts have been undertaken to identify children with handicaps who are in need of special education. Conventional techniques include census surveys, mass media, parent questionnaires, agency and physician contacts, and parent-teacher contacts. Many local education agencies have developed attractive and interesting 10- and 30-second television ads. In addition, other creative ideas have been used, including the distribution of child-find information with regular bills by General Telephone in the state of Washington.

In general, there seem to be two approaches to child-find: referral and screening. An example of a brochure used in the referral method is shown below. Basically, this approach uses the mass media or the mail and relies on public response to identify individuals in need of services. The screening method, which is seemingly a more active approach and consequently more costly, looks at a large number of individuals in a given area and tries to identify those people at risk. A relatively common example of a screening technique is yearly hearing examinations administered to elementary school students at the beginning of each school year. With both referral and screening, more thorough assessment follows the initial identification of the child.

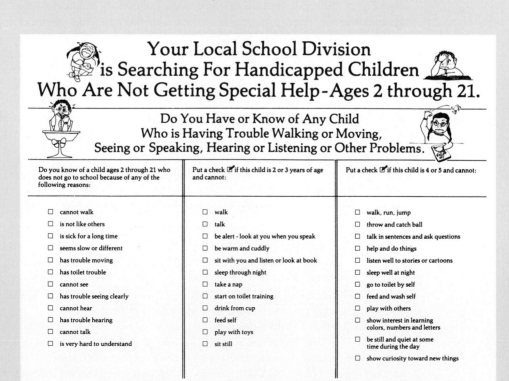

## Your Local School Division is Searching For Handicapped Children Who Are Not Getting Special Help - Ages 2 through 21.

### Do You Have or Know of Any Child Who is Having Trouble Walking or Moving, Seeing or Speaking, Hearing or Listening or Other Problems.

| Do you know of a child ages 2 through 21 who does not go to school because of any of the following reasons: | Put a check ☑ if this child is 2 or 3 years of age and cannot: | Put a check ☑ if this child is 4 or 5 and cannot: |
| --- | --- | --- |
| ☐ cannot walk | ☐ walk | ☐ walk, run, jump |
| ☐ is not like others | ☐ talk | ☐ throw and catch ball |
| ☐ is sick for a long time | ☐ be alert - look at you when you speak | ☐ talk in sentences and ask questions |
| ☐ seems slow or different | ☐ be warm and cuddly | ☐ help and do things |
| ☐ has trouble moving | ☐ sit with you and listen or look at book | ☐ listen well to stories or cartoons |
| ☐ has toilet trouble | ☐ sleep through night | ☐ sleep well at night |
| ☐ cannot see | ☐ take a nap | ☐ go to toilet by self |
| ☐ has trouble seeing clearly | ☐ start on toilet training | ☐ feed and wash self |
| ☐ cannot hear | ☐ drink from cup | ☐ play with others |
| ☐ has trouble hearing | ☐ feed self | ☐ show interest in learning colors, numbers and letters |
| ☐ cannot talk | ☐ play with toys | ☐ be still and quiet at some time during the day |
| ☐ is very hard to understand | ☐ sit still | ☐ show curiosity toward new things |

tors, and special-interest groups such as the Council for Exceptional Children. Most persons who make or affect policies related to people who are mentally retarded are not professionals. All of them, however, are involved in making decisions about the relative importance of different goals and deciding the appropriate expenditures of resources to meet each goal. It is important that policymakers identify the most beneficial set of goals and allocate the necessary resources. The prudence and the equity of policy decisions affecting those with mental retardation depend heavily on the decisionmakers' understanding of the demography of this group. In 1978 the National Institute of Handicapped Research funded a project to establish a means of providing national estimates of the incidence, prevalence, and other demographic characteristics of disabled Americans. The purpose of this effort was to provide an adequate statistical base for policy. Roistacher, Holstrom, Cantril, and Chase (1982) noted that by 1978 more than 80 federal agencies (plus many more state and local agencies) were providing services to people with disabilities. Many of the agencies collected incidence, prevalence, and demographic data, but most agencies had different legislative mandates, which resulted in different purposes for collecting data. Ultimately, the collected data lacked comparability across agencies. Roistacher et al. (1982) noted that different definitions and data collection methodologies made aggregation of data impossible. While definitional and methodological problems can be reduced, Roistacher et al. (1982) stated that developing an adequate statistical base for policy- making would be beneficial. Furthermore, while knowing the numbers of people identified as mentally retarded is important, we are only beginning to know about their demographic and clinical characteristics, attitudes and aspirations, service experiences, and adult outcomes. Collecting such information is important, but data at the national level are needed if policymakers are to make informed decisions.

**SUMMARY**

To understand the term *mental retardation,* we must begin by establishing a definition. Historically, a variety of attempts has been made to concisely state the condition implied by this term and its precursors. The AAMR definitions of Heber and Grossman have most recently reflected the essential dual dimension of the concept of retardation, with the second definition being most widely accepted now. Nevertheless, professionals continue to question and suggest alternatives, and further evolution is probable.

Classification involves delineating specific subgroups of persons who are retarded. This task has given rise to a variety of systems and a host of specific terms. The most commonly used approaches are categorization according to level of severity (e.g. the AAMR system). Although varied terms for retardation in general and levels of retardation in particular continue to be adopted and rejected, we must assume that this process will eventually be less and less fruitful.

Prevalence figures in mental retardation have proven to be difficult to establish; significantly wide ranges have been reported in the literature. Although 3% has been used by the government as an estimate of the prevalence of retardation, there is little consistent support for this figure. Additional concerns in prevalence relate to variations based on age, gender, community environment and sociopolitical factors.

# CHAPTER 3

# Assessment of Mental

# Retardation

E ducational assessment of students who are exceptional may be performed for one of two reasons: classification or educational programming. Wallace and Larsen (1978) capture the essence of this distinction when they state that educational assessment techniques are administered

1. To identify and sometimes label for administrative purposes those children experiencing learning problems who will probably require special educational help, and
2. To gather additional information that might be helpful in establishing instructional objectives and remedial strategies for those children identified as handicapped learners. (p. 5)

Administratively, **assessment** implies collecting information on an individual for the purpose of making decisions about that person. The assessment process, as described by Salvia and Ysseldyke (1985), refers to the comprehensive gathering of data.

Assessment in educational settings is a multifaceted process that involves far more than the administration of a test. When we assess students, we consider the way they perform a variety of tasks in a variety of settings or contexts, the meaning of their performances in terms of the total functioning of the individual, and likely explanations for those performances. Good assessment procedures take into consideration the fact that anyone's performance on any task is influenced not only by the demands of the task itself but also by the history and characteristics the individual brings to the task and by factors inherent in the setting in which the assessment is carried out. (p. 5)

The first goal of assessment may be to identify a child as handicapped—for instance, to find out whether his intellectual performance and adaptive

*Individualized education is crucial for students throughout their schooling.*

behavior fit the definition of mental retardation. Students who are mentally retarded may be assessed in order to classify them or to determine current strengths and weaknesses. Regardless of the immediate intent, the ultimate goal of educational assessment is to provide an appropriate program and/or treatment plan for the students.

Tests have historically been used for the purpose of making classification and placement decisions. Specific criteria establish the nature and degree of retardation of individual students. Many state education agencies recommend that children receive individual psychoeducational evaluations and be classified before they are placed in special education, and most states prescribe the nature of the evaluation for different categorical placements. For example, as we have seen, one criterion for mental retardation is an IQ of 70 or below on such standardized measures of intelligence as the Wechsler Intelligence Scale for Children—Revised (WISC-R) or the Stanford-Binet along with impairments in adaptive behavior, as clinically determined. What follows is a conceptual look at intelligence and adaptive behavior accompanied by examples of commonly used assessment instruments.

## THEORIES OF INTELLIGENCE

Intelligence can be called the ability to adapt, achieve, solve problems, interpret incoming stimuli to modify behavior, accumulate knowledge, or respond to items on an intelligence test. When psychologists and educational specialists were asked to identify the important elements of intelligence, the respondents listed as important (Snyderman & Rothman, 1987; numbers represent the percent of respondents checking the item): abstract thinking or reasoning (99.3), problem-solving (97.7), capacity to acquire knowledge (96.0), memory (80.5), adaptation to one's environment (77.2), mental speed (71.7), linguistic competence (71.0), mathematical competence (69.9), general knowledge (62.4), creativity (59.6), sensory acuity (24.4), goal-directed (24.0), and achievement-motivated (18.9). Diverse concepts of intelligence have been formulated by theorists in the field. Robinson and Robinson (1976) analyzed theories and found three themes common to most definitions of intelligence.

1. The capacity to learn
2. The total body of acquired knowledge
3. Adaptability to environmental demands

*Capacity to learn* refers to an individual's ability to benefit from education. *Acquired knowledge* includes all the concepts and information that the individual has learned up to this point, as well as that person's ability to learn. *Adaptive aspects of intelligence* are those that enable people to fit themselves into their environment and to adjust successfully to environmental changes. Theories that describe intelligence as a learning capacity or as the ability to adapt assume that intelligence is an innate quality—an inborn aptitude or potential for intelligent behavior. But equating intelligence with acquired knowledge emphasizes previous achievement, not potential. The difference between the instruments used to measure these two types of attributes, both called *intelligence,* is the difference between an aptitude test and an achievement test—a significant variation.

Early theorists posited several important definitions that have influenced what we believe about intelligence today. Terman (1921) believed that intelligence varies directly with the ability to think abstractly. In his words

> It cannot be disputed . . . that in the long run [those who] . . . excel in abstract thinking . . . eat while others starve, survive epidemics, master new continents, conquer time and space, and substitute religion for magic, science for taboos and justice for revenge. [Those who] excel in conceptual thinking could, if they wished, quickly exterminate or enslave all [those] . . . notably their inferiors in this respect. (p. 128)

Most early definitions of intelligence described it as a unitary trait, that is, a single, indivisible factor. David Wechsler (1944), author of the four Wechsler intelligence scales (1955, 1966, 1974, 1981), broke with this viewpoint when he described intelligence as an aggregate phenomenon composed of many discrete mental abilities. He also proposed that other factors such as purposiveness, drive, and incentive influence people's level of intellectual functioning and, therefore, their scores on an intelligence test.

Wechsler's scales, which are based on his particular view of the nature of the intellect, assess a variety of specific abilities and yield subtest scores as well as a global index.

In discussing theories of intelligence, it is important to mention that a theory has three functions: to make sense out of chaos, to assist in predicting outcomes, and to facilitate change. A theory about intelligence takes the complex behavior of human beings and tries to make some sense out of it, e.g., "They do that because they are not very intelligent." As the theory develops and solidifies, predictions may be made: "This person is functioning in the dull normal range of intelligence and will probably experience difficulty learning through traditional instruction." A viable theory of intelligence not only helps to explain and predict behavior or events, but also may suggest ways to change things, e.g., "This individual, placed in a more stimulating yet controlled environment, might acquire more knowledge and develop more skills than in a traditional learning environment."

Until research unearths additional information about cerebral functioning, we must realize that intelligence is only a hypothetical construct. It does not exist in any concrete form; it cannot be located by probing around in the body. Positing a construct called intelligence gives theorists a conceptual framework within which to explain individual differences and measure them. The construct is, as Maloney and Ward (1978) explain, a "shorthand way of classifying or grouping a set of behaviors which may be broadly labeled 'intelligent'" (p. 88). Accordingly, intelligence tests sample a cluster of behaviors from which we infer the presence and level of intelligence, and the IQ score is an index of how well these behaviors were performed. An IQ score is neither a brain cell count nor the measured amount of some wondrous substance embedded between layers of gray matter. Yet most people would place IQ in the same class as birthdates and fingerprints—as a personal description that does not change. This is an unfortunate misinterpretation of a scientific theory with colloquial connotations. For one thing, the validity of IQ tests as measures of intelligence is questionable. For another, intelligence per se has never been adequately defined. Consequently, there is little reason to regard an *IQ* as anything more than a score on an *IQ test.*

Still, if we keep in mind its limitations, the concept of intelligence is a valuable theoretical tool. Speaking directly to educators, Edwards and Scannel (1968) emphasize that it is important for teachers to understand that intelligence refers to two aspects—"the innate potential of the individual and the functional expression of the potential as usable and used ability" (p. 7). They further emphasize that innate potential is physiological, while the functional aspects are behavioral. Educators must concern themselves with the behavioral domain, since only in this arena do educational diagnosis and treatment occur. Regardless of the preponderance of definitions of intelligence, intelligence is still a hypothetical construct; it is inferred from tests and behavior. In other words, behavior reflects intelligence. An operationally defined theoretical construct of intelligence is useful to the extent that it is helpful in thinking about people. For teachers, the concept of intelligence is useful when it helps them constructively formulate teaching strategies and make placement decisions.

## NATURE VERSUS NURTURE

If teachers view intelligence as biologically based, fixed, or predominantly inherited, they may see their job as being disseminators of materials for students to consume. This position assigns learning and nonlearning predominantly to the child—if the child does not learn, it is his or her own fault. But if teachers view intelligence as something that can be cultivated, altered, or facilitated, they may see their job as being instrumental to the process. This position enables them to evaluate children's learning and nonlearning as an indication of their effectiveness as teachers.

The varying concepts of intelligence and the ways children learn are directly related to the nature-nurture controversy; that is, either intelligence is innate, or it is learned. Actually, few authorities claim that it is an either/or proposition. Most concede that intellectual functioning is shaped by a combination of biological and environmental factors. It is partly fixed and partly malleable (Snyderman & Rothman, 1987).

The bulk of the continuing debate concerns the relative proportions of the two major ingredients that combine to mold intelligence. It is generally agreed that a person's upbringing may nourish or starve his cognitive growth to any level within the constraints of his biologically endowed potential. But how rigid are those constraints? How powerful are environmental forces? How mutable are the effects of this interaction? Ingalls (1978), for one, says that it is useless to try to assign percentages to the relative influences of heredity and environment. Even the most genetically promising mind can have its development retarded if the environment provides no stimulation. Ingalls illustrates with an analogy of plant growth.

> The height of a given plant is a result of the particular gene type of the seed, the quality of the soil, the amount of rain, and numerous other factors. If a given plant grows to be four feet tall, it makes no sense to say that it achieved this height because of the seed variety. It is equally nonsensical to say that 80% of the height was due to the genes. (p. 41)

Even though the logic of this approach seems irrefutable, Jensen (1966, 1969, 1980, 1981) has insisted that genes and prenatal development account for 80% of the variance in intelligence, while only 20% of the variance can be accounted for by the environment. Citing research studies, growth figures, and models of intelligence, Jensen has presented a convincing case. He

*Arthur Jensen is a leading advocate of the genetic view of intelligence.*

objects to the philosophy that cites environmental deprivation and test bias as the reasons for IQ variance between cultural groups. He believes that the major determinant is genetic, not environmental, input. From examining such compensatory education programs as Head Start, Jensen has concluded that growing up in a severely impoverished environment can stunt a child's intellectual growth, but that no amount of enrichment can make him more intelligent than his potential allows. Additional mental abilities other than those normally tapped by intelligence tests, however, are malleable and deserve attention from those who wish to equalize educational opportunity.

Thus far, we know that environmental influences have a substantial impact on measured intelligence (Hunt, 1961). This finding, coupled with theories of intelligence like Feuerstein's (1979; Feuerstein et al., 1981) theory of cognitive modifiability (which suggests ways of facilitating the behavioral change associated with intellectual growth), compels educators and social scientists to arrange environments that stimulate intellectual growth. If measured intelligence is sensitive to environmental influence, it is imperative that learners be tested and observed periodically so that the educational program may allow for changes in their intellectual and adaptive growth.

## INTELLIGENCE TESTING

The earliest attempts to measure cognitive functioning were tests of sensory abilities assumed to indicate the presence or absence of the single entity called *intelligence.* in the 1890s, for instance, James McK. Cattell devised a mental test that appraised such discrimination abilities as estimating the length of a 10-second interval and distinguishing tactile sensations. These early tests, though able to sort out certain measurable differences between individuals, failed to provide any worthwhile measure of cognitive ability largely because they lacked **validity**. That is, the results of these tests were poor predictors of school achievement, success in life, and other ostensible indexes of intelligence.

## BINET

The first effective test of intellectual ability was devised in the early 1900s by French psychologist Alfred Binet. In 1904 the Minister of Public Instruction in Paris appointed Binet to a commission to study the problem of educating subnormal children. It was believed that children who were failing in school and disrupting normal classrooms would profit more from slower-paced instruction in special classes. Binet and his colleague Theodore Simon set out to devise an instrument to sift children who are mentally deficient out of the school age population. Their first test, the 30-item Measuring Scale of Intelligence, was published in 1905, then revised in 1908 and in 1911. The Binet-Simon Scale far surpassed any of the earlier measures in predicting school achievement because, instead of assessing sensory functions, it tested such mental abilities as comprehension, memory, and reasoning, which are necessary for scholastic success. Binet's early work had been in the study of individual differences, and he had criticized the use of sensory tests to discriminate between bright and dull people. He did not agree with his predecessors that slow reflexes were sufficient grounds for concluding that a person was lacking intelligence. Nor did he find it necessary to examine all areas of interindividual differences. Consequently, the Binet-Simon Scale sampled those higher level, complex processes that the authors believed to be the essential elements of intelligence.

Initially Binet considered memory and judgment to be the most essential elements. He later discovered, however, that those with good memories are not always the most intelligent. "One may have good sense and lack memory. The reverse is also common" (Binet & Simon, 1916/1961, p. 94). The first Binet scale dealt heavily with the assessment of judgments. Poor judgment was considered to include not just simple response errors but also absurd errors.

Binet and Simon went to great lengths to differentiate between the concept of general or natural intelligence and that of acquired intelligence, the knowledge gained through instruction. They sought to measure raw intelligence or capacity to learn and were not interested in measuring what had been learned or the "degree of instruction which the subject possessed" (Binet & Simon, 1916/1961, p. 93). Because reading and writing are learned skills, their test of intelligence was constructed so as not to measure reading and writing. The initial version, for example, instead tested the child's ability to identify pictured objects, repeat a three-digit series, reproduce geometric figure drawings, define abstract words, and perform similar nonacademic tasks. The following case study, cited by Binet and Simon (1916/1961), illustrates their concern with tapping natural over acquired intelligence.

> One of the cases, to us a very striking one, was that of little Germaine, a child of 11 years who came from a Paris school. Her parents, having carried their Penates to Levallois-Perret, had sent their child to one of the schools for girls in that city. But the directress refused little Germaine under the pretext that her school was full; in reality, because the child was extremely backward. In fact, the retardation was at least 3 years; her reading was hesitating, almost syllabic; faults of orthography spoiled her dictation exercise. She wrote the following phrase under our eyes: The pretly litl grils stude the flwr that the gathrd yesty (which signifies: "The pretty little girls studied the flowers that they gathered yesterday"). Her number work was equally poor. She was asked, "If I have 19 apples, and eat 6 of them, how many have I left?" The child, reckoning mentally, said "12" which is inexact but reasonable. Trying it on paper, she was lost; she made an addition instead of subtraction and found 25. In other calculations she showed that she had the power to reckon mentally, but not on paper; in the last case she made the addition correctly when she should have subtracted. It is, however, a frequent, not to say constant, rule that those backward in arithmetic do the operations better than the problems, and do more easily operations of addition and multiplication than those of subtraction and division. In short, this child had a retardation of 3 years; but knowledge of her scholarship was lacking. On the other hand her wide-awake and mischievous air and the vivacity of her speech made a favorable impression on us. We made the test of intelligence and that showed us that her intelligence was normal; she was backward scarcely a year. This is a characteristic example which shows the use of our measuring scale. (p. 110)

*Mental age.* The 1908 revision of Binet and Simon's scale introduced the notion that children gain in cognitive ability as they mature—hence, the concept of **mental age** (MA). Essentially, MA is a reading of the child's intellectual level (as gauged by his performance on a mental measurement test) recorded independently of chronological age. A child who passed on the Binet scale only those items that an average 5-year-old should pass would earn a mental age of 5. A 7-year-old child with a mental age of 5 would be considered intellectually subaverage; a 3-year-old with the same MA would be regarded as bright. To arrive at this statistic, the revised Binet test items were arranged by age levels from 3 to 10, with five additional problems each for the ages of 12, 15, and adult. The computation of MA is simple; a basal level (level on test where all items are passed) and a ceiling level (level on test where all items are failed) are determined. The MA score is obtained by adding to the basal level a specified number of months' credit for each item passed above the basal item. For instance, if an 8-year-old child solved all the problems through age 8, passed two out of five tests at age 9, one out of five tests at age 10, and failed all at age 12, the MA after all credits were assigned would be 8⅗ years, or 8 years and 7 months.

*Intelligence quotient (ratio).*   In the 1916 revision of the Binet test, Terman, influenced by Stern (1912), introduced the concept of an **intelligence quotient** (IQ) as a better scoring index than mental age. Binet had proposed that a 2-year lag in mental age, as defined by performance on his test, be the criterion for judging a child mentally retarded. But Stern explained that the absolute difference between MA and chronological age (CA) meant a greater mental deficit for younger than for older children. A 1-year delay is much more serious for a 4-year-old than for a 15-year-old. To account for this, Stern suggested the computation of a **ratio IQ score**, which Terman incorporated into his test. The intelligence quotient is found by dividing an individual's mental age by his chronological age and multiplying the quotient by 100. The formula is:

$$\frac{MA}{CA} \times 100 = IQ$$

In the previous example, the 8-year-old child with an MA of 8 years 7 months (96 + 7 months) would have an IQ of 107.

$$\frac{96+7}{96} \times 100 = 107$$

The theoretical average child, whose MA equals his CA, will have an IQ of 100. Using this method, the absolute difference between MA and CA has a diminishing influence on IQ as the child gets older. To return to our example of a 1-year deficit, the 5-year-old with an MA of 4 has earned an IQ score of 80 (20 points below average), whereas the 1-year deficit in the 15-year-old's MA gives him a score of 93 (only 7 points below average).

   The major advantage of ratio IQ over simple MA is that it gives an index of a child's IQ test performance relative to others in his age group. As the child grows, he gains in cognitive ability, but as long as his gains are average for his age, his IQ score will not change. The problem with this statistic, as with any ratio using CA as the divisor, is that most people's mental development slows to a halt at some time in their late teens, while their chronological age continues to increase. As a result, the ratio MA/CA progressively decreases as the average person ages past 18, and his intelligence quotient diminishes accordingly. To avoid implying that adults become more feebleminded with every passing day, CA must be held at some point between 16 and 18 when computing ratio IQ for adults; yet the fact that mental age plateaus at different times for different people makes choosing a universally valid cutoff CA impossible. Stern's ratio IQ is an appropriate tool for measuring the intelligence test performances of children and early adolescents, but its use for adults is questionable.

*Intelligence quotient (deviation).*   David Wechsler, author of the intelligence scales that have replaced the Stanford-Binet as favorites for school and psychological use, corrected this flaw by devising a new index—the **deviation IQ score**.

The Wechsler IQ is not found by applying a derived MA to a ratio formula, but by converting the raw scores on each subtest to standard scores normalized for the examinee's age group, and adding them for a total standard score, called the *deviation IQ*. Wechsler reasoned that intelligence is normally distributed; that is, the majority of people will score at or around the mean, and progressively fewer people will achieve scores that spread out in either direction from the mean. Thus, a group of IQ scores can be portrayed as a normal curve with an average (mean) of 100 and a standard deviation that is the same (15) at every age level. The normal curve is sometimes also referred to as the *bell-shaped* or the *Gaussian curve*.

Terman and Merrill (1960) adopted the deviation IQ as a scoring standard for the 1960 revision of the Stanford-Binet, though they chose a standard deviation of 16 rather than 15. The 1960 Stanford-Binet manual includes tables for converting MA to deviation IQ. The WISC and the Stanford-Binet (Terman & Merrill, 1973) were mathematically constructed to fit the percentages indicated within the curve.

The advantage of the deviation IQ is that the standing of an individual child can be compared with the scores of children of the same age, and the intervals from age to age remain the same. That is, the differences disclosed at each age level all fall under the percentages and percentiles shown under the normal curve. For instance, a child of age 5 who scored one standard deviation below the mean would earn an IQ on the WISC of 85 and would score roughly at the 16th percentile; therefore, appproximately 84% of the 5-year-olds would score above him (34.13 + 34.13 + 13.59 + 2.14 + 0.13 = 84.12%). The same would hold true for a 7-year-old who scored one standard deviation below the mean.

## WECHSLER

Wechsler incorporated the notion of a general intelligence consisting of specific intellectual abilities into the development of a series of intelligence scales beginning in 1939 with the Wechsler-Bellvue scales for adults. In 1949, he published his Intelligence Scale for Children (WISC) ages 6 through 16, which he revised to its present form (WISC-R) in 1974. The Wechsler Adult Intelligence Scale (WAIS) first appeared in 1959 to replace the original Bellvue Scale for use with individuals 16 years and older and was revised to its present form (WAIS-R) in 1981. For children between 4 and 6½ years old, Wechsler published the Preschool and Primary Scale of Intelligence (WPPSI) in 1966. The Wechsler tests are the mental measurements most often encountered by school administrators and classroom teachers.

When they first appeared, the Wechsler scales were distinguished by several unique features generally considered to be changes for the better (Ingalls, 1978). For one thing, every Wechsler scale is subdivided into smaller tests. The WISC, for example, consists of 10 subtests with two alternates, five verbal subtests with one alternate and five performance (nonverbal) subtests with one alternate. Each subtest is treated separately and is theoretically said to measure a different ability. Combined they assess global intellectual capacity. Wechsler (1939) believed that the Binet test does not tap performance, an important facet of intelligence. He developed a performance scale with problem-solving items that require judgment, reasoning, foresight, and planning but depend little on verbal ability.

Generally speaking, the verbal portion of the Wechsler tests requires more communication and interaction between the person taking the test and the test administrator than the nonverbal portion. On the performance section, the examinee works more independently of the examiner, and relatively little social interaction is required. The WISC-R provides estimates of the individual's levels of functioning in verbal and nonverbal ability as well as an estimate of overall intelligence in the form of a Verbal IQ, a Performance IQ, and a Full Scale IQ. The subtests of the WISC-R are listed and described in Table 3.1.

## STANFORD-BINET

Lewis Terman adapted the Binet scale for American use in 1916 while at Stanford University, and his version has since been revised in this country four times—in 1937 and 1960 by Terman and Maud Merrill, in 1973 by R. L. Thorndike (Terman & Merrill, 1973), and in 1986 by Thorndike, Hagen, and Sattler. The 1937, 1960, and 1973 forms of the Stanford-Binet included such materials as toys and miniature objects (beads, balls, cars, and dolls), which examinees were instructed to manipulate in various ways, and booklets and pictures (of animals and household objects, and so on) about which they had to answer questions. Examinees were also required to draw geometric figures and to respond to questions and problems presented orally. The 1973 Binet was difficult to administer, time-consuming, and often frustrating for the subject to take. Although a classic in its time, it began to lose its share of the market, which led to its revision as the Fourth Edition, more commonly known as S-B IV. According to Thorndike, Hagen, and Sattler (1986a), the S-B IV was developed "*(a)* to help differentiate between students who are mentally retarded and those with specific learning disabilities; *(b)* to help educators and psychologists understand why a particular student is having difficulty learning; *(c)* to help identify the gifted; and *(d)* to study the development of cognitive skills of individuals from ages 2 to adult" (p. 2).

In the Stanford-Binet Intelligence Scale: Fourth Edition (Thorndike et al., 1986a), the term *intelligence* has been replaced by *cognitive development*. The terms *intelligence, IQ,* and *mental age* are not used in the Fourth Edition anywhere in the administration or technical manual (Thorndike, Hagen, & Sattler, 1986b). The term *Standard Age Score* (SAS) replaces IQ. Five SASs, are obtained, one for each of the four areas measured (Verbal Reasoning, Abstract/Visual Reasoning, Quantitative Reasoning, and Short-Term Memory),

TABLE 3.1    WISC-R Subtests

| Subtest | Content | Correlates or Performance Requirements |
|---|---|---|
| Information | Questions of fact; general knowledge | Rote memory; educational level; early experience |
| Similarities | Questions requiring grouping | Verbal reasoning; abstract thinking; concept formation |
| Arithmetic* | Questions requiring mental calculations | Recent memory; concentration; ability to calculate |
| Vocabulary | Defining words | Word knowledge; early experience and education |
| Comprehension | Questions requiring judgment and practical decision-making concerning problems of everyday life; proverbs | Judgment or common sense; emotional control; socialization |
| Digit Span (Optional) | Repetition of numbers presented orally forward and backward | Immediate recall; passive attention |
| Picture Completion | Requires identifying missing parts in line drawings | Concentration; visual discrimination; logical thinking |
| Picture Arrangement* | Requires ordering of cartoon frames presented out of sequence | Visual organization; social awareness or competence |
| Block Design* | Requires reproduction of abstract | Visual organization; planning; visual-motor coordination |
| Object Assembly* | Requires assembling puzzles representing real objects | Visual organization; visual-motor coordination |
| Coding* | Requires copying symbols in order | Psychomotor speed; concentration; associative learning; visual-motor coordination |
| Mazes | Requires solution of maze puzzles | Planning; visual-motor coordination |

Asterisk indicates timed test.

and the Test Composite. The Composite SAS is a deviation score that is similar, if not identical, to the deviation IQ score.

The S-B IV is an individually administered test based on a three-level hierarchical model of cognitive abilities. At the top of the model is *g*, the *general reasoning* factor. The next level builds on the work of Cattell (1963) and divides *g* into three broad factors: Crystallized Abilities, Fluid-Analytic Abilities, and Short-Term Memory. Crystallized Abilities are cognitive factors needed to acquire and use information in order to deal with verbal and quantitative concepts; Fluid-Analytic Abilities are the cognitive skills needed for solving new problems involving nonverbal or figural stimuli; and Short-Term Memory is a measure of the individual's ability to retain

*Lewis Terman conceived of intelligence as a unitary factor and incorporated that concept into his Stanford-Binet Intelligence Tests. (Courtesy of The Archives of the History of American Psychology)*

information until it can be stored for long-term memory. The third level of the model divides Crystallized Abilities into Verbal Reasoning and Quantitative Reasoning, while Fluid-Analytic Abilities are identified by Abstract/Visual Reasoning. Short-Term Memory has no comparable third-level division. Figure 3.1 illustrates the model and the tests that measure each of the areas.

Each of the items represented in the 15 tests of the S-B IV is arranged in levels of increasing difficulty and designated by the letter *A, B, C,* etc. Each level has two items of approximately equal difficulty. For each test the examiner must establish a basal and a ceiling age. The multistage format begins with the Vocabulary Test, a routing test that determines the entry level for the other tests. From the results of the Vocabulary Test, the examiner finds the entry level for the remaining tests in the Entry-Level Chart on the back cover of the record booklet. The intersection of the appropriate row (chronological age) and column (highest pair of vocabulary items administered) determines the entry level (A–Q) for the remaining tests.

No more than 13 tests are given to any subject, and the authors recommend several abbreviated versions. The raw scores of each test item are converted to SASs. The Composite SAS has a mean of 100 with a standard deviation of 16 (so comparisons can be made with the Form L–M scores),

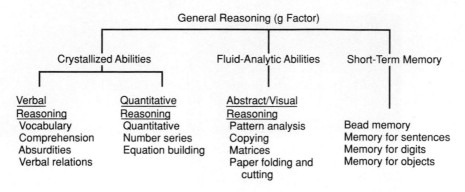

FIGURE 3.1    S-B IV Model

while the individual test SASs have a mean of 50 and a standard deviation of 8.

The S-B IV was anxiously anticipated, in the hope that it would be a superior instrument, but it has been received with mixed reviews. In its first published form it contained inaccuracies, and replacement manuals for it did not appear until a year after the kit itself was released for use. What was expected to be additional help, an expanded guide by Delaney and Hopkins (1987), for the greater part only replicated the Administration, Scoring, and Technical manuals (Thorndike et al., 1986a, 1986b). Hopkins (1988) tried to defend S-B IV by citing the response of Elizabeth Hagen (one of the coauthors of S-B IV): "It reminded her of the words on a tee shirt worn by a burly construction worker—I'm *not* Perfect, but I Have Many Parts That Are *Very Good*" (p. 44). Reynolds (1988) suggested that the Binet tradition should die gracefully. Walker (1987) ends his review of the S-B IV with, "Under the circumstances it would have seemed more fair to Alfred Binet to rename the test altogether." But Spruill (1988) adds, "In spite of numerous problems the Fourth Edition will continue to be around for many years—after all it is still THE BINET."

## OTHER INTELLIGENCE TESTS

Although the WISC-R and Stanford-Binet individual tests of intelligence have become very popular within the schools, there are also other intelligence tests for individuals. Many of these are readily available, easy to give, and require only 15 or 30 minutes to administer. These advantages increase their popularity, but test administrators and interpreters have a responsibility to remember such factors as the standard error of measurement, the standard deviation, the testing conditions, the socioeconomic level of the examinee, the standardization sample, and the purpose of testing. Those who use the results of intelligence tests must keep in mind the specific functions of the tests: to predict school performance, to classify individuals for instruction and research, or to discover patterns of abilities and disabilities that have *educational* relevance (Smith, 1968).

One of the most widely used individual intelligence tests other than the Binet and Wechsler scales is the Slosson Intelligence Test (SIT) (Slosson, 1971). The SIT is a relatively quick screening test that requires little psychometric training to administer or score. It is similar in design and content to the Stanford-Binet (many of the items are identical) and uses a comparable scoring procedure. A basal and a ceiling level are determined, and correctly answered items in between are credited to the basal score. The age score obtained may be converted to a ratio IQ. The SIT is a popular instrument, and some states permit its use in placement decisions. The problem with this procedure is that its function as a screening device is to draw out of a larger group those who need a closer look—that is, it should *overselect* candidates for special attention. In contrast, instruments used for judging whether or not a child requires special class placement should tend to *underselect*. According to the prevailing educational philosophy today, any error in the placement process should be in favor of keeping the student in the regular education classroom, the mainstream of services.

The Kaufman Assessment Battery for Children (K-ABC) (Kaufman & Kaufman, 1983) has gained acceptance as a viable instrument for measuring intellectual functioning. It is an individually administered norm-referenced assessment battery, measuring both intelligence and achievement in children whose CAs are between 2.5 and 12.5.

The theoretical basis for this instrument is closely tied to concepts of information-processing that have been derived from the work of cognitive psychologists and neuropsychologists. According to this theory, two different processing abilities make up intellectual ability: sequential processing and simultaneous processing. Sequential processing involves dealing with items of information one after another. In simultaneous processing, however, one takes care of items of information at one time and as a whole. Subtests based on this conceptualization have been developed to assess the different abilities. Besides the two scales that measure these abilities, there are two additional scales: an achievement scale and a nonverbal scale. The nonverbal scale provides another way to assess children who are atypical by combining certain subtests that can be administered nonverbally and require nonverbal responses from the child.

The three major scales and their corresponding subtests are:

Sequential Processing Scale
   Hand Movements
   Number Recall
   Word Order
Simultaneous Processing Scale
   Magic Window (partial picture is presented)
   Face Recognition

    Gestalt Closure (partially drawn figure)

    Triangles

    Matrix Analogies

    Spatial Memory

    Photo Series

Achievement Scale

    Expressive Vocabulary

    Faces and Places

    Arithmetic

    Riddles

    Reading/Decoding

    Reading/Understanding

The K-ABC has become popular with many psychometrists across the nation, even though it requires them to adjust their diagnostic and interpretive skills. Salvia and Ysseldyke (1985) have some cautionary notes about the K-ABC:

> Simultaneous and sequential processing are proposed as measures of intelligence. However, such an orientation to intellectual assessment is quite revolutionary. For many diagnosticians, acceptance of the K-ABC's orientation will require a considerably larger base of research support. We believe that the way to cope with novel theoretical orientations is to defer acceptance until a firm base of research indicates their validity. Until such research is available, patience and skepticism may serve the tester well. (p. 458)

Readers are referred to the fall 1984 issue of the *Journal of Special Education,* which is devoted to the K-ABC.

Inappropriate placement of children from bilingual and minority backgrounds in classes for the mentally retarded is one very unfortunate outcome of basing placement decisions upon single scores from intelligence tests, particularly tests that require a great deal of knowledge derived from white, middle-class American culture. Children who grow up in non-Anglo subcultures will naturally score lower on such tests than children from the dominant cultural group. Concern with this type of test bias has sparked the development of a number of "culture-free" measures, which attempt to eliminate all cultural factors that might favor one group over another. One such test is Raven's Progressive Matrices (Raven, 1958). This device attempts to measure pure abstract reasoning ability uninfluenced by prior knowledge. The test items all follow the same format: The child is shown a matrix of abstract designs with one missing element, which he must supply. Raven's and tests like it (Cattell's Culture-Fair Intelligence Test, Porteus Mazes) use no language, except for the instructions, in order to eliminate the cultural influences inherent in language.

Handicapping conditions present another set of influences limiting the usefulness of conventional intelligence scales. Adapting items from traditional tests to accommodate test-takers who are handicapped—for example, reading test questions to examinees who are blind—is only half the solution. The results will remain somewhat biased if the subject who is handicapped is compared to a standardization sample that is nonhandicapped, whose acculturation is different. The most appropriate measures for populations that are special are those few that are designed for and have as their norm groups with specific handicaps. The Nebraska Test of Learning Aptitude (Hiskey, 1966) is designed to assess the learning capacity of children ages 3 to 16 who are deaf and hearing impaired, and it provides separate normative data for each group. The examiner, who must take care to use the appropriate set of norms when administering the test, pantomimes instructions to the subjects who are deaf and reads aloud to the children who can hear. The Arthur Adaptation of the Leiter International Performance Scale (Arthur, 1950) is an untimed, entirely nonverbal device for assessing the intelligence of children 2 to 12 years old who are hearing impaired, verbally handicapped, or not facile with the English language.

Several devices currently on the market attempt to appraise the mental capacity of infants or those functioning below a two-year-old level. The Bayley Scales of Infant Development (Bayley, 1969) assess three ability areas for infants from birth to age 30 months. The mental scale tests sensory perception, language, and discrimination abilities, among others. The motor section measures the child's gross motor development. Each of these scales yields a developmental quotient similar to a deviation IQ. The third part is a personality rating that produces a description of the infant's temperament instead of an overall index. Other commonly used infant scales are the Denver Developmental Screening Test (Frankenburg & Dodds, 1967) and the Cattell Infant Intelligence Scale (Cattell, 1947).

*While these scales have been used to evaluate older children who are severely retarded, this use is not recommended.*

Thus far, infant assessment scales as a class have failed to provide any reliable measure of intelligence for children under age two. The results do not correlate with the IQ scores obtained as the child gets older. Because these children are too young to be tested through language, intelligence in infants is inferred through achievement of psychomotor milestones. Mental and motor abilities, however, need not develop simultaneously, and a test that presumes to measure one by observing the other cannot be valid. Youngsters who are physically handicapped naturally perform poorly on infant motor tests and run the risk of being labeled mentally retarded, often to the detriment of any serious efforts toward their education. Developmental scales for this group should be administered and interpreted only by professionals well acquainted with the scales' limitations.

## SOME CRITICISMS OF GENERAL INTELLIGENCE TESTING

There is considerable controversy about the issue of intelligence testing in the schools. Some critics of intelligence testing find fault with the tests, pointing out that experts disagree about how intelligence is defined and how it is best measured. They further argue that test scores are subject to various forms of statistical and administrative error and that they can vary considerably from time to time. This point is well taken. The concept of intelligence or IQ was introduced at a time (1916) when the prevailing belief held intelligence to be hereditary and therefore constant. Laypersons and professionals alike generally think of intelligence as a basic, enduring attribute of an individual. But if intelligence is a basic, constant quantity, why do IQ scores fluctuate? When a child scores a 95 IQ at age 6, an 89 IQ at age 13, and a 105 IQ at age 16, does this mean that he or she had average intelligence at first but lost intelligence between ages 6 and 12 and became brighter again by age 16? Not really. Most likely what happened was that the child was influenced on the repeated tests by emotional or motivational factors or variations in experience at these different points in life. Or perhaps the examiner's behavior and the test instrument were more or less appropriate to the youngster on these different occasions. The basic problem is that, although the word *intelligence* is used to refer to the totality of a person's ability and potential, no finite behavior sample can possibly demonstrate everything that is worth knowing about that person's capabilities. Therefore, there are no completely adequate measures of intelligence, but those in use do have a purpose. Some seem to do a better job than others, depending on the reasons for the administration of the test.

Other critics of the use of intelligence tests in the schools argue that the tests are culturally biased and discriminate against students from ethnic and minority backgrounds. These critics point to the fact that such groups, and children who are economically disadvantaged, tend to score lower on the Wechsler and Stanford-Binet tests than students drawn from middle- and upper-class homes in the dominant culture group (Jencks, 1972). Attempts to explain these group differences in IQ test performance take many directions. Scholars have argued that the differences are essentially genetic (Jensen, 1969, 1980), that they are attributable to different culturally conditioned cognitive styles (Golden & Berns, 1976), and that they reflect a multitude of environmental differences.

Regardless of the origin of group differences in IQ test scores, some assert that to continue basing placement decisions on measures with demonstrated cultural bias perpetuates inequities in the cultural and economic system by tracking students from ethnic, minority, and disadvantaged backgrounds into low-level employment. How the psychoeducational community and advocates of testing in the schools will respond to their critics' challenges is not yet clear. Of course, IQ test scores alone are not the only criteria for placement decisions or decisions concerning provision of special services. Usually teacher ratings, achievement scores (which are open to some of the same criticisms as IQ scores), classroom performance, and social adjustment are considered as well. Some have suggested less reliance on test scores and more reliance on such measures as adaptive behavior ratings (Mercer, 1973a) and social competence. Another alternative is decreased emphasis on tracking and increased concentration on student-oriented pacing with **mastery learning** (Guskey, 1980). This approach involves presenting the material to the student at whatever rate he can incorporate it satisfactorily. Thus, there is less emphasis on forcing everyone to cover the subject matter at the same speed. Although this is not a new idea, it may be one with new promise.

One thorough and innovative approach to equality of opportunity in testing is Mercer's proposed System of Multicultural Pluralistic Assessment (SOMPA) (Mercer & Lewis, 1977a). Her approach starts from the assumption that a number of cultural groups are present in this country. She proposes to establish norms for several generally accepted psychological tests (including the WISC-R) for Blacks, Anglos, Chicanos, and Latinos. This will allow for comparisons of the individual's test performance with norms for persons with similar ethnocultural backgrounds. A 1977 civil rights mandate outlawing discriminatory testing in the schools has opened up the market for measures like Mercer's; California and Louisiana already require its inclusion in the special placement eligibility process.

As Hutt and Gibby (1979) point out, SOMPA will no doubt produce more valid test scores for members of the various subgroups. However, some problems are raised by the assumption that subcultures are homogeneous—just as the original assumption of cultural homogeneity underlying the standardization of the WISC-R and Stanford-Binet results in test norms that place members of a subculture at a competitive disadvantage. Will four sets of norms be enough to provide equality of test opportunity for everyone? There are many more than four definable social, cultural, and economic groups in the population. SOMPA also sidesteps the question of predictive validity where the criterion to be predicted is success in the prevailing culture.

Another response to criticisms of test fallibility and bias comes from the growing body of research in neuropsychological testing. Neuropsychologists are adding new dimensions to traditionally held views of intelligence. Monitoring the electrical activity of the brain is a technique long used by researchers to measure the extent of retardation in brain-injured children. Now neurometric specialists are suggesting the use of electroencephalograph (EEG) readings as part of intelligence test batteries for children whose neuromotor handicaps rule out conventional forms of mental measurement. Specifically, scientists speak of measuring the brain's "evoked potential," measurements that are said to produce "a fingerprint of the brain" (Beck, 1979). This fingerprint is the EEG recording of the brain's characteristic response to interruption of a predictable sensory stimulus pattern. For example, the subject may be shown a series of lights flashed in a Morse code–type sequence and repeated until the brain becomes acclimated and ceases to attend. Once the pattern is broken, however, the brain snaps back to attention, and its recorded response to this interruption—its "evoked

See Reitan & Davison (1974) for an overview.

potential"—can be charted against the EEGs and IQ scores of a normal standardization group. Similarly, registering the rate of cardiac responses to stimulus pattern interruptions has been proposed as a cognitive ability index unbiased by handicapping conditions or cultural factors (Kearsley, 1979). Both of these methods were initially devised for use with subjects who are handicapped, but they have added potential for testing subjects who do not speak English and children who are preliterate.

There are, of course, drawbacks to modern neurometric techniques. Like the patriarchal, pre-Binet sensory tests of intellect, they tap only a limited number of mental functions. One may rightly wonder why reaction speed recorded by tracing brain waves should be any more a valid measure of overall intelligence than is reaction speed gauged by Cattell's early mental test. Furthermore, the validity of these tests is evaluated in terms of correlations with the results from IQ tests, whose own validity has also yet to be proven. Neurometric study represents a step in the right direction toward correcting traditional intelligence testing flaws, but right now it is too experimental, costly, and lengthy for general use. Nonetheless, psychological research seems destined to change the way we think about intelligence.

### STAGES OF LEARNING ABOUT INTELLIGENCE TESTING

Teachers seem to progress through specific developmental stages in learning about intelligence testing. The first stage is ignorance. Teachers in this stage have never seen the inside of an intelligence testing kit and know only that they have been warned not to become involved. They see intelligence testing as a mysterious process by which an IQ is extracted from a child's head. At this level, their concept of intelligence is somewhat rigid, and the term *learning* is separate and apart from intelligence theory. The next stage is fascination. It accompanies some understanding of a theory or theories of intelligence and a look inside an intelligence test kit, and it resembles a child's opening a present and being fascinated with its contents: "Boy, that's really a neat idea, who would have ever thought of such things as how are a fly and a tree alike!" Fascination is quickly followed by disillusionment. During this stage the teacher learns about poor sampling conditions, cultural biases, standard error, and some basic elementary measurements and can see no value in tests of this type. The last stage is that of appreciation, when the test is seen for what it is actually worth. It is neither good nor bad, perfect nor imperfect, but only a tool—a tool to be used while constantly remembering that it is the child who is important, not the testing tool. At this stage two things happen: First, the teacher tends to use *parts* of tests rather than complete ones, for by using only essential parts of tests, sought-for strengths and weaknesses are accentuated; second, the teacher is constantly amazed at how many different children keep giving the same answers, and when on occasion a different or unusual answer is given, it is a surprise to find it listed as a possible response (correct or incorrect) in the answer section at the back of the manual. After testing hundreds and hundreds of children, one cannot keep from being impressed with this fact. Sometimes a teacher is working with an individual child and seems to know exactly what that child is going to say in advance. This phenomenon reveals the extensive amount of careful work that the authors of the test have done in collecting samples of children's responses.

Teachers enrolled in test and measurement classes learn a great deal about sampling, mean, median, mode, standardization, normal distribution, standard deviation, correlation, reliability, validity, mental age, and IQ. In a course on individual intelligence testing they are taught the theory of testing and its historical development, with emphasis placed on administration and scoring. All these aspects of testing are important and must continue to be taught. For teachers, however, the importance of testing lies not in a score or multiple of scores but in the analysis of the child's specific behaviors. See how the child responds to the test, and derive what you can from it for remedial purposes.

## ADAPTIVE BEHAVIOR

Before intelligence tests were developed, social incompetence was the main characteristic for judging individuals to be mentally retarded (Nihira, 1969). As we have seen, recent definitions of mental retardation emphasize, or at least consider, individuals' capabilities to adjust and function adequately within their environments. This concept of social competence or **adaptive behavior** is a person's ability to cope with the social demands of the environment. According to Leland (1978), the ability to deal effectively with social demands is "the reversible aspect of mental retardation, and it reflects primarily those behaviors which are most likely to be modified through appropriate treatment or training methods" (p. 28).

In highlighting impairment in social adaptation as an inherent dimension of mental retardation, Dunn (1973b) cites the 1944 amended Education Act of Great Britain. This act abolished scholastic inability as the basis for the use of the terms *mental deficiency* and *mental subnormality*. Only persons designated as socially incompetent or destined to be socially incompetent could be legally classified as mentally subnormal. Children who are intellectually inadequate and need special academic education may be more appropriately referred to as **educationally subnormal**. Dunn concludes, "Perhaps, more than 25 years later, it is time the United States and Canada followed the lead of Great Britain and divorced scholastic inability from mental retardation" (p. 67).

When individuals develop and function as their peers do, they are considered normal. Only when a person's behavior lags behind that of his peers does mental retardation become a possible consideration. During infancy and early childhood, mental retardation is suspected when the child is slow in developing sensory motor skills, communication skills, self-help skills, and socialization skills. During childhood and early adolescence, mental retardation is suspected primarily when there is some deficiency in basic learning, that is, academic learning, reasoning, judgment, and social perception. The greatest incidence of mental retardation is reported during this period. In late adolescence and adulthood, persons are looked upon as mentally subnormal when they repeatedly prove themselves incompetent in handling vocational and social responsibilities. But social and occupational problems need not grow directly out of academic ineptitude. It is common to find adults who were identified during their school years as mentally retarded functioning satisfactorily and adjusting adequately in their postschool environments. Most adults who are mildly retarded and many adults who are lower functioning and multiply handicapped move from institutions to make a relatively successful community adjustment (Edgerton, 1980; Seltzer & Seltzer, 1978).

We should note two important aspects of the assessment of mental deficiency. During infancy, early childhood, childhood, and early adolescence, cognitive deficits are suspected when a child's behaviors seem subnormal in comparison with norms for the age group, but during late adolescence and adulthood, retardation is determined by comparing behaviors not with standards for a particular age group, but rather with broader community and social expectations. Remember that we are referring to *speculated* or *suspected* mental deficiency and not actual classification or diagnosis. Unless a person behaves subnormally in some way, retardation is never suspected. Moderate and severe to profound handicapping conditions are usually identified during infancy and early childhood because these children differ to such a degree that something is obviously wrong. This is not true of mild retardation. Children who are mildly retarded generally function on a par with their peer group during infancy and early childhood, in the absence of heavy intellectual demands. When they enter school, however, these children fail to keep pace academically with their schoolmates. A dilemma of classification develops, because children may be seen as retarded during school, but may function normally with peers in the neighborhood.

This problem affects many bilingual and ethnic minority children. See the discussion of the ABIC system later in this chapter.

Such is the problem of the "six-hour retarded child" (President's Committee on Mental Retardation, 1970). Does academic slowness per se constitute mental retardation? If children score in the significantly subaverage range of a standardized intelligence test and fail to learn in school, yet perform competently in a nonscholastic environment, are they retarded? It would not be unusual for them to be classified and diagnosed as mentally subnormal, but by most current definitions, including the one incorporated in P.L. 94-142, and, more recently, P.L. 98-149, they should not be so classified because they have not demonstrated social incompetence in all settings. According to most definitions, for individuals to be labeled retarded, they must exhibit problems in social adaptation. In theory adaptive behavior has emerged as an important index in the identification of mental retardation, but in practice its usage has been limited because of its imprecision (Frankenberger, 1984; Patrick & Reschly, 1982).

## DEFINITIONS

The definition of adaptive behavior currently used by the AAMR has undergone several revisions. The current manual, entitled *Classification in Mental Retardation* (Grossman, 1983), describes adaptive behavior as "the effectiveness or degree with which an individual meets the standards of personal independence and social responsibility expected for age and cultural group" (p. 157).

While this definition presents the concept in general terms, adaptive behavior can also be expressed as the sum of several components. A classic study by Sloan and Birch (1955) proposed three areas under which impairments in adaptive behavior could be measured: maturation, learning capacity, and social adjustment. These same areas are still associated with adaptive behavior (Grossman, 1983, p. 157).

Leland (1978) also looked at adaptive behavior in terms of discrete elements. In his attempts to develop a scale to measure it, he defined the construct as "the ability to adapt to environmental demands . . . represented by three behavioral formations," that is, independent functioning, personal responsibility, and social responsibility. Other research efforts have identified various dimensions of adaptive functioning by examining scales that purport to assess it. Studies by Nihira (1969) and Lambert and Nicoll (1976) analyzed the AAMD Adaptive Behavior Scale to isolate its components. Nihira's study of an institutional population using the scale extracted three facets: *(a)* personal independence, *(b)* social maladaptation, and *(c)* personal maladaptation. Lambert and Nicoll based their investigation on a public school population and derived four related dimensions: *(a)* functional autonomy, *(b)* social responsibility, *(c)* interpersonal adjustment, and *(d)* intrapersonal adjustment. Nihira's most recent definition of adaptive behavior acknowledges its multidimensional nature: "a composite of many aspects and a function of a wide range of specific abilities and disabilities" (1976).

Each of the factors that researchers claim to be a component of adaptive functioning—personal independence, social responsibility, and so forth—is a skill required for adjustment in society at large. When assessing adaptive ability, however, we must remember that very few people behave, or are expected to behave, in the same manner in all places at all times. Most individuals have a number of different roles they are expected to fulfill that vary according to the different social contexts in which they find themselves. For instance, when the president of a large investment bank is at home drinking beer and watching Monday night football with a gang of old fraternity brothers, he will probably exhibit behaviors that are suitable to that

**Observe the negative orientation of the terms used with the subjects perceived as deviant—the institutional population—as opposed to those describing the largely normal public school subjects.**

# TWO VIEWS OF ADAPTIVE BEHAVIOR

In 1972, *The Journal of Special Education* devoted an issue to articles discussing the definition of mental retardation. Principal attention was given to the concept of adaptive behavior. Two contributors to this symposium, Henry Leland and John Clausen, expressed strikingly different views of adaptive behavior and its significance in the definition of mental retardation. Many of the issues that they raised remain controversial today, and their viewpoints are worth looking at. Here are excerpts from those articles, reflecting their opinions (in part).

### Clausen

The problem with "adaptive behavior" is that it is an ill-defined elusive concept, the inclusion of which results in added confusion, rather than increased clarity, regarding the condition of mental deficiency. (p. 52)

My position is that the concept's inclusion introduces an element of subjectivity which is detrimental to work in the field. (p. 52)

Scales must be adjusted to the demands of the community of which the individual is a member. . . . None of the attempts to develop a scale for adaptive behavior . . . seems to include an assessment of the community in which a person lives. (pp. 53–54)

Let is be kept in mind that I am not arguing against the significance of adaptive behavior, only against the appropriateness of its inclusion in the definition of mental deficiency. (p. 53)

### Leland

Considerations of subaverage intellectual functioning and adaptive behavior should be based on the generalized impressions of what the child is doing in those specific activities essential to his survival in a particular setting, rather than on abstract estimations of his ability to do things in no way related to that survival. (p. 74)

The issue is not and cannot be whether the child is "really retarded," but rather how society has defined him and what particular behaviors led to that social definition. Once we know which of the child's behaviors is interfering with his ability to survive in his social unit and what types of behaviors are creating this unpleasant visibility, we are in a position to know which behaviors are most in need of modification, on a priority basis. . . . We can create an "invisibility" by reversing the elements about which society is most upset. (p. 75)

There are no generalized behaviors specific to mental retardation. There are, rather, behaviors that a specific social unit describes as retarded under specific demand situations. (p. 76) setting but would be inappropriate at an executive board meeting. Further-more, the pluralism in a society like ours, the diversity of ethnic, cultural, religious, and social groups that thrive autonomously within the confines of our common culture, creates endless possibilities for different values to dictate dissimilar degrees of acceptability for common behaviors. A Hawaiian who happened to bring Kalua pig to a potluck supper at the local orthodox Jewish synagogue would experience a different reaction to his choice of dishes than he might from relatives and friends at a family outing. Clearly, situational and cultural factors exert a great influence over a person's behaviors and thus compound the complexity of the adaptive behavior concept. Few researchers have been more concerned with this contextual aspect than have Mercer and her colleagues. Recognizing the pluralism of society, Mercer (1977) perceives adaptive behavior from the standpoint of the way an individual performs in various social systems: the family, the peer group, the community, the school, and the economy. Every person must adopt different social roles in each of these settings, and performance in these contexts determines adaptability. Although many definitions, dimen-sions, and interpretations of adaptive behavior have been recognized, a useful way to consider this concept might be to look at how a person copes with life.

From a review of the adaptive behavior sections of the Heber and Grossman manuals and from an analysis of recent developments, it appears that there have been four major influences in the formulation of our current thinking on adaptive behavior: Sloan and Birch's (1955) article, "A Rationale for Degrees of Retardation"; Doll's (1965) Vineland Social Maturity Scale; the Parsons State Hospital project from which the AAMD Adaptive Behavior Scale (Nihira, Foster, Shellhaas, & Leland, 1969) eventually evolved; and an extension of the Pacific State Hospital project from which the System of Multicultural Pluralistic Assessment (SOMPA) (Mercer & Lewis, 1977a) was developed. One subscale of the SOMPA is the Adaptive Behavior Inventory for Children (ABIC). The combined impact of these has been most significant for both definition and assessment.

## THE MEASUREMENT OF ADAPTIVE BEHAVIOR

All educational assessment can serve two primary functions: identification and placement, and intervention and educational programming (Coulter & Morrow, 1978). When reviewing adaptive behavior instruments, these two functions of assessment should be kept in mind.

The use of adaptive behavior measures has been, and most certainly will continue to be, controversial (Clausen, 1972b; Leland, 1978). Some of the debate focuses on conceptual issues, while other concerns center around practical matters. Many of the conceptual problems derive from the multiple dimensions of the concept, which we have already discussed, suggesting that maybe "the term 'adaptive behavior' actually encompasses more than one concept" (Coulter & Morrow, 1978, p. 216).

Grossman (1973) has acknowledged the difficulty of measuring adaptive behavior and emphasizes that

> Measures of adaptive behavior cannot be administered directly in offices, but must be determined on the basis of a series of observations in many places over considerable periods of time. For this reason, rating scales or interview data usually make up the data from which levels of adaptive behavior are inferred (p. 16).

In the most recent AAMR manual on definition, Grossman (1983) has highlighted some of the major differences between measures of intelligence and of adaptive behavior. First, adaptive behavior measures attempt to obtain an index of persons' usual behavior patterns; intelligence measures are designed to obtain the highest levels of potential ability. Second, adaptive behavior measures tap a number of different everyday living areas, while intelligence tests typically focus on language and reasoning abilities. Third, adaptive behavior information is obtained usually, but not always, through interviews with people who know the person being assessed; intelligence testing is regularly administered in a standardized way in a controlled testing setting.

Keeping in mind some of the problems, let us now examine several instruments currently used to assess adaptive behavior. We also look at some instruments that demand further explanation in the next sections.

## AAMD ADAPTIVE BEHAVIOR SCALES

In 1965, the American Association on Mental Retardation developed a project to study the broad dimensions of adaptive behavior. The project produced two adaptive behavior scales (Nihira et al., 1969), one designed for children aged 3 through 12, and the other for people 13 years of age and older. The scales have since been revised in a combined form called the AAMD Adaptive Behavior Scale, 1974 Revision (Nihira, Foster, Shellhaas, & Leland, 1974). The purpose of the 1974 scale is to provide objective descriptions and evaluations of an individual's effectiveness in coping with the natural and social demands of the environment. A public school version of this scale was also developed in response to the need for an instrument appropriate to the school setting (Lambert, Windmiller, & Cole, 1975).

The 1981 revised AAMD Adaptive Behavior Scale, School Edition (ABS-SE) is significantly different from the 1974 Public School Version. The two major purposes for which it is used are: *(a)* screening, instructional planning, and evaluation of student progress; and *(b)* diagnosis and placement decisions. Although the same instrument is administered for both purposes, the way in which the raw data are scored and interpreted differs.

Like the earlier version, the ABS-SE consists consists of two parts. Part one is organized along developmental lines and evaluates individual skills in nine behavioral domains related to personal and community self-sufficiency and personal-social responsibility. The nine domains are further divided into subcategories. Figure 3.2 lists the domains and subdomains. Part two of the scale measures maladaptive behaviors related to social and personal adjustment. There are 11 domains in this part of the scale. One more domain is somewhat autonomous—Use of medications (Domain 21).

| Part one domains and subdomains | Part two domains |
|---|---|
| Domain 1  Independent Functioning | Domain 10  Aggressiveness |
| Eating | Domain 11  Antisocial vs. social behavior |
| Toilet use | Domain 12  Rebelliousness |
| Cleanliness | Domain 13  Trustworthiness |
| Appearance | Domain 14  Withdrawal vs. involvement |
| Care of clothing | |
| Dressing & undressing | Domain 15  Mannerisms |
| Travel | Domain 16  Interpersonal manners |
| Other independent functioning | Domain 17  Acceptability of vocal habits |
| Domain 2  Physical development | |
| Sensory development | Domain 18  Acceptability of habits |
| Motor development | Domain 19  Activity level |
| Domain 3  Economic activity | Domain 20  Symptomatic behavior |
| Money handling & budgeting | Domain 21  Use of medications |
| Shopping skills | |
| Domain 4  Language development | |
| Expression | |
| Comprehension | |
| Social language development | |
| Domain 5  Numbers & time | |
| Domain 6  Prevocational activity | |
| Domain 7  Self-direction | |
| Initiative | |
| Perserverance | |
| Leisure time | |
| Domain 8  Responsibility | |
| Domain 9  Socialization | |

FIGURE 3.2   ABS-SE domains and subdomains

This scale can be administered by either first-person assessment or third-party assessment. In first-person assessment, someone who knows the person being assessed fills out the scale. The limitation of having the evaluator use the first-person method should be obvious: *(a)* the responder may not have access to all the information necessary to answer the questions adequately; or *(b)* the responder may have a biased view of the person being assessed. For a third-party assessment, the evaluator asks an informed observer questions directly from the scale and records the responses.

The results of the evaluation are used in two different ways, depending upon the purpose. Both techniques produce various derived scores and graphic profiles. If the purpose of the assessment was to gain information for instruction, the total raw scores for each domain are converted to percentiles, using either regular education, educable mentally retarded (EMR), or trainable mentally retarded (TMR) referent groups. After this is done the percentiles can be graphically displayed on the profile (see Figure 3.3).

If the purpose of the evaluation was to obtain information to make an eligibility or placement decision, then a different procedure is followed. Here the various domains of both parts of the instrument are organized into five factors: personal self-sufficiency, community self-sufficiency, personal-social responsibility, social adjustment, and personal adjustment. A factor score is determined (total of raw scores from each domain). The next step is to take

*Competence in using money is one aspect typically examined in adaptive behavior assessments.*

**Figure 4 Completed Instructional Planning Profile**

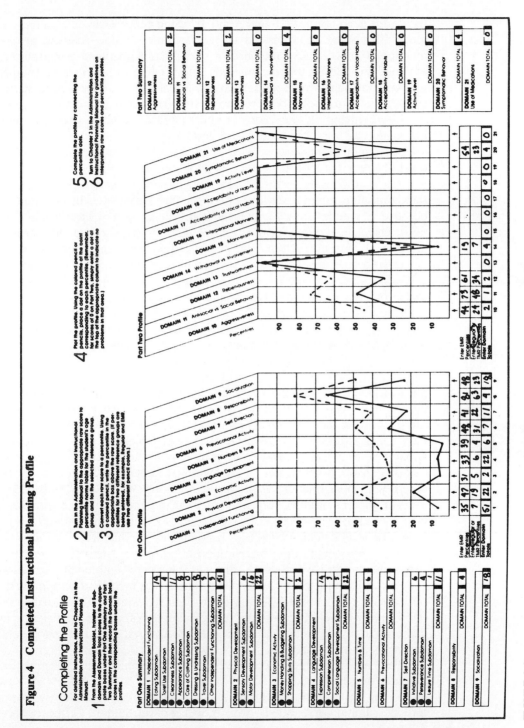

FIGURE 3.3

105

the scores from factors 2, 1, and 3 and, by using tables, obtain a comparison score. This score is compared to norms for the same referent groups mentioned above, and a measure of overall comparison (a percentile) is obtained. In addition, the total raw scores for each factor can be converted to scaled scores (again related to a given referent group); these scaled scores are then used to display performance levels graphically in a profile.

Interpretation of the scores requires practice and a good working knowledge of this instrument and test construction. General rules for selecting cutoff points are provided. These cutoffs can be used to determine critical ranges that indicate significant problems in adaptive behavior.

This revision is distinctly different from its earlier version. The size of the standardization sample was increased, but the sample is still problematic because it includes only individuals from California and Florida. Another major change is the development of two different ways to use the obtained information: for instructional purposes and for placement decisions. Of particular note is the comparison score, which attempts to help practitioners and decisionmakers determine how a person's overall functioning compares to that of other members of various groups. The revision straightens out the confusion between the instructional profiles for parts one and two that existed in the earlier version, as well as including a guide designed for parents that helps explain the instrument and its results.

## THE VINELAND SOCIAL MATURITY SCALE

The Vineland Social Maturity Scale was developed in 1935 by Edgar A. Doll at the Training School at Vineland, New Jersey. Since then it has undergone three revisions, the most recent in 1964 (Doll, 1965). It has been translated into Italian, Spanish, Swedish, German, and Japanese, and adpated for application with such diverse cultures as Hawaii's and Australia's. The most comprehensive presentation of the Vineland scale can be found in the complete manual, entitled *Measurement of Social Competence* (Doll, 1953).

The author's original purpose in constructing the scale was to provide a means of measuring social competence or "social maturity," which would help diagnose mental deficiency. Recognizing the need for an adaptive behavior component in the classification of persons as mentally subnormal, Doll sought to devise a measure "distinguishing between mental retardation with social incompetence (feeblemindedness) and mental retardation without social incompetence (which is often confused with feeblemindedness)" (Doll, 1965, p. 2). He defined the conditions of mental deficiency as demonstration of intellectual inadequacy, of arrested mental development, and of social inadequacy.

The Vineland scales were recently revised substantially and renamed the Vineland Adaptive Behavior Scales (Sparrow, Balla, & Cicchetti, 1984). Now there are three versions of the scale: Interview Edition, Survey Form; Interview Edition, Expanded Form; and Classroom Edition. Of these three,

*Edgar A. Doll constructed the Vineland Social Maturity Scale, one of the first attempts to measure what we now call "adaptive behavior."*

the Survey Form is most similar to the earlier Vineland scales. The purpose of each of these versions is indicated in its title. The first two scales are administered to individuals who know the person being assessed, usually parents or caregivers. The classroom scale is typically filled in by the teacher. There are five major domains (one optional) of adaptive behavior that these scales assess: communication, daily living skills, socialization, motor skills, and maladaptive behavior (optional).

Administration and scoring of the scales also differ from earlier versions, where the different skill domains were intermixed. These new scales follow a domain structure where only items related to one domain (e.g., communication) are together. Raw scores are converted to standard scores, percentiles (both national and supplementary, which include norms of different groups of people who are disabled), stanines, age equivalents, and an indication of adaptive level. A sum of all domain standard scores can be converted to an adaptive behavior composite score (mean = 100, standard deviation = 15). By using the standard scores for each of the domain areas, a graphic representation of performance can be produced in profile form.

The Vineland has always been a popular measure of social competency (Coulter & Morrow, 1978); the new versions improve on the earlier scales. For instance, problems with the limited standardization population of the earlier scales have been corrected.

# DECISIONS CONCERNING THE CLASSIFICATION OF STUDENTS AS MENTALLY RETARDED: THE IMPORTANCE OF ADAPTIVE BEHAVIOR

As previously mentioned in this chapter, levels of adaptive behavior functioning must be considered by those who decide if a person is mentally retarded. The recent AAMR manual *Classification in Mental Retardation* (Grossman, 1983) presents a number of case studies. Here are two of those in which adaptive behavior functioning is an important consideration. Read each one carefully and then decide if the individual should be classified as retarded. The decisions of the AAMR can be found at the bottom of this page.

### Case Study #1: Bill

Bill, age 5, was evaluated after selection during kindergarten screening. Family is "poverty level" and has 6 children. Mother reported that Bill feeds self and dresses self except for shoe tying, that he tries to help around the house and with younger children (e.g., makes bologna sandwich for little sister); she says he watches TV a lot, but not Sesame Street; she has little time for reading to children or taking them to museums, etc. and says the home is busy and noisy. Psychologist reported Binet IQ of 68, with range of 4 testing levels, and Vineland of 78. He conversed with the psychologist freely, asked many questions about objects in room. He can count to 5 and recognizes words that are the names of commercial items, saying he learned them from TV.

### Case Study #2: Camilla

Camilla, age 8, youngest of 3 children. Parents have been concerned about her development since Camilla was 4 years old, primarily because of slow language development and slowness in development of self-help skills. Mother works part time, but has spent a lot of time with Camilla from infancy, reading to child, playing with her, and attempting to stimulate language. Camilla now feeds herself with spoon and sometimes uses fork. Gross motor skills appear to be good, but fine motor skills are delayed. Camilla has good articulation, uses short sentences with correct grammar, but vocabulary is limited for age (e.g, failed vocabulary task on Binet for 6-year level) and is below developmental norms in language development. Has short attention span for age and requires many trials to master new material. Binet IQ was 70. Criterion-referenced test indicates recognition of about 25% of basic sight words; she recognizes functional words in context (LADIES, STOP, etc.) for very common words, but not such terms as ENTER HERE. Counts to 20 and understands concept of 4 objects. Repeated kindergarten and standardized achievement tests at school have consistently been 1½ to 2 grades below expected for age. In class and in everyday life, she appears to perform at a lower level than indicated by latest standardized test scores.

AAMR decisions:
Case study #1—Bill: NOT RETARDED
Case study #2—Camilla: RETARDED

## BALTHAZAR SCALES OF ADAPTIVE BEHAVIOR

The Balthazar Scales of Adaptive Behavior (BSAB) were developed in 1971 by Earl E. Balthazar at the Central Wisconsin Colony and Training School in Madison, Wisconsin, for use with individuals who are severely and pro-foundly retarded. This instrument has two sections, which together are designed to "measure the effects of treatment and training, and other types of programs for individuals in residential institutions, day-care centers and clinics" (Balthazar, 1971, p. 3). Section I of this instrument focuses on the assessment of self-care skills, while Section II deals with social behavior. The subscales of this instrument include

Section I (Scales of Functional Independence)
1. Eating-drinking scales
2. Dressing-undressing scales
3. Toileting scales

Section II (Scales of Social Adaptation)
(Social Scale Categories)
Unadaptive Self-Directed Behaviors
    Scale  1: Failure to respond
    Scale  2: Stereotype (stereopathy), posturing, including objects
    Scale  3: Nondirected, repetitious verbalizations: smiling, laughing behaviors
    Scale  4: Inappropriate self-directed behaviors
    Scale  5: Disorderly, nonsocial behavior
Unadaptive Interpersonal Behaviors
    Scale  6: Inappropriate contact with others
    Scale  7: Aggression, withdrawal
Adaptive Self-Directed Behaviors
    Scale  8: Generalized exploratory, recreational activity
Adaptive Interpersonal Behaviors
    Scale  9: Fundamental social behaviors: Noncommunication
    Scale 10: Fundamental social behaviors: Social vocalization and ges-tures
    Scale 11: Appropriate response to negative peer contact
Verbal Communication
    Scale 12: Nonfunctional, repetitious, or inarticulate verbalizations
    Scale 13: Verbalization
Play Activities
    Scale 14: Object relations
    Scale 15: Playful contact
    Scale 16: Play activities
Response to Instructions
    Scale 17: Response to instructions
    Scale 18: Response to firmly given instructions
    Scale 19: Cooperative contact

Checklist Items

(Personal care, Assisted or unassisted, and Other behaviors)

The developers of the BSAB believe that it should be administered by direct observation in the subject's natural environment. They emphasize the importance of assessing the person engaging in typical daily activities in familiar conditions. Section II can be scored by recording either the frequency of a given behavior or the occurrence of the behavior in a specified period of time (one-minute intervals).

The strength of the BSAB rests in the fact that it is minutely task-analyzed—each behavior required of the subject who is retarded is broken down into its smallest components. Table 3.2 illustrates the fastidiously detailed definition of terms that precedes each subscale of the BSAB, Sections I and II.

Such precise detail is vital to the successful implementation of training strategies for populations that are severely and profoundly handicapped. When this instrument is administered properly, it is easy to proceed from testing to teaching—the trainer knows exactly at what point to begin programming for acquisition of a skill. The authors of the Balthazar Scale emphasize the intervention and programming function of the instrument over its identification and placement function. As do the AAMR scale developers, they recognize that the data derived from a measure like this provide only part of the necessary information about the subject's total adaptive functioning. For this reason, "the scales are best utilized in an interdisciplinary setting offering a number of available services and disciplines" (Balthazar, 1973, p. 6).

TABLE 3.2  Balthazar Adaptive Behavior Scales: Definition of Items for the Eating Scales

**Class I: Dependent Feeding**

1. Mouth is open. Subject is fed orally. (The exception would be intravenous feeding.)
2. Opens mouth voluntarily. Subject opens his mouth, but might have to be reminded or encouraged.
3. Opens mouth without physical stimulation. Subject opens his mouth voluntarily at the sight of food coming toward his mouth.
4. Removes food with mouth. Subject removes food from the spoon with his mouth.
5. Removes food with lips. Subject removes food from spoon with his lips.
6. Allows spoon to be removed from mouth. Subject does not bite or retain spoon, but allows it to be withdrawn.
7. Retains food. Subject retains all food from a spoonful without spitting or drooling (regardless of position).
8. Retains food in upright position. Subject eats in sitting position and does not spit or drool.
9. Manipulates food in mouth. Subject in some manner moves food in his mouth (chewing, biting, etc.).

## ADAPTIVE BEHAVIOR INVENTORY FOR CHILDREN

The Adaptive Behavior Inventory for Children (ABIC) is one component of the System of Multicultural Pluralistic Assessment (SOMPA) developed by Mercer and colleagues (Mercer, 1977; Mercer & Lewis, 1977a, 1977b). Several assumptions implicit in the development of the SOMPA can be seen in its name. First, assessment is conceived of as a system rather than as isolated, disjunct measurements. Second, the developers acknowledge that American society is multicultural and pluralistic, regardless of the Anglo influence or status quo. In other words, other, non-Anglo cultures need to be recognized. The SOMPA attempts to consider the major implications of such a multicultural, pluralistic society, as reflected by the words of Mercer (1977):

> The SOMPA presumes that all languages and cultures are of equivalent value and that linguistic and cultural differences must be taken into account when interpreting individual performance. The SOMPA assumes that the dominant Anglo core culture will continue to be perpetuated through the public schools as a matter of public policy and will continue to dominate the major economic and political institutions of American society. (pp. 187–188)

The Adaptive Behavior Inventory for Children is the section of the SOMPA designed to assess adaptive functioning of children 5 to 11 years old. The ABIC attempts to screen out of the school age population those children whose adaptive behavior skills lag behind the skills of their larger peer group. It looks at the child's role performance in a variety of social contexts. Because it is normed on a typical school age sample, the meaning of *adaptive behavior* in this scale varies somewhat from the definition used by institution-based measures such as the Balthazar. Instruments of the Balthazar type view adaptive behavior in terms of skills for which children and adults who are institutionalized need to be programmed. In contrast, the ABIC treats adaptation as "an important component for an assessment of populations that exist in the mainstream community" (Coulter & Morrow, 1978, p. 116).

The ABIC measures a child's adaptive functioning through a questionnaire completed by the child's mother (or other primary caretaker). Its 242 items are grouped within six subscales.

1. Family role performance
2. Community role performance
3. Peer group role performance
4. Nonacademic school role performance
5. Earner/consumer role performance
6. Self-maintenance role performance

The questionnaires are then rated, and the raw scores are converted to scaled scores and plotted on the comprehensive SOMPA profile, along with scores from the other SOMPA subscales, without reference to the child's cultural background.

*Jane Mercer and other advocates believe that a child's adaptive behavior must be evaluated in the context of his or her social and ethnic background.*

Clearly, the value of the ABIC lies in the fact that, as part of the SOMPA, it relates performance to ethnicity and culture. It attempts to minimize cultural bias not by posing as a "culture-free" device but by analyzing children's adaptive behavior in the appropriate social-cultural context. The ABIC truly "operationalizes the two-dimensional definition of mental retardation advanced by the American Association on Mental Deficiency" (Mercer, 1977, p. 204). But be aware that the ABIC has received some criticism from practitioners. (See Reschly, 1982, for a discussion of this criticism.)

## CURRENT ISSUES RELATED TO ADAPTIVE BEHAVIOR

As we have mentioned, controversy still surrounds the concept and measurement of adaptive behavior. While much of the hands-on information concerning the assessment of adaptive behavior has already been presented in this chapter, there are still a number of unanswered questions related to both conceptual and practical issues. Coulter and Morrow (1978), in a most interesting discussion, have categorized some of the issues related to adaptive behavior measurement according to the two dimensions of psychological assessment. Most of the questions that these authors raise are not readily answerable, and they point out the need for further clarification through research.

Read page 100 for two experts' differing views on adaptive behavior.

Adaptive Behavior and Identification/Placement:
1. Does the use of adaptive behavior measures reduce the bias toward minority groups?
2. What happens to those excluded from special services due to the inclusion of adaptive behavior measures?

3. Can the measurement of adaptive behavior become the more important factor in identifying mental retardation?
4. Should adaptive behavior be a determinant in the identification of other exceptionalities?
5. Is there any difference between intelligence and adaptive behavior between the ages of 0 to 5?
6. Does the concept of adaptive behavior have different meaning for the severely and profoundly handicapped?
7. Some practical issues:
   a. Should specific norms for various minority groups be used?
   b. How should adaptive behavior be measured for those 13 to 21 years of age?
   c. Who is the most appropriate source of information?
   d. Who should collect the data?
8. How should the validity of adaptive measures be examined?
9. Should a single, global score be adequate for the purposes of identification?

Adaptive Behavior and Intervention/Programming:
1. Is the measurement of adaptive behavior realistic, i.e., is it too vague a concept to measure?
2. How should adaptive behavior be envisioned? (e.g., how many domains?)
3. How extensively do we need to measure adaptive behavior?
4. Can those adaptive behavior skills that are lacking be acquired through training?
5. Can we define adaptive behavior in adulthood?
6. What behaviors from a social and prevocational perspective are important at the adolescent or upper functioning levels? (Coulter & Morrow, 1978, pp. 216–223)

As these and other issues are addressed, we will gain a better understanding of an often confusing concept, but we are not at this point yet.

## ASSESSMENT FOR INSTRUCTION

Although the use of adaptive behavior as a criterion for classification is questionable, it is common practice to use information from adaptive behavior scales for instructional purposes. This is largely because the scales have a minutely detailed task-analysis format. By studying individual student responses to most adaptive behavior scales the teacher not only can determine strengths and weaknesses but also identify what skills need to be addressed and where to start instructional programming. This is not so readily apparent with intelligence tests, yet once one has some familiarity with the concepts of subsets of types of intelligence, intelligence tests can also be used to help the teacher determine areas for remediation. What follow are examples of the ways performance on an intelligence test may lead to instructional programming.

A kindergarten student failed items dealing with visual-motor activities and pictorial similarities and differences. If a child did poorly on these items, the teacher might first check the child's vision. If the child's sight was within normal limits, the teacher could begin teaching these concepts without teaching the actual test items. Common activities for facilitating visual-motor development at kindergarten age are stringing beads, pegboard work, parquetry blocks, lacing a shoe, tracing, or direct copying. A sequence of activities from simple to complex for developing skills in this area using beads could be:

1. Just get the beads on the string.
2. Put the same number of beads on the string that the teacher has put on a model string.
3. Copy the teacher's simple design by color, e.g., red, blue, red.
4. Copy the teacher's simple design by shape, e.g., sphere, cylinder, cube.
5. Copy the teacher's design, but now mix color and shape.
6. Next make the design longer and more complex.
7. Copy the teacher's design from memory. The teacher's design is shown for only a few seconds and then hidden. When the child has finished, the teacher lets the child compare the copy with the original to determine its correctness.
8. Show two strings of beads and have the child tell whether they are the same or different.
9. Have the child tell how two strings of beads are the same and different, e.g, same color but different shapes.

The point of this illustration is that the teacher, by viewing a demonstration of the child's intelligence in small parts like those involving visual-motor skills, can then develop specific activities to facilitate skill acquisition.

A child who exhibits visual-motor difficulty will have trouble copying. Since copying is such an important skill for a child to develop, it may be advantageous to discuss copying in some detail. If a normally sighted child has difficulty copying from the chalkboard, one of the first things that can be done is to find out if that child can trace. Attach commercial onionskin paper with a paper clip at each corner over some design to be traced. If the child is not motivated to do this task, try to find appealing designs—simple designs of cars, hot rods, dogs, or cats might work. A child who is able to trace adequately could go on to copying simple designs from a sheet of paper placed directly above the paper to be copied. If the child experiences difficulty here, then practice on this task is recommended.

Sometimes just encouraging the child to copy simple designs and allowing time for practice and development of this skill is all that is necessary. But if the child shows little or no progress, additional aids may be used—perhaps dots or points placed on the paper showing where to start and stop. For some children many dots or even a fine line is needed as a guide in copying. When many dots or a line are used, the dots or lines are gradually phased out until the child is copying without aids. Sometimes it is helpful for the teacher to hold the child's writing hand, actually copying the design for him or her until the child gets the idea. As the child develops copying skills, the teacher gradually releases pressure so the child is doing more and more work, until the teacher's hand is just barely touching the child's. Finally the teacher lets go altogether. After the child has mastered copying independently from a paper on the desk, the teacher moves the desk to a position facing the chalkboard. The design or material to be copied is taped or written on the board. As the child's copying skills develop, the teacher gradually moves the desk away from the board until finally the child is copying things from the board as the other children do.

Step-by-step procedures taking the child from tracing to copying from the board are quite successful for the child who can trace, but if the child had difficulty tracing, the teacher must help develop readiness skills for tracing. Such skills include the development of eye-hand coordination, and activities requiring the child to reach, touch, grasp, release, and in general manipulate items are invaluable.

An example of an eye-hand coordination activity is to have a child pick up pieces of cheese and eat them, then gradually reduce the size of the pieces. As the skill improves, the teacher places toothpicks in the small pieces of cheese and asks the child to pick up the cheese using the toothpicks as handles. Next the teacher gives the child one toothpick and instructions to spear each piece of cheese before consuming it.

One activity included in almost every elementary or early childhood methods text is drawing or tracing in sand. Because of the expense, size, and cost of maintaining sand tables and various apparatuses involving sand work, many teachers are not attracted to activities of this kind. We have found that wood shavings placed in a shoebox lid also make excellent tracing devices, and writing on clay with a stylus helps some children.

Children who fail to respond well to verbal instructions are common among high-risk children, i.e., children referred for testing because they seem to be significantly behind others in their classes. Examples of things typically taught and discussed in educational programs for children of this age are: What do we do when we are tired, thirsty, hungry? What do we do with our ears, eyes, nose? Identification of pictures in books and magazines is another tool. Usually the teacher tells the child to identify nouns like *boy, girl, dog,* or *cow.* Action verbs—*hopping, running,* and *skipping*—are used later, and the exercise often culminates in discussions of what is happening in the picture. At this level the description of similarities and differences, opposites, and the classification of such objects as animals and vehicles are taken into account. No program would be complete without some work on instructions like "stand up," "sit down," "put your name on the top line." The instructions gradually become more complex, with the teacher giving more than one instruction at a time: "Close the door and hang up your coat." Any child scoring poorly on these items should first have his hearing tested, and if there is no hearing problem, the teacher can begin with traditional activities. Once again the approach is simple: Analyze the child's test results, attend to the items missed, and determine appropriate activities for remediation.

Many nonintellectual factors influence a test, and the teacher should constantly be aware that just because a child scored low on a certain set of items, it does not necessarily mean that he or she does not know the concept under consideration. Performance on test items should be viewed as nothing more than *possible* indicators of strengths and weaknesses in various academic areas. The test itself is only a series of questions and problems designed to help the teacher know a little more about the child's functioning than day-to-day contact with the child ordinarily reveals.

**SUMMARY**

This chapter introduces the major theoretical influences shaping our current notions of how to define and assess intelligence. The debate concerning the relative impact of heredity and upbringing on intellectual ability leads only to the tentative conclusion that there is no conclusion. Intelligence testing has evolved from early tests of sensory abilities, through tests of intelligence as a single factor, to tests of intelligence as comprising many different abilities.

Although mandated by professional guidelines and by law, the use of adaptive behavior as a criterion for determining mental retardation is clouded by confusion. The available scales for assessing adaptive behavior are all based on different theories and all evaluate different skills. We are confident that much of the confusion surrounding the conceptual and practical problems of adaptive behavior can be alleviated. As this decade progresses, we must work toward uniformity of definition and more attention to adaptive behavior considerations on a statewide and national basis.

Although the tools designed to assess intellectual functioning and adaptive behavior are useful for classification and placement purposes, and new developments like neurometric research are promising for the future, educators must remember the ultimate goal of assessing any student: *to gather information that can be used in planning instructional programs for individual children.*

# CHAPTER 4

# Biological Causes of Mental Retardation

T he task of sorting out the causes of mental retardation is a formidable one. From the relatively primitive beginnings of the study of retardation in previous centuries to the more advanced efforts of the late 20th century, the search for causation has been a complex and continuing challenge for professionals from many disciplines. The goal of this chapter is to lay a firm foundation for an understanding of the many complexities of biological causes, known as **etiologies**, of retardation.

Biological causes have traditionally been most often associated with relatively severe retardation. While we have identified hundreds of specific factors as causative agents, the number of unknown or at least unspecifiable (Maloney & Ward, 1978) causes of retardation still dwarfs those known and specifiable. In fact, we know the causes in less than 50% of cases of retardation, and a key problem is that cause has most rarely been established for the large group of persons who are mildly handicapped.

For purposes of this text, causes of retardation and related developmental disabilities have been divided into two categories: biological (or physiological) and psychological-sociological. Biological causes are discussed in this chapter, with psychosocial causes emphasized in the next.

Known and specifiable biological causes are often referred to as **pathological, organic**, or **clinical**. Although such causes may result in cases of all levels of retardation, most attention in the past went to their etiological roles in the more severe cases of retardation. Pathological factors can be identified in from 60% to 75% of cases where the individual's IQ falls below 50 (McLaren & Bryson, 1987). But the traditional assumption of a single,

This chapter was contributed by Edward A. Polloway and James R. Patton.

organic cause with severe retardation is too simplistic—many individuals with mild retardation may also be affected because of such etiologies. The other traditional assumption—that mild retardation is associated with multiple, unspecifiable environmental events—has gradually given way before the fact that from 25% to 40% of all cases of mild retardation have an identifiable cause (see McLaren & Bryson, 1987).

Given its bewildering complexity, why should educators, psychologists, and other behavioral scientists spend time on the study of causation? Kolstoe (1972) noted that familiarity with etiological factors facilitates multidisciplinary communication, is an essential element of professionalism in the field of mental retardation, and is important in giving professionals the ability to make accurate information available to parents. In certain situations, etiological information can contribute to more accurate diagnosis. Such information can assist in identifying high- and low-risk individuals, prescribing treatment through biomedical and, in some instances, educational intervention, and conveying to family members data on the possible hereditary and nonhereditary transmission of specific disorders (Chaney & Eyman, 1982). The role of teachers could include monitoring the effects of ongoing or progressive disorders that may hinder daily performance, preventing future occurrences through parent counseling, or effecting immediate change, as with child abuse.

While a general awareness of etiological influences is necessary for all professionals, the mechanisms of the specific causes discussed in this chapter may often prove too complex for someone without training in medicine or biology. Input from various disciplines is essential to determine whether a cause can be specified or is relevant to treatment. That many etiologies cannot be identified should act as a spur to future research. Meanwhile we must acknowledge our limitations in this area.

Finally, while reviewing this information on causation, it is important that the reader not lose sight of the fact that behind these data are persons affected by various causative agents. As Blatt (1987) cautions, "Treatises that deal with etiological conditions rarely recognize the **human being** [in] the superficially unattractive trappings of the condition" (p. 128). The reader should be sure not to forget that we are talking about people.

This chapter is divided into five major sections. First comes a discussion of biomedical terminology, then a brief interpretation of the role genetics plays in development. The third section gives examples of specific causes, while the fourth looks at preventive and treatment measures. The final section explores ethical issues.

## TERMINOLOGY

To the student of biological causes of mental retardation and developmental disabilities, the translation of specific names for known causes into useful information can be most difficult. This section offers ways to understand the labels ascribed to the various **syndromes** most often associated with retardation.

The terminology used to identify various syndromes comes primarily from three sources: *(a)* conventional wisdom, or practices often related to a specific historical era, *(b)* names of persons who initially identified or described the condition, and *(c)* biomedical terms describing the cause or the resultant effects.

Several examples illustrate historical names for syndromes. Perhaps best known is the term *mongolism,* coined by J. Langdon Down in 1866, two decades after the discovery of the condition by Seguin (Menolascino & Egger, 1978). For 100 years this term, assigned simply because of Down's observations that one frequent characteristic of the syndrome was facial similarity to Asians, prevailed. Jordan (1976) has suggested that the term's popularity can be traced to the 19th-century idea of the "white man's burden," epitomized in those words by Rudyard Kipling, which associated mental inferiority with the alleged general inferiority of non-Caucasian races. As Kolstoe (1972) noted, realization that the syndrome is found in all racial groups (including even persons from Mongolia) aided in the withdrawal of the term from most professionals' vocabulary, although its use unfortunately persists in some popular media.

Another example of a term with a past is *cretinism.* Its source has been variously attributed to a Teutonic word for *chalky,* to the French word *chrétien,* stemming from the church's care for those affected, and to the island of Crete (Jordan, 1976). In spite of its colorful past, it is to be hoped that *cretinism* will soon join *mongolism* on the shelf of retired, stigmatizing labels.

A second, more direct way to identify a clinical syndrome is to attach the name of the researcher who contributed to an understanding of the specific disorder. For instance, professionals now identify as *Down syndrome* the condition formerly called *mongolism.* Other relatively well known syndromes so named include *Tay-Sachs disease,* after the British and American physicians who described the characteristics in the 1880s, and *Lesch-Nyhan syndrome,* named for the researchers who identified this severe disorder in 1964.

The third source of syndrome labels is biomedical terminology. Although some of these terms are frequently used by laypersons, the meanings often seem obscure because of the length of the words. Many of the labels, however, can by themselves convey some of the primary features of the disorder, causal or characteristic. Table 4.1 lists some of the more common terms used to identify clinical disorders. For each entry, the specific derivatives are noted along with their usual meaning and examples of their use.

Although labels are only an attempt to refer to complex medical, biological, or behavioral phenomena simply, being familiar with the derivatives can be of great assistance in understanding the nature of various

TABLE 4.1  Biomedical Terminology

| Stems and Affixes | Meaning | Example(s) |
| --- | --- | --- |
| ab-, abs- | from, away | abnormal, abscess |
| amnio- | pertaining to embryonic sac | amniocentesis |
| anomalo- | irregular | chromosomal anomaly |
| auto- | self, same | autism, autosomes |
| -cele, -coele | sac, cavity | meningocele |
| -cephalo- | head, brain | hydrocephalus |
| -encephalo- | head, brain | encephalitis |
| endo- | inner, inside | endogenous |
| ex-, extra- | outside, away from | exogenous |
| fibro- | connective tissues | neurofibromatosis |
| galacto- | milk | galactosemia |
| glyco-, gluco- | sweet, sugar | glycogen, hyperglycemia |
| hydro- | water | hydrocephalus |
| hyper- | over, more than usual | hyperkinetic |
| hypo- | under, less than usual, lowered | hypothyroidism |
| -lepsy | seizure | epilepsy, narcolepsy |
| lipo- | fat | lipids |
| macro-, mega- | large | macrocephaly, acromegaly |
| meningo- | central nervous system membranes | meningitis |
| micro- | small | microcephaly |
| myelo- | marrow, spinal cord | myelomeningocele |
| neuro- | nerve | neurofibromatosis |
| -osis | condition of | toxoplasmosis |
| -plasia | cellular growth | skeletal dysplasia |
| -plasma | blood | toxoplasmosis |
| -plegia | paralysis | monoplegia, paraplegia |
| -semia | sign, symptom | galactosemia |
| -somy, -some, soma- | body | chromosome, trisomy |
| toxo- | poisonous | toxemia |
| -trophy | nutrition, nourishment | atrophy, dystrophy |

From *Introduction to Military Medicine and Surgery,* Study Guide 6, 1975, Fort Sam Houston, TX: Academy of Health Sciences, U.S. Army.

disorders and terms related to them. Several specific terms illustrate the system. For example, *toxoplasmosis* indicates a condition *(-osis)* of poisonous *(toxo-)* blood *(-plasm)*. Although the clinical definition of toxoplasmosis is much more specific, the word, when analyzed, gives a fair suggestion of what the disease is about. Another example is *hydrocephalus*. The term refers to a disorder resulting from a blockage of cerebrospinal fluid, and breaking the word down into water *(hydro-)* and head or brain *(cephalo-)* again illustrates the condition. A third clear example is the disorder called *myelomeningocele*. As the term suggests, this condition is characterized by a saclike mass *(-cele)* on the spinal cord *(myelo-)* containing membrane tissue of the central nervous system *(-meningo-)*.

Another stumbling block to a clear understanding of etiological processes is the science of genetics. The next section is a primer of genetic principles and deviations.

## AN INTRODUCTION TO GENETICS

**Genetics** can be defined as the study of heredity and its variation. As such, its scope is enormous and its complexities great. Advances in genetics in the past 150 years rival those in any area of science. The contributions of geneticists to understanding the causes of developmental disabilities are particularly noteworthy. The increasing attention devoted to genetic causes is clearly demonstrated by the fact that between 1971 and 1983, the number of genetic disorders (with identified loci) doubled to reach 1600 known and an additional 1700 suspected disorders (McKusick, 1982).

The study of heredity begins with the study of **genes**. Genes are the basic biological unit carrying inherited physical, mental, or personality traits. Perhaps millions of genes are present in every complex living organism— thousands in each cell. Genes occupy specific positions on **chromosomes**, the threadlike or rodlike bodies that contain genetic information and material.

Chromosomes vary widely in size and shape, but for human cells, the normal pattern is consistent. Each cell contains 23 pairs of chromosomes. The embryo initially receives one member of each pair from each parent. There are two types of chromosomes—**autosomes** and **sex chromosomes.** Autosomes are matching pairs and constitute 44 of the 46 chromosomes within the usual human complement (that is, 22 of the 23 pairs). Sex chromosomes make up the other pair. The letter *X* is used to represent the female sex chromosome, and *Y* to represent the male sex chromosome. While the X chromosome contains a substantial amount of genetic information, the Y functions primarily as a determinant of male sex. At conception, an X chromosome is contributed by the mother, while an X or Y is contributed by the father. The XX combination creates a female, and the XY a male.

The precise and rather fragile roles of genes and chromosomes as building blocks of development is dramatically represented in mental retardation research. The two most prevalent general groups of biological causes of retardation are *genetic transmission of traits* and *chromosomal abnormalities.* But even in these clear-cut cases of genetic disorders, development is still shaped significantly by environmental influence.

## GENETIC TRANSMISSION

Traits are transmitted from one generation to the next according to the makeup of a specific gene pair on a given chromosomal pair. We can trace many specific characteristics to the presence or absence of a single gene. Transmission can occur through autosomal dominant or recessive inheritance and through sex-linked inheritance. **Dominant inheritance** means that an individual gene can assume "control" over or mask its partner and will operate whether an individual gene pair is similar or dissimilar. **Recessive inheritance** indicates genes that cannot control their partners. In a sense they "recede" when paired with a dissimilar mate and become influential only when matched with another recessive gene. Pairs of genes carrying the same trait are called **homozygous**; pairs carrying different traits are **heterozygous**.

The mechanics of dominant and recessive inheritance are illustrated in Figure 4.1. Capital letters indicate dominant traits; lowercase letters, recessive traits. In the typical case of dominant inheritance illustrated in Example A, only one parent would have the specific dominant trait in question, which is theoretically transmitted to two of four children of these parents. In the common case of recessive inheritance illustrated in Example B, probability suggests that at each conception, chances are one in four that the child will be homozygous and will manifest the recessive trait (hh), two in four that he or she will be a carrier for the succeeding generation (Hh, hH), and one in four that he or she will lack the recessive gene altogether (HH).

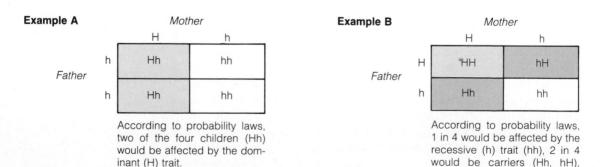

FIGURE 4.1   Dominant and Recessive Inheritance

Dominant inheritance operates in a variety of common traits, including brown eyes and premature white patches of hair. Its role as a cause of genetic transmission of retardation, however, is quite small. Some specific examples include tuberous sclerois and neurofibromatosis, which are discussed later in the chapter.

Recessive inheritance is commonly associated with blue eyes and a variety of other innocuous traits. But other recessive traits include a substantial number of very rare disorders capable of producing severe handicapping conditions. Examples include phenylketonuria, Tay-Sachs disease, and galactosemia. Since transmission of recessive traits is primarily a function of the union of two carriers (see Figure 4.1), controlling these disorders would entail using genetic screening measures to identify unaffected carriers.

A third type of genetic transmission is through sex-linked (or X-linked) inheritance. The name derives from a variety of recessive traits carried on the X chromosome. The problem is particularly significant for males and, indeed, is one reason that more males have retardation and other related disabilities. The female has two X chromosomes, and a specific weak gene can be dominated by its mate. But the male (XY) will inevitably be affected by a single recessive gene carried on the X chromosome, because there is no additional X whose genes could dominate the pathology-producing recessive trait. Instead he has a Y chromosome, which does not carry genes that will counterbalance the X-linked gene. A female can be affected only if her father is affected and her mother is a carrier. X-linked recessive traits include color blindness, hemophilia, Duchenne muscular dystrophy, Lesch-Nyhan syndrome, and a variety of other conditions that are as much as 10 times more common in males than in females. X-linked dominant disorders, which are mostly less prevalent than X-linked recessives, also exist, and these affect females who are heterozygous.

To complete the discussion of genetic transmission, we must mention five concepts that can greatly influence it: penetrance, expressivity, age of onset, mutation, and polygenic inheritance. **Penetrance** refers to the proportion of persons within a particular population who exhibit a given genetic trait. Many genes show incomplete or reduced penetrance. That is, for genes with low penetrance, relatively few of the people who have the gene manifest the outward trait or symptom it causes. This factor can have significant implications for genetic counseling, since it may be unclear whether an individual has the disorder in question. **Expressivity** refers to the severity of the trait. The symptoms produced by a gene may vary in severity of their expression in different people. Because genes have varying penetrance and expressivity, syndrome variations are more often the rule than the exception. This fact further accentuates the complexity of determining etiology, since individuals with similar genes can have widely varying physical and mental characteristics (see Hashem, Ebrahim, & Nour, 1970).

Scarr and Carter-Saltzman (1982) have referred to penetrance and expressivity as "fudge factors" because they are "concepts invoked to explain why the same gene, for the same disorder, fails to produce the same [outcome]" (p. 814).

**Age of onset** may also vary widely for different disorders. In the case of Huntington chorea, for example, onset may be as late as age 40 to 45, which means that the disorder may already have been transmitted to the next generation. Only recently has a test been developed that can tell whether an individual has the gene for the disorder. Finally, new **mutations** may occur that introduce a syndrome into a family where it would not have otherwise existed. For example, autosomal dominant disorders can be introduced as mutations and may be associated with paternal age.

The discussion above was about single gene anomalies, reflecting the concept of one gene for one trait. Most traits do not fit these simple Mendelian laws but are transmitted through **polygenic inheritance**—that is, more than one gene pair affects the appearance of a particular genetic trait. In these cases, "genetic predictions . . . have to be based on empirical data from population statistics. Simple genetic models just do not apply" (Scarr & Carter-Saltzman, 1982, p. 804). Polygenic or multigenic inheritance has particular importance in the discussion of cultural-familial retardation and is discussed at greater length in chapter 5.

## CHROMOSOMAL DEVIATIONS

A second major source of biological causes of retardation is chromosomal anomalies. Although these disorders are rare in the general population, their numbers are significant among cases of developmental disabilities where cause can be specified.

The intensive research on chromosomes that began in the late 1950s and early 1960s has provided us with an increasingly detailed portrait of both typical and atypical chromosomal patterns. These patterns are clarified through the use of **karyotypes**. The process of karyotyping includes taking a picture of the chromosomes in a human cell, enlarging it, cutting the chromosomes out, and then charting them from the largest (pair 1) to the smallest (pair 22). In the discussions concerning chromosomes and chromosomal abnormalities, examples of specific karyotypes are given.

Engel (1977) noted that at least 10% of pregnancies begin with some chromosomal imbalance, but most of these abort spontaneously during the first three months of pregnancy. A small number of these pregnancies do go to term, and the children born illustrate the potential effects of irregularities in the arrangement or alignment of autosomes or sex chromosomes. Chromosomal errors can be identified in approximately 1 in 200 live births (Engel, 1977).

While genetic disorders are classified as hereditary, chromosomal problems are more accurately termed *innate,* since an abnormal chromosome arrangement is present from the moment of conception but most often is not the product of hereditary exchange. Disorders of this type usually result from abnormalities in the process of *meiosis*. During meiosis, individual reproductive cells divide and then pair up to form the genetic foundation for the embryo. The normal process includes 23 chromosomes from each parent, which are paired to form the new organism's complement of 46 chromosomes. Figure 4.2 illustrates the karyotypes for a male and a female with normal chromosomal patterns.

Several specific abnormalities that can occur during the process of chromosomal arrangement and alignment result in either too much or too little chromosomal material's being present. In **nondisjunction**, a given parental pair of chromosomes fails to unjoin, or split, at conception, causing the formation of a group of three chromosomes, called a *trisomy,* in lieu of the normal pair. Trisomy 21, a trisomy on chromosome 21, produces Down syndrome and is the most common cause of this condition. In **translocation**, a fragment of chromosomal material is located across from or exchanged with another chromosomal pair. For example, a translocation that results in

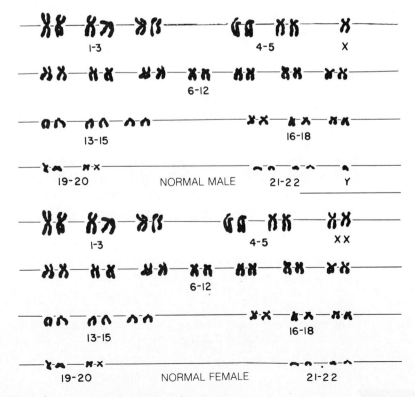

FIGURE 4.2   Normal Chromosomal Karyotypes

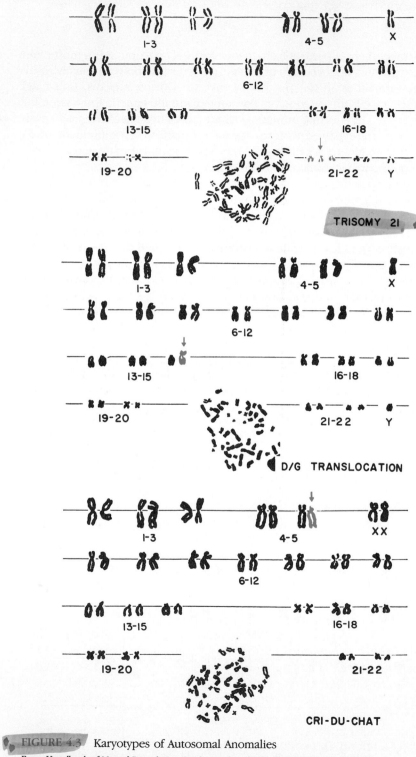

**FIGURE 4.3** Karyotypes of Autosomal Anomalies

From *Handbook of Mental Retardation Syndromes* (pp. 47, 49, 58) by C. H. Carter, 1975, Springfield, IL: Charles C Thomas. Reprinted by permission of Charles C Thomas, Publisher.

Down syndrome occurs when a fragment broken off from chromosome pair 21 attaches to a chromosome from group 15. In **deletion**, a portion of the original genetic material is absent from a specific chromosome or pair. Finally, **mosaicism** is an uneven division in mitosis that creates a mosaic pattern of dissimilar cells of 46 or 47 chromosomes. Figure 4.3 shows the karyotypes for Trisomy 21, for a translocation, and for cri-du-chat, a syndrome caused by deletion. Examples of the consequences of chromosomal irregularities are discussed later in this chapter.

## ETIOLOGICAL CLASSIFICATION

The recent manual on classification of the AAMR (Grossman, 1983) provides a functional model for etiological classification. The Grossman system divides the many specific causes of retardation into 10 broad categories. This system has been tied both to the generic International Classification of Diseases system developed by WHO and to the APA's *Diagnostic and Statistical Manual*.

The specific examples given here to illustrate Grossman's categories are only representative samples and are by no means an all-inclusive listing. Table 4.2 presents an adaptation of this classification system. The AAMR's Committee on Terminology and Classification, under the direction of Ruth Luckasson, has begun the process of revising the manual and the classification system.

### INFECTIONS AND INTOXICANTS

The first category underscores the variety of harmful substances, or **teratogens**, that can significantly affect pre- and postnatal development. The first widespread public exposure to the awesome power of teratogenic agents came from the thalidomide tragedy of the 1960s. Intended as a relaxant during pregnancy, this chemical caused severe physical deformities in many unborn children. The discussion below focuses on some of the specific infections and intoxicants that have proven teratogenic effects.

The brain is especially susceptible to malformation through infection or intoxication during the first three months of pregnancy. Infection of the mother by rubella (German measles) early in pregnancy has been found to result in fetal defects in up to 50% of cases. This is particularly significant because rubella has historically been a disease of epidemic occurrence. Recently developed immunization procedures are helping to limit its incidence. In addition to retardation, congenital rubella can result in heart disease, skull deformities, blindness, and deafness. It has been one of the primary causes of severe multiple handicaps among children.

Congenital syphilis (and other venereal diseases) is another maternal disease that can damage the central nervous system and cause severe

TABLE 4.2   Etiological Classification System

| | |
|---|---|
| Infections and intoxicants | Nutritional disorders |
|   Prenatal infections | Gross postnatal brain disease |
|     Congenital rubella |   Neurofibromatosis |
|     Congenital syphilis |   Tuberous sclerosis |
|   Postnatal cerebral infection | Other prenatal influences |
|     Viral, bacterial |   Microcephaly |
|   Intoxication |   Hydrocephalus |
|     Fetal alcohol syndrome | Chromosomal anomalies |
|     Exposure to other drugs, poisons |   Down syndrome |
|     Lead poisoning |   Fragile-X syndrome |
| Trauma or physical agent |   Sex chromosome disorders |
|   Prenatal, perinatal, postnatal injury |     Klinefelter syndrome |
| Metabolic and nutritional factors |     Turner syndrome |
|   Lipid (fat) storage disorders |     XYY syndrome |
|     Tay-Sachs | Gestational disorders |
|   Carbohydrate disorders |   Prematurity |
|     Galactosemia |   Low birth weight |
|   Amino acid disorders | Following psychiatric disorder |
|     Phenylketonuria (PKU) |   Autism |
|   Endocrine disorders |   Rett syndrome |
|     Lesch-Nyhan | Environmental influences |
|     Hypothyroidism | Other conditions |
|     Prader-Willi | |

From *Classification in Mental Retardation* (pp. 130–134) by H. J. Grossman, 1983, Washington, DC: American Association of Mental Retardation. Adapted by permission.

For additional discussion on AIDS, see Chapter 15.

retardation in the offspring. Perhaps the most alarming feature of this disorder has been its increasing prevalence in recent years—after it had nearly been eradicated. Research in the late 1980s has now also included the possible effects of maternal acquired immune deficiency syndrome (AIDS) as a handicapping agent.

One other significant possible cause of retardation through infection is blood-group incompatibility between mother and fetus. Most commonly, the condition occurs as a result of the Rh factor, a special protein on the surface of red blood cells. Rh-positive blood cells contain this protein; Rh-negative cells do not. When an Rh-positive male and an Rh-negative female conceive an Rh-positive child, neither mother nor fetus is adversely affected. At birth, however, the mother's immune system will react to the fetus's Rh-positive blood by forming antibodies to the Rh factor. These antibodies remain in the mother's system and will enter the blood stream of the next Rh-positive baby conceived, attacking its central nervous system. Rh incompatibility causes some 10,000 stillbirths yearly, while another 20,000 babies so affected are born with hearing impairments, epilepsy, cerebral palsy, and/or retardation

(Menolascino & Egger, 1978). Treatment of this immune response focuses on preventing the destructive antibodies from forming. One technique is to vaccinate the mother with Rh immunoglobulin serum within 72 hours after termination of the first pregnancy (whether by birth, miscarriage, or abortion) and of each subsequent Rh-positive pregnancy. This serum destroys the Rh-positive cells that pass from the infant's to the mother's bloodstream, inhibiting the development of antibodies that would otherwise attack the next fetus carried. This procedure does not alter the mother's immune response mechanism, but can remove the stimuli that engage it.

A substantial amount of research has investigated the effects of drugs and industrial chemicals on the fetus. Particular attention has gone to smoking, caffeine, lysergic acid (LSD), and other related drugs. The results of exposure to these substances are clear, and we should assume that any other powerful chemical substance should also be avoided by pregnant women.

The most significant breakthrough within this domain has been with alcohol consumption. Problems associated with alcohol have been generally acknowledged for years. For example, Haggard & Jellinek (1942) noted that "infants born to alcoholic mothers sometimes had a starved, shriveled and imperfect look" (p. 165). But despite this longstanding suspicion of teratogenic effects, only relatively recently has the nature of the fetal alcohol syndrome (FAS) been documented (Delaney & Hayden, 1977). Researchers have postulated that it is the third most common known cause of retardation (Smith, Jones, & Hansen, 1976; Umbreit & Ostrow, 1980), with conservative estimates standing at 5,000 children born with FAS each year in the United States (Stark, Menolascino, & Goldsbury, 1988).

In FAS, the mother's heavy alcohol consumption has direct toxic effects on the fetus. Exact levels of consumption that cause FAS are not known, but those mothers who are alcoholic, who have several drinks per day, or who engage in binge drinking run a confirmed, significant risk of damaging their unborn children. Effects can include retardation, which may be severe, cranial and skeletal anomalies, and heart defects. Research continues on the risks of moderate drinking.

While research on the nature of and effects of fetal alcohol syndrome has progressed in the last 20 years, the commitment to its prevention has been somewhat less dramatic. Baumeister and Hamlett (1986), reporting on a national survey, have indicated that, in spite of some exemplary programs, efforts to prevent FAS have not been extensive. They conclude:

> Of all the major known specific causes of severe mental retardation, FAS is, in principle, preventable with knowledge currently at our disposal. The most direct course of action would appear to be abstinence or, at least, reduction of alcohol consumption during pregnancy. Even though there are some workable ways to approach this problem, we do not have a national program to prevent this preventable disease. A coordinated prevention and evaluation program should be initiated that involves federal and state government. (p. 173)

# LEAD

# POISONING

Most of us have the misguided notion that the causes of lead poisoning and the resultant harmful effects (e.g., neurological impairment) are realities of the past. The fears of drinking from ceramic cups treated with a lead-based glaze or ingesting lead-based paint chips seem to have waned, although some of us have purchased far fewer coffee mugs at craft fairs. Unfortunately, many individuals are affected by this environmental hazard of lead poisoning every day. New sources of concern have been identified recently. One example of ways lead can get into a person's body is depicted in the drawing below. While this example is specific to Hawaii similar mecha-

nisms can be found in other locations, especially where old building materials such as gutters include lead. These materials may contact water that is later imbibed. Another source of possible lead poisoning that is getting much attention is contaminated water fountains, particularly in schools. A number of schools across the United States have identified this as a critical problem. The message from these examples is clear: the problem of lead getting into the body, especially the bodies of young children, has not gone away. It may be valuable to look into possible mechanisms of lead poisoning that exist in your area.

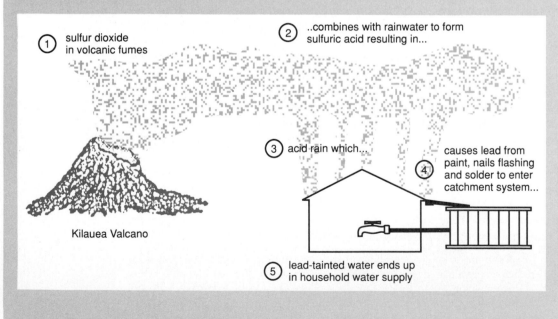

① sulfur dioxide in volcanic fumes

② ..combines with rainwater to form sulfuric acid resulting in...

③ acid rain which...

④ causes lead from paint, nails flashing and solder to enter catchment system...

Kilauea Valcano

⑤ lead-tainted water ends up in household water supply

From the *Honolulu Star-Bulletin & Advertiser*, Sept. 18, 1988, p. A-7. Advertiser Graphic by Greg Taylor.

*Children who live in substandard housing may be tempted to eat peeling lead-based paints.*

Lead poisoning, which leads to encephalitis, is permanently and progressively toxic to the central nervous system. It can cause seizures, cerebral palsy, and retardation. Although commercial paints no longer contain lead, poisoning is still a factor in residences where an infant has access to old, peeling paint. Conscious urban renewal is eliminating this problem through repainting with unleaded paints. Increased blood levels of lead can also be caused by old lead waterpipes, by prolonged breathing of polluted air, as in towns with lead smelters and heavy traffic congestion, and by the young child's mouthing and eating other objects containing lead. The President's Committee on Mental Retardation (PCMR, 1976b) has estimated that in high-risk areas up to 50% of all children have elevated lead levels in their blood. Analysis of metal concentrations for lead and other elements has indicated higher levels for children who are mildly handicapped than for their peers who are not (Marlowe, Errera, & Jacobs, 1983). There may be no such thing as a safe level for heavy metals in the body (Stark et al., 1988).

## TRAUMA OR PHYSICAL AGENT

Insult to the brain during the prenatal, perinatal, and postnatal periods falls within the category of traumas and physical agents. Particular examples include oxygen deprivation, accidents, and child abuse.

Oxygen deprivation, often referred to as *hypoxia* or *anoxia,* can result from such birth difficulties as a knotted umbilical cord, extremely short or long labor, or breech birth. Anoxia has been associated with pronounced deficiencies in the affected infant, including lower IQ scores (Graham, Ernhart, Thurston, & Craft, 1962) and is one causative agent in more than 18% of cases of mild retardation (McLaren & Bryson, 1987). The deficiencies it produces may vary greatly and are often unstable, so it is difficult to give an accurate prognosis for an anoxic child (Robinson & Robinson, 1976). Other problems at birth that can be traumatic include the delivery itself and the specific anesthetic procedures used.

A variety of postnatal traumatic events leading to disabilities can occur throughout early childhood. McLaren and Bryson (1987) have estimated that the prevalence of mild retardation stemming from trauma and neglect is as high as 15%. Head injuries account for the greater part of such cases. As MacMillan (1982) noted, the two most frequent causes of injuries are car accidents and child abuse. The relationship of the former to brain injury has spurred the passage by many states of mandatory seat belt laws. Child abuse is of special concern, particularly because of the relationship between children who are both handicapped and abused, since child abuse can aggravate primary handicapping conditions (Soeffing, 1975; Zantal-Weiner, 1987; Zirpoli, 1986). Zantal-Weiner (1987) noted in her review that children with handicaps are less able to defend themselves, have greater difficulty telling anyone of the abuse and determining appropriate and inappropriate contact, are more dependent on those who abuse them and less likely to report abuse, and are seen as less credible when they do report it. In addition to the striking of children, other disciplinary measures like vigorous shaking can play a role in brain hemorrhage and retardation.

## METABOLIC AND NUTRITIONAL FACTORS

The greatest number of specified causes of retardation fall into the category of metabolic and nutritional factors. The category includes those disorders that can be traced to dysfunction in the body's mechanisms responsible for the processing of food — so-called inborn errors of metabolism. In particular, imbalances related to fats, carbohydrates, and amino acids have been well established as causative agents. Endocrine disorders and nutritional deficiencies are also classified in this category.

Metabolic disorders resulting from an increase in lipids, or fats, in the body's tissues are frequently progressive, degenerative diseases. The developmental profile is typically a normal progression until onset of the disorder, from which point the condition rapidly worsens. Tay-Sachs disease is inherited as an autosomal recessive trait. It is disproportionately prevalent among persons of Ashkenazic Jewish backgrounds, although recent findings have shown that it occurs more frequently among Gentiles than originally thought. Infants with Tay-Sachs disorder appear normal at birth. The disease typically appears late in the child's first year, following a course of severe retardation, convulsions, blindness, paralysis, and finally death by the age of four. Tay-Sachs disease has no cure. Related disorders like Batten-Spielmeyer-Vogt syndrome begin later but have a somewhat similar profile.

An example of a carbohydrate disorder is galactosemia, a recessive condition characterized by inability to metabolize galactose, a form of sugar found in milk. The physiological changes occurring in galactosemia are biochemical rather than structural, a feature common with recessive disorders. Manifestations of the syndrome can include retardation, liver and kidney dysfunction, and cataracts, although these effects vary greatly. Following identification of the disorder, the removal of dairy products from the child's diet has proved successful in interrupting the process of deterioration, although documentation of what treatment does for intellectual functioning is limited (Schultz, 1983). But Koch and colleagues (1988) have recently reported on longitudinal research indicating that early treatment generally leads to satisfactory intellectual development. The mean IQs of children treated early (prior to four months) are virtually normal.

Diet control can also overcome the effects of genetic transmission of the amino acid disorder phenylketonuria (PKU). PKU is caused by an autosomal recessive gene, and if left untreated, it produces retardation and is frequently associated with aggressiveness, hyperactivity, destructiveness, and other disruptive behaviors (Davis, 1981). Since it was first described by Folling in 1934, PKU has been virtually eliminated as an etiological factor in severe retardation despite its incidence of 1 in every 12,000 to 15,000 births. Menolascino and Egger (1978) noted that PKU has played a significant role in the field of mental retardation because it was the first inborn metabolic anomaly proven to cause the condition. Its discovery led to both increased research into etiology and a pronounced change in the aura of hopelessness that once surrounded retardation. Figure 4.4 illustrates the discovery process for PKU.

The early results of treatment for PKU were most encouraging. Johnson and his colleagues (Johnson, Koch, Peterson, & Friedman, 1978) reported that a group of 148 treated PKU children did not significantly differ from the general population in the prevalence of congenital anomalies or major neurological defects. Intellectual level near or within the normal range was considered achievable. Children treated very early—before they were a month old—had significantly higher IQs than those whose treatment began in the second month (Koch et al., 1988); continued adherence to the diet had positive results as well.

Two major problems remained, however. The diet prescribed for PKU can be unappealing and hard to follow, and it may be difficult to balance protein control against the protein needs of developing children. For years the special diet was generally discontinued by approximately school age, but this practice has caused concern. For example, Matthews, Barabas, Cusack, and Ferrari (1986) have reported decreases in social quotients for individuals for whom the diet was discontinued at age 5½ years. In children who maintained their diets to the age of 10 instead of stopping it at 6, Fishler, Azen, Henderson, Friedman, and Koch (1987) found higher school achievement, intellectual level, language, and perceptual skills. Clarke, Gates, Hogan, Barrett, and MacDonald (1987) concluded:

> The bulk of evidence now appears to indicate that older children with PKU allowed access to unrestricted diets do experience some deterioration in intelligence, that this is associated with specific neuropsychological deficits that are not attributable simply to their intellectual handicap, and that this deficit is at

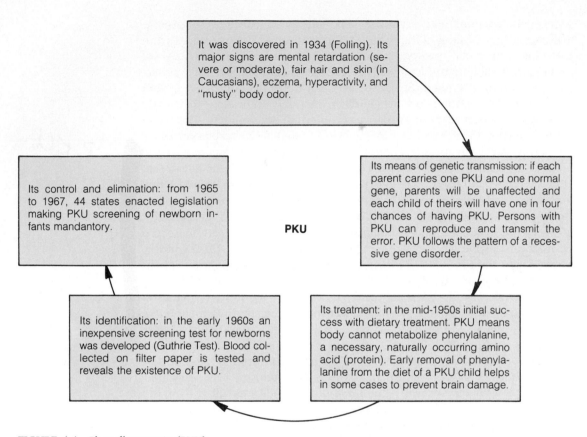

FIGURE 4.4   Phenylketonuria (PKU)

From *Mental Retardation: The Known and the Unknown* (p. 25) by President's Committee on Mental Retardation, 1976 Washington, DC: U.S. Government Printing Office.

least partly reversible by a return to carefully regulated dietary phe restriction. On the other hand, although the effects of a return to the diet are statistically significant, they are apparently not clinically significant in the short term. Therefore, although the data would support efforts to maintain older children with PKU on phe-restricted diets for as long as possible, the meager short-term clinical benefits, along with the well-known difficulty of re-introducing the therapeutic diet in older children . . . suggest that long-term return to dietary treatment is unlikely to succeed except in unusually highly motivated patients. (p. 260)

A second problem concerns women who were treated in childhood for PKU. These women's metabolic imbalances can harm their unborn children. Consequences can include retardation, heart disease, and microcephaly (Schultz, 1983). Berg and Emanuel (1987) have stated that such women should reinstate their diet during pregnancy, although it is not yet clear how successful reinstatement will be in alleviating risk. Unless pregnancy is avoided, Koch et al. (1988), citing Kirkman (1979, 1982), indicated that the effect of maternal PKU could offset the preventive benefits of screening programs and dietary treatment interventions. Blatt (1987) noted that this presents a difficult argument: "At what point does the welfare of society intrude upon the welfare of the individual, and vice versa?" (p. 130).

Lesch-Nyhan (L-N) syndrome, a disorder identified in 1964 (Lesch & Nyhan, 1964), is inherited as an X-linked recessive and thus is much more common among males. According to Nyhan (1976), this syndrome is the second most common metabolic disorder after PKU. The most striking manifestation of L-N syndrome is an apparently uncontrollable urge to cause injury to oneself and, to a lesser extent, to others.

Typically, L-N children will begin extreme self-injurious behavior (SIB) after initially acquiring teeth. They may bite ferociously and, in their frenzy, rip and tear tissue (Libby, Polloway, & Smith, 1983). In fact, as Nyhan, Johnson, Kaufman, and Jones (1980) stated, almost all L-N children can be recognized by their "distinctive loss of tissue around the lips or fingers" (p. 26). Aside from SIB, L-N children may hit, pinch, and bite others, use obscene language, spit, and engage in a variety of disruptive actions because of their inability to control their behavior (Hoefnagel, Andrew, Mireault, & Berndt, 1965). As Fernald (1976) noted, the children are driven to such behaviors and unable to inhibit them. When unrestrained they may scream as if terrified of the pain they might inflict on themselves, while when restrained they seem more tractable.

Both biomedical and educational interventions have been attempted with L-N children. Drug treatment to alter the metabolism has proven efficacious on a short-term basis, although its effectiveness in eliminating SIB once the treatment has been discontinued has not been commonly reported. Continued work on biochemical processes in the brain also offer great promise. According to Carlson (personal correspondence, 1986), several biochemical disorders including Lesch-Nyhan and PKU are likely candidates in the future for the development of **gene therapy**—a process of cloning a gene to perform the appropriate metabolic task (e.g., the conversion of phenylalanine to tyrosine in the case of PKU). Educational interventions with children with Lesch-Nyhan have included a variety of attempts at behavioral change with differing levels of success, as reported in the literature (see Anderson, Dancis, & Alpert, 1978; Bull & LaVecchio, 1978; Duker, 1975).

Endocrine dysfunctions can also seriously affect mental and physical development. Hypothyroidism, the most common endocrine disorder, is the consequence of abnormally low levels of thyroid secretions. It has an estimated incidence of 1 in 5,000 births and is detrimental whether it is congenital or occurs postnatally. The congenital condition, caused by damage to the gland or by maternal dietary deficiencies, has often been referred to as cretinism. It is characterized by small stature, dry, grayish-white skin, a large head, poor muscle tone, sluggishness, and severe retardation. If the syndrome has not been present in utero, however, or if it is acquired (as an autosomal recessive trait), thyroid treatment can prevent or reduce the development of the physical stigmata and the onset of retardation. Inexpensive screening procedures based on the same blood sample used for PKU tests can detect this disorder at birth.

Another endocrine disorder that has received attention in recent years is Prader-Willi syndrome. The most significant characteristics of this disorder are retardation in motor and mental development, hypogenital development, insatiable appetite (and hence obesity), and small features and stature (Wannarachue, Ruyalcaba, & Kelley, 1975). The biological mechanism underlying the syndrome seems to bring about a preoccupation with eating that has prompted observers to suggest that, for a Prader-Willi child, "Life is one endless meal." This organic drive to consume may lead to the eating of nonfood items as well as to stealing, gorging, and foraging (Otto, Sulzbacher, & Worthington-Roberts, 1982).

Goldman (1988) noted that the association of Prader-Willi syndrome with obesity has led to the assumption that expected life span for individuals with the disorder is limited (death before 30th birthday), at least in part because of the physical complications of being grossly overweight. In contrast, her research indicates that older individuals do exist and may have been unidentified. Since the disorder was first described only in the mid-1950s, obviously some older persons could have escaped detection. Goldman (1988) described two adult women for whom the desire to overeat continued with no evidence of understanding the need to manage intake. Goldman's two subjects obtained food through their own devices. "Even when the environment is believed to be controlled, these persons evidently engage in some variety of successful covert foraging" (p. 101).

Recent research points to the likelihood of an aberration in chromosome pair 15 as the source of Prader-Willi (Nardella, Sulzbacher, & Worthington-Roberts, 1983). If this is confirmed, the syndrome will be reclassified as a chromosomal abnormality. Additional information on the mechanics of the disorder and the effectiveness of various treatment options should be forthcoming in the near future.

Nutritional disorders help cause developmental deficiencies when either mother or child has an inadequate diet. Malnutrition during gestation or the first six months of life hinders the development of brain cells and can lead to as much as a 40% deficit in the number of brain cells. Resnick (1988) stated that the first two trimesters may be most critical to the prevention of such lacks, although he also indicated that maternal nutrition before pregnancy may be even more important. Since later brain growth is in weight rather than in number of cells, the effects of early malnutrition have long been viewed as irreversible (Cravioto, DeLicardie, & Birch, 1966; Winick, 1969). As Cravioto et al. (1966) and Crnic (1984) have pointed out, however, it is difficult to assess the true detrimental effect of poor nutrition because it tends to accompany other unfavorable circumstances—inadequate housing, substandard living conditions, poor hygiene, and poor prenatal care. We must also consider the results of diets high in calories but low in important nutrients (Springer & Fricke, 1975).

## GROSS POSTNATAL BRAIN DISEASE

Several rare disorders carried as dominant traits come within the category of gross postnatal brain disease. An individual affected by a full-blown case of postnatal brain disease is not likely to have children, so that the incidence of this type of disease is affected by the reduced penetrance, variable expressivity, and late age of onset of the dominant trait. Some cases are the result of genetic mutation.

Neurofibromatosis is also known as Von Recklinghausen's disease, for the man who first described the disorder in 1882. It is identifiable by the light brown patches (called *café au lait*) and multiple nerve tumors (neurofibromas) that appear on the body. These growths can bring about pronounced physical deformities. It has been hypothesized that neurofibromatosis was the affliction from which both John Merrick (immortalized in the play and movie as "the Elephant Man") and Quasimodo, the Hunchback of Notre Dame, suffered (Blatt, 1987).

Neurofibromatosis varies greatly in expressivity and penetrance from case to case. The café-au-lait patches are primarily just physically unattractive, but the locations of the tumors have an effect on mental development, which will be severe if there is brain injury. Otherwise, the subject may have normal intelligence. As the story of John Merrick illustrates, his wisdom eventually became far more significant for many than his physical characteristics.

Tuberous sclerosis is another skin disease carried by a dominant gene. The two words derive from the Latin and Greek for "potato-like" and "hardening," respectively. Its tumors are similar to potatoes in density and destroy the cells in the organs where they are found (Menolascino & Egger, 1978). As with neurofibromatosis, the changes resulting from tuberous sclerosis are primarily structural rather than biochemical, a common finding in autosomal disorders. The expressivity of the gene can result in great variation in characteristics of the people who have the disease. In the mild form, no retardation or serious health problems occur; in the classical severe variety, tumors can result in dysfunction of any number of organs (e.g., brain, lungs, kidneys), followed by mental deterioration, epilepsy, and early death.

Another progressive disease is Huntington chorea, a degenerative disease that attacks brain nerves and fibers. The classical symptoms are involuntary, jerky *(choreic)* movements, which give the disease part of its name. These are accompanied by mental deterioration and eventually death. Chorea is rarely a true cause of retardation as now defined, because it begins after childhood (Grossman, 1983). Offspring may inherit the dominant gene for the disorder before symptoms appear in the parent. The recent development of a screening test to determine whether an individual has the gene should be significant in its prevention.

## OTHER PRENATAL INFLUENCES

The category "other prenatal influences" was established as "unknown prenatal influence" by Grossman to include conditions present at birth but of uncertain etiology. Medical research has now identified potential causes for many of these disorders. The category includes several cranial and cerebral malformations that have been among the most common of the clinical types of retardation.

Children who have microcephaly are characterized by a small, conical skull, a curved spine that leads to a stooping posture, and severe retardation. The condition can be transmitted genetically, probably as an autosomal recessive trait, or it can be a secondary consequence of such conditions as congenital rubella. Individuals affected by microcephaly have been characterized as imitative, good-natured, and lively.

Hydrocephalus consists of at least six types of problems associated with interference in the flow of cerebrospinal fluid within the skull. The most common blockage often results in progressive enlargement of the cranium and subsequent brain damage. Physical manifestations of this condition differ widely, and an enlarged skull is not present in all cases. Hydrocephalus may come through polygenic inheritance or as a secondary result of maternal infections or intoxications. Although the condition has historically been somewhat common, more recently its effects have been greatly reduced in many infants by draining off the fluid using shunts to decrease the cranial pressure. *Shunts* are valves or tubes surgically inserted under the child's skin to pump the fluid away from the brain and maintain proper flow. The results of early shunt treatment have been very encouraging in preventing head enlargement, the symptom most often associated with a decrease in the probability of retardation. Wolraich (1983) indicated that proper treatment can ensure the survival of affected children, although significant handicaps remain a possibility. Milder cases may escape detection, with no ill effects noted. For example, some think that Einstein may have had a mild, nonprogressive case of hydrocephalus (Beck, 1972).

## CHROMOSOMAL ANOMALIES

Before the 1950s, causes of the disorders included under chromosomal anomalies were unknown (see Heber, 1959). Research published by Lejeune and his colleagues (Lejeune, Gautier, & Turpin, 1959) and other cytogeneticists has led to a much clearer understanding of the nature of chromosomal abnormalities. As mentioned earlier, aberrations in the number or arrangement of chromosomes are likely to damage the developing organism. Down syndrome and cri-du-chat syndrome are examples of autosomal disorders;

Klinefelter and Turner syndromes come from sex chromosome abnormalities. Chromosomal errors account for between 20% and 40% of the more severe cases of retardation (McLaren & Bryson, 1987). In recent years persons with chromosomal disorders have also been found in the mild retardation range.

*Down syndrome.*   This condition is by far the best known, most prevalent, and most frequently researched type of biologically caused retardation. For many laypersons, the concept of mental retardation is synonymous with a Down syndrome child. A reasonable estimate of the prevalence of the syndrome is 5% to 6% of all persons identified as retarded.

Study of the disorder has revealed three separate chromosomal causes. The first and most common, trisomy 21, is due to the failure of one pair of parental chromosomes to separate at conception, resulting in the child's having 47 chromosomes (see Figure 4.3 p. 126). This abnormality has historically been found more often in children born to older mothers, and researchers have suggested a variety of possible causes.

Specific deleterious factors that have been suspected include medication and drugs, exposure to radiation, chemicals, or hepatitis viruses, and the possible absence of a mechanism in the mother to abort the fetus spontaneously. It is important to realize that, although risk is related to age and increases to approximately 1 in 30 at 45 years old, age per se is not the cause. Recent analyses have hypothesized a linkage of paternal age with Down syndrome. Estimates have been made that in 20% to 25% of all cases of Trisomy 21, the father contributes the extra chromosome (Abroms & Bennett, 1980), although this relationship has been disputed (Carlson, 1984). Given the increased public awareness of the correlation between age and risk of occurrence and, subsequently, the more common decision to consider abortion (see p. 154), it is not surprising that a higher percentage of Down syndrome children are now being born to younger parents (Zarfas & Wolf, 1979).

The second form of Down syndrome is caused by a translocation transmitted hereditarily by carriers. Although this translocation is usually to chromosome pairs 13 or 15, the extra material comes from pair 21 and forms in a sense a partial trisomy. Mosaicism, the uneven division that creates cells varying in chromosome numbers (47 and 46), is the third and rarest cause. Patterson (1987) has concluded that the association of Down syndrome with pair 21 is clear—there are no cases of Down syndrome in which at least a partial trisomy 21 has not been found, and no reported cases of individuals with trisomy 21 who do not have the syndrome.

Down syndrome is frequently associated with specific physical stigmata. A list of characteristics that *may be* associated with it are listed below:

☐ Short
☐ Flat, broad face with small ears and nose

☐ Short, broad hands with incurving fingers

☐ Upward slanting of the eyes with folds of skin (epicanthic folds) at the inside corner of the eye

☐ Small mouth and short roof, which may cause the tongue to protrude and may contribute to articulation problems

☐ Single crease across the palm

☐ Reduced muscle tone *(hypotonia)* and hyperflexibility of joints

☐ Heart defects (in about one third of instances)

☐ Increased susceptibility to upper respiratory infections

☐ Incomplete or delayed sexual development

These vary greatly from one individual to another. Contrary to popular opinion, the number of physical characteristics present does not predict the level of intelligence (Belmont, 1971; Shipe, Neisman, Chung, Darnell, & Kelley, 1968).

A recent change in the syndrome picture concerns life expectancy. Patterson (1987) indicated that while in 1929, expectancy for individuals with Down syndrome was only nine years, by 1980 that average had increased to over 30 years, with 25% of individuals living past 50. As age increases, association of the syndrome with Alzheimer's disease has also increased. Individuals with Down syndrome apparently run a much greater risk of Alzheimer's (Patterson, 1987; Stark et al., 1988; Zigman, Schupf, Lubin, & Silverman, 1987). Epstein (1988) has pointed out that the loss of intellectual functioning associated with advanced age will be seen more often now that life expectancies have increased.

Many of the behavioral characteristics traditionally associated with Down syndrome have generally not been documented in research. In particular, the stereotype of the young Down syndrome child who is cheerful, affectionate, rhythmic, and has unusual dexterity has not been empirically established (Belmont, 1971).

Most significant have been the data collected on the intellectual functioning of Down syndrome children. Traditionally, the syndrome had been assumed to result most often in moderate retardation, with a ceiling IQ of 70. Occasional anecdotal reports of ability and special talents (see Buck, 1955; Hunt, 1961) were considered more interesting or unique than typical.

Representative of the sentiments of many toward Down children is this statement: "You show me one mongoloid that has an educable IQ . . . . I've never seen one in my experience with over 800 mongols" (Restak, 1975, p. 92). Rynders, Spiker, and Horrobin (1978) answered with a wealth of information on the question. Their review of 15 studies provided data on the intelligence test scores of Down syndrome children that indicated a significant range in level of functioning. The alleged ceiling IQ levels appear to be invalid, and differences across the three karyotypes are also noteworthy. Generally, mosaicism produces higher levels of functioning than Trisomy 21 or translocation (cf. Hopkins, 1982).

Optimistic data on the abilities of children with Down syndrome continue to accumulate. Early intervention seems to be the key to the future. In a most positive statement, Rynders et al. (1978) conclude by suggesting that there may be a 30% to 55% chance that Down syndrome children can function in the educable range.

Individual case histories add further fuel to the excitement building around Down syndrome. For example, an illustration of the range of effects of the mosaic form of Down syndrome was offered by Turkington (1987), who described the life of Paige Barton, a thirty-five-year-old woman who had completed an associate arts degree in early childhood education and hoped to become certified as a teacher.

In addition to the encouraging data on intellectual development, recent efforts in plastic surgery should be mentioned. Such efforts, most notably in Israel in the work of Reuven Feuerstein and his colleagues, have demonstrated that the physical stigmata of Down syndrome can be reduced. May (1988) provides a good discussion of the rationales, benefits, and cautions of plastic surgery for people with Down syndrome, and cosmetic intervention is further discussed later in this chapter.

Two facts must be made clear. First, individuals with Down syndrome are first and foremost people who have needs, desires, and rights similar to others'. Second, the effects of intensive interventions with young children who have Down syndrome are only now being evaluated, and historical descriptions of the syndrome are no longer accurate.

*Other chromosomal anomalies.*    A chromosomal anomaly that has recently been documented is *fragile-X* or *Martin-Bell syndrome* (Richards, Sylvester, & Brooker, 1981). After Down syndrome, this may be the most common clinical type of retardation and may represent one reason that retardation is more common in males (de la Cruz, 1985).

The disorder is caused by a deficiency in the formation of the X chromosome. Figure 4.5 shows a karyotype of fragile-X syndrome. The fragile site is the lower arm of the X chromosome.

According to Rogers and Simensen (1987), common characteristics of fragile-X include prominent jaws, macro-orchidism, long and thin faces, soft ears, soft or fleshy hands, prominent forehead and enlarged head, long ears, hands, and palms. The syndrome has been associated in males with severe and profound levels of retardation, although reports of its occurrence in individuals with various levels of retardation (and also with normal intelligence) suggest the need for caution and for careful consideration of environmental experiences (Daker, Chidiac, Fear, & Berry, 1981; Pueschel, Hays, & Mendoza, 1983; Rogers & Simensen, 1987). Women who have the fragile-X chromosome are clinically viewed as carriers; an estimated one third may be partially affected by at least mild retardation (de la Cruz, 1985; Rogers & Simensen, 1987). The discovery of the syndrome provides an exciting direction for further research, because it seems likely that many

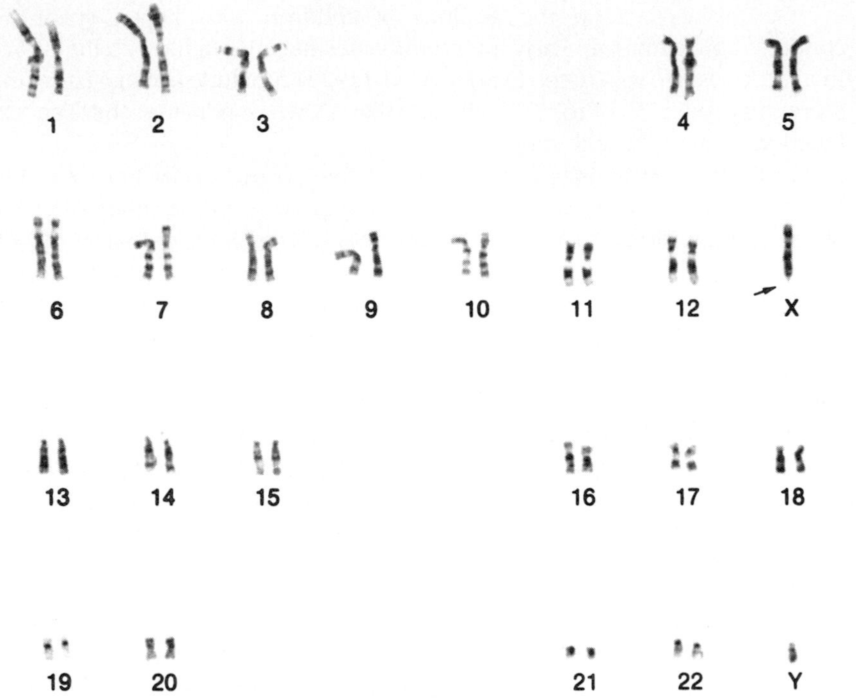

FIGURE 4.5    Karyotype of Fragile-X Syndrome

From *Counseling Aids for Geneticists* (p. 27) by W. E. Potts, R. J. Schroer, and H. A. Taylor, 1984, Greenwood, SC: Greenwood Genetic Center.

cases of retardation for which no cause was previously specifiable may have been victims of this disorder.

A third type of autosomal abnormality is known as *cri-du-chat* (cat's cry) syndrome, from the high-pitched crying of the child, caused by a related larynx dysfunction. This disorder is the consequence of deletion of chromosomal material from the short arm of a pair 5 chromosome and can be viewed as a partial monosomy. It generally results in severe retardation.

Abnormalities in the sex chromosomes have also been found to affect development adversely. Three such conditions are discussed below; their karyotypes are shown in Figure 4.6.

*Klinefelter syndrome* is a condition in which males receive an extra X sex chromosome, so that they have an XXY arrangement. The clinical pattern of the syndrome includes frequent social retardation, sterility and underdevelopment of the male sex organs, and the acquisition of female secondary sex characteristics. The syndrome is often associated with borderline or mild levels of intellectual retardation. Deficits increase with the number of X chromosomes (XXXY, XXXXY). Incidence is relatively high: 1 in 400 male

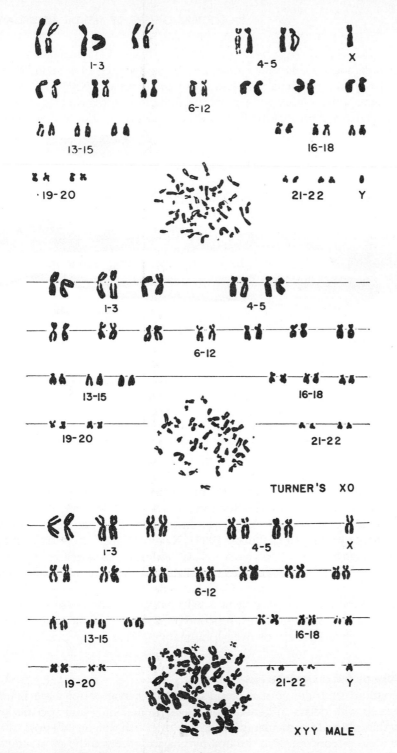

**FIGURE 4.6** Sex Chromosomal Abnormalities

From *Handbook of Mental Retardation Syndromes* (pp. 39, 43, 45) by C. H. Carter, 1975, Springfield, IL: Charles C Thomas. Reprinted by permission of Charles C Thomas, Publisher.

births. Although no specific cure exists, physical aspects of the condition can be alleviated through surgery and hormonal treatment. XXY boys can have problems with auditory perception, receptive and expressive language, and a general deficit in processing linguistic information (Bender, Fry, Pennington, Puck, Salonblatt, & Robinson, 1983).

A sex chromosomal disorder in females, *Turner syndrome,* results from an absence of one of the X chromosomes (XO). It is the only syndrome with a true monosomy and thus the only one with fewer than 46 chromosomes. Its rarity is underscored by the fact that over 95% of fetuses conceived with the XO pattern are spontaneously aborted. Although Turner syndrome is not usually a cause of mental retardation, it is worthy of mention because it is often associated with learning problems, especially spatial and organizational difficulties. As with Klinefelter syndrome, Turner syndrome produces deviations from normal development, with lack of secondary sex characteristics, sterility, and short stature as common features.

One other abnormality of sex chromosomes that has attracted substantial attention is *Jacob* or *XYY syndrome*. Although not often a direct cause of retardation, this disorder has been popularly indicted for causing behavior deviations. As Engel (1977) stated,

> The discovery of the XYY deserves special mention, having been marred by the much overstated notion that bearers of two Y's were tall, dull, antisocial, aggressive beings compelled to perpetrate murder and larceny. As if to prove the point, a drunken murderer—made notorious by the senseless killing of eight women nurses—was reported by the press all over the world as the bearer of such an anomaly, a statement untenable in light of actual chromosome test results. (p. 113)

Although XYYs have been thought to be overrepresented in prison populations, there is no clear support for this belief, and research indicates that their crimes are more often against property than people, as had been commonly assumed (Kauffman, 1989). XYY boys may show difficulties in some language skills (e.g., auditory discrimination or word retrieval), but may not differ significantly from individuals who are not handicapped (Bender et al., 1983). Carlson (1984) has indicated that XYY may not even be a true syndrome, since only a small percentage of persons with this chromosomal arrangement express one or more of the symptoms associated with the clinical pattern or behavioral manifestations.

## GESTATIONAL DISORDERS

Deviations from the normal prenatal developmental period have been associated with delays in general intellectual functioning and specific learning difficulties. In particular, prematurity, low birth weight, and postmaturity are areas of concern, with the first two having received the most attention. Potential correlates of prematurity and low birth weight are illustrated in Figure 4.7, although no simple, cause-effect relationship exists for any of

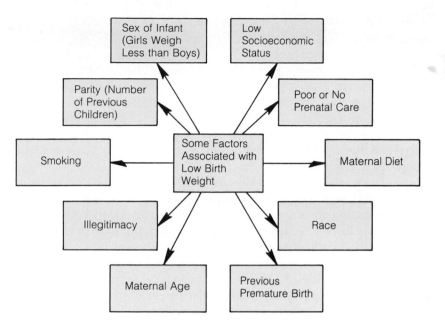

Prematurity: Gestation time of less than 37 weeks.
Low Birth Weight: Weight at birth equal to or less than 2,500 grams

FIGURE 4.7   Low Birth Weight and Prematurity

From *Mental Retardation: The Known and the Unknown* (p. 31) by President's Committee on Mental Retardation, 1976, Washington, DC: U.S. Government Printing Office.

these factors. Perhaps most notable in light of recent demographic trends is teenage pregnancy—a phenomenon on the rise (Hodgkinson, 1985)—and one that clearly increases risks low birth weight (Berg & Emanuel, 1987).

Determining the effects of prematurity has been a difficult task. Extremely short pregnancies (less than 28 weeks) or very low birth weights (below 1,500 grams, or 3½ pounds) are frequently problems, but for less substantial deviations, the results are not so clear. Data indicate that the relationship between prematurity, low birth weight, and mental retardation is most significant for very low birth weight (Berg & Emanuel, 1987).

Menolascino and Egger (1978) further discussed the relationship between prematurity and retardation when they noted a combination of conditions that could produce retardation. They stated:

> A complex, but not unusual, example would be an infant born at 32 weeks gestation, weighing 4 pounds (1,800 grams), and displaying cyanosis and respiratory distress at birth, whose mother is a short, unmarried 17-year-old female from a low socioeconomic class. So many variables are present, and many of them are so difficult to quantify, that is no wonder that consistent answers regarding prematurity and mental retardation are difficult to derive. (p. 230)

In addition to low IQ, prematurity has also been linked to increased occurrence of cerebral palsy and lack of ability to concentrate.

Some of the deficiencies that premature children develop can be attributed to life in an incubator. Exposing the children to sounds, fondling, and rocking while in the incubator may help overcome this sensory deprivation by resulting in improved sucking ability, attention skills, and, eventually, test scores. But the efficacy of these techniques has been questioned. The beneficial effects may dissipate over time, so that the techniques may not really offer as much benefit as initially ascribed to them (Robinson & Robinson, 1976).

## RETARDATION FOLLOWING PSYCHIATRIC DISORDER

The relationship between retardation and psychiatric disorders is hazy when the disorder occurs during childhood. As Benton (1964) noted, their association has four interpretations: *(a)* the two may occur coincidentally; *(b)* a single, basic process may result in both the intellectual subnormality and the behavioral disorder; *(c)* the retardation may be primary, with a stressful environment causing the psychiatric disorder; and *(d)* the psychological disturbance may be primary, resulting in intellectual deficiency. The fourth interpretation, retardation caused by disturbance, is the one that specifically applies to this etiological category.

Several syndromes are particularly apt examples of the interaction between behavioral disorders and mental retardation. *Autism,* classified by DSM-III-R as a severe form of pervasive developmental disorder, begins in infancy or early childhood. Characteristics of autistic children include impairments in social interactions and in verbal and nonverbal communication, and a limited repertory of activities and interests. Manifestations of autism are most often long term, although there is significant variation in severity (Board of Rights of the Disabled, 1987). Most significant for the purposes of discussion here is that most children with autism are functionally retarded (Rutter, 1988).

*Rett syndrome,* originally described by Andreas Rett in 1966, is another serious disorder. Affected individuals display behavior similar to that of persons with autism. Al-Mateen, Philippart, and Shields (1986) indicate that the syndrome is characterized by three phases of onset. Manifestations, including progressive mental deterioration, often begin between 3 and 18 months of age. Loss of purposeful use of the hands and legs and epilepsy occur as well. Al-Mateen et al. (1986) say that the cause is unknown, but involvement of multiple levels of central nervous system dysfunction is likely.

These two syndromes illustrate the historical dilemma of distinguishing between retardation and behavioral disorder, often a monumental problem. In many situations it is decided more by the bias of the professional making the diagnosis than by clinical agreement.

Although debate will probably continue on the potential of children with severe disturbances, in reality they are often functionally retarded (Baker,

1979). As Maloney and Ward (1978) state, "One thing is . . . clear: the earlier the disturbance occurs (providing it is of significant duration), the higher the probability that it will interfere with intellectual development" (p. 250). Similarly, Russell and Tanquay (1981) report that, while episodic psychotic illness may result in transient functioning in the mild or moderate ranges of intelligence, prolonged problems may depress intelligence permanently.

Regardless of the exact relation between the two disorders, behavioral and emotional disturbances do occur more often among those who are retarded than in the general population (Beier, 1964; Epstein, Cullinan, & Polloway, 1986; Forness & Polloway, 1987; Polloway, Epstein, & Cullinan, 1985; Szymanski, 1980). Of particular interest are the data reported by Forness and Polloway (1987) based on referrals to a tertiary care center in California that served approximately 1 in 10 of all students with mild retardation in the local catchment area. Of the students, 77.3% qualified for a psychiatric diagnosis, with disorders identified as conduct, affective, schizophrenic, personality, and autistic spectrum.

Of particular importance is the realization that behavioral disturbance is very often a concomitant problem leading to public school referrals for special class services and to residential facilities. This fact increases the likelihood that the population of persons with retardation will frequently include many who might more appropriately be identified as multiply handicapped.

## ENVIRONMENTAL INFLUENCES

Although the categories discussed so far represent hundreds of specific *causes* of mental retardation, the majority of *cases* of retardation are classified as having environmental causes and fall into the familial rather than an organic or a pathological group. This category of environmental influences includes negative experiences (or the absence of positive interactions) that the child has encountered. The two terms used most frequently to describe this group have been **cultural-familial retardation** and **psychosocial disadvantage**. Although these terms carry somewhat different implications, the assumptions underlying both are that cause cannot precisely be specified and that the condition is the result of the interaction of a myriad environmental variables and genetic factors. The next chapter delves more deeply into causal factors that relate to the interaction of heredity and environment.

## PREVENTION AND TREATMENT

The above discussion of biological causes of retardation and their results may seem to present a bleak picture. The purpose of this section is to document the tools, techniques, and procedures that prevent, ameliorate, or treat biomedical retardation. Progress has been particularly significant during the last 35 years. Inspired by a government commitment to prevent the

The issues associated with prevention are discussed again in chapter 15.

occurrence of 50% of all cases of retardation by the end of the century (PCMR, 1976b), researchers have tackled virtually all known causes of retardation. In every case a specific preventive measure has been found. Despite the pessimism of some about the goal of preventing retardation, within the biomedical domain substantial increases in knowledge have taken place. The reader who is interested in a more detailed review is referred to Menolascino and Stark's (1988) excellent text.

## BIOMEDICAL INTERVENTION

*Preconception.*   Preventive measures taken before conception can avert hereditary, innate, congenital, and other constitutional disorders. One basic tool is genetic counseling, an attempt to determine risks of occurrence or recurrence of specific genetic or chromosomal disorders. The tools of the genetic counselor include the family history and personal screening. Study of the person's genetic and general medical history is particularly concerned with evidence of spontaneous abortions or stillbirths, age and causes of death of relatives, and the existence of any intrafamily marriages that might bear on the presence of specific genetic disorders. Screening is primarily for carriers of recessive trait disorders. Blood samples can be analyzed rather easily and inexpensively; for example, Tay-Sachs screening cost about $20 in the 1980s. Based on an understanding of the mathematical probabilities associated with recessive, dominant, or sex-linked inheritance, prospective parents can make an informed decision about the risks of having a child who may be developmentally disabled.

Other specific means of prevention are also available during this period. Immunization for maternal rubella can prevent women from contracting this disease during pregnancy. Blood tests can identify the presence of venereal diseases. Adequate maternal nutrition can lay a sound metabolic foundation for later childbearing. Family planning in terms of size, appropriate spacing, and age of parents can also affect a variety of specific causal agents.

*During gestation.*   Two general approaches to prevention are appropriate during pregnancy: prenatal care and analysis for possible genetic disorders. Numerous prenatal precautions can be taken to avert congenital problems. Adequate nutrition, fetal monitoring, and protection from disease are certainly the foundations of prenatal care. Avoidance of teratogenic substances resulting both from exposure (e.g., radiation) and from personal consumption (e.g., alcohol and drugs) also relate specifically to this period.

Analysis of the fetus for the possible presence of genetic or chromosomal disorders is a key component of genetic counseling (see box for a full discussion of genetic counseling services). This analysis includes amniocentesis, chorion villus sampling, fetoscopy, fetal biopsy, and ultrasound. *Amniocentesis,* which has become an almost routine medical procedure in the past decade, involves drawing amniotic (embryonic sac) fluid for

# GENETIC
## SERVICES AND
## COUNSELING

Genetic counseling is actually one part of what more properly may be called *genetic services* available throughout the nation. Genetic counseling refers specifically to communication, which is a most important part of the process of dealing with genetic disorders in a family. Genetic services offered by different agencies typically focus on a wide range of objectives, presenting a number of options to families and individuals. This list shows genetic services available through the Department of Medical Genetics at the University of Virginia.

☐ Evaluation of children with suspected mental and/or growth retardation

☐ Diagnosis, coordination of care, and genetic counseling for children with congenital anomalies

☐ Cytogenetic confirmation of a suspected chromosome abnormality

☐ Genetic counseling for couples with a family history of a possible genetic disorder

☐ Tay-Sachs carrier screening for Jewish couples

☐ Genetic counseling and arrangements for prenatal diagnosis for chromosome abnormalities, neural tube defects, inborn errors of metabolism

☐ Diagnosis and management of problems with short stature and skeletal dysplasias

☐ Evaluation and counseling of adults with medical disorders seeking assistance in family planning

☐ Counseling of Black families concerned about sickle cell disease

☐ A source of assistance and/or information for any questions related to human genetics.

As is apparent from this list, nearly all of the services involve counseling. This process requires knowledgeable, skilled people who are qualified to deal effectively with different situations, with various types of people, and with a myriad emotional crises. Counselors in general and genetic counselors in particular must be careful and sensitive to the needs of their clients. This process may involve

1. Discussion of the problem (i.e., the genetic disease)
2. Fundamental lessons in genetics
3. Explanation of the mathematical probability of the risk or occurrence or recurrence
4. Presentation of the options that are available
5. Decision-making (i.e., acting on a given decision)
6. Follow-up support

Without question a number of moral (e.g., abortion) and ethical (e.g., who should use this service) issues are connected with genetic counseling; however, we must face these issues realistically and attempt to find solutions. We encourage you to find out more about genetic services available in your community. Additional information about where genetic services may be located can be obtained from the National Foundation/March of Dimes.

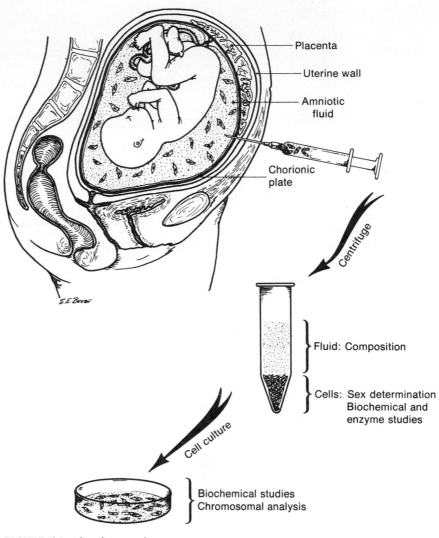

Placenta

Uterine wall

Amniotic fluid

Chorionic plate

Centrifuge

Fluid: Composition

Cells: Sex determination
Biochemical and
enzyme studies

Cell culture

Biochemical studies
Chromosomal analysis

FIGURE 4.8    Amniocentesis

From *Fetal Monitoring and Fetal Assessment in High-Risk Pregnancy* by S. M. Tucker, 1978, St. Louis: C. V. Mosby. Reprinted by permission.

biochemical analysis of fetal cells. It is usually performed during the 14th to 16th week of pregnancy. This procedure is depicted in Figure 4.8. In the majority of cases where amniocentesis is used, its primary purpose is the detection of such chromosomal errors as Down syndrome.

Generally the technique is safe. However, Tucker (1978) contends that the patient should be informed of certain risks. They are:

1. The risk factor to the mother and fetus is approximately 1%.
2. The culture of fetal cells may not be successful.
3. Repeated amniocentesis may be required.
4. Chromosome analysis, biochemical analysis, or both may not be successful.
5. Normal chromosome results, normal biochemical results, or both do not eliminate the possibility that the child may have birth defects or mental retardation because of other disorders.
6. In the case of undiagnosed twins, the results pertain only to one of the twin pair. (p. 38)

A more recent technique for prenatal diagnosis is *chorion villus sampling* (CVS). This can also provide information on chromosomal and biochemical anomalies. In CVS, chorionic tissue (material that forms the placenta) is withdrawn. The test can be performed after approximately nine weeks of gestation with initial results (chromosomal analysis) back within two days and a full culture two weeks after the sampling. The most significant advantage of the process is that it allows an earlier analysis of fetal status. It has been estimated that CVS is associated with a spontaneous abortion rate of 1–2%, and although it has been used extensively, it is still considered experimental.

These two analytical techniques have three purposes. Most encouraging, of course, is that negative tests assuage parental fears or anxieties. Second, the results can confirm suspicions of disorders and give the parents a chance to find out what to expect. They also alert the physician to the need for careful monitoring prenatally, perinatally, and postnatally. Finally, the information can be used as a basis for therapeutic abortion. The use of these techniques along with elective abortion has significantly reduced the occurrence of specific disorders like Tay-Sachs disease (Scheiderman, Lowden, & Rae-Grant, 1978) and Down syndrome (Hanson, 1978), although obviously it has also generated much controversy. Selective abortion is discussed later in this chapter.

One other technique that has contributed to an understanding of the prenatal environment is *ultrasound,* or *sonography.* It can be used for possible determination of hydrocephalus, some central nervous system disorders, and limb anomalies. The technique is also used to determine the location for amniocentesis, to assist in delivery, and as a common adjunct to *fetal therapy,* which seeks to correct conditions existing in utero.

*At delivery.* Prevention at delivery is based on anticipating possible problems. MacMillan (1977) suggests that a pregnancy be considered high risk deserving of special attention whenever

1. The mother is under 20 or over 40 years of age;
2. There is a combination of low economic status and closely spaced pregnancies;

3. The expectant mother has a history of miscarriages, stillbirths, premature infants, and previous children with significant birth defects;
4. The expectant mother has chronic conditions such as diabetes, hypertension, and alcoholism;
5. The mother has Rh negative blood or her blood is otherwise incompatible with that of the fetus. (p. 145)

Several specific measures can be used to avert significant problems during the perinatal period. The most common is the Apgar test of vital signs (Apgar, 1953), an evaluation routinely given in American hospitals at 1 and 5 minutes after the birth of a child. On a scale of 0 to 2, the physician rates each of the following factors: heart rate, respiratory effort, muscle tone, skin color, and reflex response. An Apgar score of 8 to 10 suggests the newborn is healthy and responsive; scores of 5 to 7 and 0 to 4 indicate moderate depression and severe depression, respectively. Initial screening using such a scale can assist in preliminary decision-making about children who may be at risk for specific disorders, and more comprehensive assessment then follows. Intensive intervention can begin almost immediately for premature and other infants identified as having a particular difficulty.

Computer-assisted obstetric measures assist in the close monitoring of both mother and child, and another helpful measure during the first 3 days after birth is injection of gamma globulin, which can prevent Rh-negative mothers from developing antibodies that might affect subsequent children. If a child is born to a mother who did not have the necessary injection at the time of an earlier birth (or abortion), a complete transfusion of the newborn's blood can prevent the destruction of its blood cells by the mother's antibodies.

***Early childhood.***   Although prevention in the postnatal period is primarily achieved through environmental intervention, several biomedical interventions continue to be important. Proper nutrition is of importance throughout childhood, and particularly so during the first six months. Dietary restrictions for specific metabolic disorders should be maintained until no longer needed. Finally, avoidance of hazards in the child's environment can prevent brain injury and its result, retardation, from such causes as lead poisoning, ingestion of chemicals, or accidents.

## COSMETIC INTERVENTION

We have just looked at some of the avenues open for biomedical prevention or amelioration, but the sad fact remains that disorders with biological causes currently exist and will continue to be a problem in future generations. This section spotlights measures that can be taken to reduce the additional detrimental effects on development and socialization attributed to physical characteristics common to these biologically caused disorders.

Neisworth, Jones, and Smith (1978) have presented an interesting perspective on cosmetic intervention in their discussion of the problems of somatopsychology (the study of body variations related to psychological status) from a behavioral orientation. They suggest that atypical physical attributes such as facial disfigurements can serve as specific cues that influence the behavior of others and affect the behavior of the individual who is disabled.

In pursuing this argument, Neisworth et al. (1978) suggest that body-behavior cues can set the stage for a variety of environmental interactions. Those that are most common include ignoring, punishment through ridicule or assault, or reinforcement of inappropriate behaviors related to the specific handicaps. These reactions would be somewhat consistent with the radical behaviorist concept that retardation of any type is primarily the result of environmental variables, specifically a lack of stimulation and experiences and inappropriate or noncontingent reinforcement.

The implications of such a model for treatment are clear. They are direct extensions of Leland's (1972) concept of "invisibility," that is, the goal of having persons who are retarded blend into their environment so they are not treated as retarded. The principle has validity for a variety of changes—from simple elimination of tongue protrusion (Leland, 1972) to complex language interchanges (Schiefelbusch, 1972).

*Cosmetic prostheses.*    Prosthetic devices are most often associated with the functional purpose of reducing or eliminating a specific handicap. Examples include glasses, hearing aids, or artificial limbs. However, prostheses can also serve cosmetic goals, acting primarily to alter other people's perceptions of an individual. In an interesting study related to this idea, Shushan (1974) designed a before-and-after experiment using naive observers to evaluate photographs of persons who were retarded or not retarded. He found that, by adding cosmetic aids like sunglasses and fashionable hairstyles to the people photographed, he could influence the observers to perceive them more normally.

Plastic surgery has achieved similar successes with dramatic changes in appearance. Of course, many well known celebrities have sought and undergone a variety of cosmetic changes. A strong case can therefore be made for making these procedures available to persons who are handicapped. May (1988) provides an analysis of the use of plastic surgery on individuals with Down syndrome, focusing on specific surgical procedures, as well as on their effectiveness and implications. Her conclusion highlights the ambivalence concerning such surgery:

See pages 220–221 for a discussion of the issues relating to this topic.

> It is still necessary for us to work to improve the negative attitude demonstrated by many members of society towards individuals with mental retardation or other

handicaps. Most handicapping conditions cannot be eliminated or made less visible by surgery; educating children and adults about the abilities and needs of exceptional individuals will have a greater impact on society than will surgery on a relatively few individuals. This is a less extreme approach to the normalization of individuals with Down syndrome and other handicapping conditions. (p. 19)

*Cosmetic learning.*   A related concept is that of cosmetic learning, which Neisworth et al. (1978) describe as

> teaching children ways of behaving that reduce the amount of attention they may call to themselves. Here, concern is not with physical features, but the focus is on behavioral characteristics that could contribute to a stereotype or cue too much attention and eventually devaluation. (p. 269)

Again, the principle of invisibility is relevant. Specific techniques that might be effective would include teaching children to close their mouths, avoid drooling, walk without a shuffle, smile, and speak in a "normal" tone of voice.

## ETHICAL CONCERNS

The almost incredible advancements in the medical technology of the past several decades have enabled doctors and other professionals to sustain the lives of many people with handicaps who in an earlier time would have perished. As a by-product of these medical advances, however, both the medical profession and society in general have been confronted with the need to evaluate both the proactive and passive measures now available. It is critical to consider carefully the actions that can be taken before and after birth, once a specific handicapping condition has been identified.

Our earlier discussion of amniocentesis focused on its use to detect specific genetic disorders, especially Down syndrome. Gradually this practice has come under increased scrutiny. Public encouragement to screen for the disorder has led to an increase in the number of abortions. As Smith (1981) noted,

> The ease with which the abortion of Down syndrome fetuses is accepted as the best alternative, even by people who otherwise oppose abortion, may be related to the conventional wisdom or popular misunderstanding of the level of mental retardation or other disabilities associated with this condition. (p. 9)

Smith questioned whether Down syndrome children had become defined as an out-group, something less than human, through the process of *pseudospeciation,* that is, placing certain human beings in a separate species on the basis of group characteristics like race or handicap.

The question of selective abortion of individuals with handicaps concerns more than just Down syndrome cases. Lehr and Brown (1984) have

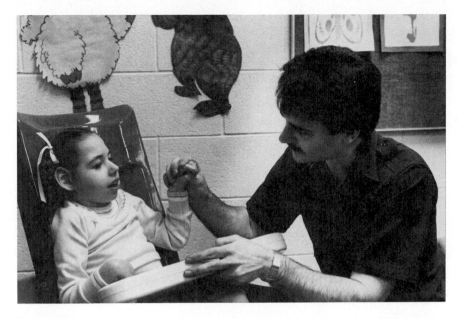

*Some children will always be recognizable as being different. However, this fact should not interfere with their being accepted.*

summarized the arguments in favor of the practice as including the possible need for intensive medical surgery, the potentially negative effects on the family (e.g., financial ability to care for the child and sibling resentment), and the drain of valuable resources from society. Included in the sentiments against the practice are basic refutation of abortion for all, presumed devaluation of the humanness of persons who are handicapped, and possible spillover effects into services for young children (if the fetus does not have the right to life, why should the child be entitled to support?). Ultimately, as Lehr and Brown (1984) noted, the resolution of the issue has come down to the legal right of parents to make the decision about whether or not to give birth to the child.

The second major ethical concern is the question of the right to life after birth of children who are disabled. Newspaper accounts of the cases of Baby Doe in Indiana, Baby Jane Doe in New York, Phillip Becker, a California teenager with Down syndrome, and Baby Gabriel in Canada have sensitized the public to issues that for years have been quietly debated in professional circles. Data suggest that cases of infant euthanasia are not at all rare; for example, Duff and Campbell (1973) reported that, of 299 deaths of infants recorded in a New Haven hospital from 1970 to 1972, 43 (or 14%) could be attributed to withdrawal or withholding of treatment. In most cases, the argument is whether a child's handicapping condition should be a primary factor in the decision to provide maximum medical care. In addition to the important legal questions involved (see chapter 13 and Turnbull, 1983), philosophical issues are also significant in this arena.

Orelove and Sobsey (1984, pp. 341–343) have summarized the debates surrounding ethics and moral values as reflecting several positions in reference to individuals with severe disabilities. These positions include:

☐ **Treat all nondying newborns**, with focus only on medical indications for treatment.

☐ **Terminate the lives of selected nonpersons**, with the justification that nontreatment is appropriate if an infant is defective and thus not counted as a person.

☐ **Withhold treatment according to parental discretion**, on the assumption that care could be withheld as an act of mercy to the infant and for relief to the suffering parents.

☐ **Withhold treatment according to quality of life**, with decisions based on the potential for so-called meaningful life.

☐ **Withhold treatment judged not in the child's best interests**, under the presumption that the treatment would maintain a burden of existence for the infant.

As Polloway and Smith (1984) have noted, much of the debate on "right to life" has focused on two diametrically opposed perspectives: "quality of life" versus "sanctity of life." From the first perspective, individuals with severe handicapping conditions are viewed as leading lives of meaningless existence full of suffering. Fletcher (1975), for example, posited that personal integrity should be placed above absolute biological survival. The quality of life concept was most dramatically revealed by the case at Johns Hopkins University Hospital involving a child with correctible duodenal blockage. Medical intervention was withheld because of the presence of Down syndrome. The child's anticipated quality of life was deemed insufficient to justify life-saving medical intervention.

The alternative position challenges the ethics of euthanasia for individuals with handicaps and defends an unconditional right to life for all persons. The basic policy statement of the American Association on Mental Retardation (1975) reflects this position: "The existence of mental retardation is no justification for the terminating of the life of any human being or for permitting such a life to be terminated either directly or through the withholding of life sustaining procedures" (p. 8). Consistent with this position, Walmsley (1978) has questioned the notion that persons who experience severe handicaps could be evaluated for their "essential lack of humanness":

> It is necessary that our society cease deluding itself by believing it can make a measure for humanness. . . . A creature is a human being who is the product of the union of a man and a woman, is conceived by woman and born of woman. (p. 388)

It is of interest to note that these divergent positions have been confirmed in attitudinal research with persons in the field of mental retardation. Polloway and Smith (1984) surveyed over 180 staff members in a large residential institution, asking them to determine whether individuals represented by five case-study examples should be provided full care and treatment, provided care without extraordinary treatment, have care and treatment withheld, or whether active measures should be taken to bring about cessation of life. They reported that while the majority favored full care and treatment, a sanctity of life position, nevertheless a distinct minority—most often those without direct care responsibilities and with less daily contact—did consider the evaluation of quality of life and thus selected either the option of withholding treatment or taking active measures.

Another related issue receiving recent attention is that of using the organs of infants born with *anencephaly*—a condition of absence of the cranial vault and virtual absence of the brain except for the brain stem—for transplantation to young children with heart or kidney disorders. Coulter (1988a) discusses the unique issues that surround the practice of transplanting organs from infants who are virtually but not technically brain dead. Again the ethical and legal dilemmas stemming from medical advances are well illustrated.

See box material in
Chapter 7, page 235.

Orelove and Sobsey (1984) have written an apt summary of the issues that surround both treating and educating infants or children with serious genetic or health impairments and accompanying (or presumed) multiple disabilities, stating that such debates are:

> by-products of our progress. Without recent and dramatic progress in prenatal care, modern techniques in surgery and treating infection, and the like, the discussion over whether to save severely handicapped newborns would be moot. Similarly, new instructional technologies, particularly those derived from behavior analysis, have made it possible to argue whether all individuals can be educated.
>
> At another level, however, the issues . . . are timeless and predictable. Our technologies can solve only practical, tangible problems. The price we pay for this power is the creation of new ethical and moral dilemmas. We generally know what we *can* do; talented neonatologists and educators, among others, see to that. But no one professional is able to tell us what we *should* do. Through rational discourse and professional integrity, each of us arrives at a comfortable, if temporary, solution. (p. 353–354)

The increased attention to this issue demands the scrutiny and advocacy of professional educators (Cohen, 1981; Powell, Aiken, & Smylie, 1982). In fact, as Smith (1984, 1989) has noted, special educators may often be better informed than doctors concerning the possibilities and potentialities for the lives of individual children with handicaps. They are in a unique position to act as advocates. The Association for Persons with Severe Handicaps (TASH) reflected on the need for advocacy in their policy statement, which was printed in their newsletter. More recently, the Board of Directors of the

# A POSITION STATEMENT ON THE RIGHT OF CHILDREN WITH MENTAL RETARDATION TO LIFE SUSTAINING MEDICAL CARE AND TREATMENT

### Position Statement

The Board of Directors of the Division on Mental Retardation of the Council for Exceptional Children resolves that the fact that a person is born with mental retardation or acquires mental retardation during development is not a justifiable reason, in and of itself, for terminating the life of that person. Mental retardation alone is not a nullification of quality or worth in an individual's life and should not be used as a rationale for the termination of life through direct means nor the withholding of nourishment or life sustaining procedures.

### Background

The issue of pediatric euthanasia is complex and troubling to professionals in the field of mental retardation. A most basic question posed by this dilemma is that of who is to make the decision to deny treatment or nourishment to a child who has mental retardation. Most often involved in this decision are parents, physicians, and, in most cases which become public, the courts. Arguments have been made for and against the role of each of these parties in making such a decision.

Support for parents as decision makers derives from the concept that children are the property of their parents and that they have the final voice in any crucial matter concerning their offspring. Critics of this view believe that parents are often emotionally distraught and lack adequate information on which to base their decision when faced with such a dilemma. Their decision may be unduly influenced by fears concerning raising the child or of institutional placement.

Physicians often feel that they are in the best position to make an objective decision. It has been observed, however, that they often are motivated by their perception of what will prevent suffering in the family. It is argued that physicians should not be the decision makers because their duty is to preserve life, not to judge which lives deserve preservation.

Parents of newborns and physicians have rarely had the opportunity to experiene living or working with individuals having mental retardation across the course of their lives. As special educators serving children with disabilities from infancy through adulthood, the Board of Directors of CEC-MR observes that mental retardation alone does not necessarily cause a life of pain, suffering or absence of life quality for the affected persons, and that it should not imply a justification for the termination of life. Research and experience with persons having mental retardation demonstrate that all people can learn, all can participate (at least partially) in the wide range of human experiences and most become productive citizens and are valued as human beings by persons who truly know them. It is with these factors in mind that CEC-MR takes a pubic position on this issue.

From J. D. Smith, *CEC-MReport,* September, 1988. Reprinted by permission.

Division on Mental Retardation of the Council for Exceptional Children (CEC-MR) has approved a position statement (Smith, 1988b) that also supports the right to life for persons with mental retardation, encouraging professional advocacy (see also Smith, 1989a for a full discussion of this issue). CEC-MR's statement is reproduced in the box.

It is not the purpose of this brief discussion to conclude with a specific recommendation. Rather, we conclude by stressing that professionals must carefully evaluate their positions on these issues and be prepared to express and defend them.

**SUMMARY**

Hundreds of specific factors have been identified as causes of mental retardation and developmental disabilities. Nevertheless, in the vast majority of individual cases, a specific cause cannot be identified.

To understand etiology, we must first understand the principles of genetics, since a large percentage of biological causes stem from recessive, dominant, and sex-linked inheritance and from chromosomal abnormalities. Other causes include prenatal infections and intoxications, brain injury, malnutrition, cranial malformations, disorders related to pregnancy, psychiatric disturbances, and environmental influences.

Prevention of retardation due to pathological causes requires an intensive program that begins before conception and continues throughout the developmental period. Every specifiable cause of retardation has a preventive measure of one type or another. Some of the most optimistic advances in recent years include genetic counseling and the screening of carriers for various disorders, amniocentesis, chorion villus sampling, and careful perinatal monitoring. Advances in medical technology have also created difficult ethical problems that society must face.

# CHAPTER 5

# Psychosocial Factors in Retardation

I n the last chapter we discussed biological causes of retardation and related developmental disabilities. Now we shift our attention to the possible effects of environmental factors. Traditionally we would focus on the category that in Grossman's (1983) manual is designated *environmental influences*. This category has usually applied to cases of mild retardation, but such an application gives rise to two concerns. First, individuals with mild handicaps are also frequently affected by genetic and other biological causes; and second, psychosocial influences are equally important in cases of more severe handicaps.

The terms in most common use today for many individuals with mild retardation reflect the dilemma of the nature of psychosocial causation: These are *psychosocial disadvantage* and *cultural-familial retardation*. The first term has grown in popularity since its introduction by Grossman in 1973.

> Criteria for inclusion under this category require that there be evidence of subnormal intellectual functioning in at least one of the parents and in one or more siblings where there are such. These cases are usually from impoverished environments involving poor housing, inadequate diets, and inadequate medical care. There may be prematurity, low birth weight, or history of infectious diseases but no single entity appears to have contributed to the slow or retarded development. (1977, pp. 67–68)

The term *psychosocial disadvantage* has, to some degree, supplanted the more traditional *cultural-familial retardation*. As Heber (1959, 1961) indicates, cultural-familial retardation generally refers to a mild handicap in a person with no organic defects. Heber lists three basic considerations.

---

This chapter was contributed by Edward A. Polloway and James R. Patton.

1. Evidence of retardation in at least one of the parents and in one or more siblings where there are such.
2. There is usually some degree of cultural deprivation present.
3. No intent in this category to specify either the independent action of, or relationship between, genetic and cultural factors in the etiology of cultural-familial mental retardation. The exact role of genetic factors cannot be specified since the nature and mode of transmission of genetic aspects of intelligence is not yet understood. Similarly, there is no clear understanding of the specific manner in which environmental factors operate to modify intellectual functioning. (pp. 39–40, 1961)

Heber's third point is particularly cogent now. In the years that elapsed between the publication of the Heber and the Grossman manuals, research could conceivably have produced a clear analysis of the two key variables, genetics (nature) and environment (nurture). If this had happened, the adoption of psychosocial disadvantage (the definition of which makes no mention of genetics) and the rejection of cultural-familial retardation (which does not rule out genetics as a contributing factor) would have represented a logical shift in emphasis. The professional community has, however, reached no consensus on the role of genetics as a contributor to mild retardation. Robinson and Robinson's (1970) observation remains valid today: "Nowhere is the nature-nurture controversy so alive as with respect to the etiology of this disorder" (mild retardation) (p. 627). In our discussion in this chapter, we use the concept of psychosocial disadvantage in its broadest frame of reference, to include the possible role of inherited traits, keeping in mind that our knowledge base does continue to grow. The great changes in the relative importance given environmental and genetic causes are well illustrated by the following comparison, (PCMR, 1977, p. 137).

| 1912 | 1975 |
|---|---|
| Feeblemindedness in 85% of cases is inherited as a unitary characteristic, probably as a Mendelian recessive, and is not affected by environmental influences. | General intelligence is "polygenic." The genetic component of mild retardation is inseparable from the debilitating effects of the poverty in which it most frequently occurs. |

Because of the complexity of the relationships between psychosocial factors and the possible contribution of genetics through polygenic inheritance, this chapter investigates three larger conceptual perspectives on causation: (a) the view that genetic factors are the primary determinants of development; (b) the view that environmental variables play the central role in influencing development; and (c) the interaction perspective, which stresses the importance of both determinants. Although the vast majority of theoreticians and researchers subscribe to the interactive view, we look at all three perspectives to identify the basic tenets of each. Our focus is primarily on mild retardation, but we should remember that the implications of psychosocial factors are also significant for people with more severe retardation or other developmental disabilities.

## HEREDITARY POSITION

The study of the role of heredity in causing mental retardation has a long and somewhat tortuous history. Family pedigree studies at the turn of the century (e.g., Goddard, 1912) fueled the fire of the eugenics scare by initially applying Gregor Mendel's theories of the simple genetic transmission of traits to the infinitely more complex issue of human intelligence. Despite these studies' obvious flaws (see Kanner, 1964; Kirk, 1964; Smith, 1985; Wallin, 1955), the study of mental retardation and that of genetics became inexorably joined. The early 20th century assumption that intelligence was a fixed, stable trait merged comfortably with this perspective (see Smith, 1985).

See chapter 1.

The hereditary position holds that intelligence, and hence familial retardation, is determined most significantly by genetic contributions. The basis for genetic determinism is **polygenic inheritance**. Unlike the one gene/one trait pattern of numerous disorders associated with retardation (e.g., PKU), polygenic inheritance refers to the interaction of many gene pairs and networks, which in combination predispose an individual to a given level of intellectual functioning. Since the complexity of this phenomenon makes it difficult to evaluate precisely in single cases, researchers depend on statistical data from population samples in seeking to determine the merits of the hereditary position.

A number of prominent scholars have advocated the genetically deterministic position. They include Arthur Jensen, William Shockley, Sir Cyril Burt, and Richard Herrnstein. When we review the hypotheses of these powerful advocates, we must not lose sight of the researchers and theoreticians who take a more moderate position.

Much of the theoretical basis for the genetic position has relied on the interpretation of the *heritability* of intelligence. Heritability is the proportion of total trait variance of a measurable characteristic that is directly due to genetic factors. For different traits, heritability could in theory range from 0 to 1 according to what proportion (from 0% to 100%) genetics plays as a determinant. Since the heritability of skin pigmentation, visual acuity, susceptibility to optical illusions, galvanic skin response, speed of visual information processing, reaction time, and related mental abilities has been established, Jensen (1973) suggests that we should not arbitrarily choose to begin denying genetic influences with intelligence.

Proponents of a strong genetic position estimate a heritability of approximately 0.80 for intelligence, basing the estimate primarily on IQ correlations from kinship studies within families and from research with adopted children. The most critical research base derives from studies of identical twins. The heritability figure has been typically obtained most directly by examining identical twins reared apart, since these pairs are genetically similar but live in different environments. A comparison of their IQs could yield a measure of heritability for the population from which the samples are selected. The most widely cited research on twins (e.g., Burt, 1966; Shields, 1962) has been used to show that IQ correlations for twins reared apart is remarkably similar to correlations for those reared together. Although these data look formidable, the studies have engendered controversy. (A discussion of the arguments about their validity appears later in this chapter.) Heritability is specifically concerned with the range of individual differences in a trait. Low genetic variance does not deny a genetic base for the trait, but rather indicates genetic similarity. Likewise, low environmental variance does not refute the importance of environment but indicates that it is not substantially contributing to individual differences. Thus Jensen (1973) asserted that the environment acts primarily as a *threshold variable*—that is, a minimal level of stimulation is required for normal development, but beyond this threshold, environment has little importance as a basic determinant of differences in intellectual functioning.

## SOCIAL CLASS AND RACIAL DIFFERENCES

A strong genetic position has direct implications for any identified social classes and social differences noted through intelligence testing. Social classes become "breeding populations" that produce an inevitable correlation between intelligence and the genetic base for each class (Jensen, 1969). Social mobility could theoretically increase this correlation, because the more able individuals would rise in class level (taking their superior genes with them), while the least able would drop to, or remain within, the lower class. The hypothetical outcome of this mobility is *gene pools* within social classes. In theory the gene pools would determine the genetic makeup of future generations in each group.

In a highly mobile society, advocates of genetic determinism suggest that variance in intelligence *within* groups is constantly being transformed to variance *between* groups. Given equal opportunity, the differences between classes should increasingly reflect differences in biologically determined ability, as opposed to arbitrary social discrimination (Herrnstein, 1971). The resulting system would differ from a closed, "caste" system, for in the closed system artificial hindrances to mobility produce a greater within-class variance (Jensen, 1973).

Racial differences are closely related to this conceptualization of social class differences in intelligence. In asserting a genetic rationale for group differences in IQ between black and white children, advocates have relied heavily on Shuey's (1966) review of research. Shuey concluded that there is a 15-point mean IQ gap between the two races. Jensen (1973) cites isolated gene pools and assortative mating—"like marries like"—as a second factor contributing to the IQ disparity among races.

If one accepts genetic determinism, the high prevalence of mild retardation among lower class and minority children becomes a direct function of polygenic inheritance within the social group. This conclusion is compatible with the research of Reed and Reed (1965), who researched family histories and concluded that approximately 1% to 2% of the fertile family members with retardation in one generation are responsible for 30% to 40% of the persons in the next generation who are retarded. Irrespective of proven cause, the risk of retardation to children of such parents is indeed great. Scarr and Carter-Saltzman (1982) indicate that it is 75% for a child born to two retarded parents who already have a retarded child in the family.

The strong genetic stance is highly controversial. In a society dedicated to a belief in equality, adopting this position has some very powerful social implications.

A theory of a genetic basis for social class and racial difference in intelligence like the one described above leads its proponents to the prediction that higher reproductive rates in those who are at the bottom of society intellectually, educationally, and occupationally could handicap future generations by widening racial and social class gaps and thus promoting greater social inequality (Bajema, 1971). This premise is consistent with the classic opinion that real equality will come about by way of biology.

Underlying any biological intervention to promote equality would be prevention through some form of birth control or through genetic engineering. While genetic engineering offers exciting challenges for the near future, the idea of socially mandated birth control and sterilization is only a new segment in the continuing saga of the eugenics movement. Sterilization is hardly a new idea; it has historically been the treatment of choice in tens of thousands of cases throughout the country. Revelations in the 1970s in Virginia, for example, indicate that as many as 8,000 persons were legally sterilized without their knowledge in state institutions between the height of the eugenics scare in the 1920s and the early 1970s (Smith, 1989b). Although proponents of this policy urge only programs of voluntary sterilization (Shockley, 1974), the history of the use of sterilization in 20th-century America and the nebulous zone between informed consent and involuntary treatment cast doubt on whether the programs could be truly voluntary. The box discusses the United States' most famous instance of sterilization, the Carrie Buck case, eventually heard by the U.S. Supreme Court.

Although legislatures have revoked many of the laws enacted during the eugenics scare, or at least the practices have been curtailed, the specter of sterilization is bound to haunt us as long as the strongly deterministic genetic perspective receives serious attention. Informed consent is now the watch-word for such procedures, but parental approval can often supersede

*See chapter 4 for a discussion of genetic engineering.*

# THE STERILIZATION OF

# CARRIE BUCK

In 1927 a young woman named Carrie Buck was sexually sterilized. Without her understanding or her agreement to what was being done to her, Carrie's ability to bear children was taken away from her. *The Sterilization of Carrie Buck* by J. David Smith (1989b) tells her story.

Carrie was the first person to be sterilized under Virginia's law, which allowed the state to impose the surgery on people judged incompetent and likely to pass their deficiency on to offspring. Carrie had an illegitimate child, was diagnosed as being "feeble-minded," and was placed in an institution when she was 18 years old. She was then chosen as the test case of the constitutionality of the law. Carrie's mother had been institutionalized before her, and it was claimed that her infant daughter also showed signs of mental deficiency. To the physicians, lawyers, and politicians who wished to see the validity of the law upheld, she seemed the perfect test case. Their judgment proved to be sound. The Supreme Court, in *Buck v. Bell* (1927) supported the constitutionality of the law under which Virginia sterilized Carrie and thousands of others. The same law became the model for sterilization statutes in other states and in European countries, including Nazi Germany.

Justice Oliver Wendell Holmes wrote the majority opinion in Carrie Buck's case. His opinion included the famous phrase "three generations of imbeciles are enough." His reasoning was consistent with the view that mental retardation is most often hereditary and that people who are mentally retarded are a primary source of crime and social problems. The argument was made that sterilization would help stem this flood of incompetence.

After institutionalization and separation from her infant daughter, Carrie never saw her again. Carrie's child, Vivian, the "third generation of imbeciles," grew up to be an attractive child and an honor roll student. Her mother, the "second generation of imbeciles," was "paroled" to a mountain village, where she soon married the deputy sheriff. Later in her life she was entrusted with the care and comforting of elderly and chronically ill people. Friends and employers attest to the fact that she was never mentally retarded.

Carrie Buck's story is a tragic example of an injured life, but it is also a warning, for it illustrates that mental retardation is a social phenomenon that involves arbitrary definitions and value judgments. Carrie's story embodies a particularly important lesson for people working in the field of mental retardation, who most need to be sensitive to the social and political implications of their work.

individual consent. It is critical that anyone discussing so-called eugenic measures distinguish between disorders clearly associated with genetic transmission (e.g., PKU, Tay-Sachs disease) and those whose causes remain uncertain, such as familial retardation. We must also divide those who espouse a moderate genetic position from the radical, self-styled genetic "engineers."

## VALIDITY OF THE DATA BASE

A key concern in terms of the genetic position is the validity of the data base. For example, some have raised objections to the use of the figure of 0.80 for the heritability of intelligence. No trait's heritability is fixed; heritability is always bound to a distinct population, period of time, and developmental situation (Cronbach, 1969; Scarr-Salapatek, 1971a, 1971b). The trait can change greatly over generations from the influence of environment. Establishing heritability figures within a specific group does not permit assumptions to be made between groups (Gage, 1972). Since the heritability figures cited by proponents of genetic determinism derive almost solely from Caucasian populations, their generalizability to other ethnic groups is highly questionable.

Second, we must ask: How valid is the use of several of the identical twin studies (i.e., Burt, 1966; Juel-Nielsen, 1965; Newman, Freeman, & Holzinger, 1937; Shields, 1962) as a data base for generating hypotheses on the importance of inheritance? In one of the most scathing attacks on the foundations of the genetic position, Kamin (1974) questions whether many of these identical twins studied had in fact been reared apart. For example, after reviewing the original case studies from the reports of Newman et al. (1937), Kamin offers the following analysis of this specific twin pair, allegedly reared apart.

> Ed and Fred's separation is at one point in the text described as "complete until their first meeting at 24 years of age." Further, "they lived without knowledge of each other's existence for twenty-five years." Their genes, during this period, appear to have impelled them to remarkably similar experiences. They each worked as electrical repair men for the telephone company, and each owned a fox terrier named Trixie. The case study, however, reports that "they even went to the same school for a time, but never knew that they were twin brothers. They had even noticed the remarkable resemblance between them, but they were not close companions. When the twins were about eight years old, their families were permanently separated." This simply does not square with the earlier account of no knowledge of each other's existence for 25 years. . . .
>
> The case study includes a photograph of the twins side-by-side "at the time of their first meeting. . . ." The twins are remarkably alike in appearance. They are wearing identical pinstriped suits, and identical striped ties. These, of course, might have been bought "at the time of their first meeting." Perhaps it is relevant to note that Fred was unemployed at the time of the study. (pp. 53–54)

Kamin (1974) further elaborates on the possible sources of bias within the selections of subjects for the Newman et al. (1937) study.

> The twins were rewarded with considerable newspaper and magazine publicity; one threatened a legal suit because a magazine had described her as intellectually inferior to her twin. There was also a very tangible inducement offered to all twins. . . . They were treated to a visit at the Century of Progress Exposition then being held in Chicago. "Pair after pair, who had previously been unmoved by appeals to the effect that they owed it to science and society to permit us to study them, could not resist the offer of a free, all-expenses-paid trip to the Chicago Fair." To qualify for this reward, the twins had to attest to the fact that they had been separated, and that they were remarkably alike.
>
> This raises a very serious issue. The facts about separation, in all the twin studies, depend heavily upon the verbal account of the twins themselves. When there are not tangible inducements, the twins are exhorted to make themselves available in the name of science. They receive free medical examinations, and enormous amounts of detailed individual attention from distinguished scientists. They could scarcely be blamed if, in a misguided effort to cooperate with science, or to bolster a sense of their unique worth, they were to stretch a fact or two. The report that "actual facts" concerning schooling were, "difficult to obtain" does little to allay anxiety on this score. (p. 54)

The other twin studies have been criticized along similar lines. Kamin (1974) describes several of the twins, again supposedly reared apart, who participated in the Shields (1962) study.

> Bertram and Christopher were separated at *birth*. "The paternal aunts decided to take one twin each and they have brought them up amicably, living next door to one another in the same Midlands colliery village. . . . They are constantly in and out of each other's houses." Odette and Fanny were separated from birth until the age of 12. The conditions of their separation seem to have been worked out by a specialist in experimental design. From the age of 3 until the age of 8 the twins were rotated every 6 months, one going to the maternal grandmother and the other to the mother. Joan and Dinah were separated at birth, but "reunited about 5." Their entire school careers were spent together in "a small country town." Joanna and Isobel were similarly "separated from birth to 5 years," and then "went to private schools together." When tested at age 50, their scores were virtually identical, and much higher than any other scores in the entire sample.

Given these interesting revelations, we must remember that such research can be considered valid only if the data support the fact that the twins were reared in significantly different environments. Professionals have unfortunately often trivialized or even ignored this critical point (Smith, 1988b).

Finally, critics have also raised questions about the data from the studies by Burt (1966), who had been the most respected authority in this field. The most damning assertion has been that Burt's data are fictional. His official biographer, Hearnshaw (1979), suggests that Burt created many of the twins in his study from whole cloth, along with his two mysterious research collaborators, who may or may not have existed. As Hawkes (1979) concludes, this biography confirms the suspicion that Burt "engaged in deliberate deception, fabricated research data and invented nonexistent 'colleagues' to support his theories about intelligence" (p. 673). Gould (1981) explains that Burt's ruse was a way to circumvent the problem of the extreme rarity of identical twins reared apart. Readers should consult Gould's book for a thorough report on the errors in Burt's research.

Difficulties and deceptions notwithstanding, professionals continue to give considerable attention to these data bases and their implications. Scarr et al. (1982) have provided a very comprehensive review of the relation between genetics and intelligence. They noted that although removing Burt's flawed research from collections of research on kinship groups reduced the magnitude of the heritability for intelligence (correlations for identical twins apart dropped from 0.84 to 0.74), both older and newer studies attest to a moderate genetic component. They concluded that the available data on both twin studies and adoption studies support the theory that heredity plays a major role in determining differences in intelligence between individuals. Henderson (1982), in a similar vein, noted that while the earlier kinship studies allowed the hypothesis of a heritability of 0.80 for intelligence, recent data and interpretations yield a more conservative estimate, between 0.30 and 0.60.

Designing research on the inheritance of intelligence poses many problems. A perfect design would *(a)* identify x sets of twins (say, 20 sets); *(b)* separate them at birth; *(c)* place them in distinctly variant environmental settings; and *(d)* retest them periodically over an extended time. Unfortunately, in social science research, practical problems usually prevent the achievement of methodological perfection, and this is especially true in the research about twins.

As a less serious conclusion, let us consider the comments of Stephen Jay Gould (1981) in his classic work, *The Mismeasure of Man:*

> If I had any desire to lead a life of indolent ease, I would wish to be an identical twin, separated at birth from my brother and raised in a different social class. We could hire ourselves out to a host of social scientists and practically name our fee. For we would be exceedingly rare representatives of the only really adequate natural experiment for separating genetic from environmental effects in humans—genetically identical individuals raised in disparate environments. (p. 234)

Despite recent research and criticism of earlier studies, the issue of heritability of intelligence is unresolved. The moderate position, which ascribes a key role, though clearly not the only role, to the genetic contribution seems to be an accurate interpretation of currently available data.

## ENVIRONMENTAL POSITION

Historically, the environmental view derives from John Locke's concept of the *tabula rasa,* which suggests that children are born with a "blank slate" on which the environment "writes" experiences and thus develops traits. Wholehearted acceptance of this position places a heavy responsibility on parents, educators, and other agents of society, because it implies that a child's mental development can be immensely influenced by home training and educational programs.

The strict environmental position holds that the primary determinant of a child's current level of intellectual functioning is experiential background. Pasamanick (1959) has clearly stated this position.

> Except for a few hereditary clinical deficiencies . . . and for exogenous injury to neural integration, behavior variation does not seem to be the result of genetically determined structural origin. It is now possible to entertain a new tabula rasa theory hypothecating that at conception individuals are quite alike in intellectual endowment except for these quite rare hereditary neurologic defects. It appears to us that it is life experience and the sociocultural milieu influencing biological and psychological function which, in the absence of organic brain damage, makes human beings significantly different behaviorally from each other. (p. 318)

The radical behavioral position epitomized by the Bijou definition of mental retardation in chapter 2 is also consistent with this environmental perspective. From this view, all behavior (including responses on an IQ test) is learned through interaction with the environment, so that individuals become "retarded" when, because of inadequate or deficient experiences, they fail to learn appropriate behaviors—or succeed in learning inappropriate ones.

John B. Watson (1930), known as the "father of behaviorism," framed a controversial yet eloquent description of the environmental point of view.

> Our conclusion, then, is that we have no real evidence of the inheritance of traits. I would feel perfectly confident in the ultimate favorable outcome of careful upbringing of a healthy well-formed baby born of a long line of crooks, murderers and thieves, and prostitutes. Who has any evidence to the contrary?
>
> I should like to go one step further now and say, "Give me a dozen healthy infants, well-formed, and my own specific world to bring them up in and I'll guarantee to take anyone at random and train him to become any type of specialist I might select—doctor, lawyer, artist, merchant-chief and yes, even beggar-man and thief, regardless of his talents, penchants, tendencies, abilities, vocations and race of his ancestors." I am going beyond my facts and I admit it, but so have the advocates of the contrary and they have been doing it for many thousands of years. . . .
>
> The truth is society does not like to face facts. Pride of race has been strong, hence our Mayflower ancestry—our Daughters of the Revolution. We like to boast of our ancestry. It sets us apart. . . . Again, on the other hand, the belief in

*A nonstimulating environment can cause cognitive, intellectual, and physical deficits in children.*

the inheritance of tendencies and traits saves us from blame in the training of our young. (p. 103)

If an environmental position is to be scientifically supported rather than simply philosophically advanced, there must be a model for understanding the influence of sociocultural effects on the development of the young child. Coulter (1988b, pp. 121–123) provides an insightful hypothesis for considering such effects:

How can one understand the neurological basis of mental retardation resulting from adverse sociocultural influences? When one considers that neuronal connections form and are maintained as a result of appropriate input or stimulation, and that this process continued throughout childhood, one can hypothesize that inadequate or inappropriate input during childhood could result in abnormal connections in the brain. This structural defect in connectivity could then result in the functional defect of mental retardation. The clearest example of this process is in the visual system, where lack of visual stimulation during the critical period of early infancy results in defective development of the visual cortex. A similar process may occur in the auditory cortex when children are born deaf or suffer from prolonged hearing impairment due to chronic otitis in infancy. It is interesting to note that children raised in the wild, deprived of exposure to human speech and communication during early childhood, are seldom able to learn to communicate effectively through speech. These experiences suggest that there are critical periods in childhood during which effective sensory input must occur in order for the appropriate connections in the brain to develop. Deprivation of these environmental inputs would then result in inadequate connectivity. Specifically, sociocultural influences that result in diffuse environmental deprivation might cause a deficiency of connections throughout the brain. Mental retardation attributable to sociocultural influences could thus be considered as a "hypoconnection" syndrome.

Concern for the role of the environment on the developing young child emerged nationally in the 1960s with Kennedy and Johnson's "War on Poverty," particularly with the Head Start program for young disadvantaged children. In the next section, we briefly outline environmental factors that may be related to "hypoconnection" and thus may relate to retardation.

### ENVIRONMENTAL CORRELATES OF RETARDATION

Psychosocial retardation has been closely linked to a number of variables that can occur in an environment of poverty. Since we will probably not be able to pinpoint a specific etiology, however, our focus remains on a whole cluster of potentially debilitating characteristics. Demographic data from 1985, which indicate that 23% of all American preschoolers belonged to families with incomes below poverty level (Commission on Minority Participation in Education and American Life, 1988) highlight the immensity of the problem.

Three cautions are critical when we consider poverty environments. First, as Chan and Rueda (1979) have stressed, we must separate the effects of poverty from the essence of cultural differences. This distinction allows us to assess the negative effects of poverty without making judgments about cultural variance. Second, while a substantial amount of research has attempted to pick out specific environmental factors that relate to retardation, factors often act in combination. Although these variables appear more frequently in lower social class environments, we must avoid presuming that they will be present in every home situation. Table 5.1 lists some correlates of poverty that may place children at risk for school failure, and its weighting system suggests the additive effect of the variables. Third, the "vast majority of individuals who are considered poor function well within normal intellectual levels, and yet they remain poor" (Garber, 1988, p. 2). The ability to identify causative factors does not imply that we can also unravel them to improve an individual's situation.

Within the poverty environment, parenting practices are as varied as they are within the general population, but authoritarianism and inconsistency are perhaps more prevalent. Parents may emphasize external controls that inadvertently stress, for example, the problems of getting caught for stealing over the avoidance of stealing for ethical reasons. Parents' reliance on punishment for control can lead children to imitate their aggressive models. Lack of structure and disorganization can also interfere with the child's need for stability. A lack of stimulation or excessive or inappropriate stimulation (e.g., bombardment of noise) may interfere with cognitive development.

Kagan (1970) focused on several key psychological differences between lower class and more privileged children, asserting that these differences emerge during the first three years of life and are stable over time. He identifies seven such major variables: language, mental set, attachment, inhibition, sense of effectiveness, motivation, and expectancy of failure. Garber (1988) draws attention to the poverty-bound mother with low IQ and

TABLE 5.1   High-Risk Index

| Factor | Weight | Factor | Weight |
|---|---|---|---|
| Mother's educational level (Last grade completed) | | Father's educational level (Last grade completed) | |
| 6 | 8 | 6 | 8 |
| 7 | 7 | 7 | 7 |
| 8 | 6 | 8 | 6 |
| 9 | 3 | 9 | 3 |
| 10 | 2 | 10 | 2 |
| 11 | 1 | 11 | 1 |
| 12 | 0 | 12 | 0 |

Family income indexed by family size    (e.g., if a family of 2 has an income of $5,010, they receive a score of *1*.)

| Size | Weights | | | | |
|---|---|---|---|---|---|
| | 8 | 7 | 6 | 4 | 1 |
| 1–2 | ≥2,000 | 3,000 | 4,000 | 5,000 | 6,000 |
| 3–4 | ≥4,000 | 5,500 | 6,500 | 7,500 | 9,000 |
| 5–6 | ≥7,000 | 8,000 | 9,000 | 10,000 | 12,000 |
| 7–8 | ≥7,500 | 8,500 | 9,500 | 10,500 | 12,500 |
| 9–10 | ≥8,000 | 9,000 | 10,000 | 11,000 | 13,000 |
| 11–12 | ≥8,500 | 9,500 | 10,500 | 11,500 | 13,500 |

| Factor | Weight |
|---|---|
| Father absent. | 2 |
| Any member of mother's or father's immediate family required special community services provided for the mentally disabled (ranging from disability payments to institutionalization). | 3 |
| School aged siblings have repeated one or more grades or scored one or more grade levels below the norm on school administered achievement tests. | 3 |
| Payments received from welfare agencies within past five years. | 3 |
| Record of father's work indicates unstable job history or unskilled labor. | 3 |
| Records of mother's or father's IQ indicates scores of 85 or below. | 3 |
| Any member of mother's or father's immediate family required special services in school (special class placement or repeated school failure). | 3 |
| Relevant social agencies in the community indicate that the family is in need of assistance. | 3 |
| One or more members of the family has sought counseling or professional help in the past five years. | 1 |
| Existence of special circumstances not included in any of the above which are likely contributors to cultural or social disadvantage. | 2 |

Criterion for inclusion in High-Risk sample is a score of >11.

From "Project CARE: A Comparison of Two Early Intervention Strategies to Prevent Retarded Development" by C. T. Ramey et al., 1985, *Topics in Early Childhood Special Education, 5*(2), pp. 15–16.

limited verbal skills who cannot effectively mediate the environment for her child, a case that directly evokes the concept of hypoconnection discussed earlier. All these variables may directly or indirectly influence school performance, and deficits in them can also limit a child's problem-solving skills.

But inappropriate patterns of parenting and child guidance are clearly not inherent in the lower class home. As Chan and Rueda (1979) point out, these deficiencies are more likely to reflect the parent's lack of access to data on techniques for enhancing psychosocial development. They base their argument on Hurwitz's (1975) finding that many poor persons live in a "communications environment devoid of meaningful information and knowledge" (p. 2). This fact has important implications for intervention.

In a lower class environment one parent, frequently the father, is often absent, and the burden of child-rearing falls more heavily on the mother. The large number of children in many families aggravates the problem, and the potential result is a decrease in each child's direct, individual contact with adult models.

The practical problems of the poor in making ends meet are too often overlooked and must also be considered. The time and effort that middle class parents spend to motivate and stimulate children may, in a lower class home, need to be devoted to finding a job, finding suitable housing, and arranging for child care. Where poverty is the overriding concern, parents do not have the luxury of planning for the future. Both parents and children focus on the urgency of the moment rather than on setting goals for the future and planning to achieve them (Hunt, 1969). The difficulties of daily living can make people feel fatalistic about their environment and reject the value of even trying to improve their situation. A parent who is worried about finding money for daily meals will not see the problem of getting a child to a preschool program on time or of following through with a home training program as a high priority. It is not surprising that educational concerns may be neglected. Nowhere is this reality more evident than with the increasing numbers of homeless families.

Children born to teenage mothers form one increasingly researched subgroup that runs an especially high risk of subsequent difficulties. As Berg and Emanuel (1987) noted in their review:

> Teenage mothers as a group are at elevated risk for producing low birth weight babies: the younger the mother, the higher the risk. . . . A number of studies have found lower IQs among the offspring of teenage mothers and have attributed this association primarily to social disadvantages. . . . While it is not clear whether problems of adolescent pregnancies are primarily due to biological or social factors, the fact remains that pregnant teenagers as a group are at high social risk, are more apt to be unmarried and poorly educated, and as a group have poorer pregnancy outcomes than older women. . . . Even if there

is no biological hazard, the multiple social and personal problems associated with teenage pregnancy indicate the need to discourage reproduction in this age group. (pp. 50–51)

Whitman, Borkowski, Schellenbach, and Nath (1987) underscored the numerous variables affecting parenting behavior when they developed the model presented in Figure 5.1. Although their focus was on teenage parents, the model's components give an excellent idea of the constellation of factors affecting child development. As these authors noted:

It is our contention that in order to parent effectively, adolescent mothers must be cognitively and emotionally prepared. The cognitive readiness of adolescent mothers depends upon the formal and informal education they receive from the

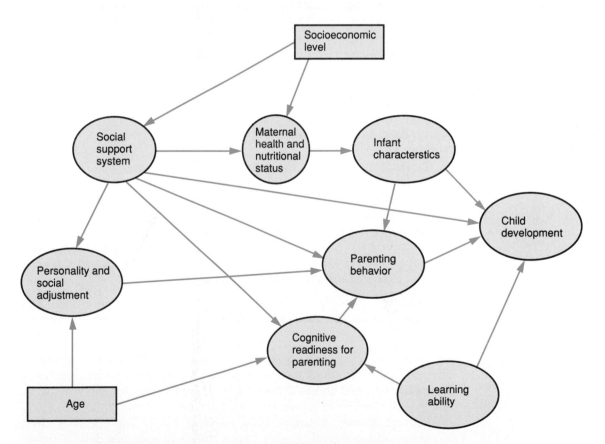

FIGURE 5.1   A Model of Teenage Parenting and Child Development

From "Predicting and Understanding Developmental Delay of Adolescent Mothers: A Multidimensional Approach" by T. L. Whitman, J. G. Borkowski, C. J. Schellenbach, and P. S. Nath, 1987, *American Journal of Mental Deficiency, 92,* p. 51.

social support systems and their ability to assimilate and utilize this information in specific parenting situations. In addition, their ability to cope emotionally with the stresses associated with parenting depend upon whether their children display deviant biological characteristics that complicate their parenting task, the type of physical and emotional assistance they receive from their social support systems and their own personal (personality) coping resources. Ineffective parenting results if external stressors are great, cognitive preparation is insufficient, and/or personal-emotional problems are overwhelming (p. 51).

National data emphasize the trend toward increased numbers of young women heading families. Edelman (1987) has reported that 85% of all Black families with a female head of the household under 25 are below the poverty rate; the rate is 74% for white families. Perhaps the most compelling statistic is that in 1983, 58% of all births to Black women were out of wedlock; for mothers under the age of 20, it was 86%. As Edelman (1987, p. 3) notes, the numbers "have now reached levels that essentially guarantee the poverty of many Black children for the unforeseeable future."

Health problems can compound the detrimental effects of living in poverty. Particular concerns include nutritional deficiencies, lack of resistance to disease, exposure to toxic substances, and inadequate medical care. Although these are biological concerns, they tend to appear with a host of psychosocial factors and may, with them, jeopardize mental development (Perkins, 1977).

Probably the clearest documentation of health problems in high-risk lower class children was Kugel's classic study (1967; Kugel & Parsons, 1967). Kugel studied 35 children and found substantial evidence of short pregnancies and long labor, infectious toxemia, anoxia, prematurity, and neurological abnormalities. Those results were seen as negating the idea of inherited factors as the basis for mild retardation and indicating that psychosocial and pre- and postnatal biological factors combine as the specific causative agents. Kugel (1967) concludes his report by stating that:

> By working diligently with this group of individuals when they are no older than 3 or 4 years of age, some of the pernicious factors can be ameliorated so that these persons need not be condemned to lifelong mental subnormality. (p. 61)

Brain-damaging child abuse can also not be overlooked as a serious physical (and psychological) health hazard. Although no social class has a monopoly on child abuse, children with cognitive impairments may be as much as 10 times more subject to abuse than are children without handicaps (Sandgrund, Gaines, & Green, 1974; Soeffing, 1975). The effects of child abuse can add to the other psychosocial causes of cognitive delay (Zirpoli, 1986).

Forness and Polloway (1987) have reported related data on students who were mildly retarded and had additional psychiatric and medical diagnoses that led to their referral for tertiary care services in their community. In reviewing the home environments of these students, the researchers found that 7.8% were victims of physical or sexual abuse. Investigation into the psychological aspects of their environments showed that 20% came from environments with moderate psychosocial stressors, 33% with severe stressors, and an additional 20% from environments with extensive or catastrophic environmental stressors. Most notably, a statistically significant correlation joined the relation, the level of stressors, and the individual student's level of adaptation.

Our enumeration of problems suggests a linkage between poverty and retardation, but since the overwhelming majority of individuals reared in lower class homes are *not* functionally retarded later, the equation is far from exact. A critical continuing need in research is to attempt to determine if specific factors or clusters of factors are most significant in their negative effect on a child's development and, if so, which these are. Trying to identify important correlates, Richardson (1981) reported that children identified as mildly retarded were more likely to come from environments characterized by the following: five or more children in the family; living in the least desirable housing areas; crowded homes (two or more people per room); and with the mother's occupation before marriage classified as semiskilled or unskilled manual job. Several longitudinal research projects have illustrated how psychosocial variables can influence early experience so that retardation becomes likely; two such projects are discussed below.

## INFLUENTIAL RESEARCH PROJECTS

The foremost name in research into early experiences is that of Harold Skeels, whose work, begun in the 1930s (when most people thought IQ was stable and genetically determined), helped lay the foundation for the massive intervention efforts of the 1960s. The importance and even the romance of this research demands that we discuss it in some detail.

The first research effort by Skeels and Dye (1939) investigated the reversibility of the effects of nonstimulating orphanage environments. Skeels and Dye based their program, unusual in its inception and implementation, on the observation of two female infants. Describing the children, Skeels (1966) wrote: "The youngsters were pitiful little creatures. They were tearful, had runny noses, and coarse, stringy, and colorless hair; they were emaciated, undersized, and lacked muscle tone or responsiveness. Sad and inactive, the two spent their days rocking and whining" (p. 5). Though their chronological ages were 13 and 16 months, their developmental levels were 6 and 7 months, respectively.

It was impractical to place these children with either foster parents or an adoption agency, so they were transferred to an institution for persons who were mentally retarded—not as residents, but as "house guests." Each girl was "adopted" by an older woman, who, under staff supervision, acted as a surrogate mother. The babies received the parental care and attention necessary for normal development, as well as appropriate levels of enrichment and stimulation. Six months after the transfer, Skeels apparently stumbled upon the two children (Bricker, 1986). He described them as "alert, smiling, running about, responding to the playful attention of adults, and generally behaving and looking like any other toddlers" (Skeels, 1966, p. 6).

Excited by this discovery, Skeels and Dye (1939) established an experimental group of 13 by selecting 11 more children from the same orphanage. The mean IQ for the group was 64, and all but two of the children were classified as within the retarded range and thus by state law unsuitable for adoption. A contrast group of 12 orphanage children under 3 years of age was later selected for comparison. This contrast group comprised four girls and eight boys with an average IQ of 86. Only two of these children were classified as mentally retarded.

While the contrast group remained in the orphanage and received minimal adequate health and medical services, each experimental subject received care on a one-to-one basis. Each "mother" (all were adolescents) was given instructions on how to care for "her" child. They were instructed and trained how to hold, feed, change, talk to, and stimulate the young children. No other direct educational experiences were provided for the children.

Two years later (Skeels, 1942) the groups were retested, and the 13 experimental children showed an average gain of 28 IQ points. Of the 13 experimental children, 11 had IQs high enough to make them eligible for adoption, and they were placed in good homes.

In 1965, more than 25 years after the original study had begun, Skeels located the subjects. His follow-up study reports that 11 of the 13 had married, and apparently all but one of the marriages were still intact. These adults had a total of nine children, all of normal intelligence. The adults' mean level of education was twelfth grade; four had completed one or more years of college. All were either self-supporting or functioning as homemakers. Their occupations ranged from professional work and business to domestic service (the two who had not been adopted), and their income was consistent with national and state averages.

The contrast group showed an initial drop in mean IQ of 26 points and as a result were generally not eligible for adoption. When he located them in 1965, Skeels found that the 11 subjects (one had died) had a mean educational level of approximately the third to fourth grade. Four of the subjects in the contrast group were institutionalized and unemployed and were costing the state approximately $200 per month each. Those who were employed, with one exception, were categorized as "hewers of wood and drawers of water." Peterson's (1987) summary of vocational outcomes for experimental and contrast subjects is presented in Table 5.2.

TABLE 5.2 Occupational Achievements of Skeels and Dye (1939) Subjects

| Experimental Group Subjects | Contrast Group Subjects |
|---|---|
| 1 elementary school teacher | 3 residents of institutions |
| 1 registered nurse | 3 dishwashers |
| 1 licensed practical nurse | 1 unskilled laborer |
| 1 beautician | 1 cafeteria worker |
| 1 clerk | 1 worked for institution where |
| 1 airline stewardess |   he had been a resident |
| 2 domestics in a private home | 1 typesetter for a newspaper |
| 1 vocational counselor | 1 had been in and out of one |
| sales manager for estate agent |   institution; during out one |
| staff sergeant—Air Force |   time lived with grandmother |
| |   doing odd jobs for her |
| | 1 died in adolescence |

From *Early Intervention for Handicapped and At-Risk Children* (p. 34) by N. L. Peterson, 1987, Denver: Love Publishing.

Skeels (1966) concludes his follow-up report with the following statement, which has served as a philosophical basis for subsequent early intervention programs.

> It seems obvious that under present-day conditions there are still countless infants with sound biological constitutions and potentialities for development well within the normal range who will become retarded and noncontributing members of society unless appropriate intervention occurs. It is suggested by the findings of this study and others published in the past 20 years that sufficient knowledge is available to design programs of intervention to counteract the devastating effects of poverty, socio-cultural, and maternal deprivation. . . . The unanswered questions of this study could form the basis for many life-long research projects. If the tragic fate of the twelve contrast group children provokes even a single crucial study that will help prevent such a fate for others, their lives will not have been in vain. (pp. 54–55)

At the height of belief in the environmental position, Skeels in the late 1960s received a Kennedy Scientific Award for his research contribution (Dunn, 1973a). The participation in the ceremony by a subject who had completed college was impressive testimony to the potential of modifications of early childhood experiences.

Kirk (1958), who was interested in measuring the effects of an enrichment program on the social and mental development of preschoolers, conducted a second major study, which also highlighted the value of early intervention. Kirk selected 81 children between the ages of three and six whose IQs ranged from 45 to 80. His two experimental groups contained 28 children living at home and attending a special nursery school and 15 children residing in an institution, who also attended a nursery school. In the two contrast non-nursery school groups were 26 children living at home and 12 children in an institution. Periodic cognitive measures indicated significant differences between the groups. Those in the enrichment nursery school program gained between 10 and 30 IQ points, while those without benefit of the stimulating environment declined in performance. Some wash-out effect was noted later, although Kirk (1958) and others have clearly interpreted the results as positive (Bricker, 1986).

The discussion of specific environmental factors and these classic studies on early intervention create a strong empirical and emotional base for the environmental position. Not only is it a stance that appeals to the principles of a democratic society; it also points the way toward a design to reduce the occurrence of retardation. Given the role of genetics, however, the most defensible position is one that acknowledges the interaction between nature and nurture.

## INTERACTION POSITION

The interaction position holds that intellectual development cannot be solely attributed to either genetic or environmental determinants and admits the importance of both variables as contributors to intelligence—and thus as possible causes of retardation. A child functions at a certain level because of the interaction of inherited abilities and biological characteristics, as modified by environmental experiences. Thus the position concedes genetic limitations but maintains that environmental variables can enhance or reduce the individual's development (Bricker, 1986). By stressing the influence of both variables, interaction avoids the oversimplification that occurs when individuals are reduced either to their genetic endowment or to the influences of their environment (Smith, 1988a).

Cancro (1971) makes the basic case for the interaction position when he states:

> The gene can only express itself in an environment and an environment can only evoke the genotype [inherited characteristic] that is present. In this sense, it may be very misleading to speak of one or other then as more important, even in theoretical terms. (p. 60)

Dobzhansky (1955) originally proposed the most commonly accepted model for examining the interaction of genetic and environmental components. He theorized that inherited characteristics and constitutional restrictions *(genotype)* create a *range of reaction* within which a human trait develops. The behavior pattern that a person develops within this genetically endowed range is a function of the environment. The behavior that results from the interaction is called the *phenotype*. As Zigler and Seitz (1982) have noted, while the nature-nurture issue has not been a fruitful debate, the concept of range of reaction does have value for understanding human development.

Gottesman (1963) molded Dobzhansky's (1955) concepts into a schematic paradigm, which is presented in Figure 5.2. Gottesman's hypothesized range for phenotypic development greatly increases as a function of genotype. Individuals with poor genetic endowment (genotype A), such as victims of recessive trait disorders or chromosomal abnormalities, would have a smaller range for phenotypic development regardless of environment. Those blessed with a richer genetic endowment (genotype D) have an extensive range for potential development.

To illustrate how the interaction phenomenon would apply, let us look at some generalized examples of the range of reaction as it relates to various situations. Consider first a child with Down syndrome, who has restricted range because of chromosomal imbalance. In an average environment, we will assume that the child will function at an IQ level of perhaps 45 to 55 points. A restrictive environment (midcentury orphanages and some current institutions) could depress the level to 35. With an enriched environment through an early intervention program, an IQ in the 60s or 70s, or perhaps higher, is quite possible.

As a second example, consider the ghetto child with parents who are mildly retarded. In the impoverished environment, we could expect the

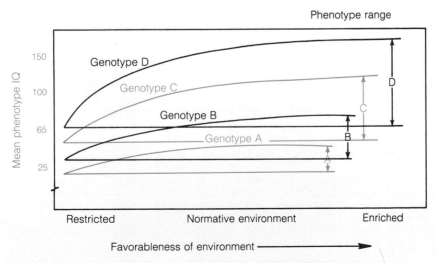

FIGURE 5.2    Estimates of Reaction Range for Hypothetical Genotypes

From *Handbook of Mental Deficiency* (p. 255) by N. R. Ellis (Ed.), 1963, New York: McGraw-Hill. Reprinted by permission.

child's IQ to range between 65 and 80 points. In a more restricted setting some further depression might be anticipated, but in an enriched one the range of reaction could include an average or nearly average level of functioning.

The magnitude of range of reaction cannot be established, particularly for an individual case, and to reduce human development to an arithmetical equation is scarcely reasonable (Lewontin, Rose, & Kamin, 1984; Smith, 1988a). Nevertheless, estimates have placed the range of reaction in the vicinity of 20 to 25 IQ points (Begab, 1981; Zigler & Balla, 1981). Accepting such a figure certainly encourages us to develop effective intervention programs, but at the same time it falls short of promising total elimination of mild retardation. As Zigler and Seitz (1982) noted, such a middle ground between dogmatic genetic or environmental positions has "the advantage of generating energetic willingness to attempt interventions without unrealistic expectations about what they can accomplish" (p. 615).

Finally, we should not forget that genetic and environmental factors also interact with a variety of other biological factors. As Graham and Scott (1988) state, multiple risk models are most productive for studying child development. They illustrate their point by stating, "If the child at medical risk is then exposed to poor environmental stimulation, the chance of subnormal intellectual performance, mild mental retardation, and school failure is increased" (p. 26).

Acceptance of the importance of environmental factors should lead to a commitment to prevention that must include nonbiological intervention. Hunt (1988, p. xxv) has described the goal well: "Attaining all of an individual's genetic potential demands providing the experience of high development—fostering quality at an early age and maintaining it continuously." The role of early intervention in the prevention of mild retardation is discussed next.

*Children from poor communities are at high risk for showing mild mental retardation.*

A broad perspective on prevention includes both the biological factors discussed in the previous chapter and the psychosocial factors highlighted here. The focus of preventive efforts is on children identified as being at risk. See the box for a discussion of this concept.

Graham and Scott (1988) have developed a comprehensive model for conceptualizing prevention (Figure 5.3). They distinguish three levels of prevention: Primary—risk conditions can be eliminated so that a condition never comes into existence; secondary—preventive efforts reduce or eliminate the effects of an existing risk factor; and tertiary—intervention assists a child who has a handicapping condition.

Below are three examples of early intervention programs that have received national attention. The focus here is on the impact of early intervention programs as a basis for the primary or secondary prevention of psychosocial variables associated with retardation and other disabilities. Because mild handicaps are usually diagnosed after the child begins school, these efforts generally concentrate not on already identified children but on children living in poverty who are "high risk" for later school-related difficulties. The reader should keep in mind that these distinctions can blur, as in the instance of a preschool handicapped child from a poverty environment.

For further discussion of early childhood intervention programs, see chapter 8.

## HEAD START

The Head Start program, a component of the War on Poverty in the mid-1960s, is a good place to begin consideration of early intervention efforts. Head Start was initiated to provide direct services to young children; it was seen as a way to close the gap between children disadvantaged by social and economic status and those not disadvantaged (Lee, Brooks-Gunn, & Schur, 1988). It can best be viewed as a major component of overall efforts to reduce school-related difficulties. As Stebbins and her colleagues have noted (Stebbins, St. Pierre, Proper, Anderson, & Cerva, 1977, p. xxiii): "Poor children tend to do poorly in school. By means of Head Start. . ., the federal government set out in the 1960s to learn what compensatory education, applied early, could do to reduce this tendency."

From its beginning, Head Start was not intended as a program for the prevention of mental retardation. Nevertheless, the program's effective-ness—or lack of it—obviously had implications for children at risk (Ensher, Blatt, & Winschel, 1977; LaVor & Harvey, 1976; Lee et al., 1988; Zigler & Cascione, 1977).

The Head Start movement has gone through three distinguishable stages of growth (Payne & Mercer, 1974). The initial stage, the halcyon period (1965–1967), was characterized by an abundance of funds, euphoria, and essentially anecdotal support of the efficiency of the program. During the

FIGURE 5.3    The Developmental Continuum of Risk

From "The Impact of Definitions of Higher Risk on Services to Infants and Toddlers" by M. Graham and K. G. Scott, 1988, *Topics in Early Childhood Special Education, 8*(3), p. 25.

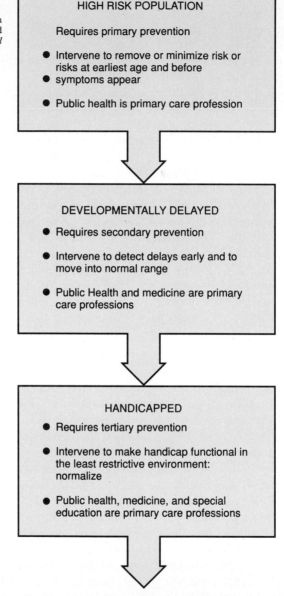

next stage, the critical period (1967–1969), the publicized "fade out" of gains and the failure of some participating children by around third grade led to criticism of the program. The Westinghouse Report (Cicirelli, 1969) heightened this skepticism. During this period, concern for empirical justification of the program overshadowed the previous reliance on descriptive reports.

Although professionals have raised serious methodological questions about this report, it led to widespread pessimism and very nearly to the termination of the program (Zigler & Seitz, 1982). A relevant point made by Hunt (Pines, 1979), one of the foremost advocates of preschool programs, was that it had been naive to assume that one summer or year of nursery school would be enough enrichment for poor children to catch up with their middle class peers. The third stage, consolidation and refinement (1969–1973), reflected the needs of the program to change purposes and procedures and to document gains in order to justify its existence. Payne and Mercer's (1974) review covered only the first decade of Head Start. Since then the program has continued to demonstrate positive research gains (Lee et al., 1988).

When the Head Start model has functioned best, it has placed primary emphasis on skills that would lead to later success in school. For example, Bereiter and Engelmann's (1966) program was based on the principles of direct instruction in basic skill areas. As a direct instruction program, their efforts relied on reinforcing children's appropriate responses and on following a structured sequence of activities to teach oral language, reading, and math skills. Significant gains were reported both in IQ and in achievement, with project children being as much as a year ahead academically at the time of their first-grade placement. Successful intervention efforts with students after their admission to school, a part of Project Follow Through, used this same methodology.

Head Start programs often serve children with great disadvantages in virtually all demographic and cognitive measures. But one-year programs, however effective, are unlikely to be sufficient to overcome school failure and poverty, and it should not be surprising that the benefits, as measured by IQ and achievement gains, have often been modest (e.g., 8–10 IQ points) and transitory (Garber, 1988).

## MILWAUKEE PROJECT

As a function of some of the limitations that Head Start and similar programs revealed, programs began that centered around younger children. As Caldwell (1970) commented, "None of the known studies that began enrichment programs as late as age 6 produced gains as large as those of either Skeels and Dye (1939) or Kirk (1958)" (p. 722). The success of infant programs produced a logical shift in emphasis toward the first years (or months) of life.

The Milwaukee Project (Garber, 1988; Garber & Heber, 1973; Heber & Garber, 1971; Strickland, 1971) received attention in professional journals as well as in the popular media. It exemplified the spirit of the infant education movement. Garber and Heber (1973) referred to the project as a habilitative effort aimed at preventing intellectual deficiencies in children identified as high risk. The project used an intensive educational program for very young children beginning during the first few months of life. After a survey of the inner city living environment, Garber and Heber concluded that poverty conditions create a high risk of mental retardation by virtue of the mother's intelligence, socioeconomic status, and community of residence. According to Garber (1988), the project

> was a longitudinal study concerned with understanding the influence of family and/or home environments on the intellectual development of normal newborns for whom the survey data indicated high risk of declining intelligence test performance and who therefore were increasingly likely to be identified as mentally retarded by school age. (p. 5)

The intervention's design included two components: maternal rehabilitation and infant stimulation. Maternal rehabilitation attempted to enable the women to provide for their families better, and infant stimulation worked toward enhancing the psychosocial and intellectual environment in the home. Mothers with an IQ below 80 were the initial focus of the project, since the researchers found that 45.4% of the mothers studied who came under this heading accounted for more than 78% of the children with similarly low IQs. The groups ultimately participating in the full project included 17 experimental and 18 control subjects whose mothers had IQs below 75 (Garber, 1988).

The infant stimulation program began before the child reached the age of 6 months. Typically, a child and a teacher stayed in a one-to-one relationship until the infant reached 10 months of age; at that time, the pair joined a second teacher-infant pair. At around 15 months, the two children began instruction with only one teacher. At 18 months, groups of three were formed for teaching. Structured teaching groups continued throughout the rest of the program. The curriculum design focused on the major language, perceptive, motor, and cognitive needs that research had established for this group of children.

A detailed program of measurement included comparisons on physical and developmental measures, intelligence scores, learning tasks, and language tests. When the children reached the age of 72 months, the mean IQs of the experimental children were reported to stand about 32 points higher than the control children (119 versus 87). Also encouraging was the fact that their IQs were about 11 points above those of a contrast group whose mothers had IQs above 100. In concluding their interim report, Garber and Heber (1973) noted:

> Infant testing difficulties notwithstanding, the present standardized test data, when considered along with performance on learning tasks and language tests, indicate an unquestionably superior present level of cognitive development on the part of the experimental group. (p. 10)

To affirm that, Garber (1988) noted that 39% of the control children had IQs below 75, while *none* of the experimental children did. Similar benefits accrued in problem-solving behaviors and language acquisition.

Garber's (1988) recent data analyses, however, are not encouraging in several areas. Both experimental children and control children have tended to do poorly in school; the majority of both groups were below average achievers in reading and mathematics by fourth grade. Fewer experimental children have repeated grades or needed special assistance, but more of them have problems with "school deportment" (documented on report cards), and reports on both groups indicate continued evidence of poor self-concept and negative attitudes toward school. Nevertheless, the alluring results that Garber and Heber reported have supported the hypothesis that the declines in cognitive functioning typically prevalent in low socioeconomic populations can be reversed through early infant intervention.

Without question the "Miracle in Milwaukee," as this project became known, was very influential in resurrecting the concept of compensatory education that Jensen (1969) and others had so severely criticized. But over the years questions arose that have tarnished the miraculous appearance of the program. Even in the afterglow of the initial publicity, Page (1972) raised concerns about several aspects of the program. He questioned in particular the possible bias in sampling of the population under study, the testing procedures, and the inaccessibility of the project data to external review by professionals. Page and Grandon (1981) noted:

> The Milwaukee Project . . . seems seldom to have appeared in refereed science journals, and details remain clouded. Yet its fame has been remarkable, particularly for its central claim: Working with available materials and intensive personal attention, we may raise children 30 IQ points; indeed, we may move them from dull normal to superior in intelligence.
>
> If this claim is true then the Milwaukee Project deserves its apparent image as the high-water mark of environmentalist accomplishment. And, repeatedly, writers advocating interventions have cited this project as such, even though it only had, as it in effect still has, the status of a series of press releases supported with occasional brief, undetailed addresses to uncritical professional audiences. An event of this kind, whether or not properly understood, can take on a mythic quality and become a pillar in one's ideology about the origins of human nature and the proper directions for social reform. (p. 240)

While the Milwaukee Project stands as a symbolic representation of the value of early intervention, the research underlying it is only now emerging from a host of methodological and legal issues. The interested reader should consult Garber and Heber (1981), Page and Grandon (1981), and Herrnstein (1982), for retrospectives on the project, and Garber (1988) for a detailed description.

Burton Blatt (1987) eloquently responded to the controversies that have been associated with the work of Rick Heber on this project as well as with other researchers in the area of the inheritance of intelligence, such as Cyril Burt. He stated:

> Nowhere in the social sciences has there been more controversy, more battle, more acrimony, more scandal than in the mental retardation research connected

with intelligence, its meaning, and its modifiability. In a sense, the concept of intelligence is the quintessential social science battlefield, and the IQ is the battle cry that goads people who otherwise know better to assume extreme and untenable positions as well as to engage in foolish, unseemly, and sometimes dishonest behavior. It's a commentary on that unfortunate state of affairs, as well as a reflection of the general pessimism concerning the possibility that capability is educable, that there exists a shadow upon the work and the persons—unfortunately, also the many honest and competent persons—involved in efforts to enhance educability (p. 53).

## ABECEDARIAN PROJECT

Several other programs that focused on intervention with young children, with follow-up to school entry, have been reported in the literature. One program worthy of particular note is the Carolina Abecedarian Project (Ramey & Haskins, 1981; Ramey & Campbell, 1984). The project began in 1972 with infants and children identified as high risk for school failure. Children were placed in a prevention-oriented day care setting until the age of five. A comprehensive curriculum canted toward cognitive, linguistic, and social development was utilized (Ramey & Haskins, 1981). Data summarized a decade after the study had begun (Ramey & Campbell, 1984) indicated that the experimental group continued to score at or near the national average in academic skill areas, while the children in the control group showed a significant *progressive achievement gap,* which began after 18 months of age and persisted throughout their years of schooling. Thus, the program demonstrated success in its goal of preventing a decline in the intellectual development of the children in the experimental day care setting. Ramey and his colleagues (Ramey, Bryant, Sparling, & Wasik, 1985) have also reported comparable findings for Project CARE, a follow-up to the Abecedarian project.

## EARLY INTERVENTION: EVALUATION

Although the general concept of early intervention has received widespread support, criticisms of specific programs and of inconsistency in research findings across programs abound. The list below, based in part on Mercer and Payne (1975), Polloway (1987), and Nevin and Thousand (1988), summarizes key points concerning effective programs and practices.

1. Curricular models stressing cognitive or academic instruction yield the most significant increases in intellectual functioning.
2. The most successful programs were structured with detailed outcome objectives and a specified plan of learning sequences.
3. Although the concept of "critical periods" of development is not consistently supported in the literature, programs that focus on younger children (e.g., 2–3-year-olds) have a number of advantages over those geared to older children (e.g., 4–5-year- olds) (see Peterson, 1987).

# BURTON BLATT:

# ON THE ACADEMICS

# OF NATURE-NURTURE

Just before his death, Burton Blatt, in his book *The Conquest of Mental Retardation* (1987), shared his thoughts about the field of mental retardation. One subject to which he returned several times was that of the academic warriors in the nature-nurture controversy.

Much has been written, and much has been ignored, concerning the work of scholars who have assumed polarized positions on the nature/nurture controversy. Burt was disgraced for alleged fudging or presenting nonexisting data. Heber apparently committed more financially oriented indiscretions. Skeels was once castigated and made the pariah, and years later Arthur Jensen found himself in similar circumstances. It almost appears as if those who insist on engaging in IQ controversy will get dirty—at least on the outside, and, so it seems, once in a while on the inside. The Harvard psychologist R. J. Herrnstein (1982) has claimed that the press and other media distort the controversy entirely in favor of the environmentalists. He has plaintively recounted the rigorous manner in which every unseemly element of Cyril Burt's life, time and time again, came out in the magazines and newspapers; on the other hand, he found it less than amusing that hardly a word was mentioned in those same journals and newspapers concerning Heber's fall from grace. Herrnstein has expressed concern about why the *New York Times* never asks a psychometrist to review books on the nature/nurture controversy, warning us that an antitesting bias has infected the media and many leftist organizations and their contributors. He has claimed that powerful pressure groups in politics, education, and the judiciary seek to contain the knowledge that science could bring to this controversy. There are anti-psychologists, egalitarians, sociologists, and other citizens who do not like testing—who do not like pitting white capability against black capability, the socially disadvantaged against the affluent. Of course, while Herrnstein's view must be examined seriously, environmentalists might make the same case of media neglect and distortion of their work. And so the controversy continues—fueled not only by the prejudices sustaining the principals engaged in the battle, but also by the prejudices of those who observe it, those who write about it, those who influence the larger society. (p. 314)

4. Home intervention complements short-term preschool programs. Although findings are equivocal regarding the degree of effectiveness in terms of child variables from specific program components focusing on parents, family involvement is a key to successful early intervention in a global sense (A. P. Turnbull, 1988).
5. Instructional activities should be selected and implemented based on their maximum contribution to a child's learning.
6. Programs of longer duration are warranted because children progress beyond the initial year of programming. Short-term efforts cannot be presumed to result in long-term change.
7. Primary school programs should be modified to capitalize on the skills that children who have benefited from early intervention bring to the classroom setting.
8. The most appropriate evaluation measures include academic and communication skills assessment and the ability to cope with later environments, *not* IQ gains. Such skills are not only more responsive to intervention but also most relevant to school performance.

A key evaluative question is the possible wash-out of effects after several years in school. Students who have received early intervention may, by late first or second grade, have lost their original advantage. Early intervention does not provide an "inoculation effect" against future problems and the challenges of adulthood (Garber, 1988). One example of an effort to carry gains into later situations is Project Follow Through, which was funded by the federal government. Included within Follow Through was a large-scale comparison of early intervention programs for disadvantaged children. According to the data, students who participated in programs based on direct instruction of school-related skills fared better in terms of later academic achievement (Polloway, Epstein, Polloway, Patton, & Ball, 1986), and it may be safe to conclude that such programs best prepared young children for these environments. Follow Through's comparison indicates that those pupils exposed to such programs demonstrated the most substantial gains in basic skills as well as being among the most effective models for enhancing affective and cognitive development (Becker, 1977; Becker & Carnine, 1980; Stebbins et al., 1977). Stebbins and colleagues (1977, p. xxvi) noted this point, stating, "Improved basic skills scores, where they have been achieved, do not seem to have been bought at the price of reduced scores in the domains of feelings and motivations."

What is the status of the efficacy of early intervention preventive efforts? Nevin and Thousand (1988) have recently reviewed the early intervention literature, drawing in particular on the efforts of the Utah State University Early Intervention Research Institute (EIRI) (e.g., White & Casto, 1984; Casto & Mastropieri, 1986). Most significant is their finding that early intervention programs for children identified as handicapped or high risk have had immediate positive benefits. For children with handicaps, longitudinal follow-up data are limited, but more support for positive long-term outcomes is available for high-risk children. In spite of the possibility of a wash-out effect, several projects have proven long-term outcomes. An appropriate place to conclude the discussion is with mention of the Perry Preschool Project (Schweinhart, Berreuta-Clement, Barrett, Epstein, & Weikart, 1985). This project resulted in substantial reductions in the number of children subsequently placed in special class programs. As Peterson (1987) noted in relating the results of the project to cost-benefit analysis:

> Graduates of the preschool intervention programs required less special education and none were placed in institutional types of care. . . . Thus the expenditures for initial preventative programs appeared to increase the chance that costs would be lessened later when the children entered public school programs. (p. 50)

Table 5.3 summarizes the major findings about long-term benefits associated with this project. It also provides an excellent concluding statement on the potential benefits of psychosocial change as a basis for improved life outcomes.

TABLE 5.3   Major Findings About Students of the Perry Preschool Study at Age 19

| Category | Number[a] Responding | Preschool Group | No-Preschool Group | $p$[b] |
|---|---|---|---|---|
| High school graduation (or its equivalent) | 121 | 67% | 49% | .034 |
| College or vocational training | 121 | 38% | 21% | .029 |
| Functional competence (average or above score) | 109 | 61% | 38% | .051 |
| Ever classified as mentally retarded | 112 | 15% | 35% | .014 |
| % of years in special education | 112 | 16% | 28% | .039 |
| Ever detained or arrested | 121 | 31% | 51% | .021 |
| Females only: teen pregnancies, per 100 | 49 | 64 | 117 | .076 |
| Employed at 19 | 121 | 50% | 32% | .031 |
| On welfare at interview | 121 | 18% | 32% | .044 |

[a]Total $n$ = 123

[b]Two-tailed probability that the group difference occurred by chance. For functional competence and teen pregnancies, the chi-square test was used; for the rest Fisher's exact test was used.

From "Effects of the Perry Preschool Programs on Youths Through Age 19: A Summary" by L. J. Schweinhart, J. R. Berreuta-Clement, W. S. Barrett, A. S. Epstein, and D. P. Weikart, 1985, *Topics in Early Childhood Special Education, 5*(2), pp. 26–35.

## PREVENTION: PERSPECTIVE

Chapter 4 discussed various biomedical preventive procedures that sound promising because of increasing scientific knowledge and its better application by biological researchers and medical practitioners. In this chapter, we have highlighted preventive programs related to psychosocial causes.

Although we have reason to be optimistic about the strides made to combat psychosocial retardation, clearly the successes that have been achieved are tempered by the obvious need for greater commitment in this area. Whether our society is willing to devote the necessary resources to breaking the poverty cycle and altering the effects of psychosocial causes with the goal of reducing the prevalence of retardation is still an unanswered question. Governmental commitment, especially at the federal level, is especially important. A most cynical comment published during President Reagan's administration was the remark by Clarence Pendleton, Reagan's choice to head the U.S. Commission on Civil Rights, that "the best way to help poor folks is to not be one" (Osborne, 1982, p. 25, cited by Blatt, 1987, p. 127).

Let us restate the basic premises of this chapter. Although advocates of the genetic stance have been active in proffering ideas concerning the bases for individual differences, it is clear that children who grow up in restricting conditions do not develop and mature as well as their more privileged peers. The negative consequences of an unstimulating environment must be diminished through the most promising intervention strategies. As Baroff (1974) writes, "Equality of opportunity is a ghastly charade if individuals are so stunted by early experiences as to be unable to take advantage of the opportunities our society offers" (p. 116). By facilitating children's cognitive, academic, social, and emotional development, we increase the chances of having a future population of healthy, self-sufficient, mature adults. Intervention strategies with a preventive aim must work to identify high-risk children and establish strategies designed to facilitate the development of each child.

---

## SUMMARY

Despite the numerous specific biological factors that can cause mental retardation, many cases stem from unknown causes within the environment or from polygenic inheritance. The terms *cultural-familial retardation* and *psychosocial disadvantage* refer to retardation associated with these factors.

The hereditary position is based on assumptions about the frequency of mild retardation found in families from lower social class backgrounds. Support for the genetic viewpoint has come from the study of parents and their children, siblings, and, most strikingly, from identical twins. This position carries implications for such controversial, biologically oriented intervention measures as sterilization. The reasoning behind it must be carefully weighed.

The environmental position claims that a number of specific external factors may negatively affect development. Hypoconnection is a possible explanation for the effects of such factors. Correlates of retardation encompass a host of variables related to poverty, from parenting practices to health problems and daily living difficulties. Such classic early intervention studies as the longitudinal research of Harold Skeels have given this position an empirical grounding.

Accepting either the environmental position or the concept of the interaction between heredity and environment demands a commitment to intensive intervention with young children in order to prevent learning problems from beginning. Achieving a significant reduction in mild retardation presents a continuing challenge to our nation.

# PART TWO

# INTRODUCTION TO THE DIFFERENT LEVELS OF MENTAL RETARDATION

# CHAPTER 6

# Mild and Moderate

# Retardation

**B**y definition individuals with mental retardation are distinguished from people who are not retarded on the basis of intellectual functioning and adaptive behavior. Significantly subaverage intellectual functioning is described along a continuum of mild, moderate, severe, and profound, according to the degree to which a person's measured general intelligence deviates from the normal range. The term *adaptive behavior* refers to the amount of personal independence and social responsibility the person demonstrates at various stages; deficits in these areas also can be placed along a continuum.

In both of these domains, the amount or degree of deficit is of prime importance. By demarcating levels of retardation, we emphasize the wide range of behaviors and abilities found among those identified as mentally retarded. On our continuum, we might place students who are mildly retarded and having difficulty with the academic and social demands of the regular classroom at one end and youngsters with profound retardation who might be immobile, noncommunicative, and unresponsive to their surroundings at the other. This chapter examines the characteristics and needs of individuals in the upper range of the continuum, who are placed in the mild and moderate categories. Chapter 7 takes a closer look at the lower range of the continuum (severe and profound levels).

Those who are considered mentally retarded are part of a heterogeneous group, and we should exercise caution when discussing any group in general. The reader should not come away from these two chapters thinking that every person with retardation displays all of the characteristics we enumerate.

---

This chapter was contributed by Carol H. Thomas and James R. Patton.

But generalizations based on research with individuals who exhibit deficits in intellectual and social functioning are worth propounding and can serve as a framework for furthering our understanding of this population.

One erroneous generalization is commonly applied to people who are mentally retarded. It implies that these individuals are "childlike." In numerous instances adults with mental retardation have been treated like children. Referring to 30-year-old adults as "kids" is not appropriate. Langness and Levine (1986) point out that this misguided perception allows us to consider persons with retardation "to be irresponsible . . . to categorize them as incompetent . . . to assume they inevitably have bad judgment, do not know what they want, and cannot be trusted . . . to overprotect them and on the other hand to ignore them" (p. xi).

The characteristic behaviors discussed in this section are frequently observed among people with retardation of various levels at different stages of life. As previously mentioned, many factors influence individual functioning and behavior. Some of these variables are evidence of organic involvement; additional handicapping conditions such as sensory or orthopedic impairments; problems relating to health; concern and resources of the family; availability of services, both medical and educational; and how early the retardation was diagnosed and intervention begun.

## MILD RETARDATION

Individuals with *mild retardation* demonstrate adaptive behavior and intellectual functioning at the upper end of the retardation continuum. According to the most recent AAMR definition (Grossman, 1983), assessed intellectual functioning of individuals with mild retardation is within the IQ range of 50–55 to approximately 70 points, with concurrent deficits in adaptive behavior. This category encompasses the majority of those who are usually classified as mentally retarded.

Evidence implies that this mild group varies greatly from one locality to another. As discussed at length in chapter 2, there has been an appreciable decrease in the number of students classified as mentally retarded since 1977, when P.L. 94-142 went into effect. This change affects the mild group most dramatically. The suggestion of those who have been studying this phenomenon (MacMillan & Borthwick, 1980; Polloway & Smith, 1983) is that a "new" group of students is being classified as mildly mentally retarded, and that this group is characteristically "more disabled." It is not advisable to compare research results of ten years ago with those that are more recent, as the subjects may differ in many important independent variables. Similarly, many conclusions made about the "traditional" group may not hold for the "new" group of students classified as mildly retarded.

The cause of most cases of mild retardation is unknown. While hereditary factors are an etiological consideration at any level, other variables such as nutrition, health care, and environmental stimulation play important roles as

This generalization relates to problems associated with handicapism, discussed in Chapter 2.

See Polloway & Smith (1983) for a detailed discussion of this issue.

well. Indeed, a disproportionate number of children identified as mildly retarded are from lower socioeconomic status families.

While the slower rate at which these children develop motor, social, and language skills may be noticeably different from their peers', mild retardation is often not suspected until the children enter school. Often a combination of difficulty with academic subjects and behavioral problems generates concern. Learning problems sometimes appear to be specific to one subject area, such as reading, but more often they are recognized across subjects.

Children who do not have the verbal and communication skills of their age mates may withdraw from interpersonal relationships or seek attention in a variety of inappropriate ways. These children may misbehave because they cannot clearly distinguish between acceptable and unacceptable standards of behavior. Problem behavior can also result from the frustrations of scholastic failure or as an attempt to gain acceptance from other children, who might encourage deviant behavior. Much inappropriate social behavior that occurs is a result of repeated failures.

A number of terms refers to students formally identified as mildly retarded and provided with special education and related services designed to meet their needs. One term, *educable mental retardation* (EMR), is used frequently in educational settings. It reflects the student's ability to profit from an academically-oriented curriculum. Students with mild retardation can, in many cases, be educated within the regular classroom by using materials and methods proven effective for learners with special needs. The "new" population referred to above, however, may not possess the skills necessary to handle the regular education curriculum. Nevertheless, our goal is for students to remain in regular education wherever possible.

While some data support the contention that individuals with mild retardation display more secondary problems than the population as a whole (Chinn, Drew, & Logan, 1979; Forness & Polloway, 1987; Polloway, Epstein, Patton, Cullinan, Luebke, 1986), most of these people can lead satisfying and productive lives, as attested to in such biographical works as *Like Normal People* (Meyers, 1980). Adults with mild retardation are capable of securing and maintaining employment and becoming economically self-sufficient, but the large amount of unemployment and underemployment in the disabled adult population is a chilling fact. With increased knowledge about how individuals with retardation learn and with more effective methodology for improving their performance, we should be able to provide even better programs that are sensitive to both current and future needs.

## MODERATE RETARDATION

Children who function below a mild level of retardation are usually identified prior to school entry. Individuals with *moderate retardation* are those who display significant deficits in adaptive behavior and are functioning intellectually within the 30–35 to 50–55 IQ range (Grossman, 1983). Various clinical

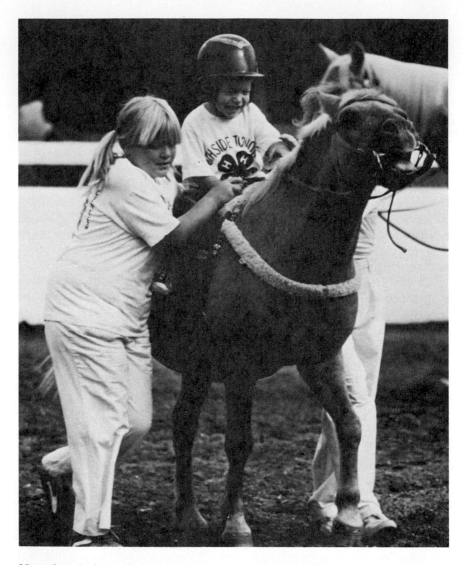

*Mental and physical limitations do not imply that children cannot participate in exciting activities.*

syndromes, notably Down syndrome, are often associated with moderate retardation and produce distinct physical characteristics. In addition, a higher percentage of children with moderate retardation than those with mild retardation have multiple disabling conditions.

Very young children who are moderately retarded will demonstrate developmental delays in such skills as sitting, crawling, walking, and especially language. Families of children with developmental problems often require support and assistance from physicians, health care workers, nutritionists, social workers, teachers, and home trainers. The recent amendments (P.L. 99-457) to the Education for All Handicapped Children Act ensure that appropriate services will go to individuals with special need and to their families. The support and services that are now available help families to deal with the problems presented by an exceptional child and to enhance the child's developmental progress.

Institutionalization is still an issue with regard to individuals functioning at the moderate level and below. At one time, residential placement was a frequently used option. Many factors are necessarily involved in the decision to institutionalize a child. One might be the specialized care and training felt to be needed for the child—and assumed to be provided by institutional placement—which would place both a physical and an economic strain on the family. Because of the former attitude that individuals who were moderately retarded could not benefit from attending public schools, relatively few communities provided educational services for them. In more recent years, however, advances in understanding of and methods for teaching this group, as well as federal legislation (P.L. 94-142, 99-457), have vastly increased educational opportunities for these students. While educational programs must be provided even for those individuals in residential placements, far fewer children who are moderately retarded are institutionalized than in the past, and many remain at home or in the same community all their lives.

Educators generally refer to children at this level as *trainable mentally retarded* (TMR), emphasizing the training aspect of their education over the more academically oriented programs for those in the educable group. Even this aspect is currently being debated, however, as some youngsters with moderate retardation have been able to benefit from academic experiences (Apffel, Kelleher, Lilly, & Richardson, 1975; Fink & Sandall, 1980; Litton, 1978). For the most part, however, emphasis is on self-help skills (dressing, eating, grooming, and other aspects of daily life), functional academics (making change, purchasing goods), and prevocational skills.

The last several years of school usually stress vocational preparation. Programming includes experiences at school as well as community-based settings. Later, employment is definitely possible in competitive settings. While individuals with moderate retardation may require a certain amount of supervision, many can achieve independence and lead satisfying lives.

## DEMOGRAPHIC CHARACTERISTICS OF INDIVIDUALS WITH MILD RETARDATION

Information about the characteristics and background of a given population enables us better to understand, prepare for, and serve the needs of that group. The following discussion focuses primarily on the demographics of individuals with mild retardation for two reasons. First, this segment of the population appears to have changed the most in the past few years. Second, individuals with moderate to profound retardation are generally not overrepresented in any given socioeconomic or racial group; they are fairly evenly distributed throughout the general population.

## GENDER

More boys than girls bear the label *mentally retarded.* In Dunn's review of the literature on persons who are mildly retarded and his subsequent description of that population in 1973, he stated that EMR students were more likely to be male. This apparently still holds true for the EMR population, if figures in recent studies characterizing individuals who are mildly retarded are indicative of the population as a whole (Epstein, Polloway, Patton, & Foley, 1989; Polloway, Epstein, Patton, Cullinan, & Luebke, 1986).

Males predominate at other levels of mental retardation as well. Abramowicz and Richardson (1975) reviewed 10 studies of children with IQ scores below 50 and in all 10 found a higher prevalence of males. Reasons given for a preponderance of males include: greater role expectations placed on males; aggressive behavior more often exhibited by males as leading to referral and subsequent labeling, and a higher probability of such biological factors as sex-linked influences affecting male children (Robinson & Robinson, 1976).

## ETHNICITY

Reviewers of demographic data have historically reported a disproportionate number of racial and ethnic minority children being labeled as mildly mentally retarded (Doll, 1962; Dunn, 1973a). During the 1960s and 1970s the imbalance in the makeup of EMR classes became the focus of much litigation, which in part led to changes in the procedures for identifying and labeling children as mentally retarded. But even with definitional changes and more stringent identification procedures, the same trend continues in evidence today.

A study conducted by the New Jersey State Department of Education (Manni, Winikur, & Keller, 1980) reported that 43% of the public school population labeled EMR were Black and 13.3% were Hispanic, although they accounted for only 17.8% and 7.4% of the school population, respectively. Polloway and colleagues (1986) reviewed information on elementary and secondary students labeled EMR who were receiving services in several medium-sized cities in northern Illinois. They, too, found a disproportionate number of nonwhite students in EMR programs. A follow-up study, also in Illinois but with different subjects, utilized data from IEPs of 107 elementary school students labeled EMR (Epstein et al., 1989). The authors found that nonwhite representation was approximately twice that of the total school population. While these studies represent only a limited geographic area, they fuel the continuing concern about racial overrepresentation in programs for students with mild retardation. Additional study is needed to evaluate compliance with identification procedures and definitional requirements designed to limit discrimination (Brady, Manni, & Winikur, 1983).

## SOCIOECONOMIC AND FAMILY PATTERNS

Environmental influences as a variable in the etiology of mental retardation are recognized by the AAMR in its inclusion of "psychosocial disadvantage" as an etiological classification. The description of this category includes the statement that "these cases are usually from impoverished environments involving poor housing, inadequate diet, and inadequate medical care" (Grossman, 1983, p. 149). Factors sometimes associated with low socioeconomic status, such as a preponderance of single-parent homes, children raised by people other than their natural parents, and family involvement with one or more community agencies for support services, have been substantiated as causes in at least one recent study describing this population (Epstein et al., 1989).

The higher prevalence of mild mental retardation among low-income families has been acknowledged for some time (Westling, 1986). This disproportionate representation, however, appears to be almost entirely limited to mild retardation. Socioeconomic conditions do not seem to affect the prevalence of moderate to profound retardation (Conley, 1973).

## MOTIVATIONAL AND BEHAVIORAL CHARACTERISTICS

Children who are mentally retarded have the same basic physiological, social, and emotional needs as children who are not. Because of their experiences in dealing with an environment in which they are less able to cope, however, they often develop patterns of behavior that serve further to distinguish them from those who are not retarded. For example, emotional and behavioral problems show a higher prevalence (Balthazar & Stevens, 1975; Polloway, Epstein, & Cullinan, 1985; Robinson & Robinson, 1976). The motivational and behavioral characteristics presented in this section are generalizations supported by studies of groups of individuals who are retarded. Because individuals are unique, and there is at least as much variability among those who are retarded as among persons who are not retarded, the following generalizations may not fit every individual.

### MOTIVATIONAL

The following motivational orientations are taken from research in the field of social learning theory. Many early investigations concentrated on distinctions between individuals who were mildly retarded and those who were not. This discussion, however, has relevance for those with moderate retardation as well.

***External locus of control.*** Locus of control refers to how one perceives the consequences of one's behavior. Individuals who operate primarily from an internal locus of control see events—both positive and negative—as results of their own actions. Those who see positive and negative events as primarily controlled by such outside forces as fate, chance, or other people have an external locus of control.

Young children tend to be externally oriented, perceiving many circumstances and events in their lives as being beyond their control. As the child matures, however, he becomes more aware of the influence of his own actions. As a result, he gradually shifts to a more internal locus of control (Lawrence & Winschel, 1975). External control, therefore, is considered a more debilitating orientation, as it keeps the child from accepting responsibility for his or her own successes and failures and impedes the development of self-reliance. *Learned helplessness* is another term sometimes used to reflect the belief that failure will crown even the most extraordinary efforts (Seligman, 1975).

Mercer and Snell (1977) reviewed the results of locus of control studies that involved subjects who were retarded. The studies indicate that such subjects are more externally oriented than their nonretarded peers. Mercer and Snell conclude that "the consistent finding that mental retardates are external and that external orientation tends to be handicapping challenges us to explore techniques for promoting internal orientations" (p. 190).

***Expectancy for failure.*** *Expectancy* refers to the reinforcement that is anticipated as a result of a given behavior. Rotter (1954) postulates two types of expectancies. The first is the expectation of a particular type of reinforcement, such as a tangible reward or social approval. The second involves expectations generalized from the results of past experiences with particular types of problem-solving activities. In other words, a new task is approached with either the expectation of success or the expectation of failure, based on what the individual has experienced in the past.

Studies by Cromwell (1963) that involved subjects who were retarded found them to have a high expectancy for failure. Zigler (1973) and Balla and Zigler (1979) noted that an individual who has accumulated failure experiences sets lower aspirations and goals in an effort to avoid additional failures. Heber (1964) pointed out that this fear of failure may become circular: The expectation of failure lowers the amount of effort put into a task, performance of the task is thus below what might be anticipated from the capabilities of the individual, and the expected failure becomes a reality.

***Outerdirectedness.*** Another result of attempts to avoid failure is a style of problem-solving called *outerdirectedness*. Instead being self-reliant in problems, the outerdirected individual imitates the behavior of others or looks to others for cues or guidance.

While this type of behavior is certainly not limited to those who are retarded, Zigler (1966) has suggested that it prevails among them because they have learned to distrust their own abilities, again because of the frequency with which they have failed in the past. Efficient problem-solving necessarily involves using both external cues and one's own cognitive resources. Relying too heavily on external cues could result in a dependence upon them even for a task well within one's own capabilities (Balla & Zigler, 1979).

In the three motivational orientations discussed (locus of control, expectancy for failure, and outerdirectedness), one recurring factor is the detrimental effect of repeated failures. Perhaps the most important implication, then, is the necessity of providing children who are retarded with tasks in which they can succeed. This holds true for both social and academic settings. Allowing the child to be successful is an invaluable motivational tool. Yet all children, handicapped and otherwise, need to learn to deal with failure as well. A sensitive teacher can shape classroom experiences in such a way that the child gains enough self-confidence through repeated successes to be able to rebound from an occasional inevitable failure. Parents and teachers need to be sensitive to their own expectations for the child, so that they do not inadvertently reinforce the child's expectation for failure. They must take care to avoid conveying the idea that they think the child is not competent to handle simple tasks. Rather, parents and teachers should require all children to assume the responsibilities that are within their grasp and should make it clear to them exactly what is expected of them.

Other ways to increase the chances of success are setting specific, realistic goals, providing immediate feedback for specific behavior, and rewarding accomplishments. If the child has repeatedly failed at a certain task, the situation should be restructured to present a novel approach to the problem that makes success possible. Finally, while it is desirable to help children who are retarded become more innerdirected and self-reliant, their tendency to rely heavily on external cues should be used to advantage. Teachers and parents should provide appropriate behavior models for children (Kauffman & Payne, 1975; Mercer & Snell, 1977).

## BEHAVIORAL

*Mild mental retardation.* While children and adolescents who are mentally retarded have historically been described as displaying more social and behavioral problems than their nonhandicapped counterparts (Balthazar & Stevens, 1975; Robinson & Robinson, 1976), more recent studies focusing on the child who is mildly retarded confirm this as well (Epstein et al., 1986; Polloway et al., 1985; Russell & Forness, 1985). Some of the specific problem areas include disruptiveness, attention deficits, low self-esteem (Polloway et al., 1985), overactivity (Polloway et al., 1986), and distractability and other attention-related problems (Epstein et al., 1989).

# SCOUTING FOR BOYS WHO ARE

## MENTALLY RETARDED

An example of the increasing integration of persons with mental retardation into the mainstream of society is a policy of the Boy Scouts of America, which authorizes such participation as depicted below.

In addition, this organization has developed a resource specifically directed at accommodating youths with retardation: *Scouting for the Mentally Retarded* (1987). This material includes a number of suggestions for working with these youngsters and for assisting them in the attainment of the advancement awards in this organization. The re-source offers examples of ways to substitute requirements when appropriate or to utilize modified approaches. The Boy Scouts has also developed a "Special Advancement and Recognition Program" designed specifically for scouts with moderate retardation. This program includes 10 Scout badges that have requirements developed with these special scouts in mind. This type of integrative effort on the part of the Boy Scouts of America is laudable and represents the type of effort that should be available in other community organizations and activities.

### ARTICLE XI, SECTION 3, CLAUSE 19 OF THE
### *RULES AND REGULATIONS OF THE BOY SCOUTS OF AMERICA*
### NOW READS AS FOLLOWS:

Clause 19. Mentally Retarded or Severely Physically Handicapped Youth Members. In the discretion of the Executive Board, and under such rules and regulations as it may prescribe upon consultation with appropriate medical authorities, registration of boys who are either mentally retarded or severely physically handicapped, including the blind, deaf, and emotionally disturbed, under age 11 as Cub Scouts and under age 18 as Boy Scouts or Varsity Scouts, and registration of young adults who are either mentally retarded or severely physically handicapped, including the blind, deaf, and emotionally disturbed, under age 21 as Explorers, and the participation of each in the respective advancement programs while registered, is authorized.

From *Scouting for the Mentally Retarded* by Boy Scouts of America, 1987, Irving, TX: Author.

*Moderate mental retardation.* It has been generally accepted that the lower the intellectual level the more pronounced the behavioral deviations. This would imply that individuals with moderate retardation would exhibit more behavior disorders than those with mild retardation. There does appear to be a higher incidence of behavioral and psychiatric disorders in this group, particularly among persons whose moderate retardation is associated with central nervous system dysfunction (Robinson & Robinson, 1976; Russell & Forness, 1985). A wide range of behaviors may be evidenced in such individuals, including distractability, hyperactivity, mood disturbances, and stereotypic behaviors. Health-related problems as well as the effects of medication may affect attention and concentration, leading both to a slower and more limited acquisition of social skills and to an increase in inappropriate behaviors.

Since being able to meet more normal behavioral expectations is often a consideration in the decision to integrate special children into regular programs, social skill problems may contribute to placement. Also, a great many variables influence the learning process. Better social, motivational, and behavioral adjustment is likely to relate to better academic functioning. Another major consideration is that independent living as an adult has many social and behavioral demands. Curricular attention to this area would help a more successful integration into community life.

Further implications extend into higher education, where professionals are being trained to work with exceptional students. In the area of mental retardation, teachers need to prepare themselves for a diversity of social and behavioral problems and receive training in appropriate intervention and management techniques for dealing with them (Epstein et al., 1986). Training is also needed in ways to incorporate social skills into the curriculum and in methods and materials by which such skills may be taught.

## LEARNING CHARACTERISTICS

We may think of *learning* as the process whereby practice or experience produces a change in behavior that is not due to maturation, growth, or aging. The definition implies *(a)* that the changed behavior is relatively permanent, as distinguished from responses to drugs or fatigue, and *(b)* that the learner is involved and participating, not just changing because of physical growth or deterioration (Bower, 1978).

Learning is a hypothetical construct and, as such, cannot be measured directly. How much or how little learning has actually taken place can be inferred only from performance. If a child points to the object the teacher has just named or spells a word correctly, we assume that learning has taken place. If the child performs the task incorrectly or does not attempt the task at all, we assume that learning has not occurred. Since learning can be measured only indirectly, we must be cautious in interpreting performance levels as direct indicators of it. A great many factors influence whether and how a child responds in any given situation. They include the physical and social setting, types and contents of materials, procedures being used, and incentives.

We have implied that physical maturity can result in behavior changes. The development of such motor skills as walking appears not to be influenced by training or experience until the child has the necessary physical maturity. Delayed development, however, is a characteristic of people with retardation, and the degree of delay is generally related to the severity of the retardation and the presence of other handicapping conditions. People who expect a person with disabilities to acquire skills at the normal rate may end up frustrated and may fail in their attempts to teach new skills. Training and practice will not supplant the maturation process; but studies of infant stimulation provide enough encouragement to justify training and practice in order to enhance development.

## COGNITIVE DEVELOPMENT

*Quantitative versus qualitative perspectives.*    Use of the concept of mental age (MA) to express the level of cognitive functioning of a given individual has given rise to differing orientations from which to view the cognitive development of persons who are retarded. For example, cognitive development may be viewed as quantitative and comparable among children of similar mental age, regardless of chronological age. This perspective, the *developmental* position, assumes that cognitive development, at least for the youngster who is mildly retarded, is similar to that of the younger, nonretarded child. According to Zigler (1969), such children progress through the same developmental levels in the same sequence as do nonretarded children, although at a slower rate and lower level of ultimate functioning.

Proponents of this point of view believe that children who are retarded fail because they are presented with tasks beyond their current ability level. Educational programs based on a developmental model would, therefore, use traditional teaching strategies but be geared primarily to the mental age (MA) of the individual. The developmental view of cognitive growth can be thought of as a series of steps or stages in which new tasks are presented only when the child reaches the mental age appropriate to that task.

Proponents of the *difference* position, however, view the cognitive development of persons with retardation as qualitatively different from that of the nonretarded. Ellis (1969) contended that there are differences in the way in which these people process information, and that the main task of research is to describe these areas of difference. The implications for teaching are that unique teaching methods and materials are needed to overcome or lessen the effects of the deficiency.

Research favoring one orientation over the other is plentiful. Firm conclusions, however, are difficult to reach because of the many variables that can affect cognitive development, for example, etiology of the retardation, motivational differences, and problems associated with matching on MA. Regardless of position on this issue, the research in this area adds to our larger understanding of how children who are retarded learn.

Since much of the developmentally oriented research is based upon Piaget's carefully sequenced stages of development, we briefly present this theory along with its application for learners who are retarded. This section describes some learning processes where distinctions have been noted between learners who are retarded and learners who are not.

*Cognitive-developmental theory.* The original tenets of **cognitive-developmental theory** were formulated by Jean Piaget, based on observations of his own ("normal") children. He viewed mental development as a result of continuous interaction with and adaptation to the environment or the child's perception of it. According to Piaget (1969), each child progresses through stages of development where various cognitive skills are acquired. The main stages of development, along with approximate age norms, are

1. Sensorimotor stage—birth to 2 years
2. Preoperational stage—2 to 7 years
3. Concrete operations—7 to 11 years
4. Formal or abstract operations—11 years and older.

The **sensorimotor stage** is characterized by sensory experiences and motor activity. As young children become more aware of the surrounding environment, they begin to distinguish between themselves and other persons and objects. The second stage, **preoperational**, involves more than purely physical operations. Children begin to use symbols for the people and objects around them, to assimilate customs, and to acquire new experiences by imitating the actions of others. During the **concrete operations** stage, children develop further abilities to order and classify objects. While mental operations are more highly developed, children are usually limited to solving problems with which they have had direct or concrete experience. The ability to perform abstract thinking and reason by hypothesis is said to develop around the age of 11 or 12, and characterizes the **formal operations** or **abstract** stage.

Piagetian theory has been related to children with mental retardation by Inhelder (1968) and Woodward (1963, 1979) who view the child who is retarded as progressing through the same stages of cognitive development as the nonretarded, with the major differences being in rate and highest level achieved. The age at which a child who is retarded would reach each stage would be later, and the more severe the retardation, the slower the progression through the stages. In addition, individuals who are mentally retarded may not achieve all stages of development. According to Inhelder, children who are mildly retarded may reach the concrete operations level, but individuals who are moderately retarded will go no further than the preoperational stage. Those with severe and profound retardation remain at the sensorimotor level.

According to Piagetian theory, mental development progresses as a result of children's interactions with their surroundings. The role of the educator, therefore, is seen as that of a provider of materials and opportunities appropriate to children's stage of development and with which they can interact. Teachers of mentally handicapped students need to be aware of the developmental sequences in order to determine a child's readiness for a particular task, and to consider the slow rate and the expected optimal level of functioning when planning curricula for children with varying levels of retardation.

## PROCESSES INVOLVED IN LEARNING

Individuals with mental retardation by definition perform below average on tests of intelligence and are slow and inefficient learners. Whether you subscribe to the developmental or difference model of the cognitive functioning of people with retardation, the practical issue of providing the optimum learning environment remains. Toward this end, a vast amount of research has been conducted in the area of learning and applied to those with retardation. Most theorists have concentrated their efforts on one aspect of learning, such as attention or memory. In generalizing the findings to educational programming, however, we must emphasize that implications from various theories relating to separate aspects of learning may be used in combination to offer learners who are retarded the best opportunities for realizing their potential.

## ATTENTION

In any learning situation attention to the task at hand is critical for successful learning. Zeaman and House (1963) did much of the early work in the area of attention. Their experiments involved two-choice visual discrimination tasks where subjects were rewarded for selecting the dimension (color, shape, size) that the investigator had previously selected as the correct choice. Responses were recorded and translated into learning curves or graphs illustrating the percentage of correct responses upon each trial. Analysis of the curves revealed that learning the discrimination tasks had two stages. In the first, subjects responded correctly about 50% of the time, or at about chance level. During the second stage, however, correct responses increased dramatically, resulting in a sharp rise on the learning curve. Zeaman and House have suggested that the first stage is an attention phase, where the subject *randomly* attends to various aspects of the task. Once the subject has focused on the key features of the task, or *selectively* attends to the stimuli, the second phase begins.

Zeaman and House compared the learning curves obtained from performances of children with and without retardation whose MAs varied. They found the two stages in the curves of all groups, as well as the sharp rise in performance at the beginning of the second stage. The difference between the groups was the number of trials composing the first stage. Children with lower MAs required more trials in the attention phase than did children with higher ones. Zeaman and House therefore concluded that subjects with retardation needed more time to learn to attend to the relevant dimensions of the stimuli.

In updating their theory, Zeaman and House (1979) also noted a relationship between MA and the number of dimensions that a subject could attend to simultaneously. Learners who were retarded could not attend to as many dimensions simultaneously as could those who were not retarded. In addition, some learners with retardation seem to prefer some dimensions over others, which may also affect their response. This is particularly relevant if, as Brooks and McCauley (1984) maintain, such learners have less attention to allocate and that "attentional allocation is a problem in general for mentally retarded people that may extend to all domains of information processing" (p. 482).

The initial research by Zeaman and House continues to generate investigations, but we can already draw implications from the work in attention for teaching students who are retarded. Among them are that the teacher should *(a)* present stimuli which vary in only a few dimensions, *(b)* direct the child's attention to these dimensions, *(c)* remove extraneous stimuli that may distract the child from attending to the task at hand, and *(d)* reward the child for attending to the task (Mercer & Payne, 1975).

## ORGANIZING INFORMATION

Once an individual has attended to a specific stimulus, he or she must organize and store it so that it can be recalled when needed. Spitz (1966) refers to this process as *input organization* and has conducted research to determine the functioning in this area of persons who are mentally retarded.

Spitz's (1966) research led him to theorize that the input step in the learning process was more difficult for subjects with retardation than for other subjects, because of a deficiency in their ability to organize the input stimuli for storage and recall. This finding has generated a great deal of research into strategies for enhancing a student's ability to categorize incoming data. Two such methods are grouping and mediation.

**Grouping,** or clustering material prior to its presentation, is seen by Spitz (1973, 1979) as more beneficial to the learner with retardation than presenting material in random order. Restructuring the perceptual field for individuals who characteristically have difficulty at this stage of the learning process should facilitate memory and recall. Grouping is perhaps the simplest method of organizing information. Material may be grouped spatially, presented in different visual arrangements; temporally, by presenting the material with a pause or time lapse between items; perceptually, by enclosing certain items in a shape or configuration; or categorically, by content or commonality of items.

Stephens (1966) has further broken down this grouping by content into physical similarity (items of the same color), function (articles of clothing), concepts (plants, animals), and sequential equivalence (subjects and objects as used in grammatical arrangements). Work by Stephens (1972) in presenting stimuli according to types of grouping indicates that the most basic type of grouping is that of physical similarity. As a child increases in mental age, more advanced grouping strategies are used. This same progression was reported for normal subjects as well as subjects with mild retardation.

A mediator is something that goes between or connects. In verbal learning, **mediation** refers to the process by which an individual connects a stimulus and a response. One approach to the study of verbal learning, *paired associate learning,* focuses on verbal mediation as a means of learning responses to stimulus words or elements. In this technique, the subject is generally presented with pairs of words. Then only the first word in each pair is presented, and the subject tries to recall the second. Verbalizing the connection between the two stimulus words seems to enhance performance. Studies reviewed by Meyers and MacMillan (1976) note marked improvements in tasks of this type even by subjects with retardation, when the subjects were instructed in mediation strategies or provided with such mediators as sentences relating the stimulus to the response. The meaningfulness of the material and the use of stimulus words or objects familiar to the subject (Estes, 1970) also facilitated learning in paired associate tasks.

Several inferences for teaching can be drawn from this research. First, materials presented to learners who are retarded should be familiar or have some relevance for them. Second, information should be grouped or organized into meaningful parts. Finally, such learners should be instructed in mediational strategies.

## MEMORY

**Memory,** the ability to retrieve information that has been stored, is one of the most heavily researched components of the learning process. A distinction is usually made between **short-term memory** (STM) and **long-term memory** (LTM). Information recalled after a period of days or months or longer is usually referred to as being in long-term memory, while data stored from a few seconds to a few hours is in short-term memory (Ellis, 1970). Most researchers contend that once learned, information is retained over the long term about as well by those with retardation as by those without (Belmont, 1966; Ellis, 1963). In the area of short-term memory, however, learners who are retarded appear to have considerable difficulty (Borkowski, Peck, & Damberg, 1983; Ellis, 1963).

Ellis (1970) and his associates consider that the short-term memory problems characteristic of people who are retarded arise primarily from their inability to use rehearsal strategies or adequate rehearsal activities. Some success has been reported (Belmont & Butterfield, 1971; Brown, Campione, & Murphy, 1974) in efforts to improve short-term memory performance among these learners by direct teaching or rehearsal or practice procedures, although the effects of the training appear to be specific to the training task and not readily transferable (Belmont & Butterfield, 1977). The major rehearsal strategies noted by Mercer and Snell (1977) in their review of studies of STM were verbal rehearsal and image rehearsal. *Verbal rehearsal* refers to labeling aspects of a task and verbalizing these labels aloud or silently while the task is being performed. For example, verbal rehearsal might be used to help a worker learn the steps of a complex assembly task: "Pick up one nut; pick up one bolt; put the bold into the nut," and so forth. In using *image rehearsal,* the individual is taught to associate aspects of a task with pictures of events that will help him to recall them. For instance, a youngster might be taught to tie shoelaces by making one rabbit ear, making another, and tying the two together.

*Executive control* or *metacognition* are terms applied to the process one consciously goes through in order to analyze a problem, anticipate outcomes of various actions, decide how the problem should be solved, and monitor progress toward the solution (Campione, Brown, & Ferrara, 1982). Researchers have noted that learners who are retarded generally do not spontaneously employ executive control processes (Brown, 1974; Sternberg & Spear, 1985), but that they can be taught to use them effectively (Borkowski et al., 1983). Other teaching techniques to facilitate recall include *(a)* organizing material into meaningful segments, *(b)* using reinforcement and incentives for remembering, *(c)* using repetition and drill, and *(d)* reminding and encouraging the child to use rehearsal strategies.

## OBSERVATIONAL LEARNING

*Imitation, modeling,* and *learning through observation* are the terms most often associated with **observational learning**, which refers to learning from demonstrations by others. Much of the research in this area has been done by Bandura (1969) and his associates. It substantiates the important role that observational learning plays in acquiring social behaviors, sex roles, language, and religious and political practices. In addition, imitation and modeling are involved in the development of new behaviors and the modification of existing ones, and it may result in the learning of inappropriate as well as appropriate responses.

While there is not a great deal of research concerning the use of observational techniques with children who are retarded, certain of their characteristics give support to the use of this tool. The tendency of these learners to be outerdirected or to look to others for cues or guidance in

*Kitchen skills can be taught through the modeling and imitation process.*

problem-solving (Turnure & Zigler, 1964) and their suggestibility (Zigler, 1973) indicates that modeling could be effectively used for acquiring or changing behavior. Suggestions for using observational learning include: *(a)* being aware that any behavior may serve as a model; *(b)* calling attention to students exhibiting desirable behavior; *(c)* ignoring undesirable behavior so that others do not model it in an attempt to gain attention; *(d)* rewarding modeling of appropriate behavior; and *(e)* using audiovisual as well as live models to facilitate learning (MacMillan, 1977).

# EDUCATIONAL CHARACTERISTICS

## PLACEMENT

This section examines various facets of the educational programs of students with mild and moderate retardation. Specifically, it focuses on placement options, curricular and service issues, and performance characteristics.

*Students with mild mental retardation.*    The diagnosis of mild retardation and any subsequent placement in a special program typically takes place after a student has encountered difficulty with the academic, social, or behavioral requirements in the first few regular grades in school (Dunn, 1973a). As evidence for redefining this population as being less able and having more accompanying disabilities than similarly labeled students of a decade ago accumulates (Gottlieb, 1981; MacMillan & Borthwick, 1980), we can expect earlier diagnosis and placement. Support for this is evidenced by the results of a recent study by Polloway et al. (1986) of the IEPs of 234 EMR public school students. The average age at the time of placement for the younger students in the study (ages 6–11) was 5½ years, as opposed to 7½ years for the older students (ages 12–18). The earlier diagnoses imply that special education placement and related services are being provided earlier in their school careers than in the past for children with mild retardation.

For many students with mild retardation, placement has been in regular education for the majority of the school day, with a smaller proportion of the time being spent in a special education setting. With the decreased ability being reported for this group comes the suggestion that the population may now not be so well suited to mainstreaming as in the past (MacMillan & Borthwick, 1980). Polloway et al. (1986) have attested that the vast majority of students with mild retardation spent less than 50% of the school day in the regular classroom. Additional research, however, is necessary in order to confirm that more limited integration of pupils who are mildly retarded into regular programs is a trend.

Students who are mildly retarded at the junior and senior high level may be assigned to resource sections of academic subjects. Special educators usually teach these classes and focus on the academic goals specified in the IEPs. Other periods in the school day may be spent in such classes as health, physical education, athletics, vocational classes, or any one of a number of elective subjects if these are considered appropriate for the individual student.

*Students with moderate mental retardation.*    With the lower intellectual and adaptive functioning of children with moderate retardation comes an earlier recognition of the retardation and its accompanying problems. The more exaggerated developmental delays in motor and language skills and/or physical and health problems are usually responsible for early contacts with medical personnel and community agencies (Bricker & Dow, 1980). With early identification comes a greater chance for eligibility for services and for infants or toddlers to receive assistance with adaptive skills and health or related problems (Bricker & Bricker, 1976). Clear measures of the effectiveness of such programs are difficult to come by (Baer, 1981; Bricker, 1987), but substantial documentation exists for the positive affects of early intervention with Down syndrome infants (Clunies-Ross, 1979; Hanson & Schwarz, 1978).

School programs for students with moderate retardation began in the 1950s and 1960s. These children traditionally work in a segregated setting, for example, a self-contained special education class. Their placement in a self-contained class, however, does not exclude integrating them with other children in nonacademic classes and other school activities (Haring & McCormick, 1986). Snell and Renzaglia (1986) stress the importance of placement that is chronologically age appropriate. Students should attend schools that serve students of their chronological age who are not handicapped.

Secondary education for the student with moderate retardation usually involves some class rotation during the school day. For example, students might change classrooms for academic and other school subjects as well as for vocational training and adapted physical education. Such an arrangement allows students to spend time with various special and regular educators trained in specific program areas as well as to conform to a traditional secondary schedule. These students, however, usually remain as a group with their peers rather than being integrated into mainstream classes.

## PROGRAMMATIC REALITIES

***Students with mild mental retardation.*** Preparation for independent living as an adult is the general goal for the student, and curricular content focuses on developing intellectual, personal, social, motor, vocational, and home management skills (Kolstoe, 1976). A curricular model, adapted from Campbell, divides the curriculum needs of the mildly retarded student into four areas: "basic readiness and practical academic development; communication, language, and cognitive development; socialization, family living, self-care, recreation/leisure, and personality development; and career and vocational development" (Patton & Payne, 1986, pp. 258–259). It is interesting to note, however, that while the literature favors a broad-based curriculum recent studies of IEP goals for students with mild retardation indicate a strong emphasis on academic goals (Epstein et al., 1989; McBride & Forgnone, 1985). In light of the more recent descriptions of this population it is not surprising that professionals in the field are calling for a more comprehensive approach to the education of these students, one that includes social skills training (Gresham, 1982; Polloway et al., 1986) and vocational and life skills (Brolin & Brolin, 1979; Edgar, 1987; Jaquish & Stella, 1986; Polloway, 1987).

Related services are provided to students who have been identified as handicapped to enable them to benefit fully from their educational program. With the change in the population of students with mild retardation, we can anticipate the appearance of more secondary handicaps and a need for additional related services to serve this population appropriately. While limited at present, research is under way on the growing prevalence of handicaps accompanying mild retardation. In the study by Epstein et al. (1989), the majority of the IEPs for the students with mild retardation listed secondary handicaps. Nearly 90 percent of the students had speech and language disorders; and sensory disorders (particularly visual impairment), convulsive disorders, and emotional and behavioral disorders were more common than in the general population. This study is consistent with other research (MacMillan, 1982; MacMillan & Borthwick, 1980) that characterizes individuals with mild retardation as evincing multiple handicaps and therefore being in need of more related services and support personnel.

*Students with moderate mental retardation.* The school program for those who are moderately retarded deviates markedly from the regular school program because of the more obvious needs of this group. Programs should reflect both the developmental age (level of ability) and the chronological age of the student in selecting goals leading to self-sufficiency (Brown, Nietupski, & Hamre-Nietupski, 1976). The curriculum for this group usually includes: self-help, basic readiness, independent living, communication, socialization, recreation and leisure skills, and cognitive development (Geiger, Brownsmith, & Forgnone, 1978; Snell et al., 1986). Age-appropriate materials should be utilized to teach functional skills that relate to the present or anticipated environmental needs (Brown, Branston, Hamre-Nietupski, Pumpian, Certo, & Gruenewald, 1979).

As independent living is a realistic goal for this population, the school program should concentrate on developing skills that will facilitate later adjustment into residential and vocational settings. Such skills might include interpersonal communication, personal grooming and hygiene, tasks related to shared daily responsibilities in a group living arrangement, and job-related behaviors required for a vocational/work environment.

Because the group tends to be more disabled than the group of those who are mildly retarded, secondary handicaps are more in evidence. (These are more fully discussed in the section Physical and Health Characteristics.) A wide range of related services—speech and language therapy, adaptive physical education, physical and occupational therapy, special transportation, and health-related services—may be needed to serve this group/adequately.

### ACADEMIC ACHIEVEMENT

Students with mild or moderate retardation will show deficits in all academic areas. The majority of students who are mildly retarded read at a level lower than would be expected for their MA, and of the various aspects of reading, comprehension appears to be the most difficult for these students (Carter, 1975; Dunn, 1973a). The child who is mildly retarded may attain some understanding of phonics skills in order to decode unfamiliar words, but the student with moderate retardation typically recognizes only those words committed to memory through the whole- or sight-word approach to reading. Many students who are moderately retarded acquire a relatively extensive sight-word vocabulary of functional and protective words, which are usually taught through a task-analysis approach (Snell, 1983).

In mathematics, the majority of students with mild retardation can learn the basic computations. Mathematical reasoning and appropriate application of concepts, however, is a more difficult task for this group (Dunn, 1973a). Students with moderate retardation, again through a task-analysis approach, may also learn the basic mathematical computations but will have considerably more difficulty with application. Functional arithmetic skills involving money, time, and measurement, because they are important for community living, are an integral part of the curriculum (Westling, 1986).

## SPEECH AND LANGUAGE CHARACTERISTICS

Speech and language problems occur with greater frequency among the population identified as mentally retarded than among those not so identified (MacMillan, 1982). This is not unexpected, since cognitive ability and language development are closely related. The speech problems most often seen are difficulties in articulation, or the pronunciation of words (Dunn, 1973a). Common articulation errors include the substitution, omission, addition, or distortion of sounds, which decrease the intelligibility of speech. Language disorders that commonly accompany mental retardation include delayed language development and a restricted or limited active vocabulary (Spradlin, 1968). Language is so important to independent functioning that prospective parents, parents of high-risk children, and day care personnel should be trained in formal and informal means of encouraging language development.

### MILD RETARDATION

As corroboration of the evidence that students now labeled mildly retarded display lower overall functioning than those classified according to the same label before the passage of P.L. 94-142 (Dunn, 1973a), we see an increasing occurrence of secondary handicapping conditions (MacMillan & Borthwick,

1980). For example, Epstein et al. (1989) gathered information from the IEPs of 107 children identified as mildly retarded in special education in northern Illinois. Speech and language problems were the most frequent secondary handicap; well over half the children were eligible for and receiving speech and language therapy as a related service. Where environment appears to play a large role in the etiology of the retardation, as it does for many who are mildly retarded, language deficits may be related to such factors as absence of or limited adequate speech and language models and less encouragement to use language. That a disproportionate number of students who are mildly retarded are also members of cultural or ethnic minorities (Dunn, 1973a; Polloway et al., 1986) may also play a role in the language deficiencies found in this population.

## MODERATE RETARDATION

Among those who are moderately retarded, speech and language disorders are even more common, not only because of their decreased intellectual development, but also from the increased possibility of concomitant handicapping conditions. The motor dysfunction accompanying cerebral palsy, for example, can seriously impede the ability to produce intelligible speech. A higher prevalence of hearing impairment also exists in this population, and poor hearing may both contribute to a further delay in the acquisition of language and affect articulation. Many children in this category, especially those with Down syndrome, have frequent bouts of otitis media, or middle ear infection, during their childhood years (Brooks, Wooley, & Kanjilal, 1972). The conductive hearing loss these infections can cause also delays language and creates speech problems (Balkany, Downs, Jafek, & Krajicek, 1979).

One of the characteristics typically attributed to the Down syndrome child is a protruding tongue. Tongue reduction surgery, often in combination with facial surgery, has become increasingly common as a means of diminishing some of the obvious characteristics. The use of such surgery as a means of improving speech, however, is dubious. Lemperle and Rada (1980) reported more intelligible speech after surgery for a majority of 63 Down syndrome children undergoing surgery, although no formal speech evaluations were conducted. In other studies Olbrisch (1982) and Lemperle (1985) sent questionnaires to families of children who had received tongue reduction surgery and reported that 88% and 68%, respectively, of the parents perceived speech improvement. Parsons, Iacone, and Rozner (1987) took formal speech assessment measures before surgery, four weeks after surgery, and again six months after surgery with 27 Down syndrome children. The number of articulation errors did not differ significantly across time, although the parents were almost unanimous in perceiving speech improvement after surgery.

The protruding tongue is caused by the smallness of the person's mouth.

# CHANGING THE LOOK OF MENTAL RETARDATION

Plastic surgeons can straighten the slanted eyes, build up the cheekbones and minimize the protruding tongue commonly found in children with Down syndrome. But should they? Plastic surgery remains the most controversial treatment offered Down syndrome children.

The 1½- to 2½-hour operation is fairly straightforward. Surgeons can build up the bridge of the nose, cheekbone and chin with bone grafts or synthetics, change the slant of the eyes and cut fat from the lower eyelids. There are usually no facial scars because the work is done through the mouth or by cutting skin flaps behind the hairline. The tongue, which appears too large and protrudes from an unusually small oral cavity, is reduced by about one-fifth.

Advocates of surgery believe that children with Down syndrome are rejected partly because of their physical features, and that improving their appearance may result in greater social acceptance. Critics respond that there is little hard evidence that the surgery has these effects. In fact, it has to be admitted that even the most gifted plastic surgeons can't make a child with Down syndrome look entirely normal. After surgery, the gait, neck and body proportions are still unusual. Even the face remains clearly different. "I've yet to see a child after the operation," says Diane Crutcher of the National Down Syndrome Congress, "who doesn't look like a child with Down syndrome." Moreover, say some critics, the surgery is itself a kind of rejection, a message that the children are not acceptable as themselves. It is society's preoccupation with "good looks" that should change, these critics argue, not the faces of Down children.

Even those who advocate the operation admit that not every child with Down syndrome is a good candidate for surgery, and both parents and child must go through an intensive screening process before their surgeon lifts a scalpel. "The surgery should only be performed in children whose quality of life can be improved by the procedures," cautions Garry S. Brody, clinical professor of plastic surgery at the University of Southern California. Surgery is immediately ruled out if the child is profoundly retarded or has life-threatening physical problems. In addition, parents must be realistic about what the surgery will and won't do. "If you think the child is going to roll out of the operating room with 20 more IQ points," says Crutcher, "you're going to be disappointed."

While controversial, plastic surgery remains an option for those willing to try every avenue. The American Society of Plastic and Reconstructive Surgeons operates a toll-free number (800/635–0635) for information on reconstructive and cosmetic surgery for Down syndrome and offers a referral list of board-certified plastic surgeons qualified to perform the operation.

From *Psychology Today,* September 1987, p. 45.

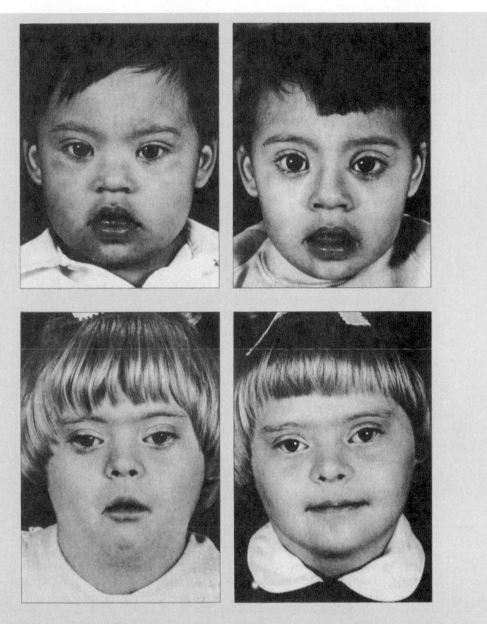

*Photos courtesy of Dr. Kenneth Salyer, Dallas, Tx.*
*Before and after. Advocates of surgery say it reduces the stigma often associated with Down syndrome. Critics say it sends the message that the children are unacceptable in appearance as they are.*

# PHYSICAL AND HEALTH CHARACTERISTICS

In general, the physical and health characteristics and needs of persons who are mildly retarded do not differ dramatically from those of other individuals. Greater retardation, however, tends to co-occur with more pronounced physical defects and health concerns. The following discussion highlights some of the health problems of individuals who are mildly and moderately retarded, as well as general health considerations that have specific implications for this population.

## SPECIFIC HEALTH PROBLEMS

As an example of a specific health problem, we begin with motor development, which even in those who are mildly retarded may be delayed and markedly less perfect than in the child who is not retarded. Motor deficits include problems of balance, locomotion, and manipulative dexterity (Bruininks, 1974). The growth rate may be slower, and these individuals are generally shorter and lighter than normal children (Bruininks, 1974; Mosier, Grossman, & Dingman, 1965).

Sensory defects are also more common among individuals who are retarded, with visual and auditory problems frequently noted (Barlow, 1978). Color blindness appears to be more prevalent among individuals with moderate retardation than among those who are mildly retarded or normal (O'Connor, 1975). Early screening for sensory defects is essential, for correctional devices or surgery may be indicated. In fact, early identification of any health problems may be critical to the total development of the child. While the retardation itself may obscure or impede efforts to diagnose additional problems, early intervention and treatment may lessen the effects of the disability and influence the rate and level of development the child may attain.

*Down syndrome.*    A child with retardation may be classified as a "clinical type." In order to be regarded as a specific clinical type, an individual must show certain facial, body, and disease characteristics relating to a particular syndrome associated with mental retardation. While there are a number of these syndromes, the one most frequently associated with mental retardation is Down syndrome, accounting for approximately 10% of the moderately and more severely retarded population.

**For more discussion of Down syndrome, see chapter 4.**

Besides their distinct physical appearance, Down syndrome children frequently have specific health-related problems. Many have structural defects of the heart that may threaten their survival, although surgical procedures are sometimes successful in correcting the defect. Lung abnormalities are also frequent in Down syndrome children, resulting in susceptibility to upper respiratory infections. The incidence of leukemia is higher than in the normal population. Other common health problems of

Down syndrome children are eye and ear infections, obesity, skin problems, (primarily due to their characteristically rough and dry skin), problems of the teeth and gums, and hearing impairments (Smith & Wilson, 1973).

Individuals working with Down syndrome children should be alert to signs of infection, particularly ear and upper respiratory infections, so that early medical treatment can prevent more serious problems. Physical education and exercise programs should also be provided, although the type and amount of activity required of a particular child should be planned with the guidance of medical personnel.

*Cerebral palsy.*   Not all children with cerebral palsy (CP) are mentally retarded, however, a child who does have this condition presents a number of health-related problems. Cerebral palsy is a neuromuscular disability that may result from damage to the brain at birth or during the early years of life. While the condition may include any number of intellectual, sensory, and behavioral disorders, the motor disability presents several potential problems. Limbs that are not exercised may lose their usefulness altogether. Some children may be on movement or exercise programs that need to be repeated at certain intervals during the day. If a child wears a cast or a brace, those working with that child should be alert to such signs of circulation problems as swelling, coldness, change of color, and evidence of infection, as well as other skin problems (Robinault & Denhoff, 1973).

Individuals working with youngers who have retardation and cerebral palsy should be aware of a number of other problems that sometimes accompany the disorder. Speech difficulties complicated by lack of muscle control are common and often require speech therapy or other special educational measures. Visual and auditory problems are also seen more frequently in the CP child, and corrective measures to improve vision or hearing may be warranted. Difficulties with chewing and swallowing may present real hazards if the child is given such foods as hard candy, popcorn, and chewing gum. Consult the parents for specific instructions about eating and drinking. As with other disabilities, upper respiratory infections are common, and early symptoms should be reported, since the consequences of such infections may be severe.

*Seizures.*   Another health problem often associated with cerebral palsy, but also characteristic of other conditions that may accompany mental retardation, is seizures (Neisworth & Smith, 1978). Since convulsive disorders are significantly more common among those who are retarded than among those who are not, teachers working with these individuals should be trained to respond appropriately and to be aware of possible side effects of seizure control medication (Epstein et al., 1989).

Seizures vary from momentary disturbances, which may go unnoticed *(petit mal),* to episodes involving jerking of the muscles and loss of consciousness *(grand mal).* Some children experience an *aura* or sensation just before a seizure begins and may be able to give some indication that it is imminent. In some children, the likelihood of a seizure is increased by external factors like flickering lights or loud sounds, or the physical condition of the child, as when he is highly excited, ill, or fatigued. By being aware, teachers can be alert to circumstances that might precede or precipitate seizures. Once a seizure occurs, it should not be interrupted. The major concern is to keep the child from injuring himself. During a grand mal seizure, the child should be eased to the floor, furniture and other objects pushed away from him, and if possible, restrictive clothing loosened and the child turned on his side to aid breathing. Someone should remain with the child until the seizure ends, and then allow him to rest.

## GENERAL HEALTH CONSIDERATIONS

*Nutrition.*    Proper kinds and amounts of food are necessary for the general well-being of all children. Poor diet not only arrests biological development and diminishes resistance to disease and illness, but is also a negative factor in social adjustment and academic learning (Paige, 1975). Inadequate or unbalanced diets may be a result of insufficient food, poor supervision of meals and snacks, or lack of understanding of the importance of proper nutrition and how to provide it.

*Illness and disease.*    As might be expected, children who are retarded are more susceptible to disease and illness than are children who are not. Poor nutrition and lack of adequate health care (which should include an immunization program) appear to be major factors in promoting retardation among children from lower socioeconomic classes. Children who are moderately retarded, and some who are mildly retarded, have additional handicapping conditions or health problems that account for their relatively poor health. The frequency of heart and lung disorders among Down syndrome children is just one example.

   Several specific problems are commonly noted among children who are retarded. Cold symptoms and upper respiratory infections are frequent and often last longer than in other children. The seriousness of the symptoms can be compounded by the presence of other disorders such as cardiac conditions.

   The incidence of dental problems is also relatively high among children with retardation. Dental problems are often due to poor nutrition and failure to practice daily dental hygiene or have routine dental checkups.

*Accidents and injury.*    Developmentally delayed children are likely to be poorly coordinated and awkward. Add to this the poor judgment and impaired reasoning that may come with subaverage intellectual ability, and a higher than average accident rate can be predicted. Conditions accompanying the retardation—limited vision, muscle weakness, motor disabilities, and seizures—may also contribute to increased injuries.

*Physical activity.* A certain amount of exercise and activity is necessary to the total well-being of any individual. For the child who is mentally retarded, a planned program of physical activity is essential for a number of reasons. Individuals with mild retardation may not differ appreciably from those who are not retarded in physical and motor skills, and sports and other physical activities may provide an opportunity for expression and achievements as well as an outlet for tension. Gains in physical strength and motor coordination as well as feelings of accomplishment often enhance social and personal adjustment.

For those individuals who are mildly or moderately retarded and deviate more markedly from the nonhandicapped both mentally and physically, planned physical education and recreation programs offer enjoyment and a productive use of leisure time as well as the typical benefits associated with physical activity. Adaptive equipment and materials enable individuals with many handicapping conditions to participate in a wide variety of games and activities.

While opportunities for physical education and recreation have represented an area of neglect with respect to people who are mentally retarded (Chinn et al., 1979), the outlook for the future is far more encouraging, as shown by recent studies (Beasley, 1982; Halle, Silverman, & Regan, 1983). Provisions of P.L. 94-142 include not only physical education but recreation and leisure education as related services that must be extended to all children. Community agencies and citizens' groups are becoming more actively involved in providing opportunities for recreation and competitive events like the Special Olympics. Programs offered by colleges and universities designed to train professionals in techniques for working with the handicapped in the area of physical education and recreation are increasing in number and scope.

---

**SUMMARY**

The best way to gain an understanding of individuals classified as mildly or moderately retarded is to spend time with those so labeled. We recognize, however, that many students enrolled in an introductory course in mental retardation may not have had this opportunity. With this in mind, we designed this chapter to give the reader an understanding of the characteristics of these groups.

The chapter provided an overview of mild and moderate retardation, highlighting some nationally identified changes. The second section described the demographic characteristics of those with mild retardation based on recent research. The next section discussed the motivational and behavioral features typically associated with individuals who have mild or moderate retardation. The fourth section focused on important learning characteristics and their implications. The next section concerned recent findings on placement of these students and types of programs provided for them. The last two sections highlighted speech/language and physical/health characteristics of these individuals.

As with any discussion of characteristics, overgeneralization can occur— that is, not every individual who is mildly or moderately retarded may display all of the characteristics presented. This chapter's intent is to note those characteristics commonly observed in these populations, recognizing that variation is always the case.

# CHAPTER 7

# Severe and Profound Mental Retardation

F or those who have not had the opportunity to know individuals with severe or profound mental handicaps, the mere thought of this type of handicapping condition conjures up thoughts of state hospital wards or county homes filled with low-functioning people who sit motionless, if nonambulatory, or wander aimlessly, if ambulatory, around white-walled day rooms with little to do. Though these nightmarish settings may still exist in some parts of the world, this chapter shows that persons with severe or profound handicaps can be viable members of today's society. The pictures mentioned above come in the majority of situations only from bad dreams or from memories of bygone days, when our technology and educational prowess were more primitive.

## PROFILE 1

Jeff is 24 years old. He shares an apartment on Gotham's east side with two other individuals, one of whom has a disability. Jeff gets up each weekday morning and assists in meal preparation, eats breakfast, and helps clean up. He walks with one of his roommates to the bus stop and takes a city bus about two miles to his place of employment —the Washington Park restaurant. There at 9:30 a.m. he cleans the floor and tables and sets up each table in preparation for the restaurant's 11:30 a.m. opening. He also stocks the bus stations with silverware, cups, glasses, ice, and napkins, following the picture chart of the stations' layout. He stacks the cooking area with dishes and

This chapter was contributed by John A. Nietupski and Greg A. Robinson.

takes a short coffee break with his co-workers. Once the lunch crowd arrives, he serves ice water to customers and buses tables, sometimes with assistance from the person primarily responsible for the salad bar. At about 1:30 he leaves the Washington Park restaurant with the lunch all employees receive (Jeff's is a light one—he's watching his weight). He meets a friend for lunch in the park across the street and then walks with his friend to his second job at Winnebago Stencil and Lithographics. There he works alongside his fellow employees stenciling T-shirts. At about 5:00 p.m. he gets a ride home from one of his co-workers who also lives on the East Side. Jeff pays his partner 50¢ per day from his earnings for this carpool arrangement.

At home, Jeff's duties vary—sometimes he sets the table, at others he assists in meal preparation or works on cleaning up. After supper he participates in any number of activities: going to a movie or a sporting event with a friend or roommate; playing catch or frisbee with his roommates in the common area of his apartment complex; swimming in the pool; or just being a "couch potato" when the weather is not conducive to outdoor activities. During the summer, Jeff plays on Winnebago's coeducational softball team and is known to drink a beer or two after the game with his teammates. Jeff recently joined the YMCA with his roommates and exercises there twice a week.

With his earnings, Jeff has been able to do a lot of interesting things. He attends professional baseball and college football and basketball games, has a great stereo, and last year took his first plane trip with one friend to a wilderness retreat in Canada in a program offered by a Canadian outdoor association.

## PROFILE 2

Marty also is 24 years old. She lives on Gotham's west side in a residential center housing 45 other individuals, each of whom shares a room in one of the center's two wings. Each morning, Marty and her peers get up and are escorted to the dining hall where breakfast is served. Following breakfast, Marty and about 30 residents board a bus donated to the facility by an area church and are taken to their place of employment—Hope Opportunity Center—located in Gotham's South Side industrial park. Marty takes part in a number of activities designed to prepare her for the world of work: sorting nuts, bolts, washers, paper clips, and sandpaper; making block and bead patterns based on a model, screwing together and unscrewing hog watering valve subassembly units, and sanding wood. Occasionally she assists individuals in the higher functioning unit of the center doing subcontract collating and packaging tasks. Marty also attends home services their child received, looking instead to school and, later, adult service personnel, for guidance in determining each child's needs. Both had fears about what the future would hold for Marty or Jeff, yet both were open to ideas about how best to help the child.

*Hypothesis 3.* The availability of particular kinds of adult services might explain the differing lifestyles. Many communities have only one model for residential or vocational services. Often such services segregate large numbers of persons with handicaps and require them to demonstrate readiness for more normal residential and vocational services. Like a growing number of communities, however, Gotham has a variety of options available. In the residential area, for example, a community might have both larger congregate facilities, smaller group homes, and supervised/supported apartment living options. Vocationally speaking, the same community might offer sheltered work or work activity programs like Marty's and supported community employment (see below) services like Jeff's. If Gotham had not provided residential and vocational services like those Jeff received, his lifestyle might have resembled Marty's. But since adult service systems—at least theoretically—are supposed to be developed on the basis of identified needs, a lack of integrated, normalized options need not preclude the development of service delivery models like the ones that benefited Jeff. Communities throughout the country are slowly changing their array of services as they witness the success of fewer models and as advocacy groups, families, and professionals push for these options.

*Hypothesis 4.* The school program through which Marty and Jeff progressed had an impact on their adult lives. Here this hypothesis is the most accurate. Marty's program, which she went to merely by the chance of her home's location, was segregated—she seldom had contact with peers who were not handicapped. She was taught only readiness skills and was never deemed ready for more challenging, normal life experiences. The staff accepted the commonly held view that persons with severe handicaps require congregate living and vocational environments and imparted that view to Marty's parents. When the time came for Marty to graduate, the school recommended that she attend Hope Opportunity Center and, if her parents wanted residential services for her, live in the community's large residential center. Jeff, unlike Marty, was always integrated into regular schools. He came to know his peers who had no handicaps and they came to know and understand him. His program focused on teaching the skills needed to participate more fully in community life. He had frequent community instruction including vocational training at a variety of different job sites. His staff believed that he deserved a chance to live and work in the community despite his severe mental retardation. They felt that with the right support, Jeff could live and work in the community and have a more normal life. They

living classes and goes on weekly community outings (supermarket, movie house, park, bowling) with about 15 of her peers. Marty and her co-workers are served lunch each day at the center and have both a morning and an afternoon break period in which they are free to socialize. Last year Marty earned $259 for her work at the center.

When Marty returns home from work, she engages in any of a variety of training opportunities. On some days she participates in leisure arts and crafts activities under the direction of the recreation specialist or of university practicum students under his charge. Occasionally training is provided in home living skill objectives developed for Marty.

Dinner is served promptly at 5:30 p.m. After dinner, residents retire to the day room to watch television or play games or do other leisure activities with staff and peers. About once a week a group of residents is transported to a sporting event, a concert or other performance, a mall, a park, or some other area attraction. On Saturday mornings Marty and her peers attend special recreation at the high school along with other area children and adults with disabilities. Last year Marty made it to the state Special Olympics meet held in the capital city. She, a number of peers, and chaperon volunteers from the university's special education teacher preparation program made the two-day trip and had a great time.

*Discussion.* As the reader will already have surmised, the young woman Marty described in Profile 2, has severe mental retardation. Perhaps the reason one is not surprised by this revelation is that Marty's lifestyle is typical for many people with severe handicaps. Most who live outside the family home *do* live in larger, handicapped-only residential centers. Most receive door-to-door transportation services from their place of residence to handicapped-only work and developmental centers. Most have things done for them by others. Most have fairly regimented and sedentary home lives. Many participate in work readiness training for what seems like forever. The majority attend predominantly handicapped-only recreational activities or descend en masse into the community. Most earn very little for their work. Finally, most have little contact with people who are not handicapped other than their paid caregivers. It would be wonderful if all this *were* a surprise to most readers of this chapter. Unfortunately, the commonness of such a lifestyle makes the information about Marty's severe disability something less than newsworthy.

What might surprise the reader, however, is the revelation that the young man Jeff described in Profile 1 also has severe mental retardation. How can this be, some enterprising university student (having taken the prerequisite course "Introduction to Exceptional Persons") might ask? Very little of the description of Jeff fits the perception of a typical life for a person with severe handicaps. Jeff lives with two friends—one of them not disabled, instead of living with an armada of like-minded peers. He works at a job, in fact two jobs, in the community. He contributes to the functioning of his home. He takes public transportation—something only the bravest of us nonhandicappers would dare to do. Jeff apparently earns decent money for the work he does (his is a subminimum wage based on productivity; $3.50 per hour at Winnebago and $2.52 per hour at the restaurant—almost $5,000 a year). He plays ball with his co-workers who are not handicapped and their spouses and drinks beer afterwards! He even has taken a vacation to Canada (where he attended an integrated wilderness camping experience in which a minority of those involved had disabilities). No, this is not what many readers would consider typical for a person with severe disabilities. It is too normal, too integrated, too close to a lifestyle that one might expect of and even value in a person who is not handicapped.

Why is Jeff's life so different, so much more *normal* than Marty's? How can two individuals with severe mental retardation have such radically different adult lifestyles? The reader might be able to suggest several reasons for the different outcomes. Below is a list of four such hypotheses. Let us examine each one in more detail.

1. Differences in functioning level
2. Differences in parental involvement and attitude
3. Differences in available adult services
4. Differences in the type/quality of school programs

*Hypothesis 1.*    Perhaps Jeff's intellectual functioning level is more advanced than Marty's despite the severe handicaps label. At face value, such an explanation might have merit. Certainly functioning level and lifestyle usually go together. But in this particular case and often in general, such a hypothesis does not explain the differences. Marty and Jeff have identical IQs, are nonverbal, follow two-step directions, and have simple motor imitation skills. Examples are numerous in the professional literature and experientially of persons who are presumably less severely retarded but lead more restricted lives than others with more significant handicaps. Functioning level alone does not always constitute an adequate explanation.

*Hypothesis 2.*    Parental involvement may account for differing life outcomes. Such an assertion is not implausible. Parents who advocate for their children often obtain better services and, hence, better chances in life for their offspring than parents who are not so actively involved. In our two cases, however, parental involvement was not the overriding factor. Both Jeff's and Marty's parents wanted what was best for their respective children. Both attended school conferences. Neither was adamant about the kinds of

shared this belief with Jeff's parents. When the time came for Jeff to graduate, staff and parents together recommended integrated vocational and residential services.

*Conclusion.*    Many individuals with severe and profound mental retardation (hereinafter termed *severe disabilities*)—far too many—have lives more like Marty's than Jeff's. A growing number of individuals, however, are receiving more normal, fulfilling opportunities. Our position is that life outcomes for persons with severe disabilities: *(a)* are not primarily dependent upon functioning level (though it may have some bearing); *(b)* are not primarily the result of parental involvement or attitude (though this certainly can have an effect); and *(c)* are not solely dependent upon availability of services. We believe that life outcomes are *primarily* a function of a student's educational program. School programs can either prepare students with severe disabilities for a life of integration, normalization, and competence or for a life of segregation, less meaningful activity, and incompetence at activities that society values. School programs can either shape pessimistic, protective, and uninterested parental attitudes or optimistic, risk-taking, and involved ones. They can either preserve that status quo with regard to adult services, or they can choose to demonstrate the need for service changes and become advocates for them.

After we try to define what constitutes a person with severe disabilities, we will describe the key elements of quality educational services for this population. Once in place, these elements can contribute to more Jeffs and fewer Martys. The chapter closes with a discussion of challenges facing the field of special education in its attempt to bring about more integrated, normalized outcomes for all individuals with severe disabilities.

## WHO ARE STUDENTS WITH SEVERE DISABILITIES?

Before enumerating key elements of quality services for a particular group, we should define the group for which these elements are intended. As readers think back on their own experiences of contact with other persons throughout their lives, they will see that persons with severe disabilities have been few. Since this group is relatively small, it should be easy to define the characteristics or similarities of its constituents. Although logical, this is unfortunately not true.

One problem of definition is whom to include or exclude. For years discussions have centered on whether the term *severe disabilities* relates only to mental retardation, or whether it includes persons with emotional disabilities or multiplicative disabilities (one or more additional impairments) as well. Complicating the issue further is the lack of uniformity in terminology (e.g., *severe mental retardation, severe and profound mentally handicapped, severely disabled*) and in definitional parameters (only for mental retardation, includes or does not include moderate/trainable population, deaf/blind, emotional variables), which vary from state to state.

States are asked to report numbers of handicapped children served under Chapter 1 Handicapped Programs of the Education and Consolidation Improvement Act—State Operated Programs (ECIA [SOP]) and Education of the Handicapped Act (EHA-B), but severe handicaps or severe disabilities is not one of the ten handicapping conditions listed. Categories include mentally retarded, multi-handicapped, deaf/blind, and other health impaired, yet how states report their numbers differs widely because of varying interpretation. Some states place students with severe disabilities under the category of mentally retarded; others categorize these students as multihandicapped (unless the handicapping conditions are deafness or blindness, in which cases the students are in the deaf/blind category!). One dramatic example of these differences can be found in the *Tenth Annual Report to Congress on the Implementation of the Education of the Handicapped Act (1988)*, by the U.S. Department of Education. The data presented in the report show that Wisconsin had an increase of 2,061.1% in students being served under the category multihandicapped between school years of 1985–1986 and 1986–1987. Multihandicapped students account for 23% of the total students with disabilities being served in Wisconsin. Contrast with these numbers the data from Wisconsin's neighbor to the west, Minnesota, which in 1986–1987 categorized a total of 19 students as multihandicapped (0.02% of Minnesota's total students with disabilities). It is doubtful that students in these two states differ as dramatically as the identification and labeling of them for federal purposes does. Is one state right and the other wrong? Not necessarily, as it becomes apparent that Wisconsin has included students with milder but multiple disabilities under the category multihandicapped. This is just one reason that the needs of persons with severe disabilities are sometimes misunderstood, duplicated, or ignored, when the governing bodies that allocate funds for instructional and support use cannot agree on definitions.

As with other handicapping conditions, initial definitions for this group focused on identification for classification purposes. Sontag, Burke, and York (1973) developed a definition based on characteristics common to students with severe handicaps. The characteristics they chose centered on those students

> who are not toilet trained; aggressive toward others; do not attend to even the most pronounced social stimuli; self-mutilate; ruminate; self-stimulate; do not walk, speak, hear, or see; manifest durable and intense temper tantrums; are not under even the most rudimentary forms of verbal control; do not imitate; manifest minimally controlled seizures; and/or have extremely brittle medical existences. (p. 21)

*Students with severe retardation often have significant physical problems, too.*

This definition is not appropriate for our two cases, Jeff and Marty.

In 1974, the Bureau for the Education of the Handicapped provided a more detailed and flexible definition that described a child with severe handicaps as one

> who because of the intensity of physical, mental, or emotional problems, or a combination of such problems, needs educational, social, psychological, and medical services beyond those which have been offered by traditional regular and special educational programs, in order to maximize his full potential for useful and meaningful participation in society and for self-fulfillment. (p. 73)

# ORGAN DONATION

One of the most controversial issues being addressed by professionals who work with individuals who are profoundly retarded is the practice of terminating the lives of infants born with anencephaly (part of the brain missing) and donating their organs to other babies. The ethical, moral, and professional issues surrounding this practice are far from being solved, and the article below is typical.

## BABY WITH NO BRAIN MAY BE RECORD DONOR

### by Sally Ann Stewart USA Today

LOS ANGELES—When Airman 1st Class Todd Keys and wife Judy found out their first baby would be born without most of her brain, they decided to donate her organs.

Baby Evelyn was born Saturday and could become the first USA anencephalic baby whose heart, liver and kidneys can be donated, says Todd Keys, 21.

Evelyn is on a respirator at California's Loma Linda University Medical Center.

"The only thing wrong with her was anencephaly," says Keys, who lives with his wife in San Antonio. "All her organs are in top shape."

If doctors pronounce her brain dead by Saturday, her organs will be donated, says Loma Linda's Anita Rockwell. After Saturday the organs may not be healthy enough for transplant.

Organ donation from anencephalics— born without most of their brain, making life outside the womb impossible—is an issue that splits the medical profession. One side questions the ethics of keeping an infant alive to use its organs; the other cites a great need.

About 3,500 anencephalics are conceived every year in the USA. Only half are born. Many die in the womb and others are aborted.

In Loma Linda's first effort in December, the baby was stillborn. The corneas and heart valves were usable.

A second anencephalic baby died at Loma Linda last week; one heart valve was healthy enough to donate.

Lawrence Platt, a University of Southern California obstetrics-gynecology professor, says doctors should continue "forwarding babies to Loma Linda. The fact that they are able to use even one valve is more than they would have gotten."

From USA Today, February 2, 1988.

Included in this group were children with serious emotional disturbances (e.g., schizophrenic and autistic), those with severe or profound mental retardation, and children with two or more serious handicapping conditions (e.g., mentally retarded deaf).

The problem with definitions used for identification and classification is that they tend to focus on what students are *unable* to do rather than on the interventions that allow such students to learn. A better approach to the definitional question is one that focuses on service needs. An example of a service definition was developed by Bellamy (1985). He defines persons with severe disabilities as those "who require ongoing support in several major life areas in order to participate in the mainstream of community life, and who are expected to require such support throughout life" (p. 6).

Such a definition has the advantage of portraying persons with severe disabilities as capable of learning life skills. It is more suited for use by human services professionals because it focuses on skills and the training and support required for participation in society.

But this definition does not assist us in determining the prevalence of severe disabilities: the percentage or number of persons within a given category at a given time. For such estimates, definitions based on intelligence (IQ) test scores are often used. According to the American Association on Mental Retardation (Grossman, 1983), individuals who score below 50–55 on an IQ test are considered to have a severe disability (moderate, severe, or profound mental retardation). The AAMR breaks this broad category down further by specifying that those with IQ scores between 35 and 50–55 have moderate mental retardation, those in the 20–35 IQ score range have severe retardation, and those below 20 have profound mental retardation.

Clinical definitions are covered in chapter 2.

The AAMR definition makes estimating prevalence easier because it relies on a theoretical distribution of IQ scores based on the normal curve. Using the normal curve, it is predicted that 0.13% of the total population has severe mental disabilities (IQ scores 50–55 or below). Given the estimated 1980 U.S. population of 222,000,000 people, a prevalence figure of 0.13% predicts that 288,600 persons have severe disabilities. To confuse the issue, however, discrepancies between predicted and actual prevalence figures are not uncommon. Haywood (1979) has indicated that of the 222,000,000 persons in the United States in 1980, 554,000, or 0.20%, will have severe disabilities, which is almost twice as many as the normal distribution predicts. But however it is calculated, the number of persons with severe disabilities is relatively small.

From the practitioner's perspective, perhaps the best approach to the definitional question is to ignore it. To many in the field, it often seems that the time spent on attempting to define this group could better be spent attempting to develop more effective intervention strategies. The category of persons with severe disabilities is small in numbers compared to other handicapping categories and consists of individuals with diverse abilities and service needs. There is neither a clear definition for this group nor a consistent data base at the state or federal level. Yet the change in tone of definitions from identification and classification to service needs should demonstrate to the reader that many educators and parents feel persons like Jeff who have severe disabilities can learn and should be afforded the opportunity.

## UNIQUE CHARACTERISTICS OF STUDENTS WITH SEVERE HANDICAPS

Students with severe disabilities exhibit characteristics that require special consideration. In this section we treat three kinds of characteristics: *(a)* communicative; *(b)* motor involvement; and *(c)* medical.

### COMMUNICATION

One of the most striking characteristics of persons with severe disabilities is the extent of their deficiency in communication (Falvey, 1986). Upon meeting such students for the first time, individuals without handicaps are often unsure how and what students are attempting to communicate and how, in turn, to communicate with them. People frequently come away with the erroneous impression that limited verbal communication skills or the use of nontraditional communication means that these students cannot communicate or comprehend communicative attempts.

This population is highly diverse in communication skills. Some students speak, some do not. Those who speak may do so in single words, short phrases, whole sentences, or rather complex conversations. Many individuals who can speak have articulation difficulties that make inexperienced listeners unable to comprehend. Research has provided practitioners with many strategies for improving communication skills. Several principal areas to consider when working to enhance communication skills are highlighted below.

*Reasons to communicate.*   Often well-intentioned educators, citizens, and parents, assuming that students cannot communicate, anticipate so many of their needs that little need to communicate exists. A stand-up comedian several years ago related how he had surprised his parents at the age of nine by speaking for the first time. When asked by his father why he had never spoken earlier, he replied that until then his parents had done just fine in meeting his every need, so why should he have put himself to the effort? While this story is exaggerated, the point is that educators must create situations that motivate students to communicate (Gruenewald, Schroeder, & Yoder, 1982), such as presenting a preferred object, person, or activity and allowing access to it only after some communicative attempts by the student.

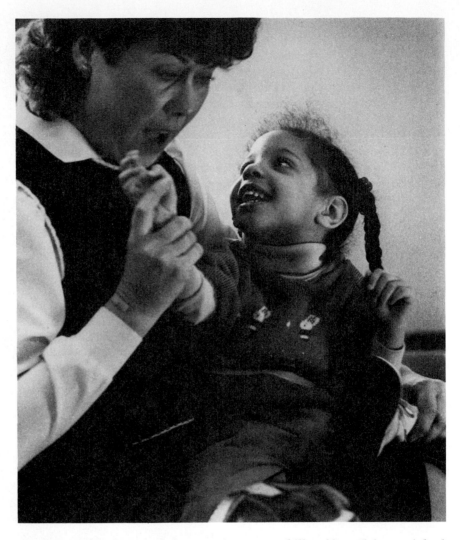

*Communication is one of the most important skills addressed in special education settings.*

***Something to communicate about.***   The content of communication needs to be based on students' daily experiences. Instead of teaching students in an urban area to make the sign for farm animals, programs should encourage communication around the play, social interaction, and domestic, community, and vocational activities in which students participate in and outside of school.

***A mode/means of communication.***   In addition to having a reason to communicate and something to communicate about, students need a way to communicate. The typical communication mode for individuals who are not handicapped is speech. Students who have intact oral motor systems, produce or show evidence of potential speech production, or progress in speech programs should be encouraged to use speech, for the general audience needs little training to understand or communicate with speech users (Nietupski & Hamre-Nietupski, 1979).

Students for whom speech is not indicated still can learn to communicate, but they require an augmentative system. One such mode is **sign language**. *Manual signing* is the use of fingers, hands, and arm movements to communicate. The various forms of sign language include Signed English, American Sign Language, and American Indian Sign Language (Amerind). Manual signing has the advantage of portability, wide vocabulary, and visual cues. Its drawbacks are its motor requirements and the limited signing audience in the community.

**Communication aids** offer a third way to make oneself understood. Communication aids are display devices that contain pictures, objects, symbols, or printed words. Students can activate them by touch, eye pointing (when students look or "point" at something with their eyes instead of their fingers), using a head wand (a prosthetic device like a light rod or stick attached to the head of a student; the student uses the wand to point at things by positioning the head so that the wand is directed at the object), or operating switches. Some sample aids are: *(a)* picture cards in binders or attached to a binder ring; *(b)* lap trays operated manually or electronically; and *(c)* computer or electronic displays. The advantages of communication aids are the relative ease of audience comprehension and reduced motoric complexity (almost any motor movement can activate a system). But these devices have to be with students at all times and, in the case of electronic and computer aids, can be very expensive.

*Appropriate training technology.*   In the past, communication skills were taught in an artificial manner. Teachers and students would sit across a table from each other; the teacher would hold up an object or a picture, and the student would speak, sign, or use a communication device. Such training does not provide sufficient motivation to communicate and often does not generalize to real-life settings (Nietupski & Hamre-Nietupski, 1979). To promote more widespread communication, training should be a natural part of everyday domestic, vocational, community, and recreation or leisure activities (Sailor & Guess, 1983). For example, when teaching a student to drink from a cup, the cup should occasionally be withheld until the student indicates a desire for more to drink. As another example, when working in the cafeteria wrapping silverware in napkins, some napkins could be withheld to encourage student requests for additional ones. In these ways students see the purpose and power of communication and become more likely to make communicative attempts. Those around the student should be alert to recognize and respond to those communicative attempts.

Communication is a high-priority need for students with severe disabilities. Communication skills vary widely across this population. Speech, manual signing, and communication aids are options practitioners can consider. To facilitate communication, students need a reason to communicate, something to communicate about, a way to express themselves, and techniques that encourage and reinforce communication in the context of daily activities.

## MOTOR INVOLVEMENT

Many students with severe disabilities have physical (or motor) handicaps as well. The severity of involvement varies greatly: some students exhibit minimal impairments in one or more limbs, while others require extensive assistance and/or adaptive devices for mobility, manipulating objects in their environment, performing such daily activities as dressing, eating, toileting, and communicating.

The most frequent cause of motor handicaps is *cerebral palsy,* a nonprogressive disorder resulting from damage to the brain and resulting in abnormal posture or movement. Eighty-six percent of cases of cerebral palsy result from injury or oxygen deprivation during pregnancy or birth (Bleck & Nagel, 1975).

Cerebral palsy takes many forms. Some students exhibit *spasticity,* extreme tightness of joints and muscles. Others exhibit *hypotonia,* a general lack of muscle tone, resulting in "floppiness" or insufficient muscle tightness. Still others show *athetosis,* writhing movements resulting from alternating tightness and floppiness.

Another condition that contributes to motor involvement is *epilepsy.* In epilepsy, fluctuations in brain patterns or functions result in seizures. Like cerebral palsy, epilepsy often results from prenatal trauma or problems during the birth process. Occasionally postnatal head injuries or childhood diseases can cause epilepsy. Seizures resulting from epilepsy often can be controlled, and sometimes entirely eliminated, by medication.

Seizures may be either *grand mal* or *petit mal.* During grand mal seizures a person loses consciousness for several minutes, falls, and exhibits relatively violent body tremors. About 60% of seizure activity is grand mal (Orelove & Sobsey, 1987). Petit mal seizures are more common in children and tend to be outgrown before adulthood. The student typically loses consciousness for several seconds but does not become rigid or exhibit tremors. Often students simply stare into space without moving or make repetitive movements like lip-smacking, eyelid-fluttering, or chewing.

Severe *scoliosis* is another condition that results in motor involvement. Scoliosis refers to a lateral curvature of the spine, which can become almost S-shaped. Scoliosis affects the ability to sit, walk, and use the hands. It can be treated through use of an upper body brace, adapted chairs that foster better upright posture, and surgery to stabilize the spine.

Students with motor involvement often require adaptive devices in order to perform functional life skills. Such equipment as crutches, leg braces, manual or automated wheelchairs, or scooter boards may be needed for mobility. Corner chairs, side lyers, prone standers, and wedges can help position a student to allow for use of hands and fingers. Often materials need to be adapted to be used. For example, thicker utensil handles may allow a student to grasp them more easily; shoes with velcro straps may be needed rather than tie shoes; pressure sensitive, wide paddles in water fountains may be easier to operate than buttons; battery-operated toys can be connected to pressure sensitive, electronic microswitches, allowing for activation through light touch. These and other creative adaptations can make it possible for students with motoric involvement to participate more fully in normal activities.

In order better to serve students with motor involvement, the expertise of physical and occupational therapists is essential. These professionals can be invaluable in terms of developing: *(a)* adaptive or assistive devices; *(b)* positioning recommendations; *(c)* strategies to promote motor development in the context of normal activities; and *(d)* medical and physical management techniques. Several writers have suggested that, to maximize the talents of teachers and therapists, an *integrated therapy model* be used. Integrated therapy is based on a team approach. Therapists and teachers together plan ways in which a student's motor skills can be developed and used in the context of everyday activities. Therapists primarily act as consultants to teachers regarding the motor component of instructional programs. Two-way communication and frequent interaction allow the student to derive the maximum benefit from professional expertise in the various disciplines.

Students who have severe disabilities and motor involvement present unique challenges. But the combined expertise of teachers, parents, therapists, and medical personnel is allowing us to meet these challenges better.

## MEDICAL NEEDS

With the advances in medical technology, children are being born into today's world who would not have survived five or ten years ago. With our successes in technology comes the realization that more children are also being born with severe medical conditions that produce medically complex long-term needs as the children grow older.

*Medically fragile children* are technologically assisted children who are dependent on life support equipment. The uniqueness and the severity of these children's handicaps require that they be educated on a case-by-case basis (Great Lakes Area Regional Resource Center, 1986). Orelove and Sobsey (1987) have written that students with multiple disabilities almost always present two or more of the following conditions: *(a)* restricted movement, *(b)* skeletal deformities, *(c)* sensory disorders, *(d)* seizure disorders, *(e)* lung and breathing control difficulties, and *(f)* other medical problems (e.g., ears, bladder, skin, ulcers).

Teachers and families are faced with learning to understand and assist with the medical problems of individuals who are ventilator dependent, tracheotomy dependent, oxygen dependent, experiencing nutritional difficulties that force the use of gasterostomy tubes, suffering from congestive heart problems, apnea-monitored, and in need of kidney dialysis (Great Lakes Area Regional Resource Center, 1986). These medical needs require the collaborative expertise of professionals in the medical field. Preservice and inservice programs must change dramatically for these students to get an opportunity to participate in less restrictive environments. Some people argue that taking unneeded risks is unwarranted with these types of individuals, yet proponents of integration maintain that the quality, not just the longevity, of life is an aspect that must be considered and is typically ignored with this small population. This problem will not diminish in the near future; difficult decisions lie before us.

## EDUCATIONAL PROGRAMMING

### EARLY INTERVENTION

The success of recent efforts in the provision of educational services for students with severe disabilities could not have occurred without the increased emphasis on early identification and intervention. Not long ago, no public school educational services were available for students with severe disabilities. If services were available in a community it was because concerned parents had started their own programs. Often these programs were segregated in nature and were conducted in church basements, out of private homes, or as part of private day care programs. The passage of P.L. 94-142 and, more recently, P.L. 99-457 has changed all that. Under P.L. 94-142, school districts were required to serve all children, regardless of the degree of handicapping condition, from ages 6 through 21. Under this law, states could also choose to serve students from birth, which, for example, Michigan and Iowa chose to do. The passage of P.L. 94-142 resulted in massive campaigns to identify and serve students at an early age. Identification activities included public awareness campaigns, the establishment of hospital-based screening and follow-up programs, intermediate or local district screening and referral systems, tracking systems, and registries. As students were identified, programs were developed to serve this population.

Public Law 99-457 established two new components as part of the reauthorization of the discretionary programs of P.L. 94-142. First, for those states who have not provided services for children ages three through five with disabilities, strong financial incentives are available to pursue this type of programming. Second, an additional new state grant program is available for infants and toddlers, ages birth through two years, who have disabilities. The implementation of these components allows for early intervention for children with severe disabilities throughout the nation. The existence of such early intervention programs can make a tremendous difference in the life outcomes of persons like Jeff and Marty.

## INVOLVEMENT OF FAMILIES IN PROGRAMMING
## FOR STUDENTS WITH SEVERE DISABILITIES

Although P.L. 94-142 legislates a free and appropriate education for all children with disabilities, educators have had their best successes when the targets of their services have been the families of which the children are a part (Bennett, 1986; Education Commission of the States, 1988; Rich, 1985). Even though the involvement of specific educators in a student's educational career is intense and aimed at attaining instructional goals, the educators' involvement is brief when compared to the amount of time parents and siblings spend with a family member who has severe disabilities. These other family members are the permanent advocates for individuals with severe disabilities. These are the people with whom they spend most of each day even when school is in session.

Sailor et al. (1986) have stated that education for students with severe disabilities may occur in a combination of the following environments: classroom; the school, or nonclassroom areas; and the community at large, or nonschool areas. Included in these nonschool areas are the family home and the homes of relatives. Other nonschool areas in the community are places frequented by family members—a mall, a theater, or a place of worship. Because of the greater knowledge that family members possess about their child's or sibling's participation in these nonschool environments, it is essential for educators to get input from family members when developing instructional program goals.

What separates the Jeffs from the Martys? We have hypothesized that it is differences in the type or quality of school programs. If that is so, why are we talking about family involvement? Special educators cannot do everything. They develop areas of expertise, and so do others around them . . . including family members. By combining their areas of knowledge and expertise with the family members', educators are able to be of greater help to their students who have severe disabilities. Success for these students comes from how well educators and significant others can determine which are the critical skills, how to teach them, and what is the best place to provide them. To do this educators must elicit information from those who know what students with severe disabilities do out of school.

There are many ways to form relationships with family members when the common bond is a person with a severe disability. Families of children with severe disabilities spend a great deal of time with educators. Their interactions are usually intended to be supportive, but in many cases they do

Family issues are discussed in depth in chapter 12.

not result in positive experiences for parents (Gallagher, Beckman, & Cross, 1983). Family members should be allowed to talk about their loved one as they wish. Educators must convey that family members, too, are specialists. Many times new teachers or support service personnel feel uncomfortable talking with parents, and their conversational patterns belie their apparent sincerity and willingness to work together. They want to come off as being all-knowing and in command. Telling parents of a completely dependent teenage boy with multiple disabilities that you "know how they feel," when you have no children and limited experience in special education, is a statement far too many new professionals make. Talking constantly and not allowing a comfortable silence—family members may need to think of responses to questions, after all—is another skill that takes time to develop. Finally, some parents may not want to be as active as educators may want them to be or feel they should be. This does not mean that they fail to appreciate the actions of the professional staff, and professionals must realize and accept this as a fact.

For those parents who want to furnish information, there are several avenues. Browder and Sullivan-Fleig (1987) report, in a study conducted by the Iowa Department of Education of approximately 3,000 parents of children from preschool to high school age with disabilities, that a majority of the respondents indicated a preference for written communications and phone calls rather than face-to-face sessions. One of the more common written forms of communication with parents of students with severe disabilities is an inventory form that asks families what kind of activities students do and how independent they are in tasks unconnected with the school environment (home setting, community, recreation, leisure). Perception questions may also be asked about what family members may think are potential vocational (competitive employment, sheltered workshop, adult day activity) or domestic (supervised apartment, group home, family home) outcomes for family members with severe disabilities. These inventories come in many forms: the reader may wish to consult Maurer, Teas, and Bates (1980); Turnbull et al. (1985); and Vincent, Davis, Brown, Broome, Miller and Gruenewald (1983). For more information on family involvement when working with persons with severe disabilities the reader should feel encouraged that many sources are becoming available (Bronicki and Turnbull, 1987; Carney, 1987; Fewell and Vadasy, 1986; Healy, Keesee, and Smith, 1985; Turnbull and Turnbull, 1985).

## TEACHING FUNCTIONAL, AGE-APPROPRIATE, COMMUNITY-REFERENCED ACTIVITIES

Curriculum is a critical factor in producing normalized outcomes. Teachers and families of students with severe disabilities face the question of *what to teach* on a daily basis. How this question is answered affects whether students have adult lives more like Jeff's or like Marty's.

In order to give students with severe disabilities the best opportunity to enjoy a life like Jeff's, the educational program must focus on teaching *functional, community-referenced,* and *chronologically age-appropriate activities. Functional* activities are those that are needed in everyday home, community, vocational, and recreation and leisure environments. Often teachers of students with severe disabilities answer the question what to teach by teaching students to put pegs in pegboards, match shapes and colors, string beads, complete worksheets, feel different textures, and so forth. These are examples of nonfunctional activities; they are not needed in the real world. Functional activities are practical. A simple test to see if an activity is functional is to ask the question: If (student) doesn't do this activity, would someone have to do it for him/her? If the answer to this question is yes, the activity is probably functional for that student. If the answer is no, the activity is not functional. Table 7.1 is a list of activities. See if you can determine whether they are functional or nonfunctional.

In addition to being functional, activities should be *appropriate to a student's chronological age.* Often students who have severe disabilities are treated like small children—even if they are adolescents or young adults. Usually this happens because some teachers believe that instruction needs to be geared to a person's mental age. The problem with this approach is that students seldom learn activities that other people their age are learning, and they are made to look very different from the people around them. Think about it: Would a university student want to hang out with someone whose primary leisure pursuit is putting together Big Bird puzzles? Probably not. Most would be more inclined to want to get to know people who like to play video or computer games, go to sporting events, or "shop till they drop." The activities that are taught must be similar to those that people in the student's age group do.

Finally what is taught must include activities that are *community-referenced;* those needed in specific home, community, vocational, and

See Brown, Nietupski, & Hamre-Nietupski (1976).

---

TABLE 7.1   Functional or Nonfunctional Activities

---

1. Counting little plastic teddy bears.
2. Counting dollars to make a purchase.
3. Putting quarters into a vending machine to buy something.
4. Putting poker chips into a slot cut into a coffee can lid.
5. Grasping a dowel (wooden cylinder).
6. Grasping a bathroom grab bar as parent/teacher transfers student from wheelchair to toilet seat.
7. Putting pictures of food, clothing, toiletry items into pictorial replicas of supermarkets, department stores, and drugstores.
8. Selecting the correct store to enter and search for food, clothing, or toiletry items.

recreation or leisure environments and taught in the environments in which the student now functions or might function in the future. Community-referenced instruction is important, because no teacher who does not know the demands of specific environments can prepare students for a life in the community. Once the teacher knows the requirements of specific settings, instruction must be conducted in such real-world environments. One cannot assume that what is taught in school will prepare these students for a normal or near-normal adult life (Brown et al., 1976). Teachers must determine specific performance requirements in community sites and teach specifically to those requirements in those locations.

## HOW TO IDENTIFY FUNCTIONAL, AGE-APPROPRIATE, COMMUNITY-REFERENCED INSTRUCTIONAL ACTIVITIES

How do teachers determine the specific instructional activities that will prepare students for a life in the community? Brown, Branston, Hamre-Nietupski, Johnson, Wilcox, and Gruenewald (1979) and Brown, Branston-McLean, D. Baumgart, L. Vincent, M. Falvey, and J. Schroder (1979) recommend an *ecological inventory* as a way to generate a curriculum tailored to the needs of particular students in particular communities. This process involves setting educational goals on the basis of careful observations of nonhandicapped performance in real-world settings. The steps in this process have been outlined by Nietupski and Hamre-Nietupski (1987) and are contained in Table 7.2. Several of the key steps are discussed briefly below.

*Step 1: Identify domains.* An ecological inventory process involves generating instructional activities in four domain areas considered crucial for integrated adult life: *(a)* vocational; *(b)* domestic living; *(c)* community living; and *(d)* recreation and leisure. These four areas represent persisting life

TABLE 7.2    Steps in an Ecological Inventory Curriculum Development Process

---

Step 1 Identify curriculum domains (vocational; domestic; community; recreation and leisure).

Step 2 Describe the present and future environments in each domain in which students function or might function.

Step 3 Inventory and delimit the subenvironments within each environment.

Step 4 Inventory and detail the activities persons perform in those subenvironments.

Step 5 Prioritize activities in order to set IEP goals.

Step 6 Describe the skills needed to perform the activities.

Step 7 Conduct a discrepancy analysis in order to determine required skills not currently in the student's repertoire.

Step 8 Determine necessary adaptations.

Step 9 Develop an instructional program.

---

needs for all individuals in our society. As a nation, Americans value the ability to work (vocational domain); to live on one's own (domestic domain); to make use of stores and services in the community (community domain); and to use free time wisely (recreation and leisure domain). Curricula divided up in this fashion, therefore, should make educators strive to teach functional, real-world activities.

*Step 2: Describe environments.* For each domain, teachers conducting an ecological inventory identify specific environments or places that a student currently experiences or might possibly experience in the future. For example, in the domestic domain, the current environment might be a student's family home. The next domestic environment for that student might be a supervised or supported apartment or a group home. Focusing on the present environment helps identify activities that assist a student to be more independent and capable *now.* Focusing on future environments helps ensure targeted instructional activities that will prepare students for life away from school.

*Step 3: Inventory and delimit subenvironments.* Each environment has specific areas, or subenvironments, in which certain activities typically take place. For example, the vocational environment of a Dairy Queen restaurant has an entranceway, a seating area, a customer-counter area, a front counter work area, a fryer area, a storage area, and so forth. Identifying subenvironments allows a teacher to organize activities by location.

*Step 4: Inventory and detail activities.* This step is the heart of the ecological inventory process. It involves carefully observing people who are not handicapped in these environments and subenvironments and writing down the specific activities they perform. In this way, teachers know precisely what activities are necessary in particular settings. Table 7.3 provides a partial inventory of vocational domain activities at the Dairy Queen. As the reader can see, an inventory yields many possible activities for consideration as instructional targets.

*Step 5: Prioritize activities.* As Table 7.3 illustrates, inventories yield a large number of possible instructional activities. Astute readers of this chapter may wonder how all such activities can be taught within the framework of a six-hour instructional day. Obviously, no teacher could possibly teach students all activities in all environments. Some method of prioritizing activities in order to identify those that are critical is needed.

Ford and Miranda (1984) and Wuerch and Voeltz (1981) outline a number of crucial considerations for determining priority IEP objectives. Considering a number of factors can narrow the list of possible activities to teach. Six factors to keep in mind are *(a) family preference,* activities most valued by a student's family; *(b) student preference,* activities the student most enjoys; *(c) instructor preference,* activities the teacher thinks most meaning-

TABLE 7.3    Partial Inventory of Vocational Domain Activities

Domain: Vocational
  Environment: Mineral City Dairy Queen
    Subenvironment 1: *Fryer Area*
      Activities
        1. Deep fry chicken nuggets.
        2. Deep fry french fries.
        3. Deep fry fish fillets.
        4. Deep fry onion rings.
        5. Stuff cardboard fry trays into paper bags.
        6. Stack "5" into bins.
        7. Put french fries into trays and bags.
        8. Put onion rings into trays and bags.

    Subenvironment 2: *Broiler Area*
      Activities
        1. Place hamburger on broiler or brazier.
        2. Set out buns on foil wrap (silver = hamburger; gold = cheeseburger).
        3. Construct and package hamburgers.
        4. Construct and package cheeseburgers.

    Subenvironment 3: *Seating Area*
      Activities
        1. Clean table with spray cleaner and towel.
        2. Pick up trash from/under tables and seats.
        3. Deposit trash into swing-door receptacle.
        4. Sweep floor.
        5. Change trash receptacle liner.
        6. Wipe off seats, seat backs, and windowsills with towel.

    Subenvironment 4: *Washrooms*
      Activities
        1. Replace toilet paper.
        2. Replace paper towels.
        3. Clean urinal (men's).
        4. Clean toilet.
        5. Clean mirror.
        6. Sweep floor.
        7. Wet-mop floor.
        8. Clean stainless steel stall door.
        9. Replace paper towel receptacle liner.
        10. Fill sanitary products dispenser (women's).
        11. Fill liquid soap dispenser.
        12. Clean sinks.

ful; *(d) frequency of occurrence,* activities that happen most often, thus placing frequent demands upon students and offering substantial practice opportunities; *(e) safety concerns,* activities that, if performed competently, promote the safety of the student (e.g., crossing a street); and *(f) social significance,* activities that increase a student's social acceptability, promote interactions with peers, and project a more normal image for the student.

Nietupski and Hamre-Nietupski (1987) discuss these six considerations in greater detail. Application of these factors facilitates identification of priority IEP goals.

***Step 6: Describe the skills needed to perform the activities.*** Once an activity is targeted for instruction, it must be broken down into its component steps. This process, called *task analysis* (Gold, 1976), involves listing the specific actions that an activity comprises. Table 7.4 contains a skills breakdown of one activity, table cleaning, from the Dairy Queen inventory. As is evident, table cleaning involves many small steps. Breaking an activity into smaller steps makes it easier to teach it to students with severe disabilities. Think of it this way: College students faced with learning to use a computer for the first time, say for word processing purposes, are often overwhelmed. The task becomes much more manageable, however, if assistance is provided first on simply activating the computer; then loading the program; then creating a file; then entering material; and, finally, printing that incomparable essay on mental disabilities. Likewise, since many activities as a whole prove difficult for students with severe disabilities, teaching small steps of the process is more effective.

***Step 7: Conduct a discrepancy analysis.*** This step simply refers to finding out the specific steps a student does or does not already know how to perform. Sometimes referred to as a *baseline,* a discrepancy analysis involves having a student perform the activity and noting which steps he or she does correctly or incorrectly.

TABLE 7.4   Task Analysis of Table Cleaning

| | |
|---|---|
| Step 1 | Obtain pump-spray cleaner bottle and towel from storeroom. |
| Step 2 | Stand next to table. |
| Step 3 | Squirt one pump spray on upper left table corner. |
| Step 4 | Squirt one pump spray on upper right table corner. |
| Step 5 | Squirt one pump spray on lower right table corner. |
| Step 6 | Squirt one pump spray on lower left table corner. |
| Step 7 | Set cleaner bottle on seat. |
| Step 8 | Wipe back and forth across table, starting at top and proceeding to bottom. |
| Step 9 | Turn cloth over. |
| Step 10 | Repeat step 8. |
| Step 11 | Pick up spray bottle. |
| Step 12 | Go on to next table or put materials away. |

*Step 8: Determine necessary adaptations.* This step is critical for many students with severe disabilities. Often the challenges a task presents to a student's cognitive, motor, or sensory abilities make it difficult to perform activities in a typical manner. In the table-cleaning example from the Dairy Queen inventory, some students may have difficulty finding the spray bottle in the storeroom because of visual or cognitive disabilities. Others may find it difficult to operate the pump spray because they lack hand strength or coordination. Still others may have difficulty remembering to spray only four times on the corner areas of the table.

Educators must decide whether students can be taught the problem steps through extensive instruction and practice. This decision often relies on the teacher's judgment. If, on the basis of extensive experience with a student, a teacher determines that one or more task steps are impossible for that student to perform in a typical manner, the teacher must develop some form of adaptation.

Adaptations take several forms. One type of adaptation is *adaptive/prosthetic aids,* or portable materials that compensate for skill deficits. In the table-cleaning example, students might match a picture of the spray bottle to the same picture attached to the storeroom shelf in front of the spray bottle to aid in obtaining this item.

Another type of adaptation involves *modifying existing activity materials.* For example, if students cannot push the pump spray, a rigid tongue depressor could be attached to the spray button for better leverage. As a second example, the "play" and "eject" buttons on a cassette player can be color coded to help nonreading students operate the equipment.

A third type of adaptation is to modify the *skill sequence.* This may involve changing the way to do an activity, such as using a bucket of soapy water instead of a spray cleaner, if it is not possible to teach a student how much spray to use. Another skill sequence modification is reordering steps. For example, students with dexterity difficulties can take out their money before ordering at a fast-food restaurant to save time and not delay impatient customers.

A fourth type of adaptation is *adapting rules,* the formal or informal guidelines that govern an activity. This adaptation typically is used in the recreation and leisure domain to simplify game activities. For example, a student in a wheelchair who does not have the motor ability to throw a beanbag can still play Toss-Across with peers who are not handicapped by being allowed to move next to the game board and push the beanbag over the edge of the wheelchair lap tray.

If none of these adaptations works, the final adaptation is *providing personal assistance.* This involves having a teacher, a peer, or someone else do the step or assist the student through the problem step. In the table-cleaning example, this might mean having a peer with more advanced motor or cognitive skills spray the table with the student wiping the table off.

This kind of adaptation results in only partial participation in an activity, so it is used only when direct training or other adaptations prove ineffective.

*Step 9: Develop an instructional program.* Developing a program is the culmination of the inventory process. Not until the teacher has identified domains, conducted inventories, prioritized and analyzed activities, and considered adaptations can the training plan (instructional program) be developed. The reader interested in a detailed discussion of instructional programs should consult Williams, Brown, and Certo (1975).

## SYSTEMATIC INSTRUCTION

Once the teacher has identified tasks, broken them down by task analysis, and developed adaptations, instruction can begin. As Snell (1987) indicates, systematic instruction is required in order for students with severe disabilities to meet the performance demands of the real world. *Systematic instruction* refers to a well defined, replicable teaching process. It involves precise delineation of what to teach, where to teach it, how to promote skill acquisition, maintenance, and generalization, collecting data on student performance, and using the data to modify the program. The inventory process answers the "what to teach" question. We discuss where to teach and how to promote skill acquisition and generalization below.

*Where to teach.* Until very recently, students with severe disabilities received almost all their instruction in the classroom. The assumption seemed to be that training in school would result in performance in the real world. Professional experience and a growing body of research (e.g., Stokes & Baer, 1977) have demonstrated that this assumption is incorrect. Our current thinking is that school-based training alone is insufficient to prepare students for a productive life in the community (Brown et al., 1983). Instruction needs to be in realistic settings, many of which are outside the school, and programs around the country have begun to expand their *community-based* training efforts. In these, students of elementary school age might receive most of their instruction in school, with once weekly training in the community (e.g., domestic skill training in a student's or teacher's home; shopping in a grocery store). As students move to middle school age, the proportion of nonschool instruction should increase, with students receiving 50% or more of their training outside the school (Sailor et al., 1986). By high school age, 85% or more of a student's school week should be devoted to nonschool instruction. Table 7.5 lists settings in all four domains in which students might receive nonschool instruction.

*How to promote skill acquisition.* Fifteen years ago we knew very little about effective techniques for teaching skills to persons with severe disabilities. Fortunately, research and practice have yielded considerable information on effective teaching strategies.

TABLE 7.5  Selected Nonschool Instructional Settings

| Domains | | | |
|---|---|---|---|
| Domestic | Community | Recreation and Leisure | Vocational |
| 1. Student's home | 1. Supermarket | 1. Library | 1. Restaurant |
| 2. Local group home | 2. Department store | 2. Movie theater | 2. Motel |
| 3. Staff member's home | 3. Drugstore | 3. Arcade | 3. Hospital |
| 4. Home of person in school neighborhood | 4. Public transport | 4. YMCA or YWCA | 4. Insurance office |
| | 5. Restaurant | 5. Bowling alley | 5. Government office |
| | 6. Various types of intersections and streets | 6. Park | 6. Greenhouse |
| | | 7. Swimming pool | 7. Laundry or dry cleaner |
| | 7. Shopping mall | 8. Fitness center | 8. Factory |
| | 8. Discount store | | 9. Church |
| | 9. Laundromat | | 10. Supermarket |

*Response chaining* is a technique in which an activity is broken down into smaller response units (task analysis), and each unit is taught in order. In *forward chaining,* the student learns to perform the first step in a chain, with assistance on the remaining steps (Spooner & Spooner, 1984). Once the student reliably performs the first step, the teacher goes on to the first two steps, continuing to assist with the remaining steps. This process of gradually exposing a student to one more step eventually should result in performance of the entire sequence. *Backward chaining* reverses the order of instruction: The last step is taught first, then the last two steps, and so on (Spooner & Spooner, 1984). Finally, in *total cycle chaining* students perform the entire sequence of steps on each trial (Spooner & Spooner, 1984). In general, total cycle chaining is used with older or more skilled students. Students who need more training and assistance are often taught through backward or forward chaining.

*Prompting* procedures occur frequently in conjunction with chaining. Prompts are assists that are provided either before a behavior occurs (antecedent prompts) or after (consequent prompts/correction procedures) to assist a student in performing the correct behavior. Prompts typically are arranged in a hierarchy. A most-to-least assistance hierarchy generally is employed when antecedent prompts are used and a least-to-most assistance order when consequent prompts are used. The various types of prompts are listed in Table 7.6 in a most-to-least assistance hierarchy.

*Shaping* is another commonly used teaching procedure. In shaping, the teacher gives the reinforcement (rewards) for gradual improvement in a behavior (Snell, 1987). For example, suppose one is teaching a student to make the sign for "help" (left hand palm up directly in front of body midline, fisted right hand resting on palm of left hand, both hands moved upward together). Shaping would involve first reinforcing students for making any

TABLE 7.6  Prompt Levels

| | |
|---|---|
| Full physical assistance | Manual guidance through a behavior or sequence |
| Partial physical assistance | Manual guidance through a partial behavior or sequence |
| Modeling | Teacher demonstrates a behavior |
| Verbal | Teacher gives verbal direction to perform the specific behavior |

gesture in which the two hands are in contact at midline. Later, the teacher would try to encourage closer approximations of the true sign by reinforcing a student only when the right hand rested on the palm of the left. Once a student reliably performs this approximation, reinforcement might be forthcoming only if both hands were lifted up. Finally the student would have to make the true sign to receive reinforcement. These strategies form the basic methodology for teaching new skills (acquisition). The reader is referred to Snell (1987) for a more in-depth discussion of these and other teaching techniques.

*Promoting generalization.*   *Generalization* refers in this context to the performance of a skill in a wide variety of places, with different materials, and in the presence of different people and different cues. Generalization does not magically happen for students with severe disabilities, but must be systematically inculcated. One way to do this is to change materials, settings, persons, and cues frequently. In our Dairy Queen example, this might mean having a student use different spray bottles and washcloths while cleaning; rotating instructors (teacher, aide, student teacher, co-worker); varying the setting (Dairy Queen, school cafeteria, classroom, home); and changing the cues used to direct a student. By constant alteration of the conditions in which activities occur, teachers can help students be more likely to perform the correct activities in novel or unexpected situations.

## INTEGRATION WITH PEERS WHO ARE NOT HANDICAPPED
Another critical factor in promoting postschool success is integration (Wehman, Wood, Everson, Goodwyn, & Conley, 1988). In 1978, Kenowitz, Zweibel, and Edgar estimated that approximately 70% of all students with moderate, severe, or profound disabilities were served in segregated, special schools. Recently Fredericks (1987) and Meyer and Putnam (1988) have reported that the percentage of students with severe disabilities served in regular public schools ranges from less than 50% in some states to more than 90% in others. This variability in placement rates has also been established in a recent analysis of federally reported placement data by Danielson and Bellamy (1989). To illustrate the movement toward integrated education, take the case of one state, Iowa. In 1976, Iowa had 35 segregated schools serving

*[handwritten margin note: Prompt fading provide any asses. to perform the task, then gradually fade as learner does more and more for himself]*

approximately 90% of all students with severe disabilities. By 1988, only 11 segregated schools remained, and these facilities housed approximately 30% of all public school students with severe disabilities. Why has this move toward integrated education occurred? What has prompted the phenomenal growth of the integration movement? One factor undoubtedly has been the passage of landmark federal and state legislation. In 1975, Congress passed P.L. 94-142, one of whose key provisions (copied by parallel statutes in each of the 50 states) is the least restrictive environment clause. This provision requires districts to educate students with disabilities to the maximum extent possible with their peers who are not handicapped. Laws like P.L. 94-142 have laid the groundwork for more integrated educational opportunities.

Beyond legislation, the integration movement has grown as the result of persuasive philosophical arguments and studies demonstrating the benefits of interactions between students with and without handicaps. Table 7.7 briefly describes these arguments and research findings.

Integration of students with severe disabilities has taken two forms. The predominant model features a self-contained classroom within a regular school but offers frequent chances for social interaction (Blackhurst &

TABLE 7.7   Philosophical Arguments and Research Evidence Supporting Integration

### Philosophical Arguments

☐ If students with severe handicaps are to live in the community as adults, they need to learn to interact with peers who are not handicapped as they grow up (Brown et al., 1976).

☐ Since people who are not handicapped will eventually encounter persons with severe disabilities, they too must be prepared during their formative (school) years (Brown et al., 1976).

☐ The only way to break down prejudices and stereotypes and promote a more positive attitude toward people with disabilities is to provide longitudinal opportunities for citizens without handicaps to get to know their peers with disabilities (Brown et al., 1979).

☐ Segregation has no place in an egalitarian society.

### Research Findings

☐ Attitudes toward and perceptions of persons with disabilities improve through integration (Certo, Haring, & York, 1984).

☐ Students with disabilities show gains in communicating, social skills, recreation, and domestic skills as a result of structured interactions with peers without handicaps (Certo et al., 1984).

☐ Integrated students with severe disabilities have greater academic progress than segregated students (Brinker & Thorpe, 1984).

☐ Academic achievement of students who are not handicapped does not decline as a result of integration (Jenkins, Speltz, & Odom, 1985).

Berdine, 1981). Advocates of this approach feel that it balances students' needs for a functional curriculum with their need for social interactions. More recently, efforts to develop regular class placement with support as an option have begun (Forrest, 1987; Strully, 1986, 1987). Preliminary results from programs in Canada, Vermont, Minnesota, New York, Wisconsin, and Iowa suggest that they have promise as viable placement options.

For a discussion of dealing with geographical and funding restrictions, see Blackman (1989).

A key component to any integration effort is careful planning. If the potential benefits of integration are to accrue, administrators, teachers, and parents must take steps to make it work. Nietupski, Hamre-Nietupski, Schuetz, and Ockwood (1980) have described strategies used in Milwaukee to integrate 76 students into regular elementary, middle, and high schools (see Table 7.8).

Integration is a key to successful postschool life. It opens the door to better understanding, close personal relationships, and increased social competence. One might go so far as to say that integration is the most important factor in allowing people with disabilities to assume their rightful places as partners beside peers without disabilities in vocational, recreational domestic, and community environments.

## TRANSITION TO THE WORLD OF WORK

A final area we must address if we want to empower outcomes like Jeff's is the transition from school to adult vocational services. It does very little good for a student to receive functional, chronologically age-appropriate, and community-referenced instruction in a systematic manner in integrated environments if, upon graduation, that student goes on to perform only meaningless activities in segregated settings. The bad news is that this is an all-too-frequent occurrence; the good news is that professionals have recognized this problem and are beginning to deal with it through transition planning.

*Transition* here refers to a carefully planned process to implement a plan to achieve employment upon graduation for a student with severe disabilities (Wehman, Kregel, & Barcus, 1985). Typically, formal transition planning occurs two to five years before graduation. At that time, parents, teachers, and adult service system representatives meet to establish vocational goals, decide upon vocational training experiences, and make arrangements for transferring responsibility for the student's services from the school system to the adult vocational system.

In a sense, transition has always occurred in the past. The problem has been that transition for students with severe or profound handicaps has always been into one of the vocational options described in Table 7.9. These options have come under increasing criticism over the past five years (see Table 7.10).

Supported employment is also discussed in Chapter 11.

As a result of growing criticism, a new model for adult vocational services has taken form: *supported employment.* Supported employment has four key

TABLE 7.8    Strategies for Promoting Successful Integration

☐ Regular schools are selected on the basis of principal and staff receptivity, accessibility, geographic location, and age of students.

☐ Prior to integrating, staff and students are sensitized to integration and the reasons for it and given information on the students to be integrated. At such sessions, seek ideas about ways to make students with severe disabilities part of the school.

☐ Preintegration planning between teachers, administrators, and parents is needed to ensure use of gym, lunchroom, library, playground, and other school facilities, appropriate classroom location, similar arrival and departure times and routines, and scheduling.

☐ Once programs are integrated, students who are not handicapped and staff receive ongoing information about students with severe disabilities. Such information should focus on demonstrating similarities among all students, promoting understanding of differences, and facilitating positive interaction.

☐ Teachers of students with severe disabilities must become full-fledged staff workers. This means attending meetings, assuming the school duties expected of regular teachers, getting to know other teachers and students, and serving on committees.

☐ An open-door policy should be practiced in order to encourage staff and student interest and understanding of students with severe disabilites and their program. Not closing the door to the special education classroom makes opportunities for visitations and peer interactions with other students possible.

☐ Teachers of students with disabilities should develop structured interaction programs. These can take the form of peer tutoring in which students who are not disabled teach skills to peers with severe disabilities. Assigning peer partners or special friends is another approach, one in which students who are not disabled interact in mutually enjoyable social and recreational activities.

☐ Students with severe handicaps should share the school roles other children participate in—office assistant, messenger, lunchroom helper, lunch or milk slip collector, audiovisual equipment person, library helper.

☐ Ongoing efforts should be made to integrate students in naturally occurring activities that are enjoyable and pertinent for all students. Examples are holiday parties, assemblies, school-sponsored programs, field trips, after-school drop-in centers.

☐ Teachers of students with severe handicaps need to support and assist regular staff in integrated activities and keep the lines of communication open. Such communication needs to be both ways—asking as well as answering.

components: (a) real jobs in community business; (b) wages for the work performed; (c) integration within the general workforce; and (d) long-term, possibly lifelong, support in order to learn and maintain the job. The basic assumption behind supported employment is that persons with severe disabilities can successfully get and keep employment in the community if they, their employers, and their co-workers have ongoing assistance.

TABLE 7.9   Traditional Adult Vocational Service Options

☐ *Sheltered workshops* are segregated settings that provide job training to clients with disabilities through subcontract or salvage operations. An individual must usually perform at 50% of productivity level or above (in comparison to nonhandicapped norms) in order to gain access to a sheltered workshop.

☐ *Work activity centers* provide some work training, often unpaid, but also train for such presumed prerequisites to work as grooming, home living, socialization, and academics.

☐ *Development centers* are exclusively nonvocational in nature. Generally, self-maintenance and craft actvities are the focus of such programs.

A key person in the success of supported employment is the employment training specialist, who is responsible for: *(a)* getting to know the client/student; *(b)* working with employers to design a job that includes tasks the client can do that meet essential business needs; *(c)* learning the job duties and then training the client; and *(d)* working with client, employer, and co-workers to maintain employment and a positive work environment as long as such assistance is necessary.

Supported employment is a flexible model that benefits both clients and employers. Clients with severe disabilities have numerous options under this model: *(a)* individual placement; *(b)* complementary job sharing; *(c)* placement in a small group distributed within a single business; or *(d)* being a member of a work crew. Clients also benefit by having job duties tailored to their abilities; they are not required to perform the whole job. The advent of supported employment has allowed people with severe disabilities to work in an unprecedented variety of community jobs, including the food service, janitorial, clerical, manufacturing, insurance, retail, telecommunications, lawn and garden, hotel, child care, animal care, and government sectors of the economy.

TABLE 7.10   Criticisms of Traditional Adult Vocational Service Options

☐ *Segregation is no longer justifiable,* particularly since most graduating students have had integrated school programs.

☐ *Wages are low,* on the average of $268/year in work activity centers and $1,175/year in sheltered workshops.

☐ *Few people ever move up* through the three-tiered system into competitive community employment. Once one is in a program for more than a year, the chance of moving on is only about 3%.

☐ *Human dignity and self-worth are not enhanced* through participation in handicapped-only, meaningless activity for little or no pay.

☐ *Low parental and societal expectations* are engendered (and justified) when persons with disabilities are segregated from other citizens and involved in nonproductive activity.

# A PERSONAL PERSPECTIVE ON SEVERE/PROFOUND

# MENTAL RETARDATION

For many institutionalized individuals with severe or profound handicaps the most important persons in their lives are the direct care staff who tend to their daily needs. These employees typically have more physical contact with these residents than any other human being. Heidi, a member of the direct care staff of a large residential facility for mentally retarded people, depicts the importance of this type of employee. Most importantly, she demonstrates what we think is a healthy attitude toward her charges.

Heidi is an older woman of German background who works in a unit of very low functioning residents. Every day she wakes up her assigned group, attends to their immediate needs, cleans their beds, bathes, dresses, and feeds them. While she is doing the tasks most of us would find less than enjoyable, she is talking to these uncommunicative and mostly unresponsive persons, as if they were her best friends or close relatives, about all sorts of topics. The fact that none of them ever contributes to the conversation does not seem to affect her at all.

After witnessing these events on more than one occasion, I asked her why she carried on the way she did with people who probably don't understand a word she was saying. She looked at me strangely and said, "Got to be a person in there somewhere."

I left that particular unit very humbled but with a renewed respect for those who mean so much to those we actually know so little about. It was particularly struck by the idea that we don't know what is going on inside these individuals who perform so low on our existing measures of ability. Perhaps they hear and understand everything that is said to them but just can't communicate their feelings to us. (For a related example, read the book *Johnny Got His Gun,* by D. Trumbo [1959, Bantam Books]). On this particular day, I was also reminded of something that I tell students every time we visit such residential facilities: These individuals are much more like us than unlike us.

I also realized one other thing—to a small number of people, Heidi is more important than the president, the governor, Elizabeth Taylor, Don Johnson, or Eddie Van Halen.

From *Exceptional Children in Focus* (4th ed., pp. 69–70) by J. R. Patton, J. S. Payne, J. M. Kauffman, G. B. Brown, and R. A. Payne, 1987, Columbus, OH: Merrill Publishing.

Employers benefit as well from supported employment. Persons with severe disabilities: *(a)* are loyal, competent workers; *(b)* help reduce staff turnover; *(c)* have excellent safety records; and *(d)* have low absenteeism rates. Further, supported employment services; *(a)* reduce employer hiring, training, and supervision costs; *(b)* offer financial incentives through tax credits for hiring people with disabilities; and *(c)* increase the productivity of more skilled employees by removing entry-level duties from their job descriptions and assigning these to supported employees.

Because of supported employment, transition planning now has new meaning. The role of the schools becomes one of providing gradually more involved, community-based vocational training, with the student's goal being to get a job upon graduation. One of the roles of such adult service agencies as divisions of vocational rehabilitation and departments of human services is to provide funds for supported employment opportunities for former students who have completed their schooling. Vocational service agencies provide the supports necessary for success on the job. Transition planning brings together these various agencies in the hope of carrying out responsibilities in a coordinated fashion, resulting in life outcomes like Jeff's.

**SUMMARY**

In this chapter we have attempted to present a vision of what life could hold for persons with severe disabilities: meaningful participation in integrated home, work, recreation, and community life. We have discussed factors that can contribute to the realization of this vision. Finally, we have outlined the unique characteristics of the population and the tremendous challenges that face the field as it strives to assist more individuals to achieve fulfilling lives, as the Jeffs of this world have done.

Clearly, many individuals with severe handicaps have not had the opportunities available to individuals like Jeff. This should not deter us from striving for such outcomes for all students. Worthwhile achievements start with a vision. But vision alone will not allow us to accomplish our goal. Visions of a society in which each of us belongs and participates to the maximum of our ability must be combined with the technology and the process that allow such aspirations to be realized. Services for people with severe disabilities have improved dramatically in the past 15 years. Applying and extending that technology while maintaining our vision should make the next 15 years ones of expanding opportunity for persons with severe disabilities.

# PART THREE

# PROGRAMMING AND ISSUES ACROSS THE LIFESPAN

# CHAPTER 8

# Infancy and
# Early Childhood

B irth through early childhood is a critical period of development for later learning. Infants and young children who have difficulties during these formative years may face a lifetime of problems. Researchers have shown that early identification and appropriate early intervention are both beneficial to the intellectual, social, and emotional growth of young children and economical in terms of reducing or alleviating the need for later special education services (Bailey & Wolery, 1984; Fallen & Umansky, 1985). But identifying infants and children at risk for school-based problems is often not easy. Many infants and young children have indicators of multiple disabilities, and determining the single cause or primary handicapping condition at this age is no simple matter. For this reason, professionals responsible for the education and training of infants, toddlers, and preschoolers, including children with mental retardation, hesitate to label these youngsters in the traditional special education manner. Early childhood special educators believe in a noncategorical approach to identification and intervention for young children with special needs. They recognize the multidimensionality of early childhood special education and the problems inherent in labeling young children.

This chapter presents information about the many facets of early childhood special education. Because the field takes a noncategorical approach, this chapter, unlike others in the book, is written from that perspective. The focus of the chapter is on educational programming for infants, toddlers, and young children. Individual topics address the rationale for early childhood special education, legislation affecting programs for

---

This chapter was contributed by Mary Beirne-Smith and Richard F. Ittenbach.

infants and young children, early identification and assessment, service delivery, curriculum, and program implementation.

## RATIONALE FOR EARLY CHILDHOOD SPECIAL EDUCATION

Just a quarter of a century ago educational programs for infants and children with handicaps were virtually nonexistent. Today the focus in special education is clearly on programming for children in the birth-to-five age range who are developmentally delayed (including the cognitively impaired) and at risk. Most special educators now agree that appropriate early intervention significantly impacts a child's intellectual capacity and potential to learn.

In recent years early childhood special education has experienced phenomenal growth. According to U.S. Department of Education statistics, in 1985, 25 states had legislated that children under age five should receive services. In addition, 29 states had developed personnel preparation programs for early childhood special educators (Blackhurst, Doty, Geiger, Lauritzen, Lloyd, & Smith, 1987). In October 1986 Congress passed P.L. 99-457, which extends the rights and privileges afforded individuals with handicaps under P.L. 94-142 to three-to-five-year-old children with handicaps and provides for voluntary development of programs for birth to two-year-olds who are developmentally delayed and at risk.

**P.L. 99-457 is discussed in detail later in this chapter.**

The importance of the early childhood years to later learning has been noted by a number of scholars and researchers. Among the first to draw attention to the significance of the early years were Maria Montessori, Friedrich Froebel, and G. Stanley Hall. Other researchers have added their support. For example, Benjamin (1964) found that children develop 50% of their total intellectual capacity by age four and 80% by age eight. White (1975) concluded that the period between eight months and three years is of utmost importance in the development of intellectual and social skills. In addition, Hayden and Pious (1979), McDaniels (1977), and Smith and Strain (1984) have argued that for children with physical, social, emotional, or mental handicaps, educational programming should begin shortly after birth. Recently, Bailey and Wolery (1984) summed up the case for early childhood education. According to them, early intervention can successfully detect problems when they are distinct and remediable, change the behavior of children in different areas of development, prevent the secondary consequences of a primary disability, reduce the cost of serving these children at a later age, and provide assistance and training to families in need.

**See chapter 5 for a discussion of early intervention in the prevention of mental retardation.**

# CHILDREN AT RISK

Most of us are aware of the constant reminders telling us that we are "at risk" for something harmful to us. Those who smoke are at risk for lung cancer or respiratory problems; people who don't wear seat belts or shoulder harnesses are at risk for serious injury if they are involved in an accident. Recently we have heard and read that our nation is at risk because of the state of our educational system. These are adult realities, but other circumstances, also quite serious, affect a much younger group. Thousands of children across the nation are at risk for school failure and possible classification as mildly retarded, but many of these young children do not necessarily display overt signs at an early age.

One of the major dilemmas in implementing early intervention programs is knowing which children are at risk. Unfortunately, some confusion exists about what professionals mean by *risk*. One definition says: "A risk factor is any ascertainable characteristic or circumstance of a person or group of persons that is known to be associated with increased probability of having, developing, or being adversely affected by a process producing a handicapping condition" (Garber & McInerney, 1982, p. 134). Common examples of risk factors include the socioeconomic status of the family, the intellectual abilities of the

parents (especially the mother), and the number of children in the family (see Table 5.1).

Keogh (1983) concluded that three types of children are at risk. Her categorization highlights the point that there are important differences in the way we should conceptualize at-risk children.

1. Established risk: Children in this category have known medical conditions that affect their lives.
2. Suspect risk: These children have developmental histories that suggest presence of a biological problem, but it is not apparent.
3. Environmental risk: Children who fit this group have no known medical or biological problem, but they do experience life situations (e.g., family, school) that can give rise to problems.

When considering whether children are at risk or not, it is important not only to evaluate the children but also to investigate external factors like their homes and life events. If efforts to identify and provide services to at-risk children and families are well designed and systematically implemented, fewer children should fail at school, and consequently fewer will be identified as in need of special services.

# LEGISLATION AFFECTING EARLY CHILDHOOD SPECIAL EDUCATION PROGRAMS

A number of legislative directives and mandates have contributed to the field of early childhood special education. We present a chronology of these legislative actions in this section.

## ELEMENTARY AND SECONDARY EDUCATION ACT

The Elementary and Secondary Education Act (ESEA) was passed by Congress in 1965. This act turned over substantial amounts of money to local education agencies for the purposes of establishing educational programs for children who are handicapped, disadvantaged, and between 3 and 21 years old. The Head Start programs were funded under ESEA. In 1972 Congress amended the act to require that 10% of the enrollment capacity of these programs be reserved for children with handicaps.

## HANDICAPPED CHILDREN'S EARLY EDUCATION ASSISTANCE ACT

In 1968, Congress enacted P.L. 90-538, the Handicapped Children's Early Education Assistance Act (HCEEP). This was the first law designed specifically to deal with the needs of preschool children with handicaps. Most consider it the beginning of the field of early childhood special education as we know it today.

Incentive grants are awarded with the expectation that at the end of the funding period, the project will secure other support to continue operation.

Under P.L. 90-538, three-year incentive grants encouraged the development, implementation, and replication of model programs for young children. Early projects funded under HCEEP legislation tended to focus on children in the three-to-five-year age range. More recently funded projects have developed programs for children in the birth-to-two-year age group.

Public Law 90-538 has had a great impact. The first year after passage of the act was devoted to planning implementation strategies. In 1969, 24 demonstration projects were funded, and many of these continue to operate today. To date, every state has received grants for at least one project, and over 400 demonstration projects have been funded (Karnes, 1986).

## PUBLIC LAW 94-142

As other chapters have related, P.L. 94-142, the Education for All Handicapped Children Act of 1975, for the first time provided for free appropriate public education to all children aged 3 through 21 with handicaps. Although P.L. 94-142 included children in the 3-to-5 age range, services for this group were not mandatory if the individual state did not require preschool services for all children or if such services were inconsistent with state law. In the language of the law:

> [A] free appropriate public education will be available for all handicapped children . . . between the ages of three and twenty-one . . . except that, with

respect to handicapped children aged three-to-five and aged 18 to 21, inclusive, the requirements of this clause shall not be applied in any State if the application of such requirement would be inconsistent with State law or practice, or the order of any court, respecting public education within such age groups in the State. (Education for All Handicapped Children Act of 1975, P.L. 94-142, in *Code of Federal Regulation,* 1986).

That is, P.L. 94-142 allowed states discretion in serving three-to-five-year-old children with handicaps. In addition, the law provided Preschool Incentive Grants to encourage states to identify and serve three-to-five-year-olds in need of special education. None of the regulations or recommendations accompanying P.L. 94-142 addressed the special service needs of infants and toddlers under three with handicaps.

## PUBLIC LAW 98-199

Public Law 98-199, the 1983 Amendments to the Education for All Handicapped Children Act, extended many of the requirements of P.L. 94-142. Two aspects of P.L. 98-199 that pertain specifically to preschool children with handicaps are: (*a*) the granting of permission to use federal funds under the Preschool Incentive Grant to identify and serve children below age three with handicaps, and (*b*) the establishment of state grants to develop and implement comprehensive plans for providing early childhood education to all children handicapped from birth.

## PUBLIC LAW 99-457

Public Law 99-457, the Education of the Handicapped Amendments, was signed into law on October 8, 1986. As mentioned, P.L. 99-457 extends all rights and privileges under P.L. 94-142 to infants, toddlers, and preschoolers from birth to five years old, and to their families.

Readers interested in more comprehensive information on P.L. 99–457 should consult Ballard, Ramirez, & Zantal-Veiner, (1987.)

In order to meet its objective of serving the educational needs of preschool children with handicaps, the new law is structured around two components. The *Preschool Component* is mandatory and it requires that by the school year 1990–1991 any state receiving funds under the law must have provided free appropriate preschool education with related services to all children aged three to five with handicaps. The *Infant Component* of the law is voluntary and it provides individual states with incentive grants to assist in the development of an interagency council whose purpose is to ensure planned, coordinated services for children aged birth to two with handicaps. A unique feature of the new law is the recognition of the need for parental involvement in the education of their children. Under P.L. 99-457, parents must be given assistance in determining their child's needs and obtaining services.

While the purpose of P.L. 99-457 is to extend the parameters of P.L. 94-142 to younger children with handicaps, the regulations for its implementation differ significantly from those of P.L. 94-142. In addition, regulations for implementing the law's Preschool Component differ from the requirements for the Infant Component. See the following sections for a consideration of these differences.

***Preschool Component.***    This component of the law is mandatory. Regulations accompanying P.L. 99-457 that differ from those of P.L. 94-142 are:

1. Individual states that serve three-to-five-year-old children with handicaps are not required to report child count figures by existing disability categories.
2. Each Individualized Education Plan (IEP) for children in the three-to-five age group must include instructions for parents.
3. In order to allow local education agencies to use a variety of service delivery options, including full- or part-day, center-based, home-based, and combination programs, the length of the school day and school year may vary.
4. Preschool education programs for three-to-five-year-olds are administered through the state education agency; local education agencies may, however, contract services from other programs (e.g., Head Start) or other agencies (e.g., Department of Social Services) in order to meet the requirement for provision of a full range of services.
5. Failure to comply with the new law results in loss of federal funds generated by the Preschool Grant, funds generated under the larger P.L. 94-142 formula for three-to-five-year-olds, and federal grants and contracts for preschool education programs.

***Infant Component.***    Requirements accompanying the voluntary component of P.L. 99-457 differ both from those of P.L. 94-142 and from the mandatory component of P.L. 99-457 in the following ways:

1. States applying for grants to serve infants and toddlers aged birth to two with handicaps must establish an Interagency Coordinating Council to assist parents in determining needs and obtaining services. Such Council must be composed of service providers and agencies that routinely serve children in this age range.
2. Criteria for classification of infants and toddlers with handicaps age birth to two are to be established by the individual state. Eligible children include those who: (*a*) are developmentally delayed, (*b*) have conditions that typically result in developmental delays, or (*c*) are considered at risk for substantial developmental delay (from poor prenatal care, low socioeconomic status, or other potentially confounding variables).
3. Every eligible child and his or her family must be assigned a case manager whose responsibility is to ensure that child and family receive appropriate services.
4. Except where federal or state law sets a schedule of adjusted fees, services are gratis.

5. Services must include: (*a*) multidisciplinary assessment, (*b*) a design to address the child's developmental needs, and (*c*) a written Individual Family Service Plan (IFSP) developed by the multidisciplinary team with assistance from the parents.
6. The IFSP must include:
   a. A statement of the child's present level of functioning in cognitive, speech and language, psychosocial, motor, and self-help skills.
   b. A statement of the family's strengths and needs.
   c. A statement of expected outcomes, including criteria, procedures, and time lines.
   d. A description of the services that the needs of child and family demand, including their method, frequency, and intensity.
   e. Projected initiation and termination dates for all services.
   f. The name of the case manager.
   g. Procedures planned to ensure successful transition from infant services to preschool programs.
   h. Procedures in place for reviewing the IFSP every six months and evaluating its appropriateness once a year.

## IMPLEMENTING P.L. 99-457

The purpose of P.L. 99-457 is to encourage states to provide free appropriate early intervention services to a diverse population of young children with handicaps. Implementation of the act, however, raises a number of issues that special educators must address if the intent of the law is to be fulfilled. Professionals in early childhood special education have begun a dialogue intended to ensure that the new legislation brings about quality services for young children. Issues include: funding, eligibility, integration of services, transition, family involvement, interagency collaboration, and necessity for qualified personnel.

*Funding.*  Insufficient funding is a critical concern in implementing educational programs. It is difficult to expand existing programs, establish new programs, or ensure the quality of programs when services mandated are inadequately funded.

The federal allocations to programs for three-to-five-year-olds are intended as incentives to states not currently serving this age group. A funding formula has been developed for phasing in services to preschool children with handicaps. Under this schedule, proposed authorization levels increase from $300 per previously served child and $3,800 per newly identified child for the 1987–1988 and 1988–1989 school years to $500 per previously served child and $3,800 per newly identified child for the 1989–1990 school year. For the 1990–1991 school year and thereafter, the authorization level is $1,000 per child served. The Congressional Budget Office and the U.S. Department of Education estimate the total cost of serving children under P.L. 99-457 at $2.6 billion, of which the federal government will absorb only $330 million (U.S. House of Representatives, Committee on Education and Labor, 1986).

While the proposed federal allocations are significantly larger than current ones, they do not nearly cover the cost of the programs. State and local education agencies will have to make up the difference. States that are unwilling or unable to do this will lose all federal dollars they would receive under P.L. 94-142 for three-to-five-year-old children with handicaps, the new Preschool Grant for birth to two-year-olds, and all other grants and contracts for preschool special education.

In an effort to encourage states to make better use of existing funds, P.L. 99-457 requires that existing federal, state, and local resources be used in early intervention services. Specifically, Part H, the Infant/Toddler Component, emphasizes the need to coordinate existing resources. According to *House Report 99-860:*

> It is the Congress' intent that other funding sources continue; that there be greater coordination among agencies regarding the payment of costs; and that funds made available under Part H be used only for direct services . . . that are not otherwise provided from other public or private sources. (U.S. House of Representatives, 1986, p. 15)

The issues involved in funding P.L. 99-457 are complex. As Barnett (1988) points out, the true cost of educating preschool children with handicaps may exceed the estimated cost. According to Barnett, estimates used to determine proposed federal allocation levels failed to account for the possibility of population growth among preschool children with handicaps or for inflation. Estimates also failed to consider that cost per child varies by handicapping condition. The more severely handicapped the child, the more costly the education (Kakalik, Furry, Thomas, & Carney, 1981).

Part H, the Infant/Toddler requirement for sharing resources, presents additional problems. Compliance with this provision of the law may necessitate interagency assessment of available funds and revisions or amendments to existing federal or state laws that currently prohibit sharing of funds and personnel (Smith & Strain, 1988).

Clearly, these issues are not going to be easily resolved. Barnett (1988) recommends that state agencies systematically experiment with alternatives in order to lower costs and increase benefits. Smith (1986) and Smith and Strain (1988) advocate cooperative interagency agreements about fiscal responsibility for services, personnel, and monitoring. How states elect to treat these matters is up to the individual state. But unless programs are implemented, young children with special needs will not receive services;

*More programs are now available to younger students with mental retardation.*

and failure to comply with the law will result in loss of a considerable amount of federal education funds.

***Eligibility.***    In addition to expanding services for three-to-five-year-olds, P.L. 99-457 provides for comprehensive interdisciplinary services for children from birth to two years. Children eligible to receive services under the Infant Component of the law include those who have a developmental delay in one or more of the following areas: cognitive development, speech and language development, psychosocial development, motor development, self-help skills, or a diagnosed physical or mental condition which has a high probability for such developmental delay. Each state has the discretion of serving children at risk for substantial developmental delay if such services are not now provided.

As of this writing, all states have indicated that they intend to implement both components of the law (Garwood, Fewell, and Neisworth, 1988). With implementation, however, comes the problem of identification. For the three-to-five-year-old population, states must decide whether to report children noncategorically or by disability. For the infant and toddler population, states must determine which children are at risk for developmental delay. For both populations, procedures are needed to determine which children are not eligible for early intervention (Smith & Strain, 1988).

To clarify some of the difficulties of eligibility and identification decisions, the National Executive Board of the Division for Early Childhood of the Council for Exceptional Children recently issued a position statement on the definitions of categories of children to be served (Smith et al., 1987). Part of their statement follows.

1. Developmental delays include children who have been diagnosed by a multidisciplinary team as having a significant delay in one or more of the following areas of development: cognitive, speech/language, physical/motor, vision, hearing, psychosocial, and self-help skills. Significant delay can be a 25% delay in one or more developmental areas or a 6-month delay in two or more areas.

See chapter 4 for a discussion of the biological causes of mental retardation.

2. Diagnosed physical or mental condition which has a high probability of resulting in a developmental delay includes infants and young children who have identifiable conditions but who may not be exhibiting delays in development at the time of diagnosis. Examples of such conditions include, but are not limited to: (1) Down's syndrome and other chromosomal abnormalities associated with mental retardation; (2) congenital syndromes and conditions associated with delays in development such as Fetal Alcohol Syndrome, Cornelia de Lange Syndrome, severe microcephaly and macrocephaly (3rd percentile or 97th percentile), metabolic disorders, intracranial hemorrhage (subdural, subarachnoid, intraparenchyma, and grade III or IV intraperiventricular hemorrhages), malignancy of brain or spinal cord, neonatal seizures, asphyxia, and respiratory distress syndrome with prolonged mechanical ventilation; (3) sensory impairments; and (4) maternal Acquired Immune Deficiency Syndrome (AIDS).

3. At-risk of having substantial developmental delays if early intervention services are not provided includes children who are: (a) medically or biologically at-risk because of early health factors which are known to produce developmental delays in some children; this term includes, but is not limited to, the following examples of health factors: significantly premature birth, low birth weight, and infants of mothers who are chemically dependent or who were exposed to medication or other teratogens known to cause developmental risk, who are admitted to a neonatal intensive care unit for at least seven days, who had complications at birth or who have significant medical problems, chronic otitis media, or failure to thrive; and (b) environmentally at risk because of physical or social factors in their environment which pose a potential threat to their optimal development; this term includes, but is not limited to, the following examples: parental mental retardation or psychiatric disorder, parental substance abuse, suspected child abuse or neglect, maternal age less than 15, and children who are economically disadvantaged and whose caregiver(s) has (have) less than a 12th grade education, or children whose parent(s) or regular caregiver have significant concerns regarding their development. (pp. 5–6)

Another eligibility issue under P.L. 99-457 concerns those children categorized as at risk under Part H of the current regulations. Children served as at risk are not handicapped and thus lose their eligibility for services at 3 years of age. As Smith and Strain (1988) have pointed out, the need for early intervention does not end at 2 years 11 months of age. These authors have recommended that the mandatory portion of the law be extended to include the birth-to-two-year-old population.

*Integrated services.*   P.L. 94-142 requires that , so far as possible, children with handicaps be educated with peers who are not handicapped. The doctrine of least restrictive environment (LRE) has long been an issue in education. With the passage of P.L. 99-457 the confusion surrounding the appropriateness of the educational setting reaches the preschool handicapped population as well.

With regard to the legal aspects of the integration issue, Edmister and Ekstrand (1987) have noted that, because the LRE clause of P.L. 94-142 does not specify any particular age group of children with handicaps, we must assume that it includes preschool children with handicaps. Further, Johnson (1976) pointed out that in the effort to integrate children who are handicapped with children who are not handicapped, "the state (as represented by individual school districts) bear[s] the burden of proof when making placements or when applying treatments which involve partial or complete removal of handicapped children from their normal peers" (p. 60).

The LRE clause as it has been applied in the past refers, then, to removal of children from regular education settings. The complexity of the issue for preschool children with handicaps becomes apparent when one realizes that for the birth-to-five age child there is no such setting. Strain and Cardisco (1983) have suggested that a reorganization of traditional administrative arrangements could result in better integration of children who are handicapped and nonhandicapped in preschool programs. Included in their list of suggestions are enrollment of children who are handicapped in family day care or center-based preschool programs, enrollment of children who are not handicapped in specialized programs (e.g., Head Start), and enrollment of children with handicaps in school-sponsored preschools and kindergartens.

Clearly we will not easily resolve the difficulties attendant on integrating preschoolers who are handicapped with those who are not, and the long-term benefits of such integration are uncertain. Turnbull (1982) noted that a relatively restrictive early placement for some preschool children with handicaps may facilitate later functioning in a less restrictive environment. The child's individual needs may preclude placement in the regular class setting.

Efficacy research on the social advantages of integrating preschool children with handicaps shows that the results are equivocal. Research corroborates social benefits to the child who is handicapped (Strain, Guralnick, & Walker, 1986), but it has also shown that the more severely handicapped the child, the less likely social interaction is to occur between the child who is handicapped and the child who is not handicapped (Guralnick, 1981). Smith and Strain (1988) caution that to be successful, the integration must be carefully planned. These authors recommend that early childhood regular and special educators share their knowledge.

*Transition.*    Changes in age, abilities, or programming needs may result in a number of transitions within the service delivery system for young children with handicaps and their families. For example, children may move from home-based to center-based programs or from programs sponsored by health agencies to others sponsored by local education agencies. According to Fowler (1988), the changes caused by transition can create a number of problems for both child and family.

Families and children must adjust to new locations, to new teachers and staff, and to changes in program format or curriculum. The level of parental involvement, intensity of parental contact, or even availability of services for parents may also change. Such changes may adversely affect the child's ability to adjust to new settings or to acquire new skills. Differing eligibility requirements and lack of interagency coordination may result in loss or delay of services (Johnson, Chandler, Kerns, and Fowler, 1986) and parental anger or distrust of service providers (Harbin, 1988).

A critical issue, then, in the implementation of P.L. 99-457 is how to reduce the risks of transition for young children with handicaps and their families. One solution involves careful planning at the agency, service provider, and family levels. Hains, Fowler, and Chandler (in press, cited in Fowler, 1988, p. 62) provide the following guidelines for facilitating transitions between programs:

1. *Interagency planning.* Each agency should develop a written transition plan outlining the activities involved in changing the placement of a child and family. The plan should contain a suggested timeline for each activity and staff assignment for ensuring completion of each activity. The sending and receiving agencies should communicate and coordinate this plan with one another. After the transition is completed, the agencies should evaluate the quality of the transition from the program's and family's perspective.

2. *Program planning.* The sending program staff should obtain basic information regarding the next placement in order to prepare the child and family for the new program. Such information might include the program's philosophy, schedule, routines, curriculum, and skills expectations. Exchange visits between programs are one way to gather this information and make the planning easier. When possible, the sending program should introduce the child to skills that will be needed in the new program as well as new routines. Staff should also prepare the family for differences in the level of family contact or support.

3. *Family planning.* Families should have the option to participate in all phases of transition planning and should be provided with the anticipated sequence of activities and a timeline for completing the transition. Families can be encouraged to visit the new placement option and meet with the new staff. Families should be included when the child and family needs are identified and prioritized at the placement conference, and they should participate in any decisions regarding child placement. They can help prepare the child for the transition by taking the child for a visit to the new program, discussing the change, and including skills and routines expected in the new program in their daily home activities.

A second solution involves the dissemination of exemplary practices from model programs with transition components. Four such programs, developed in part under HCEEP legislation, are described below:

1. PROJECT BEST

   Advance planning and communication between the sending and receiving programs and the home are emphasized in the BEST model (Building Effective School Transitions). A manual includes guidelines and sample formats for (a) developing interagency agreements, (b) communicating between the home and service program, (c) involving families in decision making, (d) constructing a timeline for each child's transition, (e) identifying local agencies for referral, (f) preparing the child for a change of programs, and (g) evaluating the family's and program's satisfaction with the transition process.

   A three-part conversation guide, the Transition Planner, assists families in identifying and prioritizing child and family needs related to the transition. A skills readiness survey is completed by the sending and receiving teachers to identify similarities and differences in program expectations several months prior to the transition. The materials have been developed and field-tested with children moving from preschool programs to elementary school programs.

2. PROJECT STEPS

   The STEPS model (Sequenced Transition to Education in the Public School) presents a community-wide interagency approach to helping children with handicaps and their families make a successful transition from a preschool program to the least restrictive environment in the public schools at the kindergarten or elementary level. The model was developed among seven diverse preschools working in active collaboration with the public school system. The preschools included specialized preschools for the handicapped, integrated preschool programs, Head Start, and community agencies serving at-risk children.

   The project replication manual describes procedures for establishing an interagency group and negotiating and implementing transition timelines and procedures. Sample procedures and forms for this administrative component are provided. Strategies for staff development in the sending and receiving schools are identified. These include training and cross-program visitation. The Helpful Entry Level Skills Checklist is a quick screening device that staff can use to identify social and behavioral skills that help children to be independent and enhance their successful placement. An instructional strategies document correlating to this checklist is also available. The parent involvement component presents a multilevel approach ranging from one-on-one counseling to group training.

3. PROJECT TEEM

Project TEEM (Transitioning into the Elementary Education Mainstream) has developed a model that enables school systems to establish and implement a transition planning process. The model is designed to address the concerns expressed by families and professionals regarding entry into the public school, promote the implementation of best practices, and facilitate the transition of all children with handicaps from preschool into the regular kindergarten and elementary school mainstream.

There are two major components of the model. The first component delineates best practices across the following steps: (a) establishing a transition planning team comprised of all key individuals, (b) informing and involving the child's family, (c) preparing the child and local elementary school prior to placement, (d) planning the child's social and educational integration, (e) monitoring and supporting the child's placement, and (f) planning future transitions.

The second component provides guidelines for systems to develop a transition process. Included are guidelines for (a) eliciting system-wide commitment and involvement, (b) developing written procedures that encompass the best practices and promote timely and systematic transitions, and (c) identifying and obtaining the training and resources to establish and support the transition process.

4. INTERAGENCY TRANSITION MODEL

The objective of this is to ensure a planned transition for young children with special needs who are moving from one primary service provider to another. The model provides direction to administrators, assessment and direct service personnel, and parents as they plan and carry out transitions.

The Troubleshooting Guide assists model users with identifying problems related to their current transition practices. Completion of this guide results in a prioritized list of issues, which then directs users into the strategy section of the model. Strategies are presented in six issue areas: transfer of records, timing of transition events, awareness of programs, parent involvement, decision-making process, and postplacement communication.

Required actions, guidelines, and necessary forms are included with each strategy. Participating agencies are encouraged to modify strategies and forms to fit their specific needs and existing practices. An evaluation plan assists users with examining overall outcomes as well as the effects of individual strategies. Model procedures have been field-tested and replicated by numerous early intervention programs, school districts, and Head Start programs representing urban, suburban, and rural locales. (Adapted from Fowler, 1988, pp. 62–63)

*Family involvement.*    While special educators have long acknowledged the importance of family involvement in the education of children with handicaps, legislation has primarily focused on the needs of the child. With enactment of P.L. 99-457, the focus has shifted, and the relationship between the family and the service provider has changed dramatically. The IEP and IFSP provisions of the law require that family needs and resources be assessed and that parents be counseled and instructed about their child's needs and be assisted in getting services for the child. These new features of the law challenge service providers to adapt and extend the range of services currently offered under P.L. 94-142.

The needs of children with handicaps and their families are complex. Recent data from the U.S. Bureau of Census (1985) indicate that the structure of the American family has changed since the early 1970s. Divorce, widowhood, teenage pregnancy, and births out of wedlock mean that approximately 67% of the children born in American today will be raised in single-parent households, usually in mother-child relationships, for at least part of their life. The median income of households headed by single female parents is characteristically lower than that of two-parent households. Women and children are now the majority of Americans living below the poverty level. The challenge to service providers becomes clear when these data are coupled with research that indicates higher than expected incidences of developmental delay among children of low socioeconomic status and from single-parent homes (Peterson, 1987).

The economic realities of single parenthood have caused an increased number of women with children under 18 to go to work (Klein & Sheehan, 1987) and consequently the number of children served in day care outside the home is greater (Sells & Paeth, 1987). Sells and Paeth estimate that 30% of the children now in day care are under 3 years of age. Halpren (1987) predicts that in 1990, 75% of children under age 6 will require child care services outside the home. At the same time, as the stability of family life has decreased, incidences of child abuse have increased. Recent reports indicate that, nationally, child abuse has doubled since 1976, and research shows that children with developmental delays or behavior problems are at increased risk for abuse (Zirpoli, 1986.)

These factors and the added stress on the family of raising a child with a disability have led a number of professionals to recommend a family systems approach to early intervention (Berger & Foster, 1982; Bristol & Gallagher, 1982; Fewell, 1986; Salisbury, 1986; Turnbull, Summers, & Brotherson, 1986). According the A. P. Turnbull (1988), a family systems perspective addresses the interrelationships of family members, the contribution each member can make, and the partnership between families and professionals. Turnbull describes the four components of the family systems approach as:

1. *Family resources*—the variables involved in the family's ability to address the individual and collective needs of its members. A major assumption of a systems perspective is that each family is unique in the variety of resources it has available for coping with the child's exceptionality.
2. *Family interactions*—the relationships that occur between individuals and subsystems within the family system. Families have been members whose

needs must constantly be addressed. These needs compete with each other for the time and resources of the family unit.

3. *Family functions*—the different categories of needs for which the family is responsible. Because of the comprehensive and multiple nature of these needs it becomes obvious that families are extremely busy trying to attend to all of their tasks and responsibilities.

4. *Family life cycle*—the sequence of changes that affect families as they pass through different time periods. These changes include both developmental and nondevelopmental transition (such as divorce). (p. 82)

A. P. Turnbull (1988) notes that the family systems perspective, illustrated in Figure 8.1, provides a means of viewing the child as a member of the family unit and aids professionals in understanding how a family uses its resources. According to Turnbull, professionals who recognize and act on this information are more competent in assisting families to enhance their quality of life.

In general, research supports the systems approach for families with children who are handicapped. In a review of the literature, Dunst, Trivette, and Cross (1986) concluded that intrafamily role-sharing and help from extrafamily sources affect family and child functioning. Dunst (1986) found that change among children with severe or multiple disabilities depended on home environment, family characteristics, family support systems, and professional intervention. Harbin (1988), however, points out that some types of family intervention may be detrimental, especially to poor or minority families. Harbin notes that technical assistance to service providers in designing IFSPs that meet the needs of the family yet are not intrusive is needed.

*Interagency collaboration.*    A number of agencies, services, and programs are available to meet the needs of young children with handicaps and their families. Each of these may be essential to the growth and development of the child who is handicapped. Yet parents seeking to coordinate services from several service providers are often frustrated by differing eligibility requirements, limitations on service agency roles because of mission, funding, or political influences, and lack of communication or coordination between programs. The result for the parents and the child is unnecessary duplication of some services and fragmentation or lack of others. Professionals often find the situation as annoying as do parents.

Many have suggested interagency collaboration as a means of providing comprehensive, coordinated, and multidisciplinary services to young children with handicaps and their families. The purported advantages of collaboration are more and better services, cost-effective programming, and improved communication among professionals. Where this arrangement is feasible, a coalition of public and private health, mental health, social, and educational service providers cooperate in identifying all eligible children

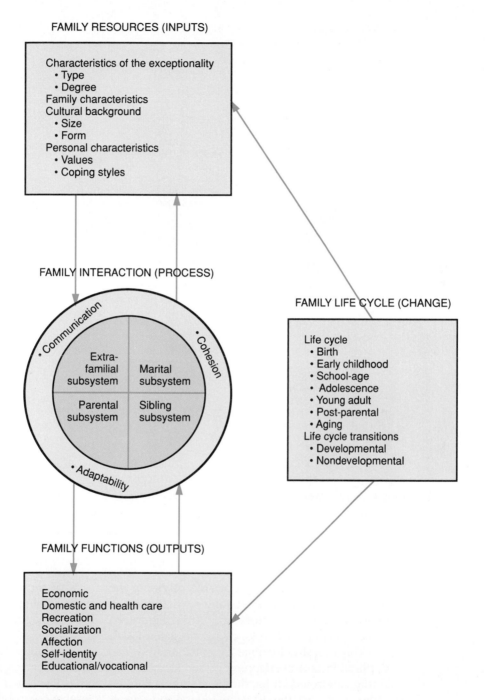

FIGURE 8.1   Family Systems Conceptual Framework

From *Working with Families with Disabled Members: A Family Systems Approach* (p. 60) by A. P. Turnball, J. A. Summers, and M. J. Brotherson, 1984, Lawrence, KS: Kansas University Affiliated Facility.

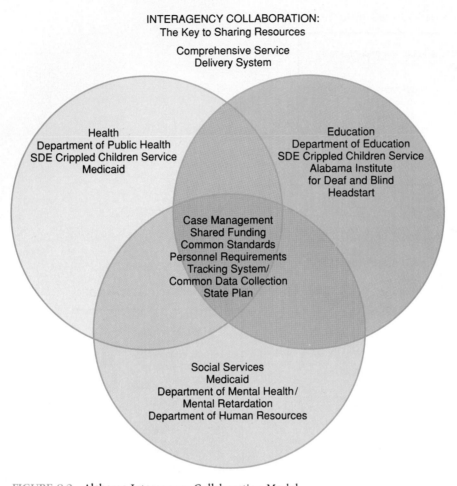

INTERAGENCY COLLABORATION:
The Key to Sharing Resources

Comprehensive Service
Delivery System

Health
Department of Public Health
SDE Crippled Children Service
Medicaid

Education
Department of Education
SDE Crippled Children Service
Alabama Institute
for Deaf and Blind
Headstart

Case Management
Shared Funding
Common Standards
Personnel Requirements
Tracking System/
Common Data Collection
State Plan

Social Services
Medicaid
Department of Mental Health/
Mental Retardation
Department of Human Resources

**FIGURE 8.2**   Alabama Interagency Collaboration Model

From *A Vision for the Future* by Alabama State Department of Education, April, 1987, Montgomery, AL: AL
SDOE.

who are handicapped and at risk; assessing the needs of these children,
developing IFSPs, implementing service plans, and coordinating transition
between programs (Houston, 1987). Figure 8.2 depicts the interagency
collaboration plan developed by the state of Alabama.

Theoretically, interagency collaboration leads to elimination of costly
duplication and overlapping of services and more and better services for
young children with handicaps and their families. But as Flynn and Harbin
(1987) point out, the disparate federal and state policies that control many of
the affected agencies may be difficult to coordinate. In addition, competition
among existing programs may be difficult to resolve (Harbin, 1988).

*Qualified personnel.* Implementation of P.L. 99-457 is impossible without trained personnel. Yet research conducted shortly before enactment of the new law indicates a serious shortage of qualified personnel to work with young children with handicaps (McLaughlin, Smith-Davis, & Burke, 1986). With passage of the law and the corresponding expansion of services to younger children with handicaps, personnel shortages become even more critical. Besides teachers, the personnel needed include such related service providers as nurses, social workers, occupational therapists, physical therapists, speech and language pathologists, psychometrists, and psychologists.

In special education, qualified personnel are individuals trained and certified to work in an area of speciality. Training is provided by institutions of higher learning. For teachers, state education agencies (SEAs) generally set standards and certify. Certification may be *generic,* enabling personnel to serve a wide range or ages and handicapping conditions, or *specific,* restricted to a limited age range or category of handicapping conditions. For many related service providers, such as speech and language pathologists or occupational and physical therapists, certification standards are set by national boards, and SEAs that employ them and determine the competencies needed by these workers have little control over the setting of standards or awarding of certification (Burke, McLaughlin, & Valdivieso, 1988).

State education agencies attempting to respond to the need for early childhood special educators face a number of problems related to the availability and certification of qualified personnel. Foremost is the relationship between certification standards and program quality. As Burke et al. (1988) have pointed out, comprehensive certification requirements tend to promote high program quality but may restrict the number of personnel. More lenient certification standards allow for greater flexibility in hiring or reassigning personnel but may result in less well trained service providers.

Quality programming is certainly important for preschoolers, but such early childhood educators as kindergarten teachers, may reasonably be expected, with a minimum of additional training, to acquire the skills necessary to teach a slightly younger group of children. Temporary or provisional certification leading to reassignment of available personnel, coupled with continuous evaluation and monitoring of the effectiveness of this approach, may be a viable short-term response to the personnel shortage at the preschool level. The advantages of this solution are that retraining available personnel and awarding temporary or provisional certification would allow local education agencies to meet the immediate need for early childhood preschool special educators. Continuous monitoring and evaluation would provide data from which to judge how well the solution works. The danger is that a short-term stopgap may become a long-term response, and program quality may suffer.

For infants and toddlers no such simple solution is advisable. The competencies needed for quality programming of children younger than three with handicaps come only from more extensive training. As Geik,

Gilkerson, and Sponseller (1982) have pointed out, an effective infant and toddler interventionist must be able to act as teacher, program developer, advocate, team member, and consultant. Such a specialist must have knowledge of age-appropriate assessment techniques and instruments, age-appropriate teaching techniques, curriculum and materials, and child development. Reducing training or certification requirements for infant and toddler specialists will produce trainers who lack essential skills and contribute to poor program quality.

# ASSESSMENT

The quality of assessment information obtained about a child is directly related to the integrity of both the instruments and the methods used to obtain that information. Two basic approaches to assessment have predominated in early childhood special education, formal methods and informal methods. Although both approaches are necessary to a comprehensive multidimensional approach to intervention, neither alone can provide all the information needed.

### FORMAL ASSESSMENT

Formal assessment procedures are those with specific guidelines for administration, scoring, and interpretation (McLoughlin & Lewis, 1986). Formal assessment procedures generally include such standardized, or norm-referenced, tests as intelligence tests, achievement tests, interest inventories, and so on. The term *standardized* refers as much to the rigors of administration and scoring as it does to the scores. Each child's performance on a given test or task is compared to the performance of other children in a reference group by using a *standardized score*. The normative group forms the basis for all comparisons in norm-referenced testing. Although most norm-referenced tests do not provide the classroom teacher with guidelines for intervention, they do allow a teacher to compare a child's test performance with those of other children of similar age and under known conditions.

Neisworth and Bagnato (1988) have identified three principal purposes for norm-based assessment: (*a*) to describe a child's level of development, (*b*) to place a child in a diagnostic category, and (*c*) to predict a child's future level of development. Well designed tests with a representative reference group (age, race, sex, residence, geographic region, and socioeconomic status) allow educators to do more than just compare a child who is handicapped with other children on general measures of aptitude or ability; they allow them to estimate the child's unique skills and abilities as well.

If describing a child's skills and abilities well enough to meet the qualifying criteria for placement is the letter of the law, describing that child's strengths and weaknesses well enough to design effective interventions is its spirit. School age children must have a diagnostic label before they can receive services, but preschoolers, infants, and toddlers need only be at risk for substantial developmental delay. Early childhood educators are now being required to meet both the spirit and the letter of the law by designing interventions based more on the needs of the child than on the stereotype of a label. Well designed standardized tests can perform that function.

These tests' potential to help predict future academic performance is now more an ideal than a reality. Standardized test scores for children under two years of age demonstrate little, if any, predictive ability (Anastasi, 1988). Bracken (1987) investigated the psychometric properties of 10 frequently used standardized preschool instruments and found that "many of these tests designed for preschool use are severely limited in floor, item gradient, and reliability, especially at the lower age levels" (p. 325). This evaluation, combined with the relatively small number of preschool children who are developmentally delayed per standardization sample, requires us to be cautious about making long-term predictions.

Tables 8.1 through 8.5 illustrate formal tests commonly used in preschool programs. These tables are organized by the domains specified in P.L. 99-457.

## INFORMAL ASSESSMENT

Informal assessment methods are similar to formal methods in that they are designed to elicit educationally relevant information; they differ because they obtain the information under less stringent and more flexible conditions. Because external guidelines or criteria against which to compare the child's performance are absent, the teacher is free to design techniques and methods of assessment based on hypotheses about the preschool child's learning pattern. What these techniques lack in normative data they make up for in their relevance to instruction. Using informal methods has several advantages: (*a*) test items may be designed and administered by the teacher; (*b*) test items may coincide with instruction; (*c*) the teacher can revise both the items and the overall format as testing progresses; and (*d*) the teacher can assess the child before, during, and after each lesson or set of lessons, depending on the type of information wanted.

Although many different types of informal assessment exist (observations, work-sample analyses, task analyses, inventories, interviews) (McLoughlin & Lewis, 1986), a frequently used in-class method is *criterion-referenced testing* (CRT). In CRT, the teacher attempts to measure the child's skills against preestablished levels of mastery (Salvia & Ysseldyke, 1985). CRT is based on the premise that a child's performance may be best understood in the context of what a child can do within a given content area, instead of simply how well a child performs relative to other children (Anastasi, 1988). A fundamental prerequisite to CRT is defining a content area well enough to represent it with prespecified questions. CRT is versatile enough to be appropriate for everything from school readiness to self-help skills.

TABLE 8.1  Measures of Socioemotional Development

| Instrument | Age Range | Domains/Areas | Scores Provided | Standardization Sample Size & Model | Median Scale Reliability Estimate |
|---|---|---|---|---|---|
| *Behavior Evaluation Scale* (McCarney, Leigh, & Cornbleet, 1983) | K to 12th | Learning problems Interpersonal difficulties Inappropriate behavior Unhappiness/depression Physical symptoms/fears | Behavior quotient scores (M = 100, SD = 15) Scaled scores (M = 10, SD = 3) | Not reported (N = 1,018) | 0.88 |
| *Burks Behavior Rating Scale: Preschool and Kindergarten Edition* (Burks, 1983) | 3-0 to 6-0 | 18 scales | Raw scores | Not reported (N = 464) | Not reported |
| *Children's Apperception Test* (Bellak & Bellak, 1974) | 3-0 to 10-0 | Reality testing Regulation of drives Object relations Thought processing Ego functioning Defense mechanisms Stimulus sensitivity Autonomy Integrative ability Mastery competence | Not applicable | Not applicable | Not applicable |
| *Test of Early Socioemotional Development* (Hresko & Brown, 1984) | 3-0 to 7-11 | Parent rating scale Sociogram Student rating scale Teacher rating scale | Scaled scores (M = 10, SD = 3) Percentile ranks Deviation quotients (M = 100, SD = 15) | 1983 statistical abstract (N = 1,006 students & teachers) (N = 1,773 parents) | 0.89* |

Asterisk denotes values calculated from standardization data for preschool ages only.

TABLE 8.2 Measures of Motor Ability

| Instrument | Age Range | Domains/Areas | Scores Provided | Standardization Sample Size & Model | Median Scale Reliability Estimate |
|---|---|---|---|---|---|
| *Bruininks-Oseretsky Test of Motor Proficiency* (Bruininks, 1978) | 4-6 to 14-6 | Fine motor<br>Gross motor | Standard scores ($M = 50$, $SD = 10$)<br>Battery composite<br>Gross motor composite<br>Fine motor composite<br>Subtest scores ($M = 15$, $SD = 5$)<br>Age equivalents<br>Percentile ranks<br>Stanines | 1970 census ($N = 765$) | Not reported |
| *Peabody Developmental Motor Scales and Activity Cards* (Folio & Fewell, 1983) | Birth to 6-11 | Fine motor<br>Gross motor | Standard scores ($M = 100$, $SD = 15$)<br>Developmental motor quotient<br>Gross motor composite<br>Fine motor composite<br>Age equivalents<br>Percentile ranks | 1976 census ($N = 617$) | Not reported |
| *Test of Gross Motor Development* (Ulrich, 1985) | 3-0 to 10-0 | Gross motor | Composite quotient ($M = 100$, $SD = 15$)<br>Subtest standard scores ($M = 10$, $SD = 3$)<br>Percentile ranks | 1980 statistical abstract ($N = 909$) | 0.86* |

Asterisk denotes values calculated from standardization data for preschool ages only.

285

**TABLE 8.3** Measures of Self-help Skills

| Instrument | Age Range | Domains/Areas | Scores Provided | Standardization Sample Size & Model | Median Scale Reliability Estimate |
|---|---|---|---|---|---|
| *AAMD Adaptive Behavior Scale—School Edition* (Lambert & Windmiller, 1981) | 3-0 to 16-0 | Personal self-sufficiency Community self-sufficiency Personal-social responsibility Social adjustment Personal adjustment | Comparison scores Scaled scores Regular, EMR, TMR | Not reported (N = 6,500) | 0.83* |
| *Normative Adaptive Behavior Checklist* (Adams, 1984) | Birth to 21-0 | Self-help skills Home skills Independent living skills Social skills Sensory-motor skills Language concepts | Standard scores (M = 100, SD = 15) Age equivalents Percentile ranks Performance rankings | 1980 census (N = 6,014) | 0.94* |
| *Vineland Adaptive Behavior Scales: Survey Edition* (Sparrow, Balla, & Cicchetti, 1984) | Birth to 18-11 | Communication Daily living skills Socialization Motor skills | Standard scores (M = 100, SD = 15) Adaptive behavior composite Domain scores Age equivalents Adaptive level norms Composite and Domains Percentile ranks Stanines | 1980 census (N = 3,000) | 0.89* |
| *Scales of Independent Behavior* (Bruininks, Woodcock, Weatherman, & Hill, 1984) | 0-3 to 29≤ | Motor skills Social & communication skills Personal living skills Community living skills Broad independence | Standard scores (M = 100, SD = 15) Broad independence Domain scores Age equivalents Functional performance level Instructional range Normal curve equivalents Percentile ranks Relative performance index Stanines | 1980 census (N = 1,764) | 0.90* |

Asterisk denotes values calculated from standardization data for preschool ages only.

TABLE 8.4   Measures of Speech and Language Ability

| Instrument | Age Range | Domains/Areas | Scores Provided | Standardization Sample Size & Model | Median Scale Reliability Estimate |
|---|---|---|---|---|---|
| *Peabody Picture Vocabulary Test—Revised* (Dunn & Dunn, 1981) | 2-6 to 18-0 | Receptive language | Standard score ($M = 100$, $SD = 15$) Age equivalents Percentile ranks Stanines | 1970 census ($N = 4,200$) | 0.76* |
| *Preschool Language Scale: Revised Edition* (Zimmerman, Steiner, & Pond, 1979) | 1-6 to 7-0 | Auditory comprehension Verbal ability | Standard scores ($M = 100$) Language quotient Auditory comprehension quotient Verbal ability quotient Age-equivalents | Not reported | Not reported |
| *Receptive-Expressive Emergent Language Scale* (Bzoch & League, 1971) | Birth to 3-0 | Expressive language Receptive language | Standard scores ($M = 100$) Combined language quotient Expressive language quotient Receptive quotient Combined language age | Not reported | Not reported |
| *Test of Early Language Development* (Hresko, Reid, & Hammill, 1981) | 3-0 to 7-0 | Expressive language Receptive language Syntax & semantics | Language quotient ($M = 100$, $SD = 15$) Age equivalents Percentile ranks | 1979 statistical abstract ($N = 1,884$) | 0.88 |
| *Utah Test of Language Development—Revised* (Mecham & Jones, 1978) | 1-0 to 15-0 | Expressive language Receptive language | Language age equivalents Percentiles Stanines | Not reported | 0.94 |

Asterisk denotes values calculated from standardization data for preschool ages only.

TABLE 8.5  Measures of Cognitive Ability

| Instrument | Age Range | Domains/Areas | Scores Provided | Standardization Sample Size & Model | Median Scale Reliability Estimate |
|---|---|---|---|---|---|
| *Kaufman Assessment Battery for Children* (Kaufman & Kaufman, 1983) | 2-6 to 12-6 | Sequential processing Simultaneous processing Achievement Nonverbal | Standard scores ($M = 100$, $SD = 15$) Mental processing composite Sequential processing Simultaneous processing Nonverbal Socio-cultural Subtest scores ($M = 10$, $SD = 3$) Age-equivalents Percentile ranks Stanines | 1980 census ($N = 2,000$) | 0.90* |
| *Stanford-Binet Intelligence Scale: Fourth Edition* (Thorndike, Hagen, & Sattler, 1986a, 1986b) | 2-0 to 23-11 | Verbal reasoning Abstract/visual reasoning Quantitative reasoning Short-term memory | Standard scores ($M = 100$, $SD = 16$) Test composite Verbal reasoning Abstract/visual reasoning Quantitative reasoning Short-term memory Subtest scores ($M = 50$, $SD = 8$) Percentile ranks | 1980 census ($N = 5,013$) | 0.91* |
| *Wechsler Preschool and Primary Scale of Intelligence* (Wechsler, 1967) | 4-0 to 6-6 | Verbal Nonverbal | Standard scores ($M = 100$, $SD = 15$) Full scale IQ Verbal IQ Performance IQ Subtest scores ($M = 10$, $SD = 3$) Percentile ranks | 1960 census ($N = 1,200$) | 0.94* |

Asterisk denotes values calculated from standardization data for preschool ages only.

*Curriculum-based assessment* (CBA) is one type of criterion-referenced testing. CBA test items are drawn directly from the teaching materials and are considered to be a highly effective way of monitoring and modifying methods of instruction. Fuchs and Fuchs (in press) have identified two specific forms of CBA, precision teaching and mastery teaching. In precision teaching a lesson or program is broken down into a hierarchy of skills. Measurement

*Although the needs of younger children are as great as those of their school-age counterparts, the training of professionals to work with this group differs.*

procedures analyze the child's performance for each step in the skills hierarchy. In mastery learning, the smaller parts of each instructional unit are the principal focus of routine assessment. Mastery assessment is highly dynamic; the teacher tests a concept, gives feedback, and then tests the concept again until the child has completely mastered the task. Precision teaching and mastery teaching share a number of elements (Fuchs & Fuchs, in press): (*a*) progress is assessed on short-term objectives; (*b*) measurement focus shifts upon mastery; and (*c*) the teacher designs assessment tasks.

*Judgment-based assessment* (JBA), though relatively new in name, actually consists of time-honored clinically useful techniques. JBA provides a structured framework within which a teacher or examiner may include and quantify the opinions and impressions held by primary caregivers (Neisworth & Bagnato, 1988). In JBA the examiner constructs a scale or checklist designed to measure abilities not typically mentioned in standardized tests. The individual is the sole referent for each analysis. The principal advantage of JBA is that it provides a type of social validity (Wolf, 1978), a means of linking traits and behaviors with results from other, more formal tests.

## ISSUES IN PRESCHOOL ASSESSMENT

Assessing young children who are handicapped presents a number of problems not always encountered when working with similar older children. For the educator working with infants and toddlers the difficulties become even greater. Educators must be aware of the multifarious issues that impact on the assessment process, issues that we can divide into five broad areas: (*a*) developmental, (*b*) idiographic, (*c*) technical, (*d*) ethical, and (*e*) procedural.

### DEVELOPMENTAL

Preschool children in general, and preschool children who are handicapped in particular, have a number of characteristics that set them apart from school age children. One is their short attention span. Preschool children are willing participants as long as they are interested, but as their interest wanes, so does their willingness to cooperate. Their physiological needs are also different. A preschool child who begins an assessment period sleepy, tired, hungry, or needing to go to the bathroom will probably not participate for very long. The same principle holds for mental and physical ability. Young children do not generally have the stamina or endurance to respond for extended periods of time. Two other phenomena affect many infants and toddlers: stranger anxiety, a generalized fear of strangers and new environments, and separation anxiety, a fear of being separated from their parents. Parental encouragement to the contrary, young children commonly fail to respond to others outside the home; there seems to be no real need to perform just because an adult has asked. Many of these children have simply not yet learned the role of test-taker, which seems to come more naturally to older children. For the child who is developmentally delayed or at risk, essential developmental steps may be incomplete or even missing, making many of these tasks more difficult, if not impossible.

## IDIOGRAPHIC

Idiographic approaches to assessment seek to describe an individual's behavior in the context of what is uncommon or unique about that person (Rychlak, 1981). All individuals are unique because they represent one permutation of all possible interactions between demographic, genetic, environmental, and personality factors. Attempts to study or understand the individual without considering each variable and its impact on development are unhelpful at best, damaging at worst.

From the moment of conception, each individual organism has a unique combination of genes that will serve as the developmental framework for the rest of the organism's life. This genetic code regulates the rate and sequence of all phases of development. But as important as this genetic code is, it is only a skeleton; other variables give it flesh. Such chemical and environmental factors as altitude, illness, infections, physical activity, radiation, temperature, and toxins can have a profound impact on the developing infant. For the older preschool child, demographic variables—age, gender, geographic region, race, religion, and socioeconomic status—also affect development. In addition to these pervasive and long-lasting influences is a plethora of situation-specific variables such as family dynamics, the child's playmates, physical health, area of residence, and so on.

For the child who is handicapped, however, there is one more critical component—the impact of the disability. The greater the handicap, the more likely the developmental process will be altered. Understanding how children grow and develop relative to their own unique conditions and abilities is essential to designing sound intervention strategies (Reynolds & Clark, 1983).

The reader is referred to Marci Hanson's (1984) book, *Atypical Infant Development*, for a thorough discussion of the impact of handicaps on the developmental process.

## TECHNICAL

Preschool instruments do not possess the same psychometric integrity found in instruments typically used with school age children (Bracken, 1987; Weger, Tschantz, & Walters, 1986). Preschool instruments generally consist of fewer items, take less time to administer, and, as a result, have lower estimates of reliability and validity. When these instruments have more items, they also have higher estimates of reliability and validity. But preschool instruments are shorter by design, for ($a$) the children have short attention spans, ($b$) their abilities are in the earliest stages of development, and ($c$) their fund of information is generally so small that it limits what the teacher can elicit. A major criticism of today's preschool instruments is that they do not discriminate effectively at the lowest levels of ability. Given that very few children below the age of six can read, spell, or do simple mathematical problems, this comes as no surprise, and many preschool instruments tend to emphasize instead perceptual, memory, and visual-motor types of tasks. Very few instruments have norms representative of the entire preschool population; even fewer have norms that include preschool children who are handicapped or mentally retarded. Many instruments in use today were not designed for use with children with handicapping conditions (Reynolds & Clark, 1983). Valid measures require more than just alternative guidelines for administration; they require alternative norms for samples that are exceptional. Comparing the performance on a given task of a child who is handicapped to a set of norms derived predominantly or wholly from children who are not handicapped offers a distorted picture of the child's ability relative both to all children in general and to all children with a similar handicapping condition.

### ETHICAL

Fundamental to the idea of special education services is the assumption that all service providers are trained and qualified to serve as necessary. The training and abilities needed to evaluate preschool children effectively differ substantially from those needed to evaluate school age children. A number of investigators have collected evidence to suggest that many examiners lack training and/or ability and that traditional methods of early childhood assessment are less than optimal (Dillon & Stevenson-Hicks, 1983; Johnson & Beauchamp, 1987; Schakel, 1987). Technical and professional standards governing preschool assessment are identical to the standards for all age groups, but in early childhood special education a wide variety of tests and techniques is used, administered, and interpreted by individuals with vastly different areas of expertise; and the potential for misuse is great (American Educational Research Association, American Psychological Association, & National Council on Measurement in Education, 1985). To offset the risk of misuse, then, individuals conducting or using assessments of preschoolers, infants, and toddlers should have formal education in such areas as child development, assessment of mental and special abilities, and educational interventions, as well as supervised experience working with young children who are handicapped. Those who have not had these experiences should refrain from offering assessment services (National Association of School Psychologists, 1983). Lack of appropriate training affects all areas of assessment: selection of a test or technique, administration, scoring, and interpretation.

### PROCEDURAL

Preschool assessment is plagued by many of the problems of school age assessment, not the least of which is identifying the child who is at risk. Identification criteria vary from state to state, just as for the school age child.

For instance, in some states a developmental delay of 25% in one area is all that is required; in other states a delay of 25% in two or more areas is required; in still others, a 35% delay in a single area is necessary for qualification. As with other exceptionalities, states are free to use multiple criteria such as standardized test scores, discrepancy formulas, or simple percentile ranks. A second problem is the mechanism for meeting the needs of the family and those of the child who is developmentally delayed or at risk. For the birth-through-two group, a case manager must be assigned to each family to help coordinate and implement educational services. Although how to select the case manager varies from agency to agency, the potential better to address the educational needs of the child, the family, and the entire educational community through more appropriate distribution of services has increased. Third are the problems of generalization from isolated observations. P.L. 94-142 and its newest amendment, P.L. 99-457, have attempted to address this concern through nondiscriminatory assessment, an approach that seems to unite practitioners and researchers. Fourth is the validity and reliability of group decisions. In multidisciplinary team meetings, group decisions can result in anything from static, categorical placement to innovative educational alternatives. Professionals should make decisions based on the unique needs of the child, using sound logic and valid reasoning, and not simply to meet the needs of the group making the decision or because it was the most cost-efficient and expedient route to take.

Many of the issues mentioned here and elsewhere will continue to surface and resurface over time just as they have with P.L. 94-142. What is different from the past decade, however, is that special educators now have a wealth of information on which to build and base their decisions as they begin their evaluation of America's youngest school age children.

## SERVICE DELIVERY MODELS

The educational needs of young children with handicaps differ from those of their school age counterparts. In order to meet the diverse needs of younger children, greater flexibility and variety in service delivery options are needed. Some options are variation in the length of the school day and the school year, joint service provisions with existing preschool programs, and use of space, personnel, and equipment other than that typically found in public school classrooms. Educators responsible for planning and implementing appropriate early intervention services must identify current resources, coordinate existing programs, and develop innovative service delivery models. Four service delivery models that have proven successful in the education of young children are home-based, center-based, a combination of the two, and consultation (Bailey & Wolery, 1984). Table 8.6 details the advantages and disadvantages of each model.

TABLE 8.6    Service Delivery Models for Young Children with Handicaps

| Model | Advantages | Disadvantages |
| --- | --- | --- |
| Home-based | Rapport with family is more easily established. | Parents who may lack skills are responsible for implementing much of the intervention. |
| | Family routines are less likely to be disrupted. | Teachers spend potential planning and instructional time traveling from site to site. |
| | Children are more at ease, less frightened in familiar surroundings. | No opportunity exists for peer interaction and socialization. |
| | Materials can be designed to meet the needs of the natural setting. | |
| | Building and maintenance costs are unnecessary. | |
| Center-based | All primary and support services are housed in one location. | Cost of providing facilities and range of services is high. |
| | Teachers have more time for planning and instruction. | Center may need to provide transportation and bus aides, which increases cost. |
| | Situation promotes peer interaction and socialization. | Families may move and time be lost in reorganizing bus routes or locating the family. |
| Combination | Greater flexibility in delivering services is possible. | Same as with home- and center-based models. |
| | Same as with home- and center-based models. | |
| Consultation | More efficient use of staff time. | Parents are responsible for implementation of the intervention. |
| | | Imposes on parents to transport children. |
| | | Limited amount of service can be provided to child or family. |

## HOME-BASED SERVICES

As the name implies, home-based services take place in the home. Home-based programs are most appropriate for the birth-to-two-year-old child who may not yet need to develop peer interaction skills. Home-based programs are also good when the family is the focus of the intervention. For logistical reasons, these programs are more common in rural areas, where there are fewer children to be served and where transportation is more likely to be a problem.

Home-based intervention seeks to assist families in setting goals and acquiring the skills they need to meet them. A teacher or consultant visits the home on a regular basis and helps the family to develop an appropriate home intervention program for the child who is handicapped. Depending on the needs of the child and the family, visits may occur as often as several times weekly or as infrequently as once monthly. During visits the teacher or consultant may assess the child and/or the family situation, review the child's progress since the last visit, observe parent-child or family-child interactions and offer suggestions, demonstrate activities, or aid the parent in designing materials or developing activities.

One well known home-based program is the Portage (Wisconsin) Project. This program serves children up to age six who show at least a one-year developmental lag. Approximately half the children served are mentally retarded (Karnes & Zehrbach, 1977). The program uses both professional and paraprofessional home teachers, who usually visit the homes once a week. The emphasis is on teaching parents to use behavior modification techniques with their children. The project uses the *Portage Guide to Early Education,* a curriculum that includes 450 skills organized by normal developmental sequence. In addition, the staff works with other community agencies to serve the child and the family.

A slightly different approach is taken by the Regional Intervention Program (RIP) in central Tennessee (Eller, Jordan, Parish, & Elder, 1979). In this program, parents come to the Nashville center for an initial individualized training program that meets five days a week for as long as necessary. This training program is run by other parents who have been through the program with their children. Parents learn to record data, choose instructional goals, reinforce desirable responses, and teach their children. Instruction of the child also begins at the center, and staff members watch the parents work with the children and help them improve their teaching skills. At the end of the parent training program, parents return home as the sole service providers for their child. In order to enter the program, parents must agree to work in the center for six months after intensive intervention with their child has ended. Once this intensive work is completed, the center acts as a liaison to follow the child's educational placement and progress. RIP focuses on children under age five, and over half the children begin the program at age three or younger. It has the extra advantage of being an informal parent support group.

## CENTER-BASED SERVICES

Services in center-based programs take place in a single location. Professionals consider center-based programs most appropriate for preschool age children who require services from a team of specialists, for children who need peer models or peer interaction, and for children whose parents are not always available to participate in their education. Some programs accommodate only children who are handicapped, and others mix children who are handicapped with others who are not. Usually the children attend the center for three to five hours per day, four to five days per week. Family participation in the programs varies and may include observation or classroom participation, scheduled meetings to review progress or receive instruction for home implementation of center activities, and parent support groups.

One example of a center-based program is the Model Preschool Center for Handicapped Children at the University of Washington in Seattle. This center offers a variety of programs, including (*a*) an infant learning program for infants with Down Syndrome; (*b*) an infant program for other infants at risk; (*c*) programs for preschoolers with Down Syndrome—an early preschool for children aged 19 months to 3 years, an intermediate preschool for those aged 3 to 4, an advanced preschool for children aged 4 to 5, and a kindergarten for 5 and 6-year-olds; and (*d*) preschool programs for children with severe handicaps (Karnes & Zehrbach, 1977). These developmental programs all work toward helping the children function as normally as possible, with the eventual goal of placement in programs in their home communities.

## COMBINATION SERVICES

Combination service models offer various configurations of home- and center-based services. Some programs are organized so that younger children receive services at home and older children receive them in a center. In other programs, the specific needs of child and family dictate where the services will be provided. For example, an older child with severe physical involvement who may be difficult to transport may be served in the home, whereas a younger, more mobile child might be a candidate for center-based services. In addition, combination service programs allow some children to receive all services at home while others receive all services at a center.

The Teaching Research Infant and Child Center in Eugene, Oregon, is an example of a combination program. This program serves children aged 1 to 18 who are moderately to profoundly handicapped (Fredericks, Baldwin, Moore, Templeman, & Anderson, 1980). It includes a classroom for children aged 1 to 3 and one for children aged 3 to 6, as well as classes for older children. The curriculum is based on the *Teaching Research Curriculum for the Moderately and Severely Handicapped* (Fredericks et al., 1976), which uses developmentally sequenced materials and task analyses of skills. Daily center teaching involves both individualized and group instruction. Teachers also train parents to work on jointly chosen instructional programs coordinated with the school programs and designed to extend the school day. Home teaching periods last from 10 to 30 minutes each day.

Another example of a combination program is the Saginaw D.O.E.S. Care Program in Saginaw, Michigan. This program serves children with handicaps, including those who are mildly and moderately retarded, from birth to age 8. In the D.O.E.S. program, home trainers, working under the direction of professional staff, visit the home until the child reaches the age of 3. From 3 to 8, the children attend classroom programs focusing on individual learning needs.

## CONSULTATION SERVICES

In the consultation service model, parents bring the child to the center, and professionals provide instruction for training. As with home-based programs, this method of service delivery relies on parents to implement the recommendations of professionals.

## CURRICULUM

Most early childhood special education programs employ a variety of approaches to teaching infants and young children. Generally the curriculum is based on the needs of the infant or child and derives from one of three theoretical perspectives on learning—developmental, behavioral, or functional.

Developmental curricula are based largely on the work of Piaget. According to this theory, skills develop hierarchically, and children pass through developmental stages in a highly predictable fashion. Development of high-level skills is inextricably bound up with development of lower level skills. The teacher following the developmental curriculum matches tasks to normal developmental milestones, identifies deficits and gears instruction to accelerating the rate of development of the child or infant who is handicapped to the nonhandicapped norm. Fewell and Kelly (1983) have pointed out that an advantage of developmental curricula is that their teaching of clusters of interrelated behaviors encourages generalization of skills. The disadvantage, according to Fewell and Kelly, is that overemphasis on readiness skills may lead to placing the blame for any failure to learn on low developmental level rather than on the design or implementation of the curriculum.

Behavioral curricula are based on the theory of operant learning. Their proponents believe that children learn best by experiencing repeated reinforcement for responses to environmental stimuli. Skills are taught in the behavioral curriculum according to the child's or infant's needs in the present or projected future environment. The model defines skills precisely in behavioral terms and states criteria for performance clearly and quantitatively. In contrast to the developmental curriculum, the behavioral curriculum teaches skills directly and independently of one another. According to Fewell and Kelly (1983), opponents of the behavioral approach argue that it inhibits the cognitive and emotional development of young children with handicaps by prohibiting interaction with the environment. Its supporters maintain that children who lack essential skills require a highly structured approach to learning and that the structure can be relaxed as learning progresses.

The functional curriculum is a hybrid of the developmental and the behavioral curricula. It attempts to incorporate the best features of the two. Insofar as it emphasizes teaching interrelated classes of behavior and generalization within task classes, it is developmental, but it is behavioral in its emphasis on teaching skills that the infant or child needs now or will need.

Research has not demonstrated that any one curricular approach excels. In practice, the approach must meet the needs of the individual child who is handicapped and of that child's family. To assist practitioners in the selection process, Fewell and Kelly (1983) have drawn up questions to use in evaluating and analyzing curricula for young children with handicaps:

1. Is the curriculum based on a theory of early development and learning? If a particular theoretical perspective has not been identified and, instead, an eclectic approach has been used, are the various perspectives openly acknowledged? If an eclectic approach has been used, it is essential to include specific guidelines (e.g., for instructional strategies, teachers' roles), so that staff understand why they are to respond in certain ways and how they can generalize behavior to situations not described.

2. Do the goals of the curriculum complement the existing goals of the program? For example, if one of the program's major goals is facilitation of parent-child interaction, how are parents included in the curriculum?

3. Can the goals and objectives be assessed? Entry and exit levels must be determined so that programs can be individualized and child progress can be measured.

4. Are the objectives designed to accomplish the terminal goals of the curriculum? . . . A rationale for coordinating immediate and long-term goals is often missing, making empirical evaluation difficult. This question, therefore, is an important one for program evaluators to consider in assessing program validity.

5. Does the curriculum focus on the skill domain that is most critical for the target population? If, for example, the children to be served are deaf or language-delayed, a curriculum that carefully addresses communication needs should be selected. This would not preclude inclusion of other skill domains, but strategies for facilitating language while addressing other target skills should be reviewed.

6. Are the instructional objectives and activities broken down into small workable statements appropriate for use with the target population? If the children are severely handicapped, a finely sliced curriculum with several activities for each objective might be appropriate. If the children are not handicapped or only mildly delayed, fewer items might be required for each domain. A program that serves children with several types of delays (e.g., deaf, blind, communication-delayed) might require a variety of curriculums to develop individualized programs.

7. Are the items developmentally relevant and logically sequenced? A current emphasis in assessment and curriculum materials for children who are

handicapped is the inclusion of only those items that are functional (skills that enable a child to perform in the environment).

8. Does the curriculum include techniques for attracting and sustaining a young child's attention? These techniques are likely to include methods for reinforcing attention and responses, then gradually fading reinforcement as the child acquires the skill and exercises it freely in several settings.

9. Does the curriculum include ways to build and maintain appropriate social interactions between the adult and the child? Whether the child is mildly or severely handicapped, learning should be as enjoyable for the child and parent or teacher/therapist as possible. This requires a curriculum that fosters reciprocity, permitting the child and adult to form a natural and enduring relationship.

10. Does the curriculum allow for skill generalization? As early as 1962, Taba emphasized that generalization occurs through either content or methods used in learning. Does the curriculum address how learning is to be generalized? More recently, Brown, Nietupski, and Hamre-Nietupski (1976) suggested that skills be taught in reaction to or in the presence of at least three different persons, in three natural settings, in response to three difference appropriate language cues.

11. Has the curriculum been tested on the population it was designed to serve? For example, if the curriculum is designed for children who are blind, has its success been documented with this population? Empirical evidence of curriculum validity and reliability are critical if staff are to be accountable for designing and implementing appropriate educational plans.

12. Does the curriculum include procedures for collecting and recording data as the curriculum is implemented? Is the system described in a way that would allow paraprofessionals to use it?

13. Have the authors drawn on the expertise of different kinds of specialists in preparing the curriculum or suggested guidelines for deciding when to turn to specific professionals?

14. Is the curriculum easy to implement and export? This requires written instructions that are easy to follow, as well as clearly defined parent, teacher, and child expectations.

15. Does the curriculum allow for formative and summative evaluation of the child's performance and of the curriculum's impact on the entire program? As a critical element in any program, the impact of the curriculum must be measured to determine its contribution in the program's success. (pp. 428–430)

## PROGRAM IMPLEMENTATION

Programs for infants and preschoolers differ from programs for school age children in the amount of time spent in school and the goals and objectives for learning. Yet teachers of young children face similar challenges in arranging the classroom and scheduling the school day. Workable classroom arrangements and effective scheduling are crucial to the success of infant and preschool programs. We discuss principles that apply to these variables in this section.

## CLASSROOM ARRANGEMENTS

Organizing the physical space in the classroom is the first step in facilitating learning. Designing the optimal classroom arrangement for infants and preschoolers requires careful planning. Among the factors teachers must consider are:

1. *The space available.* State education agencies usually dictate the minimum allowable space for infant and preschool classrooms. But the shape of the room and the presence of fixed features like windows, sinks, and toilets sometimes inhibits optimal classroom arrangements. Polloway, Patton, Payne, and Payne (1989) suggest that teachers begin planning room arrangement by drawing a rough sketch of the room, then adding in basic equipment like tables, desks, and chairs.

2. *The physical needs of the students.* The physical needs of preschool children who are handicapped often differ from those of their peers who are not handicapped. Children in wheelchairs or walkers or on portable stretchers, for example, require carefully planned room arrangements. At the very least, the teacher must consider fixed barriers (e.g., doorways) and movable barriers (e.g., tables). For children who are not toilet trained or are incontinent, the teacher must consider the need for and privacy of changing tables. Finally, as with all children, the size of the furniture must match the size of the child. Gray (1975) has pointed out that chairs, desks, and tables that are too large or too small are uncomfortable and inhibit learning.

3. *Group arrangements.* Infant and preschool programs use a variety of group arrangements during the school day. Quite obviously, the space and location requirements vary for one-on-one, small group, and large groups instruction. Lund and Bos (1981) recommend that, to encourage attending, quiet and individual work areas be placed together out of the line of traffic. They also recommend designating a fixed area in the classroom for group activities.

4. *The purpose of instruction.* Lesson objectives frequently suggest the location and type of space needed. Activities that involve direct teacher instruction, for example, language learning, require a more structured, quieter setting than activities that involve only teacher supervision, for example, free play. Lund and Bos (1981) suggest arranging group areas so students can move easily from one to another and using pictures or colors to code different classroom areas.

5. *Material accessibility.* Searching for materials stored in out-of-the-way places can waste valuable teaching time, and materials that are not readily available are less likely to be used to enhance lessons. Also, because

fostering independence is an important goal of early childhood special education programs, teachers should avoid making materials difficult for children to locate and secure on their own. Lund and Bos (1981) suggest placing instructional areas close to material storage places, keeping frequently used materials close together to facilitate accessibility, and labeling or color coding storage areas for aides and volunteers.

6. *Personal territory*. Like their school age counterparts, children in preschool arrive with a variety of personal possessions. A safe and accessible space is needed in the classroom to store outerwear, story-books, and toys, etc. Gray (1975) points out that personal space in the classroom contributes to the child's sense of belonging. Lund and Bos (1981) suggest cubbies or lockers for children's personal belongings and picture cues to assist students in identifying their personal space.

## SCHEDULING

Many preschool programs provide for a half day of direct instruction services. The teacher may spend the rest of the day in planning, case management, consulting with other professionals, or meeting with parents. Other programs provide for a full day of services. Regardless of the length of the school day, the daily schedule is an important ingredient in the effectiveness of the service. The daily schedule sets the tone for learning. A well planned schedule considers the individual needs of the children, promotes accomplishment of IFSP goals and objectives, allows for different activities and group arrangements, realistically reflects the time needed for transition between activities, and is structured for routines but is flexible enough to meet situations that arise unexpectedly in the course of a school day.

Polloway et al. (1989) point out that the first step in developing a daily schedule is to determine how many hours the child is in school and how much of that time is available for instruction. Such events as snack or lunch, related services (e.g., physical therapy), sharing-time, and so forth, must be scheduled in and deducted from instructional time. Once these factors are accounted for, the teacher should consider high-probability and low-probability activities. Low-probability activities require direct teacher instruction in a skill or concept (e.g., classifying words into the categories food, animals, transportation). The most difficult low-probability activities should be taught early in the day when children are most alert and, for variety, interspersed with high-probability activities like story time or work centers designed to develop different skills. Next the teacher must consider how or whether to schedule small group or one-on-one instruction. As O'Connell (1986) has made clear, this can be difficult for several reasons: (*a*) in integrated preschool programs the children who are not handicapped may not exhibit skill deficits, and direct instruction for them would be restrictive; (*b*) with only a teacher and an aide in the classroom the number of children in two small groups may still be too large for effective teaching; (*c*) one-on-one instruction presents the problem of what to do with the other children in the classroom. If the teacher decides that the need for small group or one-on-one instruction is overriding, then alternative, productive activities must be provided for the rest of the class. One possible solution is for the teacher to conduct the direct instruction while the aide supervises one or two groups of children involved in activities designed to promote cognitive, motor, perceptual, language, or creative skills. Figures 8.3, 8.4, 8.5, and 8.6 illustrate possible full and half-day schedules.

| | |
|---|---|
| 8:30–8:50 | Interaction with children and parents, hang up coats, etc. |
| 8:50–9:10 | Circle time (days of the week, months, colors, etc.; varies with need). |
| 9:10–9:20 | Group 1 with teacher for direct instruction. Groups 2 and 3 with aide for activities. |
| 9:20–9:30 | Group 2 with teacher for direct instruction. Groups 1 and 3 with aide for activities. |
| 9:30–9:40 | Group 3 with teacher for direct instruction. Groups 1 and 2 with aide for activities. |
| 9:40–10:10 | Free play or outdoor play. |
| 10:10–10:20 | Transition, bathroom, etc. |
| 10:20–10:40 | Snack. |
| 10:40–11:00 | Circle time (language, cognitive development, etc.). |
| 11:10–11:20 | Story time. |
| 11:20–11:30 | Interact with children and parents, put on coats, etc. |
| 11:30 | Dismissal. |

FIGURE 8.3   Half-Day Preschool Schedule with Direct Instruction

| | |
|---|---|
| 8:30–8:45 | Interaction with children and parents, hang up coats, etc. |
| 8:45–9:05 | Circle time (days of the week, months, colors, etc.; varies with need). |
| 9:05–9:35 | Free play (activities designed to develop various areas—cognitive, motor, etc.). |
| 9:35–9:50 | Story time. |
| 9:50–10:00 | Transition, bathrooms, etc. |
| 10:00–10:20 | Snack. |
| 10:20–10:45 | Outdoor play. |
| 10:45–11:00 | Circle time (language, cognitive development, etc.). |
| 11:00–11:20 | Free play (as above). |
| 11:20–11:30 | Interaction with children and parents, put on coats, etc. |
| 11:30 | Dismissal. |

FIGURE 8.4   Half-Day Preschool Schedule Without Direct Instruction

| | |
|---|---|
| 8:00–8:30 | Teacher planning. |
| 8:30–9:00 | Arrival, self-help (undressing). |
| 9:00–11:00 | Individual activities: physical management, gross motor, fine motor, cognition). |
| | 9:30–10:00 Language group 1 (augmentative). |
| | 10:00–10:30 Language group 2 (3–4 word utterances). |
| | 10:30–11:00 Language group 3 (imitation). |
| 11:00–12:00 | Lunch; self-help (eating, brushing teeth, toileting). |
| 12:00–1:00 | Nap. |
| | Arrival of nonhandicapped students. |
| 1:00–1:30 | Self-help (dressing) self-directed activities. |
| 1:30–2:00 | Individual language activities (groups 1, 2, 3). Language group 4 (integrated). |
| 2:00–2:30 | Snack and socialization groups (integrated). |
| 2:30 | Departure. |
| 2:30–4:00 | Teaching planning. |

FIGURE 8.5   Full-Day Preschool Schedule

| 8:00–8:30 | Teacher planning. |
| 8:30–9:00 | Arrival and interaction with families. |
| 9:00–11:00 | Individual activities.** Physical management. Motor development. Language development. Cognition. |
| 11:00–12:00 | Lunch; oral motor skills, self-help (eating, brushing teeth, toileting). |
| 12:00–1:00 | Nap. |
| 1:00–1:30 | Self-help (dressing, toileting). |
| 1:30–2:00 | Sensory activities, individualized within group setting to enhance social skills. |
| 2:00–2:30 | Interaction with families. |
| 2:30–4:00 | Teaching planning; case management activities, home visits. |

FIGURE 8.6    Full-Day Infant Schedule*

*The infant schedule must be flexible to take into consideration each child's schedule of eating and sleeping.
**These activities match the overlap between domains during infancy. Emphasis is placed on developing skills across domains to encourage the infant to interact with all facets of the environment.

**SUMMARY**

With enactment of P.L. 99-457, special education services have become mandatory for three-to-five-year-old children with handicaps; voluntary programs are encouraged for birth-to-two-year-olds. The new law emphasizes the importance of including the family in educational decisions and provisions for the child. Efficacy studies generally support the positive efforts of early intervention for handicapped children. Implementation of P.L. 99-457 raises a number of difficult issues, including funding, eligibility, integration of services, transition, family involvement, interagency collaboration, and shortage of qualified personnel.

Assessment of infants and preschoolers employs both formal and informal procedures. It may, however, be less practicable than for school age children because of developmental, idiographic, technical, ethical, and procedural problems. Infants and young children receive services through home-based, center-based, combination, and consultation programs. Curriculum approaches to early childhood special education programs are designed to meet the unique needs of the child and family and are based on developmental, behavioral, or functional theories of learning. Organizing classroom space and scheduling the school day are important considerations in implementing early childhood special education programs.

# CHAPTER 9

# Educational Programming—
# School Years

W e have already dealt with the causes, characteristics, and assessment of various levels and types of mental retardation. Now it is time to go a step further to focus on the critical task of developing and implementing educational programs that give all individuals who are mentally retarded, regardless of their limitations, the opportunity to participate in the activities of their daily environment as much as possible.

We discuss below a number of key aspects of the educational programming process. First we look at placement alternatives for school age learners who are mentally retarded. Second we go on to ponder the complementary roles of teacher and learner in special education. Third is a discussion of the critical task of selecting appropriate learning objectives for students who are mentally retarded, followed by a look at a sampling of curricular objectives geared to meet the needs of students who are classified at the general levels of mental retardation—mild, moderate, and severe and profound. Fourth we describe the components of the educational programming process in detail. And finally we focus on specific instructional methods that are often useful for working with learners with handicaps.

## PLACEMENT ALTERNATIVES

The trend today toward providing appropriate, beneficial, humanistic services to persons in our society who are retarded has led to changes in the structure of American schools as well as to the development of entirely new educational alternatives. The goal is no longer to hide the handicapped from view, but to habilitate them. A guiding principle is *normalization*—the idea that people who are mentally retarded should lead lives as much like yours and mine as possible. For children this principle is reflected in part by P.L. 94-142's mandate for education in the least restrictive environment.

This section deals with various program alternatives for individuals who are mentally retarded. We look at placement alternatives for school age children and youth and also at the statements of proponents and opponents of the Regular Education Initiative (REI) about the issues surrounding proposals for more integrated systems of education for students with mild learning handicaps.

*One very important aspect of adaptive behavior is social interaction.*

## PROGRAMS FOR CHILDREN AND YOUTH

The free public school system was established in the United States shortly after the War of 1812 (Pulliam, 1968). Before that time, education was mostly limited to church-sponsored programs for which the provision of equal education for all children was not a concern. During the early part of the 19th century, state enacted laws that required communities to offer educational opportunities but did not make attendance mandatory. These efforts at mass education emphasized the importance of curricular content and not the needs of individual children. For the most part, children with mental and physical limitations were kept out of school. This situation changed with the advent of compulsory attendance, which began in Rhode Island in 1840. The entry of youngsters who were retarded into the public schools meant that the public schools had to offer a greater array of programs. We can group the current program alternatives used for educating school age youngsters who are retarded into 16 types. The programs are divided into four major categories: those based in regular classrooms, in special classrooms, in special schools, and in other settings (see Table 9.1).

During the last few years, the trend has been to serve children with special needs without segregating them from students who do not have

TABLE 9.1  Models for Educating Retarded Pupils According to Level of Program Segregation and Degree of Retardation

| | |
|---|---|
| Children with mild retardation | *Regular class-based programs* <br> Special materials and equipment <br> Special materials, equipment, and consultation <br> Itinerant services <br> Resource room with special education teacher <br> Diagnostic-prescriptive teaching center |
| Children with mild and moderate retardation | *Special class-based programs* <br> Special education class <br> Part-time in regular class <br> Full-time in special class |
| Children with moderate and severe retardation | *Special school-based programs* <br> Special day school <br> Special residential school |
| Unless temporary, children with severe and profound retardation | *Nonschool-based programs* <br> Hospital instruction <br> Homebound instruction |

# MAINSTREAMING REVISITED

Since the implementation of the Education for All Handicapped Children Act of 1975, there has been much mention of the concept of mainstreaming. Often associated with the notion of placing students in the least restrictive environment, mainstreaming implies the integration of students who are handicapped into regular education. Some authorities, however, point out that some regular education settings may be more restrictive rather than less restrictive. Regardless of the restrictiveness debate, other important issues are relevant to the practice of mainstreaming students who are retarded. The following list includes some of the major concerns facing educators and researchers dealing with this topic.

☐ In light of the presumed benefits of having students who are handicapped educated as much as possible with their nonhandicapped peers, we still lack a solid research base that supports this idea.

☐ There may be more interest in mainstreaming students than in what happens to them afterward.

☐ What are the practical and financial implications of mainstreaming preschool age children?

☐ If the mildly retarded population has changed over the last few years, then there are two notes of caution: *(a)* earlier research on mainstreaming students who are mildly retarded is probably not applicable to the present population; and *(b)* this new, lower functioning group is probably not so capable of being mainstreamed as the earlier one.

☐ No definite conclusions about the success or failure of mainstreaming efforts can be drawn from the existing corpus of research.

☐ If suitable retarded students are to be successfully integrated into regular education settings, they will have to

acquire the classroom-related survival skills and behaviors required in these settings;

develop appropriate social skills (i.e., social competence); and

participate in cooperative ventures with peers who are not retarded so that they can be perceived as performing reasonably well.

☐ There is a great need to *(a)* identify programs that seem to mainstream students successfully; *(b)* examine the components of these programs; and *(c)* disseminate information.

learning problems. This trend, which encompasses mainstreaming and integration, envisions teaching all children who are exceptional (including those who are mentally retarded) in the regular education classroom or integrating them into regular education settings whenever possible (see box).

MacMillan (1982) has stated that the child who is retarded should be placed in the program alternative closest to the regular class that the student's needs and characteristics will allow, and that arrangements for instruction should be flexible to allow as much integration of the student who is retarded into mainstream education as possible. When establishing objectives for any child who is retarded, it is important to make only a tentative commitment to a program level, not considering placement in any program as permanent or terminal. Educators should provide students who have handicaps with programs that will maximize their potential and allow them to function in society. Opportunities for moving children who are retarded from more segregated programs to more integrated programs should constantly be considered, and changes made whenever feasible.

## PUBLIC LAW 94-142

The 1975 Education for All Handicapped Children Act (P.L. 94-142) has been, to date, the most significant piece of legislation for the education of children and youth who are handicapped. In educational placement for this population, two of its legal guarantees are relevant:

1. Assurance of the availability of an appropriate public education for all children who are handicapped at no cost to parents.
2. Assurance that special education will be provided to all children who are handicapped in the least restrictive environment.

These assurances compel educators to ensure that no child is rejected from services on the basis of handicap and that every child is integrated with normal peers to the maximum extent possible. Several specific alternatives are available for placement of students who are retarded.

## REGULAR CLASS PROGRAMS

The goal of placement is to provide the most beneficial services to children who are retarded with minimal segregation from their peers. Some students can reach this goal in regular class programs that have a variety of instructional arrangements. The needs of all the children in the class dictate which arrangement should be used. Constant review keeps the placement appropriate and based on the changing needs of the child with handicaps.

*Special materials and equipment.* Occasionally regular education teachers are able to teach pupils who are retarded in their classrooms with the help of some special education materials. The material may be a high-interest, low-vocabulary reading series, a programmed reader, a job-related mathematics book, or any material or hardware that allows the teacher to individualize instruction. This level of special education support requires a highly skilled regular education teacher who is sensitive to the needs of learners who are retarded.

*Special materials, equipment, and consultation.*    In this plan, limited consultation from a special education teacher supplements the regular education teacher's special materials and equipment. Consultation may consist of demonstrating materials or equipment, assessing the child's needs, developing teaching strategies, or providing an inservice training program. This level of support also requires that the regular education teacher be highly skilled and sensitive to the needs of children who are retarded. In either of these plans, the regular education teacher should be working with a moderate to small class (approximately 5 to 12 students).

*Itinerant services.*    An itinerant services program supplies regular education teachers with regular consultative and instructional services for their pupils who are retarded. An itinerant teacher operates from a central office and visits the school periodically, usually working in individualized or small group instruction with students who have special needs that hamper their scholastic progress. This alternative is especially popular for students who have vision or language disorders. Since these services are limited (visits are typically weekly or biweekly), responsibility for the children's education rests with the regular education teacher. Occasionally school-based tutors, who are either volunteers or teacher aides, bolster up the itinerant services. Student tutoring helps teachers to individualize instruction; it is gaining popularity as a technique for assisting regular education teachers with learners who are retarded. Peer tutoring has also been successfully used to improve academic skills, foster self-esteem, help the shy youngster, help students who have difficulty with authority figures, improve race relations, and promote positive relationships and cooperation among peers (Mercer & Mercer, 1989).

*Resource room with special education teacher.*    In the resource room plan, the pupil who is handicapped remains in a regular education class and receives special education through the coordinated efforts of the regular education teacher and the resource room teacher assigned to that school. Models for resource instruction vary substantially from school to school. For example, Roger and Koppman (1971) note, "Resource room programs for children with problems are not new, but there seems to be a large degree of variation among programs and there is not universal understanding of this kind of approach" (p. 460).

The child may be placed in the resource room for all academic instruction, returning to the regular education class only for lunch, art, and physical education, for instance, or may have resource room instruction only

for particular problem areas like reading and language arts. The flexibility of
the resource room plan allows it to accommodate the different needs of both    See Figure 9.1
teachers and children.

One trend is to have resource teachers provide their services in the
regular education classroom, not in a separate resource room. This promotes
greater transfer of learning and greater maintenance of learned concepts than
if resource help is given in a special setting (Gearheart, 1980).

Although the resource room is gaining popularity as an instructional plan
for educating children with special needs, its efficacy is rather presumed than
well documented. But in one study of children with learning disabilities,
Sabatino (1971) found evidence indicating that daily contact (40-minute
sessions) with the resource room teacher was more effective than semi-
weekly 30-minute sessions. Until research suggests otherwise, the resource
room will probably remain a model for educating children with special needs
within the mainstream.

*Diagnostic-prescriptive teaching center.*    The idea of a diagnostic-prescriptive teaching center is relatively new. In this plan, children are taken for short
periods of time to in-school centers staffed by a team of special educators and
diagnosticians. The center staff members assess the child's performance and
develop an individualized educational strategy. The child returns to the
regular education class, but instruction is based on the program the center's
staff recommends.

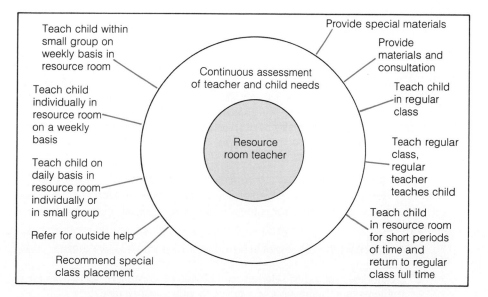

FIGURE 9.1    Service Alternatives for the Resource Room Teacher

## SPECIAL CLASS PROGRAMS

Special class programs provide a self-contained instructional environment for the child who is unable to profit fully from education in the regular classroom. Classes of this kind are usually no larger than 10 to 15 students and often have an aide for the teacher.

*Special education class.*  Self-contained special classes are designed for children who cannot keep up with the pace of instruction in a regular education classroom. Generally, the special education class consists of a group of children identified as exceptional and in need of extraordinary treatment, for instance, students who are mentally retarded, emotionally disturbed, or learning disabled. Children may receive all their academic instruction in the self-contained class or they may divide their academic day between self-contained class instruction in some subjects and regular class instruction in others. Although special class students usually participate in regular physical education, art, and music classes, they are segregated from the mainstream of education.

For years, studies and reviews (Cassidy & Stanton, 1959; Dunn, 1968; Johnson, 1962; Rubin, Krus, & Balow, 1973) have been questioning the efficacy of special class programs for children who are handicapped. In recent years a strong movement has been afoot to keep students out of special classes, since these classes do segregate the special student from the regular education students (Lyssky & Gartner, 1987; Skrtic, 1986; Stainback & Stainback, 1984; Wang, Reynolds, & Wahlberg, 1986; Will, 1986). But the special class may be the only public school setting that is educationally appropriate for some students. Commenting on the special class, Dunn (1973b) has stated:

> The self-contained special-class plan has been most severely criticized when used with slow-learning and disruptive children. Too often the plan has been used to put out of sight pupils the regular teachers do not want. It is to be hoped, however, that this practice will not disguise the appropriateness of the plan, especially for children with severe learning disabilities and for younger children. Certain of these children may need an intensive, specialized curriculum to learn specific skills so as to take a greater part in the regular school program later in their school careers. (p.28)

In other words, when used to educate those students who require it, the self-contained program is a viable service delivery model. Mercer (1987) has set the following criteria for times when the special class is deemed appropriate.

1. The special class teacher should be trained to teach the types of students in the class.
2. The students should be selected on the basis of learning or social-emotional problems, not on the basis of socio-economic status or race.
3. Each child should receive intensive and systematic instruction tailored to his unique needs.

4. A wide variety of teaching materials and resources should be available to the teacher.
5. The class size should be considerably smaller than a regular class.
6. A variety of teaching styles is needed to accommodate the different needs of the pupils.
7. Each pupil's progress should be constantly monitored. Reintegration into the mainstream should be considered when it appears feasible.
8. The class should have administrative support. (p. 167)

## SPECIAL SCHOOL PROGRAMS

In the past, school districts placed the majority of their students who were mentally retarded in special schools. Under this arrangement, students were bused to a day school whose sole purpose was to serve exceptional students. The chief advantage of such special schools is that they exert complete control over the child's curriculum and daily life. They can arrange all the variables in the learning environment—scheduling, physical facilities, instructional climate, and so forth—to benefit the individual student most. But the absence of contact with normal peers presents an unrealistic picture of the world and eliminates the benefits that exceptional children could gain through modeling and socialization with other children. As a result, few school districts continue to use special schools for students who are mildly or moderately handicapped (although some districts still have special schools for students who are severely and multiply handicapped).

*Special day school.* A child whose handicap is so severe as to prevent functioning in a regular school may attend a special day school on either a part-time or full-time basis. In systems combining regular and special day schools, the children who are the most severely disabled are bused to a central school for part of the day for essential educational services not provided in their home schools. In systems where services for students who are retarded are not available in the regular school, they may receive their entire educational program in a special day school. In sparsely populated regions, it may be economically impractical to set up special classes in each local school, and the district may feel that it is "necessary" to use a special school instead.

Some educators would claim that all students—no matter how severe the handicap—should be placed in regular education schools (see Brown, et al. 1979).

*Special residential school.* In cases where a child who is retarded has educational and social disabilities so pronounced as to warrant round-the-clock attention, the child might attend a special residential school. Facilities of this kind have very low pupil-staff ratios, which benefits the students by allowing intensive instruction. Such segregated schools, however, deny pupils who are retarded the opportunity to interact with peers who are not handicapped, and in so doing contradict the principles of normalization and least restrictive environment of P.L. 94-142. Nonetheless, there are, and will continue to be, certain persons with severe handicaps who require the highly specialized treatment offered in residential facilities. Many of these children have physical disabilities that demand close attention. The environment of a residential school may, then, for some children who are severely retarded and multiply handicapped, be the least restrictive environment in which they can function effectively. Even then, according to P.L. 94-142, educators must monitor each child's progress in case a move to a less restrictive environment becomes possible.

## OTHER PROGRAMS

Hospital tutelage and homebound instruction are the two most common alternatives for school age children who are physically unable to be transported to school.

*Hospital instruction.*   Hospital instruction is usually temporary and limited to students who are recovering from an illness or accident. For children confined to a hospital or convalescent home for serious, chronic afflictions, however, hospital instruction is a continuing process. Itinerant or regular education teachers normally teach such children.

*Homebound instruction.*   Homebound instruction is similar to hospital instruction in that it is provided for students who are temporarily unable to attend school. Itinerant or regular education teachers usually furnish the instruction. Since it is costly and segregates the child, it should be a last resort.

As noted by Dunn (1973b), the characteristics of the child, the school, the parents, and the community influence a child's assignment to an educational program. Child-related variables include the nature of the disability, motivation, academic skills, and behavioral characteristics. School variables include the nature of the regular education class program, the availability of appropriate special education facilities, and the competence of special educators. Parental and community factors include parental support, home environment, and community services.

Although these factors influence placement decisions, the strongest determinant in keeping with the prevailing trend toward integration should be the attempt to educate children who are handicapped in as normal a setting as is feasible. The child should be integrated as much as possible within the school, the home, and the local community. In essence, programs that segregate children with handicaps from the normal environment are the least desirable expedient.

## REGULAR EDUCATION INITIATIVE

As previously mentioned, researchers and educators have long questioned the efficacy of special class placement for students with handicaps. Recently, the entire system of delivering services to students with handicaps has come under fire. Under the auspices of the U. S. Department of Education, Office of Special Education and Rehabilitation Services (Will, 1986), a proposal called the *Regular Education Initiative* (REI) is being advanced that recommends fundamental changes in the ways to educate students with mild learning handicaps, including those categorized as educable mentally retarded. The REI proposes a merger of special and regular education services to cause students with handicaps to receive educational services within the framework of the regular education system.

Proponents of the REI argue that current special education practices, particularly identification, categorization, and separation of services, have proven ineffective in meeting the needs of large numbers of students with mild learning handicaps. Specifically, proponents of the initiative state that children identified as having a mild handicapping condition are increasing at an alarming rate (Reynolds et al., 1987); that data are accumulating to indicate that methods used to classify students are questionable and arbitrary (Algozzine & Ysseldyke, 1981; Lakin, 1983); that teaching technologies and methodologies used by special educators are becoming less "special" and more like those of regular educators (Lilly, 1986); and that resource room placement, which is the most frequent placement, is no more effective than regular class placement (Glass, 1983).

Opponents of the REI argue that diluting or eliminating hard-won services for students who had been poorly served in or excluded from regular education programs without analysis of what will happen is dangerous (Keogh, 1988); that the potential of the regular education system to serve students with handicaps is untested; and that the resources to serve these students in regular education settings are not now available (McKinney & Hocutt, 1988). They also point out that charges that special education programs serving students with mild handicaps are inefficient and have failed to increase skills and achievement significantly in these students are based on research that is less than substantial and methodologically flawed (Hallahan, Keller, McKinney, Lloyd, & Bryan, 1988; Kauffman, 1987; Schumaker & Deshler, 1988).

What the initiative will do to alter service delivery models for students with mild learning handicaps, including those who are mildly retarded, remains to be seen. One positive outcome of the REI and the debate about it has been that, more than a decade after implementation of P.L. 94-142, special educators have begun to evaluate the effects of the law and the services students receive under it. If reevaluation results in improved services for students with handicaps in either special or regular education settings, the initiative will have provided a valuable service to all education.

## THE ROLES OF THE TEACHER AND THE LEARNER

The educator's goal in teaching is to identify adaptive behaviors for each individual and structure the educational environment carefully so that students will learn. Meeting this goal involves going through the steps in the educational programming process detailed later in this chapter so that the

In this chapter, the
terms *behavior*,
*skill*, and *objective*
are used
interchangeably.

student who is retarded *(a)* acquires a wide variety of adaptive skills; *(b)* learns when and where to use them; *(c)* generalizes specific skills to other settings; and *(d)* maintains the skills over time. The educator must keep these four objectives for the learner in mind. In this way, the tasks of teacher and learner will be complementary.

### ACQUIRING A WIDE VARIETY OF ADAPTIVE BEHAVIORS

Persons who are mentally retarded must function successfully in school, home, job, and community settings. To do so, they need skills in many areas, including self-care, mobility, communication, social interaction, academics, health and safety, leisure, and vocational pursuits. Teachers have to target useful learning objectives in all of these areas rather than focusing solely on traditional academic subjects. When teaching students who are severely and profoundly developmentally delayed, teachers often find that academic skills are neither relevant nor adaptive learning objectives and may concentrate entirely on skill areas like self-care, motor, and nonverbal communication.

### LEARNING WHEN AND WHERE TO USE THE SKILLS

Students who are retarded must learn to observe and respond to environmental cues which signal that a particular behavior is adaptive and appropriate in that setting. Along with being able to perform a skill to a certain level of mastery, students must recognize the proper conditions for its performance. For example, when is it appropriate to approach, shake hands, and introduce oneself to another person? At a party when a new person arrives, on the street to a complete stranger, or in a work setting while in the midst of completing a task? Or when is it appropriate to add? When making a withdrawal from a checking account, when estimating the total cost of groceries to be purchased, or when asked to find the product of two numbers? Or when should one reach and grasp an object? When handed a soft toy, a bowl of hot cereal, or when within reach of another person's hair or eyeglasses? Discrimination tasks like these require learners who are mentally retarded to observe each setting to determine relevant cues and then quickly and reliably decide which behavior from their repertoire is appropriate. The teacher must structure the educational program so that students learn to attend to relevant cues, make adaptive responses, and receive positive reinforcement for their efforts.

### GENERALIZING ADAPTIVE BEHAVIORS TO OTHER APPROPRIATE SETTINGS

Generalizing behaviors is a corollary of learning skills. The person who is retarded must be able to identify similar settings in which a behavior is appropriate and respond correctly in those settings as well. For example, obtaining lunch in a variety of fast-food restaurants, repotting several types of plants and flowers, and filling out job applications for different clerical jobs all (within each kind of situation) have similar but not identical elements that a person should recognize as cues for a particular set of adaptive behaviors. Also, the person must be able to generalize responses from the training situation to the real-life environment in which the behavior should occur. Many practitioners and researchers are paying more attention to this instructional challenge, as the increasing number of articles in the *Journal of Applied Behavior Analysis* and other journals shows. These articles focus on the use of generalization training techniques as integral parts of their programs.

## MAINTAINING THE PERFORMANCE OF NEW BEHAVIORS OVER TIME

Behaviors must continue in the persons' repertoire past formal training into future environments and situations that occur throughout life. Here again, the structure of programs can facilitate both generalization and maintenance of new behaviors through systematic manipulation of such program variables as training materials, instructors, and reinforcement schedules.

## SELECTING FUNCTIONAL BEHAVIORS

One key to successful educational programming is the selection of functional behaviors (Guess et al., 1978). A functional skill or behavior is one useful to students that gives them some control over their environment in terms of obtaining positive and consistent results. A student will probably not maintain a nonfunctional behavior over time. For example, the teacher may need to decide whether or not it is functional for a high school student who is mentally retarded to be able to identify Roman numerals (M, C, L, etc.) or to be able to name the parts of a sentence (simple subject, indirect object, etc.). Is it functional for junior high students who are moderately retarded who already have good fine motor skills to spend time randomly stringing beads? Teachers must ask if their particular students would benefit in the long run from this type of specialized training. Is the skill likely to be useful in the students' real-life environments? Is it age appropriate? Will students retain the skills over time? If the answer is no, teachers must choose more useful behaviors upon which to focus their students' time and attention.

Regardless of the student's level of functioning, the educator should ask the following questions when selecting each target skill for an individual's educational program.

1. Is it a functional skill? Is the skill one that will be useful and adaptive for that individual?
2. Will the learner be able to use the skill in the immediate environment(s)? Will use of the skill produce positive environmental consequences for the learner in daily interactions?
3. Will the learner be able to use the skill often? Often-used behaviors are likely to be maintained over time.

4. Has the student demonstrated an interest in learning the skill? If a student can demonstrate, verbally or nonverbally, a preference for learning a particular skill, this motivation increases the probability of carrying out a successful instructional program.

5. Is success likely in teaching this skill? The successful acquisition of a new skill is rewarding to both teacher and learner, and can make future success more likely.

6. Is the skill a prerequisite for learning more complex skills? For example, the fine motor skills of reaching, grasping, and releasing are prerequisites to various self-help skills like self-feeding and hair-washing as well as the skill of writing. The ability to identify different denominations of coins is prerequisite to paying for purchases in a store and verifying that the correct change has been given.

7. Will the student become more independent as a result of learning this skill? People who are mentally retarded have traditionally been primarily dependent on others' care for their needs. But most individuals with mild retardation can learn to lead totally independent lives; individuals who are moderately retarded can become productive and semi-independent in their daily living skills; and even individuals in the severe and profound categories can often learn some basic skills that make them less dependent upon others—for instance, using the bathroom independently, manipulating toys and other objects, moving around a room, or using a six-picture communication board (Gruber, Reeser, & Reid, 1979). Teaching independent skills means helping individuals exert the greatest degree of control possible over their environment and hence their lives.

8. Will the skill allow the student to qualify for improved or additional services, or services in a less restrictive setting? Frequently, specific criteria must be met for admission to a particular educational program. For example, young children may have to be toilet trained for admission to a day care program; adults may need to demonstrate good self-care and homemaking skills to be admitted to a group home in the community; and adolescents may need to demonstrate mastery of basic functional academic skills in order to be considered for enrollment in a vocational training program.

9. Is it important to modify a behavior because it is harmful or dangerous to self or others? Some individuals who are mentally retarded (usually individuals in the lower functioning levels) have learned maladaptive behaviors like rocking, hand-wringing, head-banging, or hitting by which they may not only interfere with learning other adaptive skills but also physically harm themselves or others. In structuring an educational program, teachers must use procedures to reduce these undesirable behaviors when they occur and to teach substitutes that will get the student social attention, stimulation, or another positive consequence in a more normal, productive way.

## CURRICULUM AREAS

The term *mental retardation* is used for children and adults with a very wide range of skills and needs. Therefore, curricula designed for individuals who are mentally retarded necessarily cover a wide range of content areas and levels of difficulty, even within each of the major subgroupings: severely and profoundly mentally retarded, moderately or trainably mentally retarded, and mildly or educably mentally retarded. Curricula designed for individuals who are moderately, severely, and profoundly retarded often work from cradle to grave, not just during the typical school age period of 5 to 18 years. With the recent emphasis on transitional planning, the concept of lifelong learning and programming is now being implemented with individuals who are mildly retarded.

### CURRICULUM FOR INDIVIDUALS WHO ARE SEVERELY AND PROFOUNDLY MENTALLY RETARDED

In the past, many people assumed that people who were severely and profoundly mentally retarded could not learn, and that their only needs were for physical protection and custodial care. Now we recognize that, given an appropriate instructional program, these persons can learn both to take an interest in and respond to their environment and to master basic skills in many areas.

One behavior prerequisite to learning almost all other skills is attending. Attending is actually a category of behaviors. It can include such skills as focusing the eyes, turning the head, and orienting the body toward a stimulus for a particular amount of time. Since much learning takes place through imitation, it is obvious that focusing attention is a critical first step in the learning process. Along with attending, typical curricular objectives for students who are profoundly retarded may include responding to stimulation, familiar people, and objects by cooing, smiling, relaxing, or moving body parts; such social skills as making eye contact or touching another person; motor and verbal imitation; gross and fine motor movements—head control, reaching, grasping, sitting, and protective behaviors; and following simple directions. Teachers try to increase and improve the variety, rate, and quality of the adaptive responses the child or adult can make.

Since many individuals who are profoundly retarded also have severe physical handicaps that limit voluntary movement, a comprehensive curriculum usually involves putting them into proper positions for work, play, and rest, passive exercise to encourage and permit functional use of their bodies and prevent further deformities from developing, and a variety of auditory, tactile, and visual stimulation that they would not normally have access to because of impaired mobility or sensory deficits. This group of learners is particularly challenging to teachers as they choose appropriate objectives, devise and select adaptive equipment (easy-to-grip eating utensils, communication boards, mobility aids), use appropriate rewards, and find ways to record each learner's progress toward objectives that reflect and highlight even very small improvements.

A curriculum for learners who are severely mentally retarded can include the elements described above along with more advanced skills in physical development, self-care, and communication and socialization. Often gestures, signs, or symbols are the preferred communication mode.

See chapter 8 for a discussion of early childhood special education service delivery models.

Since most persons who are severely and profoundly mentally retarded are identified at birth or soon after, educational programming can begin early, in either a residential (institutional) placement, day program, or home setting. School age and adult programs are also important in teaching daily living skills and in ensuring that the learner continues to use the adaptive behaviors previously learned.

Because of this population's special needs and medical problems, services often come not only from teachers and home trainers but also from occupational therapists, physical therapists, language specialists, and prosthetic equipment experts. All the service providers need to work as a team to create a coordinated, useful educational program for these students.

## CURRICULUM FOR INDIVIDUALS WHO ARE MODERATELY MENTALLY RETARDED

Learners in this category can benefit from multifaceted training that will eventually prepare them for semi-independent or supervised living and working situations. Self-care skills like toileting, dressing, self-feeding, and grooming are often worked on first, along with physical development and oral or signed communication. As students progress through a school age educational program, such areas as interpersonal interaction and social behaviors (in school, home, work, and community settings), functional academics like writing one's name, address, and telephone number, recognizing survival words like "exit," "ladies' room," and "poison," basic money use, counting, telling time, and constructive leisure activities (sports, crafts, gardening, puzzles) are included. For older students, the emphasis shifts toward acquiring good work habits (being on time, completing tasks), social skills critical for vocational success (Rusch, 1979), specific job skills, housekeeping chores (preparing simple meals or making beds), community-access behaviors (using public transportation and eating in restaurants), and human sexuality.

Postschool placement opportunities for learners who are moderately retarded often involve work activity centers or sheltered workshops, and , as more facilities become available in the community, placement at a group home (Janicki, Mayeda, & Epple, 1983). Educational programming continues in these settings to help individuals cope with the changing demands of their environment (Schulman, 1980).

## CURRICULUM FOR INDIVIDUALS WHO ARE MILDLY MENTALLY RETARDED

The mildly mentally retarded category represents the largest group of learners who are retarded and probably the widest range of skills and needs. Most learners who are mildly retarded are identified at school and not before, and they do not usually have significant physical or sensory impairments. The majority go on to live independent lives in the community involving home, marriage, job, and family. Few attend college, but some obtain postsecondary vocational training. Their home environments and causes of developmental delay vary widely; the teacher must consider them when structuring an educational program.

Curricular objectives in a program for children who are mildly handicapped are often similar to those found in a regular classroom. Academic subjects like reading, writing, and mathematics are normally taught, with the focus on functional academic skills that will enable the student to succeed in the community and at home. Reading is taught primarily for protective and informational purposes (reading food labels and recipes, newspaper ads, and signs) and secondarily for enjoyment as a constructive leisure activity. Writing involves such useful everyday tasks as filling out employment applications and writing business and social letters. Mathematics emphasizes all aspects of money handling, including budgeting. Other subjects include science, social studies, effective oral communication, health, and human sexuality. Older students learn about apartment living, marriage and family responsibilities, and community resources. All this is in addition to a heavy emphasis on job preparation, including skills like locating job openings in newspapers and displaying correct behavior during a job interview (Kelly, Wildman, & Berler, 1980). Many high school students who are mildly retarded have the opportunity to learn a trade through specialized, school-sponsored vocational training or on-the-job training in the context of a full- or half-day work-study program.

One additional skill area to target for students who are mildly retarded is assertiveness. Most adults who are mildly retarded live unsupervised in the community. Because they may interact at times with people who attempt to take advantage of them financially, socially, or sexually, they need to be able to refuse to do things that are against their wishes or judgment and follow through on their refusal. Instructional programs can give students the opportunity to learn and practice assertive behaviors for many occasions through role-playing and other techniques (Bregman, 1984).

The instructional materials commonly used in programs for students who are mildly handicapped, especially at the younger levels, often are similar to or even the same as those used in regular education classrooms. For example, learning centers can be used effectively with these students to individualize instructional tasks and promote active learning and independent functioning. Materials for older students with handicaps, especially print materials, are generally "high interest, low readability." These written materials are geared toward the more sophisticated interests of older students but are written at a lower grade level so that students can understand them more easily.

In all three of these curricular categories, objectives and materials frequently cut across categories. Even though guides to many excellent curricula for learners who are retarded state that they are geared to one category of student, they may also be very useful for students in the other classifications.

# EDUCATIONAL PROGRAMMING

Educational programming for students who are mentally retarded involves many related components. Educational programs must be designed, implemented, and evaluated systematically so that educators make decisions that have an optimal effect on the development of each learner.

The programming process we describe below can work for all educational programs, regardless of the learner's age, placement, or level of retardation. Based on an assessment of an individual's current skills and needs, the process first determines what specific skills the individual needs to learn to make successful functioning possible. Then it fixes on the best arrangement of the teaching-learning environment for facilitating acquisition and maintenance of adaptive behaviors.

## ASSESSMENT

The first step of the assessment process is determining exactly what skills the student already can do in each important area of functioning. Educational assessment techniques should obtain information about the learner that leads directly to development of an appropriate educational program (see chapter 3).

A comprehensive educational assessment should have several outcomes. First, it should give an overall picture of the student's functioning level. Second, it should pinpoint the specific strengths and weaknesses in the student's behavioral repertoire. Third, it should clarify the logical next steps in the student's development—often the next steps on the assessment scale. Instead of coming up with a single score or label, the assessment should yield many individual items of information and point to many different areas where instruction would be beneficial in moving the person toward more independent functioning.

A criterion-referenced or curriculum-referenced measurement of a student's mastery of specific, observable behaviors is usually more program-oriented than a norm-referenced measure of behavior (Howell & Morehead, 1987). Criterion-referenced assessments elicit specific information leading to the formulation of instructional objectives, while norm-referenced assessments are more useful for obtaining information for placement decisions. Many standardized achievement and intelligence tests are norm referenced.

Hundreds of behavioral criterion-referenced assessment tools are available. They include either a range of skill areas or a focus on one or two discrete areas (e.g., sight-word vocabulary, mathematical facts, and dressing behaviors). Tools vary in usefulness and objectivity, and the prospective users must examine them carefully and individually (Walls, Warner, Bacon , & Zane, 1977). Special care must be taken when selecting an assessment instrument for use with individuals who are profoundly retarded or multiply handicapped. Testers should use instruments that credit individuals who are lower functioning with rudimentary behaviors and slight improvements in skill levels. Many teachers choose to develop their own assessment tools as well. Several disciplines (for example, language therapy and physical therapy) have highly specialized but useful tools. In selecting one or more assessment tools, the professional must take care to match their complexity and difficulty with the functioning level of the student, so that the data collected are usable.

## GOALS AND OBJECTIVES

Teachers can draw on a number of sources to determine appropriate educational goals and objectives, remembering that a goal is relevant only to the degree to which it is functional for each individual. Goals and objectives can be drawn from curriculum guides geared for a particular population or from assessment tools that measure important adaptive behaviors, or one may develop them through careful observation of a learner's needs in everyday settings.

*Goals* usually refers to the broader, long-term purposes of educational programs. Examples of long-term goals might include improving self-care skills like clothing selection, learning a trade, say, furniture refinishing, or learning to make a weekly home budget. *Instructional or behavioral objectives* usually refers to logically arranged sequences of specific, short-term steps toward meeting a program's goals. These objectives are important so that educational programs can be not only planned but also evaluated on the basis of learner progress toward meeting specific criteria. Behavioral objectives are statements that specify an observable behavior, the conditions under which it will occur, and the acceptable standard for accuracy against which to measure performance. Sample behavioral objectives for students at four different functioning levels might be:

☐ Given a help-wanted newspaper ad, the student will say the meanings of four abbreviations with 100% accuracy (mild).
☐ Given five coins of five different denominations, the student will arrange them in order from most valuable to least valuable at least four out of five times (moderate).

☐ Given a toothbrush, toothpaste, and a cup of water, the student will brush teeth, moving brush along all surfaces and using a circular brushing pattern for at least 2 minutes (severe).

☐ When his name is called, the student will maintain eye contact with the teacher for at least 2 seconds within 5 seconds of the cue (profound).

## METHODS

Instructional methods involve actively structuring the learning environment to promote learning of targeted objectives. Specifically, the teacher is concerned with choosing appropriate antecedents and consequences of behavior so that learning can take place efficiently and effectively. These variables and corresponding instructional strategies and techniques are discussed later in this chapter.

## MATERIALS

The teacher should choose instructional materials that help promote active learning of targeted skills. Materials can run the gamut from texts and other print materials, workbooks, dittos, audio- and videotapes, records, films, models, realia, and games and toys, to teaching machines, computers, programmed learning materials, and prosthetic equipment. Teachers should use materials that closely match the student's ability level and lead directly to skill acquisition. Materials geared for regular education classrooms can often be used or adapted, particularly for students who are mildly handicapped. Many teachers and other specialists develop their own instructional materials, which are usually less expensive than commercially produced materials and often motivate their students more because they can be personalized.

## ACTIVITIES

Teachers also plan individual and small and large group activities that help in the acquisition of target behaviors. Activities can involve performing motor behaviors, talking, gesturing, writing, role-playing, sorting, counting, and so on. Activities should be varied to add interest to the curriculum and should provide many opportunities for learners to make active responses. Whenever possible, they should take place in the real-life environment (such as a store or laundromat), so that the transition from the simulated to the real-life environment is easier.

## EVALUATION

Learners' progress toward targeted objectives needs to be measured regularly. Progress—or lack of progress—signals teachers when to move on to more complex objectives and when to change instructional methods, materials, and activities to avoid failure situations and facilitate success. Progress data to guide educators in the decision-making process may be obtained in many different ways and can be collected on a daily or a weekly basis.

The six-step educational programming process we have described helps achieve an integrated educational program based on individual students' needs. It is closely related to the process and requirements P.L. 94-142 mandates for the Individualized Education Plan (IEP).

## THE INDIVIDUALIZED EDUCATION PLAN

Every child who is handicapped has an Individualized Education Plan, which outlines and integrates the educational programming process we have discussed. Programs that serve adults who are mentally retarded or preschoolers with handicaps sometimes call their plan by a different name, such as *Individual Habilitation Plan* (IHP) or *Individual Family Service Plan* (IFSP), but these plans usually contain components similar to the IEP's.

IEPs contain seven major elements:

1. *Statement of present levels of functioning.* The assessment process determines these levels.
2. *Prioritized annual goals.* Goals may be selected and arranged in order of importance using the criteria for selecting functional behaviors discussed earlier in this chapter.
3. *Short-term instructional objectives.* Short-term objectives should be behavioral objectives that provide a clear direction for instruction and ongoing evaluation of student progress. Many references are available that identify and discuss suitable learning objectives for a wide range of learners who are mentally retarded (Haring, 1977; Kolstoe, 1976; Snell, 1987; Stephens, Hartman, & Lucas, 1978; Van Etten, Arkell, & Van Etten, 1980).
4. *Special education and related services.* Especially for students with more severe handicaps, services in addition to those of a classroom teacher are needed in order to have a program that meets all of the child's educational needs. Services may go directly to the child (speech or physical therapy or special transportation), or they may take the form of family services delivered by a psychologist or parent trainer.
5. *A statement describing the extent of the child's participation in regular educational programs.* The extent of participation (which can legitimately vary from no participation to almost full-time involvement) varies according to the child's special needs and limitations and is determined by the expected benefits on a case-by-case basis.
6. *Time line of the initiation and duration of services.* Services must occur as much as and in the order that the interdisciplinary team schedules.
7. *Objective criteria and evaluation procedures.* By fixing on salient behavioral objectives, gearing instruction directly toward their acquisition, and using reliable and valid devices to record behavior regularly, the requirement of objectivity and evaluation can easily be met.

**THE INTERDISCIPLINARY TEAM**

The interdisciplinary team has the task of providing a comprehensive, appropriate educational program. According to P.L. 94-142, the role of the interdisciplinary team includes making placement decisions and formulating and implementing IEPs. The rationale behind the use of an interdisciplinary team is that students who are mentally retarded (as well as students with any type of handicapping condition) have a wide variety of needs that can best be met through input from people with a broad range of training, experience, skills, insights, and perspectives. Team members can be, for example, teachers, psychologists, school administrators, parents, student advocates, nurses, social workers, physical, occupational, and language therapists, and even the student affected. Each has an important contribution to make to the team effort. The needs of the individual student determine the exact composition of the team. Often the team grows in size with the severity of a student's handicaps. The team must make a coordinated effort to decide about such critical areas as assessment tools and methods, instructional objectives, educational placement, instructional strategies, and evaluation. To maximize effects and avoid duplication of efforts, teams should meet regularly to plan and review programs and should carefully delineate each person's responsibilities. Unfortunately, teams do not always function as smoothly in practice as they do in theory, in part because of the very heavy case loads that many professionals carry. One recent development that is a potential time-saving device for interdisciplinary teams is the use of microcomputers. Microcomputers enable team members to collect and store student data efficiently, analyze these data rapidly and accurately, and produce multiple, legible copies of reports easily for use in educational planning (Smith & Wells, 1983; Nolley & Nolley, 1984). Microcomputers have the additional advantage of freeing team members from routine, time-consuming paperwork, allowing more time for direct service to handicapped individuals.

# CHARACTERISTICS OF STUDENTS WITH MENTAL RETARDATION AND IMPLICATIONS FOR EDUCATIONAL PROGRAMMING

In earlier chapters we saw that several characteristics are typical of many learners who are mentally retarded and should be considered when structuring educational programs. The first characteristic is the tendency to have an external locus of control; that is, individuals who are mentally retarded may think they have little control over the environment or the consequences of their actions. The teacher can use several strategies to help students become more internally oriented. First, students must acquire skills that are adaptive and functional, so that they actually achieve a measure of control over their environment. Second, instruction should teach the students to associate their actions with their consequences, and then to anticipate probable consequences so that they can choose appropriate behaviors. A very effective strategy for teaching this type of skill is role-playing, which allows the student to practice repeatedly, in a nonthreatening situation, choosing and using suitable adaptive behaviors. Another strategy involves the use of a social learning contract that spells out, in writing or in pictures, the environmental factors linking various situation-specific behaviors and their possible positive, negative, and neutral results.

*A variety of adaptive techniques can help students who are mentally retarded.*

A second characteristic to consider is the high expectancy for failure shown by many learners who are mentally retarded. This negative orientation is readily understandable, as many people who are mentally retarded have long histories of failing to learn new skills, usually as a result of poor (or nonexistent) educational programming. Not only may they anticipate failure when trying to learn new tasks; they may even refuse to attempt them at all.

Teachers can counteract this nonproductive trait in several ways. First, they should look closely at the results of their assessments and set reasonable, achievable goals and objectives based on the student's demonstrated level of functioning in each skill area. Second, they should structure the instructional program for success by breaking down objectives into small learning steps (via task analysis) and using a rich schedule of positive reinforcements. Third, they can reward effort and improvement as well as perfect performance. These and other similar strategies can help to make students more willing to try new tasks and lead to positive comments—"I can do it"—which indicate that the student expects to succeed, not fail.

A third characteristic of learners who are mentally retarded is outer-directedness, or a tendency to rely on external cues or instructions for behavior. For example, a student who needs help with work, may always wait for the teacher to notice the problem and give advice and instructions. Teachers can reward more inner-directed behaviors such as actively asking the teacher for help or independently identifying several possible solutions to the problem and then trying each one until the solution is reached. In every case, teachers must look beyond general characteristics to plan programs based on each individual's characteristics.

## INSTRUCTIONAL METHODS

In this section we describe methods to help students learn new, adaptive behaviors and eliminate inappropriate ones from their repertoires. After a look at the principal environmental variables that affect learning, we briefly review several educational techniques. Before teachers decide to try one or more of these techniques, however, especially those designed to reduce inappropriate behavior, they should read and study further to ensure that each technique is correctly used.

Many of the methods below are characteristic of good educational programming in general and are not by any means the sole property of special education. But some of the strategies are particularly effective with students who are mentally retarded, and their effectiveness stems from their having been developed to address learning problems of this group of students.

## LEARNING

The past decade of research in special education has seen the discovery of some important relationships between teaching and learning. These findings are shifting attention from speculation about the internal circumstances of learning to systematic studies of the effect of environmental conditions on learning. Learning is an extremely complex process; yet the teacher can exercise much control over the environmental variables that affect it to make learning a more efficient and successful experience for students who are mentally retarded.

The conditions or events that precede behavior are often referred to as *antecedents* and include such things as scheduling, environmental arrangement, and presentation of materials, verbal directions, or other stimuli. All these events and conditions, when skillfully arranged, can increase learning. *Consequences* like rewards or punishments can, if made contingent on the occurrence of appropriate or maladaptive behavior, greatly facilitate learning as well. Figure 9.2 illustrates the relationship of antecedents, consequences, and behavior. The effective teacher learns and uses strategies and methods that ensure that positive behavior change, or learning, takes place. One produces such a learning system by manipulating both antecedent events and contingent consequences for each child.

Although teaching takes many skills, the true and only test of its effectiveness is whether a new skill is learned. Obviously, if the student learned, the instruction was effective; if not, it was ineffective. The interaction and relationship of antecedent and consequent events in the learning process is paramount.

Before we continue, however, one important question must be resolved. What is learning? *Learning* has been defined in many ways, as the acquisition of knowledge, skills, and attitudes, for example, or as the development of awareness and insight. In any case, a change in behavior demonstrates learning. The change in behavior may indicate the acquisition of various bits of knowledge, skills, and attitudes; without these important changes in a student's observable actions, we have no way to determine that learning has occurred. Therefore, instruction must focus on teaching observable, measurable behaviors to individuals who are mentally retarded. This orientation is commonly called the behavioral approach to teaching and learning. An abundance of further information on behavioral techniques and documen-

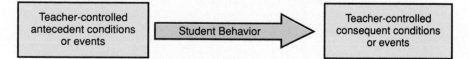

FIGURE 9.2    Paradigm of Teaching and Behavior Change

# COMPONENTS OF EFFECTIVE INSTRUCTION

Much time is spent discussing the effectiveness of programs, materials, and people. Most programs implemented today, educational or other, include mechanisms for evaluating effectiveness. However, what does "effective" instruction mean? On a general level, responding to this query is relatively easy. An answer to the question would probably imply that some type of progress or learning takes place. Reflection obscures the meaning of this question, making it difficult to answer.

Other related but more specific questions—To what specific skills are we referring: academic, social, or what? Does time come into play here; is rate of learning important?—are critical to any analysis of effective instruction. Moreover, effective instruction implies the most facile acquisition of a wide range of knowledge or skills in a psychologically healthy, appropriately structured learning environment. Furthermore, effective teachers do certain things called components of effective instruction.

The figure below highlights a number of significant facets of effective instruction (from a teacher's orientation) that helps learning occur. The essential components are divided into three phases, although some overlapping exists. For a more extensive discussion of this model, see Polloway et al. (1989).

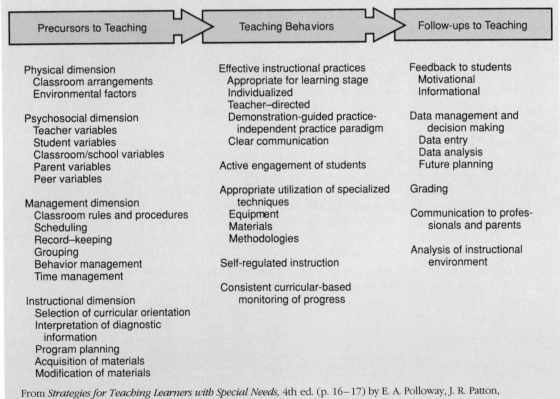

From *Strategies for Teaching Learners with Special Needs,* 4th ed. (p. 16–17) by E. A. Polloway, J. R. Patton, J. S. Payne, and R. A. Payne, 1989, Columbus, OH: Merrill.

tation of its numerous applications to teaching skills to learners who are mentally retarded is available in textbooks (Martin & Pear, 1983; Polloway, Patton, Payne, & Payne, 1989; Repp, 1983; Sedlak & Sedlak, 1985; Snell, 1987) and in professional journals *(Journal of Applied Behavior Analysis; Behavior Modification; Journal of the Association for the Severely Handicapped; Mental Retardation).*

## ACQUISITION AND MAINTENANCE

We differentiate two specific stages of learning mentioned earlier in this chapter: *acquisition* and *maintenance. Acquisition learning* refers to the initial attempts at mastering a skill or a chunk of knowledge. *Maintenance learning* refers to the ability to retain this skill or knowledge over a period of time. Maintenance learning cannot be equated with memory, because maintenance implies more than remembering. It takes the learner from the initial grasp of a fact, a concept, or a skill during acquisition to its solid establishment in the response repertoire over time. Perhaps it can best be viewed as a combination of remembering and continued use of learned materials.

The differences between acquisition and maintenance learning give rise to several important teaching considerations. These include determination of needs at each stage relative to the antecedents and consequences of the targeted behavior.

First we consider the consequences of behavior. During the acquisition stage, the production or shaping of responses requires a continuous schedule of reinforcement. *Continuous reinforcement* is a one-to-one correspondence between behavior and consequence; every time the student performs the skill to be acquired, the teacher responds with a tangible or intangible reward. Examples might include praise for each button buttoned correctly or for every word or sentence read aloud correctly, or a token for every time a child raises a hand to speak. Whether word recognition, hand-raising, self-toileting, or using sign language is the particular skill targeted for acquisition, the more immediate the reinforcement, the greater the efficiency of the learning experience.

Students acquire new skills most efficiently through continuous rein-forcement, but they maintain them most efficiently through intermittent reinforcement. Research indicates that a one-to-one correspondence be-tween behavior and consequence is not so important during maintenance as it is during acquisition. In fact, behavior that has been reinforced intermit-tently after its acquisition tends to become very firmly established in the student's repertoire over time. During maintenance, reinforcement should be varied over time and frequency of occurrences. A teacher might reward the child at the end of every two or three pages or stories read, upon completion of dressing, or occasionally at the end of the day for appropriate hand-raising.

*Specific types of con-sequences to use are discussed in greater detail later in this chapter.*

Our second consideration is the relative necessity of antecedents for learning. During the initial stage, the teacher needs to present frequent and varied stimuli to ensure that the students will acquire the skill. For example, for a student who is mentally retarded to learn a vocabulary list, the same words may have to be presented often in a variety of ways—through flash cards, via the language master or computer-assisted instruction, written as spelling words, or cut out of magazines. The teacher may present the words several different times per day for a while. Once the student has learned the words to a certain level of proficiency, they will not have to be presented as often in formal training sessions, but can be maintained through periodic reviews incorporated into the student's reading assignments.

Third, based on the importance of continuous reinforcement and frequent, varied presentation of antecedents to learning, it follows that , for learners to acquire new behaviors, the instructor must teach them directly and intentionally. Educators, especially teachers working with students who are mentally retarded, must assume the responsibility to teach actively whatever students should learn and not to rely on incidental or chance learning. Only through direct teacher-student instruction can the requirements for antecedents and consequences be fulfilled. But during the maintenance stage, techniques ranging from worksheets to student tutors can play a valuable role.

Using the example of the vocabulary list, the student could be given one-to-one or small group instruction involving modeling during the acquisition of new words. Peer tutoring is another way to help the student acquire and practice this skill (Cooke, Heron, Heward, & Test, 1982). These approaches ensure that each individual student has frequent opportunities to respond to the stimuli (flash cards, and so on) and to receive correction or reinforcement immediately. After the child has progressed to a predetermined percentage of correct responses, self-directed seatwork or large group practice periods are probably sufficient.

Whether the skill is naming colors, writing one's name, collating papers, or doing long division, this change in teaching conditions is necessary to reflect progress from the acquisition to the maintenance stage of learning.

The differences between acquisition and maintenance learning dictate teachers' approach to meeting students' educational needs and to their subsequent class and lesson plans. Misuse and confusion of the teaching techniques for these two stages can cause two obvious problems.

Lindsley (1964) discussed the first problem clearly and succinctly, and his points continue to be valid today. The problem concerns the continued use of acquisition techniques for maintenance learning. For example, after a child has learned all the primary colors, teachers sometimes continue to teach the differences between red and yellow directly, when the child could easily handle an assignment with a worksheet or educational game. This type of teaching can be counterproductive for three reasons: *(a)* it wastes teacher and student time that could be spent on acquisition of other learning tasks; *(b)* it restricts the student from getting over what Lindsley calls the "acquisition hump" to go on to further skill development; and *(c)* the time could be better spent on maintenance learning of the task. He notes that "it is almost as unkind to crutch-trap a handicapped person as it is to deny him a crutch in the first place" (p. 65). Some teachers of students who are mentally retarded are prone to this fault. Such an error is due in part to the misperception that these students need to spend extra time and effort on acquisition activities even after they have mastered the skill.

Denying the crutch to the student is the second problem. This happens when an educator uses teaching techniques geared for maintenance during the acquisition stage, and it involves attempting to teach students who are mentally retarded new skills through methods that provide them opportunities to learn and work solely on their own, such as completing worksheets, sorting items, or viewing films. Rather than carefully programming new skills, this misuse makes students try to cope for themselves, without the continuous feedback and reinforcement they usually need for acquisition learning.

Avoiding these problems involves careful assessment of the student's skill development during instruction. As the student shows evidence of learning and improvement (i.e., reaches a preestablished level of correct performance), the teacher should gradually phase out the components of acquisition teaching in favor of reliance on maintenance activities. If the student has significant trouble with the transition, the teacher can reuse more frequent reinforcement and directive techniques before trying to move the child away from the acquisition stage (Lindsley, 1964).

## ANTECEDENT EVENTS

A teacher must understand and consider a number of strategies and techniques that are antecedents to learning. These include events or activities that prepare for, facilitate, and guide learning. The person who develops and perfects an array of antecedent instructional skills is building a solid foundation for becoming an effective teacher. As antecedents to learning, we discuss task analysis, formulation of class rules, prompting, considerations of classroom environment, the planning and scheduling.

*Task analysis.* Task analysis is one of the major skills that all teachers of students with learning problems must master, particularly teachers of students with all degrees of mental retardation. Through task analysis, the teacher sets a terminal learning objective and establishes a sequence of objectives that if mastered, will lead to the attainment of the terminal objective. Task analysis is the breaking down of a large skill into its component behavioral parts. For example, using the telephone involves recognizing numbers, matching numbers on paper to those on the dial, dialing the phone, speaking appropriately into the phone, and using the phone book. Making a bed involves assembling two sheets, a blanket, a pillow, and a pillowcase and putting each one on the mattress in a particular order. In both examples, each subobjective can be broken down into yet smaller steps, and each component can be separately and directly taught. How far each task must be broken down depends upon the learning needs of the student; in general, the more severely handicapped the student, the more minutely the task must be analyzed.

In some cases, a sequence of subgoals for a particular task is available to the teacher in the form of diagnostic tests, teacher manuals, commercial teaching programs, or curriculum guides. For instance, a person who wanted to know something about the steps required for self-feeding could obtain this information from a tool like the Balthazar Adaptive Behavior Scales (Balthazar, 1971, 1973). This test breaks down self-feeding into small sequential steps that greatly help the teacher plan and execute a program to teach self-feeding. In the area of language, a teacher can obtain a sequence of steps for teaching language from a number of commercial language programs. One resource that is widely used with students who are mentally retarded is DISTAR (from Science Research Associates), which begins with something as simple as teaching single statements like "This is a cup" and moves to teaching complex statements like "Hand me all the cups that are blue and are not broken." Similar programs are also available in the areas of mathematics and reading, and many programs focusing on self-help skills for students with more severe handicaps are on the market as well. But not all of what needs to be taught is readily available in commercial form and the individual teacher must analyze various tasks and determine subgoals.

*Rules.* Another antecedent to behavior involves classroom rules. Many children, and most children who are mentally retarded, seem to function best in situations in which they know what is expected of them. Students need to be aware of what will and what will not be tolerated. Explanation, demonstration, and posting of classroom rules prior to any violations is often a sound practice in antecedent instruction. Students who are mentally retarded need not be placed in a situation of having to test limits to determine classroom rules, since the teacher can explain acceptable and unacceptable behavior. Classroom rules should be few in number, clearly defined, written or illustrated by pictures, and posted for quick referral. Consequences, both positive and negative, should follow consistently when students obey or break rules. Regular review of the rules facilitates learning them, as do immediate notification to violators after each and every infraction and frequent praise for students who obey the rules.

*Prompting.* Prompts are antecedent stimuli presented to the learner along with the task being taught in order to increase the chances of a correct response. Prompting consists of a variety of techniques, including physical prompts, verbal cues, highlighting or accenting, and imitation.

Becker, Engelmann, and Thomas (1971) have published guidelines for increasing the effectiveness of prompting. The teacher should gradually withdraw or fade out all prompts until they are no longer necessary. The prompt used should be the least possible one, in order to facilitate fading. The instructional task stimuli should precede the prompt to make sure the learner attends to the task rather than to the prompt.

*Physical prompts.*   In physical prompting, the teacher assists the child in motor movements. For example, a teacher can teach a child to raise the arm toward a toy by firmly holding the child's wrist and raising the arm until the toy is touched. In this example, the prompt can be faded as the child begins to exert some control by the teacher's just starting the arm movement and reducing the pressure of the grip to barely holding or touching the wrist. Eventually the teacher does not need to touch the child's wrist at all.

*Verbal cues.*   Verbal cues can accompany the task and assist in producing the correct response. Voice inflections and verbalization (modeling) of the correct response are two common ways to use this technique. For example, learning the names of colors can present difficulties for young children who are mentally retarded. For a child who can respond correctly to all primary and secondary colors except orange, the following procedure could be implemented. The teacher shows the child an orange block, holds it up, and asks, "What color is this?" Before the child can answer incorrectly, the teacher says, "Orange." Within a very few trials, the child should respond simultaneously. Gradually the teacher can fade the cue by reducing the vocal prompt until it is inaudible but continuing to imitate the mouth movements of the response "orange." These cuing lip movements can also be eliminated over time.

*Highlighting.*   Building cues into instructional materials can mean highlighting or accenting some critical features or dimensions of one correct response among several choices. Some of the most common ways are to make the correct response bigger, present it louder, or highlight it in a contrasting color or sound. These somewhat artificial cues should be faded as the student consistently selects the right answer in order to avoid dependence on them.

Another example of the use of accenting in the educational setting is placing lines on the floor to designate quiet study areas and play areas where talking is permitted. A similar technique can remind students of safety areas. For example, to teach a child to stay out of the way of a swing, the teacher can draw a line around the swing set and instruct the students not to cross the line while a child is seated in the swing. This technique is used at the high school level in many shop classes. Circles are drawn on the floor around the power equipment, and only one person can be in the circle at a time. In both cases, the circles or lines are antecedent stimuli used to prompt students not to get in the way of others. As students learn the safety rules through a combination of praise and negative verbal feedback, the lines are no longer needed and can be faded out.

***Imitation.***    Students who are mentally retarded learn a lot through imitating the behavior of others. It is imperative that teachers stay aware of the power of such learning and keep in mind the fact that individuals who are mentally retarded sometimes imitate inappropriate and appropriate behavior indiscriminately. Having good models—both adults and peers—is of paramount importance. Modeling involves both antecedent events (the model actually demonstrating the behavior) and consequences (positive reinforcement for correctly imitating the modeled behavior). For the teacher wishing to improve imitative learning in the student, three components need to be kept in mind: simplify, demonstrate, and repeat.

To simplify imitative movements, a teacher may need to exaggerate, to restrict actions to short time spans, or to model in some sequence moving from simple to complex. For example, in teaching a child to greet other people, a teacher initially could model the handshake and verbal hello, and later, perhaps through modeling or other means, work on the qualitative, more nuanced skills—eye contact, tone of voice, and duration of interaction.

Some children may find it difficult to imitate no matter how well the behavior is demonstrated. If the student has difficulty imitating, the teacher must actually teach imitation, either motor or verbal. Imitation usually is taught by a combination of instruction, demonstration, and prompts.

***Classroom environment.***    Lindsley (1964) coined the phrase *prosthetic environment* to refer to environments designed to facilitate learning. Without question the classroom environment should be considered an important part of the process of learning, particularly with respect to providing appropriate antecedents to learning.

Prosthetic environmental strategies can include seating (or prone position) arrangements that stimulate response and discourage distractions, audiovisual equipment that assists in highlighting and emphasizing important points, charts that constantly remind students of certain rules, furniture and areas that encourage interaction and sharing, manipulative games that promote the development of fine motor skills, and mobiles and other stimulating items that vary in color, texture, and size to attract the attention of the students with more severe handicaps. Not too long ago the majority of special education classes were small, underequipped, and located in undesirable areas of the school building. Even today, many classrooms fit this description.

Certainly all schools have physical limitations, but regardless of the physical barriers and restrictions, the teacher must create an environment that allows for small group instruction, individual work, and nonseated activities. For students with multiple handicaps whose mobility is impaired, the environment must be flexible enough to allow them to be positioned in a variety of ways and locations. Whether the classroom is small and self-contained or part of an open-classroom pod, flexible arrangements are essential for developing a prosthetic environment.

*Planning and scheduling.*    The schoolday schedule is seldom put together so as to increase opportunities for learning, but the importance of a well planned schedule cannot be overemphasized. Tempo and pace of instruction are dramatically affected by the schedule of daily events. By weaving interesting, creative, and exciting activities through the day and by alternating kinds of activities (seatwork, individual instruction, group instruction, and verbal, motor, and writing activities), teachers can plan a program that will be interesting and enjoyable as well as educationally profitable.

To schedule well, the teacher needs to develop a daily plan made up of a series of specific lesson plans. The daily schedule ensures both that there will be enough activities for the day and that there will be enough time for each activity.

*Lesson plans.*    A well planned daily schedule helps the teacher in effective instruction. After the teacher has determined students' specific needs, lesson plans slot concrete activities to meet those needs. A lesson plan focuses directly on the learning objectives in the child's IEP. In the lesson plan, the teacher states exactly what to teach to each student and how to teach it. The important aspect for teachers is not the specific plan format but the information about the skills they plan to teach. Figure 9.3 illustrates a typical lesson plan.

## CONSEQUENT EVENTS

No matter how well the teacher presents the antecedent events, learning cannot take place without consequences that signal the students whether their responses are correct or incorrect.

Consequences may be items, activities, or events. They must come immediately after the response as well as be contingent upon it. To be *contingent* means that the consequence occurs if, and only if, the behavior precedes it. It serves to increase or decrease the behavior it follows.

*The functions of consequences.*    Consequences are feedback mechanisms that predominantly serve two functions: *(a)* to motivate children, and *(b)* to control children who act inappropriately. Motivation implies the need to increase some behaviors; control implies the need to decrease certain responses. Behaviors in both situations can be either academic or social.

We must emphasize that the effect of a particular consequence on behavior is entirely an individual matter, for what seems reinforcing to one person may be neutral or even punishing to another. The educator must choose consequences on an individual basis and use them only so long as they have their intended effect. One can only know what works when detailed records are kept on each student's daily progress.

---

**Student:** Joan Boaks

**Objectives:** Long-range—Student will name all primary and secondary colors on command; e.g.,"What color is this?" "Red."

Specific lesson—The student will be able to point to the correct colored object (red and yellow) upon verbal command (e.g., "Point to the red cup") at least 90% of the time.

**Materials:** Red cup, yellow cup, shield (blotter), raisins

**Method of Presentation:** Place the red and yellow cups upside down in front of the student. Shield the cup from the student's view with the blotter. While the cup is shielded, place a raisin under one of the cups (e.g., yellow), take the shield away and say, "Pick up the yellow cup." When the child picks up the yellow cup, let the child have the raisin. If an incorrect choice is made, say, "No, this is yellow" and take the raisin and repeat the process. Be sure to alter the placement of the cups so that the student does not learn placement rather than color.

**Evaluation of lesson:** Date_____

|  | Trials correct | Trials incorrect |
|---|---|---|
| Red | | |
| Yellow | | |

Total percent correct = _____

**Projected needs:**

**Child's reaction to lesson:**

---

FIGURE 9.3    Lesson Plan Format

***Motivation.***    Motivational consequences can accelerate either academic or social behaviors. Typical types of positive consequences or reinforcers used to motivate children who are mentally retarded are praise, food, toys, and games. For example, a student may be praised for completing a mathematics assignment, assembling a circuit board, making sure finished work is correct, keeping the head erect for 10 seconds, or following directions. Tokens, activities, or other positive consequences can also strengthen academic or social performance. General experience and an abundance of research suggest that children perform both quantitatively and qualitatively better when properly motivated by positive consequences used systematically.

Many types of positive reinforcers are available to the teacher, including social reinforcers, tangible items. activities, and tokens. Social reinforcers include such things as praise and physical contact like hugging or shaking hands (Hall & Hall, 1980). Common tangible reinforcers are food, toys, books, records, and notebooks. Recreational, sports, and even educational activities can also be positive consequences because they give students a chance to participate in something they find pleasurable. Tokens, in the form of poker chips or points, which can be exchanged for desirable tangible items and activities, can also be very effective in producing positive behavior change. Involving the student in self-charting of behavior and planning of contracts (Salend & Ehrlich, 1983) can increase the chances of success in any reinforcement program.

Several factors should be considered when using positive reinforcers. First, the positive consequences follow the appropriate behavior immediately. If there is a lapse in time, an intervening behavior, perhaps even an inappropriate one, may accidentally be reinforced. Second, in a sense, there is a continuum of types of reinforcers ranging from tangibles to activities to tokens to social. This continuum begins with reinforcers that are more artificial, in that they are not always available in the natural environment (how often will a child or adult obtain a tangible reward for doing a home or work task?). This continuum ends with more natural reinforcers like tokens (money is a token reinforcer with which most of us are familiar), praise, and attention. It is helpful to use reinforcers at the higher end of the continuum, if they are effective for a particular student, in order to prepare for the outside world. If the person responds only to lower level reinforcers, they may be used in combination with higher level ones so that the more natural consequences gradually become reinforcing. But teachers must take care in using food reinforcers to avoid such problems as allergies, weight gain, and so on (Shevin, 1982).

We need to mention one last factor about choice of reinforcers. The teacher has to be very creative in this area, especially when working with individuals who are profoundly retarded or multiply handicapped who may not be motivated by praise, tangible items, tokens, or even food (they may have eating and digestive problems). In such cases, the teacher can try auditory, visual, and tactile stimulation like music, colored lights, rubbing with lotion, and water play to see if they are effective reinforcers (Wolery, 1978).

*Control.*    Control consequences are commonly used to decrease or decelerate disruptive, disturbing, or other inappropriate behaviors. These consequences present an unpleasant event contingent upon and immediately following an undesirable behavior, causing the behavior to decrease in frequency. As for positive, motivational consequences, negative, control consequences must be chosen on an individual basis. Mildly unpleasant consequences (for example, ignoring, verbal reprimands, loss of points or privileges) should be tried before resorting to more restrictive consequences (e.g., time-out). Whenever negative consequences are used to decelerate inappropriate behavior, the teacher must always select an appropriate substitute behavior to teach to the student and use positive consequences to make this learning possible. For example, students who are frequently out of their seats may earn points exchangeable for recreational activities when they are in them and on task, while losing points for out-of-seat behavior. Or students may receive a loud no when engaging in self-stimulation like hand flapping but get praise and attention for using their hands in appropriate ways like playing with toys or feeding themselves.

The vast majority of teaching interactions with individuals who are mentally retarded should and do involve positive interventions, and only a relatively small proportion involve negative contingencies. But negative consequences are sometimes necessary.

Typical negative consequences employed in classrooms for students who are mentally retarded involve loss of points or check marks, loss of a special privilege, or loss of free time. These contingencies may be effective for reducing certain undesirable behaviors in some children.

Time-out is a procedure used to decrease inappropriate behavior. It involves withdrawal of positive reinforcement. Time-out involves the temporary removal of an individual from the setting in which the behavior has occurred, thus taking away any possibility of positive reinforcement. The student may be placed in a safe but nonstimulating area or room for a brief time. Upon returning to the original setting, the student is directed to engage in appropriate behaviors and reinforced for successful efforts. The combination of time-out and positive reinforcement is often effective in bringing about positive behavior change. One consideration in the use of time-out is that its effectiveness is due in large part to the high rate of positive reinforcement in the classroom and its complete absence in the time-out area. Without both elements, the procedure is of limited usefulness.

More aversive consequences are occasionally used with individuals who are mentally retarded and who have seriously self-destructive behaviors like head-banging, biting their own hands and other body parts, and rumination. Unpleasant tastes, smells, sounds, or sensations have been used effectively to reduce life-threatening behaviors in some individuals. Staff using these procedures must be expertly trained and well supervised during the actual implementation, and must prepare and carry out simultaneous positive programs to teach functional skills. Along with this discussion of using aversive consequences, we want to point out that many educators successfully employ only positive techniques to reduce inappropriate behaviors. These reinforce behaviors other than or incompatible with the inappropriate behavior and reinforce successively lower and lower rates of the target behavior until it is eliminated (Denny, 1980; Repp & Deitz, 1979; Tarpley & Schroeder, 1979).

Further reading and study are necessary before a teacher attempts any of the procedures mentioned in this section, particularly those involving negative consequences (Foxx, 1982).

Appropriate services for students who are retarded form a continuum ranging from regular class placement with special help to special residential schools. Effective teaching of students who are retarded requires careful assessment, detailed instructional planning, and individualized behavior and learning management—the same ingredients all good teachers use with their pupils. But in addition, teachers of students who are retarded need to choose curricula and specific educational targets that will be functional for their students and help them succeed in their everyday environments. Educational programs for students who are retarded often focus on practical daily living skills that increase students' independence rather than on academic skills. Teachers must be thoroughly familiar with the common learning characteristics of students who are retarded, and must match their instructional strategies and materials to each student's needs. It is particularly important that the teacher create a learning environment that increases students' chances for success by carefully analyzing the tasks, drawing up lesson plans and daily schedules, making students aware of classroom rules, and prompting desired responses. The consequences that students receive for making responses must be thoughtfully chosen if they are to be effective in motivating students to learn or to control behavior. The teacher must also know whether the student is acquiring or maintaining the skill. Teaching students who are retarded requires not only standard teaching skills but also specialized knowledge and careful management.

# CHAPTER 10

# Career, Life Skills, and Transitional Planning

O ur society places a great emphasis on each person's ability to support himself or herself and on that person's ability to contribute to society at large. Even people with conditions like mental retardation are not exempted from this social requirement. Yet statistics (Bowe, 1978; Hasazi, Gordon, & Roe, 1985; Levitan & Taggart, 1977; E. W. Martin, 1972; Mithaug, Horiuchi, & Fanning, 1985; Schalock & Lilley, 1986; Wehman, Kregel, & Seyfarth, 1985) have shown that many mentally retarded persons in our society are either unemployed, underemployed, or have difficulty retaining jobs. Many explanations for this vexing problem have been advanced. For example, vocational training programs for individuals who are retarded have often had a narrow focus; that is, they develop only one or two specific skill areas by design. Consequently they fail to teach the employment adaptability skills needed for independent functioning, adjustment to a variety of work environments, and maintenance of acceptable levels of performance (Gifford, Rusch, Martin, & White, 1984; Mithaug, Martin, & Agran, 1987). Some programs have prepared their clients for a job market that no longer exists. In some extreme cases, there is no career or vocational preparation program at all.

While this information is factually correct, it represents a negative or pessimistic view of career preparation for those who are mentally retarded. For instance, from Edward Seguin in the 1850s to Richard Hungerford in the 1940s to the present concern over career education, workers in the field of mental retardation have recognized the need to prepare each person with retardation to be a contributing member of society. In the 1850s, Edward Seguin firmly stated that occupational preparation should have a place in educational programs. A century later, Richard Hungerford outlined a comprehensive program of vocational education. His program, entitled

"Occupational Education," was designed to build vocational and social competence skills. The program included occupational education, vocational training, and vocational placements (Hungerford, DeProspo, & Rosenzweig, 1948). Today practitioners are seeking to provide more realistic vocational training for students who are retarded (including those who are severely and profoundly retarded), to integrate them into regular education vocational training programs, and to assist them in making a successful transition from school to the community. Whether they are optimistic or pessimistic about career programming for those who are mentally retarded, professionals in this area need to move forward in the development of stronger career preparation programs that prepare such individuals to be gainfully employed and to fit naturally into society.

In this chapter, we discuss past and present career and vocational programming practices for students who are mentally retarded. The chapter has two major sections. The first section takes a close look at the development of the concept of career education, elements of a career preparation program, transition programming, and a number of issues that the evolution of the concept of career education has raised. The second section of the chapter deals with the specifics of the later states of career education, that is, topics relating directly to vocational preparation. We explore such topics as vocational assessment, vocational placement and follow-up, and issues related to vocational education.

## EVOLUTION OF THE CONCEPT OF CAREER EDUCATION

Career education for all children became a national priority in 1971, when U.S. Commissioner of Education Sidney P. Marland called attention to the insufficient preparation of our nation's youth for careers beyond high school. Marland (1971) made three basic points: (*a*) career education is needed by all students, whether they will eventually work in a sheltered workshop or local plant or go to college; (*b*) career education should occur throughout the individual's educational career, starting in kindergarten and continuing into adulthood; and (*c*) career education is meant to give the individual a start in making a living. Marland's postulates about career education seem to have the following implications for students who are mentally retarded.

1. Since a person assumes varying roles throughout life, and these roles are a function of both the social system and the person's experiences, it is imperative that the educational opportunities of students with retardation allow them to learn to assume different roles in the society.
2. It is essential to view the person as a whole. Only by considering the varied aspects of a person's present circumstances and probable future circumstances can effective education be implemented. Thus, career education

for students who are mentally retarded requires a knowledge of each individual's career strengths *and* weaknesses.

3. Great knowledge and experience are necessary to reach specific career education goals. These goals are often complex and can be realized only through the cumulative effect of an educational program that proceeds from kindergarten through grade 12 and beyond.

4. Placement in real vocational situations is a vital part of education for each student. This situation is no less necessary for students who are mentally retarded.

5. All persons, including those who are mentally retarded, have a right to an education suited to their needs and capabilities.

## HISTORY OF CAREER EDUCATION

Writers have traced the history of career education from several different time periods preceding the rapid growth of career education in the early 1970s (cf. Cegelka, 1979; Herr, 1977; Hoyt, 1982; Kolstoe, 1981; Smith & Payne, 1980) to the contemporary concern over how to implement this concept most effectively. These authors do not always agree exactly where or when this movement began, but they generally concur that vocational education and related legislation have provided much of the framework upon

*The development of appropriate social skills is critical.*

which career education has been built. For example, Cegelka (1979) states that monies that were made available through the Smith-Hughes Act in the early 1900s secured the place of vocational education in the United States. She also states that such later legislation as the Vocational Education Act of 1963, extended vocational services to many groups who previously had not received such services, including students who are handicapped.

Smith and Payne (1980) report that events like the passage of the 1962 Manpower Development Training Act, the Vocational Rehabilitation Act (P.L. 93-112) and its accompanying Section 504 (1973) (essentially a civil rights act for the handicapped) and the concern of such major professional organizations as the Council for Exceptional Children (CEC) and the American Association on Mental Deficiency (AAMD; now AAMR) with this evolving concept have intensified its impact. They also point out that special education has played a major role in the solution of the career education movement. For example, from the early 1940s onward, special educators like Richard Hungerford and his associates have emphasized the need for students who are mentally retarded to develop occupational skills. This emphasis on providing direct work experiences led to the development of the cooperative work-study programs in the 1960s (Kokaska, 1968). These work-study programs for those with retardation proceeded from the premise that the school could provide only limited in-house work experiences. Industry in the community, educators felt, could offer much better and more realistic work experiences. Therefore, school personnel sought to establish cooperative arrangements with community industries. The schools' goal was to produce students with good vocational skills; the businesses gained people who had at least minimal job skills; and the students received educations that met their specific needs. Commenting on the merits of work-study programs, Dunn in 1973 stated that these programs had been one of the most innovative features of secondary curricula in the preceding decade (Dunn, 1973b).

While all of these movements were taking place, many people, including Marland (1972), noted with alarm that quite a few of the nation's youth were not involved in vocational preparation programs, that the dropout rate from the public school system was very high, and that most of the functional career preparation and training school age youngsters received came during the last year or two of high school. Disturbed by the lateness and brevity of programs to prepare students for different careers, Marland called for the formulation of a comprehensive, educationally based career program, and the concept of career education was born.

## DEFINING CAREER EDUCATION

Career education and vocational education are not synonymous; career education has a broader meaning. According to the Division on Career Development of the Council for Exceptional Children, "Career development is a process which facilitates responsible and satisfying life roles—that is, student, worker, family member, and citizen—through the utilization of teaching, counseling, and community interventions." Career education and vocational education both accept the idea that schools are supposed to prepare students for participation in the larger society, but they differ in their interpretation of this idea. Vocational educators attempt to prepare students to enter the job market as competent, employable wage earners. To this end, vocational education focuses on the high school student who will soon be seeking full-time employment. Vocational educators perform such functions as assessing students' work potential, helping the workers-to-be explore different work possibilities in their community, and giving a number of trial work experiences through which to identify their preferences. Career educators, on the other hand, see preparing students for participation in adult life as their mission, and career education's emphasis extends from the elementary grades through secondary school and beyond. Vocational education is actually in subcategory of career education. We can see that other aspects of the school curriculum—reading, writing, science, mathematics, family life education, consumer education, sex education—could also be subsumed under the broad heading of career education, because they are components of an educational program whose purpose is to prepare students for future life.

Yet career education is even more than the sum of these elements, because it is the unifying vehicle for ensuring that an individual has more than an even chance to become a contributing member of society. For example, in the past, most elementary pupils at some point would discuss different kinds of jobs and the workers who did them. But these discussions were often a matter of happenstance instead of part of the educational plan. With the adoption of career education, these discussions—at whatever school level—become a required part of the curriculum. Thus students will be continually exposed to different careers as they move up to higher grades. Career education also helps youngsters to see how such basic subjects as reading and mathematics will enable them to succeed at certain jobs.

## MODELS OF CAREER EDUCATION

Brolin (1978, 1986; Brolin & Kokaska, 1979) has described one of the most comprehensive career education models developed to date. This model is three-dimensional and consists of competencies, experiences, and stages. Brolin describes 102 subcompetencies that comprise 22 major competencies. These 22 major competencies are clustered into 3 curriculum areas: daily living skills (e.g. buying and preparing foods), personal-social skills (acquiring self-confidence), and occupational guidance and preparation (exhibiting sufficient physical-manual skills). The student can develop each competency during the four career education stages: career awareness, career exploration, career preparation, and placement and follow-up. In the career awareness stage, which extends through elementary school, the child learns about the value of working toward a goal and developing academic and social skills, and is introduced to 15 different career clusters. According to Herr (1977), these 15 clusters include the 20,000 job titles listed in the *Dictionary of Occupational Titles*. The 15 clusters are:

1. Construction occupations
2. Manufacturing occupations
3. Transportation occupations
4. Agribusiness and natural resources occupations
5. Marine science occupations
6. Environmental occupations
7. Business and office occupations
8. Marketing and distribution occupations
9. Communications and medial occupations
10. Hospitality and recreation occupations
11. Personal service occupations
12. Public services occupations
13. Health occupations
14. Consumer and homemaking occupations
15. Fine arts and humanities occupations

The career exploration period is devoted to studying examples of jobs within these clusters and measuring the child's interests and skills against the demands of specific careers. One goal during this stage is to demonstrate to each pupil that a range of possibilities exists within any job cluster. A file clerk, a secretary, and an administrative assistant are all office workers. Brolin sees this stage as occurring during late elementary school. Kolstoe (1975) argues, however, on the basis of his experience, that exploration should not be implemented until secondary school, probably late in junior high.

In the career preparation stage, students learn the actual competencies required in their chosen line of work. For pupils who are mentally retarded, the development of performance skills and attitudes for an actual job are stressed. The placement and follow-up stage involves placing students in a job and providing the assistance necessary for their success. These final phases require much coordination between the school and the community. As students pass through these stages, they should become increasingly able to assume the many roles that will be required of them at school, in the family, and in the community.

Clark's (1979) School-Based Career Education model consists of four elements: (*a*) values, attitudes, and habits; (*b*) human relationships; (*c*) occupational information; and (*d*) acquisition of job and daily living skills. Career awareness begins in kindergarten and continues through elementary school. Curricula for grades K–9 delineate specific goals for each of the four elements during this stage. Career exploration occurs during junior high school, and career preparation begins in high school and continues to postsecondary settings. Figure 10.1 illustrates Clark's career education model.

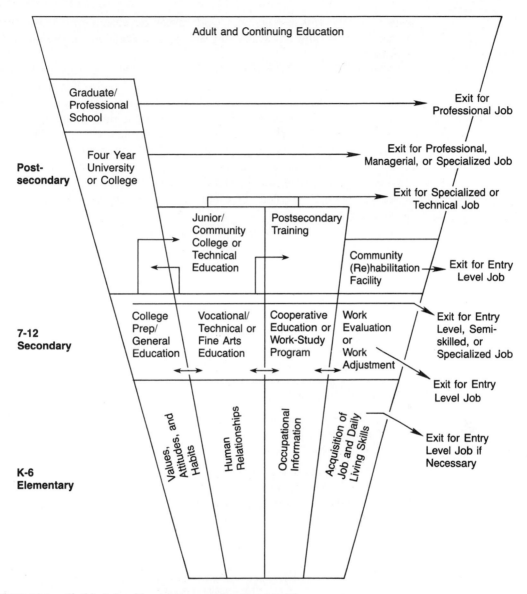

**FIGURE 10.1**    Clark's School-based Career Education Model

From *Career Education for the Handicapped Child in the Elementary Classroom* (p. 19) by G. M. Clark, 1979, Denver: Love Publishing. Reprinted by permission.

## TRANSITION PROGRAMS

Recently, local educational agency personnel have recognized the need to prepare students with retardation better for life after high school. The literature has documented this need, and it has been targeted nationally as a top priority (Will, 1984). This process has three major phases: (*a*) secondary level curricula, IEP management, and career development; (*b*) transition-al management; and (*c*) availability and appropriateness of postsecondary operations.

The prospect of adjustment by adolescents who are retarded to the world of work and community living depends greatly on how well various groups function. The cooperative efforts of local education personnel, vocational rehabilitation counselors, postsecondary education staff, adult service providers, and various community agencies that assist such young adults are vital to this transition process. There has been too little cooperation among these important groups, and there have been too few attempts to study the entire transition process (Johnson, Bruininks, & Thurlow, 1987; Polloway, Patton, Payne, & Payne, 1989; Peters, Templeman, & Brostrom, 1987; Stodden & Boone, 1987).

Figure 10.2 schematizes the transition process. The middle phase, transitional management, includes three alternative pathways:

1. No special services: Some students simply find their own way to the world of work, relying on their own resources. Some students have no other choice!
2. Transition with time-limited services: This option refers to short-term services (e.g., vocational rehabilitation, postsecondary vocational training) that lead to employment.
3. Ongoing services: This linkage refers to some type of employment with ongoing support for the worker and the employer. This concept of *supportive employment* is relatively new.

The Office of Special Education and Rehabilitative Services (OSERS) has identified transition as a national priority and has funded several major transition projects. Types of projects within each category are:

1. Service demonstration model projects
2. Youth employment projects
3. Postsecondary demonstration projects
4. Cooperative model projects
5. Personnel preparation projects

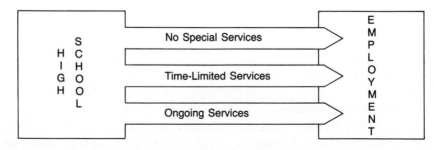

FIGURE 10.2   Major Components of the Transition Process

The goals of these transition projects are to: (*a*) maximize students' performance and movement through programs, (*b*) increase awareness of their interests, aspirations, and educational needs, and (*c*) increase availability by appropriate programming options. Generally, these programs are designed to identify appropriate interventions and provide training to facilitate the transition from school to life after school. According to Mithaug et al. (1987), model transition programs have four common elements: "(a) a range of services from generic to specific, (b) coordination of transition outcomes, (c) implementation of transition programs to prepare students for post-school life, and (d) instruction starting at early ages in community sites" (p. 500).

## MODELS OF TRANSITION PROGRAMS

Polloway et al. (1989) note that two key areas that models of transition programs can address are *life domains,* which include community involvement and citizenship; education and training in preparation for work, home and family, and leisure and recreation; and *support domains,* which include emotional and physical health and financial support. Figure 10.3 illustrates these areas of transitional planning.

Although there is some overlap, in practice transitional program models address these domains in two ways: (*a*) through models of career preparation and (*b*) through models of life skills preparation. Whatever the model selected, Patton and Browder (1988) have suggested that transition planning should involve families; and that secondary level curricula should reflect the availability of services and adult outcomes, involve interagency collaboration and cooperation, and be comprehensive, flexible, and responsive to changes in values, goals, and experiences.

Some exemplary career and life skills programs are discussed in the following sections.

*Career preparation.*   The Hawaii Transition Project (1987) is a multiyear project that encourages active parent participation in planning postschool options for individuals who are mentally retarded. A key feature of the project is the individualized transition plan (ITP). Depending on local needs, the ITP may be incorporated into the IEP, but unlike the IEP, which is a plan for acquiring skills and knowledge, the ITP is a plan for services. Figure 10.4 illustrates a typical ITP form.

Readers interested in a more comprehensive description of the Hawaii Transition Project are referred to Polloway et. al. (1989).

During the first year of a student's enrollment in the project, *initial transition planning* takes place. School representatives, the parent(s), and the student identify potential postsecondary services and placements and begin to match the student's needs with available community resources. Information about the student's transitional needs is communicated to appropriate community agencies. In the middle years, *active transition planning* occurs. School representatives and a transition team conduct

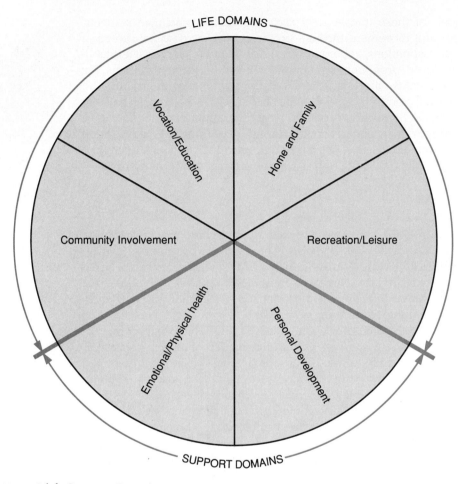

FIGURE 10.3   Adult Outcome Domains

From *The Hawaii Transition Project: Major Areas of Transition*, 1987, Honolulu: University of Hawaii,
Department of Special Education. Reprinted by permission.

vocational assessments and determine appropriate community agency referrals. Together, the parent(s) and the student investigate enrollment (e.g.,
Social Security Insurance [SSI], wait lists), while school representatives and
the transition team review programming implications and initiate IEP
planning to support the transition plan. In the final year, school representatives, the parent(s), the student, and adult service providers *facilitate
transition planning* through such activities as arranging cooperative programming, identifying transition coordination responsibilities, and finalizing
enrollment of the student in an appropriate postsecondary education
program or work setting.

| Individualized Transition Plan | | |
|---|---|---|
| Student _____ School _____ Grade _____ Student # _____ Date of Birth _____ Date of expected Graduation _____ | | |
| Transition Service Areas | Person Responsible | Time Line |
| Vocational/educational service goal: _____<br>Plan for this year*:<br>Residency/work documents:<br>____ Social Security     ____ Health certificate<br>____ Work permit     ____ State ID<br>____ Green card     ____ Bus pass<br>Transportation/mobility: | | |
| Community service goal: _____<br>Plan for this year:<br>Transportation/mobility: | | |
| Recreation/leisure service goal: _____<br>Plan for this year:<br>Transportation/mobility: | | |
| Home and family service goal: _____<br>Plan for this year:<br>Transportation/mobility: | | |
| Financial support service goal: _____<br>Plan for this year:<br>Transportation/mobility: | | |
| Health service goal: _____<br>Plan for this year:<br>Transportation/mobility: | | |
| *Place a check mark by all plans that will be addressed in the student's IEP.<br>Date of ITP meeting _____    ITP coordinator _____<br>Persons agreeing to ITP (signatures) _____    _____<br>_____    _____<br>_____    _____ | | |

FIGURE 10.4   Sample Format for an Individualized Transition Plan

From *The Hawaii Transition Project*, 1987, Honolulu: University of Hawaii, Department of Special Education. Reprinted by permission.

# EMERGING TRENDS IN TRANSITIONAL PROGRAMMING

In a recent special issue of *Exceptional Children* on the transition from school to adult life, guest editors Gary M. Clark and H. Earle Knowlton interviewed four respected authorities on transitional planning. In the following excerpt from that interview, Lou Brown, Andrew S. Halpern, Susan Brody Hasazi, and Paul Wehman respond with their personal views to a question about emerging trends in transitional programming.

*Guest Editors:* What trends do you see emerging now for the field in transitional programming?

*Wehman:* I see four trends, all of which seem to be developing at different rates. The first is that more and more parents and advocates are going to insist on real employment before students leave school. Prevocational, simulated, or other pretend types of work are increasingly in disfavor in many school systems; this will continue. Second, the segregated adult centers which have been spawned over the past decade and a half are now and will continue to change rather dramatically in the nature of services they offer. Center-based options will be rejected by students and parents, thus forcing local programs to become more industry-based in nature. Third, the eligibility requirements for vocational rehabilitation services are beginning to blur tremendously as more and more students, previously thought to be ineligible because of functioning level, are exhibiting vocational competence, thus placing greater pressure on rehabilitation agencies to provide services. Finally, more students are moving into better paying manufacturing positions and are less concentrated into the entry level service positions such as dishwashers or potscrubbers.

*Hasazi:* The recent focus on transition programming has led to a number of promising practices from both a learner-centered and systems perspective. First, during the high school years, students are having increased opportunities to acquire and use occupationally specific and social skills in a variety of paid and unpaid jobs in the community. This will allow students with handicaps to build a work history prior to graduation and increase their prospects for employment following high school.

Second, parents and professionals are spending a great deal more time together planning from a future-oriented perspective. Goals and objectives will be developed and implemented that address outcomes, such as building and maintaining a friendship network, planning for a place to live in the community, and placement in a job or postsecondary education program.

Third, because of the enthusiasm about and successful demonstrations of competitive and supported employment, adult services agencies are developing vocational service options that focus on employment as an outcome. These options will gradually replace day and work activity centers, and change the way sheltered workshops operate.

Finally, there is a trend in awareness of a need to train special educators and adult services professionals as employment specialists for placing, training, and maintaining individuals with handicaps in supported and transitional employment. This trend will require specialty concentrations in secondary special education and rehabilitation training programs.

*Brown:* I think several trends can be delineated.

First, unlike school, adult services are not guaranteed. Parents have become more aware of the vulnerability of their children and are more involved in lifelong planning. Second, the very nature of secondary education is changing dramatically for the better. In the past, many people were spending the adolescent years trying to take students with disabilities through normal infant development stages and phases. This, of course, resulted in 21-year-old people acting like young children. The trend now is to look at the requirements of adulthood and then devote the last 10 years of education to teaching students to behave as adults and to function as effectively as possible in integrated environments and activities.

Third, in the past, the goal of public school personnel was to prepare people with disabilities to spend the years from age 21 to 70 in segregated activity centers or sheltered workshops. If someone goes through an integrated school program at an immense cost and is then locked up in an activity center, a workshop, or an institution ward, we have failed that person, that family, and the taxpayers.

In my opinion, there are fewer obstacles to overcome in the process of securing integrated post-school services. More adult service agencies are providing integrated options and more professionals have the values, skills, and experiences necessary to provide quality services therein. Parents are playing a stronger role in advocating for integrated work options due to their increased involvement in integrated services throughout the school years.

Finally, there is a trend for people with disabilities to be afforded a wider range of work options as we move beyond the limited and stereotypic jobs currently offered. Ultimately, paid work and affirmative social relationships with nondisabled others will evolve if we professionals do our jobs proficiently.

*Halpern:* The first of two main trends that I see emerging in the field of transition is a broadening of the goals to include residential, social, and leisure dimensions, in addition to the vocational dimension. In fact, if we consider adjustment from the perspective of client satisfaction, it may turn out that vocational adjustment is less consistently valued by people with disabilities than are the other dimensions of community adjustment. Furthermore, it appears that the various dimensions of community adjustment are relatively uncorrelated with one another, meaning that success in one area does not guarantee success in any of the others. This implies that transition programs will have to be individually tailored to each dimension of community adjustment that is a desired outcome, and that the OSERS policy guiding the transition movement will also have to be broadened to accommodate the nonvocational dimensions as valued in themselves.

A second major trend that should emerge soon is a reawakening of concern for people with mild disabilities. During the past decade, there has been a clear and understandable focus of attention and resources on serving people with the most severe disabilities. Unfortunately, this has occurred somewhat at the expense of services for those with milder but still significant disabilities. As a consequence of this shift in emphasis, many people with "mild" disabilities are falling far short of their potential for achieving satisfactory levels of community adjustment. Transition services will have to be reoriented somewhat toward this group, which outnumbers those with severe disabilities by a ratio of at least 10 to 1.

From "From School to Adult Living: A Forum on Issues and Trends" by G. M. Clark and H. E. Knowlton, 1987, *Exceptional Children, 53*, pp. 546–554. Adapted by permission.

*Life skills preparation.*   The Adult Performance Level (APL) model was developed by the University of Texas at Austin as an adult basic education program and later adopted by LaQuey and colleagues (1981) for use in secondary special education settings. The APL is a two-dimensional model that integrates basic skills (reading, writing, speaking/listening/viewing, interpersonal relations, and computation) into the functional skills, termed *content/knowledge domains,* needed for daily living (consumer economics, occupational knowledge, health, community resources, and government and law). Table 10.1 provides some examples of tasks in the APL model of functional competencies.

See LaQuey (1981)
for a description of
adapting the APL
model to meet gradu-
ation requirements.

A distinct advantage of the APL model is that it can be used, with school system approval, to meet graduation requirements. Cronin (1988), however, cautions that the model is only a guide to programming. Educators must augment it in the areas of social skills and vocational training.

## CAREER EDUCATION AND MENTAL RETARDATION

Since the goals of career education are appropriate for all students, career goals for people who are mentally retarded are similar to goals for those who are not. How these goals become realized is the difference between the two types of students and is a function of the individual's general and specific characteristics.

To discuss this process for students who are mentally retarded, we need to distinguish between career education for those with mild and for those with moderate to profound retardation. The behavior of children and adults who are mildly retarded only minimally reduces their career options. The vast majority of them will be capable of independent living as adults, and many will no longer be labeled or recognized as mentally retarded after they leave school. (Individuals who are mildly retarded make up approximately 80% of those labeled "mentally deficient.") In contrast, those who are moderately to severely retarded often exhibit patterns of behavior that disrupt their learning and interaction with others so much that their career options are sharply limited. As adults, they will frequently be dependent upon support from others in order to function within the community. Throughout their lives, they are likely to be perceived as mentally retarded, or, at best, as different from their neighbors. (This group constitutes approximately 20% of the population of individuals with mental retardation.) Given these distinctions, we can see that the knowledge and skills each group masters will greatly differ, as will their particular career capabilities and needs.

Research on their community and postschool adjustment strongly supports the need for career education for students who are mentally retarded. The data for postschool adjustment come from studies employing different sampling techniques, different definitions of adjustment, and different statistical techniques. Consequently, inconsistencies of interpretation are common among these studies. Results show that persons with mental

TABLE 10.1   Tasks in the APL Model of Functional Competency

|  | Consumer Economics | Occupational Knowledge | Health | Community Resources | Government and Law |
|---|---|---|---|---|---|
| Reading | Read an ad for a sale | Read a job description | Read first aid directions | Read a movie schedule | Read about rights after arrest |
| Writing | Fill in income tax form | Complete a job application | Write a menu | Complete an application for community service | Write your congressman |
| Speaking, listening, viewing | Ask questions of IRS | Listen to an employer talk about a job | Listen to a doctor's directions | Use the telephone | Describe an accident |
| Problem-solving | Decide which house to rent | Decide which job suits you | Decide when to call a doctor | Use stamp machines in the post office | Decide which candidate to vote for |
| Interpersonal relations | Relate to a sales clerk | Be successful in a job interview | Interact with hospital personnel | Ask directions | Interact with police successfully |
| Computation | Compute sales tax | Calculate paycheck deductions | Decide how many times a day to take a pill | Calculate the time it takes to travel a distance | Calculate the cost of a speeding ticket |

From APL Model of Functional Competency, 1981, Austin: University of Texas. Reprinted by permission.

retardation have varying degrees of success in adjusting to life following school. Generally, though, most studies indicate that adults, even those recently released from institutions, can adapt to community life if given proper training. Below is a synopsis of information derived from reviews and studies of workers with mild retardation conducted by Brolin, Durand, Kromer, and Muller (1975), Heber & Deyer (1970), and Kokaska (1968).

1. Job success is a function of attitudes and personality, rather than IQ. Intelligence is not a significant reason for job success.
2. Adults who are retarded seem particularly susceptible to changes in the economy; their rate of employment is closely tied to economic situations. When the economy is in a downward cycle, these workers seem to get and hold fewer jobs. The converse is also true.

3. Since employees who are mentally retarded are often the last hired and the first fired, they often cannot afford better than substandard dwellings.
4. Workers with retardation tend to hold unskilled or semiskilled jobs. Brolin et al. (1975) report that 50% of their sample held jobs in service occupations (dishwasher, waitress, maid, janitor); 12% were in clerical and sales work; 9% in structured occupations like shop work, carpentry, and maintenance. The remaining workers held jobs in such areas as farming and fishing, machine trades, and benchwork occupations. While these are low-level jobs, they do illustrate what a wide variety of jobs adults with retardation can hold.
5. Persons who are mentally retarded tend to hold unrealistic career goals. Most see themselves in skilled and professional occupations. This finding is in marked contradiction to their actual job status.
6. Such individuals are often underemployed. They are not attaining their occupation potential, and they work at jobs below their ability level. This may be due to employer attitudes, supervisors' concerns for high production rates (Payne & Chaffin, 1968), or to poor vocational training programs.
7. A great many people who are mentally retarded get married and raise families. Their marital success seems comparable to that of the population that is not handicapped.
8. Individuals who have participated in work-study programs tend to respond better to occupational demands and are more employable than those who have not.

These findings clearly indicate that adults who are mildly mentally retarded are capable of being successful workers and making successful community adjustments. They also suggest that being a successful worker and adapting in the community is a consequence of learned behaviors. We can analyze these learned behaviors in terms of the requisite skills and knowledge needed for successful functioning and teach them as part of a comprehensive career education program.

Information from studies by Gertsen, Crowell, and Bellamy (1986) and Hill, Hill, Wehman, and Banks (1985) indicate that individuals who are more severely retarded can likewise make successful adjustments to society and become contributing members of their communities. Recently, for example, workers with moderate and severe retardation have been successfully placed in competitive employment, performing such jobs as kitchen utility worker, porter, elevator operator, dishwasher, groundskeeper, janitor, and assembly line worker (Rusch, 1983; Vogelsberg, 1986; Wehman, Hill, & Koehler, 1979; Wehman & Kregel, 1985).

The key to the success of competitive employment for individuals who are severely handicapped appears to be appropriate training and ongoing job support. Rusch (1983) recommends that training include a *survey-train-*

*place-train model*. Using this model the job counselor would: "(a) survey potential employers to determine important skills that need to be trained, (b) train students to perform these skills, (c) place trained clients in nonsheltered settings, and (d) provide long-term follow-up training" (p. 503). Although programs differ in the type of ongoing work support provided, Bellamy and Horner (1987) note that successful programs usually have four common elements: They (*a*) use systematic approaches to training and maintaining work behaviors; (*b*) focus on work opportunity over work preparation; (*c*) emphasize social integration with co-workers, customers, and others in the workplace; and (*d*) define program success in terms of wages and work benefits. These authors also note that ongoing support in the form of retraining, contingency management, and crisis intervention may be needed for workers who are severely handicapped for as long as they are employed.

## CAREER EDUCATION ISSUES

We have now looked at our conceptions of the nature of career education, its current status, and its value for people who are mentally retarded. While many other educators share these views, you should not infer that these views are universal or that all debate regarding these matters has ceased. In fact, Brolin and D'Alonzo (1979) state that many of the points we have already discussed in this chapter are issues that must be resolved if students who are handicapped are to receive the major benefits of the career education movement. The six critical issues they enumerate are: (*a*) Should career education be primarily job-centered or life-centered? (*b*) Should career education be infused into all levels of the curriculum, or should it be a separate program? (*c*) Who should be responsible for ensuring that students who are handicapped are included in career education? (*d* ) Can the goals of mainstreaming and career education be accomplished at the same time? (*e*) What will happen to ways of teaching that do not emphasize career education, and to courses and materials associated with them? (*f* ) How will teacher preparation programs give new teachers career education skills?

Obviously, we do not have the last word on any of these issues, but we do have some reasoned opinions about each one .

***Should career education be primarily job-centered or life-centered?*** Career education, in our opinion, should be life-centered as well as job-centered. Past and present evidence indicates that too heavy a reliance on a job-centered perspective to the exclusion of such aspects as attitude training has caused many of the problems (such as underemployment and unemployment) that adults who are mentally retarded or otherwise handicapped presently face.

*Should career education be infused into all levels of the curriculum, or should it be a separate program?*   One of the problems with current school curricula is that they contain no mechanism to prepare each student for life. Most children in our schools learn to read, write, and compute. A few even learn some vocational skills. We believe that career education can provide the comprehensive framework to bring all of these educational elements together so that the individual can more easily move through different life experiences. To do so means infusing career education throughout the curriculum; if students see the functional uses of the skills they learn they will get a more integrated, realistic view of their skills.

*Who should be responsible for ensuring that students who are handi-capped are included in career education?*   Special educators, now and for some time in the future, must be responsible for ensuring the inclusion of students who are mentally retarded in career education programs. Since special educators are moving away from providing direct services to all handicapped students, career education opens another avenue to them for making certain that students who are handicapped receive an appropriate education.

*Can the goals of mainstreaming and career education be accomplished at the same time?*   As Brolin and D'Alonzo (1979) have pointed out, main-streaming and career education can greatly enhance the chances of success for all students who are handicapped by providing them with more lifelike experiences and by relating instruction to real-life existence.

*What will happen to ways of teaching that do not emphasize career education, and to courses and materials associated with them?*   More career-oriented substitutes will supplant many courses, materials, and teaching approaches just as, in their time, these formerly useful mechanisms superseded earlier courses, materials, and teaching approaches. Our concern should be how to get the most out of the things that will change as a consequence of career education.

*How will teacher preparation programs give new teachers career educa-tion skills?*   Ensuring that career education concepts are systematically included in teacher preparation programs is a difficult goal, compounded by the fact that many teacher preparation programs are still struggling with the task of teaching general educators to deal with students who are handi-capped. MacArthur, Hagerty, and Taymans (1982) have made a proposal that integrates program changes with service delivery systems, coordinates efforts of educational specialists with those of other professionals, involves the business community and the public sector in developing community-based programs, analyzes and demonstrates cost effectiveness, and disseminates information about effective programs. As this approach is refined and others develop, career education will become an integral component in teacher education programs.

# CRUCIAL ELEMENTS OF A CAREER PREPARATION PROGRAM

Whether you rely on the tenets of career education (for example, see Brolin and Kokaska, 1979) or some other vocational preparation model to develop a systematic view of how ultimately to prepare students who are mentally retarded for the world of work, your model must contain several crucial elements for any career preparation to succeed. Among those elements are adequate program objectives, provision of counseling services, and a distinct stage for developing specific vocational skills. These three elements are not the only ones that can cause a career preparation program to succeed or fail, but if one or any combination of them is missing, then the program will be less than optimal. Without clear program objectives, it will lack direction; without counseling services, program participants will not always make the best choices when they are confronted with career decisions; and unless they learn some specific vocational skills, many participants will leave the program without skills that they can put to use.

## DEVELOPING PROGRAM OBJECTIVES

A first priority in the development of a comprehensive career preparation program is the development of a set of program objectives (Smith & Payne, 1980). While not all career preparation programs will have the same objectives because of differences in students' characteristics, jobs available in the community, and so on, certain objectives should be almost universal. The objective that should lead off any career preparation program is to develop a continuing career profile of the student's skills and interests. Since students enter a program with different skill and interest levels, the program coordinator must assess these skills and interests to determine the appropriate beginning training level for each student. For example, if a young man is interested in auto mechanics and has been working in this area already, he would probably be placed ahead of others just beginning an auto mechanics training program. As the student moves through the program, the instructor should gather and record additional information that reflects the trainee's changing or developing skills and interests. This information can then be used to motivate the student, as well as to convince employers that he is a desirable candidate.

A second program objective should be to engage each student in actual or direct job experiences and activities. This objective is important because, as the National Association for Retarded Citizens has stated, many programs that attempt to train persons who are retarded for different kinds of work have been too academically oriented. Such programs have tended to stress reading, writing, and other "school" skills over "life" skills (Payne, Polloway, Smith, & Payne, 1981). This oversight can be corrected by allowing the student on-the-job training opportunities in any reasonably safe environment, whether it is a typical school, a factory, or a sheltered workshop. A third, related objective for all career preparation is to develop entry level job skills for every student. For this, students work on actual job sites both to learn how to adjust to the demands of the job and fellow workers and to begin building a repertoire of the requisite skills for employment in the area of work. For instance, the best way for aspiring cement masons to learn the latest mortaring techniques is to apprentice with a skilled craftsman under whose direction they can handle genuine masonry tools and do the actual cementing. Concrete experiences of this kind are particularly crucial for students with mental retardation. For them modeling and imitation are among the most effective teaching techniques (Payne et al., 1981).

The fourth important objective of all programs is to provide job placement and follow-up services for students who have completed or will complete the preparation program. Since many of the persons we are concerned with will qualify for services from vocational rehabilitation or other agencies, personnel from those agencies can often provide placement and follow-up services. In other instances, public schools may have their own vocational placement facilities. What is important here is to make placement and follow-up one of the goals of the career preparation program.

## PROVIDING COUNSELING SERVICES

Another essential ingredient in a career preparation program is the availability of counseling services. Before discussing the two primary kinds of counseling (personal and career counseling) to use with students who are mentally retarded, we should first define the term *counseling* and describe the counseling process. According to Hansen, Stevic, and Warner (1972), counseling is:

> A process that assists an individual in learning about himself, his environment, and methods for handling his roles and relationships. Although individuals experience problems, counseling is not necessarily remedial. The counselor may assist an individual with the decision-making process in educational and vocational matters, as well as resolving interpersonal concerns. (p. vii)

The elements of this definition indicate both a number of roles that the counselor plays and a number of counseling goals. A major goal of the counseling process is to help the client become more self-sufficient and independent. The counselor helps clients to achieve this goal by showing them that they can shape many of the circumstances that affect their lives. One of the counselor's specific roles is to help the individual develop and explore alternative ways and means for dealing with problems or conflicts; a second role is to help the client overcome obstacles to progress in an area. As a result of counseling, the client is better able to make decisions that will lead to a resolution of uncertainties and conflicts. The vocational counseling process follows this general format.

Counseling is usually divided into a number of different sub-areas such as personal counseling and career counseling. But as Hansen et al. (1972) point out, the process remains much the same. A crucial difference between career counseling and personal counseling, however, is that career counseling calls for a substantial knowledge of occupational materials, options, and other concerns. For example, a career counselor must be knowledgeable about career and vocational assessment, the local job market, and the characteristics and needs of local employers, as well as the characteristics of the client population.

## DEVELOPING VOCATION SKILLS

The culminating phase in the career education process involves the development of some specific vocational skills. We explore this topic more extensively in the next section, but we want to give you an overall view of what should take place at this time. Initially, as we have already seen, all students' skills should be assessed. Next, present and projected jobs should be analyzed to determine what skills are necessary to perform these jobs. Once this is done, students should be trained on the basis of their present skill level, their interests, and the projected job availability. Following training, students should be placed on permanent job sites. Worker and employer should receive follow-up services to minimize the consequences of any problems. Finally, professionals should evaluate the program for how well it has prepared the student for employment.

# VOCATIONAL PREPARATION

We now focus on the events that take place during the period when the student who is mentally retarded is actually preparing for gainful employment, competitive or otherwise. In this section we discuss topics ranging from traditional vocational options for those who are mentally retarded to program evaluation to issues related to vocational education.

## TRADITIONAL VOCATIONAL OPTIONS

*High school work-study programs.* The high school work-study program is used most frequently for teaching vocational and occupational skills to students who are mildly mentally retarded. According to Kolstoe (1975), the high school work-study program usually runs over a 3-year period that encompasses the 10th, 11th, and 12th grades. In the first year of the program, lessons emphasize things like transportation, budgeting, peer relationships, personal hygiene, and measurement. Units are usually part of the academic portion of the program, which covers half of the school day. The student spends approximately half the day in the formal classroom setting and half in

*Giving students exposure to the experiences with jobs that are available in their communities is a key element in good programs.*

more practical instruction. In this part of the program, job analysis and job explorations, as well as specific assessment of the student's vocational skills and interests, begin. During the second year of the program, students refine their skills by learning how to complete job applications and how to behave in a job interview. At this time they should develop some rudimentary skills in a number of areas, such as clerical work, food service, carpentry, or automobile repair. During the third year of the program, students begin to concentrate on work skill refinement in one or two specific areas, spending part of the day on an actual job and the remaining time in school. As the third year draws to a close, students spend more time on the job and less in school.

See Figure 10.5.     There are five phases in the special education and work program: vocational exploration, vocational evaluation, vocational training, vocational

FIGURE 10.5   Phases in the Special
Education Work-Study Program

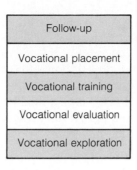

| Follow-up |
| Vocational placement |
| Vocational training |
| Vocational evaluation |
| Vocational exploration |

placement, and follow-up. These phases are incorporated into a work-oriented special education curriculum of skill training experiences and job-related classroom instruction. In the first phase, vocational exploration, the instructor familiarizes the student with various occupations and their skill requirements. During this prevocational stage, two separate sets of assessment take place. One evaluation determines students' vocational capabilities and the types of jobs that may interest them. Simultaneously, a job analysis is performed within the community. Lawry (1972) defines job analysis as "a systematic way of observing jobs; determine the significant worker requirements, physical demand, and environmental conditions; and reporting this information in a concise format" (p. 27). In addition, Brolin (1982) stated that a job analysis is concerned with what, why, and how a worker fulfills job requirements. Vocational evaluation, the second step, involves experiences with different job skills prescribed in order to determine the student's vocational abilities and preferences. The vocational training stage is designed to develop job skills in the pupil's general area of preference. To help prepare for a variety of occupations, training covers a wide range of job skills, usually at the semiskilled level. The choice of such specific job skills as typing or bricklaying is based on the previous assessments. In the next stage of the program, the person is exposed to a variety of actual on-the-job experiences under the supervision of the special education faculty. An individual who has tried several jobs for brief periods will begin to seek permanent employment. Vocational placement consists of locating a job for the student upon graduation from high school. Follow-up entails counseling to help the newly employed person deal with any difficulties encountered on the job. This phase may also involve further training or replacement if the student is unable to adjust to the first assignment.

***Sheltered workshops.***   The vocational education option that is traditionally used with individuals who are moderately to severely retarded has been called the *sheltered workshop, rehabilitation workshop* (Brolin, 1982) or *community work center.* Regardless of which name is used, these facilities have several common characteristics.

1. Clients/employees usually work on contract jobs.
2. The contract jobs are usually of short duration, and a staff person is needed to bring in new ones.
3. Most tasks are broken down into small steps.
4. Jobs usually proceed in assembly line fashion; one part is added at each step of the process until a final product is completed.
5. The facility may or may not provide vocational assessment and training for persons outside the center.

In order to attain the goal of employment for people who are retarded, a workshop essentially delivers four services: work evaluation, work adjustment, work experience, and placement and follow-up. Individuals are given evaluations of their basic abilities and are assessed in various work settings to determine work limitations and capabilities. A work adjustment program trains the adolescent or adult in general work skills—"punctuality, dependability, personal habits, cooperation with supervisors, cooperation with fellow employees, proper use of materials and equipment, and the ability to work under pressure" (Cohen, 1971, p. 423). The work experience phase is the progressive development of specific work skills needed for successful employment. This phase usually follows a step-by-step procedure from simple to complex tasks. At each skill level, a staff member observes the individual's work to determine the level of functioning. The purpose is to match the worker's aptitudes as closely as possible to an appropriate occupation. To this end, work experience training covers a wide spectrum of work skills ranging from unskilled assembly line tasks to highly complex assignments. The placement and follow-up services offered in a sheltered workshop parallel those furnished by special education work-study and vocational education programs. Cohen (1971) has described the placement and follow-up stages as follows:

> During this crucial period, the individual should be provided opportunities for selective job placements, either within the workshop or within the community. Appropriate ongoing services should be available to ensure his successful adjustment to the community working situation. (p. 423)

The considerable variety of services and facilities needed in a sheltered workshop requires a large budget. While it is possible in theory for an industry of this nature to be economically self-sufficient, it has proved impossible in practice. Because of the time it takes to train individuals for job success, workshops rarely become self-sufficient. Massie (1962) has said that, in order for such businesses to be self-supporting, they must accept only the higher IQ applicants. Since the sheltered workshop is an effective means of training workers of almost all intellectual levels, that admission criterion would severely limit workshops' potential to serve all people who are retarded. For this reason, they rely on various sources of assistance: federal, state, and local grants; community resources; foundation grants; and individual contributions.

The two major obstacles to the success of the sheltered workshop are its economic dependence on outside sources (Kolstoe & Frey, 1965) and a general inability to provide a wide scope of occupational tasks for the varied skills of the workers. Gold (1973) points out that most contracts received from the participating local industries engage the workers only in menial, monotonous tasks for notoriously paltry wages. This limits the possibility for maximizing the potential of all the clients in the workshop. He offers suggestions for future workshop policy that might reverse this trend, recommending that industrial contracts be required to have the following characteristics:

1. Tasks should challenge workers to learn new skills.
2. Adequate time must be allowed for production and training of workers for the tasks.
3. Full-time human labor, rather than automation, should be emphasized.
4. A variety of skills should be required to fulfill the contract.
5. Both workshop and worker should profit from the contract.

Finding suitable contracts and training the workers requires thought and planning. Brown, Wright, and Hitchings (1978) have suggested a variety of sources from the state directory of manufacturers to community service clubs like the Kiwanis as sources of potential contracts. They further suggest that workshop staff visit the potential contractor, task-analyze the jobs to be done, train their workers to do them, and continually evaluate ongoing job performance.

With the recent emphasis on transition planning and integration of individuals who are severely handicapped into competitive work settings, the concept of the sheltered workshop has come under fire. Criticism centers around its segregated approach to employment, low wages, and general failure effectively to move clients into competitive work environments. Reform, however, is under way. Results of recent studies indicate that one third of sheltered workshops have significantly increased the provision of services that lead to competitive employment, and another third are in the process of redesigning their programs for this purpose (Whitehead, 1986).

## VOCATIONAL ASSESSMENT

An individual's occupational aptitudes can be assessed either by using written tests or by observing work samples. We can group written assessment devices into at least two categories: aptitude tests and interest inventories. Aptitude tests measure the abilities and traits of an individual in a certain area. For example, an aptitude test that measures typing abilities should indicate whether or not a person can type or learn how to type. Educators most often use results of these tests to predict an individual's chances for success in a stated field. Examples of aptitude tests that measure career-related skills are the General Aptitude Test Battery and the Nonreading Aptitude Test Battery (U.S. Department of Labor, 1970). Interest inventories assess the student's feelings and preferences about types of occupations rather than measuring potential proficiency. The Gordon Occupational Checklist (Gordon, 1967) and the Minnesota Vocational Interest Inventory (Clark & Campbell, 1966) are two such devices. Another currently popular interest inventory is the AAMD-Becker Reading Free Vocational Interest Inventory (R-FVII) (Becker, 1975). This test comprises sets of three pictures from which the individual must choose one that shows the activity he or she would most like to do. The sets give scores for 19 different interest areas, for example, food service, clerical, and laundry service, 11 of which typically appeal to males and 8 of which are usually chosen by females. The test takes less than an hour to administer and is especially appropriate for use with individuals who have low verbal and reading skills.

Another way to assess work skills is though a work sample or job simulation. This procedure evaluates each individual's rate of production and general job-related behaviors. Brolin (1982) has offered the following suggestions for making the most of this procedure. The job sample or work sample should be written up and organized in such a way that the tasks required are in order, from the least demanding to the most. The students should be allowed to practice each task and master it completely before proceeding to the next one; in this way, they can master each task necessary for the production of a particular good or service.

One example of a job simulation device is the Jewish Employment and Vocational Service Work Samples (JEVS) package. Brolin (1982, 1986) has described these work samples as being composed of 28 tasks that measure worker skills in 14 general industrial categories. During the evaluation, which covers a 2-week period, the person being evaluated is required to perform work-related tasks that vary from simple (lettering signs) to complex (disassembling and rebuilding equipment).

While these instruments and procedures do yield valuable information about students' vocational capabilities, they have frequently been criticized for several reasons. First, the reading level for many of the paper-and-pencil tests is too high for many students with retardation (reading levels for these instruments are usually at or around a sixth-grade level). Second, few if any items relate directly to females. Third, socioeconomic differences are ignored (the preponderance of items reflects a middle class orientation). Finally, the racial and cultural diversity of the population of this country is not taken into account. Work sample evaluations are criticized because they are expensive and time-consuming, often requiring extensive travel to and from the work site.

## VOCATIONAL PLACEMENT

Once a student has acquired some vocational skills, either the school or some other agency such as a vocational rehabilitation agency seeks to place the student on a permanent job site. Smith and Payne (1980) suggest a number of procedures to aid the placement specialist. The list below summarizes these procedures.

1. Make as many personal contacts with local employers as possible.
2. Use local clubs to advertise your program, as well as to secure information concerning placement sites.
3. Become more selective in the use of job sites as the program grows.
4. Consider employers an integral part of the program. Use them at different levels of the program, for example, the prevocational as well as the vocational level.

Additionally, such technological advances as computerized occupational information systems (Kruger, 1980) can provide job placement specialists with easy access to information about job possibilities and requirements.

## FOLLOW-UP AND EVALUATION

Once students are placed on a permanent job site, the placement specialist has the responsibility of following their progress to ensure that they are successful on the job. Brolin (1982), as well as Phelps and Lutz (1977), have noted that initially follow-up services should be frequent and then become less so. For a short period, the follow-up services to the student and the employer may occur daily, then once a week, and finally on a monthly to yearly basis. Much of the information gained during this period can also be used to assess the effectiveness of the program in preparing the student for the present job. The relationship between follow-up and evaluation makes it possible for future as well as present program participants to benefit.

Follow-up and evaluation services continue to be one of the weakest links in the vocational preparation program for people who are mentally retarded. The provisions of P.L. 94-142 calling for annual review and an increase in communication between school personnel and state vocational rehabilitation personnel (Capobianco & Jacoby, 1966) have proven to be insufficient to alleviate the problem. But we can reasonably assume that as school programs continue to improve and job counselors refine both their own job placement skills and the job-seeking skills of individuals with mental retardation, follow-up services will be increased or greatly strengthened.

## PROGRAMMING ISSUES

Vocational preparation of students who are retarded has come a long way, but we do not have all the answers yet. Two problem areas demand special attention.

The first problem is the difficulty of the written material used in vocational programs for students who are mentally retarded. The reading level of much of this material is too high even for those with mild retardation. Vocational and special educators have struggled with this problem for some time without being able to reach a workable solution. Coleman (1977) has outlined one possibility. His preliminary research indicates that a modification of Basic English, developed by Ogden (1934) and his associates, enables retarded readers to understand vocationally related materials. Coleman has translated materials from a standard form into Basic English, using only the 850 words of that system. The readability level of the material he has developed is third- or fourth-grade level and below.

Problem number two relates to what to do when a person who is mentally retarded resigns or is fired from a job. A similar event would not cause too much concern with a person who is not retarded, but it does seem to cause consternation on the part of family, friends, and professionals who work with people who have handicaps. Should a job termination be more of an issue for workers who are retarded than for the rest of the labor force? We believe that an employee who is mentally retarded has as much right as the next person to like or dislike a job or co-workers and to leave an unpleasant or unproductive situation if necessary. To deny this is to deny equal rights (and responsibilities) to the adult who is mentally retarded, and it runs wholly contrary to the idea of normalization.

## SUMMARY

In this chapter we have taken a broad look at career and vocational programming for students with mental retardation. Career education is aimed at helping students prepare for life as well as for a job and should extend throughout schooling and beyond. Traditionally, career education programs for individuals who are mildly retarded have differed from those for more severe cases. Earlier vocational preparation programs for students with mild retardation prepared them to enter the job market after high school, whereas programs for the more severely affected presumed placement in sheltered environments or rehabilitation workshop programs. Recently, however, studies have shown that with systematic training and ongoing support many individuals who are moderately and severely retarded can succeed in integrated, competitive work settings. To be successful, a career education program for any student should include specific program objectives, counseling services, and the development of specific vocational skills.

# CHAPTER 11

# Adult Years

I n recent years we have witnessed dramatic changes in the lives of adults who are mentally retarded. Although referring to the more generic classification of developmental disabilities, Castellani (1987) believes that these changes are mostly positive and that they have significant implications: "There is simply no other area of human services in which fundamental changes in the context and structure of services, finance, clientele, and organization have been so dramatic and far-reaching in such a short period of time" (p. 149). One of the most striking movements has been to integrate more adults into community settings. Many persons who are retarded are now living in community environments and dealing with the same scenario of adulthood that all of us face, with its problems, pleasures, and complexities. For some, community living is not too difficult; for others, everyday life poses major challenges that are not being handled well. This chapter highlights some issues of adulthood and community living.

One of the purposes of the institutions established in the mid-1800s was to train those with greater limitations so that they would acquire the skills necessary for successful reintegration into community life. As we saw in chapter 1, the backlash to integrative efforts stemmed in part from the fact that so few individuals were able to adjust to community living successfully. At the same time, powerful efforts to keep this group away from society were being exercised. This situation lasted for many years and remains with us to some degree today.

Now, however, people have a heightened interest in removing individuals from institutional settings and creating community settings for them. Many factors are responsible for this, including: emphasis on individual and civil rights; evidence of successful community experiences of adults with mental retardation; and attempts to provide living situations (i.e., employment, residential, educational, social, family) as close to what is considered normal as possible. The principle of normalization is usually associated with the work of Nirje (1969) and Wolfensberger (1972), although Wolfensberger (1983) now espouses the use of the phrase *social role valorization* over its predecessor, *normalization*. This new concept implies "the use of culturally valued means in order to enable, establish, and/or maintain valued social roles for people" (Wolfensberger, 1985, p. 61).

Although most professionals in the field of mental retardation advocate the development of programs and services to initiate and maintain people in the community, most would agree that it is shortsighted to deny the complexity of the issue. Adulthood *is* complex, and so are the lives of those who are mentally retarded (Edgerton, 1984). Kleinberg and Galligan (1983) remarked that "the view that community-living arrangements are necessarily more 'normalizing' than are traditional institutions is too simplistic" (p. 21). They emphasized that programmatic intervention is critical to successful adjustment, implying that without it community placement may not be much better than institutional placement. In addition to the systematically determined criteria for successful community adjustment, professionals should consider what this concept means to those who are retarded. Research by Lovett and Harris (1987) has shown that the areas of importance identified by adults who were retarded were similar to the areas ranked by professionals.

It has become increasingly clear that the status of adults with disabilities can be described in the following ways: high rates of unemployment, part-time employment, and underemployment; less education; low income levels; lack of mobility; and inadequate preparation for adulthood. These descriptors hold for those with mental retardation as well.

## TRANSITION FROM SCHOOL TO COMMUNITY

Chapter 10 discussed the importance of preparing adolescents for life after high school. Since the outcomes of transitional planning relate so closely to the focus of this chapter, we should show how transition links adolescence and adulthood. As all of the transition literature points out, the process has three major components:

☐ assuring that certain school-related activities occur early during the secondary careers of students who are retarded
☐ establishing linkages between schools/students/families and employers, postsecondary educational facilities, and other community agencies so that needed intervention is not interrupted when formal schooling ends
☐ creating and maintaining appropriate adult services that will support quality adult living and encourage community participation, independence, and productivity

One of the most important considerations in this process is the involvement of families. Patton and Browder (1988) have stressed that transitional planning should be performed *with* parents, not *for* them. Parents need to become intimately involved in this process, as they may be the only advocates or case managers for their children once formal assistance ends. We encourage professionals to involve parents and be sensitive to cultural values, family values, and individual family situations (e.g., resources) in all situations.

There is some question of what transitional planning should be. Certainly it should involve developing a plan for the future, usually through drawing up an individual transition plan (ITP). The ITP should help families make contact with adult services that will be needed. It also should begin preparing students and their families for the realities of community living for their particular young adult. This last point raises two questions: How should we prepare students? What are the curricular implications of transitional planning?

The manner in which we prepare students is being addressed better than the question about curricular implications. Many new training programs stress community-based instruction and focus on getting students into competitive jobs and helping them stay there. There has been a decided movement away from sheltered employment when possible. The results of various competitive and supported employment projects around the country are encouraging.

What we should teach (i.e., curriculum) students who are retarded is not so clear. Much emphasis has been on vocational preparation. Training in this area is very important, but other functional areas must be addressed as well. If we look back to Figure 10.3, we can see that the vocational/educational domain is only one of six major areas needing attention. Close, Sowers, Halpern, and Bourbeau (1985) present 51 behavioral domains that they derived from analyzing assessment devices for adolescents and adults who are mentally retarded. These domains, which are organized into 15 content area clusters (4 major content dimensions) and presented in Table 11.1, can serve as a guide for identifying the range of skills that must be taught to students during transitional preparation. This list is not exhaustive and can be extended (see Knowles, 1984), but it underscores the point that adulthood places complex demands on all of us. It is far from straining at conclusions to suggest that these pressures may fall more heavily on those who by definition have more difficulty coping with the demands of everyday living.

Curricular innovation at the secondary level is receiving more attention these days. Halpern and Benz (1987), in their study of secondary-level special education teachers in Oregon, found that curricular factors could play the greatest role in improving programs at this level. When we couple this finding with the alarming statistics about students who do not complete their high school education (Edgar, 1987; Office of Special Education Programs

TABLE 11.1   Content Clusters and Domains

I. Foundations of Achievement
   A. Basic development skills
      1. Sensory development
      2. Motor development
      3. Cognitive development
   B. Survival numerics
      1. Basic mathematics
      2. Time management
   C. Survival reading
      1. Basic academic skills
      2. Functional reading
   D. Communication
      1. Expressive language
      2. Receptive language
      3. Writing and spelling skills
II. Foundations of Adjustment
   A. Knowledge of self
      1. Self-awareness
      2. Self-concept
   B. Emotional and personal adjustment
      1. Acting out or withdrawal
      2. Self-stimulation
      3. Coping
   C. Social and interpersonal skills
      1. Basic interaction skills
      2. Group participation
      3. Play activities
      4. Social amenities
      5. Sexual behavior
      6. Responsibility
III. Community Adjustment Skills
   A. Self-help skills
      1. Dressing
      2. Eating
      3. Toileting

   B. Consumer skills
      1. Money handling
      2. Banking
      3. Budgeting
      4. Purchasing
   C. Domestic skills
      1. Kitchen skills
      2. Household cleaning
      3. Household management, maintenance, and repair
      4. Laundering and clothing care
   D. Health care
      1. Treatment of various health problems
      2. Preventive health measures
      3. Usage of medication
      4. Corrective devices
   E. Knowledge of community
      1. Independent travel skills
      2. Community expectations
      3. Community awareness and use
      4. Telephone use
IV. Prevocational and Vocational Skills
   A. Job readiness
      1. Job awareness
      2. Job application and interview skills
      3. On-the-job information
   B. Vocational behavior
      1. Job performance and productivity
      2. Work habits and work attitudes
      3. Work-related skills
      4. Specific job skills
      5. Learning and transfer of job skills
   C. Social behavior on the job

From "Programming for the Transition to Independent Living for Mildly Retarded Persons" by D. W. Close, J. Sowers, A. S. Halpern, and P. E. Bourbeau, 1985, in K. C. Lakin and R. H. Bruininks (Eds.), *Strategies for Achieving Community Integration of Developmentally Disabled Citizens* (pp. 161–176), Baltimore: Paul H. Brookes. Reprinted by permission.

[OSEP], 1988), we are further encouraged to reexamine the nature of secondary-level programming. Polloway, Patton, Payne, and Payne (1989) suggest that innovative programming for students with mental retardation should be adult-referenced or community-referenced (Smith & Schloss, 1988); comprehensive or broad in scope; relevant and appealing to students; empirically and socially valid; flexible enough to accommodate a range of differing student needs; and community-based (that is, much of the training should occur outside the classroom). Edgar (1987) advocates the development of a meaningful and valued alternative program for the large number of secondary-level students who are not college-bound.

## COMMUNITY ADJUSTMENT

When we speak of community adjustment, we are referring to three major factors: *(a)* characteristics and behaviors of the individual; *(b)* demands placed upon the individual to live and function adequately in the community setting; and *(c)* interaction between the two. A fair amount of research has gone into studying individuals before and after they move into community settings. While some researchers (Hull & Thompson, 1980; Willer & Intagliata, 1981) have emphasized the importance of environmental factors for this process, relatively little systematic consideration and examination of community settings has taken place. Even less research has been directed at inspecting what Rappaport (1977) referred to as the "person-environment fit." Heal, Sigelman, and Switzky (1978) have highlighted the situation.

> What has not yet been systematically considered is the possibility that one residential environment might be optimal for a client with one set of characteristics, while another is optimal for a client with a different set of characteristics. Suggestive evidence from related fields pinpoints the interaction of person and environment as a significant determinant of behavior. (p. 240)

In the past, most students classified as mildly retarded in school environments were likely to adjust to life in the community without too much difficulty. But more recent findings about students in school settings (including those who are mentally retarded) are more alarming (Hasazi, Gordon, & Roe, 1985; Mithaug, Horiuchi, & Fanning, 1985; Wehman, Kregel, & Seyfarth, 1985). Some indications suggest that adjustment is more problematic for a large number of individuals who have spent a considerable amount of time in special education. As mentioned, transitional efforts have emerged in great part to address this need.

Researchers use two general approaches in studying community adjustment. One is follow-up studies of previously institutionalized people or of students who have left formal schooling. Institutional follow-up research dates back to the early part of this century. The second approach involves the attempt to predict successful community adjustment and is typically based on the individual's characteristics. These studies are sometimes called *prognostic* studies (Rosen, Clark, & Kivitz, 1977).

### FOLLOW-UP STUDIES
Over the years many follow-up studies have been performed. In general these studies suggest that individuals who were either deinstitutionalized or

"graduated" from school settings were able to adapt successfully to community living. When adults who were retarded did not succeed in community settings, it was usually because of maladaptive behavior (Intagliata & Willer, 1982). Keep in mind that community adjustment is complex and that simple descriptions of it may be inadequate. It is also worth noting, as McCarver and Craig did in 1974, that much of the follow-up research has methodological flaws (Heal et al., 1978).

***Criteria for successful community adjustment.***   One of the methodological problems of the follow-up studies has been their inconsistency in selecting and defining criteria for successful adjustment to community life. Although much of the research has used similar criteria, there has been no effort to standardize criteria, making comparisons between studies difficult. On the other hand, it *may* be necessary to vary some specific criteria to understand the idea of "person-environment fit."

Researchers have defined successful community adjustment in so many ways that Craig and McCarver (1984) have suggested that outcome measures be considered "researcher specific." The growing literature on transition seems to indicate that new conceptualizations of adjustment are now available. We give examples of the factors that some researchers have considered viable criteria.

Willer and Intagliata (1981) have presented five areas of functioning that are related to adjustment: self-care, community-living skills, behavior control, use of community resources, and social support. McCarver and Craig (1974) have identified eight major criteria by which to gauge community adjustment. Within each of these major categories, more specific variables may be considered. Rosen et al. (1977) summarize the adjustment variables identified by McCarver and Craig as follows.

1. Living environment (type of residence, amount of rent or mortgage payments, residential stability, satisfaction with living quarters);
2. Type of employment (place of work, skill level, job requirements);
3. Job changes (general stability, mobility up or down);
4. Savings and money management (debts, bank accounts, budgeting, installment buying);
5. Sexual problems (venereal disease, promiscuity, prostitution, homosexuality, illegitimacies, marital adjustment, exploitation);
6. Antisocial behavior (legal problems, arrests, delinquency, acts of violence);
7. Marriage and children (sexual adjustment, contraception, parental responsibility, health of children);
8. Use of leisure time (social contacts, recreational activities, hobbies, reading, travel). (Rosen, Clark, & Kivitz, 1977, pp. 142–143)

To some professionals, the primary criterion for successful adjustment, in terms of persons who were being deinstitutionalized was whether or not they were reinstitutionalized. Analysis of the community integration process forces us to adopt a more sophisticated model. Although a generally accepted model does not yet exist, understanding the complexity of the issue will help us move toward developing one. Haney (1988) has examined research into many factors of community adjustment and provided a graphic summation of these various factors and their relationship to successful community living. This information is presented in Table 11.2.

TABLE 11.2    Potential Factors in Successful Community Adjustment

**Individual Characteristics**

*No relationship with success:*
Diagnostic category
Racial or ethnic background

*Mixed findings:*
Sex
Age
IQ
Adaptive behavior
Academic ability
Physical handicap
Health problems

*Some relationship with success:*
Personal appearance
Vocational skills
Personality
Social skills

*Best individual-level predictor of success:*
Maladaptive behavior

**Small Group Characteristics***

*Mixed findings:*
Number of dependents in setting

*Association with success:*
Caregiver age
Psychological well-being
Overprotection
Religion
Vocational orientation
Experience
Support from relatives
Relatives in the home
Peer group composition
Family involvement
Treatment milieu—training, restrictiveness of movement, structure, household responsibilities, activities promoting social integration, resident-staff interaction, and some aspects of the social environment

**Organization Characteristics***

*No association with success:*
Short-term institutionalization

*Association with success:*
Setting type
Geographical location
Facility size
Normalization in facility design
Staff training
Parent counseling and training
Normalization and research policies
Quality of life

**Community Characteristics***

*Association with success:*
Community-provided training, support, and case management
Caregiver supervision
Existence of residential alternatives
Caregivers' financial needs
Community response

*No comparison studies:*
Advocates or benefactors
Self-help groups

*There has been little research and frequently only a single study on many of the factors in these areas.

From "Toward successful community residential placements for individuals with mental retardation" by J. I. Haney, 1988, in L. W. Heal, J. I. Haney, & A. R. Novak Amado (Eds.) *Integration of Developmentally Disabled Individuals into the Community* (2nd ed.), Baltimore: Paul H. Brooks.

*Cloak of competence.*    An example of the institutional follow-up study is a classic study initiated during the early 1960s. It involved 53 persons with mental retardation who were released from Pacific State Hospital between 1949 and 1958 (Edgerton, 1967). Actually, 110 individuals successfully completed a vocational training program at Pacific State Hospital, but for practical purposes 53 people were selected to be contacted personally. This study was designed to gain a greater appreciation of the everyday lives of persons who had been released from an institution. In this study, Edgerton and his colleagues decided to focus on the following areas, which they believed to be factors in community adjustment.

1. Where and how the ex-patients lived,
2. Making a living,
3. Relations with others in the community,
4. Sex, marriage, and children,
5. "Spare time" activities,
6. Their perception and presentation of self, and
7. Their practical problems in maintaining themselves in the community. (Edgerton, 1967, pp. 16–17)

Subjects in this study ranged in age from 20 to 75, with an average age of 35. The distribution of men and women was even, and the mean IQ of all subjects was 64.

Through interviews with the subjects and other people who associated with them (neighbors, relatives, friends, and employers), Edgerton and colleagues gained much information about the subjects' everyday lives. Approximately 17 hours of investigation were devoted to each of the 53 people involved in the study. Overall, Edgerton's subjects were coping with life in the community; however, there were some areas that were troublesome. The authors point out that many of the subjects had a difficult time dealing with the stigma related to the label mental retardation. They spent a great deal of energy and time "denying" their retardation and attempting to "pass" as normal. Major areas in everyday life that were problematic for the subjects centered on *(a)* making a living; *(b)* managing sex, marriage, and reproduction; *(c)* using leisure time. To cope with these problems and to help pass as normal, many of the subjects developed relationships with "benefactors." The benefactor, like today's advocate, would assist the person who was retarded in coping with problems of everyday living.

In 1972 and 1973, 12 years after the original study, Edgerton and Bercovici (1976) were able to locate 30 of the original 53 subjects. Again using interviews and participant observation, the researchers focused on factors of community adjustment as they had in the 1960–1961 study. This time subjects were also asked to compare their present lives with their situations 10 years before. Researchers rated each subject's present adjustment with that of 1960–1961 and found that 8 subjects had improved, 12 had not changed, and 10 seemed to have regressed. While the researchers noted that they were not able to predict very well from their original data how a person would be doing at a later date, some general statements could be made. As length of time in the community increased for the subjects, they seemed to have fewer feelings of stigmatization, less concern with trying to deny their retardation, and less need for benefactors.

A number of points the researchers raised are worth reiterating. First, adjustment is a multidimensional and complex concept. Second, as Edgerton and Bercovici point out, "Social adjustment . . . may fluctuate markedly, not only from year to year, but from month to month or even from week to week" (1976, p. 495). Third, perhaps what constitutes good social acceptance from the viewpoint of the person with mental retardation may differ significantly from the criteria used by professionals. The following statement corroborates this.

> After many years of community living, persons once institutionalized as mentally retarded could . . . develop their own collective and individual views of what constitutes good social adjustment. If, as we suspect, our criteria of adjustment will continue to emphasize competence and independence while retarded persons themselves emphasize personal satisfaction, then our dilemma is even worse than we had all previously recognized. (Edgerton & Bercovici, 1976, p. 495)

In 1982, 20 years after the original study, Edgerton and his associates again set out to locate and examine the lives of the people they had previously studied (Edgerton, Bollinger, & Herr, 1984). Of the original 53 subjects from whom information was gathered in 1960–1961, only 15 were identified as being able to provide adequate data in 1982. This group was now much older, with an average age of 56 years. We are just beginning to know about older people who are retarded, especially those who live in community settings, and these data, while limited, provide some information. Using data-gathering techniques similar to earlier ones, the researchers ranked the subjects in the following areas: life satisfaction, social competence, life stress, relative dependence on benefactors, quality of life, and degree of improvement in life circumstances over the last 10 years. In the last category, 5 were stable, 4 had gotten worse, and 3 had improved. About the other 3 no agreement could be reached. Overall, the subjects conveyed a sense of hope, as reflected in Edgerton and colleagues' comments: "They [the subjects] believed that the future could be better and that their efforts could make a difference; they would pursue a better life by a variety of means" (1984, p. 350).

***Other follow-up studies.*** Over the years researchers have conducted many different follow-up studies of individuals who have been deinstitutionalized. This section summarizes the findings of three recent studies of students who have exited from formal schooling. Two of these studies (Hasazi et al., 1985;

Wehman et al., 1985) focused more on the employment outcomes for this group, while the other one (Mithaug et al., 1985) examined other domains as well. It should be noted that *(a)* some of these follow-up studies were not limited to individuals who were mentally retarded, and *(b)* their findings should not be generalized beyond the locations where they were conducted. Nevertheless, the results illustrate the current state of affairs.

☐ Hasazi et al. (1985)
—50% of special education graduates were unemployed.
☐ Wehman et al. (1985)
—60% of young adults with mental retardation were unemployed; this figure rises to 70% if part-time and sheltered employment are omitted.
—75% of the subjects in the Virginia study (Wehman et al., 1985) earn less than $500 per month.
—adult services were not being used.
—68% of young adults used friends, parents, or themselves as primary agents in the initial process of locating jobs.
☐ Mithaug et al. (1985)
—at the time of the study, 31% of subjects were unemployed; of those employed, only 32% were full-time workers.
—43% of those employed earned less than $3 per hour.
—50% of the respondents had not taken any courses after high school.
—42% of this group could be considered socially inactive.
—64% lived at home.

## PREDICTING SUCCESSFUL COMMUNITY ADJUSTMENT

It would be wonderful to be able to predict successful and unsuccessful adjustment outcomes for individuals who are retarded upon their leaving either an institutional or a school setting. As Rosen et al. (1977) state,

> The fact that some retarded persons can succeed in the community while others fail suggests the need to determine, before their discharge from institutional or special school programs, which persons have the greatest potential for successful adjustment to independent living. (p. 171)

A number of researchers have had precisely this goal in mind. Unfortunately, the results of research into predicting community adjustment have not supported any one combination of predictor variables. It would seem that IQ might be useful as a predictor variable, but studies have not confirmed this hypothesis (Willer & Intagliata, 1981).

Typically, prognostic studies have concentrated on characteristics of the individual, which can include such variables as IQ and age, institutional-related factors (age at admission, training received, length of institutionalization), personality, emotional status, physical status, academic ability, vocational skills, and physical appearance. Until now, most research has prized cognitive variables over some of the others. To be able better to predict the outcome of community adjustment, we need to consider some alternative approaches to this type of research. Future researchers may do well to study social skill and personality variables in more detail for their prognostic value. It also seems prudent to consider factors that are community-related. That is, it may prove to be very helpful in predicting community adjustment to know something about the community an individual is entering.

Heal and colleagues (1978) have identified five areas that should be carefully considered in preparing individuals for adaptation to the community environment. They are

☐ community attitudes and behaviors toward residential facilities and their residents;
☐ zoning controversies and regulatory obstacles;
☐ availability, adequacy, and access to community resources/support services;
☐ role of benefactors, friends, or advocates;
☐ characteristics of the residential service system itself. (p. 229)

The overwhelming theme that we can discern from information about community adjustment is that the process is extremely complex both conceptually and practically. To prepare individuals best for community life, it is essential that appropriate programming occur while they are still at school or residing in more sheltered settings. We must look more closely at *(a)* what are being defined as key areas of transition; *(b)* those factors associated with successful adjustment (see Table 11.2); and *(c)* community-specific factors. The next section elaborates on the major features of community living.

## CHARACTERISTICS OF LIFE IN THE COMMUNITY

Where do they work and sleep? What do they do? How do they spend their day? Some persons with mental retardation are fully integrated and actively involved in their community: working and receiving paychecks, establishing a home, entertaining friends, and participating in local events. Others spend much of their time alone or involved in activities that serve only to occupy time.

The complexity of each person's life, the variety of experiences, and the opportunities to develop and assume responsibilities all depend on the availability of appropriate community resources, public and private attitudes, and the strengths and weaknesses of the individual.

Work, home, and play comprise the major endeavors of adult life. Community options prompted by the goal of providing lifestyles that are as normalized as possible are increasing in each of these areas. Great effort has gone into facilitating the participation of adults with mental retardation in ways that resemble normal rhythms and routines. The following discussion highlights features of adult living that most would consider important (see

# INDEPENDENT  LIVING

Timmy and Carol Savage presently live in an apartment, on their own and as independent as any couple could possibly be. Tim spent 37 years of his life in the state's institution for those who are mentally retarded, after which he lived in a group home. Tim now works full time sanding picture frames for ACME Industries, while Carol performs routine maid services for the Best Western Inn. According to Tim, and incidentally confirmed by the landlord, "We pay on time, every time. We don't get behind."

Tom Houston, housing developer for the handicapped with Mental Retardation Services, explains it has been a long process of educating landlords and neighbors alike that those who are mentally retarded are more similar to than different from those pegged as normal. "Many landlords have very legitimate concerns about disabled individuals, because if a tenant is impeded in his performance of his duties as a tenant, it could result in a loss to the landlord."

The Savages have access to a Citizens Advocacy program that matches a volunteer from the community with a "special-friend," a process by which the program hopes to develop lasting friendships. The layperson acts as an advocate for the human and legal rights of the person with retardation. It is simply one more way that differences can be diminished; volunteers grow in their understanding of the handicapped.

Houston feels compelled to assure a prospective landlord that where a tenant who is handicapped has inadequacies, there will be a professional, or a layperson like a Citizen Advocate, to compensate. Some people like the Savages need little supervision. They have demonstrated a consistency of behavior that assures a landlord of their ability to handle most of their duties as tenants with little guidance from others.

When a client is deemed ready for independent living, Houston helps him work out an agreement for monthly rent payments, including utilities, which are not to exceed ¼ of the individual's gross income.

Once an apartment is found to suit everyone's purposes, a 1-year lease is signed. The client is guaranteed that his rent subsidy will be renewed annually for the next 5 years.

"Some landlords are very responsive," says Houston. They call him up when they have a vacancy because they like the program and go out of their way to help the tenant. For our landlords, "It's just a cut-and-dried agreement, strictly business. He wants to know, 'Am I going to get my checks on time? Is my lease going to be violated?' "

Houston says over and over again that these tenants are turning out to be reliable. They like structure and adhere rather consistently to a routine once good habits are taught them. But Houston is quick to point out that "it's not a humanitarian thing. It's a good business deal."

"I wouldn't be on the phone to you," he tells a landlord, "if I didn't feel it was good business."

Figure 11.1). The choice of topics presented in this section is somewhat arbitrary, but major demographic considerations underlie the topics and overlap with the major areas of transition as identified by various research endeavors. Our intent is not to give specific standards or criteria by which to evaluate these components. You should, however, consider the expectations and constraints inherent in each and how these affect the lives of adults who are retarded.

## EMPLOYMENT

The routine and rhythm of work, the work tasks, the socializing associated with work, all these become part of the pattern of normalizing living. For instance, it is common for people to leave where they live each morning, board the bus, punch in, take coffee breaks, talk with co-workers, have lunch, go back to work, and then return home—another day passed and another dollar earned (Wolfensberger, 1972).

Work is no less significant for the person who is retarded than for anyone else. Social changes, as well as changes in public policy, have allowed more such people to enter the workforce and share in the benefits of gainful employment. During the past few years, advances in task analysis and vocational prosthetics have greatly revised the employment forecasts for people with retardation. Although they were once thought to possess little potential for gainful employment, even individuals with the most severe retardation are now demonstrating the ability to perform complex vocational tasks when provided with appropriate and systematic training (Bellamy, Sowers, & Bourbeau, 1983). In addition, federal legislation—the 1986

FIGURE 11.1    Characteristics of Life in the Community

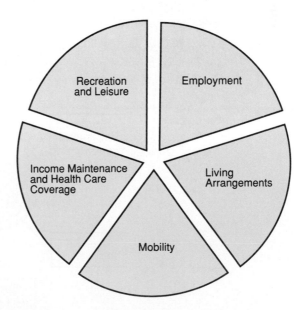

amendments to the Rehabilitation Act, the 1983 amendments to P.L. 94-142, the Carl D. Perkins Vocational Education Act of 1984—have greatly expanded vocational possibilities for many individuals who are mentally retarded. New alternatives have been created within the community for vocational training and job placement.

Vocational programs need to build on values that attend to the current and future needs of individuals. Most training programs are transitional, emphasizing skill acquisition and eventual placement in more independent settings. Some programs tend to serve as long-term sites for persons who cannot work in more demanding and less structured situations. Although the ultimate goal of habilitation is placement in a regular, competitive job, some adults who are retarded cannot always meet this goal.

*Employment options.* Today a number of employment options are available for adults with mental retardation (see Figure 11.2). Economic conditions, the extent and adequacy of systematic training, the flexibility of the employment sites to facilitate adjustment, and an individual's character- istics interact to determine which option is most appropriate for a specific person at a given time.

*Nonemployment.* This category is appropriate for three groups. The first group is those who are so profoundly involved or whose skills are so minimal that it is unlikely that vocational training can be undertaken and employment secured. The second group is those who are capable of working but choose not to. This group includes people who are influenced by disincentives that create compelling reasons for not seeking employment. The third group is those who want to work but cannot find employment. It can also include workers who have been laid off.

*Unpaid employment.* Some adults who are retarded may have opportuni- ties to work but not receive pay. In some instances this situation is positive: The individual is participating in an ongoing activity, and income is neither

FIGURE 11.2   Employment Options

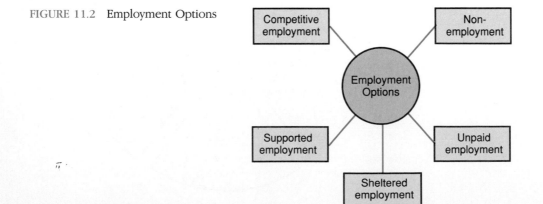

necessary nor expected (e.g., volunteer work). In other situations this option may reflect unfair treatment, as when a person is not paid for work that usually generates income. As some (Brown et al., 1984) have argued, however, placing a person in a job, even without pay, may be preferable to more restrictive sheltered services.

*Sheltered employment.*    One of the most traditional employment options for adults who are retarded is sheltered employment. This practice, which is associated with settings like activity centers or sheltered workshops, is what many laypeople consider the model for employment of adults with retardation. In recent years movement away from sheltered employment has been discernible, but there are many sheltered settings in communities around the country. Sheltered settings will continue to be a viable option for some persons who cannot be placed on regular job sites.

Sheltered employment is also discussed in chapter 7.

In many areas, local associations for citizens who are retarded, church groups, and other private organizations have developed programs to provide daytime activities for those who require continuous supervision. These activity centers serve persons with severe retardation who are older than school age and considered to be too handicapped to meet production criteria within workshop settings, though some may move on to these settings. Many of these individuals lack the behavioral and motor skills required in sheltered workshops. Activity centers provide training in such prevocational and vocational skills as simple assembling tasks. They stress increased self-sufficiency over employability and place a greater emphasis on teaching daily living skills—travel, safety, grooming, and communication. They also typically include recreational and socialization programs, as well as opportunities for work and pay.

Sheltered workshops, usually located in one large facility, offer an assortment of job experiences to train vocational skills and behaviors within simulated work situations. These workshops are generally comprehensive, providing both long-term and transitional placements, and they may serve individuals who are mildly, moderately, and severely retarded, as well as individuals with other handicapping conditions. Although activity centers are sometimes considered to be a form of workshop, sheltered workshops are usually of two types: transitional and long-term. Transitional workshops train clients for eventual competitive employment and often place a strong emphasis on production; clients in these settings may have to meet established production quotas. Long-term or extended workshops (Heward & Orlansky, 1988) provide training to clients who are likely to continue in this setting indefinitely, and they place less emphasis on rate of production. Some workshops offer both types of training.

Most sheltered workshops provide basic rehabilitation services, including screening, evaluation, training, placement, and follow-up. Programs focus on developing individual competency in a variety of tasks and the personal behaviors and attitudes associated with good working performance: promptness, attention to task, sociability, grooming, safety, and so on. Assignments within a workshop may include refinishing and restoring used goods, crafts, or contract work like cleaning headphones for airlines. As workshops strive to expand an individual's abilities and potentials and develop a repertoire of marketable job skills, the quality of the services offered depends on the number and variety of outside contracts the workshop can procure. This need requires that one or more of the staff members devote much time to securing contracts. These staff members must be knowledgeable about local businesses and aware of the workshop's production capabilities. Their job is to sell the services of the workshop to business and industry (Brolin, 1982). Long-term contracts are desirable because they provide a steady, reliable source of work and income to the workshop. Workers within sheltered workshops are usually paid on a piece-work basis at rates comparable to other local rates.

**Why are workers in sheltered workshops usually paid on a piece-work basis instead of at an hourly rate?**

An example of a successful attempt to train and employ severely handicapped workers in a long-term workshop setting is the Specialized Training Program (STP). This model was originally developed at the University of Oregon and has been replicated in six western states (Bellamy et al., 1983). Although workers in these settings do possess acceptable behavior and motor skills, they are both severely handicapped and considered inappropriate recipients of vocational services. Yet, the clients in the STP programs are capable of productive work.

*Supported employment.*    Although the goal of most programmatic efforts is to place clients or students on their own in a competitive job, this is not always immediately possible. An attractive intermediate option that has shown repeated success is the supported employment model. Buttressed by initiatives from the Office of Special Education and Rehabilitative Services, supported employment exemplifies the movement away from sheltered settings toward more integrative ones.

In general, this intermediate option allows for decreasing supervision and segregation and increasing autonomy and integration through structured support given to the individual in competitive settings. Persons with retardation who are placed in supported employment may work *(a)* individually at regular job sites with varying amounts of special support, *(b)* in small groups within a regular industrial setting *(enclaves)* and receive more continuous support and supervision, or *(c)* in a group that resembles a work crew.

Bellamy, Rhodes, Mank, and Albin (1988), in analyzing the definition of supported employment presented in the Developmental Disabilities Act (1984), have outlined its three major components: paid employment, continuing support, and integration. Figure 11.3 shows the relationship of these three features. All three must be present. One other feature of the definition of supported employment is that it is appropriate for those

FIGURE 11.3  Components of
Supported Employment

Supported employment can exist only when paid
employment, ongoing support, and integration are
present.

From *Supported Employment: A Community Imple-
mentation Guide* by G. T. Bellamy, L. E. Rhodes,
D. M. Mank, and J. M. Albin, 1988, Baltimore: Paul
H. Brookes. Reprinted by permission.

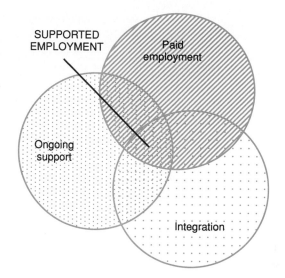

individuals for whom employment in competitive settings (i.e., for pay at or
above the minimum wage) is not likely.

Supported employment can be conceptualized as a more attractive
alternative to sheltered employment and, for many, as a transitional phase to
competitive, nonassisted employment. It approximates competitive employment in that *(a)* individuals are paid for work performance and not skill
development—although this may be at minimal levels (Bellamy et al., 1988);
*(b)* structured support is given to clients who by virtue of their skill levels
need further training by employment specialists (who are not paid employees of a given company and thus relieve employers of this task); and *(c)*
clients work beside persons who are not disabled (see Table 11.3).

The supported employment concept has been applied in different ways,
but the three most frequently discussed models are the supported job, the
enclave-in-industry, and the mobile crew. Schutz (1988) has summarized
these three models' differences (see Table 11.3). Note that terms are often
used interchangeably (e.g., employment specialist = job coach), and that
implementation of these models may vary somewhat from the descriptions in
the table.

One example of the supported employment model that involves the use
of employment specialists is described below (COMTEP, n.d.). After a suitable
place of employment has been secured for a client, job coaches go with the
client to the job site and provide any assistance the worker may need in
adapting to the new situation. Coaches are gradually withdrawn so that the
worker is able to function independently. This model increases individual
workers' chances to adjust to their jobs. Because the coaches offer the
necessary assistance, the employer does not have to, but no matter who

TABLE 11.3    Supported Employment Models

| Services | Program Model | | |
|---|---|---|---|
| | Supported Work | Enclave | Mobile Crew |
| Primary jobs targeted | Job types vary | Manufacturing contracts | Service contracts |
| Organizational structure | Nonprofit support to individuals and employers | Nonprofit support to host company | Nonprofit |
| Number of workers per job site | 1 per job site | 6–8 per site | 4–6 per crew |
| Assessment | Conducted at job site, based on ecological inventory approach | Conducted at job site, based on ecological inventory approach | Conducted at job site, based on ecological inventory approach |
| Training | Individual training at placement site in:<br>☐ job tasks<br>☐ social survival skills | Individual training in:<br>☐ production tasks<br>☐ social survival skills | Individual training in:<br>☐ service tasks<br>☐ community integration activities |
| Amount of support | Time-limited follow-up continuous initially, decreasing support over time | Enduring, continuous | Enduring, continuous |
| Supervisor | Supervision shifts from job coach to employer over time | Continuous supervision by job coach; host company may assign employee as backup supervisor | Continuous supervision by job coach |
| Staff to worker ratio | 1:8 to 1:10 | 1:6 to 1:8 | 1:4 to 1:6 |

From "New Directions and Strategies in Habilitation Services: Toward Meaningful Employment Outcomes" by R. P. Schutz, 1988, in L. W. Heal, J. I. Haney, and A. R. Novak Amado (Eds.), *Integration of Developmentally Disabled Individuals into the Community* (2nd ed., pp. 193–210), Baltimore: Paul H. Brookes. Reprinted by permission.

assists the person, supervision shifts from skill training to monitoring of performance and satisfaction. Some school systems are also using this model in work-study programs with high school students, placing them in garages, hospitals, or good service programs, for example. These intermediate positions are significant in helping individuals advance to independent employment, as they lessen the differences between sheltered work and competitive job sites, and facilitate the transfer of skills. The last point is especially important, because research on the success of individuals' movement from sheltered programs to competitive ones is disappointing (Stodden & Browder, 1986).

*Competitive employment.*    More adults with mental retardation are taking their places in independent, competitive employment settings. Unfortunately, some of these jobs involve only unskilled or semiskilled labor, and many of them are part time. Some individuals are self-employed and hire themselves out as yard workers or housekeepers. These persons obtain positions through their vocational programs or, as is more often the case, locate jobs independently through friends, family, or their own efforts. In the past, most adults who were retarded and who found competitive jobs were mildly affected; however, this has changed in recent times, as more individuals who are moderately or severely retarded are finding success in competitive settings. Numerous variables dictate whether competitive employment is feasible for a particular client: individual abilities, personality, and preparation; employer attitude and willingness to consider the person a capable worker; and flexibility within the work environment.

*Comparisons of employment options.*    Table 11.4 summarizes the different employment options we have presented in this section. It integrates information found elsewhere (Schutz, 1988; Vogelsberg & Schutz, 1988) with the points highlighted above. The organization of the table suggests a sequence of preference from left to right, indicating that competitive settings are preferred to other options if appropriate. One could assert that unpaid or volunteer employment is preferable to sheltered employment if it takes place in integrated environments, but it is given the less preferred position in the table, just as it has in the discussion. What becomes obvious from this comparative table are the attractive features of the supported employment option. The growing amount of research validating supported employment corroborates this position.

*Issues.*    Although many issues are related to the employment of adults with mental retardation, three selected ones are highlighted here: characteristics of employability, maintenance of employability, and disincentives to employment.

   Many studies have been conducted to identify the *characteristics of employability* that accompany successful work performance. The results of

TABLE 11.4    Analysis of Employment Options

| Dimension | Employment Option | | | | |
|---|---|---|---|---|---|
| | Nonemployment | Unpaid | Sheltered | Supported | Competitive |
| Pay for work | no | no | below minimum | minimum or more | minimum or more |
| Ongoing support | none | no special | continual | continual at first; faded over time | no special |
| Integration | | | | | |
| a. contact | no | yes | no | yes | yes |
| b. setting | — | usually community | segregated | community | community |
| Production of valued goods | no | possible | unlikely | yes | yes |
| Population served | profound to mild | severe to mild | severe to moderate | severe to mild | severe to mild |

From "New Directions and Strategies in Habilitation Services: Toward Meaningful Employment Outcomes" by R. P. Schutz, 1988, in L. W. Heal, J. I. Haney, & A. R. Novak Amado (Eds.), *Integration of Developmentally Disabled Individuals into the Community* (2nd ed.), Baltimore: Paul H. Brookes; and from "Establishing Community Employment Programs for Persons with Severe Disabilities: Systems Designs and Resolutions" by R. T. Vogelsberg and R. P. Schutz, 1988, in M. D. Powers (Ed.), *Expanding Systems of Service Delivery for Persons with Developmental Disabilities,* Baltimore: Paul H. Brookes. Adapted by permission.

this research indicate that personal and social skills are more directly related to employability and job stability than measured intelligence or physical dexterity. The characteristics that tend to predict job success include (Kolstoe, 1961; Sali & Amir, 1970):

☐ Positive attitude toward the work sites
☐ Motivated behaviors—promptness, pride
☐ Ability to get along with supervisors and co-workers
☐ Ability to communicate with more than one-word responses
☐ Physical attractiveness—grooming, good health, appropriate height-to-weight ratio
☐ Fair motor coordination

   The ability to adjust socially to the work environment is the crucial factor in acquiring and maintaining a position. Occupational failure may be caused by inability to get along with employers and co-workers, poor attendance and punctualilty, poor personal appearance and manners, and irregularity of moods and behaviors. Environmental constraints like problems of obtaining reliable transportation, family difficulties, and lack of appropriate referrals and support also hinder successful employment for some individuals.

   Successful competitive employment appears to be directly related to motivation and the ability to adjust and respond to the vocational and social demands of the job situation. In 1969, Kantner again confirmed that IQ was not a significant predictor of success and that, of 82 subjects studied, only 6% lost their jobs because of inability to perform some of the skills necessary for the job. This and other studies strongly imply that vocational programs must emphasize the development of good personal adjustment and general job skills if they are to be effective. Employability must be strengthened by providing training in such areas as interviewing skills, social and conversational skills, using transportation services, and reporting in when sick or late, in addition to developing task-oriented manipulative skills. Rusch and Mithaug (1985) argue that more attention must be given to the social context in which a person must function. They advocate a systems-analytic approach to competitive employment preparation, which in principle is based on the concept of *criterion of ultimate functioning* (Brown, Nietupski, & Hamre-Nietupski, 1976).

School systems are also incorporating career development exercises into their curricula for special classes to help build realistic job aspirations and awareness of responsibilities (see Brolin & Kokaska, 1979). Too few training programs are attempting to seek better "fits" between the social demands of a particular work setting and the personal and communication skills of the individual. Improvements in early and well focused programs should better the possibility of competitive employment for most persons with retardation.

One topic that is receiving some attention in the training and instructional literature is the need to maintain performance over time (skill demonstration). Rusch, Martin, and White (1985) emphasize that maintenance should not be considered a given and that cueing strategies (both external and internal) may need to be taught to individuals to ensure appropriate long-term performance. Mechanisms must capitalize on cues in situ, particularly as more supported and independent models of competitive employment take root.

Forces still act against job attainment. Castellani (1987) notes that employment is often at odds with certain community services, particularly income support and health care programs, which many adults who are retarded receive. Conley, Noble, and Elder (1986) identify three major obstacles: *(a)* reduction of net gain from work; *(b)* development of dependency and negative attitudes toward work; and *(c)* greater income security for those who continue to receive the services than their working peers achieve. In the first case, for some individuals work may result in a net loss in income and an additional tax burden. Next, a person who qualifies as being unable to earn above the Substantial Gainful Activity (SGA) level and therefore receives monthly benefits has little incentive to disprove this determination. The third factor works on a simple principle—it's better to be safe than sorry. Conley et al. (1986) describe this scenario:

> It is not reasonable to expect these beneficiaries to give up easily what appears to be a secure monthly cash income and assured medical care in exchange for jobs that are often temporary or insecure and that may pay little more (or possibly less) than their monthly benefit. (p. 73)

## LIVING ARRANGEMENTS

*Where* people live determines to a great extent *how* they live. This seems obvious when one thinks of persons in institutions, and it is also true of those residing in the community. For some people who are mentally retarded, living in the community may mean having a local address and a neighborhood, yet spending hours alone in a room not knowing anyone or how to occupy the time. Or it may mean a very active life that includes interacting with neighbors, catching a bus to work or to shop, planning meals, and maintaining an apartment. Community living is more than just physical location. It demands involvement and interaction with the immediate surroundings and should be preceded by appropriate training. Often interaction with the community has been negative. Zoning laws that regulate the establishment of group homes have discriminated unfairly against adults who are retarded. Community opposition to the establishment of group

*Shopping skills are essential to community living.*

homes has also been documented (Kastner, Reppucci, & Pezzoli, 1979; Lubin, Schwartz, Zigman, & Janicki, 1982; Seltzer, 1984).

The factors introduced earlier in this chapter to explain the community movement are largely responsible for the development of community residential facilities (CRF). It is interesting to recognize, as Lakin, Hill, and Bruininks (1988) have pointed out, that this movement has occurred in the absence of any national program focused on residential services. Nevertheless, almost every state and the District of Columbia have shown increases in the number of adults with developmental disabilities who are living in smaller residences. Figure 11.4 shows these changes (in terms of percentages) by state over the course of a five-year period.

Wolfensberger (1969) has strongly advocated establishing small residences in neighborhood settings, having live-in houseparents and a family orientation, and using generic community services. He also suggests using foster care and adoption as means to mainstream those with retardation individually. Others still believe that people who are retarded need to be protected and benevolently guided on a day-to-day basis, limiting their exposure to the community from fear of the risks involved. Still another view focuses on establishing alternative community environments by organizing residents into a cohesive and independent group—in settings apart from the general public. Emphasis on acquiring daily living skills through planned activities defines still other settings as having a training orientation and function.

The dominant orientation that a CRF has is a function of the characteristics and needs of its residents. CRFs vary in size, location, number of residents, staffing patterns, and degree of handicapping conditions residents have. But level of retardation does not invariably determine the most appropriate residential setting. The underlying orientation and operating procedures of a CRF greatly influence for whom it is best suited and how the following areas are addressed.

☐ Degree of autonomy allowed or developed within the residents
☐ Restrictions placed on residents: required activities, curfews, etc.
☐ Residents' role in determining house or facility policies
☐ Residents' responsibilities within the facility
☐ Degree of privacy allowed
☐ Sexuality of residents
☐ Residents' length of stay: long-term or transitional
☐ Emphasis on community involvement
☐ Atmosphere created through decorations and furnishings
☐ Actualizing the normalization principle

Some persons who are mentally retarded remain in their families' homes instead of moving to alternative community arrangements. Yet many of these same issues and perspectives—specifically those affecting autonomy and responsibility—are pertinent to the home setting also. Whether the locus is

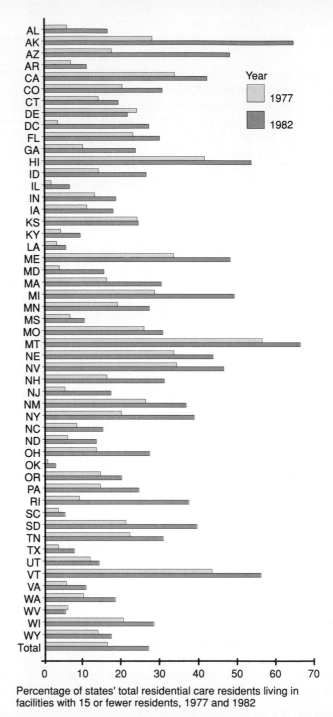

Percentage of states' total residential care residents living in
facilities with 15 or fewer residents, 1977 and 1982

FIGURE 11.4   Data on the Community Residential Movement

From "Trends and Issues in the Growth of Community Residential Services" by K. C. Lakin, B. K. Hill, and R. H. Bruininks, 1988, in M. P. Janicki, M. W. Krauss, and M. M. Seltzer (Eds.), *Community Residences for Persons with Developmental Disabilities: Here to Stay* (pp. 25–43), Baltimore: Paul H. Brookes. Reprinted by permission.

a private home or a community facility, the match between an individual's needs and the setting's emphasis ultimately defines the quality of the living arrangement.

A number of community living arrangements have been developed, although a generally accepted taxonomy of them does not exist. Examples of various systems are available (Baker, Seltzer, & Seltzer, 1977; Hill & Lakin, 1986; Scheerenberger, 1982). We use a different system here. Although the residential options described below are on a continuum of sorts, their availability in some locations, particularly rural settings, may be limited. And quality can vary greatly from one setting to another.

*ICF-MR programs.* Intermediate Care Facilities for the Mentally Retarded (ICF-MR) provide 24-hour care, including nursing, medical support, training, and therapeutic support to the residents. Theoretically, these facilities provide necessary services to a more involved clientele in a less restricted environment—the community. Some observers (Taylor, McCord, & Stanford, 1981), however, have suggested that certain states have used the federal Medicaid monies allocated for these facilities to create "mini-institutions."

*Group homes.* The group home is the most common community living arrangement that social services or private organizations establish for adults who are mentally retarded. In these homes, a group lives within a residential neighborhood, receiving support and supervision from live-in counselors. Some homes are transitional in focus; others serve as long-term residences. Sometimes several homes are near each other and staffed by a single resident manager. These settings, known as congregate homes, provide a living environment suited for more capable residents because supervision, counseling, and assistance is less intensive. Many evoke images of comfortable family settings—using large old houses where possible, decorating them with the memorabilia and belongings of the residents, and encouraging a sense of responsibility and contribution by household members. Most are in sharp contrast to sterile, institutional settings.

These homes usually attempt to give training in daily living skills and community awareness through direct experiences. Areas emphasized include self-help skills, household management, basic academics, socialization, leisure activities, and travel and safety skills.

The everyday life in such settings resembles that of other adults who are not disabled. During the day house members may participate in activities like work, school, or training; at night they are likely to be involved in preparing dinner, cleaning up, watching television, receiving instruction, or enjoying a social or leisure activity. Figure 11.5 shows the weekly schedule at one group home.

Group homes can be categorized according to size and population. The number and characteristics of the residents may also affect the degree of

FIGURE 11.5 — Weekly Resident and Staff Schedule at One Group Home

All clients are at work or school during the day

4–5 p.m. Clients arrive home. Work on personal hygiene, socialization, and daily living skills.

**EVENING**

| MONDAY | TUESDAY | WEDNESDAY | THURSDAY | FRIDAY | SATURDAY | SUNDAY |
|---|---|---|---|---|---|---|
| 5–6 p.m. Dinner Preparation and Table Setting | | | 5–7 NIGHT COLLEGE | 5–6 p.m. Dinner Preparation and Table Setting → | | |
| 6–7 p.m. Dinner and Clean-up | | | 7–8 p.m. Dinner and Clean-up | 6–7 p.m. Dinner and Clean-up → | | |
| 7–9 Coffeehouse (every other week) Individualized Tutoring by House Staff | 7–9 p.m. Free Time | 6:30–9:30 p.m. TUTORS (with clients from 7–9 p.m.) | 8–9 p.m. Free Time | 7–9:30 p.m. Recreational Activity → | | 7–9 p.m. Free Time  Individualized Tutoring by House Staff |
| 9–10 p.m. Personal Hygiene, Daily Living Skills, Socialization | Throughout Evening Personal Hygiene, Daily Living Skills, Socialization | 9–10 p.m. Personal Hygiene, Daily Living Skills, Socialization | | 9:30–10 p.m. Personal Hygiene, Daily Living Skills, Socialization → | | 9–10 p.m. Personal Hygiene, Daily Living Skills, Socialization |

**DAY**

| SATURDAY | SUNDAY |
|---|---|
| Residents sleep in. | Church (optional) |
| Residents prepare and clean-up breakfast and lunch (with staff help as needed) | |
| Shopping or Group Activities or Individual Activities | 3–5 p.m. Required Activities  Meal Selection |
| *Residents usually plan and implement their own weekend schedule as much as possible. | Housework  Food Shopping |

FIGURE 11.5   Weekly Resident and Staff Schedule at One Group Home

personalization, socialization, training, and integration the residents get. Some features of group homes are listed below.

☐ Most group homes have 15 or fewer residents, an in-house staff, and a relief staff.
☐ Others offer more specialized services and have additional professional staff (e.g., nurses) on duty.
☐ Opportunities for resident autonomy, decision-making, and contact with adults who are not retarded vary greatly.
☐ Some mixed group homes are transitional and serve individuals other than those with retardation, often providing a place for convalescing rather than training.
☐ An increasing number of group homes serve or are capable of serving older adults who are retarded.

Group homes have often been controversial. Community opposition, usually from neighbors, is a common, major barrier to providing less restricted living options. Although neighbors fear that their property values will decrease if a group home is established in their neighborhood, their fears are unfounded, as real estate values of homes in the same communities as group homes do not seem to decrease (Wiener, Anderson, & Nietupski, 1982). Interestingly, Seltzer (1984) has found that efforts to educate the public about retardation and group homes correlated positively with community opposition. She observed that "opposition is less likely when the community becomes aware either after the residence begins operations or more than 6 months before it opens" (p. 7). The implication of these findings is that it might be better to adopt a "low-profile" entry strategy rather than a "high-profile" (i.e., intensive community education programs) one when establishing a community residence.

*Protected settings.* Certain community living arrangements afford adults who are mentally retarded protected settings with varying degrees of support and supervision. The most notable organizational structures in this category are the foster home and boarding settings. These arrangements are designed to maintain individuals in a family-oriented setting. The quality of care, support, and supervision can range from excellent to abusive, as the person who manages the home exercises an extraordinary amount of power. Because these providers are reimbursed for each adult in their homes, their motivations for offering their services can be misguided and sometimes malevolent. Three different settings are described below.

☐ Care homes—licensed family or residential homes that provide room, board, and personal care
☐ Boarding homes—licensed homes that provide room and board to ambulatory individuals needing minimal care and supervision

# THE CAMPHILL COMMUNITIES

The Camphill movement, and others like it throughout the world, strive to adapt the environment to the individual. These programs create discrete societies where persons with retardation may live sheltered from the rejection and failures they too often experience in society. Although this type of placement differs markedly from the community-based models we describe in this chapter, some would argue that they offer a setting that is normal in the same way that an ethnic community is a normal, though different, segment of the larger community.

In all respects, Camphill is more than just a program—it is a philosophy. Camphill villages are based on the thinking of Rudolf Steiner, who provided the basic tenets of the Camphill movement. Today Karl Konig and Carlo Pietzner are the most prominent proponents of Steiner's thinking.

Steiner, an Austrian, was deeply influenced by the philosophical writings of Goethe, who believed in a spiritual realm beyond man's sensory experiences. Steiner believed that these psychic forces must be used to restore a sense of humanistic values to a materialistic world and that latent in every person is an enhanced consciousness that proper training can develop.

In 1939, Konig began the Camphill movement in Aberdeen, Scotland, in the form of a school for children with physical, emotional, and mental handicaps. The initial success of this school led to the establishment of similar schools throughout England and Europe. Concern for the students after they passed school age was behind the establishment of the first Camphill village, Botton, in Yorkshire, England, in 1954. Pietzner (1966) has said that the most striking aspect of the movement is its concern for the adult who is retarded. The first such village in the United States was founded in 1961 by Pietzner.

Steiner, Konig, and Pietzner have implied that the purpose of Camphill is to cure those who are retarded, but in actuality the "cure" lies in providing a tolerant, sympathetic, and compromising minisociety.

Each member of these villages produces according to ability and receives according to needs. There is no staff-client dichotomy, and the emphasis in on forming healthy interpersonal relationships. All members of the community share the ownership and the profits of labor as equal partners. Staff members are referred to as *co-workers* and are fully committed members of the community. The staff consists primarily of adults, who usually receive assistance from local volunteers functioning as temporary workers. Each co-worker is houseparent to a group of villagers, who together represent a family unit, and every "family" has a house of its own.

Adult villagers must be able to care for their own physical needs and require no medical or custodial care. Those who can meet the social standards of the normal community are not permitted to be villagers. This attitude derives from the belief that the best place for adults with retardation is in the security of their own homes. Konig realized that a Camphill village "family" is only a substitute for the natural security of an individual's own family; he has recommended that an adult who is retarded be kept at home if at all possible (Konig, 1966).

The goal of each village is economic self-sufficiency; to this end, each community has its own livestock and vegetable garden. Surplus food and products manufactured in the village are sold to neighboring communities. Although the objective is to be self-sufficient, tuition is charged to the villagers' parents, and outside donations are accepted to reduce operating costs.

☐ Companion homes—licensed private family homes that provide a homelike environment and an active program of training for adults; a similar setting is available for children and is called a *teaching home*

***Community training programs.*** Workshop dormitories have been developed in some areas as boarding-school type models for individuals working in sheltered workshops. These dormitories are programmatically or administratively attached to the workshop. Although they stress community living skills, vocational training usually receives a greater emphasis. These training programs and dormitories are generally transitional.

Similar training models also exist on the grounds of some institutions. These are frequently called *community preparation programs* and are designed to give residents some controlled, structured experiences with the increased independence, risks, and responsibilities they will encounter if and when they are deinstitutionalized. Such programs typically use a cottage or building located somewhat apart from other institutional facilities, and they offer training in telling time, managing money, using public transportation, doing household chores, using social skills, and exercising one's legal rights. Participants may also commute daily to an employment site within the community. The quality of these settings as preparation for community living depends on their ability to approximate and progressively involve residents in the circumstances they will encounter when they move beyond the institutional grounds and shelter.

***Apartment programs.*** Apartment programs represent the least restrictive alternatives within community residential programming. The degree of supervision, support, and training residents get depends on individual needs. Some residents need support in money management, cooking, or household skills. Others may demand services only during times of crisis. Residents in these programs are usually less severely handicapped than those in other models and have better personal and social adjustment skills. Variations of this service model include

☐ Apartment clusters—several apartments in close proximity to each other, sharing the supervision of a central staff person
☐ Single or resident apartments—a live-in arrangement in which a person who is not retarded shares a home or apartment with one or more individuals who are.
☐ Independent apartment living—one or more individuals who are retarded living in an apartment and receiving support and assistance on a periodic basis from a nonresident staff person.

## INCOME MAINTENANCE AND HEALTH CARE COVERAGE

Many adults who are mentally retarded benefit from certain entitlements that exist to guarantee that their needs are taken care of. Here we offer only a brief introduction to the history, national fiscal commitment, and intricacies of these programs. Figure 11.6 is a matrix that shows the four major programs of interest. The accompanying descriptive information helps to explain the purpose of each program. The two programs with the greatest effect on adults who have mental retardation are supplemental security income (SSI) and Medicaid.

As a way to provide regular income to those in need, SSI is available to persons who are disabled before the age of 22 and who are incapable of gainful employment. It is a federally funded program that is augmented by state contributions in all but 7 states. The actual amount each person receives varies and is tied into the individual's income as well as other factors (e.g., amount in savings account). Boggs (1988) noted that in 1987 an eligible adult living independently could receive federal SSI benefits if the monthly income was less than $360 and assets were less than $1,800. Other conditions can affect the monthly benefits. If residing in a publicly supported setting, the person is eligible to receive only a $25 per month personal needs allowance. A person living in a family setting receives only one third of the full SSI allowance. Once individuals meet the eligibility criteria, they are entitled to monthly benefits as long as they remain eligible. Castellani (1987) has pointed out the dual importance of SSI: It not only directly assists individuals but also is a source of funding through these adults to community-based services.

Medicaid is a state-federal health care program largely for people who cannot afford private insurance or pay cash for medical services. Adults with

FIGURE 11.6    Matrix of Entitlement Programs

Matrix representing relationships among Social Security (SSDI, ADC), Medicare, Supplemental Security Income (SSI), and Medicaid for persons with disabilities. The criteria for eligibility based on disability are uniform for all programs in all states. The economic criteria differ. Social Security and Medicare are federally administered according to uniform rules in all states. SSI basic entitlements are federally administered according to uniform rules; most states provide state supplementation under state-specific criteria. Medicaid is a federally assisted, state-administered program. In most states, SSI-eligible persons are also eligible for Medicaid. In addition, some persons who meet the disability criteria may meet the economic criteria (means tests) for Medicaid even if ineligible for SSI. Children with disabilities may be eligible for SSI, Medicaid, or both.

From *How to Prepare for Their Future* by Association for Retarded Citizens of the United States, 1984, Arlington, TX: Author. Reprinted by permission.

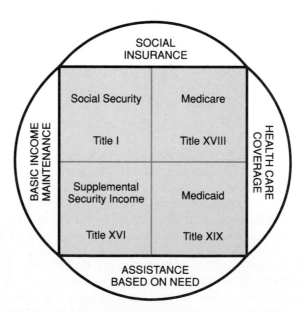

mental retardation typically qualify for Medicaid. Stone and Newcomer (1985) have described the Medicaid program as follows:

> Medicaid operates as a third-party insurance coverage program. The state, in other words, pays bills for services rendered to individuals eligible for the program. The services received are determined by the provider and patient rather than by Medicaid staff, thus creating a largely open-ended entitlement program. (p. 30)

Under medicaid, the federal government reimburses states for 50%–77% of the total costs.

Ironically as discussed earlier in this chapter, the receipt of benefits like SSI can be a disincentive to seeking and obtaining employment. An individual's SSI benefits could be stopped if that person's income from employment exceeded the monthly criterion level. Nevertheless, programs like Medicaid and SSI are extremely important to many adults who are mentally retarded.


## RECREATION AND LEISURE

Like all people, those who are retarded need recreational and leisure activities to balance the rigors of daily living. Unfortunately, far too many individuals with mental retardation remain outside the mainstream of community life in these areas. Yet evidence shows that health and physical fitness, language, social skills, and self-esteem can be enhanced through participation in various recreational and leisure pursuits (Wilson, 1974).

Though many persons who are mentally retarded express interest in a wide range of activities, the recreational repertoire of most of them consists of passive activities like watching television or the movies, listening to records, and looking at magazines. If special bus passes are available, some will ride buses for hours on end. Few adults who are retarded go to parties, plays, or initiate social get-togethers. Sometimes this is because of overprotection by families or benefactors. Their activities are restricted to those they can do alone or with family members, and to those that avoid contact with strangers or new places (Katz & Yekutiel, 1974). This uncreative use of leisure time results from factors associated with both the individual and the community. Although difficulties in these areas are not inherent in mental retardation, many do not have recreational skills because of limited experiences or instruction, slow or uneven physical development, or a lack of friends with whom to learn or play. Shortness of community funds, trained personnel, and until recently awareness of the need for recreation has also contributed to the problem, which may also be compounded by transportation difficulties. These difficulties may be more pronounced for persons living in more independent settings, as they may have less accessibility to peer groups or transportation than persons living in group or family homes.

Recreation programs have existed for many years in institutions, though they have been more concerned with keeping residents occupied and providing relief for staff than with developing skills. Advocates for those who are retarded, however, have demanded that community recreational opportunities available to normal individuals be extended to other persons also. Communities have begun responding publicly and privately by developing special programs and modifying regular services. Examples include

☐ Special overnight or day camps for people with special needs
☐ Special Olympics programs
☐ Therapeutic recreation classes and programs
☐ Mainstreaming into regular recreation facilities and classes

Other innovative projects have sprung up over the past few years. Individuals who are retarded in Milwaukee have formed a group to publish a local newspaper—the *Milwaukee Citizens*. The Mohawks and Squaws, a social organization in Massachusetts, was developed to provide a club atmosphere—a place to belong. Recently, the Mohawks and Squaws have begun successfully to hire themselves out as consultants specializing in mental retardation. Rec Clubs have begun in some areas of the country (Schloss, Fodor-Davis, & Moore, 1986). Drama groups, craft guilds, jogging clubs, cooking groups, and other activities have increased over the past few years. Parents, teachers, and service providers have realized the importance of developing home-centered hobbies and have included instruction in card games, checkers, plant growing, stamp collecting, and other leisure projects in their curricula or service plans. Manufacturers have begun to produce games that do not rely on reading skills, but use color codes and shapes to facilitate play. The development of special equipment like modified bowling balls and walkers for ice skating has broadened opportunities to participate in sports. Specialized curricula such as *Ho'onanea Program: A Leisure Curriculum Component for Severely Handicapped Children and Youth* (Wuerch & Voeltz, 1981) have been developed specifically to address this area. The removal of physical and attitudinal barriers has also expanded the options available to adults who are mentally retarded.

Until recently, use of leisure time by those with retardation was characterized more by a lack of choice and knowledge than an expression of true interest. As with other skill areas, persons who are retarded need intentional and systematic instruction in the use of leisure-time skills in order to develop hobbies and participate in activities with confidence. Communities are beginning to respond with preparation and opportunities enabling these individuals to make choices and to gain personal and social enrichment through recreational activities.

## MOBILITY

Travel develops an awareness of other people and places, facilitates a sense of personal control over the environment, and is something most adults do. The ability to move from one place to another is essential, and remaining in one fixed location is viewed as odd and limiting.

Mobility is complex for persons who are mentally retarded. Most do not have driver's licenses or cars. They must walk, depend on others for rides, or use public transportation systems. Independent travel skills also require certain intellectual and physical abilities.

Each of these options presents its own limitations and requirements for these individuals. Always riding with friends or caretakers forces one to be dependent on other people. Walking limits destinations to relatively short distances. An individual must also know how to cross streets, as well as knowing where and how to go. Public transportation systems can present a complex array of limitations and requirements. They limit destinations to routes covered, and travel must be within the system's hours of operation. Use of public transport may thrust individuals into a world that relies on reading, telling time, determining correct change (if passes are unavailable), and discriminating locations quickly. Individuals who are retarded generally have difficulty under these circumstances.

Safety is another concern in independent travel. What if persons with retardation get lost? Being in public places like bus stops, or walking on streets, may expose them to perplexing situations, and they may become disoriented and confused. Even though traveling in groups may offer more safety and security for the individual, proponents of normalization discourage having small "packs" of individuals, all of whom are retarded, walk or ride together, as this tends to isolate and mark them (Wolfensberger, 1972).

These limitations, difficulties, and dangers are real issues that can restrict ability to travel and ultimately confine people to home. But many of these problems can be overcome through sequential systematic training. Other concerns take community awareness and a willingness to change existing formats.

Many educational, vocational, and residential programs now include instruction in street safety and mobility skills as components of their total treatment services. Individuals learn general safety rules such as crossing only on green lights and at crosswalks and looking both ways; they also develop a repertoire of known paths to points of interest. Persons at all levels of ability are being taught how to use public transport. They initially receive close supervision and guidance, which is phased out until they use the skill independently. They are taught how to recognize buildings and environmental cues as destination points and how to determine whether they are lost. Practice in asking strangers for help, in locating the police, in using identification cards and the telephone, and in responding to harassment is also included in the curriculum. Money skills are taught in conjunction with riding public transportation. The social skills and etiquette of being a passenger, such as appropriate conversation or responses to strangers, are covered. Some communities have begun special transit services to aid those who are physically and severely handicapped. These offer wheelchair lifts and supervision.

The advances in mobility instruction have encouraged and enabled individuals who are retarded to enjoy their lives more, but there is still room for improvement. For instance, the hours that buses run to certain areas within a city need to be extended so that those who rely on this transportation are not restricted to a limited schedule (e.g., 7:00 a.m. to 7:00 p.m.). Coding strategies (colors, symbols) for bus routes and other compensatory techniques would also facilitate mobility. The mobility issue and attempts to address it are not problems of urban centers alone; they exist in more rural areas as well.

Although traveling out of town by oneself may not be difficult for many adults who are retarded, it does present a challenge for some. Making reservations, changing connections or terminals, managing schedules, taxis, hotels, tips, luggage, and many other intricacies of long-distance travel by bus or plane can overwhelm any traveler. These common problems are exacerbated for a person who is mentally retarded. Some airlines do provide special services for these passengers, but this again places them in the position of being singled out as different from and dependent on others. Costs often keep these individuals from enjoying this kind of adventure. Out-of-town travel still presents many difficulties for those who are mentally retarded, yet it is an interesting and exciting challenge for educators and professionals to analyze and break into manageable parts.

## ISSUES RELATED TO COMMUNITY LIVING

Frustrated, puzzled, jubilant, overwhelmed, bored, or busy people who are mentally retarded react to their environments like everyone else. Their work experiences, use of leisure time, relationships, decisions, competencies, and self-images are determined not only by the opportunities available to them but also by their individual aspirations, needs, and interpretations of these interactions. Descriptions of their lifestyles must include personal as well as environmental variables. Several areas have been identified in which the variety, nature, and quality of an individual's development as a community member is significantly affected by the mix of these two dimensions.

### PUBLIC ACCEPTANCE
Public acceptance and understanding are interrelated processes that are crucial for the successful and active integration of adults who are retarded

into our communities. The public in general and communities in particular support the deinstitutionalization movement. The degradation and the pathos of institutions, as reported by Blatt and Kaplan (1966) and Rivera (1972), have angered many. People also support the need for having persons with retardation live in communities as an extension of social equality, equal opportunity, and humanitarian rights (Gallup, 1976). But these attitudes are abstractions; when the time comes to hire a person with retardation or watch a house down the street become a group home, attitudes not infrequently change.

Once in communities, many persons who are retarded encounter resistance and discrimination in employment, housing, education, and public service. Reports have circulated of neighbors' verbally and physically opposing the construction of group homes on their blocks. Zoning ordinances have been quickly enacted or rediscovered to prevent such moves in many communities.

Public attitudes toward those who are retarded vary in their intensity and content. Yet most people seem to want answers to several questions when having adults who are retarded living in their own communities becomes a real possibility. People are often concerned about tax increases that might be required to support group homes and other needed services, declines in property value, the safety of their children, and proper behavior upon meeting such an individual on the street or in a store. Wolpert (1978) has shown that people's fears are generally unfounded in his studies of the effects of group homes in New York City's neighborhoods. If ignored, however, such questions can prevent the acceptance and active social integration of the persons with retardation; anger and fear can be self-perpetuating. These concerns and feelings can develop into legal battles holding up the opening of group homes or into cold stares and avoidance of persons who are retarded in the neighborhood.

Fortunately, fears and reactions can be prevented or changed. Most stem from a lack of public understanding of what mental retardation is and is not. Most people view mentally retardation in general terms, believing that those affected are unable to live independently and require close and constant supervision. These low expectations and the fears associated with them often dissipate when individuals get to know persons who are retarded and recognize their abilities and potential. Several studies have shown that public attitudes and acceptance of those with mental retardation improved after expected undesirable consequences of integration did not occur (Ebron & Ebron, 1967; Hamilton & Bishop, 1976; Hollinger & Jones, 1970; Jaffe, 1966; Semmel & Dickson, 1966). This research indicates that positive experiences in living with people who are retarded promotes more positive attitudes toward them (Kastner, Reppucci, & Pezzoli, 1979).

To facilitate acceptance of persons who are retarded, professionals must address the need for public education. Efforts must be made to inform the

Note Seltzer's (1984) admonitions, presented earlier in this chapter.

public about the nature, causes, and implications of retardation and how to respond and react to those who have this condition. These educational efforts must provide opportunities for interaction that is positive and progressive. Because not all persons adjust successfully to community living, service providers must assure the public that adequate support is available.

The deinstitutionalization project of New York state serves as a model of comprehensive community education and involvement. Public media displays providing information on the needs and nature of mental retardation, task forces comprising community members who locate appropriate group home sites, and speakers' bureaus to address community concerns form the basis of this campaign to educate and obtain support.

> Nothing is more essential to the eventual success of the community mental retardation services movement than the good will, acceptance, and support of the general public. Whether directly as neighbors or employers of retarded persons, or indirected as voters guiding public officials with regard to zoning issues, program proposals, and agency budgets, the general public's knowledge and attitudes are largely responsible for the nature of the community in which retarded people live. That community can accept or reject, help or impair. While the effects of mental retardation on instrumental and expressive functions is real, the extent to which mental retardation constitutes a daily problem for an individual depends heavily on the extent to which other people are tolerant, helpful, and adjustive to the differences of mentally retarded persons. (Kastner et al., 1979)

Other efforts foster acceptance of students with mental retardation in the schools. These programs can serve as models for adult programs as well. Programs that provide structured interactions between children who are not retarded and those who are, especially those with severe retardation, have increased the social acceptance of these students (Voeltz, 1982). The literature suggests that positive outcomes are likely when planned, cooperative opportunities are created. Although we do not yet know the long-term effects of these interactions, positive attitudes established during childhood may well carry over into adulthood.

For a discussion of integration see Chapter 7.

## QUALITY OF LIFE

According to one person's point of view, "It seems funny and ironic . . . that most people spend an exorbitant amount of time trying to distinguish themselves as unique and different while all that a handicapped person wants is to be just like everyone else" (A citizen advocate, 1978). This phenomenon has two different interpretations. In 1967, Edgerton used the phrase *cloak of competence* to describe the lives of 53 newly deinstitutionalized persons. He was referring to their efforts to pass as normal through the assumption of the roles, behaviors, expressions, and mementos of their neighbors, denying to themselves the reality of their label and previous years in isolation. As we saw earlier in this chapter, these individuals were aware of the negative connotations society has attached to the label mentally retarded. They considered public disclosure of their condition devastating, because it would result in their segregation and exclusion. They would not even admit that they were, or had been, "retarded." They devised excuses and pretenses, or "cloaks," for covering up their deficits in an attempt to acquire and maintain acceptance.

Bogdan (1980) offers a perspective that focuses on the individual and promotes the notion that retardation does not exist. Based on his interviews with adults who were considered retarded, he found that many of them did not think they were retarded. He emphatically states:

> Rather than seeing the denial of retardation as part of a client's cloak of competence, I want to suggest that the use of the term "retardate" provides labelers a cloak of competence—calling a person a retardate gives a false impression of knowledge. In research and service delivery it clouds rather than clarifies the nature of the clients. (p. 76)

The terms our society uses to define adulthood—*independence* and *productivity*—and the roles we expect adults to assume—worker, partner, parent, and household manager—contrast sharply with the public images and expectations the term *mental retardation* evokes. In fact, the expression *adult with mental retardation* seems contradictory to many misguided people who think that adults with retardation are childlike, dependent, and unable to make decisions. They are not children; they are adults attempting to establish themselves in their communities and to form their own self-images.

For most people, the criteria by which to judge personal value and competence are achievement measures and material attainment: having a job, meaningful relationships, a home, and personal possessions. These have become the hallmark of normalcy, and many adults with retardation aspire to these goals.

An adequate definition of quality of life is elusive, and while it is discussed regularly, it still wants clarification. Blunden (1988) proposes that quality of life is related to four factors: physical well-being, material well-being, social well-being, and cognitive well-being. Physical well-being corresponds to health and physical condition. Material well-being in this context refers to pecuniary acquisitions as well as to the material environment in which one lives. Social well-being implies opportunities for relationships and the skills to achieve them. Cognitive well-being, perhaps the most important component, is concerned with how adults who are retarded perceive their own quality of life. Too often, we fail to consider this idea.

Adults who are retarded want to be part of a system that is hesitant to welcome anyone who is different. Whether it is more accurate to describe these adults as fighting exposure of who they are or as not thinking of themselves as retarded to begin with, it is safe to say that the label of mental retardation is not a comfortable one. The development of a positive sense of self is a lifelong endeavor for adults who are considered retarded, as it is for everyone, but for people who are retarded the stakes are a bit higher—and the cards are slightly stacked against them.

## FRIENDSHIP

A sense of belonging, of feeling accepted, and of having personal worth are qualities that friendship brings to a person. Friendship creates an alliance and a sense of security. It is a vital human connection.

People who are mentally retarded want and need friendship like everyone else. Yet they typically have few opportunities to form relationships or to develop the skills necessary to interact socially with others. Their exposure to peers may be limited because they live and work in sheltered or

*It's important for people with retardation to have a variety of friends.*

isolated environments. They usually lack a history of socializing events like school clubs, parties, or sleepovers that help to develop or refine personal skills. They may not know how to give of themselves to other people and may be stuck in an egocentric perspective. Persons who are retarded may also respond inappropriately in social situations. Many people shun adults with retardation who freely hug or kiss strangers when greeting them. Some persons with retardation have speech problems, making communication difficult. Other factors may further hinder their ability to attract and keep friends. Some (particularly those who are higher functioning) often avoid associating with others who are also retarded but lower functioning for fear of emphasizing their own stigma.

Because of their few contacts and opportunities, persons with retardation may attempt to befriend strangers or unwitting individuals. Many attempt to become social acquaintances with their professional contacts. In their effort to maintain the contacts and relationships they have developed, some individuals will overcompensate: calling their friend too many times, talking too long on the phone, demanding attention, and not being able to let up. Unfortunately, these behaviors tend to make people uncomfortable and hesitant to interact with them for fear that they will have to hurt their feelings at some later date. Some persons who are retarded have also been victimized or exploited by some "friends"—a situation that is usually blown out of proportion but remains a risk.

Friends can play a vital role in the adjustment to community living of adults who are retarded by providing emotional support and guidance through the exigencies of daily life. Certain organizations have begun to address this need for friendship by initiating social opportunities. One example of this includes the Mohawks and Squaws mentioned earlier. This is a social club for adults with retardation in which members plan their own parties and projects. Some programs offer supervised dating; others establish one-to-one relationships between volunteers and clients for the purpose of aiding adjustment.

One of the biggest hurdles to developing stable friendships is the lack of appropriate social skills for such relationships. A number of suitable social skill programs have been developed and are now available commercially. It is an unforgivable oversight to fail to teach these skills systematically to those who need them.

## SEXUALITY

Sexual expression, marriage, and parenthood may be the most controversial issues surrounding the discussion of adults with mental retardation. The sexual development of persons who are retarded is usually no different from that of others who are not retarded, although they may have some problems understanding and reacting to it. Perception of their sexuality by parents, some professionals, and the general public, however, is laced with misconceptions. Some of the myths include:

- ☐ They are not interested in sex.
- ☐ They are oversexed.
- ☐ They lack the ability to comprehend information regarding their sexuality.
- ☐ They lack the ability to control their sexual desires responsibly.
- ☐ They have enough difficulties without becoming involved with the risks of a sexual relationship.
- ☐ They will reproduce their kind.
- ☐ They cannot adequately care for a child.

Refer to page 166 for an example of how this happened

Because of these fears on the part of caretakers, many people who are retarded have been "sheltered" from sex education, references to love or dating, and opportunities to interact with members of the opposite sex. More invasively, thousands of these adolescents and adults have been sterilized to avoid the consequences of their sexuality, if not the issue itself.

With the movement toward less restrictive living conditions, persons with retardation are returning to or remaining in the community. Many professionals would argue that sexual development and interaction be part of their lives and that the right to sexual expression not be prohibited. The increased independence and patterns of social interaction now available in the community necessitate, in practical terms, that this issue no longer be ignored. Parents, public school systems, group homes, and training programs are beginning to provide those who are mentally retarded with sex education.

*Underlying concerns.* It is impossible to characterize the degree of sexual interest and capabilities of individuals by virtue of the mental retardation classification itself. But the nature of the retardation may have both direct and indirect effects on sexual awareness, knowledge, and expression.

- ☐ It does seem that individuals who are retarded generally have limited information about sex, and the attitudes they do have may lead to problems later on in their lives (Branlinger, 1985, 1988).
- ☐ Persons with retardation usually are not involved in such interpersonal activities as clubs, parties, and dating in which they could develop appropriate social skills for dealing with persons of the opposite sex and make contacts.
- ☐ Their sexual activities are more likely to be considered inappropriate because of their visibility. This is generally because they live under close supervision, in goldfish-bowl circumstances, not because of innate perversity (Johnson, 1971).
- ☐ Normal sexual expression may be difficult to achieve in settings that are considered abnormal, for example, institutions (Blatt, 1987).
- ☐ People with retardation generally lack the outside sources of information

that supplement direct instruction about sex because they do not have an informed peer group (there is little "locker-room talk"), and they may not be able to read printed materials or have access to them.

☐ They tend to be more affected by their inhibition or imposed prohibitions of sexuality than their own need for expression and often have extremely straitlaced views about sex (Rosen et al., 1977).

☐ Sex roles within marriage are defined in terms of providing shelter and support to children, rather than in the sexual relationship between husband and wife (Rosen et al., 1977).

☐ Sex role development may be impaired for persons who have lived in institutions and were exposed only to persons of the same sex.

*Sex and family education.*   More parents and educators are recognizing that sex education is needed for adolescents and adults who are retarded, particularly with the increasing threat of AIDS. Yet sex and family education programs, adequate materials and curricula, and qualified instructors are still too few. Branlinger (1988) found that only limited programming in essential sex education areas was occurring. Many programs emphasize hygiene, morality, and prohibitions (Rosen, 1970, 1972) while omitting such topics as sexual awareness, behaviors, and social and emotional development. Some innovative approaches have, however, begun to help these adults explore and enjoy this aspect of their humanity responsibly. Systematic instruction— using discussions, role playing, and programmed experiences—should be provided in the following areas:

☐ Issues related to anatomy—health care, bodily processes and changes, conception, pregnancy

☐ Means of sexual expression—masturbation, heterosexuality, homosexuality

☐ Sexual responsibility—birth control, venereal disease, parenthood

☐ Interpersonal relationships—appropriate behaviors with strangers, friends, boyfriends and girlfriends

☐ Values, morals, and laws—emphasizing responsibility and possible restraint in certain instances

☐ Decision-making skills and practices

☐ Realities of communicable diseases—especially AIDS

The scope and depth of what to present should be individually determined on the basis of a person's intellectual abilities, physical development, and social needs. Contrary to earlier beliefs, most adults with mental retardation are able to learn socially appropriate sexual behaviors and to demonstrate responsibility and self-control (Johnson, 1971). Some methods of birth control are difficult for some persons with retardation because of their complexity or the requirement for daily attention and responsibility; nevertheless, many are able to use these techniques with much success.

Other methods, such as monthly injections (DepoProvera) that run the risk of serious side effects, should be undertaken very cautiously. The ultimate indignity of sterilization is unnecessary.

***Marriage and parenthood.***   The issues of marriage and parenthood are closely allied with sexuality and elicit similar concerns about the rights of those who are retarded. Laws in many states still restrict and prohibit marriage between "feebleminded" persons and allow the courts to remove a child from a mother who is retarded on the grounds that her condition renders her unfit to be a parent. As with sex, most people with retardation do not receive instruction in the responsibilities of marriage and child-rearing or how to initiate or maintain these roles. Some advocates are beginning to accept marriage for individuals with IQs over 50 (Rosen et al., 1977).

Ingalls (1978) has estimated that the marriage rate among persons with mild retardation is only slightly below the national average. They appear to marry persons of higher intellect, to complement the skills of their partners, and to depend on each other for companionship and support. Women marry more frequently than men. Previously institutionalized persons have a lower incidence of marriage than individuals who remained in the community and progressed through special programs or classes (Rosen et al., 1977). Some of the problems encountered by couples in which both members are retarded include low income, difficulties managing money, erratic employment or low job status, limited social skills or outlets, and difficulties in planning for the future. Though little research has been conducted on the long-term status of these persons, "appropriate preparation, training and continued understanding help . . . mildly retarded adults . . . make as good a marital adjustment as nonretarded persons in the same socioeconomic circumstances" (Katz, 1972).

Many individuals who are retarded view marriage as an important part of life—a symbol of acceptance and normalcy and a needed means of belonging and sharing. In addition to desiring marriage, a few individuals also wish to have children. Of all the issues in the field of mental retardation, this one still evokes the most stringent taboos, the strongest fears, and the hottest debates. Two major concerns arise regarding parenthood: *(a)* Will parents who are mentally retarded pass on their condition? and *(b)* Can they be suitable parents?

To answer the first question, very few cases of mental retardation are directly attributable to genetically known factors, and thus very few are transmittable. Parents—retarded or not—who have few economic resources, limited cognitive abilities, and few skills to call upon to deal with the demands of daily life often produce children who are at high risk for future problems. Youngsters require adequate health care, sound child-rearing practices, and much stimulation to ensure normal development. The limitations mentioned above may interfere with the ability to provide this kind of care even when outside support is available.

Can people who are retarded be good parents? There are no ready answers to this question. Scholars have done little research on their ability to be adequate parents. Individuals have speculated that parents with retardation may be prone to abuse their children because they are frustrated. Others have wondered how grown children who are not retarded will view their parents. Attempts to find answers to these questions will have to take into account the economic constraints faced by most of these adults. The criteria used to evaluate effective parenting will need to reflect the values of their low socioeconomic group rather than those of the middle class. The availability of support and training in infant stimulation and mothering techniques will also affect competence to function as parents.

The rights of individuals who are retarded to express themselves sexually, to marry, or to reproduce will remain controversial for some time. However, our past means of coping with these issues—isolation, mass sterilization, and legal and physical prohibitions—have proven to be largely ineffective, dehumanizing, contradictory to our belief in normalization, and damaging to the individual and possibly to society. People with mental retardation are sexual beings. Given their intellectual limitations, they need support and guidance in this area. Appropriate training, information, and an awareness of alternatives are all necessary if such individuals are to direct their sexual needs and energy into personally and socially constructive channels.

## LIFELONG LEARNING

That learning continues well beyond formal schooling is no earthshaking fact. Continuing education, whether formal or informal, is receiving growing emphasis as a means toward professional advancement, a recreational outlet, and an opportunity for personal enrichment. It has become a necessity as our society becomes more complex and demanding. Institutions of higher education have begun offering many credit and noncredit courses at low fees to encourage the participation of the general public. For the most part, such opportunities have been limited to the intellectually "normal."

Recently, however, professionals have recognized that those who are retarded not only have a right to continue their education beyond the mandatory school years—they cannot afford not to. Continued learning is essential to adapt to change and to reach maximum levels of independence. Lifelong learning is a logical endeavor for adults who are retarded.

Instruction can occur in a number of different settings. Often it takes place at the employment site or training center. The place of residence can also provide it; educational programs are often part of the weekly schedules of group homes. Another setting sometimes used for continuing education is the community college. McAfee and Sheeler (1987) found that one third of the community colleges they surveyed had students with mild mental retardation on their campuses. Some have established special programs for adults who are mentally retarded, and others meet the needs of this group by providing counseling and supplemental services.

Adult education programs for adults with mental retardation have also been established. Many of them follow the programs developed at the Metro College for Living in Denver, Colorado, and Night College in Austin, Texas. These types of programs have been developed across the country since 1970. They emphasize and enact the concept of normalization—many are held on college or university campuses and operate during normal school hours. Students select their classes, register and pay fees, arrange their own transportation as independently as possible, and have a responsibility to attend. Although most programs are still coordinated and funded by special (not generic) services, impetus for their adoption by regular continuing education facilities is growing.

These colleges are a meaningful leisure time activity for adults who are retarded. They emphasize daily living skills and functional academics such as those outlined in Table 11.5. They also provide an opportunity for socializing and developing a group of college friends. Teachers are usually volunteers from local universities or the community in general and are trained in the basics of classroom management and the learning characteristics of students with retardation.

The College for Living and Night College programs have broadened the opportunities for these adults to expand their behavioral repertoires and to participate in activities that foster dignity, responsibility, and contribution. They are a source of pride for the participants and provide firsthand experiences for persons interested in pursuing careers in the human service field. Because they use regular college campuses and community resources, they also help educate those who are not retarded about the potential of those who are. In the words of a Night College teacher from Charlottesville, Virginia,

> When I took my legal rights class on the bus to go register to vote for the coming election, we got the usual stares from the other passengers as two of my students had Down syndrome and elicited the "Ah, yes, that one's retarded" looks. Yet the stares really increased as my students' discussion on pari-mutuel betting and the zoning ordinance was overheard. Intelligent words from faces thought to hold blank minds—that was a real education for those people on the bus!

Some more capable individuals enter military service as a means of pursuing postsecondary training. How they do in their military occupations is not well documented, but they may encounter problems, as Patton and Polloway (1982) describe:

> For those not familiar with military service, some of the more recognizable military demands placed on the person involve organization, discipline,

TABLE 11.6  Types of Advocacy

| | |
|---|---|
| **Systems (Corporate) Advocacy** | |
| Advocacy by: | An independent collective of citizens |
| In order to: | Represent the rights and interests of groups of people with similar needs |
| | Pursue human service system quality and progressive change |
| **Legal Advocacy** | |
| Advocacy by: | Attorneys-at-law |
| In order to: | Represent individuals or groups of individuals in the litigation or legal negotiation process |
| **Self-Advocacy** | |
| Advocacy by: | Individuals whose rights are at risk of being violated or diminished |
| In order to: | Represent one's own rights and interests; speak on one's own behalf |
| **Citizen Advocacy** | |
| Advocacy by: | A mature, competent, volunteer citizen |
| In order to: | Represent, as if they were his or her own, the rights and interests of another citizen |

acceptance and thus help change public attitudes toward persons with disabilities.

Several types of advocacy now exist (see Table 11.6). Systems and legal advocacy have been instrumental in effecting legislation such as P.L. 94-142 and in altering the nature of many institutions and improving the quality of the rest. Citizen advocates have played a major role in the lives of many persons with retardation, helping them to get jobs, stay in school, learn to ride the bus or use the bank, and providing a sense of caring and companionship to individuals who often have few friends. Self-advocacy is a newer and very important concept that is growing throughout the country. One excellent example of an organized effort of self-advocacy is People First, a movement in which individuals with retardation have organized themselves on local, state, and national levels to identify common needs and develop lobbying power.

Though a relatively new social movement, advocacy has been heralded as the major force that can and will assure success for the individual within our communities who is mentally retarded.

# GROUPS OF PARTICULAR INTEREST

This section focuses on two groups of adults who are retarded: those who are elderly and those who have come into contact with the criminal justice or socialization, and following directions and orders. In addition, various academic skills may be necessary, depending on the soldier's duties or military occupational speciality [MOS]. (p. 81)

## ADVOCACY

*Advocacy* has been defined as the representation of the rights and interests of oneself or others in an effort to bring about change that will eliminate barriers to meeting identified needs. During the past two decades, advocacy has become a popular and potent consumer movement.

Social services have been criticized for being resistant to change, bogged down in red tape, inaccessible, slow to move, and impersonal (Wolfensberger, 1972). Many communities are still raising legal and social bulwarks against citizens who are retarded. These oppressed individuals, their parents, interested friends, and concerned others have actively attacked these barriers by investigating existing services, evaluating their effectiveness and appropriateness, and acting as catalysts for change. Operating on a one-to-one basis or as a group, through long-term relationships or in times of crisis, in the courts or at the supermarkets, advocates identify, protect, and assert the rights and interests of those in our society who are retarded. In addition to helping them get needed services and opportunities, advocates also serve as models of

TABLE 11.5   Course Offerings—Night College, Charlottesville, Virginia

| I. Communication | IV. Community Education |
|---|---|
| Talk and Say a Lot | Riding the City Bus |
| Keep On Talking | How to Find and Keep a Job |
| Community Checklist | Know Your Community I |
| For Your Own Writing | Know Your Community II |
| Using the Telephone | Living on Your Own |
| The Communication Workshop | First Aid and Home Safety |
| II. Money and Money Management | Driver's Education |
| Money Skills Assessment | What's Cooking: The Basics in |
| Simple Money | Good Eating |
| Money I | V. Leisure Time |
| Money II | Fun in Your Free Time |
| Using Your Money | Bicycle Safety |
| Community Checklist | Swimming and Water Safety |
| Budgeting | Art and Nature |
| Opening a Checking Account | Photography |
| III. Sex Education, Hygiene, and Personal | |
| Adjustment | |
| Looking Good | |
| You and Others I | |
| You and Others II | |
| Understanding Yourself | |

correctional systems. These two groups have been chosen because they display unique needs that require unique solutions.

## OLDER ADULTS WITH MENTAL RETARDATION

Although no exact age has been agreed upon for determining who is "elderly," many sources use 55 as a ballpark figure. Jacobson, Sutton, and Janicki (1985) break down old age into two categories: individuals who are "aging" (55–64 years) and those who are "elderly" (65 years or older). Regardless of the criterion used to identify this group, these adults have for a long time remained a somewhat invisible group. Community programs typically have emphasized serving the young adult. This is in part because many elderly individuals were in institutions; only small numbers lived in the community. Recently we have begun to get a clearer picture of what this group looks like and how they live (Hauber et al., 1985; Janicki & Jacobson, 1986; Seltzer & Krauss, 1987).

Demographic characteristics of elders who are retarded are found in various studies. Seltzer and Krauss (1987) have summarized these data from a number of such studies, and this information is presented in Table 11.7. Comparable data are not available for all of the descriptive variables.

With knowledge of the community adjustment patterns of adults with retardation and of the experiences of elderly people who are not retarded, and referring to the emerging information about elders with retardation, we can begin to describe their lifestyles.

☐ This group is quite heterogeneous, a fact that has major implications for service delivery (Seltzer & Krauss, 1987).

☐ They are likely to be unemployed.

☐ They are likely to have significantly reduced incomes and assets.

☐ Their interaction with the community is usually minimal.

☐ For the group in general, intellectual abilities do not seem to decline markedly (Janicki & MacEachron, 1984); however, this does not hold for certain subgroups (e.g., Down syndrome).

☐ The percentage of females increases with age (Seltzer & Krauss, 1987). This can be seen from the Janicki and MacEachron (1984) and Sutton (1983) findings listed in Table 11.7.

☐ Life expectancies are shorter than the general population's (Eyman, Grossman, Tarjan, & Miller, 1987). This finding is influenced greatly by those who have Down syndrome; however, these rates are increasing (Jacobson et al., 1985).

☐ Some of their behavioral capacities begin to decline at an earlier age (in their fifties) (Puccio, Janicki, Otis, & Rettig, cited in Seltzer & Krauss, 1987).

☐ Most members of this group tend to live in sheltered settings, often institutions (Jacobson et al., 1985). Seltzer and Krauss (1987) in their study

TABLE 11.7  Demographic Characteristics of Elders Who Are Mentally Retarded

| | Age | | Sex | Level of Retardation | | |
| Study | Range | Mean | % Female | Mean IQ | % Mild/ Moderate | % Severe/ Profound |
|---|---|---|---|---|---|---|
| Baker, Seltzer, & Seltzer, 1977 | 50+ | 59 | 66 | | | |
| Carsrud & Carsrud, 1983 | | 61 | 0 | 32 | | |
| Cotton, Purzycki, Cowart, & Merritt, 1983 | 60–87 | 69 | | | | |
| Cotton, Sison, & Starr, 1981 | | | 32 | | | |
| Edgerton, Bollinger, & Herr, 1984 | 47–68 | 56 | 47 | 62 | | |
| Hauber, Rotegard, & Bruininks, 1985 | | | | | | |
|   a. community-based facilities | 40–62 | 45 | | | 69 | 31 |
| | 63+ | 50 | | | 88 | 12 |
|   b. public residential facilities | 40–62 | 47 | | | 30 | 70 |
| | 63+ | 64 | | | 38 | 62 |
| Janicki & Jacobson, 1984b | 50–99 | | | | | |
| Janicki & Jacobson, 1986b | 45–94 | | | | 46 | 53 |
| Janicki & MacEachron, 1984 | 53–62 | | 48 | | 41 | 51 |
| | 63–72 | | 51 | | 42 | 48 |
| | 73+ | | 61 | | 38 | 50 |
| Krauss & Seltzer, 1986 | 55–91 | 63 | 49 | | | |
| Reid & Aungle, 1974 | 45+ | | 59 | | 80 | 20 |
| Seltzer, Seltzer, & Sherwood, 1982 | 55+ | 64 | 64 | 49 | | |
| Sherman, Frenkel, & Newman, 1984 | 46–92 | 63 | 58 | | 67 | 33 |
| Snyder & Woolner, 1974 | 70–88 | 75 | | | | |
| Sutton, 1983 | 53–62 | | 49 | | 58 | 42 |
| | 63–72 | | 53 | | 60 | 40 |
| | 73+ | | 60 | | 53 | 47 |
| Wood, 1979 | 41+ | | 40 | | 85 | 10 |

From *Aging and Mental Retardation: Extending the Continuum* by M. Seltzer and M. Krauss, 1987, Washington, DC: American Association on Mental Retardation. Reprinted by permission.

of elders with retardation found that over half of them lived in group homes or ICF-MR settings.

☐ The programming and daytime activities for those who live in community settings vary but for the most part are not vocationally oriented. Table 11.8 (taken from Seltzer and Krauss [1987]) illustrates this observation.

It is interesting that so little attention has traditionally been directed toward the needs of this group. Possible explanations for the neglect are:

☐ Relatively few professionals are familiar with the gerontological aspects of mental retardation.

TABLE 11.8   Typology of Community-Based Day Programs For Elders with Mental Retardation

| Type | n | Percent | Characteristics |
|---|---|---|---|
| Vocational day activity program | 35 | 25.9 | MR program<br>Full time (21 hours/wk or more)<br>Some vocational component |
| Day activity program | 37 | 27.4 | MR program<br>Full time (21 hours/wk or more)<br>No vocational component |
| Supplemental retirement program | 30 | 22.2 | MR program<br>Not full time (less than 21 hours/wk)<br>No vocational services<br>Center-based |
| Leisure and outreach services | 17 | 12.6 | MR program<br>Not full time and atypical scheduling<br>Not a regular day program (e.g., summer camps, courses, community outreach)<br>May not be center-based |
| Senior citizens' program | 16 | 11.9 | Not an MR program<br>Primarily serves elderly nondisabled or disabled nonretarded elders<br>Center-based |
| TOTAL | 135 | 100.0 | |

From *Aging and Mental Retardation: Extending the Continuum* by M. Seltzer and M. Krauss, 1987, Washington, DC: American Association on Mental Retardation. Reprinted by permission.

☐ The elderly are often dependent on others for transportation, and service locations are often not accessible.
☐ Funding is scarce.
☐ No agency coordinates existing services.
☐ Generic service programs are reluctant to view elders with retardation as clients.
☐ Community attitudes toward this group tend to be negative.
☐ Most people are unaware of the problems of elderly retarded people.

Because elders who are retarded remain a relatively underidentified and underserved group without a strong cohesive consumer voice, some communities do not address their needs by generic or special services. In other communities, however, innovative programs have been developed, including specialized employment opportunities, self-awareness and assertiveness groups, and social and recreational programs. Janicki, Otis, Puccio, Rettig, and Jacobson (1985) point out that this older group has service needs similar to other adults' except that the "structure and manner" of the services needed may differ. A range of special needs must be taken into account. The four major service areas for this group are: residential care, day services, health services, and support services (e.g., income maintenance, case management) (Janicki et al., 1985).

Seltzer and Krauss (1987) suggest that three options are now available for delivering services to elderly individuals who are retarded:

☐ Including them in programs for younger adults who are retarded
☐ Including them in programs for the general elderly population
☐ Developing specialized services

The first option is most commonly used for providing services, although the second choice comes into play for residential placement (e.g., nursing homes). As time progresses we will probably see more specialized services for this group.

Persons who are retarded are now living longer because of advances in medicine, technology, social practices, and their good fortune to benefit from them, yet we are just beginning to address their right to age with dignity. Much still needs to be done. It is not clear what the goal of intervention should be with this group. Seltzer and Krauss (1987) found that opinions differed as to whether programs should stress skill maintenance over skill development. This issue raises some intriguing questions and influences the nature of certain services. Other areas like professional knowledge, community awareness, and personnel preparation must be improved if we are to recognize our responsibility to those of all ages.

## OFFENDERS WHO ARE MENTALLY RETARDED

One area worthy of study that has drawn only scant professional attention concerns the problems arising when persons with retardation encounter the criminal justice and correctional systems. In general, studies indicate that the majority of those incarcerated in state prisons are "undereducated, under-skilled, and come from culturally and financially impoverished backgrounds" (Marsh, Friel, & Eissler, 1975, p. 21).

Some previous studies have estimated that close to 10% of the total prison population could be classified "legitimately" as mentally retarded (Brown & Courtless, 1967). If we extend this consideration to those individuals who are in the borderline range of retardation, then estimates of "exceptional offenders" in the penal system increase to 40%. A special article in the *Washington Post,* while suggesting a conservative estimate of 5% of the prison population as mentally retarded, highlights the extent of the problem.

> There are at least 25,000 retarded people in the nation's prisons, and some studies suggest that the number may be double that, or triple. This means that possibly one out of every 20 of the 500,000 prisoners in the United States is mentally retarded. Their crimes include murder and armed robbery, but many are more innocuous offenses, such as "cheating" cab drivers because they didn't understand about paying. (DeSilva, 1980)

Although there definitely seems to be a disproportionate number of people who are retarded in the penal system, the implication that mental retardation causes criminality should be avoided. Biklen (1977a), in reference to these high estimates, suggests that "the figure may not reflect any greater propensity of the mentally retarded than other segments of the general population toward crime" (p. 52). Then what explanation might there be for this disproportionality? The hypotheses offered to account for this overrepresentation revolve around two major domains: *(a)* certain characteristics of those who are mentally retarded and *(b)* procedural realities of the legal-correctional system. The problems encountered by the exceptional offender are not limited to the criminal justice system but extend into the correctional system as well.

*The criminal justice system.*   Just how an individual enters the criminal justice system varies from case to case. Biklen (1977a) presents three plausible explanations why a disproportionate number of adults with retardation wind up in prison.

1. They may be at risk of being easily influenced by delinquent peers;
2. They may have far fewer occupational roles available to them and so may choose crime as an available activity;
3. They may experience greater frustration than the average person in a highly competitive society and thus may choose delinquency as an act of rebellion. (p. 52)

Another hypothesis suggests that they lack many of the skills necessary for avoiding being caught. In addition, some professionals suggest that being a criminal may give some individuals a status that they would not achieve from normal community living. Finally, many individuals may not comprehend that they are breaking the law and that their actions may carry certain unpleasant consequences. Another relevant consideration may be their low socioeconomic status.

After a person allegedly has committed a criminal act and is apprehended, some type of intake procedure ensues. At this point, problems can develop. First, many law enforcement officials are not able to recognize that a person is retarded, sometimes resulting in the unfair handling of such a suspect. McAfee and Gural (1988) in their study involving state attorney generals found that the arresting officer recognized individuals as being retarded less than 30% of the time. Second, often confessions are obtained quite readily from these individuals, who want to please authority figures or are intimidated by threatening language used in interrogation. Third, even though programs have been designed to inform these adults of their legal rights, few individuals who are arrested are aware of their constitutional rights.

Even more problems emerge at the adjudication stage. The following list summarizes these obstacles to justice.

☐ Preconviction assessment—Individuals have a right to request that an assessment be conducted to determine competence. The techniques used in this process are of questionable validity.

☐ Competency to stand trial—A person found incompetent to stand trial may be receiving the equivalent of a life sentence without parole, as the trial is merely delayed until competency is achieved. For all practical purposes, many persons so identified probably will not become competent. In *Jackson v. Indiana* (1972), the Supreme Court ruled that an individual could be held only for a "reasonable" length of time, at which time either civil commitment procedures must be initiated or the person must be released.

☐ Insanity plea—This plea actually pertains to the issue of culpability for one's actions. At the present time, much confusion still remains over the suitability of the insanity defense with offenders who are mentally retarded. Even if a person is relieved of criminal culpability by virtue of insanity, commitment proceedings would most likely be initiated.

☐ Plea bargaining—It is not uncommon for the sake of expediency to plea bargain many cases (that is, the offender agrees to plead guilty to a lesser charge). In effect, rather than going to trial with a plea of not guilty or attempting to establish an insanity defense (which are both time-consuming and expensive), a plea bargain is obtained, most likely resulting in parole or imprisonment.

☐ Court-appointed counsel—Marsh and colleagues (1975) capture the essence of this problem: "Court appointed attorneys often do not have the time to expend as much effort on an indigent as a regular client" (p. 24).

☐ Probation—In many areas, to be placed on probation rather than be incarcerated it is necessary for an individual to have or gain steady employment. For many individuals with mental retardation this may not be likely (Marsh et al., 1975).

*Recently, the Supreme Court ruled that the constitution does not forbid the execution of convicted persons who are mentally retarded.*

With these and other obstacles facing the offender who is mentally retarded, it is no wonder that an inordinate number of them enter the penal system.

***The offender with mental retardation who is in the correctional system.*** For most, if not all, of those individuals imprisoned, the experience is one of brutality, degradation, frustration, helplessness, and loneliness. Individuals who are placed in harsh prison environments can be quite susceptible and vulnerable to this institutional lifestyle.

To this day, very few prison programs have been designed for the exceptional adult offender. Marsh et al. have recognized this problem and offered a reason for it.

> Since prisons are not designed to treat the mentally retarded, it is no surprise that little programming exists that attends to this group's special needs. Furthermore, the low funding priority of most correctional systems insures that programs must be geared to the average rather than the retarded inmate. (1975, pp. 24–25)

To maximize treatment and habilitation of those in the correctional system who are disabled, Menolascino (1974) has stated that it is necessary to consider three major areas: *(a)* classification and diagnosis; *(b)* treatment; and *(c)* prerelease planning and parole. He goes on to explain the implications.

> With early identification of the degree of retardation and emotional problems (if any), a more realistic approach may be made to an individual's rehabilitation needs. The treatment of a retarded offender must include special education and vocational training so that the offender acquires the skills to get along in the outside world. Lastly, halfway houses (Keller & Alper, 1970) should be utilized for the transition from a correctional institution to the community, buttressed by a strengthened system of parole officers who are trained to manage retarded offenders with a more humanistic approach that stresses acceptance and hope. (p. 9)

But some correctional centers have developed distinct programs for offenders who are retarded or developmentally disabled. Denkowski, Denkowski, and Mabli (1983) noted that at that time 14 states reported programs for this group. The intent of these units is to provide specialized services for these offenders. Although some problems are inherent in this type of program (for instance, lack of trained staff), this is definitely a step in the right direction.

McAfee and Gural (1988) poignantly describe what adults who are retarded face.

> The lack of statutorily determined treatment for defendants and offenders with mental retardation suggests that inconsistencies will continue to occur. Courts will act according to the mood of the day. Some of these offenders will be treated with overzealous sympathy, others will effectively forfeit their rights. (p. 11)

## SERVICES IN COMMUNITY SETTINGS

It seems quite logical to say that any given community differs in many dimensions from any other community. But certain services may be universally needed for enhancing the lives of adults who are mentally retarded. Everyone needs certain services in order to maintain a certain standard of successful living. With this in mind, we can make a few observations about services.

☐ A confusing assortment of services is available (Grossman & Tarjan, 1987).

☐ Social support services are unpredictable at times and subject to change (Koegel, 1986).

☐ They can be vulnerable to both political and economic factors (Castellani, 1987).

☐ Over the course of the last few years, the private sector has become a much more important provider of services for many adults with retardation.

**TYPES OF SERVICES**

One way to conceptualize the different types of community services is to refer to a taxonomy developed by Gilhool (1976), which presents a system divided into four areas.

1. Type I services—available to all citizens; adults who are retarded would use, as would general population (e.g., garbage collection, police protection, education, employment services)
2. Type II services—available to all citizens; persons who are retarded would use in special ways (e.g., access to buildings)
3. Type III services—available only to some citizens; people with retardation would use if they qualify in some category (e.g., public assistance, SSI, Medicaid)
4. Type IV services—available only to citizens who are mentally retarded (e.g., supervised residential services)

Gilhool suggests that type I and type III services are most often the services from which people who are mentally retarded have been excluded in the past; education would fall under type I.

Regardless of the classification system used, certain basic services should be afforded those citizens who are retarded and who live in the community; furthermore, they should be taught to use them. Table 11.9 briefly explains the major areas that need to be considered. While most services presented in Table 11.9 relate to Gilhool's type IV, access to other, more common services generally available to the total citizenry is also needed. Many communities have established a system of service delivery whereby those services listed in the table are provided. Other communities, often located in less urbanized areas, suffer from inadequate and insufficient mechanisms for providing these essential services. It is of paramount importance that communities make every effort to accommodate citizens who may need special services.

**RURAL NEEDS**

Community services for citizens with mental retardation have developed rapidly in urban areas during the past 15 years or so. The development of these comprehensive services and resources, however, has not been so rapid or so extensive in less heavily populated rural areas. Rural communities, for the most part, still remain unprepared for the integration of individuals who are retarded and are often unable to maintain them within community residential facilities.

A dispersed population, distance from professional services, small base with which to fund programs, absence of private service agencies, transportation difficulties, and the rural tendency toward preference for independence and resistance to outside influence have been cited as reasons for this lag in the development of services, despite recent legal and social changes (Talkington, 1971). The number of persons with special needs identified greatly exceeds the services available for them in most rural areas. This

TABLE 11.9    Essential Community Services

| Category | Description |
|---|---|
| 1. Developmental programs<br>  a. Day activity<br>  b. Education<br>  c. Training | Includes a variety of educational and care programs appropriate for a person's age and severity of handicapping conditions. |
| 2. Residential services<br>  a. Domiciliary<br>  b. Special living arrangements | Includes out-of-home living quarters: 24-hour lodging and supervision, and less supervised living arrangements for less severely handicapped persons (e.g., supervised apartment). |
| 3. Employment services<br>  a. Preparation<br>  b. Sheltered (including work activity)<br>  c. Competitive | Includes a continuum of vocational evaluation, training, and work opportunity in supervised and independent settings. |
| 4. Identification services<br>  a. Diagnosis<br>  b. Evaluation | Includes efforts to identify presence of disabilities and their probable cause(s), and to assess and plan service needs of the disabled person. |
| 5. Facilitating services<br>  a. Information and referral<br>  b. Counseling<br>  c. Protective and sociolegal<br>  d. Follow- along<br>  e. Case management | Includes a variety of actions needed to insure that disabled persons are informed of available services, assisted in getting services, provided protection of rights and guardianship if needed, and given continued review of plans to insure that services are appropriately delivered. |
| 6. Treatment services<br>  a. Medical<br>  b. Dental | Includes appropriate medical care, prosthetic devices needed for maximum adjustment, and dental care. |
| 7. Transportation | Transportation to training, work, and other activities. |
| 8. Leisure and recreation | Structured and unstructured leisure opportunities as needed. |

From *Exceptional Children and Youth: An Introduction* by E. L. Meyen, 1978, Denver: Love Publishing. Reprinted by permission.

disparity between services needed and provided has forced many rural families to institutionalize their children. Where most communities are now institutionalizing only those with profound limitations, the admissions from rural areas still include higher functioning individuals who need special education and vocational services (Talkington, 1971).

It is critical that services be extended from the regional centers of more populated areas to these rural districts and that local rural resources be developed to serve those in need. Several projects along these lines have begun. Some institutions and social service agencies are establishing diagnostic, evaluative counseling centers in counties, and in a few instances shifting control of these centers to local agencies. Vocational training and employment opportunities have also been developed in some rural areas, although transportation and the need for extensive outreach services remain blocks to effective and far-reaching support services within these areas.

**SUMMARY**

More attention, in our opinion, needs to be directed toward the issue of community life for adults with mental retardation. This chapter has attempted to sensitize the reader to many aspects of community life. For the community integration movement to be successful, a full range of appropriate services must be available and accessible. We must recognize the major problems facing adults with mental retardation, understand the complex nature of these problems, and formulate plans for addressing them. This chapter has examined the concept of transition from school to community, the issues associated with community adjustment, the major components of life in the community, some of the problems encountered in these settings, and specific services that should be available to all persons who are mentally retarded.

PART FOUR
# CONTINUING CONCERNS

# CHAPTER 12

# Family Issues

F amilies give a lifetime of support to people who are mentally retarded. Professionals have become increasingly aware of the importance of families in the last three decades. In the 1940s and 1950s, the literature on mental retardation contained few references to parents, but since the mid-1950s, the literature on families with a member who is mentally retarded has grown vastly. Several factors have contributed to this change in professional awareness, one of which was the President's Panel on Mental Retardation, formed in 1961 by President Kennedy. This panel impelled research and development into the prevention of mental retardation, the care, education, and rehabilitation of affected individuals, and the development of more comprehensive community-centered clinical and social services. The emphasis that the panel placed on community-based services influenced the amount of attention given to parents and families.

A second major cause of increased professional attention to parents is research on the importance of early stimulation for intellectual development. The negative effects of environmental deprivation gained greater attention (see, for example, Hess & Shipman, 1965; Skeels, 1966). From this research, it became apparent that the home is a more favorable environment for child-rearing than the institution—especially for a child in the early stages of development. More recently, Nihira, Meyers, and Mink (1983) have demonstrated the influence of the home environment on the child with mental retardation. The literature also bears witness to the benefits of parent involvement in the child's educational program (e.g., Adubato, Adams, &

This chapter was contributed by Diane M. Browder, Eric D. Jones, and James R. Patton.

Budd, 1981; Cheseldine & McConkey, 1979; Miller & Sloane, 1976; Salzburg & Villani, 1983; Schreibman, O'Neill, & Koegel, 1983).

A third, and probably the most important, factor in bringing parents to the attention of professionals has been parents' enormously increased political strength. During the past two and a half decades, individual parents and parent organizations, for example, the Association for Retarded Citizens, have fought in the courts and lobbied in state and federal legislatures to secure basic legal rights for their children. (In the vast majority of cases, they have been successful.) It has taken the combination of enlightenment through research and demonstration of political clout to bring parents of individuals with mental retardation to professionals' attention.

Once the importance of families had been made clear to professionals, the literature began to reflect a surge of interest, although it still reflected a dichotomy between parent and professional priorities. Much of the literature focused on ways to "train" parents to be better educators and managers of their child with mental retardation. Some "diagnosed" parents' level of adjustment to their child's disability. The contribution of this literature was to identify and demonstrate how parents could be coparticipants in their child's education and to begin to sensitize professionals to the difficulties of coping with a family member who was disabled. More recently researchers have turned to other such important issues as factors that influence the family's stress level (Beckman, 1983).

Also, a new understanding of families in general has influenced the recent literature. Previously, parent-training literature focused on the unilateral role of the parent as trainer or child manager, but the reciprocal influence between parents and children has gained increasing attention (Baltes & Brim, 1979). Children give their parents cues about the best ways to meet their needs, and they help parents grow as well as receiving nurture. Similarly, a person who is mentally retarded affects a family's growth as well as receiving support. The chronology of the literature about families of individuals with mental retardation, which is also a chronology of the thinking on the same subject, might be summarized as *(a)* an era of underestimating family influences (1940s and 1950s), *(b)* an era of recruiting and training parents as coeducators (1960s and 1970s), and *(c)* the current era of increased understanding and nurture of the family as a social structure (1980s). As professionals have gained skill in understanding parents' perspectives, the literature has evolved to reflect increased respect for the family's challenge in nurturing each member when one has mental retardation.

## RESEARCH LIMITATIONS

Although the issues concerning families of persons with mental retardation are now receiving more attention, they frequently are accompanied by judgments and generalizations that cannot be made honestly from the existing research. In the last few years authors have noted the shortcomings of previous research and have begun to take new approaches to defining and meeting family needs (e.g., Beckman-Brindley & Snell, 1984; Blacher, 1984; Nihira et al., 1983).

One methodological problem in previous research is the tendency to make statements about "families" based on research with one family or a few parents (e.g., Emde & Brown, 1978). While the study of small samples can reveal useful insights for similar families, the findings probably are not applicable to the widely heterogeneous group of people with family members who are mentally retarded.

A second methodological problem is in conceptualizations of the family. Research has assumed that the family consists of the traditional members (father, mother, children). Further, one member, the mother, has been studied alone to make inferences about the family unit. Even when a traditional family structure exists and the mother provides most of the care for the member who is mentally retarded, the mother should not be viewed in isolation from the family unit (Beckman-Brindley & Snell, 1984). Within the family unit, relationships exist between the various family members. For example, the mother has a relationship with her spouse, her children who are not handicapped, and the child with mental retardation. Her relationship with her child who is mentally retarded is influenced by her other relationships. Besides the omission of family-centered research, studies have not kept pace with the changing demographic patterns of families in our society.

## FAMILY PATTERNS

*Single-parent families.* Most public policy is built around the image of the traditional nuclear family. The discrepancy between that image and the reality of many families seems to be increasing. Coates (1978) reported that the number of families headed by females has increased more than 250% since 1950. The number of children who live with a single mother increased by approximately 40% between 1970 and 1976. Coates predicts that "approximately 45% of the children born in 1976 will have lived with a single parent for some time before reaching 18 years of age" (p. 35). The increasing number of single-parent families appears to be an important consideration for agencies that provide services to those who are mentally retarded—especially when family intervention is involved. As there is very little research on single-parent families with members who are mentally retarded, we have no adequate means for policymakers to analyze and program for the needs of these families.

*Young mothers.* Females under the age of 15 currently constitute the only group in the United States with a significant expansion in birthrate (Coates, 1978). Mothers who are in their early teenage years contribute 20% of the live

emotions like anger or sadness can help us identify needs for change or support. Professionalism sometimes requires us to act neutral while feeling upset, but it is critical to have a supportive network for honest sharing. Parents are sometimes surprised by the intensity of their feelings toward a child with special needs. Professionals' acceptance of parents' range of feelings can foster a positive parent-professional alliance. As we mentioned previously, past literature has sometimes tried to classify parental stages of adjustment to their child with mental retardation. Blacher (1984) reviewed 24 such articles, noting their methodological flaws and questioning the usefulness of describing stages of adjustment. Similarly, Crnic and colleagues (1983) have criticized the tendency to classify families' adjustment and recommend instead that professionals look at adaptations to stress and the family's coping resources to mediate it. Having a professional with whom to share feelings and identify ways to cope with problems can be one such resource to mediate stress for the parent of a child with retardation. Some of the crisis situations for families with a member who is mentally retarded are presented below to help us consider how professionals might provide sensitive support.

## INITIAL DIAGNOSIS

In a society as complex as ours, which places such a high premium on intelligence, the realization that their child has mental retardation can come as a great shock to parents. Raech (1966) has said that one of the most trying emotional experiences a couple could ever face would be the diagnosis of their child's mental retardation. The reactions of parents to this diagnosis have been compared to the trauma of a death in the family and have been called "the grief cycle" by Turnbull and Turnbull (1985). One influence on the impact of this shock is the timing of the diagnosis. If it is presented immediately after the child's birth, as in the case of a genetic defect or an obvious abnormality, parents will not have had time to consider the possibility that their new child has special needs. Both parents are usually exhausted and under stress from delivery, and one initial reaction may be total rejection of the new infant. Roberts (1986) has described the case of one mother who had an infant with Down syndrome. Although the father had a sister with Down syndrome, the couple had never seriously considered that their child might have it. Because the mother was aware of the sacrifices that her mother-in-law had made, she felt she had been dealt a harsh blow. In confusion and anger, the couple sought counsel from a minister, whose explanation for their having had this child gave little comfort. The mother left the hospital unsure whether or not she would keep the child. An unusual event occurred that, according to the mother, "saved her life" at that critical time. A pediatrician asked to keep the infant for the first few weeks while the mother decided whether or not she could parent the child, and the pediatrician's delight in this infant and kind acceptance of the mother's

# A UNIQUE PARENTAL PERSPECTIVE

We who work with people who are retarded are always inspired by parents who do things that make their child a significant part of the family. It is typical for proud new parents to send out birth announcements of their new family member. Usually, these announcements are full of excitement and satisfaction. But how do you tell people that your newborn is retarded? Most of the time, this information is carefully disguised or withheld. To be sure, this is not an easy task, nor one that parents enjoy doing.

Sometimes interesting items come to our attention and we do not know from where they came or who gave them to us; the following material falls into this category. It is a real birth announcement, but its authors are unknown. It demonstrates one of the most positive parental attitudes we have seen. We have omitted the child's name, date, and time of birth because it is not necessary; the important message is contained in the parents' words. This child who is retarded is lucky to be introduced into a family like this one.

We invite you to rejoice with us
at the birth of our daughter

on

at

It is our belief as Latter-day Saints that we all lived a pre-earth life with our Heavenly Father. Certain valiant spirits were selected at that time for special missions during an earth life. One of these spirits has been chosen for our family. Our daughter is a child with Down's Syndrome. We feel privileged to be entrusted with the care of this special child, who will return to her Heavenly Father at the end of her earth life and resume, for all eternity, her valiant status with her body and intellect completely restored.

turmoil led the couple to bring the child home. Through the ARC's Parent-to-Parent program, this mother met another mother of a child with Down syndrome and began a friendship that became the second lifesaver in the family's history.

Most parents receive the diagnosis after they have begun to suspect that their child is different or "slow." The period of doubt preceding formal diagnosis can itself be a cause of great stress. Sometimes parents search for a diagnosis. Their search is sometimes related to the feelings of denial and anger that accompany having a child who is so different from society's expectations. Sometimes "shopping for a diagnosis" is necessary because of professionals' reluctance to dishearten parents with the full diagnosis in initial visits. Many professionals believe that families need to be given information gradually to lessen the shock, but such a tactic can lead parents to believe that professionals have not been candid with them about their child. Similarly, when a school age child is diagnosed, professionals may try to lessen the blow by using such terms as *special needs* in early conferences with parents and only later introducing the term *mild mental retardation.*

Providing early information does require sensitivity, since parents often find it difficult to absorb details when shocked by an unexpected diagnosis. Being sensitive to parents' emotional reactions should help the professional to judge how much information should be conveyed. But honesty is essential to building trust. Professionals should also make clear to parents their availability for further discussion. Offering printed information—books or pamphlets—can inform parents more gently, since they can read the information at their own pace and in privacy, where emotions need not be repressed. The best support a professional can offer may not be his or her services but a contact with other parents who have experienced the same crisis.

If parents indicate dissatisfaction with the information provided, the professional should respect their right to seek other opinions. Although some parents do indeed "shop" for more acceptable diagnoses instead of facing the reality of their child's handicap, many seek alternative opinions in order to clarify further the nature of the child's problems.

## REVISING EXPECTATIONS

Realizing that a child or other family member is mentally retarded is only one challenge families face. Next parents begin coping with the myriad expectations they had for their child. Some of the many questions that parents begin to ask appear in the feature.

All parents revise their expectations as they grow along with their children in the family's lifespan, just as in the movie *The Natural* a baseball player must cope with life's not turning out as he had expected. While a child with mental retardation may bring unique joys to a family, he or she is not what was expected. Dreams for a child's college education, marriage,

# PARENTS' QUESTIONS

When an infant with severe handicaps is born, providing the parents with support during this very emotional and stressful time is of utmost importance. There is also a need to give the parents appropriate information in response to the decisions that they may have to make. Any discussion dealing with future possibilities should include the changing attitudes toward people with disabilities, the principle of normalization, the right of a child to family life, and the many advances in educational and behavioral technology.

Parents who learn that their newborn is severely handicapped often ask questions in an effort to gain some meaning from a confusing situation. The questions asked range from life-and-death issues to financial concerns to concerns about breast-feeding. Through their questions, parents are often trying to gather the information that they will need to make major decisions that may have a significant impact on their lives and the lives of other family members.

To illustrate the many concerns with which parents must deal during this time, we have compiled a list of some of the typical questions parents ask. As you examine these questions, you will see that adequate support systems and accurate answers to these questions are essential.

Will our child always be sickly?
What can be done to optimize our child's abilities?
Will our child ever talk?
What should we tell our child about being different?
Why did this happen to us?
Where can we get help and information?
What alternative placements are available, and should we consider them?

How will our child be different from other children?
Will our child always need constant care?
What foods will our child eat?
Is there any chance that our normal children's offspring might similarly be affected?
Is there anything we can do to make our child smarter?
What do most people decide to do about placement?
Whose fault is it?
Can our child be cured?
What will happen when our child grows up?
Will the child look funny?
What will the child be able to do developmentally?
Will our child be in pain?
How should we treat our child?
Will our child need special medical care?
Will our child progressively get worse?
How long will our child live?
Will we be able to love our child?
Does anything exist that can help?
Is it safe to have other children? (Will it happen again?)
Is there an operation that might help?
What will happen to our child when we die?
Are there any parent organizations that we can contact?
How should we explain this child to our family, friends, and neighbors?
Will the child be able to go to school?
Will our child ever be independent?
What is the cause of the problem? (How did it happen?)
Should we institutionalize our child?
What will the effects of this child be on our family?

parenting, carrying on a family business, and so on often must be discarded or drastically revised. Also, a child who is mentally retarded requires a substantially greater investment of parents' physical, emotional, and financial resources than a child who is not. Olshansky (1962, 1966) calls the feeling parents have *chronic sorrow.* Parents sometimes talk about events that will trigger grief, for example, seeing a neighbor's child learn to drive and realizing that their own child will probably never drive or own a car.

In an era when parents often seek status through their children, as Elkind (1981) describes in *The Hurried Child,* it is especially poignant to have a child who simply cannot be hurried to meet developmental milestones. Phillip Roos, formerly executive director of the ARC and also father of a child with mental retardation, has summarized some of the feelings that accompany the process of revising expectations.

*Perfection and guilt.*   One expectation that is quickly revised in any parenting experience is that we can produce and raise perfect children. Similarly, in any personal experience of tragedy or disappointment, we confront the reality that life is "unfair." Human beings, when confronted with failure or disappointment, commonly seek to lay the blame at someone's door. A parent may feel ambivalent about the child who has made life so much more complicated and challenging. Personal religious beliefs are often shaken when parents feel that God has either punished them or let them down. Mothers often review every memory of their pregnancy or the child's early years, berating themselves for every mistake that might have caused the retardation. (In most cases the etiology of mental retardation is unknown, which deepens the mystery: Why do some parents have a child who is mentally retarded, and others do not?) Whether the blame is placed on the child, God, themselves, their spouse, or all of these sources, guilt may be intense, focusing on personal failure or on blaming others. Sometimes the pressures of raising a child who has special needs may make a parent long for escape and have fantasies of the child's dying, or of their abandoning the family, or of life as it would have been if the pregnancy had been aborted. Because parents also feel an intense bond of love with their child, such fantasies can produce guilt and low self-esteem.

*See chapter 4 for a discussion of etiologies of mental retardation.*

When the etiology is known and preventable, as in the case of fetal alcohol syndrome, guilt can become especially acute. A mother who knows just how she contributed to her child's mental retardation has a heavy burden to bear. Religious and/or psychological professionals may be especially important in restoring her self-esteem. All professionals can help parents burdened with guilt, whether justified or not, by affirming their efforts with their child and helping them realize that all human beings are imperfect and vulnerable to error.

*Hope and denial.*   Children are a status symbol. Parents may dress their children in designer clothes and brag about their child's giftedness while the child is still a toddler. Also, children are a beacon of hope for the future. As

Dalton and Epstein (1963) have found, parents of children with mild mental retardation may be especially prone to deny their child's handicap. The differences observed may be attributed to a speech delay or a lack of motivation. For example, the parents might assume that their child ignored rather than failed to comprehend simple instructions. To have a child fail to achieve even average expectations is a serious assault on many parents' self-concept. Parental denial may be a defense against feelings of hopelessness.

What professionals label "denial" may be a healthy and effective strategy for coping with stress. Parents sometimes need to take a breather and let go of a problem for a while when no solutions can be found. Turnbull and Turnbull (1985) call this *passive appraisal,* short-term strategy that allows parents to relax by setting aside a problem for a period of time such as their taking a vacation alone together rather than participating in a school's parent-training program. Sometimes it includes not considering the future, but just coping with problems one day at a time.

On occasion, denial helps parents maintain an idealism about their child that makes them excellent advocates for services. It has sometimes been parents' refusal to accept professionals' premise that their child with severe mental retardation cannot learn that has pressured professionals into finding more effective educational procedures. Sometimes parents are inaccurately labeled as having "denial" when in fact it is the educational system's failure, not their child's, that has created the need for special services. For example, minority group children are overrepresented in classrooms for children with mild mental retardation. Bereiter and Engelmann (1966; see also Engelmann, 1970, 1977) contend that poor teaching accounts for a substantial portion of the academic failures among minority group children. Hentoff (1977) provides a graphic illustration of a black father's anger and frustration over the failure of educators to meet the needs of his child.

At one of the first New York City Board of Education meetings I went to, a black father got up to speak. He had been a school dropout in the south, I learned later, came north, worked at a string of menial jobs, and eventually wound up in a dead-end factory slot which paid him some ninety dollars a week. His hope was his child, and he had watched her fall farther and farther behind each year of school.

The black father was very angry. "You people," he said to the board, "operate a goddamn monopoly, like the telephone company. I got no choice where I send my child to school. I can only send her where it's free. And she's not learning. Damn it, that's *your* responsibility, it's the principal's responsibility, it's the teacher's responsibility that she's not learning."

The more or less distinguished members of the Board of Education looked on impassively.

"When you fail, when everybody fails my child"—the father's voice had gotten thick with rage and no little grief—"what happens? Nothing. Nobody gets fired. Nothing happens to nobody except my child." (p. 4)

When dealing with parents who seem to deny their child's handicap, professionals need to clarify for themselves exactly what harm, if any, is done by the denial or period of passive appraisal. For example, professionals may be concerned that parents do not participate in services. If parents prefer not to participate in parent-training activities, the professional should take a good look at the myriad needs the family faces besides the special child's. If parents are refusing such important services for their child as therapy or academic remediation, it may be most beneficial to review the advantages of the services and discuss specific concerns. Professionals may want parents to use the accepted terminology to describe the child's disability. If parents prefer not to use the term *mental retardation* for their child but will accept placement in services for students with mental retardation, the professional who is wise will respect their preferences. A third concern professionals may have is that parents seem to take an adversarial stance toward them. Parents often have legitimate complaints about services—an example is the lack of integration of special education classrooms—which should be considered a problem in the service system rather than in the parents' "acceptance" of their child's handicap. Professionals may try to recruit interested parents to work with them on a plan for changes in service delivery. Finally, professionals may be concerned about parents' unrealistic expectations for their child, but they must be careful not to destroy the hopes and dreams parents have. When confronted with what seem like unrealistic parental expectations, professionals can gently present their own professional hopes for the child's achievement, at the same time acknowledging that it is impossible to know what any child may achieve.

*Legacy and chronic sorrow.*    For many families, each new child born creates an opportunity to continue and enhance the legacy of the family. Upwardly mobile families are especially hopeful that the next generation will bring further honor to the family. A new child may be given the name of the father or of some other family member as a symbol of pride and expectations for achievement. When John Smith, Jr., or Pamela Garland Smith-Jones has mental retardation, however, the family must adjust from the hope of having a corporate president or judge to the idea of having a person with special needs who, with considerable support and training, may achieve a low-status job and maintain a home with minimal supervision. Marriage, child-rearing, and a college education are much less probable. If the child has severe mental retardation, parents face the prospect of lifelong support from either the family or professionals. As we mentioned earlier, Olshansky (1962, 1966) has described the feeling that accompanies this loss of dreams for a child as *chronic sorrow.*

Professionals are sometimes too eager to convey to parents the positive qualities of children with mental retardation in hopes of convincing them to be happy with their child. Professionals who have chosen to work with people with mental retardation may indeed know these special joys, which the next section discusses. But rarely does any professional have a lifelong involvement with a person who is mentally retarded, nor do professionals ordinarily have to shape their personal lives around the challenge of nurturing a person with special needs. Some of the differences between professional and family relationships are poignantly described by Ann Turnbull, who lives both roles.

When a parent seems discouraged and sorrowful, professionals need to be especially gentle. Sometimes nonjudgmental listening is the best response. Parents who seem to be seriously depressed might be referred to professional counselors who specialize in working with families that have members with special needs. Olshansky (1966) recommends concrete services for the children of such grieving parents. Services to children may not, however, be enough. Waisbren (1980) compared the parental adjustment of Danish and American parents of children with developmental delay. Although more services were available in Denmark, there was no significant difference in the adjustment of parents in the two countries. Services designed for the parents rather than the child may be the greatest resource to combat discouragement. For example, professionals may encourage the parent to place the child in respite services for a vacation with a spouse, special time with other children in the family, or just to be alone to rest and rediscover personal interests. A permanent "adjustment" may be an unrealistic expectation for parents, since nurturing a child with special needs creates ongoing challenges.

*New hope and joy.*    Many studies of parents' experience with having a child with mental retardation convey only the trials and negative feelings. But professionals also need to be sensitive to parents' positive feelings about their situation. First and foremost, parents of children with special needs continue to have all the other things to think about and the range of interests that other families have. Parents often find that after crises like the initial diagnosis, life goes on, and paying bills, pursuing career goals, being with friends, deciding what to cook for dinner, trying to lose five pounds, and so on continue to consume as much of their daily attention as do the child's ongoing needs. Professionals who have ongoing relationships with parents can sometimes improve their rapport by discovering and enjoying common interests (e.g., discussing the increased cost of housing or swapping recipes). Second, parents are often pleasantly surprised by the delight their child takes in life. One parent noted, "Sometimes I think those of us not born with mental retardation are the ones to be pitied. I envy my son's open affection for others and joy in simple things like a new snowfall or eggs for supper." Third, parents discover new expectations and sources of pride. One father described the pride he felt when his daughter with mental retardation and cerebral palsy learned to walk at the age of five. Because her ability to learn

# FROM BEING A PROFESSIONAL
# TO BEING A PARENT

It is difficult indeed to convey adequately what it is like to have a son or daughter who is severely mentally retarded. Unless we actually are in such a situation, then we *really* can't experience the trials, frustrations, successes, and other feelings that are part of daily life with a child who is severely handicapped. The following comments of Ann Turnbull, excerpted from *Parents Speak Out*—a collection of writings by parents of children with handicaps who are also professionals in the field—express her experiences of living with her stepson, who is severely handicapped. Her words effectively relate some of her feelings concerning the ups and downs of being a parent of such a child. What makes these selections especially poignant is that Ann is an eminent special educator who works with parents of similar children. Her story illustrates the transition from being a professional to being a parent.

I can vividly recall when I spoke 3 years ago to an interagency committee in a nearby community on the topic of deinstitutionalization. At the time I was a strong advocate for the quick return home of substantial numbers of mentally retarded persons from state institutions. [At one point, Ann remarked that she couldn't understand how certain parents could oppose having their child return home.] Immediately a mother of a mentally retarded son flew to her feet and began berating me in front of the group. While shaking her finger in my face, she screamed, "Do you know what it is like to live with a mentally retarded child?" I felt both embar-

rassed and defensive. After trying to explain my comment, I responded (probably in somewhat of a self-righteous way), "No, I don't know what it is like, but in 2 weeks I will begin to find out. My husband and I will be bringing his mentally retarded son home from an institution." She smiled at me as if to say, "Are you ever in for it"; yet my confidence in approaching the new parental roles and responsibilities was unshaken. I had three degrees in special education with an emphasis in mental retardation, several years of teaching experience in public schools and a residential institution, and was on the university faculty. Being with mentally retarded children was a way of life for me. I thought to myself, "Just wait. I will show you that it really is not all that difficult to be a parent."

Rud [Ann's husband] and I took a leisurely trip through New England and picked Jay up on our return at his school in Massachusetts [Jay's first day of deinstitutionalization]. We were very happy to see him and filled with excitement and anticipation as we packed his things in the car. After a tearful good-bye to Sue and Dom D'Antuono, we started the trip back home to North Carolina. We stopped early on the first afternoon at a motel, so we could have a relaxing swim before dinner. As we approached the pool, Jay's temper tantrum started, and it did not end for a seeming eternity. He kicked and screamed and cried. Finally, when he calmed down, he got in the pool but would not budge from clenching the railing on the side. A girl much younger than Jay was swimming laps beside him. Her father, who was beaming with pride and clapping at her performance, turned to me and said, "Do you always have this much trouble with him?" I absolutely froze. I could not muster any kind of response. I wanted to shout, "Give me time. I've been his mother for less than a day." I choked my tears back and insisted that we go back to the room. Throughout the remainder of the trip home, the question kept echoing in my mind, "Do you always have this much trouble with him?"

For one who thought she knew, the last 3 years have, indeed, been a humbling experience. The 24-hour reality test has standards far higher than any examination I ever took while earning my three degrees. In fact, the three degrees may have been more a hindrance than a help in meeting my new parental responsibilities. I had always been taught to be objective and to consider the facts of a situation. All of a sudden, I had an ache in my heart, a knot in my stomach, and tears welling in my eyes. It did not take long for it to dawn on me that the mother from the interagency meeting was right—I was in for a startling experience.

In Jay's first months home, I faced many of the emotional reactions that parents typically encounter immediately after the birth of a handicapped child. Almost all of my friends were professionals whose work related to the developmental problems of children. Many of them reacted to Jay as a patient or client, rather than as a child. I became very angry at their offhand remarks, and as a result, some of my closest friendships were abruptly ended. One friend commented, "I've never seen a child with such a big head." Another said, "Doesn't Jay remind you of an autistic child, the way he stares off in space?"

I was very confused . . . and felt alienated from many of my professional colleagues who were advising me to be objective and to remove myself from the emotion of the situation. In many encounters I was getting the message that they thought I was an obnoxious and hostile parent. I had been on the inside long enough to know what professionals think about parents who refuse their advice. I could remember having those feelings myself about parents. That's what really hurt. I felt both parental anger and sorrow over some of my own professional mistakes in previous interactions with parents.

What goes on in training programs in the name of education is sometimes shocking. It has become very prevalent in special education departments of colleges and universities to offer courses on working with parents. I cringe at the thought of some of the course syllabi I have reviewed. In many of these courses, very limited attention is directed toward helping parents solve the day-to-day problems which almost invariably are encountered, yet weeks are devoted to the "psychological insight approach to parental guilt." Many such courses are a fraud and tend to insure further conflict and unsatisfactory relationships between parents and professionals. *Extended practicum with families of handicapped children and the provision of respite care for families should be standard requirements* for courses which purport to prepare students for working with parents [emphasis added].

Moving from a professional to a parental role has been a sometimes painful and difficult task for me. It has caused me to engage in tremendous self-examination. Being Jay's mother has also resulted in an extended growth process for me. As much as anything, I have learned how much I do not know. Now, I am ready to learn.

From *Parents Speak Out* by A. P. Turnbull and H. R. Turnbull (Eds.) (pp.127–135), 1985, Columbus, OH: Merrill Publishing. Reprinted by permission.

to walk had been uncertain, and five intensive years of therapy had been invested for her to achieve this difficult goal, he felt as much pride as he had the day he received his Ph.D. When she walked down the aisle as a flower girl for a family wedding the next year, the entire family felt an overwhelming joy and pride.

# GROWING AS A FAMILY

### THE DIVERSITY OF FAMILIES AND THEIR NEEDS

While all families exist to nurture the needs of individual family members, a great diversity of family structures and individual needs exists. Our society stereotypes the family as mother, father, and children, but real families often differ from this image. An aging parent who has special and increasing needs for care may live with the family. "Stepfamilies" or "blended families" may include children from both previous and current marriages. Single parents are an increasing phenomenon in American society because of both divorce and unmarried mothers, and unmarried mothers may be much younger than one expects. Very little research exists about the ways that these diverse family structures affect a child with mental retardation, and vice versa. While professionals have in the last two decades more fully researched the relationship between fathers or siblings and family members who are mentally retarded, those relationships are just beginning to be better understood and described. The relationships described here concern mothers, fathers, siblings, grandparents, and single parents. The reader is encouraged to think also of ways in which the total family unit is affected by a special member.

### MOTHERS

As mentioned earlier, much of the literature on families has focused on mothers, but often on white, middle-class mothers of young children. In her account of firsthand experiences of three mothers, Roberts (1986) notes that mothers are affected differently across the lifespan of caring for a child with special needs. In the preschool years, mothers often assume primary responsibility for child-rearing and finding additional services to meet the child's needs. This era can be a critical time for establishing a support network in friends and family. Sometimes career goals must be altered or postponed. Decisions about having additional children may be difficult, given the needs of the special child. In this era many mothers of children with more severe handicaps go through a turmoil of changing expectations as the discrepancy of development between their child and others becomes ever more apparent.

During the school years, mothers of children with mild mental retardation may experience this same turmoil as the child lags further behind

*Many programs work with very young children who are retarded.*

with each school year. At this time mothers often become effective advocates for their children within the educational system.

When the child reaches adolescence, the mother faces new problems caused by the child's awakening sexuality and the impending termination of public school services at age 21. While accepting and encouraging a teenager's independence challenges all parents, the mother of a child with special needs is especially challenged by the conflicting needs to encourage independence and to provide ongoing support. As one mother of an adolescent related:

> Monica wanted to stay home alone, and although I've left her alone for short periods of time, like half an hour maximum, I'm not ready to leave her alone for three hours. She didn't want a babysitter. She wanted to do something else. So we made other arrangements for her. That's my problem. I have to be open enough for her to make some choices. (Roberts, 1986, p. 216)

While rarely discussed in the literature, aging dependents who have mental retardation create special challenges for mothers who are themselves aging. Even if professional services provide home care for the dependent, the mother may worry about who will nurture her dependent after she dies.

## FATHERS

The literature on fathers in general has grown in recent years, but research about fathers of children with mental retardation continues to be sparse (Cummings, 1976). The literature that does exist provides valuable insights into ways that the presence of a child with mental retardation affects men in their role as fathers.

What fathers themselves have written verifies that coping with feelings is a challenge. Roos (1975), who is both a special educator and a parent, has described the anger parents experience toward professionals who treat parents as patients and who convey negative attitudes about people with mental retardation. Sometimes the stress related to the initial diagnosis is compounded for fathers because they are not included in conferences. From interviews of fathers of children with Down syndrome, Erickson (1974) found that fathers often had difficulty getting professionals to give them a straightforward diagnosis. Instead, they had to rely on their wives for all information. These fathers recommended that professionals wait to share the diagnosis until both parents are present and a person who is knowledgeable about the syndrome is available to provide further details.

Despite changes in family structures as more women work, mothers are still the primary caregivers in most families. The stress of having a child with special needs can sharpen this role differentiation. Four family styles may emerge, depending on the father's involvement with the child. In the first style, the father delegates the child's care entirely to the mother and divorces himself through pouring more energy into his traditional role of breadwinner. The added expense of a child with special needs may increase a father's perception of needing to maintain and improve the family's financial status. Also, men may be especially vulnerable to loss of self-esteem (Tallman, 1965), especially if the child with mental retardation is a boy (Farber, 1972). Too much role differentiation and obsession with work can place a tremendous strain on the marriage. Tew, Lawrence, Payne, and Rawnsley (1977) have reported higher divorce rates for families with a child who is mentally retarded.

In a second style, the mother joins the father in delegating the child's care and increases her involvement in such outside pursuits as a career. These parents may seek to institutionalize the child, or a grandparent or other family member may become the primary caretaker.

In a third style, the father devotes himself to the care of the child and makes personal and career concerns subordinate to this relationship. The whole family may join the father in making the child its center. Family members may become extremely close as they focus their energy on the joint priority of the special child. This style may have a negative impact on siblings (see next section). In some cases, the mother may assume the role of breadwinner, delegating primary responsibility for care to the father.

In a fourth style of family adjustment, the father tries to balance the child's needs with his own personal and career goals. Mothers and older siblings may also adopt this style, which provides interesting patterns of taking turns being "on call" for the special family member. Such a family may feel that the presence of the child has added strength to the family and the marriage.

The Supporting Extended Family Members project at the University of Washington has demonstrated that professionals can be supportive of fathers. The staff of this project encourages fathers to learn to be more effective in reading their child's cues and in providing appropriate activities and experiences. Fathers also have the opportunity to share experiences with other fathers and learn more about their child's disabilities (Meyer, 1986). To be successful, such a program must value fathers' input and offer flexible program scheduling to be compatible with fathers' job demands.

## SIBLINGS

Crocker (1981) has discussed the many variables that can influence the impact on siblings of a sister or brother with mental retardation. For example, the logistics of adapting family routines and resources to accommodate the child may make the sibling feel a need to compete for attention and resources like the parents' time and financial support. Siblings may feel ambivalent about a brother or sister who requires so much attention. They may feel guilty because of their negative feelings or because they feel they somehow contribute to their parents' sorrow or despair. Sometimes a brother or sister feels obliged either to compensate for a sibling's disability by excelling or to become a surrogate parent to a special sister or brother.

Research about siblings has yielded information on both positive and negative results of these potential stresses. A negative impact may be on psychological functioning—more anxiety and less sociability (Grossman, 1972), or a higher incidence of behavior problems (Gath, 1973). Other research has reported positive effects, such as an increased sensitivity to people who are different (Farber, 1963; Grossman, 1972).

Outside support for siblings can increase the likelihood of positive coping. Peer support groups for siblings, as for parents, can help them cope with feelings. Siblings also need information about the handicap and will benefit indirectly from resources that help parents meet the continuing challenge of raising a child with special needs.

## GRANDPARENTS

Current trends in American society make it less likely that grandparents will be involved in the daily life of their grandchildren than in previous generations because of the increased mobility of two-career families and the trend for older Americans to live independently for more years. But many grandparents still do maintain an active involvement in their grandchildren's lives. Robertson (1977) has described the many roles grandparents have assumed based on literature on this family role. For example, grandparents may provide baby-sitting, gifts, relate family history, take children to church, provide advice on personal problems, offer home recreation, shop, lend money, or take grandchildren on brief vacations. Given the increased needs

# CONCERNS OF NONRETARDED SIBLINGS

The effects on parents of having a family member with retardation have been documented in many different places; however, the effects on the nonretarded siblings have received much less attention. Siblings also have concerns and questions about their brother or sister who is handicapped. Unfortunately, their confusion often remains undispelled because special education professionals have not tried to explain the situation to them or answer their questions.

Powell and Ogle (1985) have identified seven major areas about which siblings may have concerns, voiced or not, and list examples of questions they might have. While Powell and Ogle were considering children with disabilities in general, their examples are appropriate to situations where a family member is retarded.

| *Concern* | *Question* |
| --- | --- |
| Cause of the handicap | Why is my sister handicapped? |
| | What caused the handicap? |
| | Will future brothers and sisters also be handicapped? |
| | Whose fault is it? |
| The child's feelings | Is my brother in pain? |
| | Does he have the same feelings I do? |
| | What does he think about? |
| | Does he know me? |
| | Does he love me and my parents? |
| | Why does he behave so strangely? |
| Prognosis | Can my sister be cured? |
| | Will she improve? |
| | Can she grow out of this? |
| | Can treatment really help? |
| Needed services | What special help will he need? |
| | Who are these professionals who work with him? |
| | What do they do with him? |
| How to help | What am I supposed to do with my sister? |
| | What can I expect from her? |
| | Can I help teach her? |
| | How can I interact with her? |
| | Should I protect her? |
| Where the child lives | Why does my brother live at home? |
| | Wouldn't an institution be better for him? |
| | Why doesn't he live at home? |
| | Aren't institutions bad for handicapped persons? |
| The future | What will happen to my sister in the future? |
| | Will she always be with us? |
| | Will she go to school? |
| | Will she get married and have a family? |
| | Will she ever live on her own? |

From *Brothers and Sisters—A Special Part of Exceptional Families* (pp. 45–46) by T. H. Powell and P. A. Ogle, 1985, Baltimore: Paul H. Brookes. Reprinted by permission.

of families with a special member, grandparents can become an invaluable resource for respite and support.

## SINGLE MOTHERS

As mentioned earlier, many family patterns exist besides that of the nuclear family, and the family comprising a single mother and a child with special needs deserves special attention. Since single mothers face alone the challenges of coping with feelings, meeting increased demands for resources, and meeting the needs of their other children, it is understandable that they will be especially under stress. This stress takes several forms, including more institutionalization of children of single parents (German and Maisto, 1982) and reports of stress in questionnaire sampling (Beckman, 1983). This personal report helps to illustrate the single parents' dilemma:

> I'm at the end of my rope. I'm not despondent, but I need to regroup my forces and pull myself together. In fact, I'm going to be selfish and insist one of my older children bail me out and take care of my son occasionally. I just wish I could have a week alone to pull myself together. (Vadasy, 1986, p. 236)

## OTHER FAMILY CHARACTERISTICS

Besides the roles of individual family members, certain general family characteristics need to be considered by professionals attempting to develop supportive relationships with parents. "Blended" families are an increasingly common pattern in our society because most people who divorce remarry. In the blended family, the professional may have more than two parents with whom to communicate, especially if joint custody has been arranged. Turnbull and Turnbull (1985) note the need for special sensitivity in working with blended families; for example, the professional must take care to keep all parents informed of the child's progress and to avoid being caught in power struggles in IEP or other meetings.

A family may also be culturally different from the professional in race, religion, social class, and so forth. The professional should try to learn more about the family's culture or religion to understand how values may differ in family structure or in education. For example, Mexican-American families may value cooperation over competition. Families from Asian cultures may have difficulty in pursuing their child's education aggressively because they are too respectful of professionals' position and expertise. Professionals who are white might underestimate how important extended family members like aunts or grandmothers can be in a family who is Black. Professionals can improve their work with families across cultures by opening themselves to information about other cultures and to opportunities for multicultural awareness.

A third characteristic to be considered is socioeconomic status, which includes income, educational level, and social status of occupations held by family members. Although financial resources can be an asset for family coping (e.g., by purchasing services like baby-sitting), it is a fallacy to assume that higher SES families therefore invariably cope better than low-SES families. Because high-SES families are achievement-oriented, the presence of a child with mental retardation can be an even more difficult challenge for them. The low-SES family may be less concerned with achievement but may need more information on ways to care for a child who is different. Besides value differences, poverty is a harsh reality for some families. Programs created for low-income families with children at risk for disabilities have often had difficulty recruiting participants. More urgent problems, such as finding housing and food or coping with serious illness, may overshadow a child's disability. The parent may also have a disability. Professionals can become especially discouraged when faced with such multiple family problems. But building rapport with the family, making realistic suggestions, and working with other agencies that provide support to the family can all be important contributions to the welfare of the child.

Whatever its SES level, a family may be in poor mental health, with incidents of child abuse or neglect. The factors that contribute to abuse are complex, but it is known that mental retardation may both contribute to and result from abuse, although the vast majority of parents of children with special needs do not abuse them. Most schools have policies for reporting suspected abuse that professionals should know and follow. While following these policies, professionals can remain nonjudgmental and respectful. Starting from the assumption that parents do not want to abuse their children can be beneficial in facilitating the family's access to resources to end abuse.

### SELF-HELP FOR FAMILY GROWTH

More and more resources for families provide strategies for meeting challenges and emerging as a stronger family unit because of common concern over a child's special needs. One such resource is the book *After the Tears* by Robin Simons (1987), in which parents offer practical advice on, for example, coping with feelings, strengthening the marriage, nurturing other children in the family, planning for the future, and working with professionals. Professionals may encourage a family's stress management and growth by conveying confidence in their ability to meet challenges and referring them to resources like other families or literature for discussing specific issues. One of our favorite quotes from Simons' (1987) book is by a parent who is reflecting on her growth in her years as a mother of a child with special needs. She says, "If you had asked me ten years ago could I do the things I've done in the last ten years, I would have said, 'No way'" (p. 78).

### PROFESSIONAL RESOURCES FOR FAMILY GROWTH

Professionals may further encourage the self-growth of families with a member who is mentally retarded. Folkman, Schaefer, and Lazarus (1979) have described five types of coping resources that can help families mediate stress. First, parents' physical and mental health can be an asset in meeting the stresses of caregiving, behavior management, school conferences, and so on. Families may benefit from professional services that are health maintenance-oriented, such as fitness clubs or support groups. Second, problem-solving skills, including the ability to search for and analyze information and plot out various courses of action, can help families cope with short- or long-term problems. School-based parent groups or counseling services might offer courses in problem-solving to enhance families' skill in meeting new challenges. Third, social networks of supportive relationships can help families maintain community involvement and cope with problems. Professionals might introduce new parents to other families who have a member with special needs or might include extended family members (e.g., grandparents) in parent-training activities. Fourth, from a strictly utilitarian viewpoint, income and education can give families more resources for coping. Some may need to focus temporarily on a parent's continued education for job advancement to meet increased expenses. The final resource Folkman et al. (1979) suggest is the individual's personal beliefs, including feelings of self-efficacy and belief in some higher purpose (e.g., religious faith). Professional respect for religious difference is important in supporting individuals' quest for the inspiration to meet daily challenges. Although this list of potential resources is far from complete, professionals may find ideas in it for helping families.

## DEVELOPING A PARENT-PROFESSIONAL PARTNERSHIP

If relationships between professionals and parents can be designed with cooperation and coordination in mind, many family needs can be met. During the initial stage of the relationship, parents and professionals should identify and agree upon *(a)* the child's eligibility and needs for service, *(b)* the short- and long-term objectives of treatment, and *(c)* the priorities for treatment. Unless parents and professionals can basically agree on the needs of the child and the objectives and priorities for treatment, the relationship will probably not be productive.

Agreement about the child's needs and about programming is necessary but not sufficient for a good working relationship. Professionals and parents must work together to maximize the child's development. Effective coordination of efforts can be more readily obtained if parents and professionals identify and agree upon their respective roles. Heward, Dardig, and Rossett (1979) list seven roles commonly assumed by parents of children with handicaps. Those roles are *(a)* teaching, *(b)* counseling, *(c)* managing behavior, *(d)* parenting siblings who are not handicapped, *(e)* maintaining parent-to-parent relationship, *(f)* educating significant others (such as relatives and neighbors), and *(g)* relating to the school and the community.

Without even listing the roles of various professionals, it should be apparent that many roles are common to parents and professionals. Most children who are retarded spend a greater portion of their time with their parents than with professionals. Since parents have access to a wide variety of potential reinforcers, the child can be provided with an effective program, if the professionals and the parents can coordinate their efforts. The child will make maximal progress if the instructional program is consistently administered in both school and home settings.

Interchange of information is extremely important to maintain a productive treatment program, as both parties need to be aware of the child's progress in each setting. When changes in the program are sought, both parties should be informed. A parent-professional relationship that meets the preceding criteria may not be easy to develop, may be difficult to maintain, and may not produce the desired results as quickly as might be wished. Despite these problems, the development of a good parent-professional relationship is advantageous for the welfare of the child. Neither professional nor parents alone can provide a comprehensive and consistent program; they must work as partners. Turnbull (1978), herself the stepmother of a son who is retarded and a professional special educator, has offered suggestions for professionals who work with parents. They include

1. Professionals must acquire humility and the honesty to say "I don't know."
2. Courses on working with families of the retarded should include a practicum with families of the handicapped and should teach skills to help parents solve day-to-day problems of living with a retarded child.
3. Respect is an essential ingredient in the parent-professional relationship.
4. Parents and professionals must work together if handicapped children are to reach their full potential.
5. Handicapped children need to have personal relationships with individuals outside the family. These relationships are also important to assure the parents that others love their child and seek opportunities to be with him or her. (adapted from pp. 136–140)

## PROFESSIONAL MISHANDLING OF PARENTS

Unfortunately, parents of retarded children have not always received the help they need from professionals. Roos (1975) contends that too often professionals deal with parents in an unproductive and pejorative manner.

***Problems of obtaining diagnosis.***    Parents frequently have difficulty with professionals when they seek a diagnosis of their child's condition. While parents may already suspect retardation, the actual diagnosis can be a very upsetting experience, as we have discussed. Diagnosticians are often keenly aware of the parents' anxieties, and they too may feel considerable anxiety when delivering the diagnosis. Unfortunately, the attempts of some professionals to reduce their own anxiety in addition to the anxieties of parents sometimes result in mishandling of the diagnostic process (MacMillan, 1982).

Roos (1975) claims that professionals, operating from the medical model, often consider mental retardation to be an incurable condition.

> They (professionals) generate self-fulfilling and self-limiting prophecies which threaten to mitigate [sic] against the development of mentally retarded persons. Parents are usually sensitive to such defeatist attitudes and either adopt similar expectations or resent those who hold negative expectations toward their child. (p. 341)

Research supports Roos's claim. Abramson, Gravink, Abramson, and Sommers (1977) surveyed 215 families whose preschool children were diagnosed as mentally retarded. Of the sample, 94% sought advice from medical doctors. Only 18% of the families in the sample indicated that they received sympathetic and informative advice. Regarding the nature of the advice, Abramson et al. report:

> For the most part advice consisted of an objective and clinical portrayal of the situation (27%), another referral (24%), or an attempt to minimize the symptoms (14%). A bleak prognosis, misinformation, and [advice to] love [and] treat the child as a normal child accounted for 9%, 5%, and 3% respectively. (p. 29)

It is not surprising that the responses of 51% of the families ranged from feelings of great dissatisfaction to uncertainty about the advice they had received. Considering that most physicians have not been given extensive training regarding the nonmedical care and treatment of persons who are mentally retarded, it is not surprising that they sometimes do not provide parents with adequate nonmedical service. Most of the problems involved in rearing such children are not primarily medical problems; yet, they are important family problems.

Abramson and colleagues (1977) did find that the parents were more satisfied with the medical services than with the nonmedical services provided by physicians; "77% of the sample was either satisfied or very satisfied with the medical treatment their child had received" (p. 29). Other writers (for example, Carr, 1974; MacMillan, 1982; Wolfensberger, 1967; Zwerling, 1954) report that callous and insensitive treatment frequently accompanies the negative and hopeless type of diagnosis. It is certainly possible that some professionals may present a stern or callous attitude as a defense against their own anxiety. In other cases, they may feel that they have to convey the diagnosis as a grim reality to the parents in order to force them into action.

In deference to medical personnel, we must acknowledge that there are many persons very knowledgeable of nonmedical matters, and some medical schools are beginning to include topics on mental retardation. We hope that there will be more interchange between the two groups in the future. We must also remember that physicians are not responsible for most diagnoses of mental retardation; educational agencies are. Physicians usually diagnose more severe cases of mental retardation, or cases accompanied by physical features or disabilities, when the child is young. Educators and administrators who represent educational agencies have also mishandled a great many parents who were seeking services for their children. They have just managed to do it with a little less notoriety.

Jensen (1950) has reported another frequently occurring error in the diagnostic process. Too often professionals encourage parents to be over optimistic. Eventually, the reality of the child's limitations becomes apparent, and the result disillusions parents. False encouragement also tends to delay diagnosis, and without diagnosis, needed services may not be available for the affected child or other family members.

There is some justification for delaying diagnosis if the diagnostician suspects, but is not certain, that the child is retarded. In those instances a reexamination or further referral is appropriate. Diagnosticians should be aware, however, that delays and additional referrals can cause parents to "shop around." Anderson (1971) defines *shopping* as

> The retarded child's parents making visits to the same professional or to a number of professionals in such a manner that one visit follows another without resolution of a resolvable problem. (p. 3)

While some professionals regard "shopping" as symptomatic of parents' inability to accept the diagnosis, others (including Anderson, 1971; Keirn, 1971; Roos, 1975) claim that shopping may indicate a search for services. Keirn (1971) arbitrarily defines a shopping parent as one who pursues a third professional evaluation. He surveyed 218 families and found that only six—less than 3%—could be identified as "shoppers." Consultations with different professionals should take place if the intent is to provide a thorough diagnosis and comprehensive services. The number of parents who shop for magic cures may be so minimal that the negative connotation of the term probably does not apply to most parents seeking additional professional services. Much assistance could be given to parents if one professional would consolidate previous evaluations and encourage them to return for services (Keirn, 1971).

*Parents as patients.*    Parents of children who are retarded operate under considerable emotional stress. Some professionals identify the parents' emotional stress as the primary problem, suggesting that parents are really patients. Instead of receiving the services and information that could be used to meet their needs and those of their children, some parents have been subjected to psychotherapy and counseling. Psychological treatment regimes are unlikely to succeed if they do not provide the parents with other benefits, including *(a)* an understanding of the nature of mental retardation and *(b)* information to help them identify and meet the needs of their children.

*Professional omniscience-omnipotence.*    An omniscient-omnipotent attitude (all-knowing and all-powerful) manifested by some professionals is another kind of inappropriate treatment of parents. Professionals have too often made important decisions affecting the welfare of a child without consulting with the parents. Some professionals have commonly withheld information from parents. Their rationale for denying parents access to information is usually based on the assumption that such information would be too threatening or destructive (Roos, 1975). Current legal provisions such as P.L. 94-142 have by no means eliminated the willful withholding of information from parents. Legislative mandates apply only to documented information, but professionals frequently maintain private notes that are not available to parents. Although there is some justification for maintaining private notes before a decision is made, there is less justification for withholding information from parents if it relates to decisions that have been or are being made regarding their child—especially in the areas of evaluation, placement, and service delivery.

Total responsibility for the success or failure of a working partnership between parents and professionals is the responsibility of both parties, demanding cooperation and coordination. While we have been stressing the professional's responsibility for making the relationship work, parents can be responsible for the failure of some relationships to become productive. Some parents have indeed denied that their child was retarded, have neglected important needs of the child, have declined to participate in goal setting and transitional planning, have rejected professional aid, have distrusted the motives of professionals, and have held unrealistic expectations for the relationship. The list of the sins of omission and commission could be expanded for each party. What is very important to note is that the development of the parent-professional partnership should be considered an ethical responsibility, a practical necessity, and, for professionals, a legal obligation.

## PARENTS AND THE RIGHT TO EDUCATION

Chapter 13 discusses the legislation and litigation that have affected the welfare of all who are mentally retarded. The Education for all Handicapped Children Act, P.L. 94-142, and its amendments, have specific relevance to the parent-professional relationship. The discussion here highlights some important points of P.L. 94-142 as it relates to parents.

Two of the expressed purposes of P.L. 94-142 are

1. To insure that a free appropriate public education which includes special education and related services is available to all handicapped children.
2. To insure that the rights of handicapped children and their parents are protected. (sec. 121a.1)

The assurance of due process for parents and child is essential to fulfillment of the handicapped child's educational and other needs. The educational agency may not unilaterally decide the needs of the child, the child's eligibility for service, or what services will be provided, but must attempt (and document its efforts) to obtain the written informed consent of the parents before any activity related to evaluation or the delivery of special education services may be carried out. The parents' consent must be obtained in all of the following situations: prior to evaluation for eligibility, before implementation of the IEP, at the completion of each annual review, and prior to any change in placement or reevaluation. In addition, parental consent may be revoked at any time.

The rights of parents are not limited to approving or disapproving proposed placements, services, and activities. Parents also have the right to attend and participate in the development of their child's IEP. They have the right to veto any decisions and to recommend activities and services for their child. They have the right to request a reevaluation of their child or a review of the child's placement and IEP. The parents' role in the development of the IEP is extremely important, because the IEP determines what constitutes an appropriate education.

According to P.L. 94-142, parents of children suspected of or identified as being handicapped have other rights as well. These additional rights include

1. The right to inspect any educational records with respect to identification, evaluation, placement, and the provision of a free appropriate education. (Sec. 121a.502)
2. The right to obtain an independent evaluation: If the independent evaluation is to be submitted at an IEP meeting or at a due process hearing, it must have been conducted by a qualified examiner who is not employed by the education agency responsible for the child's education. (Sec. 121a.503)

   If an agreement cannot be reached between the parents and the educational agency, regarding the provision of a free appropriate education and related services, either party has the right to seek settlement in a due process hearing.
3. The right to receive parent counseling and training as a related service (Sec. 121a.13(6)): If it is determined that this service is necessary to meet the special needs of the child and if the parents agree to participate, then the educational agency must provide this service. Providing parent counseling and training is not intended to allow educational agencies to train parents to shoulder the burden of educating their handicapped child themselves. The intent of that provision is: *(a)* to help parents understand their child's special needs; *(b)* to provide them with information about child development; and *(c)* to enable parents to have a method for supplementing the child's educational program whenever appropriate.

The protection guaranteed by these procedural safeguards for both children with handicaps and their parents is an essential component of the delivery of an appropriate education. The potential adversarial relationship between parents and professionals when these safeguards are applied tends to strain many partnerships. Although this type of relationship is undesirable,

*Parents' involvement in their children's programs is welcome.*

it may be unavoidable. Most important, these legal safeguards must be available to parents. Since it is possible for an adversarial relationship between parents and professionals to develop, we might ask whether it should be avoided for the child's sake. When either party—the school or the parents—becomes more concerned with its own interests than with the child's, it is the child who suffers. Sometimes differences in opinion can be worked out through mediation before it is necessary to invoke formal due process. When in disagreement, parents and professionals might be able to ensure an appropriate education for a child by working together for the child's benefit.

# ROLES OF PARENTS

### PARENTS AS MEMBERS OF ORGANIZATIONS

Parents of children with handicaps have gained important political power in recent years. Although some parents on their own have been able to obtain services for their children, it has been the collaborative efforts of parent organizations that have had a significant impact on securing services for people who are mentally retarded.

One of the largest organizations concerned with the education and care of persons with retardation is an organization founded by parents: the Association for Retarded Citizens (ARC). Although the ARC is now a large, complex, diversified organization, it had simpler beginnings. Roos (1975) has described its development from its grass-roots beginning to its present status as one of the largest and most influential organizations representing citizens who are retarded. In 1950 many local parent organizations came together to form the National Association for Retarded Children. In 1973 the name was changed to the National Association for Retarded Citizens, reflecting a change in perspective from just children to all people. It is now known as the Association for Retarded Citizens (in this country, Association for Retarded Citizens—United States). Roos has pointed out that there has been a gradual trend for nonprofessionals to become involved as members and as leaders in ARC.

The rapid growth of the ARC-U.S. attests to its ability to help meet the needs of those who are mentally retarded and their families. Roos (1975) reports that "from 125 member organizations with approximately 13,000 active members, it has grown to over 1600 state and local units and a membership of approximately 250,000 in 1974" (p. 348). As of 1980, there are approximately 1900 state and local units, with approximately 1,000,000 members.

While the ARC has always attempted to meet parents' needs for support and information, it also has expanded beyond this important self-help role. On the national and local levels, it has entered four important areas: *(a)* provision of programs and services, *(b)* political lobbying and litigation, *(c)* citizen advocacy, and *(d)* monitoring and evaluating programs. A current emphasis of the ARC is to secure the publicly supported services that persons who are mentally retarded are entitled to as citizens.

Reviewing the impact of parent organizations in general and the ARC-U.S. in particular, Roos (1975) states:

> In summary, the day of the naive parent struggling impotently to find desperately needed services for his retarded child is now past. Parent organizations in the United States, primarily under the aegis of NARC, have matured into strong, sophisticated advocates for the retarded and their families. No longer alone and

helpless, parents have demonstrated that they can be valuable assets in behalf of their own children as well as in behalf of all retarded, wherever they may be. (p. 353)

## PARENTS AS BEHAVIOR MANGERS

Parents of children who are retarded have often had to raise their own children, but they have not always been regarded as competent to do so, as Kurtz (1978) points out.

> Social forces and human service arrangements have diminished the status of parents and reduced their incentive to assume their role as powerful agents in the child's development. This is especially true for parents who feel inadequate and ill prepared. Human service agencies have communicated to parents that someone else can do the job better. By taking major responsibility for services, professionals in schools and health and social service agencies have undermined the position of parents. (p. 452)

Fortunately, parents have been receiving more recognition as key figures in their children's development and later lives. Research in the area of early childhood education with at-risk children (Bronfenbrenner, 1974) and early intervention for handicapped children (Boyd, 1979; Clunies-Ross, 1979; Shearer & Shearer, 1972) has highlighted the importance of parental involvement in early childhood developmental programs. More recently, the importance of family involvement in the transitional planning process has also been established (Patton & Browder, 1988).

## CONCLUSION AND SUGGESTIONS

Professionals have continued to develop an interest in the problems faced by families with members who are handicapped. The quality of research has continued to improve, and as a result many important issues have been identified. It is particularly important to be mindful of such indicators of future problems as demographic changes. The relevance of certain demographic changes, such as the higher incidences of teenage mothers, single parents, and working mothers, is not a problem of the future but a reality of the present. We must study the family structure rather than focusing on one member in isolation from the family.

The importance of obtaining adequate samples and conducting sound research cannot be overemphasized. Whatever services are available to persons who are retarded and their families are frequently made available by virtue of various policy-making agencies, and policymakers should be able to base their decisions on information that reflects the facts, not just on our best guesses.

# CHAPTER 13

# Individual Rights and
# Legal Issues

T his chapter details the rights of persons who are mentally retarded and the legal issues associated with these rights. The discussion includes: a review of the context for securing individual rights; an examination of the legal bases used to establish these rights; an in-depth analysis of issues in education, institutionalization, and community life; and attention to selected personal rights.

## THE CONTEXT FOR SECURING INDIVIDUAL RIGHTS

A review of the last 30 years indicates that advocates have gained a lot for persons with mental retardation. These advocates, for the most part, have attempted to establish that all citizens have certain rights; they are not privileges earned by a few. Much effort has been devoted to two fundamental activities: *(a)* establishing that persons with mental retardation are entitled to the same rights guaranteed all citizens; and *(b)* ensuring that those who are retarded are exercising these rights.

Wald (1976) has remarked that the rights to which individuals who are retarded are entitled are those that define a man or a woman as a human being. She suggests that these rights carry obligations for the individual as a member of society. The status of those with mental retardation as contributing members of society is precisely what must be accepted if the rights supposedly granted to all citizens are to be secured for this group.

To think that legal remedies alone will assure the rights of those who are mentally retarded is simplistic. The acceptance of these people is influenced by a complex set of interactive factors. Townsend and Mattson (1981) have proposed a model that reflects the interrelationships of five major factors.

Their model is presented in Figure 13.1. The factors that, according to them, crucially affect real change are:

1. *Political coalitions* (i.e., the evolution of various interest groups that advocate for resources to meet common goals),
2. *Laws and judicial interpretations* (i.e., the creation of rules which formalize and stabilize the agreements of diverse political coalitions),
3. *Science and technology* (i.e., the development of professional expertise to transform limited resources into effective practices that will meet the goals of various interest groups),
4. *Personal satisfaction* (i.e., the creation of working and living environments which allow individuals the opportunity to discover and pursue a variety of interests), and
5. *Public attitudes* (i.e., the evolution of images, ideas, words, and behaviors which express the uniqueness and similarities of human interests). (p. 77)

## LEGAL BACKGROUND AND TERMINOLOGY

Proponents of any social change movement in today's world, such as the push for individual rights, need to become familiar with the language of law, because legal remedy is often one tool through which they can legitimize change. Advocates must have an understanding of the need for legal action, the significant legislation to date, the arguments upon which court action is based, and the implications of judicial decisions and consent agreements. All these are addressed in this chapter.

One must also have some understanding of juridical language. Table 13.1 should assist the novice in legal terminology. It includes definitions of selected terms like *equal protection* and *due process,* which are frequently used in judicial procedures and to which we refer regularly in this chapter.

**FIGURE 13.1**   A Multidisciplinary Concept of Rights

From "The Interaction of Law and Special Education: Observing the Emperor's New Clothes" by C. Townsend and R. Mattson, 1981, *Analysis and Intervention in Developmental Disabilities, 1,* pp. 75–89. Reprinted by permission.

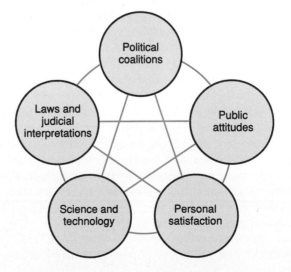

## FUNDAMENTAL ISSUES

Throughout history, people who were mentally retarded have been misperceived in a number of ways, ranging from early thinking that they were demonically possessed to Justice Holmes's infamous perception of them as social parasites (*Buck v. Bell,* 1927). As noted in chapter 1, the treatment accorded this group was much a function of the sociopolitical influences of a given time. This has been demonstrated in many ways and has included such practices as institutionalization for custodial and protective purposes, compulsory sterilization laws, exclusion from education and training, zoning ordinances that restrict the establishment of group homes, and most recently withholding treatment from severely involved infants.

***Prejudicial attitudes.*** The term *mental retardation* conjures up many misconceptions. Many of the general public associate this condition with sickness (Kurtz, 1977). All too often, individuals who are mentally retarded are perceived in negative ways and as a single homogeneous group. This happens because stereotypes are common and generalizations are easy to make. Such must be replaced by more accurate information and appropriate images.

See chapter 2 for a discussion of stereotyping.

Even professional thinking tends to accentuate the disabilities rather than the abilities of those who are retarded. Sociological perspectives are built upon deviancy models (significant variance from the norm). Legal thinking has often used "differentness" as a basis for argument, particularly in equal protection claims. Attitudes and perspectives like these can easily lead to decisions and patterns of treatment that are antithetical to both egalitarianism and social role valorization. They underscore the importance of public attitudes as important factors in the legal rights movement, as Townsend and Mattson (1981) have pointed out.

***Quasi-suspect class.*** As a group, people with mental retardation historically have been vulnerable to purposely unequal treatment (e.g., compulsory sterilization), which has brought about a need for legal action and protections. One of the most powerful arguments for redress is to establish that such people's right to equal protection is being violated. Equal protection claims cause the court to examine "the plaintiff's entitlement to judicial protection and the interest being abridged" (Bateman, 1986, p. 14). An important factor in this analysis is whether a group qualifies as a "suspect class" or "quasi-suspect class," as this determination leads to a much stricter analysis of the claim by the court. These concepts indicate that certain actions (e.g., legislation, policies, regulations, ordinances), when applied to a group that has traditionally been liable to unequal treatment, are "suspect, subject to strict scrutiny, and justifiable only by a compelling interest of the state" (Gilhool, 1976, p. 183).

The issue of suspect classification has been addressed in several court cases. Of particular note is the U.S. Supreme Court's unwillingness to grant

TABLE 13.1   Selected Legal Terms

*Cause of action.*   The legal damage or injury on which a lawsuit is based. There must be a cause of action, or legal "wrong," for a court to consider a case; (in *Wyatt v. Stickney,* denial of treatment and maintenance of harmful conditions in institutions gave rise to causes of action for violation of constitutional rights).

*Class action.*   Most lawsuits are individual actions. A class action suit is brought by one or more named persons on their own behalf *and* on behalf of all persons in similar circumstances ("similarly situated"). A court's ruling in a class action suit applies to all members of the "class." For example, the court's ruling in the Willowbrook case applied to all 5,000 people who were residents of Willowbrook State School when the suit was filed, not just the few in whose names the suit was filed.

*Complaint.*   A formal legal document submitted to a court by one or more persons (the plaintiffs), alleging that their rights have been violated. A complaint specifies one or more causes of action, names those who have allegedly violated the plaintiff's rights (the defendants), and demands that the defendants take certain corrective action (relief).

*Consent agreement (consent judgment* or *consent decree).*   A court-ratified and enforced agreement between the opposing parties in a suit, resolving the contested issues. Reached after the initiation of a lawsuit, a consent agreement, because it is ratified by a court, carries the same weight as any other court order. The Willowbrook, case, *NYARC v. Carey,* resulted in a consent agreement. For a plaintiff, a consent agreement minimizes the cost and time of continued litigation and avoids the risk of receiving an unfavorable ruling from a court.

*Due process.*   A right guaranteed under the 5th and 14th Amendments to the U.S. Constitution. The concept of *substantive due process* refers to all citizens' fundamental rights to life, liberty, and property. For example, in *Donaldson v. O'Connor,* the Supreme Court ruled that the state of Florida had deprived Kenneth Donaldson of his rights under the 5th and 14th Amendments by involuntarily confining him in a custodial institution. *Procedural due process* refers to the fairness of procedures involved in any action that deprives people of their rights. Recent court rulings and legislation apply due process requirements to educational and treatment decisions. For instance, in *Mills v. Board of Education of the District of Columbia,* the court ruled that parents or guardians are entitled to due process regarding the school classification and placement of their children. Courts have interpreted the right of due process to require at a minimum that a person receive *reasonable notice* and the opportunity for a *fair hearing* prior to being deprived of legal rights.

suspect or quasi-suspect classification status to individuals who are mentally retarded (*City of Cleburne, Texas v. Cleburne Living Center, Inc.,* 1985). In reversing the Fifth Circuit Court of Appeal's decisions to do so, the Court felt that a less strict standard could be used for determining the constitutional issues of the case (Henderson & Vitello, 1988).

TABLE 13.1  *Continued*

*Equal protection.*  A right guaranteed by the 14th Amendment. This clause of the U.S. Constitution states that all citizens are entitled to equal protection under the law—that is, to be free from discrimination in the exercise of rights except where the state demonstrates a rational basis or compelling interest for apparently unequal treatment. In *Brown v. Board of Education of Topeka, Kansas,* the U.S. Supreme Court prohibited racial segregation in schools on the basis of the equal protection clause. The concept of equal protection has served as the foundation for landmark right-to-education and right-to-treatment suits on behalf of persons with disabilities.

*Motion.*  A request to the court in the context of a specific case to take some action relating to the case.

*Ordinance.*  A local law, that is, a city, town, or county law.

*Petitioner.*  The party appealing a court's decision to a higher court. Synonym for *appellant*. Also sometimes used to identify the plaintiff in certain courts or types of cases.

*Plaintiff.*  The party who brings a lawsuit alleging a violation of rights. The plaintiff is always named before the defendant in a case title; for example, Donaldson is the plaintiff in *Donaldson v. O'Connor*. Upon appeal, the order of names is reversed.

*Precedent.*  A prior court decision in a relevant case, cited in the interpretation of law or constitutional provision. A court may or may not accept a precedent as authoritative in interpreting the law in a specific case, depending on the factual similarities between the cases and the jurisdiction in which the precedent arose.

*Relief.*  The remedy to some legal wrong or violation of one's rights. Plaintiffs seek from the court certain types of relief against defendants, such as declaratory relief, injunctive relief, writs of *habeas corpus* (release), or money damages.

*Remand.*  An order by a higher court returning a case to a lower court for further action consistent with the higher court's decision.

*Respondent.*  The winning party at the trial level in a case that has been appealed. Synonym for *appellee*. Also used to mean the defendant in certain courts or cases.

Adapted from S. J. Taylor & D. Biklen, *Understanding the Law: An Advocate's Guide to the Law and Developmental Disabilities.* Syracuse, NY: Syracuse University and the Mental Health Law Project, 1979, pp. 3–11. Reprinted by permission. The authors would like to thank Michael Lottman, Lee Carty, Harold Madorsky, and Lesley Lannan for their assistance in the preparation of this paper.

**Best interest versus legal right.**  From time to time the principles of best interest and legal rights of an individual have come into conflict. When the state acts under the best interest principle, it does so in one of two ways. If the state acts in the best interest of the individual, it does so based on the theory of *parens patriae* (that is, the state is the father of the country and of its citizens). If the state acts in the best interest of society, it does so based on the theory of police power (that is, the power to impose restrictions upon private rights that are related to the general welfare of the public). This legal principle can impose upon the rights of an individual, as evidenced in many sterilization cases, in which the state interceded on behalf of the general welfare of the public. The principle of *parens patriae* seems on face value to be harmless, but situations can arise in which its use negates the individual's right to due process under the law.

### LEGAL BASES FOR ESTABLISHING RIGHTS

Different avenues are available for securing the rights of those who are mentally retarded. Turnbull (1986) has presented a ladder model that shows three options at each level of authority (see Figure 13.2). At each level there is a fundamental governing document that is the most important source of law.

*Federal constitutional arguments.*  The 14th Amendment to the Constitution contains two frequently invoked clauses: *(a)* the *due process* clause ("nor shall any State deprive any person of life, liberty, or property, without due process of law") and *(b)* the *equal protection* clause ("nor deny to any person within its jurisdiction the equal protection of the laws"). Many of the rights secured and services established during the last few years for those with retardation have been achieved through litigation based on constitutional grounds, particularly on these two principles. Table 13.2 presents the constitutional arguments that have been used most frequently in cases involving persons with mental retardation. This table is only a brief guide to the constitutional basis for much recent litigation; it is not a comprehensive list of all previous, present, or future bases for litigation.

Since the equal protection clause of the 14th Amendment has been the backbone for many rights for persons with mental retardation, we will look

FIGURE 13.2   A Model of Public Law

From *Free Appropriate Public Education: The Law and Children with Disabilities* by H. R. Turnbull, 1986, Denver: Love Publishing.

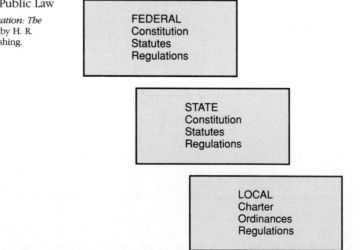

TABLE 13.2 Constitutional Arguments Frequently Used in Litigation

| Constitutional Argument | Constitutional Basis (Amendment) | Explanation | Example of Application |
|---|---|---|---|
| Equal protection | 14th | No state shall deny to any person within its jurisdiction the equal protection of the laws | Right to education |
| Due process (substantive) | 5th (federal) 14th (state) | Legislation must be reasonably related to the furtherance of a legitimate governmental objective | Right to appropriate classification Right to treatment |
| Due process (procedural) | 5th (federal) 14th (state) | Guarantees procedural fairness where the government would deprive one of property or liberty | Placement rights in the criminal justice system |
| Freedom from cruel and unusual punishment | 8th | Protection from punishment that is found to be offensive to the ordinary person, that is unfair, or that is grossly excessive for the offense | Right to refuse treatment Right to treatment Rights in prison |
| Freedom from slavery and involuntary servitude | 13th | No person shall be forced or coerced into working | Right to work (institutional) |
| Freedom of speech and the right to vote | 1st | Free exercise of basic rights | Right to education |

at it more closely. There are three types of equal protection analyses (the application of equal protection to a specific claim): *(a)* "rational basis" analysis; *(b)* "intermediate scrutiny" standard; and *(c)* "strict scrutiny" analysis. Bateman (1986) explains their differences in the context of a discimination claim:

> The court selects one of three different standards by which to judge whether the discriminatory treatment is allowable. Under the "rational basis" test the government has only to show some *rational* connection between the different treatment and a *legitimate* purpose. The "intermediate scrutiny" standard prohibits discrimination unless there is a *substantial* relationship to *important* government objectives. The "strict scrutiny" test requires the discriminatory classification be precisely drawn to further a *compelling* government reason. (p. 14)

*The inclusion of students with severe mental retardation on regular school campuses was achieved on the basis of equal protection arguments.*

When the courts apply the rational basis analysis, or traditional analysis, they use a two-pronged test. First, they ask whether the purposes sought by the state are legitimate. Second, they investigate whether there exists a "rational" correspondence between the purposes of the state action and the classification.

The intermediate scrutiny standard is used when discriminatory practices are claimed against a group of people who share some of the characteristics of a "suspect class." This standard implies a more stringent analysis than the rational basis standard. Various courts have suggested that claims made on behalf of individuals with mental retardation should be examined under this standard. In light of the *Cleburne* decision, however, the U.S. Supreme Court, as it will be composed in the near future, is not likely to invoke this heightened standard in cases using equal protection arguments (Henderson and Vitello, 1988).

If the courts apply the strict scrutiny standard, they put into motion a test that contains three major features. First, the situation must involve a suspect classification. Second, a fundamental interest must be at issue. Third, if the first two criteria are met, then the courts demand that the state demonstrate a "compelling interest" for its action, based on necessity, not convenience (Turnbull, 1975).

*Federal statutes and regulations.* Another mechanism for securing the rights of citizens who are mentally retarded that has had and will continue to have significance is federal legislation and its accompanying regulations. As more federal legislation is enacted, reference to it will occur more frequently. This is particularly noteworthy in light of the Supreme Court's reluctance to apply either the intermediate or strict scrutiny standards—standards that make it easier to win equal protection claims (Bateman, 1986).

To date, this country has enacted a number of landmark pieces of legislation. Detailed descriptions of each can be found elsewhere (see Office of Special Education and Rehabilitative Services, 1988) and are not covered here. The importance of these legislative actions is twofold comprising *(a)* the mandates they make, and *(b)* the legal basis they provide for arguing against unfair treatment.

*State constitutions, statutes, and regulations.* Since it is incumbent upon each state to provide education for its citizens by virtue of compulsory education laws, it would follow that this legislative mandate would be a strong basis for arguing that these same services be afforded to handicapped children. Although referring specifically to the right-to-education issue, Turnbull (1975) states the importance of state mandates.

> The case law on the right to an education is not based solely upon federal and constitutional arguments. And not surprisingly, the federal equal-protection and due-process arguments are not as likely to be a secure ground for establishing the right to education as is the guarantee of education imposed on the state by its constitution or statutes. (p. 6)

# UNWELCOMED IMMIGRANTS

Not long ago, there was an article in *Sports Illustrated* ("From Russia with Love") about a Soviet immigrant named Max Blank. While the *SI* article was about this 6′ 8-½″ tall high school basketball star, we were more interested in his younger brother. In describing the travels of the Blank family to the United States, *SI* reported:

> But the Blanks continued on to Italy; they spent eight months in the village of Ladispoli, west of Rome, waiting for a special waiver that would

enable Max's younger brother, Yakov, a Down's syndrome child, to enter the U.S. A 1952 immigration statute prohibits the admission of aliens who are mentally retarded without such a waiver.

We located Section 212 of the Immigration and Naturalization Act entitled "General Classes of Aliens Ineligible to Receive Visas and Excluded from Admission." The first part of Section 212 is presented below.

## GENERAL CLASSES OF ALIENS INELIGIBLE TO RECEIVE VISAS AND EXCLUDED FROM ADMISSION

Sec. 212 (a) Except as otherwise provided in this Act, the following classes of aliens shall be ineligible to receive visas and shall be excluded from admission into the United States:
(1) Aliens who are feeble-minded;
(2) Aliens who are insane;
(3) Aliens who have had one or more attacks of insanity;
(4) Aliens afflicted with psychopathic personality, epilepsy, or a mental defect;
(5) Aliens who are narcotic drug addicts or chronic alcoholics;
(6) Aliens who are afflicted with tuberculosis in any form, or with leprosy, or any dangerous contagious disease;
(7) Aliens not comprehended within any of the foregoing classes who are certified by the examining surgeon as having a physical defect, disease, or disability, when determined by the consular or immigration

officer to be of such a nature that it may affect the ability of the alien to earn a living, unless the alien affirmatively establishes that he will not have to earn a living;
(8) Aliens who are paupers, professional beggars, or vagrants;

The waiver about which the Blanks were waiting to hear is Form I-601, which is entitled "Application of Waiver of Grounds of Excludability." This form and $35.00 are submitted to the office of Immigration and Naturalization Service when applying for permanent residency. Although there seem to be supportable arguments for excluding certain individuals from becoming citizens of this country, we will let you decide whether individuals with retardation should be one group of such individuals.

Turnbull goes on to say that nearly all states have constitutions that contain provisions for educating their children, including those who are handicapped. This classification includes those children who are mentally retarded.

*Local charters, ordinances, and regulations.*    These provisions also play an important role in determining the rights of individuals who are mentally retarded. Charters typically specify the establishment of various boards (e.g., school boards) and commissions. Ordinances like those that control zoning can be critical in terms of securing opportunities for this population. Regulations that are developed and issued by people in positions of authority and that are based on policy decisions of various legislative bodies will also affect citizens who are retarded.

## LEGAL PRECEDENTS FOR INDIVIDUAL RIGHTS

### EDUCATIONAL RIGHTS

The importance of education is generally recognized and supported. The Supreme Court, in the landmark *Brown v. Board of Education* (1954) decision, clearly commented on the value that education can have in one's life.

> Today, education is perhaps the most important function of state and local governments. Compulsory school attendance laws and the great expenditures for education both demonstrate our recognition of the importance of education to our democratic society. It is required in the performance of our most basic public responsibilities, even service in the armed forces. It is the very foundation of good citizenship. Today it is a principal instrument in awakening the child to cultural values, in preparing him for later professional training, and in helping him to adjust normally to his environment. In these days, it is doubtful that any child may reasonably be expected to succeed in life if he is denied the opportunity of an education. Such an opportunity where the state has undertaken to provide it, is a right which must be made available to all on equal terms.

With the proliferation of legal cases there has been a shift in focus from a systems-centered decision-making process to a more child-centered one. Individual characteristics must be considered when educational decisions are made. Overriding concepts like appropriate education and least restrictive environment demand a child-centered perspective.

*Right to education.*    To many people, education is considered a fundamental right that the authors of the constitution definitely incorporated into their masterpiece. The Supreme Court, in *San Antonio Independent School District v. Rodriguez* (1973), stated that education is not a fundamental right, guaranteed either explicitly or implicitly by the constitution. While initially this is a shocking statement, nevertheless the *Rodriguez* decision has some encouraging implications. In *Rodriguez*, there is ostensible mention of the importance of acquiring the basic skills required for exercising the First Amendment rights of free speech and involvement in the political mechanism of voting. Denial of educational services to any individual may impede the acquisition of these skills and may consequently be a denial of constitutional rights. Although *Rodriguez* did not establish the right to education as fundamental, it did reaffirm the importance of education and implicitly denounced the denial of such services.

Table 13.3 summarizes some of the early litigation affecting special education. As can be seen from the table, the arguments most frequently employed by plaintiffs in right-to-education cases include establishing the importance of education, using equal protection and due process claims, and addressing state and federal statutory provisions. If education is provided to the public in general, these plaintiffs have argued, it should be available to all children regardless of level of ability or type of impairment. Another critical factor established in the two major legal cases described below, *Pennsylvania Association for Retarded Children v. Commonwealth of Pennsylvania* and *Mills v. Board of Education of the District of Columbia* is that all individuals with mental retardation can benefit from education or training. Without having established this fact, opponents could have put up substantial opposition against providing educational services to many children and youth who were retarded and who had been excluded from schools. The issue of educability resurfaces periodically (Kauffman & Krouse, 1981; Noonan, Brown, Mulligan, & Rettig, 1982), particularly in times of financial restraint and cutbacks.

Before the 1970s, it was a longstanding practice to keep children with mental retardation out of school, but in the early 1970s legal challenges to exclusionary policies were successful. This litigation paved the way for later federal legislation that would significantly alter the delivery of educational services.

Early in January 1971, the Pennsylvania Association for Retarded Children and the parents of 13 children who were mentally retarded filed a class action suit *(Pennsylvania Association for Retarded Children* (PARC) *v. Commonwealth of Pennsylvania)* in federal court on behalf of all persons with mental retardation between the ages of 6 and 21 who resided in the Commonwealth of Pennsylvania and who were excluded from receiving educational services. At issue was the prevailing policy that denied these school age children access to public education. Expert testimony stressing the educational benefits (i.e., attainment of self-sufficiency for many and some level of self-care for others) that all children with mental retardation could gain weighed heavily in this case.

Although settled by means of a court-approved consent agreement in October, 1971, the *PARC* case had a profound impact on special education and children with mental retardation. It established a precedent guaranteeing access to publicly supported education for all mentally retarded people. By reason of due process rights and equal protection claims, the plaintiffs were able to establish that certain Pennsylvania statutes were unconstitutional. Implications of this decision are listed in Table 13.3.

Not long after the consent agreement in *PARC* was reached, a civil suit *(Mills v. Board of Education of the District of Columbia)* was filed. In this case, the parents and guardians of seven children charged that the board of education was denying these children a publicly supported education. All the plaintiffs in this case qualified as exceptional. In August 1972, Judge Waddy ruled in favor of the plaintiffs and in effect declared that a publicly supported education was the right of all children who were handicapped, regardless of the type and severity of their disability. *Mills* actually extended many of the legal guarantees *PARC* had achieved for children who were mentally retarded to children with other handicapping conditions. The defendants claimed that funds were insufficient to provide education to all children who were handicapped. Judge Waddy's reply reflected the attitude of many concerning the exclusionary practices so long in effect.

> The District of Columbia's interest in educating the excluded children clearly must outweigh its interest in preserving its financial resources. If sufficient funds are not available to finance all of the services and programs that are needed and desirable in the system, then the available funds must be expended equitably in such a manner that no child is entirely excluded from a publicly supported education consistent with his needs and ability to benefit therefrom. The inadequacies of the District of Columbia public school system, whether occasioned by insufficient funding or administrative inefficiency, certainly cannot be permitted to bear more heavily on the "exceptional" or handicapped child than on the normal child. (*Mills v. Board of Education,* 1972)

Limited financial resources are not sufficient reason to exclude children from receiving an appropriate education. But financial resources are limited, and even with P.L. 94-142 and its recent amendments in effect, financial issues will continue to demand our attention.

After *PARC* and *Mills,* right-to-education suits were filed in many other states as well. Soon all students who were mentally retarded were to gain the right to the free, appropriate public education that had previously been denied them, as many of the provisions formulated in the *PARC* consent agreement were later incorporated into the Education for All Handicapped Children Act.

***Right to an appropriate classification and placement.*** The most frequent charges in litigation involving placement decisions have involved violations of equal protection and due process. MacMillan (1977) offers an explanation of the typical equal protection claim that can be raised in relation to special class placement for students who are mildly retarded. "The contention is made that a child placed in a special education class is denied equal educational opportunity because his options are reduced . . . and because

TABLE 13.3 Summary of Early Right-to-Education Litigation

| Litigants | Year | Highest Level of Judicial Review | Issues | Implications of Litigations | Arguments Used |
|---|---|---|---|---|---|
| *Brown v. Board of Education* | 1954 | U.S. Supreme Court | Segregation of students by race<br>Impact of racial segregation on the child's motivation to learn | Segregation by race unanimously declared unconstitutional<br>Established importance of education for advancement<br>Established policy in favor of equal educational opportunity<br>Generalized the purposes of education, not its fundamentality | Equal protection |
| *Pennsylvania Association for Retarded Children (PARC) v. Commonwealth of Pennsylvania* | 1972 | U.S. District Court (PA) | Class action suit—challenging the exclusion of mentally retarded children from free public education<br>Access to education for all retarded citizens<br>Particular learning needs of the mentally retarded | Consent agreement of both parties<br>Established a right to education for mentally retarded children<br>Established that all mentally retarded children could gain from education and training<br>Demanded appropriate education<br>Demanded preschool services if normal children received such<br>Provided tuition grant assistance<br>Provided due process mechanisms<br>Required the identification of mentally retarded children not already identified<br>Provided for education in the least restrictive setting | Equal protection<br>Due process<br>State statutes |
| *Mills v. Board of Education of District of Columbia* | 1972 | U.S. District Court (DC) | Class action suit—exclusion of all exceptionalities<br>Access to education<br>Use of waiting lists | Extended the logic of *PARC* to all handicapped regardless of the degree of the impairment<br>Gained procedural safeguards<br>Required timetable of implementation<br>Acknowledged alternatives placement | Equal protection<br>Due process<br>District of Columbia Code |

| Case | Year | Court | Issue | Decision | Basis |
|---|---|---|---|---|---|
| *San Antonio Independent School District v. Rodriguez* | 1973 | U.S. Supreme Court | Claim that a discrimination exists due to being in a poorer school district<br>Challenge to state-financing scheme<br>Assertion that education is a fundamental right | Rejected wealth discrimination claim<br>Left open the fundamentality of some identifiable quantum of education<br>Reaffirmed the importance of education<br>Indicated that denial of education could be used in terms of denial of freedom of speech and right to vote | Discrimination<br>Equal protection |
| *Lebanks v. Spears* | 1973 | U.S. District Court | Challenged Louisiana's failure to provide education/training to a large number of mentally retarded children | Consent agreement<br>Two features not found in *PARC* or *Mills*<br>(1) Education—oriented toward making every child self-sufficient or employable<br>(2) Educational services to adults who were not given services as children<br>Acknowledged additional factors for evaluation of mentally retarded besides intelligence | Equal protection |
| *Maryland Association for Retarded Children v. Maryland* | 1974 | Circuit Court of Baltimore County | Class action suit on behalf of mentally retarded and physically handicapped children being denied free public education | Began to address "appropriateness" issue<br>Required the state to provide the necessary funding | State statutes |
| *In the Interest of H.G., A Child* | 1974 | Supreme Court of North Dakota | Equal educational opportunity | Involved the highest level of judicial review prior to 1975 and P.L. 94-142 | State constitution<br>Equal protection |

the quality of the EMR program is poorer than that of the regular class" (p. 290).

The due process arguments are based on the contention that the procedures used for classifying a child or for placing a child in a special class (such as administration of certain tests) may deny substantive due process. The denial of proper procedural safeguards before and after evaluation also violates the procedural due process clause of the Constitution. The thrust of the opposition to misclassification centers on the chronic effects of labeling a child. Many people vehemently object to the stigma associated with a child's being placed in a class for students who are mentally retarded. The available research, however, offers no strong evidence that these labels have negative effects (Gottlieb & Leyser, 1981; MacMillan, Jones, & Aloia, 1974). Much of the criticism focuses on the segregation and isolation of special class placement.

The use of intelligence measures as the primary determinant for identification and placement decisions has long been under scrutiny. The problems associated with intelligence testing have come under fire in a number of legal suits. *Hobson v. Hansen* (1967), *Larry P. v. Riles* (1972), *Diana v. State Board of Education* (1970), and *PASE* (Parents in Action on Special Education ) *v. Hannon* (1980) have specifically considered the use of intelligence tests for the purposes noted above.

In *Hobson v. Hansen* (1967), the denial to poor school age children of educational services equal to those of the more affluent was determined to be unconstitutional. The court found that students were being "tracked" into ability groups on the basis of instruments that seemed to be biased against black students and those from lower socioeconomic groups. Schools in the District of Columbia were no longer permitted to use IQ measures to place children in tracks, and a close review of classification practices was ordered. This case is important to those of us interested in mental retardation because it addressed the consequences of being labeled mentally retarded.

In *Larry P. v. Riles* (1972), the Federal District Court for Northern California decided that standardized, unvalidated IQ tests could not be used as the sole determinant in the identification and placement of black students in segregated classes for students who were educably (i.e., mildly) mentally retarded. This decision was appealed, and in January of 1984 the Ninth Circuit Court of Appeals upheld by a two-to-one margin the lower court's opinion. Turnbull (1986) makes two interesting observations about this case. First, he submits that *Larry P.* was more a racial discrimination case than a special education decision.

> *Larry P.* . . . was, as much as anything, a race discrimination case that put the court in the unenviable position of choosing among three possible explanations for the over-representation of minority children in special education: (1) the tests and their invalidity, (2) the "gene pool" argument that minority children are inherently less intelligent than non-minority children, and (3) the socioeconomic explanation of low performance on standardized tests. (pp. 78–79)

The court chose to focus on the first explanation. Turnbull's second observation is that neither court actually examined comprehensively whether these tests were racially biased. Nevertheless, the outcome of this decision was that schools were enjoined from placing black students in classes for those who were educably mentally retarded primarily on the basis of IQ scores.

Just as *Larry P.* specifically concerned the problems of black children who were being misclassified, other cases brought in California have focused on the problems of other ethnic groups in placement decisions. In *Diana v. State Board of Education* (1970), the injured party, representing Spanish-speaking children, argued that many such students had been placed in classes for students with mild retardation on the basis of individual intelligence tests that were considered culturally biased. The children involved in this lawsuit primarily spoke Spanish but were given intelligence tests in English. Although *Diana* was settled out of court, it resulted in clear changes in the methods and procedures used for identifying and placing students in special classes.

It would be misleading to suggest that these were the only lawsuits involving appropriate classification and placement, or that all litigation has been decided in the same way. In a class action suit filed in an Illinois federal district court *(PASE* [Parents in Action on Special Education] *v. Hannon)*, the use of intelligence tests to place minority students in special classes designed for children with mild retardation again came into question. This time, however, the court ruled differently, declaring this practice valid when additional measures are also employed. Unlike *Larry P.,* this case closely examined specific intelligence tests for possible racial bias. So few items were found suspect that the court decided that these measures should be considered culturally neutral. The court went on to underscore the importance of clinical judgment in the interpretation of IQ results and the decision-making process.

The diametrically opposed findings in *PASE* and *Larry P.* have added more confusion to an already controversial area. The use of IQ measures continues to undergo professional scrutiny, as concern for misdiagnosis and misplacement remains a top priority in the referral and placement process. The effect of these decisions on practice has been mixed. Cordes (1984) remarked that some professionals feel there has been little change. Others (Polloway & Smith, 1983) believe that agencies have adopted a more conservative posture toward classifying minority students as mildly retarded. Certainly assessment practices leading to eligibility decisions in specific areas of the country like California have been dramatically affected by concern for misidentification and misplacement (Forness, 1985). But even in areas where a more conservative approach is evident (again, California), overrepresentation of minority students in classes for students with mild retardation continues (MacMillan, 1988). The problems are far from solved.

***Right to an appropriate education.***    Once an appropriate education was mandated by the Education for all Handicapped Children Act, it was inevitable that the question of what an appropriate education is would need to be answered. The issue is discussed routinely at IEP meetings, but it was never formally addressed until 1982. Then the U.S. Supreme Court ruled in the case *Board of Education of the Hendrick Hudson Central School District v. Rowley*—the first case argued on the basis of P.L. 94-142 to reach this highest level of judicial review.

Although the plaintiff named in this particular litigation, Amy Rowley, was a student with a hearing impairment, this case has significant implications for students who are retarded. This is so because the Court specified criteria for a "free appropriate public education" in the majority opinion written by Justice Rehnquist.

> According to the definitions contained in the Act, a "free appropriate public education" consists of educational instruction specially designed to meet the unique needs of the handicapped child, supported by such services as are necessary to permit the child "to benefit" from the instruction. Almost as a checklist for adequacy under the Act, the definition also requires that such instruction and services be provided at public expense and under public supervision, meet the State's educational standards, approximate the grade levels used in the State's regular education, and comport with the child's IEP. Thus, if personalized instruction is being provided with sufficient supportive services to permit the child to benefit from the instruction, and the other items on the definitional checklist are satisfied, the child is receiving a "free appropriate public education" as defined by the Act.

A number of important issues in interpreting the Education for All Handicapped Children Act arose in this case and they have had and will continue to have bearing on litigation. First, the Court discussed the importance of a "basic floor of opportunity" for students. The meaning of this concept is that all students should have reasonable opportunity for learning. The Court stressed that the Act intends for students to have "access to specialized instruction and related services which are individually designed to provide *educational benefit* (emphasis added) to the handicapped child." It seems that the term *educational benefit* suffers from the same ambiguity that *appropriate education* does.

Another issue, and the one that has received the most attention, involves the "level of education" to be provided to students. What type of services should be provided and to what extent must they be offered? In *Rowley* the U.S. Supreme Court reversed the Second Circuit Court of Appeals' ruling that Amy Rowley was entitled to an interpreter. The Court's interpretation of congressional intent in enacting P.L. 94-142 suggested that programs do not have to develop students to their maximum potential. The Court noted that language addressing this particular issue was "noticeably absent" in the federal statute.

The *Rowley* decision initially sent shock waves through the field of special education, as many thought that students with disabilities would suffer from school systems' taking narrow interpretations of this case. Special education professionals feared that schools would have too easy a time demonstrating that students were getting "educational benefit" in programs that were not providing needed supportive services (DuBow & Geer, 1983). Blatt's (1987) concern was that schools would: *(a)* have more freedom to decide what is acceptable for students with special needs; *(b)* no longer be motivated to provide optimal programs; and *(c)* meet a "far lesser" standard. But the negative scenario that many envisioned has not materialized.

***Right to related services.*** Under P.L. 94-142, students are entitled to related services if needed, particularly if they allow a student to benefit from a free appropriate public education. It has not always been clear, however, whether certain services qualify as "related services," especially those that are more medically oriented and that many children with severe and profound retardation need. This issue is important because purely medical services are not considered related services and therefore do not have to be provided as part of a student's individual program. For some students this could exclude them from receiving special education.

In *Irving Independent School District v. Tatro* (1984), the U.S. Supreme Court ruled that a student with spina bifida was entitled to clean intermittent catheterization (CIC) services (a procedure that empties the bladder). The Court decided that this service could be performed by a school nurse and technically did not qualify as an excludable medical service, thereby making it a related service. What is important in this case is that such services were viewed as creating an opportunity for learning that would otherwise be denied. As in *Rowley,* the message here was that a student is entitled to supportive services to guarantee access to an appropriate, but not necessarily the best possible, education.

***Right to extended school year.*** Another issue associated with the education of students with mental retardation is whether they and other students with disabilities are entitled under P.L. 94-142 to an extended school year (ESY) if it is deemed necessary to provide an appropriate education. As Sargent and Fiddler (1987) have summarized, a number of suits have focused on this topic, most of them filed in the early 1980s. While early cases took more interest in students with severe problems, other cases (e.g., *Georgia ARC v. McDaniel,* 1984) concerned students with milder handicaps.

The most celebrated case was *Armstrong v. Kline* (1979), filed originally in federal district court in Pennsylvania and later appealed to the Third Circuit Court of Appeals. The foremost issue in this litigation was whether significant gaps (e.g., summer breaks) in the educational programs of certain students cause losses in skill development *(regression)*, require an unreasonable amount of time to make up *(recoupment)*, and therefore entitle students to an extended school year. Both decisions found the defendant's policy of limiting educational services to a maximum of 180 days inflexible, thus preventing students from receiving an appropriate education. Sargent and Fiddler (1987) note that the regression and recoupment question has remained the primary determinant in deciding which students qualify for ESY, even though research has yet to validate this concept. They also point out that courts have been concerned not only with that issue but with effects on an individual's self-sufficiency as well.

## INSTITUTIONAL RIGHTS

Institutions are discussed at length in the next chapter, but this section provides an introduction to the legal maneuverings that have become the backdrop for many changes in institutional settings. Much of this section is devoted to discussing a fundamental right that had been denied many of those confined to institutions for too long: the right to treatment.

***Right to treatment.*** The terms *treatment* and *habilitation* are used interchangeably, although some professionals do make a distinction. Both imply the delivery of some type of service, and they have been at the center of much discussion concerning those living in large, segregated facilities. Baer (1981) interpreted the various courts' definitions of *habilitation* to mean "behavior change in the direction of those skills that cumulatively allow community living" (p. 91). Although this definition is very general, it does give a sense of purpose. Lakin and Bruininks (1985), analyzing the view of habilitation promoted in *Romeo v. Youngberg* (1982), have remarked that the U.S. Supreme Court defines habilitation as something that ensures "safety and freedom from undue restraint." The usefulness of this perspective is questionable.

The treatment issue revolves around the notion that if individuals are committed to institutions, often involuntarily, then constitutionally they are entitled to services. Many landmark cases have looked at this issue; a few are presented below. Most notable among them are *Wyatt v. Stickney* (1972), *New York Association for Retarded Children v. Rockefeller* (1973), *O'Connor v. Donaldson* (1974), *Halderman v. Pennhurst* (1977), and *Romeo v. Youngberg* (1982).

The legal impetus for reform was dramatized in the litigation of a landmark case, *Wyatt v. Stickney,* on April 13, 1972. This case had a direct impact on the adequacy of services in residential facilities for individuals with mental retardation. The plaintiffs in this class action suit built their case on the grounds that the residents of the Partlow State School (Alabama) were being denied their right to treatment. While this was a class action suit, it was originally filed by the legal guardian of Ricky Wyatt against the Alabama Department of Mental Hygiene in 1970. Specifically, in *Wyatt* Ricky Wyatt (named plaintiff) represented all residents in the state of Alabama who were involuntarily confined in the state's hospitals.

The decision of Judge Johnson of the District Court of the United States for the Middle District of Alabama, North Division, declared that the constitutional rights of those residents were being violated under the 14th Amendment. The failure of this state to provide proper treatment in its residential facilities moved the court to draw up a precedent-setting 22-page appendix that defined minimum treatment standards for the state school to adopt. The order and the decree of the *Wyatt* decision were comprehensive in their coverage of residents' right to treatment and habilitation, records and review, physical environment, medication, and admissions policies. Minimum treatment standards include:

1. Individuals who were borderline or mildly retarded shall not be placed in residential institutions.
2. Admission to a residential institution shall be granted following the determination that the client-environment match is the least restrictive habilitative setting.
3. Institutions must attempt to move residents in the following manner.
   a. To a less structured living environment;
   b. From larger to smaller facilities;
   c. From larger to smaller living units;
   d. From group to individual residence;
   e. From segregated to integrated community living; and
   f. From dependent to independent living.

To summarize the importance of *Wyatt,* let us look at what it achieved. First, the case applied to individuals with mental retardation residing in institutions. Second, the court issued a set of minimum standards and monitoring procedures for residential facilities that would serve as a model to other states. Third, the case recognized the constitutional rights of these residents.

Of course, many judicial proceedings deal with essentially the same issues, and they sometimes reach diametrically opposed decisions (e.g., *Larry P.* and *PASE).* This was exactly the situation in the class action suit *Burnham v. Department of Public Health* in Georgia (1972), in which a completely different decision from the *Wyatt* decision was reached. Judge Smith, presiding in the United States District Court for the Northern District of Georgia, recognized that individuals in mental institutions have a *moral* right to treatment. But he did not rule that there was a *legal* obligation for such treatment (Scheerenberger, 1976a). As a result, there was a legal discrepancy between *Wyatt* and *Burnham.* Resolution would come on appeal of *Wyatt* to the Fifth Circuit Court of Appeals (*Wyatt v. Aderholt,* 1974). The Court of

Appeals essentially upheld the earlier decision of the federal court, re-emphasizing that residents with mental retardation have a constitutional right to treatment. Furthermore, the decision allowed the federal court to set standards and monitor their implementation.

On September 22, 1986, a consent agreement was approved in federal district court in Alabama, providing a settlement to this litigation, which had been initiated 14 years earlier. Over the course of time the original *Wyatt* case had been reopened periodically to review the status of what the court had ordered in Judge Johnson's original decision (*Wyatt v. Hardin,* 1975; *Wyatt v. Ireland,* 1979). The latest action may be the end of this litigation, although the impact of the *Wyatt* case will remain. This particular agreement was conciliatory; both plaintiffs and defendants made compromises. But as Marchetti (1987) describes it, "It appeared that all parties to the litigation and the federal court were seeking a justifiable reason for returning the mental health system back to the state's 'control,' while protecting the rights of the class members" (p. 249). Marchetti provides an excellent chronology of the *Wyatt* litigation, a concise description of the consent decree, and an interesting discussion of the implications of this action.

Another case presented here because of the attention it received is *New York Association for Retarded Children v. Rockefeller* (1973). This case is commonly referred to as the Willowbrook case, since the institution under scrutiny was the Willowbrook State School. This case, like *Wyatt,* originated after reductions in staff procedures that fueled the understaffing arguments. It focused on three major issues: overcrowding, understaffing, and the absence of community alternatives to institutionalization. Even though conditions did improve, the court's rulings were not so comprehensive and powerful as in *Wyatt.* What may be most important about the Willowbrook case is the national attention it received. It made more people aware of the deplorable conditions and the lack of programming that existed in many such settings.

Another suit that had an impact on institutionalized people, decided by the Fifth Circuit Court of Appeals, was *O'Connor v. Donaldson* (1974). Donaldson (the plaintiff) had been committed to an institution in 1957 by his father. It was determined that the defendants were aware at the time of Donaldson's placement that he was neither reckless nor dangerous to himself or others. Once he was institutionalized, Donaldson received neither adequate treatment nor therapy. The decision by the court awarded the plaintiff $38,000 in compensatory and punitive damages, which were to be paid personally by the defendants. In this particular case, the defendants were held personally liable. Subsequently the case was sent to the court of appeals, where the original decision was upheld. *O'Connor v. Donaldson* is significant in that it established the illegality of involuntarily institutionalizing a person who is not dangerous and who is able to function without institutional care.

The first case concerning individuals who were retarded and residing in institutions to reach the U.S. Supreme Court was *Halderman v. Pennhurst* (1977). This case is fascinating because, in addition to the issues related to correcting unsatisfactory conditions at a large state-run facility located in southeastern Pennsylvania, it ultimately sought to deinstitutionalize all residents, thereby closing down large, segregated facilities.

In the original action, begun on May 30, 1974, Terri Lee Halderman, a 20-year-old female resident of Pennhurst, filed suit on behalf of herself and all present and future residents of the facility, alleging that subhuman conditions and the lack of habilitative programming at Pennhurst violated their statutory and constitutional rights.

In the first phase of the nonjury trial, begun in April, 1977, the court spent 32 days hearing testimony to establish the truth of Halderman's allegations. By the end of this exposition, any illusions of Pennhurst State School and Hospital as a facility for the "care and training" of persons with mental retardation were erased. These excerpts from the opinion of presiding Judge Raymond Broderick suggest the quality of "care and training" afforded to residents there.

> Pennhurst is almost totally impersonal. Its residents have no privacy—they sleep in large, overcrowded wards, spend their waking hours together in large day rooms and eat in a large group setting. . . .
>
> All residents on Unit 7 go to bed between 8:00 and 8:30 P.M., are awakened and taken to the toilet at 12:00–12:30 A.M., and return to sleep until 5:30 A.M. when they are awakened for the day, which begins with being toileted and then having to wait for a 7:00 A.M. breakfast.
>
> The physical environment at Pennhurst is hazardous to the residents, both physically and psychologically. There is often excrement and urine on ward floors, and the living areas do not meet minimal professional standards for cleanliness. Outbreaks of pinworms and infectious disease are common.
>
> Obnoxious odors and excessive noise permeate the atmosphere. Such conditions are not conducive to habilitation. Moreover, the noise level in the day rooms is often so high that many residents simply stop speaking.
>
> Residents' records commonly contain a notation that they would benefit from specific types of programming. However, such programming has, for the most part, been unavailable. The average resident receives only 1½ hours of programming per weekday and no programming on weekends. No one, except those in school, gets more than 3½ to 4 hours per day. If one factors out those programs which are not considered beneficial, the average drops to about 15 minutes per day.
>
> On the whole, the staff at Pennhurst appears to be dedicated and trying hard to cope with the inadequacies of the institution. Nearly every witness who testified concerning Pennhurst stated that it was grossly understaffed to adequately habilitate the residents.

The Broderick court held that confinement at Pennhurst clearly deprives residents of their right to nondiscriminatory habilitation, to minimally adequate care, to due process, equal protection, and freedom from harm, and to treatment by least restrictive means. Broderick ordered the eventual close of Pennhurst and the arrangement of suitable community settings to which residents could transfer. Moreover, he ordered that Individual Program Plans be developed for each remaining resident and that monitoring procedures be established for the duration of the facility's operation.

Pennhurst officials and their various co-defendants appealed this decision in 1979 to the Third Circuit Court of Appeals. The appeals court affirmed the right of every individual with mental retardation to receive habilitative care in the least restrictive setting possible as well as their private right of action to enforce this right. Although the appeals court did not mandate Pennhurst's termination, it upheld 38 of the 41 paragraphs of Judge Broderick's order, along with his belief that persons with retardation would benefit most from community placement. The Third Circuit Court of Appeals based its judgment on statutory grounds—the 1975 Developmental Disabilities Assistance and Bill of Rights Act. The court stated that this legislation created substantive rights for individuals who were retarded to habilitative services. In 1981, the U.S. Supreme Court reversed the appeals court decision. The high court recognized the inadequate conditions at Pennhurst but did not feel that the congressional intent of the Developmental Disabilities Act created rights and required adequate treatment. McCarthy (1983) summarized the Court's position: "The Supreme Court declared that the Act was not intended to create new substantive rights; it was designed to *encourage,* but not to *mandate,* better services for the developmentally disabled" (p. 519). McCarthy goes on to suggest that the Supreme Court position seems to be that it will strictly interpret funding legislation and will not demand that states provide services not explicitly stated in the laws.

In January 1984, out-of-court negotiations began between the parties involved in this case. By fall of that year, a settlement had been reached in which the state agreed to close Pennhurst, thus ending ten years of litigation. Although this famous case did not achieve some of the outcomes desired by the plaintiffs, *Pennhurst* will remain a byword in the movement to depopulate institutions.

In *Youngberg v. Romeo* (1982) the U.S. Supreme Court ruled that individuals with severe retardation who were involuntarily confined to any state facility had a constitutional right to habilitative services to ensure their safety and freedom from undue restraint—a decidedly restrictive view of habilitation. The Court reasoned that this right is based on the substantive due process provisions of the 14th Amendment. As Turnbull (1982) has indicated, the case affects professionals in significant ways. It spotlighted the roles of professionals and professional differences of opinion by acknowledging that there are various models of treatment and a lack of consensus about which is best. The Court also recognized that professionals are in much better positions than judges or juries to make decisions about treatment.

*People with mental retardation have the same community rights as other citizens.*

Lakin and Bruininks (1985) note that the Supreme Court seems to have established a more limited role for federal courts in decisions of this type.

## COMMUNITY RIGHTS

Much of the litigation that was directed at securing reasonable treatment in institutional settings also suggested that efforts be undertaken to establish living conditions in community settings for as many individuals as possible (e.g., *Wyatt*). In line with the goal of providing living conditions as close to normal as possible, advocates have championed the notion of community placement. The resultant community movement, as described in chapter 11, has taken hold, and many living arrangements are now available for this population.

The right to live in community settings has not come without a struggle in many localities. This has been most obvious in community opposition to the establishment of group homes. Henderson and Vitello (1988) state that there are three kinds of barriers that can interfere with the community living movement: *(a)* local zoning ordinances; *(b)* state legislation that requires advance notification and in some cases permission from neighbors; and *(c)* restrictive covenants (e.g., people in a neighborhood are able to enforce a specific covenant to preserve the character of the neighborhood). Of the three situations, the first has received the most attention. It is discussed further below.

The case of *Cleburne Living Center, Inc. v. City of Cleburne, Texas* (1985) illustrates the problems that arise when a community opposes a group home. The principal obstacle in this case, as well as others like it, is attempting to establish a group home in a "single-family residence" zone. In the past, group homes were commonly located in less desirable areas that were industrially or commercially zoned—areas for which permits were easier to obtain. In this case, the Cleburne Living Center, Inc., was notified that a special-use permit would have to be approved before it could establish a group home for adults with mental retardation. The city council denied this permit on the basis that such a "hospital for the feebleminded" violated a local zoning ordinance. A suit was filed in federal district court claiming that the constitutional rights of these adults were being violated. The federal court upheld the city's decision to deny the request. On appeal, the Fifth Circuit Court of Appeals reversed the district court's ruling, citing that the ordinance was unconstitutional. This case was eventually appealed to the U.S. Supreme Court, which also found the zoning ordinance to be a violation of the plaintiff's equal protection rights.

TABLE 13.4   Rights of Persons in Community-Based Residential Programs

Right to services in the least restrictive environment
Right to normalized living conditions
Right to dignity and respect
Right to freedom from discomfort and deprivation
Right to appropriate clinical, medical, and therapeutic services
Right to vote
Right to religious worship
Right to private communication
Right to free association
Right to physical exercise
Right to seasonal, clean, neat clothing
Right to manage personal funds
Right to bed, dresser, and storage area
Right to privacy
Right to access to public media
Right to adequate nutrition
Freedom from unnecessary medication and mechanical, chemical, or physical restraints
Freedom from involuntary servitude
Right to equal protection and due process

From *Staff Development in Mental Retardation Services: A Practical Handbook* by J. F. Gardner and M. S. Chapman, 1985, Baltimore: Paul H. Brookes. Reprinted by permission.

Adults with mental retardation living in community settings should be entitled to the same rights as other citizens. Gardner and Chapman (1985) have developed a list of rights that persons living in community-based residential programs should enjoy (presented in Table 13.4). This list is not exhaustive, but it does give a sense of the rights we take for granted that have not always been available to people with retardation. To this list could be added other more controversial rights like the right to marry, the right to be parents, and the right to raise children.

## LIFE AND DEATH ISSUES

Within the last few years, much media attention has been given to the issue of withholding treatment from certain individuals with disabilities. Two celebrated cases have been *Guardianship of Becker* (1981, 1983) and *United States v. University Hospital, State of New York at Stony Brook* (1983), better known as the Baby Jane Doe case. Both of these cases involve the major issues typically associated with all such cases: parental and family autonomy, appropriateness of governmental intervention, and the question of quality versus sanctity of life. What tends to be missing is concern for the best interest of the child.

The original *Becker* cases (*In re Phillip B.,* 1979) have received much publicity (see the box for background information). The earlier litigation was not successful in obtaining the corrective surgery Phillip needed to prolong his life. Parental sovereignty won out over governmental interest in such matters. Recent guardianship proceedings have allowed Phillip to have new, surrogate parents and to receive the corrective surgery that he needed. What is interesting in the Becker case is the legal means used to obtain the desired results—guardianship proceedings. Herr (1984) has noted that "the jurisdiction of state courts to resolve *Becker*-type disputes does not depend on constitutional or section 504 violations . . . the remedy . . . was established under a traditional guardianship statute" (p. 38).

The other type of "withholding treatment" case is exemplified by the Baby Jane Doe case. In this type of case, unlike *Becker,* where the child is older and his abilities are known, the individual is a newborn and typically severely or profoundly handicapped. In this particular case, the hospital, with the parents' consent, chose not to perform certain surgical procedures that were needed to correct various physical problems. The government attempted to obtain the infant's medical records to determine whether the child's rights were being violated, taking the position that the treatment program selected (or the lack of one) might be in violation of Section 504. In this case, the federal district judge denied the government access to the child's medical records.

The Baby Jane Doe case and other situations like it have caused much professional reaction. Organizations such as the American Association on Mental Retardation, the Association for Retarded Citizens—United States, and

# THE LIFE AND TIMES OF PHILLIP BECKER

Over the course of the last few years, considerable attention has been given to the situation of Phillip Becker, his natural parents, and other significant people in his life. Early events in Phillip's story highlight a number of critical issues that relate to other individuals who are retarded as well. Foremost among these issues is the elusive concept of "quality of life" and how it is interpreted by the courts.

Phillip Becker is much older now, but when his story first became public, he was 11 years old. Phillip suffered from a congenital heart impairment and needed corrective surgery. His cardiovascular system was overtaxed and was sure to continue to deteriorate, eventually leading to a sudden heart attack and an almost certain early death (probably by age 30). The crux of the problem was that Phillip's natural parents refused to allow the surgery.

Eventually, the Juvenile Probation Department (California) sought a court order to permit the surgery to take place. After testimony was given by both sides, the juvenile court judge affirmed the parents' position. His decision was based primarily on the lack of proof that Phillip would die immediately if surgery were withheld and on the principle of parental sovereignty (i.e., the parents acting in the best interest of the child—especially when making life-and-death decisions). This lower court ruling was upheld by the court of appeals, and subsequent requests by the attorney general's office to the California Supreme Court and to the U.S. Supreme Court were refused, thus letting the previous decision stand.

The courts have favored parental autonomy over the state's interest in intervening in family matters. The "quality of life" issues that are raised in this litigation stem from attitudes of the parents and several doctors in this case. Their stance was based on the following beliefs, which surfaced during testimony.

1. Phillip's life is not a "life worth living" (since he is mentally retarded).
2. If the surgery were performed, then Phillip would most probably outlive his parents and be deprived of their supervision and attention. As a result, he would not receive quality care.
3. The risk of surgery is too great.

The first two positions implied that Phillip was better off dead than alive, an opinion open to criticism. The last position was best addressed by Baines (1980): "The operation carries a 10% maximum risk of death, as compared with the 100% certainty of greatly premature death" (p. 132).

Upon reflection, two salient questions remain. They poignantly summarize the plight of Phillip and others in situations like his.

☐ Who among us is in a position to determine what is a "quality" life?
☐ Has Phillip's life received less protection because he is mentally retarded? (Baines, 1980, p. 132)

### Update

There have been some significant changes in Phillip's life since these earlier proceedings. First, custody of Phillip has been given to his foster parents (the Heaths). Second, Phillip has undergone corrective surgery.

The Association for Persons with Severe Handicaps (TASH) have taken positions against withholding of treatment. TASH (1984) has published a monograph on this topic entitled, *Legal, Economic, Psychological, and Moral Considerations on the Practice of Withholding Medical Treatment from Infants with Congenital Defects.*

Another effect of the Baby Jane Doe case is Congressional action to include "Baby Doe" provisions in amendments to the Child Abuse Prevention and Treatment Act, originally enacted in 1974. The purpose of these provisions is to protect infants with disabilities. This legislation has been supported by a large number of professional organizations, with one notable exception—the American Medical Society. Instances where treatment is withheld or withdrawn are referred to in this legislation as *medical neglect.*

## CONCLUSION: PERSISTING PROBLEMS

Much progress has been made in recent years with regard to guaranteeing the individual rights of persons with mental retardation, but the heyday of successful litigation may be over. It seems that courts have been stretched as far as they can go in certain areas (e.g., right to treatment) and that more conservative interpretations of law are being made. Blatt (1987) refers to some of the recent changes.

> More and more, the courts are (again) deciding on behalf of defendants rather than plaintiffs. More and more, the legislatures of our country are reluctant to either pass progressive legislation or to fully implement current legislation that would cost the taxpayers money—money which the legislators say the states do not have, and money which the taxpayers say they do not want to give for such purposes as providing the fullest educational opportunities for handicapped individuals. Here again, we have a situation for which nothing succeeds like failure and nothing fails like success. (p. 231)

Whether one agrees with Blatt's comments or not, they are worth considering. It also behooves us to reexamine what we have gained for those who are mentally retarded and what remains to be done.

## SUMMARY

Many of the issues in the field of special education and human services have been civil rights issues and rights have been achieved through processes other than education, psychology, or service delivery. We feel that anyone who studies mental retardation must, at some point, be able to articulate the individual rights guaranteed to all citizens who have this condition. Equally important is an understanding of the legal issues underlying these rights and the battles fought to secure them.

The first part of the chapter provided a brief introduction to legal terminology and concepts. The second part of the chapter examined the legislative and litigative developments in this field that have established individual rights for persons with retardation in the following areas: education, institution, community, and other personal matters. The last section highlighted some of the persisting legal problems affecting those who are retarded.

# CHAPTER 14

# Institutions and Deinstitutionalization

T o most people, the word *institution* conjures up a phalanx of unpleasant thoughts and scenes. Burton Blatt (1987) said it best: "It is difficult to discuss institutions without engaging in controversy. After all, the Willowbrooks and Pennhursts of the world are famous for being infamous" (p. 159). Many perceptions of institutional life have been shaped largely through exposure to the media or from third-party sources, as most people have never actually visited a state or private institution. Motion pictures such as *Titicut Follies* (a documentary) and *One Flew Over the Cuckoo's Nest* (fictional drama) have depicted some of the injustices associated with institutional settings. While there have been and still are injustices done to residents, what we read in the newspaper and watch on television emphasizes the sensationally negative aspects of institutions. We cannot defend the institutional concept from bad press, but we can recognize that there are different perspectives on the role of institutions. Mindful of Blatt's admonition, we try to present the major components, issues, and trends relevant to institutions for those who are retarded.

Much has happened since the time when Guggenbühl first founded the Abendberg in the mid-1800s, and current practices and thinking about institutions are very different. One trend illustrative of the institutional movement that gained momentum in the late 1800s and early 1900s is the amazing growth in the number of these facilities. Figure 14.1 presents data collected from various sources (Baumeister, 1970; Scheerenberger, 1976a, 1979, 1982). Facilities for those who are retarded for the most part have operated on the premise that these individuals should be removed from society. Only recently has institutional placement been questioned for its custodial nature and reevaluated on the basis of (*a*) its inhibiting and debilitating effects on residents and (*b*) its lack of adequate programming. In this chapter we look into both kinds of evaluation.

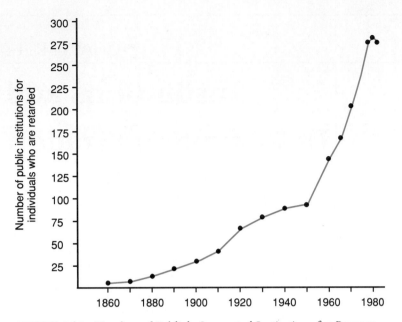

**FIGURE 14.1**   Number of Publicly Supported Institutions for Persons with Mental Retardation

From "Community Adjustment" by E. M. Craig and R. B. McCarver, 1984, *International Review of Research in Mental Retardation, 12,* p. 98. Reprinted by permission.

To appreciate the scope of the issue, it helps to look at some statistics. Not all studies report the same figures, but they are close enough to give a reliable idea of the situation. Figure 14.1 shows how many institutions are now in operation across the country. The average daily number of residents in these settings is also worth noting. This figure peaked in the late 1960s, with the first drop reported in 1968, when there were approximately 194,000 residents (Lakin, Hill, & Bruininks, 1988). This was the beginning of a steady decrease, and a more recent update is shown in Figure 14.2. Later we discuss why this has occurred, as well as elaborating on the implications of the data in Figure 14.2.

Another perspective on institutions and on the trend to move more residents into smaller, community-based settings can be gleaned from examining the spending patterns of these two different models. Figure 14.3 compares the expenditures for these two, taking into account inflation. A significant increase in allocations for smaller settings located in the community has clearly taken place. Nevertheless, it is also obvious that more money is directed toward subsidizing larger (16 persons or more) settings, including large public facilities, although we can see a very slight decrease beginning in 1982 (Braddock, Hemp, & Fujiura, 1987).

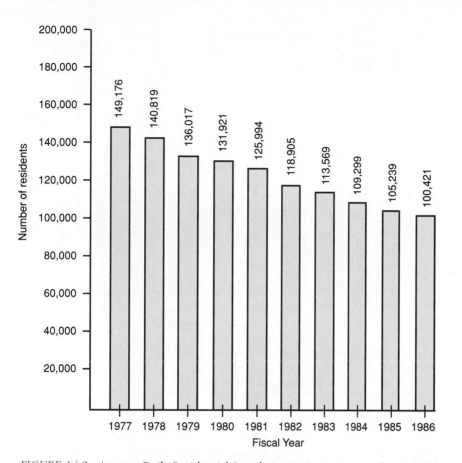

FIGURE 14.2 Average Daily Residential Population in Institutions in the United States (1977–1986)

From "National Study of Public Spending for Mental Retardation and Developmental Disabilities" by D. Braddock, R. Hemp, and G. Fujiura, 1987, *American Journal of Mental Deficiency, 92,* pp. 121–133. Reprinted by permission.

## INSTITUTIONALIZATION

Committing an individual to an institution requires legal proceedings conducted according to the guidelines established in each locality, and one should have at least a cursory understanding of this process. It is also important to consider the factors that influence the decision to institutionalize someone.

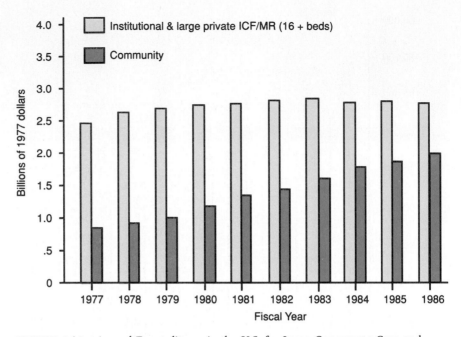

FIGURE 14.3   Annual Expenditures in the U.S. for Large Congregate Care and
Community Services

From "National Study of Public Spending for Mental Retardation and Developmental Disabilities" by D.
Braddock, R. Hemp, and G. Fujiura, 1987, *American Journal of Mental Deficiency, 92,* pp. 121–133. Reprinted
by permission.

## THE CERTIFICATION/COMMITMENT PROCESS

There are two formal procedures for committing someone to an institutional
setting: voluntary and involuntary. We explain how these two processes occur
in the state of Virginia.

*Voluntary commitment.*   In Virginia, certification for voluntary commitment is initiated when the parent or guardian of the person who is retarded
contacts the facility to seek approval for admission. Within 30 days after the
request, officials of the facility must observe the candidate for *no more than
48 hours* to determine whether or not there is "sufficient cause to believe the
person is mentally retarded or mentally ill." If the evaluators find no such
"sufficient cause," the applicant is denied admission. Otherwise, the facility
endorses his or her candidacy, and the individual's eligibility for admission
becomes a judicial matter. The parent or guardian next must petition in local
district court for eligibility proceedings, and a judge determines if the
candidate is "willing and capable of" requesting voluntary commitment. The
judge then offers the candidate admission and prescribes a minimum period
of treatment once he or she accepts. Voluntary commitment is relatively easy,

*Institutions have changed in many ways since this bulletin board was assembled in the early 20th century. The small metal tags identified the eight groups of "pupils" from left to right, top to bottom, as: "cretins, gelatinoids, hydrocephalic, isolated congenital cases, microcephalic, congenital (one of two or more cases occurring in a family), excitable, paralytic."*

since all parties apparently agree upon the desired outcome. Legal action is only a formality.

*Involuntary commitment.* Involuntary commitment is also legal, but is far more problematic—both practically and morally. Again, the Virginia Code provides an example representative of most jurisdictions. In a case of parent or guardian-initiated contact, the individual under consideration may not wish to be certified for admission to an institution. He may still be observed by the facility, found eligible by the local district court judge, and offered the opportunity to apply for voluntary admission. If, however, he does not accept voluntary commitment, the judge advises the individual of the right to a commitment hearing and to counsel, which the court provides. This process ensues.

1. A commitment hearing is held as soon as possible, allowing for preparation of defenses and witnesses.
2. The judge summons a physician licensed in Virginia and skilled in the diagnosis of mental retardation and/or mental illness.

3. The physician is given the opportunity to examine the individual personally and certifies that he or she has cause to believe that:
   a. The person is/is not mentally ill or mentally retarded.
   b. The person does/does not present an imminent danger to self or others.
   c. The individual does/does not require involuntary hospitalization.
4. The judge hears the evidence and observes the individual in question. The following factors are considered in the judge's decision:
   a. The person does/does not present an imminent danger to self or others as a result of mental retardation or illness.
   b. The person has/has not otherwise been proven to be so seriously mentally ill or retarded as to be substantially unable to care for self.
   c. There is/is not any less restrictive alternative to institutional confinement and treatment, other alternatives having been investigated.
5. If the judge finds that (a) and (b) above are true, but (c) is not, the individual shall be subject to court-ordered outpatient treatment, day treatment in a hospital, referral to a community mental health clinic, or other appropriate treatments necessary to meet the needs of the individual.
6. If the judge finds all three considerations above to be positive, the individual will be certified for admission, and removed to a facility for a designated period of hospitalization not to exceed 180 days.
7. The individual may appeal the involuntary commitment to the circuit court within 30 days of the commitment order, and is entitled to trial by jury.
8. At the expiration of 180 days:
   a. The individual may be released.
   b. The individual may be readmitted involuntarily by further petition and order of the court.
   c. The individual may be recommitted for treatment on a voluntary basis if he or she so wishes to change his or her status.

It is important to realize that the procedure described above represents only one system; notable differences are likely to be found in other locations.

***Issues.***     Several obvious practical problems arise from this process. For one, the person's right to counsel, though acknowledged on paper, is in practice abridged simply because very few lawyers to date have been trained in the field of developmental disabilities or are well-grounded in the legal rights of this group. Moreover, this procedure presupposes that the local district court judge is qualified to determine if a disabled person is "willing and capable of" seeking or refusing voluntary commitment. It further assumes that the judge has the expertise to ascertain, in the limited time spent in hearings, which type of facility best suits the individual's needs.

An ethical question arises when one considers the institutionalized person's right to treatment, first established in *Wyatt v. Stickney* (1972). Does right to treatment imply its corollary—right to refuse treatment? If so, involuntary commitment may be a violation of human rights. If not, should this not be established as a separate right? With the current trend toward deinstitutionalization, civil rights advocates have become increasingly concerned with this aspect of "disability law."

## FACTORS INFLUENCING THE DECISION TO INSTITUTIONALIZE

The actual steps toward certification for admission comprise but one facet of the entire commitment process. You may wonder what would prompt the parents or guardians of children and wards who are mentally retarded to seek institutionalization. We categorize some of these reasons into four domains: individual characteristics; family characteristics; parental beliefs and perceptions; and nonfamily factors.

*Individual characteristics.* Some combination of four different characteristics leads to certain individuals' being institutionalized: medical needs (i.e., skilled nursing care is required); nonmedical needs such as specialized therapy, need for protection from harm, and behavior problems (Spreat, Telles, Conroy, Feinstein, & Colombatto, 1987). Campbell, Smith, and Wool (1982) found more maladaptive problems in those who were being considered for institutionalization than in those who were not. The salient feature of these behavior problems is that they are of such severity that families are not able to handle the child who is retarded. MacMillan (1977) suggests that many factors other than deficient mental functioning impel the decision to institutionalize. He believes there must be an additional negative component that renders the individual "superfluous or threatening" in the eyes of his or her caretakers.

*Family characteristics.* Certain family traits may color the placement decision. One factor that may affect the decision to institutionalize is family disorganization. A large percentage of institutionalized children come from single parent homes, although it is unclear whether the presence of someone with severe retardation in the home actually disrupts marriages or whether divorce generates circumstances that make the task of raising such a child overwhelming. Another factor may be low socioeconomic status (SES). Severe mental retardation does not favor any particular social class; however, the decision to institutionalize may be skewed by SES. One study of institutional populations (Eyman, Dingman, & Sabagh, 1966) observed that residents of institutions were more likely to come from lower class backgrounds. The researchers suggest that some lower class parents perceive the institution as an environment preferable to what may be a deprived home. Eyman and colleagues (1966) also note that higher SES parents tended to place their children who were retarded sooner and that the willingness of higher SES parents to institutionalize a child is directly related to the number of normal children in the home; that is, the more normal children in the family, the more likely parents are to institutionalize a child who is retarded.

*Parental beliefs and perceptions.*    Most parents institutionalize a child out of concern for the child's welfare. This action results from concern about specific characteristics of their children in conjunction with the belief that the institutional setting is the best alternative. Some of the more common perceptions supporting this belief are listed below and derive from a number of sources (Craig & McCarver, 1984; Latib, Conroy, & Hess, 1984; Spreat et al., 1987).

☐ Beliefs about retardation and institutions:
    The idea that their child will never develop the skills needed for community living
    Institutions have proven methods
    Institutions are centers of expertise
☐ Concerns about community-based services:
    Not enough security and supervision
    Lack of adequate programming
    No assurance that community services will endure over time

In a study of family attitudes toward deinstitutionalization, Spreat and colleagues (1987) found that families with an institutionalized member generally supported this placement and disfavored community alternatives. The researchers also noted that most of these families seemed to lack adequate information about community services.

*Nonfamily factors.*    There are moving anecdotes of parents' being told not to see their newborn child who is severely involved and to institutionalize the child as soon as possible. Most of these are very sensational, but that does not mean that they are not true. In Spreat et al.'s (1987) study, 74% of respondents indicated that they were influenced to institutionalize their child by the advice of a doctor, clergy, or other professional.

Community attitudes add another dimension to the question whether or not to institutionalize a family member. If the prevailing viewpoint of the community into which a child who is severely retarded is born reflects a fear of "deviant" human beings, the parent(s) will probably be under considerable social pressure—subtle or otherwise—to separate the "deviant" from those who find him offensive; that is, to hide the child in an institution. Not all parents respond to these community attitudes, and not all public sentiment is so rejecting. But when these two variables interact, institutionalization becomes more likely.

## THE INSTITUTIONAL SETTING

This section provides an introduction to the realities of institutions and life in them. It is divided into five subsections. The first is a description of the characteristics of an institution; the second, an account of what happens in institutions; the third, examples of some of the behaviors observed in residents; the fourth, a discussion of some of the services available; and the last, an update on current thinking about this type of placement.

## ORGANIZATION OF A TYPICAL LARGE RESIDENTIAL INSTITUTION

Two types of people are needed for a large residential facility: those who are put there to live and those who are hired to manage and care for them. As in any large organization, the operation of an institution is on two levels, administration and staff. The administrative level deals with management aspects like budget, admissions, training, and coordination of services. The remaining personnel are the staff members, who implement the programs and provide the day-to-day services that the administration directs.

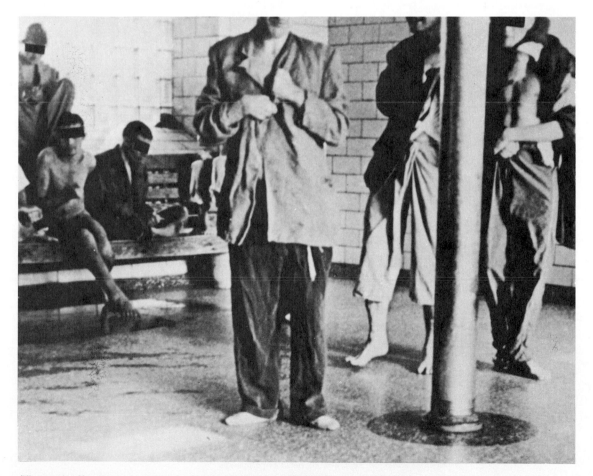

*Theoretically, programming in institutions was minimal or nonexistant.*

The size of public institutions has decreased over the course of the last two decades. In the late 1950s the average size was over 1,500 residents per institution, with some facilities housing many thousands. More recently we have seen the average size of institutions drop to a level close to 400 residents per setting. These changes are documented in Figure 14.4. It is unlikely that any large public institutions will be closed anytime soon, although there are attempts to redirect critical funding (i.e., Medicaid) to community-based settings, thus jeopardizing the continuation of these facilities. As a result, the number of institutions will probably level off in the next few years.

*One such action is the Medicaid Reform Act.*

***Administration.*** The traditional large public residential institution presents a myriad managerial problems, and the consequent reduction in the quality of care provided to residents has long been an issue. Since the 1960s, many institutions have adopted an organizational system called **unitization** in an

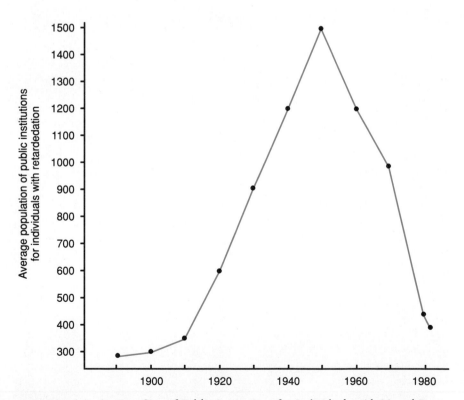

**FIGURE 14.4** Average Size of Public Institutions for Individuals with Mental Retardation

From "Community Adjustment" by E. M. Craig and R. B. McCarver, 1984, *International Review of Research in Mental Retardation, 12,* p. 100. Reprinted by permission.

effort to improve their efficiency. Unitization takes a number of different forms, but it has three basic elements (Raynes, Bumstead, & Pratt, 1974).

☐ Individual buildings are grouped into units according to certain broad attributes, such as age and severity of handicap.

☐ Unit directors assume responsibility for admission, treatment, and release of residents on their respective units.

☐ Staff members are assigned permanently by unit.

Figure 14.5 illustrates unitization in the organizational structure of a large residential facility in Virginia. Each discrete center (Child Development, Community Adjustment, and so on) represents a unit as described.

Institutions that have adopted the unit plan have generally been attempting to improve the quality of care for residents. Increasing the consistency of staff-client interactions and allocating staff time more equitably are typical objectives. Research findings, however, have turned up a substantial discrepancy between the hoped-for improvement and the actual upgrading of care. Raynes et al. (1974) have examined the effects of reorganization by units in a public facility of some 1,200 residents. Though the purpose of the reorganization was to devote more resources to the fulfillment of resident needs, the researchers found little evidence of the desired change four years later. Apparently administrative changes such as the unitization attempted in this institution were not sufficient to redirect the attitudes that determine resident care practices on the building level. For this, policies should focus not on administration, but on the institutional staff.

*Personnel.* Three types of staff are essential to the operation of a residential institution. Psychologists, teachers, therapists, and social workers comprise some of the professional staff, whose job it is to habilitate the resident toward more adaptive functioning and eventual return to the community. The direct care staff are the ward attendants, professional staff, and other employees who work in direct, continuous contact with the residents, attending to their more basic and custodial needs—feeding, dressing, toileting, medicating, and so forth. The third type are maintenance personnel—janitors, grounds-keepers, and others who concern themselves with upkeep of the physical plant, though they may have numerous contacts with residents throughout the day. These three groups of employees, particularly the direct care staff, set the tone, the psychological climate, in which daily events transpire. Their attitudes and interactions are far more powerful than upper level policy decisions in determining whether those in their care will be abused, ignored, or genuinely served.

Conflict between the goals of the professionals and those of the direct care staff often creates tension in the ranks to the detriment of joint efforts. The differing responsibilities of professionals and direct care personnel lead them to see residents in dissimilar settings, either in the office or on the ward,

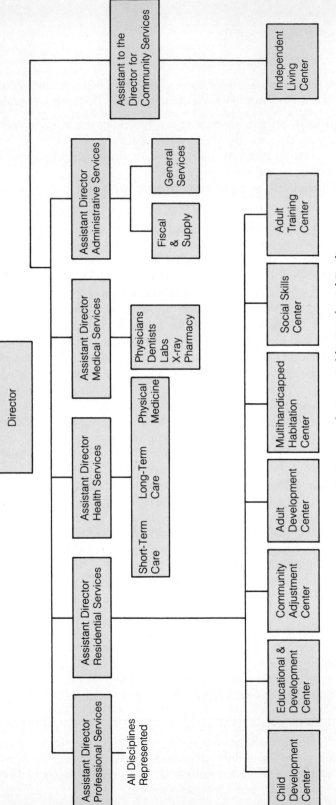

**FIGURE 14.5** Unitization of a Large Public Residential Facility

which in turn biases each group's perceptions of the resident. Whereas professionals look toward eventual habilitation for the resident, smooth operation of the ward often takes priority for the attendants. For example, a high-functioning resident from whom attendants might enlist help in cleaning bedpans or monitoring other residents can become a bone of contention between the professionals who wish to remove that person from the institution and the direct care attendants who want the individual to stay. Attendants generally frown on professional staff activities that tend to disrupt routine or agitate the residents. These forces, often combined with officiousness from the better educated professionals, can generate enough tension to contribute to what is usually a high staff turnover rate.

Personnel shortages, as reflected in the high turnover rate, present a persistent problem in institutional operation. Lakin, Bruininks, Hill, and Hauber (1982) surveyed 75 public and 161 nonpublic facilities for persons with retardation to examine staff turnover rates. They reported annual turnover rates ranging from 2% to 157% for public institutions (mean 32.8%) and from 0% to 400% for private community settings (mean 54.2%). MacMillan (1982) notes that economic opportunity in the outlying community influences the rate of staff change, as the salaries are typically low. Obviously, employees are more likely to leave the institution if other jobs are available elsewhere. In addition, attendant turnover tends to vary directly with the ratio of professionals to custodial workers; that is, the greater the proportion of professionals relative to attendants, the higher will be the turnover. Most direct care workers seem to find their jobs more palatable when supervision by professionals is kept to a minimum.

For instance, the pay scale for teachers is often considerably higher in public school settings.

In recent years professionals have been concerned about the potentially detrimental effect of high staff turnover on residents. One study, conducted by Munro, Duncan, and Seymour (1983), investigated the effect of front-line staff turnover on the behavior of 140 residents living in a unit of an institution. The investigators found, to their surprise, that staff turnover had little impact on residents' behavior. They interpreted the results as suggesting that

> retarded persons may learn to cope well with the seemingly unstable situation. Also, the most important factor affecting resident behavior may not be turnover rates, but the nature of staff residents' relationships (whether new or established), the quality of residential living environments, and the consistency by which programs are carried out. . . . Turnover can eliminate staff who are considered incorrigible, "burned-out," or abusive toward residents. (p. 331)

Underfinancing is another chronic disease of both public and private institutions, and one that exacerbates personnel shortages and low staff morale. In an economic system that maintains the notion that net price equals net worth, meager salaries mean low prestige and failure to attract the best qualified personnel. Clearly, the unfortunate outcome of relying on an underpaid, underqualified, overworked staff to conduct the daily business of

In some states (e.g., New York), salaries of direct care staff are not low.

# FOSTER GRANDPARENT PROGRAM

If you have not visited a residential facility for individuals who are retarded recently, you may be surprised to see senior citizens on the grounds of the facility. These senior citizens are foster grandparents (FGPs).

The Foster Grandparent Program, a federally supported program that began in 1965, provides an opportunity for senior citizens who are 60 years or older and who have low income to serve individuals with special needs who are no older than 21. The foster grandparents serve on a regular basis, usually four hours daily, five days a week, in such places as institutions, public schools, day care centers, and other nonprofit agencies. They bring their skills and experiences, as well as their kindness, patience, and understanding.

This program is beneficial to all parties involved. Institutions receive free assistance with their programs, and children benefit greatly from the additional attention. The foster grandparents receive the following benefits:

nontaxable hourly stipend, which is not considered wages or compensation; transportation or transportation allowances; one meal per day; annual physical examinations; accident and liability insurance while on the job; uniforms (you will see them wearing smocks); vacation and sick leave; regular training; annual recognition.

In institutional settings, it is amazing to see persons with profound retardation who are unable to communicate in any traditional fashion respond positively to their FGP. Little language is used because the physical proximity of the FGP is usually enough. FGPs are generally assigned to two children each day and may provide companionship, attend to the personal needs of the individual (dressing, feeding, or toileting), and provide social contact. If you desire more information about this program, you can either contact the regional office of ACTION or call toll-free (800) 424-8580.

a complex organization can only be to prevent the institution from fulfilling its stated purpose—service to the disabled.

*Residents.* As is the case with most descriptive statistics, there is great variation across settings. In an attempt to inform those not familiar with institutional settings, demographic data are presented in Table 14.1. These data come from two principal sources. The first is a series of studies conducted by Scheerenberger (1976a, 1976b, 1977, 1982) on more than 200 public residential facilities (PRFs). The other major source is a study of two institutions in California conducted by Eyman and his colleagues (Eyman, Borthwick, & Tarjan, 1984).

The data presented in Table 14.1 give some indication of the characteristics of residents who inhabit institutions today. As can be seen, they tend to be older individuals who are severely or profoundly retarded. The events that have produced this result are discussed later in the chapter.

TABLE 14.1    Demographics of Institutionalized Residents

| Gender: | Male | 58% | (Eyman et al., 1984) |
|---|---|---|---|
| | Female | 42% | |
| Age: | 0–11 | 4% | (Eyman et al., 1984) |
| | 12–17 | 11% | |
| | 18 and above | 84% | |
| Level of | severe/profound | 80% | (Scheerenberger, 1982) |
| functioning: | profound | 55% | (Rotegard et al., 1984) |
| | profound | (a) 83% | (Eyman et al., 1984) |
| | | (b) 48% | (Eyman et al., 1984) |

Figures in columns 1, 2, and the third entry of column 3 are from "Current Trends and Changes in Institutions for the Mentally Retarded" by R. K. Eyman, S. A. Borthwick, and G. Tarjan, 1984, *International Review of Research in Mental Retardation, 12,* pp. 178–195. The first and second entries in column 3 are from "Public Residential Services, 1981: Status and Trends" by R. C. Scheerenberger, 1982, *Mental Retardation, 20,* pp. 210–215; and from "State Operated Residential Facilities for People with Mental Retardation: July 1, 1978–June 30, 1982" by L. L. Rotegard, R. H. Bruininks, and G. C. Krantz, 1984, *Mental Retardation, 22,* pp. 69–74, respectively.

## DYNAMICS OF INSTITUTIONAL LIFE

*First impressions.*    As we have mentioned, to many people who have never seen the inner workings of a large residential facility, the word *institution* is a distasteful one that provokes images of horror and human suffering. Unfortunately, for many of those who have "experienced" an institution in one way or another, the reaction is the same. The following is a description of the scene that confronted an uninitiated visitor to a ward for 82 low-functioning residents (mean IQ of 15.4) in a 3,000-bed state facility in southern California. The authors, MacAndrews and Edgerton (1964), recount their impressions of a group that today forms the majority of the institutional population—individuals who are severely and profoundly retarded.

> Words, however well-chosen, cannot begin adequately to convey the combined sights, sounds, and smells which initially confront and affront the outsider on his first visit. What follows is at best an approximation.
>
> Despite the size of Ward Y, the simultaneous presence of its 82 patients evokes an immediate impression of overcrowding. Additionally, most of the patients are marked by such obvious malformations that their abnormal status appears evident at a glance. One sees heads that are too large or too small, asymmetrical faces, distorted eyes, noses, and mouths, ears that are torn or cauliflowered, and bodies that present every conceivable sign of malproportion and malfunction. Most patients are barefooted, many are without shirts, and an occasional patient is—at least momentarily—naked. What clothing is worn is often grossly ill-fitting. In a word, the first impression is that of a mass—a mass of undifferentiated, disabled, frequently grotesque caricatures of human beings.
>
> Within moments, however, the mass begins to differentiate itself and individuals take form. A blond teen-ager flits about rapidly flapping his arms in a birdlike manner, emitting birdlike peeping sounds all the while. A large Buddhalike man sits motionless in a corner, staring straight ahead. A middle-aged

man limps slowly in a circle, grunting, mumbling, and occasionally shaking his head violently. A shirtless patient lies quietly on a bench while a small patient circles about him, furiously twirling a cloth with his left hand. A blind youngster sits quietly digging his index fingers into his eyes, twitching massively and finally resolving himself into motionless rigidity. A red-haired patient kneels and peers intently down a water drain. A portly patient sits off in a corner rocking. Another patient rocks from a position on all fours. Still another patient, lying supine, rolls first to one side then to the other. Several patients walk slowly and aimlessly around, as if in a trance, showing no recognition of anyone or anything. A microcephalic darts quickly about, grinning, drooling, and making unintelligible noises. An early twentyish mongol wearing an oversized cowboy hat strikes about with his hands firmly grasping the toy guns in his waistband holsters. Others smile emptily, many lie quietly, still others from time to time erupt into brief frenzies of motion or sound.

A few patients approach the newcomer to say "Daddy," or "Wanna go home," or to give their name or to offer some paradoxical phrase such as "tapioca, too, ooga, ooga," One or another patient may attempt to touch, pull, or grasp the stranger, but such attempts at interaction are usually of the most fleeting duration. Others may approach and observe from a distance before moving away. Most pay no attention to a new face.

In the background, strange and wondrous sounds originate from all sides. Few words can be distinguished (although many utterances, in their inflection, resemble English speech); rather, screams, howls, grunts, and cries predominate and reverberate in a cacophony of only sometimes human noises. At the same time, loud and rhythmic music is coming out of the loudspeaker system.

There are, finally, the odors. Although many patients are not toilet-trained, there is no strong fecal odor. Neither is there a distinct smell of sweat. Yet there is a peculiar smell of something indefinable. Perhaps it is a combination of institutional food and kitchen smells, soap, disinfectant, feces, urine, and the close confinement of many human bodies.

In sum, Ward Y and its inhabitants constitute a staggering visual, auditory, and olfactory assault on the presupposedly invariant character of the natural normal world of everyday life. Here, to a monumental degree, things are different. (pp. 313–314)

Even today, this type of reaction by first-time visitors to institutions for those with developmental disabilities is not uncommon. The authors relate an honest account of their thoughts and feelings as they walked through the institution. In this account, there is no mention of abusive or cruel practice toward residents, contrary to treatment of some residents in years past. There is, however, a disservice, possibly as unjust as abuse or overcrowding occurring in institutions today. This disservice is the adherence to strict routine. Below is a description by Cullari (1984) relating the day-by-day events of residents who were severely and profoundly retarded.

It is 6:30 A.M in section D of Blossom Hall. Bobby, along with 19 other profoundly mentally retarded clients who live there, is awakened. Today three aides are working on the section. Many of the clients are nonambulatory and have a number of other physical problems.

By 7:30 A.M., all of the clients are changed, toileted, shaved, and dressed. Bobby and the rest of the section are brought down to the dining room for breakfast. Each staff person moves from one client to another feeding everyone except the handful that can help themselves. A respirator is nearby for those who are prone to choking on food. At 8:15 A.M. everyone is back on the section, and oral hygiene begins. One aide remains in the central day room with most of the clients, while the other two aides are in the bathroom brushing teeth.

By 9:00 A.M. everyone is finished, and the aides take turns for their breaks. Until these are over, only two aides remain on the section. One of them supervises the 20 clients, while the other starts the housekeeping chores, such as bedmaking, that they also must do. Bobby is quietly rocking in his chair. Many of the other clients are rolling on mats placed on the floor.

Just before lunch, one of the aides marks the "progress" that the clients made on the assigned program plan, even though she didn't have time to actually carry it out. Her supervisor is usually in the main office completing paper work and rarely does he check whether programs are carried out.

That afternoon, Bobby and the other clients are seated in the day room in front of the T.V. He doesn't seem to be too interested in the soap opera that's on. The three aides sit together and gossip about the latest rumors going around the Center. Interaction with the clients is limited to keeping everyone seated and fairly quiet. Some of the clients are leafing through Sears catalogues.

At three o'clock, the afternoon shift begins. One aide called in sick, so there will only be two assigned to the section. After everyone is changed or toileted, the ambulatory clients are prepared for outdoor activities. These consist of a 20-minute walk around the Center. The nonambulatory clients are again placed on mats on the floor.

Shortly after dinner is over, the clients are prepared for bathing. Some of them were supposed to see a movie that night, but it had to be cancelled because of the shortage of staff. At eight o'clock, the supervisor comes down to help with the bathing.

One person undresses the clients, while the other two bathe, dry, and put pajamas on everyone. Bobby is the last one to finish. At 9:30 P.M., he is put to bed. (p. 28)

A routine remarkably similar to this is adhered to in many wards nationwide. While there is nothing deliberately cruel about the practices, there is seldom any attempt to transcend the utterly custodial nature of what institutions call "treatment." Cullari (1984) noted, "In many institutions, programming is virtually nonexistent, staff interaction with clients is minimal, and activities are limited to watching T.V., looking at pictures in books and magazines, short periods of "workshops," and long periods of rocking" (p. 28).

Structure is essential in the care of persons who are mentally impaired, and routine is an effective management tactic for those charged with their care. But routine easily becomes rigidity, and the purpose is twisted from one of assistance to one of control, particularly in settings where employees regard residents as subhuman beings who require little more than to be kept alive. That such a destructive attitude has historically shaped the "treatment" of institutionalized populations is one of the major criticisms of the system.

***Means of control.*** Routinization is but one means of control regularly exercised in the institutional setting. Isolation, mechanical restraints, and aversive treatment techniques like drug therapy and electric shock are used as well, at times to an extent unjustified by any real need.

Aversive treatment techniques comprise an extreme form of behavior modification designed to eliminate maladaptive behaviors characteristic of children and adults who are retarded. In the past decade, scores of studies have demonstrated the effectiveness of various aversive conditioning techniques in suppressing such behaviors as body rocking (Baumeister & Forehand, 1972), persistent vomiting (Kohlenberg, 1970), and self-induced seizures (Wright, 1973) that impede the person's learning of adaptive skills or cause him or her physical harm. Wallace, Burger, Neal, Van Breno, and Davis (1976) surveyed 207 public residential institutions for individuals who were mentally retarded on their use of aversive treatment, defined as the "application of any of the following noxious stimuli in contingent relationship with a behavior . . . electric shock, physical punishment, chemical irritants, and auditory irritants" (p. 17). Of the 115 (56%) institutions that replied, 53 (54%) allowed aversive treatment with particular residents. Each of these 53 users, and 74% of the responding nonusers, condoned the use of aversive conditioning as a legitimate mode of treatment. Of all respondents, 87% felt that a multidisciplinary team rather than a single individual should approve or disallow the use of aversive techniques with each individual, but only 17% of aversive treatment users were found to be in compliance with the regulation by the Joint Committee on Accreditation of Hospitals Standard requiring parental approval for use of aversive treatment with legally incompetent clients.

Drugs are also widely used to pacify chronically disruptive residents. Dispensing of drugs for this purpose is legally restricted to prescription by the in-house physician. Yet institutional practices vary from administration of lawfully required dosages (for instance, for those with epilepsy) to extreme overuse. Drugs like thorazine or stelazine can become a conventional control over a wide range of undesirable behaviors, and "hyperactivity" acquires a spurious definition. Planning programs to alleviate boredom and help vent "hyperactive" energy would minimize the need for chemical control (Biklen, 1977).

Mechanical restraints provide another effective imposition of control on "hyperactive" behavior. Such devices as straitjackets *(camisoles),* restraining sheets on beds, and restraining chairs are widely used to calm recalcitrant residents or inhibit self-destructive behavior. Biklen (1977) has documented countless incidents of overzealous restraining practices.

We saw a teenage girl wearing a camisole being led into an isolation room where there was only a mat on the floor. The room was barren. One attendant spoke to another. "We took her over to the hospital this morning to give her an enema. We had to put the camisole on her in order to do it." The girl remained expressionless. I asked why she needed an enema. The attendant told me, "Well, she's on such heavy doses of tranquilizers, it's necessary." (p. 45)

Forced seclusion is another type of control justified as a deterrent to self-abuse. This involves removal of the offending resident to a solitary, locked ward or room for what may become an indeterminate length of time.

Guidelines for control of aberrant behavior are on the books. But in practice another type of seclusion—isolation of the physical plant from contact with outlying communities—typically ensures that such dicta will be roundly ignored. Most large, public residential facilities discourage inquisitiveness from the outside for much the same reason that many businesses fear IRS audits. Authorized inspection can prove disastrous for those who insist on dodging regulations. The traditional mental institution avoids this, affirming its status as a separate entity by erecting high walls and fences around prisonlike buildings remote from population centers. When the institution reinforces its public image of deviance, myths born of ignorance and fed by separation compel its continued isolation.

Isolation can be psychological and emotional as well as physical. Censorship of mail, monitoring of visits, restrictions on outside travel, and rationing of telephone privileges all cut off institutionalized persons from what Biklen calls "potential allies." Segregation by sex controls the mating of "undesirables" and prevents potentially volatile alliances between residents. The psychological isolation created by these abnormal circumstances flourishes within the impervious, obdurate, cagelike facilities that historically house institutionally retarded people. The language of architecture in such "Siberias of human service" (Turnbull, 1980) is clearly that of control.

Although aversive techniques have been widely used as a means of control, institutions have begun to use positive measures more frequently. Marks and Wade (1981), for example, found that giving praise and edibles to residents for contact with leisure-related material that they did not destroy significantly reduced the frequency of destruction of these materials. In another study, Smith, Piersel, Filbeck, and Gross (1983), eliminated food stealing by a female with severe retardation through response cost and positive reinforcement. These instances clearly support the idea that positive techniques may and should be used more often in institutional settings.

*These positive techniques are often referred to as non-aversive measures.*

## BEHAVIORAL MANIFESTATIONS

*Socialization.*    Critics of institutions have long attested to the debilitating effects of institutional life on the cognitive and social functioning of the residents. The eternal monotony of routinized feeding, toileting, dressing, and so on, the mass movements at scheduled times, the rationing of clothing and possessions, and the monumentally drab environment provide little of the intellectual challenge needed for cognitive growth. Segregation, over-crowding, and understaffing encourage routinization and preclude opportunities for positive social contact. Vitello (1976) summarizes the effects on child development as follows.

1. The earlier a child is institutionalized, and the longer he remains, the greater will be his cognitive and behavioral deficits.
2. Institutionalized children from enriched backgrounds show greater loss of cognitive and behavioral functions than do those from impoverished environments. The latter may actually demonstrate gains if the prior setting was less nurturant than the institution.
3. It is possible to increase environmental stimulation and positive social contact within institutions to promote cognitive and behavioral growth; however community alternatives are, in the aggregate, more effective.

MacMillan (1982) notes that, in tests done on institutionalized children, impairment is more pronounced for verbal IQ than performance IQ. He suggests remediation through more frequent meaningful verbal interactions between children and staff. Personality, as well as cognitive, disorders are more common in institutionalized than noninstitutionalized people who are retarded. Zigler (1966) found a common trait of young residents to be an unusually strong desire for contact with an approving adult. Yet the impersonality of institutional settings, where overworked employees have little time (or inclination) to individualize, denies warm contact to those who need it most. A debilitating cycle is then activated, in which, according to Zigler, a resident who cannot get sufficient adult attention becomes more childishly dependent and makes no progress toward acquiring independent living skills. In this case, disability is both a cause and a result of institutionalization.

*Learned helplessness.* A similar phenomenon repeatedly observed in institutional settings is known as **learned helplessness.** Are the passivity and resistance to learning characteristic of persons with retardation in institutions a cause for commitment? Or are they the product of an environment inimical to learning? Or do people with retardation in large residential facilities actively learn not to learn? Researchers have identified learned helplessness in animals (Overmier & Seligman, 1967) and in humans (Seligman, 1975) as a pattern of submissiveness that develops when the victims repeatedly discover that their actions are of no consequence, that outcomes are beyond their control.

Learned helplessness is especially common in large institutions, where residents continually see aversive stimuli meted out for no apparent reason. Attendants often punish residents indiscriminately out of their own frustration or ignorance about the needs of persons who are mentally retarded.

Residents often victimize each other in random fits of pent-up energy, for example, striking an unsolicited blow to the nearest shin. Similarly, persons suffering from seizures find themselves totally helpless in the face of recurring inexplicable and traumatic events. DeVellis (1977) observes that learned helplessness is brought on by a person's inability to predict or deter such aversive events and is abetted by frequent recurrence of outcomes over which the person is powerless. A person who has learned not to learn will be (*a*) more submissive, (*b*) less responsive to stimuli, and (*c*) less able to connect his or her actions with consequences. The syndrome can be cured by forcibly leading the afflicted individual through actions that halt particular aversive stimuli. For instance, a victim might need to be dragged several times through the motion of removing herself from the path of a hair-pulling wardmate before she realizes she can avoid that particular irritation. But she will eventually catch on. Learned helplessness is best prevented by teaching individuals at an early age that outcomes *do* follow logically from their actions, and by repeatedly exposing them to situations they can control. For institutional personnel, this involves allowing the resident opportunities to begin and end simple activities, to express a preference when choices are available, and to handle objects that can be easily manipulated. Direct care staff should be alerted to the importance of letting the residents exert some influence over their environment.

*Other behaviors.*    Many residents of institutions display maladaptive behaviors that can be very disruptive. Whether some of these behaviors are brought into these settings with the residents or whether they result from being there is debatable. Some types and extents of maladaptive behaviors are presented in Table 14.2. Critics have identified several other maladaptive behavioral syndromes that seem to be institution-induced. Levy and McLeod (1977) describe a condition referred to today as **stereotypic behavior** in which institutionalized residents react to their stressful living conditions by self-stimulating (rocking, hand weaving, and so on). They liken these stereotyped behaviors to those shown by normal individuals who have been deprived of sensory stimulation for extended periods.

Biklen, from his observation of six state schools and five mental hospitals in 1977, concludes that the rigid, condemning living environment characteristic of most mental institutions induces the very behavior it is designed to control. In the few facilities he examined with relaxed, accepting climates and no locked wards, Biklen found none of the violent acting out that calls for seclusion or restraints. But in contrast, he found that in the traditional cold, regimented institutions where locked wards were part of the aversive treatment repertoire, residents upended furniture, banged heads, bit, kicked, and screamed—quite likely in *response* to their being caged and isolated for hours with nothing to do. Logically, frustration and its manifestations that warrant restraints can be abated if residents are given meaningful ways to

TABLE 14.2   Percent of Residents Exhibiting Maladaptive Behavior As Reported by Direct Care Staff

| Category of behavior | Private Facility Residents (N = 964) | State Institution Residents (N = 997) | State Institution New Admissions (N = 286) | State Institution Readmissions (N = 244) |
|---|---|---|---|---|
| Injures self | 11.1% | 21.7% | 22.0% | 21.3% |
| Injures other people | 16.3% | 30.3% | 42.0% | 38.5% |
| Damages property | 11.1% | 17.6% | 19.2% | 23.4% |
| Unusual or disruptive behavior | 28.8% | 34.3% | 37.8% | 41.0% |
| Breaks rules; won't follow routine | 19.1% | 18.8% | 32.4% | 33.2% |
| Refuses to go to day program | 7.2% | 11.7% | 20.9% | 25.8% |
| Has spent one of last 30 days at home because of refusal to go | 2.5% | 5.7% | 9.4% | 13.8% |
| Has purposely run away | 2.2% | 3.6% | 11.5% | 13.5% |
| Has run away within the last six months | 1.3% | 2.5% | 8.7% | 8.2% |
| Has broken the law within the last year | 1.5% | .5% | 3.1% | 7.4% |
| Court or law enforcement personnel involved | .7% | .1% | 1.4% | 4.1% |
| Total with one or more types of behavior | 47.3% | 59.7% | 68.5% | 68.4% |

From *Residential Services for Adults with Developmental Disabilities* by R. H. Bruininks, B. K. Hill, K. C. Lakin, & C. C. White, (1985), Logan: Utah State University, Developmental Center for Handicapped Persons. Reprinted by permission.

spend their time and a pleasant, accepting atmosphere in which to do it. Otherwise, the natural, *normal* response is rebellion.

## SUPPORT SERVICES/LEGAL PROTECTIONS

In addition to the expected intervention and daily living services, some other services are beneficial to residents. For the most part these services are important because they safeguard the rights of this population. Three of these are discussed in this section: advocacy, human rights committees, and the ombudsman.

The primary function of an **advocate** is to help persons with retardation exercise their rights. This group as a *class* is represented by many local, state, and national organizations that lobby for such broad programs as federal aid and right to appropriate education. The President's Committee on Mental Retardation, the Council for Exceptional Children, The Association for Persons with Severe Handicaps, and the Association for Retarded Citizens are such organizations. Advocacy for those *individuals* who are retarded, both for those living in the community and those remaining in institutions, poses a different challenge. Most retarded persons in the community find the business of merely surviving sufficiently complex, much less dealing with legal rights. Three types of advocacy programs are used in different jurisdictions to protect citizens who are retarded against denial of rights: state agencies, citizen advocates, and legally trained advocates. Scheerenberger (1976b) has emphasized the role of natural parents as advocates. This has been further supported by research on transition. Though not all parents are good at this, conscientious parents are encouraged to have themselves appointed guardians if their son or daughter needs such supervision beyond legal majority.

Most of the **human rights committees** (HRCs) began in the 1970s as a result of the lawsuits and rights movement. The HRCs work within an institution and are designed to protect the rights of institutionalized persons. Kemp (1983) reports that the HRC has responsibility for a wide range of functions. Some of these include review of behavior management programs, investigation of grievances, complaints and alleged rights violations, review of research programs, investigation of abuse and neglect, advocation or protection of resident rights, and review of client care, including a humane environment and adequate services. The most commonly reported cases brought before the committees were behavior modification programs and the use of psychotropic medication to control behavior.

The **ombudsman** in public institutions is a new concept, not yet a force in residential care. Still, reform advocates look to the future possibilities of ombudsmen as major agents of change. Mallory (1977) defines an ombudsman as "one whose role is to protect the rights of individuals seeking services from government agencies and educational systems." Ombudsmen in an institution for those who are mentally retarded are charged with protecting persons hurt by rules and procedures that support institutional structure and ignore divergent resident needs. Specifically, (*a*) they address grievances a resident might have with the management and negotiate for a solution, and (*b*) through their own investigation, they identify bugs in the system and recommend tactics for correcting problem areas to administrators. Where an advocate would be an outsider and thus limited in influence over internal operations, the ombudsman works inside the institution in a position independent of administrators and other staff. For maximum effectiveness, an ombudsman should be

1. Thoroughly versed in the inner workings of the institution—fiscal policy, regulations, communication patterns, and so on

2. Secure in his or her position, so that criticisms need not be tempered by fear of reprisal
3. Afforded full investigative power within the institutional system
4. Trained in legal issues, characteristics of developmental disabilities (especially severe and profound retardation), and organization and management of residential facilities.

Ombudsman services have tremendous potential for effecting institutional reform from within. Should the concept take hold, ombudsmen will be valuable agents for increasing accountability of institutions to taxpayers, lawmakers, and human rights advocates, and for availing due process to institutionalized residents.

## CURRENT OPINION ON INSTITUTIONALIZATION

The history of institutional service has progressed along waves of widely fluctuating public sentiment and remains to this day an emotional issue. The prevailing opinion of institutionalization in its present form is that the large public residential facility is an abnormal, unhealthy environment in which efficiency of operation dominates the needs of residents as a group and of individuals in particular. For all the lip service paid to habilitation, the goal of "treatment" in most existing public facilities is permanent residence. Care is, at best, custodial. Beyond this general agreement, opinions on how best to correct an error of such magnitude vary. Wolfensberger (1975) sides with the most severe critics, charging that present-day institutions are unsalvageable and should be dismantled. This theme was prevalent in the Pennhurst case as well (see chapter 13).

The opinion of most professionals about institutions is negative. An observation made by Menolascino and McGee (1981) reflects their underlying thinking: "The new institution . . . is still a system that generally dehumanizes and depersonalizes its residents" (p. 219). When this feeling is coupled with the desire to provide valued lifestyles and living conditions as close to normal as possible, it is easy to understand how such a negative sentiment develops.

But others, for example Ellis et al. (1981), believe that with a thorough structural overhaul many institutions can be made more humane and more habilitative. They suggest that these settings should be included as a part of a continuum of services available to those with retardation and their families. Furthermore, the fact remains that some institutions are providing some very good programming, and in many institutional settings the staff are very dedicated, concerned, and hardworking.

Many families also have positive attitudes about institutional placement. This cannot be discounted in our attempts to push for institutional reform, whether that be internal changes like those Ellis and associates recommend or the more drastic wholesale abolition of these facilities argued by others.

# THE DEINSTITUTIONALIZATION MOVEMENT

Four major developments have greased the wheels of institutional reform and deinstitutionalization.

1. Widespread approval of *normalization* as a goal for those labeled *deviant.*
2. Exposure of abominable conditions in large, public, residential institutions.
3. The egalitarianism of the 1960s and 1970s.
4. Judicial backing for the rights of the institutionalized and their right to the least restrictive conditions necessary.

The first two factors have been covered previously and are not discussed here. Turnbull (1988) has discussed the third factor, egalitarianism, at some length. He has noted that the decades of the 1960s and 1970s were times of increased attention to and action for those who were at some disadvantage. They were times characterized by a "dedication to reform" and motivated by the theme of equal opportunity. Without a doubt this prevailing attitude had a major impact on the actions of many professionals in the field. Turnbull also notes that today, because of changes in public attitude and policy (i.e., budget cuts and efforts to defederalize human services), egalitarianism has faded, putting many persons with mental retardation "on the razor's edge of public selfishness" (p. 18).

The fourth factor relates to the increased use of litigation for securing the rights of those who are susceptible to various infringements of them. A number of court decisions and legal actions involving the interpretation of the constitutional guarantee of certain rights have catalyzed institutional change. Many arguments used to obtain services and privileges have been based on Section 1 of the 14th Amendment, which lends itself well to any attempt to establish rights for people who are mentally retarded.

> All persons born or naturalized in the United States and subject to the jurisdiction thereof, are citizens of the United States and of the State wherein they reside. No State shall make or enforce any law which shall abridge the privileges or immunities of citizens of the United States, *nor shall any State deprive any person of life, liberty, or property without due process of law,* nor deny to any person within its jurisdiction equal protection of the law. [emphasis added

Legal channels for creating and inspiring change have been used very effectively in the past two decades. Yet it was not until 1972 that the federal courts really opened to the crusade for institutional reform. The first major court decision, *Wyatt v. Stickney* (1972), which has had a major impact on altering conditions in institutions, was concerned with the right to treatment. Another landmark case. *Halderman v. Pennhurst* (1974), has had a significant effect on the rights of those institutionalized as well.

These cases are discussed in more depth in chapter 13.

## DIMENSIONS OF DEINSTITUTIONALIZATION

Securing the legal right-of-way for institutional reform is, as with all social change movements, only the first step in a long journey. The crucial factor—public attitudes—cannot be changed by legislation. At the heart of the movement for change must be acceptance by all parties of the legitimacy of the deinstitutionalization principle and cooperative effort toward its realization.

Successful institutional reform requires support in four different ways.

1. Community and residential personnel must provide every opportunity for clients who are retarded to be served in the least restrictive local setting.
2. A person whose condition requires residential placement should be so placed no longer than is absolutely necessary.
3. Institutionalized persons who can function in the community should be transferred there as soon as possible.
4. All phases of residential programming should emphasize independence and personal growth consonant with the deinstitutionalization principle

The linchpin of the institutional reform movement is belief in normalization, more recently referred to as social role valorization by Wolfensberger (1983). He defines the goals of socially valued roles as (*a*) reducing or preventing the differentness or stigmata that may devalue a person in the eyes of observers; and (*b*) changing societal perceptions of a devalued person or group so that a given characteristic or person is no longer seen as devalued.

Deinstitutionalization is one crucial goal of institutional reform and is a natural corollary to the normative principle. According to the National Association of Superintendents of Public Residential Facilities for the Mentally Retarded (1974), deinstitutionalization encompasses the following processes.

1. Prevention of admission by finding and developing alternative community methods of care and training.
2. Return to the community of all residents who have been prepared through programs of habilitation and training to function adequately in appropriate local settings, and
3. Establishment and maintenance of a responsive residential environment which protects human and civil rights and which contributes to the expeditious return of the individual to normal community living whenever possible.

In the language of human service, this principle translates into a continuum of residential options with a range of desirability. Appropriateness of these options is very much a function of the age of the individual, and a child-based continuum would include the following options: natural home environment, foster care, ICF-MR facility in the community, large institutional placement. Any point along the continuum may be the "least restrictive environment," depending on the needs and capabilities of the child and the family, but in general, movement along the continuum toward a more homelike environment is encouraged.

## CURRENT TRENDS

*Smaller community-based facilities.*    Large, isolated facilities still exist, but there are many smaller settings now that ensure proximity to population centers.

Scheerenberger (1976a) reported a 74% increase in the number of public residential facilities (PRFs) operating in the United States from 135 in 1964 to 235 in 1974 (see Figure 14.1). Since 1974, he (1982) has reported an additional 47 such facilities (total 282), which represents a 20% rise. This wave of new construction was offset by declining populations within existing facilities (Figure 14.2) and the consistently smaller bed capacity (Figure 14.4).

Scheerenberger's analysis of census statistics for 176 PRFs revealed an 8.9% total decrease in population over the 1969 to 1974 period, and a decrease of 15.9% for the older PRFs between 1964 and 1974. Between 1975 and 1981, based on 282 PRFs, Scheerenberger(1982) has reported an 18.09% decrease in total population. The older facilities in his study, those built before 1964, ranged in bed capacity from 169 to 3,178, with a median of 1,014. Those constructed after 1964 varied from 10 to 1,508 beds, with 318 the median.

The countermovement to the traditional isolation of large public institutions is evidenced by an increasing number of alternative services arising in and around communities—from regional centers of 200 beds and fewer (for example, in California and Connecticut) to small group arrangements like nursing homes, group homes and apartments, and foster homes, as discussed in chapter 11.

*Lower functioning population.*    Other specific changes are also apparent within existing large institutions, most notably in the characteristics of the residents (e.g., average age, multiple problems). One consequence of the push toward community-based placement has been a dramatic reduction in the number of residents who are mildly or moderately retarded. Scheerenberger (1976b, 1982) has studied this trend in terms of first admissions to institutions. His findings indicate that between 1922 and the 1950s there was a steady decrease in this group. The trend has accelerated since themid-1950s to the point where, in 1975, 63.1% of all first admissions and 71.2% of the total institutional population were severely retarded. In 1981, Scheerenberger reported that approximately 80% of the population was severely or profoundly retarded.

See Table 14.1.

Lakin, Hill, Bruininks, and White (1986), analyzing multiple data sources, have developed a table showing the inverse relationship over a number of decades between the number of residents who are mildly retarded and those who are profoundly involved. This information appears in Table 14.3.

One outcome of housing an increasingly disabled group of people is the need for more technical centralization in large institutions. Severe mental retardation is often accompanied by serious physical problems, often as part of a syndrome such as Down syndrome, a metabolic or genetic disorder, or

TABLE 14.3   Resident Population by Level of Retardation

| Year | Percent Mildly or Borderline Retarded | Percent Profoundly Retarded |
|------|---------------------------------------|-----------------------------|
| 1939 | 40% | 15% |
| 1964 | 18% | 27% |
| 1982 | 6%  | 57% |

From "Residential Options and Future Implications" by K. C. Lakin, B. K. Hill, R. H. Bruininks, and C. C. White, 1986, in W. E. Kiernan and J. A. Stark (Eds.), *Pathways to Employment for Adults with Developmental Disabilities* (pp. 207–228), Baltimore; Paul H. Brookes. Reprinted by permission.

a physical trauma. Consequently, a facility undertaking the care of a large concentration of residents with severe handicaps requires a trained medical staff as well as a substantial arsenal of therapeutic equipment and supplies. This could easily lead to a return to the medical model of institutional service, as described by Wolfensberger (1975), in which medical personnel dominate the administrative staff, hospital routines are followed, and terminology is medical ("patients," "nursing units," and so on). The difference, we hope, would be that modern institutions would not attempt to "cure" the "disease" of retardation but rather would use medical technology to mitigate the physical problems of these residents.

## REFLECTIONS ON DEINSTITUTIONALIZATION

The final goal of the deinstitutionalization process is to allow individuals with retardation to live in settings like everyone else's and to have the opportunity for a happy, meaningful life. To this end, persons who are retarded will be removed from institutions if at all possible and placed in settings that mirror home life. In the 1970s, estimates of the number of institutionalized persons who qualified for transfer ran as high as 50% of the total residential population (Scheerenberger, 1976b). Since that time, many of those have been relocated. But in many areas of the country, individuals who could be moved into the community are still institutionalized.

***Relocation concerns.***   In deinstitutionalization, people are uprooted from familiar settings and transplanted into surroundings to which they must quickly adapt. Many normal individuals do not adjust easily to new surroundings; what, then, is the prognosis for people who are retarded, who are actually identified by their deficits in adaptive behavior? Logically, for a substantial number of this group, a hasty exit from the institution will *not* mean a happy life. The rush to deinstitutionalize sometimes obscures the goal of normalization.

"The relocation syndrome" has long been a problem in homes for the aged, especially since Medicare legislation in the early 1970s began to exact

*Many institutionalized residents who are higher functioning have been reintegrated into society.*

improved care standards in nursing homes and to reduce residency where possible. Reports on the yearly number of elderly persons who die soon after moving to or between nursing homes vary from 3% (Cochran, Sran, & Varano, 1977) to 34% (Bourestrom, 1973).

The "least restrictive environment" movement has created a similar but not necessarily identical set of circumstances. Cochran and colleagues (1977) observed the "relocation syndrome" in a study of 250 former residents of a large centralized facility in Maryland who were transferred en masse to Great Oaks, one of six smaller regional centers newly erected near their family homes to serve adults who are retarded. The following account is typical of the five residents who suffered the symptoms.

Joan, a 52-year-old white, profoundly mentally retarded female, was considered normal at birth and had no serious illnesses or injuries, although her developmental landmarks were all extremely delayed. She remained at home, attended no school programs, and was somewhat overindulged until the time of her parents' death. She was admitted first to a psychiatric facility and, shortly thereafter, to Rosewood Center, where she resided for 18 years. No depression occurred at Rosewood and she was in good health. At the time of transfer to Great Oaks Center, she was rather quiet and fearful, but not particularly depressed. A few days following transfer, however, she ceased eating, became increasingly depressed, and spent a great deal of her time weeping. Her depression lasted 3 to 4 weeks, during which time she lost approximately 15% of her body weight. There was poor response to high caloric dietary supplements and antidepressant medications. She improved gradually and has done well subsequently. (p. 10)

Though only five out of the 250 relocated residents reacted in this way, they suffered severely and perhaps unnecessarily. One of the five eventually died of pneumonia. Coffman and Harris (1980) have documented a parallel set of symptoms that they call *transition shock*. This condition is analogous to the adjustment problems of recent divorcees, ex-prisoners, and returning veterans, and the "culture-shock" experienced by cross-cultural travelers like exchange students and VISTA volunteers. Certain common characteristics other than symptoms exist.

1. Cue problems—Responding inappropriately to cues that were relevant in the old environment but not in the new (e.g., bells signaling mealtime in institutions), as well as failing to respond to cues peculiar to new environment.
2. Value discrepancies—for example, personal traits developed by rigid institutional routine—sluggishness, dependence, inability to make decisions—will normally not be valued in the community.
3. Emergence over time—as with relocation syndrome, problems associated with transition shock do not occur immediately, but incubate for 1 or 2 weeks. Perhaps it is at this time that the special treatment afforded to newcomers gives way to routine.

The symptoms manifested by a "shocked" former resident attempting to adjust to a new environment—depression, withdrawal, shyness, wistfulness, irritability, sleep disturbances, incontinence—often mislead observers to ill-informed conclusions that the individual has permanent behavioral disorders. Persons unfamiliar with developmental disabilities tend to forget that people who are retarded experience the full range of human emotions; they fail to recognize that transition shock is an emotional reaction, and that despondence, loneliness, anxiety, hostility, and so on are feelings no less proper to those who are retarded than to normal persons.

Heller (1984) reviewed the literature on this relocation phenomenon and noted the following general trends:

☐ No significant increase in mortality rates
☐ Increases in physical/medical problems
☐ Some decreases in constructive behaviors
☐ Increases in social withdrawal

Noting that relocation can have negative effects, Heller also pointed out that individual reactions vary greatly according to (*a*) individual characteristics (e.g., health, age); (*b*) individual perceptions, expectations, and readiness; (*c*) nature of the social disruption and types of available support systems; and (*d*) the quality of the sending and receiving environments. Another critical factor in relocation research is timing. It seems that the impact is most debilitating during the first few weeks, which suggests that it may be a good idea to evaluate adjustment longitudinally.

*Transition process.* For the newly deinstitutionalized person, the road to social integration is full of obstacles. That these can become overwhelming is evidenced by the soaring number of readmissions that presently follow on the heels of mass exodus from institutions. It is often difficult to discern which problems are the fault of ineffective (or nonexistent) preparation by the institution, which are inseparable from the transition process as described, and which stem from deficiencies in the ability of the new setting or receiving staff to accommodate new community members. Where the institution is to blame, difficulties can be sidestepped with an extensive preparation program that involves

1. Contact with staff members from both the present and receiving facilities as proof to the client of continued interest in his welfare
2. Visits to the new residence prior to the move
3. Family participation in the moving and adjustment processes
4. Assignment of a personal advocate (chosen by the individual if possible) well before the move to advise and support the person with retardation.

Where problems arise from the individual's particular emotional response to change, patience on the part of the receiving staff and empathetic counseling from both ends are the best weapons. The person should be reassured that the depression is probably only temporary.

Expectations of success or failure heavily influence the new community member's ease of transition. The person who has thorough preparation and ample support in the new role will naturally have better expectations for adjustment. Equally important is a general public belief that individuals with mental retardation can lead meaningful lives if given the necessary training and support. This encompasses teacher expectations in school and employer expectations on the job. Public sentiment can be affected in subtle ways. If the name of a new community facility implies deviance, if residents are called "patients" or "inmates," or adults are referred to as "children," the community at large will have understandably low expectations and will behave accordingly. In such a climate, normalization is not possible.

*Readmissions.* Opponents of community placement typically raise the issue of readmission to show that deinstitutionalization is not working. As chapter 11 pointed out, this statistic has been used in the past as a crude index of community adjustment. The data on readmissions are confusing and must be interpreted carefully. Between 1963 and 1974, the number of yearly releases from public institutions rose almost 150%. While this is impressive, a more dramatic figure for the same period was the 500% increase in readmissions, As the Figure 14.6 shows, more people were being released than were being readmitted. Yet for some (more than 40% in 1973), deinstitutionalization was largely a process of shuffling residents through a devastating experience in community living and then reeling them back in. During this time, the primary reason for unsuccessful placement was a lack of supportive services in the community (Scheerenberger, 1977).

More recently, the rate of readmission seems to have decreased. Craig and McCarver (1984) analyzed 10 studies with the following characteristics: they were conducted between the mid-1970s and early 1980s; they examined deinstitutionalized residents; and they reported readmission figures. Craig and McCarver found that the median readmission rate was 19% which is similar to Scheerenberger's (1982) figure of 18%. Three major points are worth noting. First, one must be cautious about interpreting the studies reviewed, as they reflect information on just over 2,000 individuals over a number of years. Second, even though the rates have fallen, 19% still represents a considerable number of persons who are returning to large institutional settings. Third, the reason that more persons are remaining in community settings seems to be related to a deepening commitment to

**See chapter 11 for examples.**

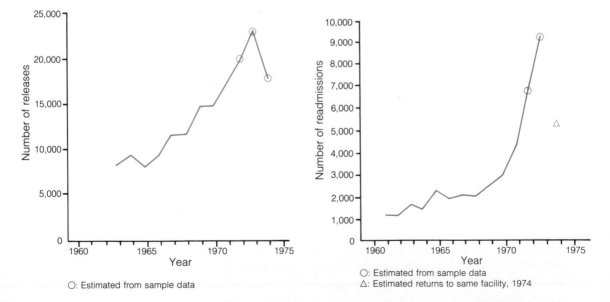

O: Estimated from sample data

O: Estimated from sample data
△: Estimated returns to same facility, 1974

FIGURE 14.6    Release and Readmission Rates of Individuals with Mental Retardation (1960–1975)

From ''Trends in the Deinstitutionalization of the Mentally Retarded'' by J. W. Conroy, 1977, *Mental Retardation, 15*(4), 44–46. Reprinted by permission.

community-based settings, with its accompanying increase in available options and services.

*Quality of life.* Too often a person's failure to adjust in a new setting is the fault of ill-conceived alternative placement by overzealous reformers. Community facilities are not inherently normalizing; in fact, they can be as restrictive as the worst institution if the setting is inappropriate and the residents are unsupported by the services they require. Until now, we have implied that smaller size means superior service. A fair inquiry into institutional reform compels that we question this blind assumption. Balla (1976) examined the impact of institutional size on aspects of care provided to residents. He attempted to determine whether certain structural elements common to large institutions foster practices that downgrade the quality of care, but found too little empirical data from which to draw strong conclusions. Balla's findings can be summarized as follows.

1. No data could be found supporting the supposition that smaller facilities return more residents to the community.
2. There is little significant correlation between the size of a facility and the adaptive behavior of residents.
3. There is no significant correlation between proximity of a residential facility to the home and frequency of visits by family members.
4. *Type* rather than *size* of an institution seems to determine the quality of care, with smaller, community-based facilities being generally more resident-oriented than large, isolated institutions.

Balla found that, of four types of residential facilities, group homes were the most resident-oriented, followed by small regional centers (10 to 116 beds), then average-sized regional centers (150 to 300 beds). Large, centralized institutions were the least resident-oriented. Orientation of care practices varied predictably across institutional types; however, within each group, the size of the facility had no bearing on orientation. Clearly, it is incorrect to presume that a person who is retarded will be better served in a smaller facility simply because it is smaller. Regional centers can easily become surrogate institutions, and nursing homes have tremendous warehousing potential. Landesman (1988) remarks that a community setting can adopt many of the negative features of larger facilities. It is equally wrong to expect that locating within a community will automatically make a facility more normalizing. Few of us have "homes" in warehouse districts. Nor should we translate removal from the institution "as soon as possible" to mean "immediately if not sooner." As mentioned previously, preparation for community life cannot be rushed; neglecting that crucial readiness period all but assures that the client will become one more casualty of institutional reform.

# SUPPORT FOR INSTITUTIONS

In contrast to what many supporters of the deinstitutionalization movement want to encourage, some families with members who are retarded have strong positive feelings toward maintaining institutions. The letter to the editor presented below demonstrates the attitudes of this other camp. (Note: Waimano Training School and Hospital is Hawaii's largest public residential facility.)

## PARENTS OF SEVERELY RETARDED FEAR BILLS WILL HURT CHILDREN

### by Ruth Butchart,
### Parents and Advocates of Waimano

The Hawaii Department of Health and its Developmentally Disabled Division are placing, over strong parental objections, profoundly mentally retarded residents of Waimano Training School and Hospital into foster homes in the community at an alarming rate.

Many of these unfortunate individuals are also multiply handicapped, non-verbal and unable to control basic body functions.

If beautiful normal children placed in foster homes can be so abused, as shown in a recent ABC news special, imagine what is in store for these mentally retarded who are unable to even protect themselves from the common dangers of life.

Would you wish to have your son or daughter placed in a relatively unsupervised community foster home in these circumstances?

The Chaffee Bill (S. 1673) now being considered in the U.S. Senate, with a companion Florio Bill in the U.S. House, would immediately reduce and ultimately eliminate Medicaid funding for any residential care facility for more than 15 residents.

These bills will virtually eliminate every state institution for the mentally retarded and developmentally disabled throughout the United States, including Waimano. Ask your congressmen and senators if they are still "signed on" as sponsors of these bills, and ask if they know the consequences to Waimano and its mentally retarded residents if they are enacted.

More than 400,000 parents of mentally retarded in the United States are united in trying to stop this insidious move to destroy the institutional "homes" where our children have been given love, care and protection over the years. Please add your voice to this effort.

From: *Honolulu Star-Bulletin,* Sept. 12, 1988.

*Economics: Community versus institution.* Existing large institutions cannot be depopulated until enough alternative sites have been constructed to absorb the new releases. People cannot merely be released from institutions and sent home. Like all worthwhile social endeavors, this takes money. Whether or not a community has sufficient revenue to build new facilities for its citizens who are retarded depends on a number of variables—the local tax base, state and federal aid contributions, the priority given to mental retardation services, and so forth. In a sense, new construction also generates money, in that employment rises and the community gains a new investment asset, but this is a separate issue. Construction costs are finite, while operational costs may continue indefinitely.

Operating costs for community-based alternatives are substantially lower than for large facilities. Earlier claims charged that the lower expense for smaller facilities was simply unsubstantiated, but subsequent findings suggest otherwise. Table 14.4 lists comparative data representing the per day reimbursement rate in 1982 for a single person across settings. This table shows great differences across the spectrum.

TABLE 14.4　Per Day Reimbursement Costs by Type of Facility

| Setting | Cost |
| --- | --- |
| Board & supervision | $15.97 |
| Specialized foster care | $16.15 |
| Personal care | $17.05 |
| Semi-independent | $27.40 |
| Small group residence (1–15) | $38.31 |
| Large private residence (16–300+) | $45.15 |
| Specialized nursing care | $49.81 |
| Large public residence (16–300+) | $85.84 |
| Total average cost | $61.89 |

From "Characteristics of Residential Facilities" by B. K. Hill, K. C. Lakin, and R. H. Bruininks, 1988, in L. W. Heal, J. I. Haney, and A. R. Novak Amado (Eds.), *Integration of Developmentally Disabled Individuals into the Community* (2nd ed., pp. 89–124), Baltimore: Paul H. Brookes. Reprinted by permission.

## FINAL THOUGHTS

As is true for any reform movement, the claims of those who seek to abolish public residential institutions are best regarded with a degree of healthy skepticism. Several points need to be stressed.

First, it is possible to abolish the residential institution. Those who now reside in institutions, however, are entitled to quality care. There will always be some individuals who are severely or profoundly retarded, have serious medical needs, and will have a difficult time living in most of the community-based options. To impose the unrealistic standards of a "culturally normative environment" on such individuals is to deny their constitutional rights. Equal opportunity may at times mean unequal treatment. To quote MacMillan (1977), "We should not get carried away with treating retarded individuals as though they were normal; because they are retarded, they have a right to special services, which may not be altogether normal" (p. 509).

Second, many advocates for persons who are retarded are deeply concerned that "the community service system will become the institutional model of the future" (Turnbull, 1988, p. 22). This concern is compounded by recent restrictions and cutbacks in federal spending on human services programs.

Third, because large, isolated institutions for those with retardation are as much a social phenomenon as any "institution" in the generic sense (marriage, baseball, whatever), to abolish such settings is to treat only the symptoms of a larger social disease. The history of residential treatment has proven that institutions basically mirror prevailing social attitudes about people who are retarded. It is much easier to charge institutions with wrongdoing than to indict a nebulous "public conscience." As Biklen (1977) says, "It would be easy to recommend that a dirty ward be cleaned or that shabby clothes be replaced by new and stylish clothing, but such changes would not expunge those forces which create dirty wards and ill-clothed inmates." (p. 35). Ultimately, the fault is not with the abusive attendant who feeds residents lighted cigarettes but with the social attitudes that allow such actions to go unpunished.

Institutions are likely to continue to be used, as is evidenced by the high levels of funding that they continue to receive. Whether it would be disastrous to eradicate institutions at a time when readmissions continue is arguable. Clearly, upgraded residential institutions are needed. We should work on changing these settings so that they can actually be part of the deinstitutionalization process—one phase in the transition to less restrictive settings.

Institutions have long been part of the field of mental retardation. For this reason, a chapter of this book has been devoted to them. The first part of the chapter looked at the process of institutionalizing someone and the factors that influence this decision. The second part focused on the institutional setting: how it is structured, who works there, what occurs within the confines of these settings. The next section examined the deinstitutionalization movement and the changes it has caused.

The goal of this chapter has been to provide an orientation to institutions in such a way that those who have never visited one would have some sense of what they are. It is important to recognize that institutions are an emotional topic and that any discussion of them leads to controversy, as Blatt (1987) has pointed out. It is important that students in the field of mental retardation be aware of these controversies and take positions on them.

**SUMMARY**

# CHAPTER 15

# Looking into

# the Future

T his chapter talks about a few of the "dots," as Linstone calls them in the following passage, that may eventually contribute to a holistic image of the field of mental retardation. This task includes both projecting present scenarios into the future and forecasting new situations.

> As futurists . . . we are like Pointillist painters of the Neo-Impressionist period. We paint large and small dots which do not provide a holistic image or "feel" for a future. The reason is clear: Unless we confine ourselves to strictly technological systems, it is exceedingly difficult to consider the tremendous number of elements and interactions between them which are characteristic of complex human and societal systems. It is not yet possible to deal simultaneously with a very large number of variables (some quantitative and some qualitative) so as to minimize disharmony or discordance in the total system. Thus our scenarios for the future are more like a series of dots on the canvas than a cohesive image. (Linstone, 1977, p. 3)

## PREDICTING THE FUTURE

As Linstone suggests, the challenge of predicting the future is a monumental one. Basically, predictions are based on what we already know. Some error must always be acknowledged in any prediction, because we cannot foresee all the variables that will affect the future.

A more appropriate name for this activity might be "probabilistic conjecture" (McHale, 1980). Nevertheless, we must persevere in our efforts and, at the very least, try "to anticipate the consequences of alternative courses of action" (PCMR, 1976b, p. 38).

The business of certain agencies, institutions, and professions is largely that of prediction. Insurance companies, for instance, rest their profit margins on their ability to predict certain statistics (life expectancies, number of auto accidents, injuries, and deaths; thefts and fires, etc.). Institutions of higher learning use certain variables such as high school grade point average and SAT scores to predict success in college. Meteorologists live and die by making predictions, since they are constantly accountable to the public. Prediction is also used in medicine when various prognoses are based on present information about a patient. In all these examples, we can see that certain events are projected from existing facts.

Those of us interested in mental retardation are very much concerned about where we have been, where we are today, and where we will be in the future, but the best we can do without the gift of clairvoyance is to base our hunches on the trends and changes that the field is presently experiencing. Social forecaster John Naisbitt (1984) based his popular, insightful *Megatrends* on this premise: "The most reliable way to anticipate the future is by understanding the present" (p. xxiii). Unfortunately, that persistent element of the unknown lurks before us; therefore, to adopt a simplistic view of the future denies the possibility of major turning points or what Kuhn (1970) calls revolutionary change in scientific thinking. Naisbitt points out that, while certain broad tendencies can be noted (e.g., the shift from a national to a world economy), no one can predict what specific form our future society will take. Attempts to describe it in detail, he feels, "are the stuff of science fiction and futuristic guessing games" (p. xxiii). A simplistic view of the future ignores the impact of sociopolitical factors that can significantly alter the course of events.

Although futurists do not always agree, they do share some consensus about certain fundamental elements that affect the future. Cain and Taber (1987) have identified three elements that have a significant impact on the future:

☐ Continuity: The future is always influenced by the past and the present.
☐ Change: The future is always influenced by unexpected events that break the continuity of history.
☐ Choice: The future is always influenced by the choices that people make when confronted with a new development.

These variables interact with one another and make it very difficult to predict the future with any certainty, particularly for situations involving complex human and social systems (Linstone, 1980).

## CHANGES IN SOCIETY

Before we can approach topical issues, it is essential that we understand the changes and influences our society will probably experience. The social and economic structure of mankind has progressed through three major stages (hunting and gathering, agricultural, and industrial) and is currently in a fourth stage (postindustrial).

The pressures placed on an individual vary significantly with the demands of a given social system and location. The ability to succeed in school was not very important in the agricultural society of the early 18th century, where manual labor was esteemed. The industrial revolution introduced new demands for semiskilled and skilled workers; ability and training for these jobs became mandatory for success in this era. As we have advanced from an industrial to a postindustrial society, the types of skills demanded by social institutions, and particularly by the workplace, have begun to change dramatically. Naisbitt (1984) presents the following information.

> MIT's David Birch has demonstrated that of the 19 million new jobs created in the United States during the 1970s—more than ever before in our history—only 5% were in manufacturing and only 11% in the goods-producing sector as a whole. Almost 90%, then—17 million new jobs—were not in the goods-producing sector. (p. 8)

Linstone (1977) posits that the years ahead will be characterized by the themes of *communication* and *information*. He states, "The change from an energy to an information society is of such depth and magnitude that it boggles the mind" (p. 5). To Naisbitt (1984), the "restructuring of America from an industrial to an information society will easily be as profound as the shift from an agricultural society to an industrial society" (p. 9). While the transition from agriculture to industry took 100 years, the shift from an industrial to an information-based society has taken only 20. Naisbitt believes the change has happened so quickly that many people are only just now realizing it.

Examples of some of the changes that one can observe in the transition from an agricultural to an informational age are presented in Table 15.1. The table focuses on work-related issues, but it illustrates the magnitude of the other changes we have experienced and adumbrates those to come.

## FUTURE SCENARIOS

*Trends.* It seems evident that everyday life will continue to become more demanding and technologically sophisticated, which will have a major effect on other specific areas as well. Some predictable changes in the near future are given below.

☐ The nature of work will be different. Jobs will be more technically demanding, and many more jobs will be automated, thus reducing the number of positions in manufacturing and agriculture.

☐ Society will experience a significant aging effect. The number of older individuals will increase.

☐ Health care will become more sophisticated and more expensive. Questions as to who will benefit from it will arise.

TABLE 15.1   Societal Changes Through the Ages

|  | Agricultural Age | Industrial Age | Information Age |
|---|---|---|---|
| Defining technology | Craftsman | Clock | Instruction-based systems |
| Strategic resource | Raw materials (seeds, water, soil) | Capital (money) | Ideas (minds) |
| Transforming resource | Natural energy (sun) | Processed energy (coal, electricity) | Synergy (minds working together) |
| Product | Food | Mass-produced items | Information |
| Organizing principle | Seasons | Product design | Inflow (information flow) |
| View of time | Cyclical | Steadily onward | Multiplexed |
| View of progress | Progress in history | Perfectibility of man and society | Merger of man and machine |
| Machine paradigm | Spindle | Heat engine | Organism (instruction-based machine) |
| Communication | Conversation (transfer ideas locally) | Face-to-face conference (transfer ideas by transporting people) | Teleconference (transfer ideas by transmitting images) |

The transition from the Agricultural Age to the Industrial Age to the Information Age has changed the means, methods, and materials with which we work. This chart notes the changes that have taken place for a number of work-related items and activities.

From "Rethinking How We Work: The Office of the Future" by S. E. Bleecker, 1987, *The Futurist, 21*(4), pp. 15–19. Reprinted by permission.

☐ Economic conditions in the United States (e.g., the federal budget deficit) will remain problematic, constraining spending in many areas, for example, services and health care (Amara, 1988).

☐ Educational systems will be different. It seems inevitable that schooling will become year round and that the school day will be longer.

Some futurists (Dator, 1988; Macarov, 1985) speak of a 21st century environment that they characterize as a "workless society." They suggest that efforts should be directed at creating a society of full unemployment. This thinking is based on various notions: (*a*) technology will make a large workforce superfluous; (*b*) resources will be abundant; and (*c*) unemployment will always be with us. Macarov (1985) describes the situation in the following way.

What is needed is a planned, conscious movement toward the highest technology possible, replacing human effort in every area for which changes in methods, machines, and materials can be found. In short, the goal should be full *un*employment. Paradoxically, the elimination of unemployment requires that it be widened to include the majority, if not nearly all, of society. This way, it will be widened to include the majority, if not nearly all, of society. This way, it will be seen as a social good rather than a social ill. When only 10% of the population produces all the goods and services needed, the remaining "unemployed" 90% will look at unemployment in a much different light. (p. 22)

Whether this scenario will come to be or not is subordinate to the implications for teaching and service delivery inherent in it. We should look beyond the present and even the near future to the distant future. If we are to prepare ourselves, our children, and their children for the future, we must start planning now. To do so, we must consider what the future might be like.

*Implications for individuals with mental retardation.* Changes in the social and economic structure as well as in our lifestyles will have a profound impact on persons who are mentally retarded. In an informational society, it will be important to use developing technology to the advantage of those with retardation, on the one hand, and to prepare them for the demands of such a society, on the other. McHale (1980) suggests that some will be able to take advantage of future changes, and some will not, so that there will be "haves" and "have nots" in the informational society as in any other. The implications of this duality are presented in Table 15.2 Without assistance (i.e., planning and preparation), most persons with mental retardation will fall into the "have-not" category if we are not careful. The paradox is that new developments, by and large, will be beneficial to this group (see the next section). But those with retardation are also at risk of being left behind as more barriers to adjustment are created.

TABLE 15.2    Implications for the "Haves" and "Have Nots"

| Information "Haves" | Information "Have Nots" |
|---|---|
| Become basis for elites in a restratified society | Training in applications of technology—how to use rather than what to use for |
| More socially mobile, with diverse career paths and life-style opportunities | Will tend to be more locked in to particular jobs—less able to change occupations |
| Their acquisition of more and new knowledge becomes progressively easier | May tend to resign themselves to helplessness and alienation—will seek and use less and less information |
| Added capacity to create their own knowledge bases | Less able to cope with perplexing changes |
| More able to organize and associate at a distance through access to new techniques | Will become suspicious and hostile to the "knowledge people" |
| May possibly have more enlightened self- interest | Limited social mobility |

From "Mental Retardation and the Future: A Conceptual Approach" by J. McHale, 1980, in S. C. Plog and M. B. Santamour (Eds.), *The Year 2000 and Mental Retardation* (p. 19–70), New York: Plenum Press. Reprinted by permission.

TABLE 15.3   Questions to Consider About the Future and Mental Retardation

☐ To what degree will individuality be cherished and what will be the degree of tolerance toward deviation from normative patterns?

☐ To what extent will individual life be valued, particularly with reference to such practices as population control, abortion, and euthanasia?

☐ To what degree will procedures designed to shape man's own destiny be sanctioned, such as psychotechnology and genetic engineering?

☐ Can we expect an integrated and comprehensive effort by the biomedical and social sciences to reduce the incidence and severity of mental retardation?

☐ What will be the state of prenatal care, nutrition, intensive care for premature infants, genetic counseling, and family planning in the year 2000?

☐ Is a centralized data system foreseeable for intervention purposes, and for tracking high-risk groups?

☐ Will there be significant shifts in demographics, including morbidity and mortality patterns?

☐ What new modes of communication may either offer opportunities or create problems in attempting to change public attitudes?

☐ Will there be a scarcity of natural resources and of funds for government services? If so, will that cause people to regard the retarded as parasites or needed contributors whose productive potential must be developed?

☐ Will the trend toward full citizenship rights for retarded people continue?

☐ What will our judicial system be like 20 years from now?

☐ What is the future of legal services to the poor?

☐ How do you reconcile the right of a mentally retarded individual to be a parent versus the right of a child to have a normal parent?

☐ If retarded people are to enjoy full citizenship status, there are three basic realizations that our society must learn to accept. To what extent can we expect the following statements to be accepted by the year 2000?

1. That retarded people can be more independent and can function more competently than is commonly believed.

2. That retarded people have the same rights, legal and constitutional, as every other U.S. citizen.

3. That full citizenship be exercised in a *community setting*.

☐ Our perception of the retarded person and his abilities is being altered. Will society reject the notion that because a person is incompetent to do one thing, he is therefore incompetent to do all things?

☐ Can the retarded person's rights of equal access to quality medical services, equal educational opportunities, equal protection in the criminal justice system, equal employment opportunities, and the rights to marry, raise children, and to vote be realized by the year 2000?

☐ What is the employment outlook for the mentally retarded?

☐ What will be the governmental emphasis on human services?

☐ What will the government emphasize in its decision-making patterns?

☐ What will be the nature of governmental funding patterns?

☐ To what degree will consumers have options for selecting among service system alternatives?

☐ How active will government be in quality control of human services and research (e.g., standard setting, accreditation, monitoring)?

☐ To what degree will education, including the impact of changing philosophy and technology, undergo significant changes?

☐ What will be the effects of the shrinking work week and increased leisure time?

☐ To what degree will the world of work and prevailing work-related ethics undergo changes?

☐ What is our society going to look like—not only in terms of the handicapped but in terms of the entire population?

Adapted from *Strategies for Achieving Community Integration of Developmentally Disabled Citizens* by S. C. Plog and M. B. Santamour (Eds.), 1980, New York: Plenum Press. Reprinted by permission.

One of the outcomes of a technologically more advanced society is that certain demands of everyday life are made easier (e.g., pocket telephones). But the limitation for many adults who are mentally retarded is that they do not know how to use these devices nor—and maybe a more fundamental issue—are they able to purchase them. This situation holds true for the ballooning computer technology in the workplace as well.

The President's Committee on Mental Retardation brought together a group of futurists to consider the impact of change on those with retardation by the year 2000 (Plog, 1980). The questions this group raised and addressed are noteworthy as a segue to the next section of this chapter. Table 15.3 lists them.

Mindful of these questions and of the necessity for caution about any prediction, let us begin our venture into the future. We make no pretense to be able to predict the future of the treatment of those with mental retardation à la Huxley, Orwell, Wells, Asimov, or Roddenberry, although some of what we suggest may seem as fantastic as their works. As the validation of many of the ideas presented in *Brave New World* proves, the distinction between fiction and reality is tenuous, and even the most extravagant predictions can become credible. Moreover, the pace at which the predicted becomes the real often is faster than we might imagine.

## LIFE IN THE FAST LANE

Commensurate with the technological advances characteristic of hypothesized postindustrial society, changes will also emerge in social attitudes and perhaps in the concept of retardation itself. Let us speculate on what we may be able to expect in the future. (Note that in the sections that follow, there is at times a fine distinction between what we predict will happen and what we would like to see happen.)

### ATTITUDES

Attitudes are eminently important because they are usually indices of behavior. Harth (1977) remarks that attitudes "represent a verbal statement about how one feels toward a particular construct" and later goes on to say that "people hold rather strong and divergent attitudes about mental retardation" (p. 4). In regard to persons with mental retardation, attitudes correlate strongly with (*a*) the availability of services and programs, (*b*) the amount of interaction between those with retardation and those without, and (*c*) the self-esteem of those who are retarded (Guskin, 1977).

Historically, social attitudes toward deviant populations or individuals have placed the blame for the deviancy upon those who, for various reasons, are different. Ryan's (1976) powerful book *Blaming the Victim* describes this phenomenon as it relates to placing the blame for poverty on its victims. As a result of this type of thinking, most intervention programs are designed to change the individual, not the system. Rappaport (1977) proposes that what is required is a paradigm that involves a "person-environment fit," emphasizing the relationship between individuals and their social and physical environment. A perspective that includes this notion of person-environment fit would benefit persons who are mentally retarded by encouraging society to look more broadly at the full range of potentialities, needs, and problems of this group. What typically happens is that "we try to fit people into existing structures, rather than evaluate what is wrong with a social system that does not accept someone as she or he is" (Amado, 1988, p. 303). Society must move away from blaming the person to a more transactional model. There are signs that this is beginning to happen.

One alternative perspective has been suggested by Bogdan (1980). He is skeptical of the concept of mental retardation and considers it a social construct. His approach is to look at mental retardation through the eyes of those who are retarded—a view seldom taken. Bogdan remarks that "this approach involves suspending, as much as possible, one's own assumptions about people one talks to and attempting to see the world from their perspective" (p. 75). Adopting this perspective, we are likely to get a very different view of what retardation is.

The media can have a major impact on people's attitudes about those who are retarded. Portrayals of persons with mental retardation in the media have changed for the better. In numerous cases, characters who are retarded are shown in positive and realistic ways (e.g. Benny in *L.A. Law*). Nevertheless, we must remain vigilant to misportrayals and stereotyping, and respond to such situations when they occur to prevent misinformation from being disseminated and misperceptions from developing.

## DEFINITIONAL ISSUES

Prevalence figures owe their existence to definitions and to other variables that may influence them (age, gender, culture). Most professionals now support prevalence figures of less than 1% over the often-cited figure of 3%. Recent data on the number of students classified as mentally retarded in the schools (refer to Figure 2.4) reflect this lower figure. Whether this decrease which we have witnessed over the last few years will continue remains to be seen, although most probably it will level off. These changes have significant implications for our conceptualization of and service provision to this population, as Polloway and Smith (1983) have clearly suggested.

It seems likely that we may need to pay more attention to those students whom we call *slow learners* for two reasons: (*a*) they have typically been in need of special assistance; and (*b*) this group is becoming more populated by students who were formerly served in special education.

There are strong pressures in the field of special education to reexamine the process and the effects of labeling individuals mentally retarded.

Although (as we saw in chapter 13) no strong evidence exists that labeling students mentally retarded has negative effects, many professionals are concerned about labeling, and efforts to evaluate its effects are warranted.

As time progresses, let us hope that classification models stress more often adaptive behavior, cultural factors, various social roles, and person-system interaction, as Hobbs (1975) described.

> The development of a classification system that takes into account (for individual children in particular settings) assets and liabilities, strengths and weaknesses, linked to specified services required to increase the former and decrease the latter. (p. 281)

In the future, definitions should recognize that individuals vary considerably and consequently have different needs. McHale (1980) offers a perspective from which to view future changes in conceptualizing and defining mental retardation.

☐ Mental retardation is more socially than biomedically determined as to numbers, causation, and incidence, therefore, more amenable to socially oriented preventive and ameliorative action.

☐ Its very definition is conceptually restrained within given sets of sociohistorical and sociocultural conditions—and is, in itself, peculiarly susceptible to future change.

☐ We must keep in our minds, therefore, that implicit within any consideration of change in relation to mental retardation is the idea that our conventional notions of normalcy, of human competency, and of human nature itself are also open to change and considerable modification. (p. 21)

Emerging definitional perspectives are likely to deemphasize the importance of test performance while emphasizing other types of competence (Adelson, 1980). The focus would be much more on how well individuals interact with their environments. The reigning position given to the intelligence criterion in present practice will not die easily. Such technological advances as computer-based diagnostic systems where a student would be tested at a computer terminal and a written diagnosis of test performance would be available immediately will be embraced by psychometrists and will probably prolong the argument for more formal procedures.

Formal assessment of individuals need not end; but its role may become more restricted. Competency should be considered situation specific, and technically adequate measures for assessing competence, beyond current adaptive behavior measures, must become available. Hallahan and Kauffman's (1976) idea of using as many behavioral descriptors as are needed to explain a person's functional ability still is appealing.

Regardless of changes in the professionally accepted *concept* of mental retardation, the *term* will probably remain in our vocabularies, although when we look at the terminology used across the United States (see Table 2.3) and in other parts of the world, we can see that other terms—no less

being born have been affected by these diseases suggests that this area will command much attention in the future. Right now, the most effective intervention is education. Affected adults must be made aware of the consequences of these conditions on the children they bear. The AIDS issue is of such severity that the American Association on Mental Retardation has issued a resolution on this topic (see Figure 15.1).

Whereas, acquired immune deficiency syndrome (AIDS) is a serious health threat to all people of the world, including people with mental retardation; and

AIDS is fatal and, during its progression, causes mental and physical disabilities in persons who have acquired the disease so that even people who did not previously have disabilities will often develop them; and

Increasing numbers of infants are being born with AIDS, and most infants who are born with AIDS will be mentally retarded and will have additional mental and physical abnormalities;

Therefore, be it resolved that the American Association on Mental Retardation urges:

a. Continued and immediately expanded research efforts for a cure for the disease and amelioration of its effects.

b. Continued and immediately expanded services to support the humanity and dignity of all people with the disease, including people with mental retardation who have the disease.

c. Continued and immediately expanded efforts for prevention of AIDS in infants and young children, including the provision of education which is accessible to people of all ages and abilities, including people with mental retardation. Women of child-bearing age and their sex partners must be provided accessible AIDS education. Adequate pre- and post-natal care for children at risk of acquiring the disease must be provided.

Whereas, AIDS is a preventable disease, and education and consequent behavior changes can protect an individual from contracting the disease; and, although people with mental retardation are no more susceptible to the disease than mentally typical people, education and training efforts must take into account the special learning needs of people with mental retardation,

Therefore, be it resolved that the American Association on Mental Retardation urges:

Education, accessible to persons of all ages and abilities including people with mental retardation, that will allow the choices and behavior changes necessary for the prevention of the disease in individual cases.

Whereas, the societal discrimination that is so prevalent in the lives of people with disabilities is amplified when the individual has AIDS, AIDS-related complex, or the AIDS virus,

Therefore, be it resolved that the American Association on Mental Retardation urges:

Nondiscriminatory and accessible services, including health care, confidential and properly consented-to testing and counseling, social services, sex education, employment, and appropriate community-based residential services for persons with mental retardation who have AIDS, AIDS-related complex, or the AIDS virus. Services must continue to be consistent with the least restrictive environment principle.

FIGURE 15.1    Resolution on Acquired Immune Deficiency Syndrome (AIDS) and Disability
From American Association on Mental Retardation, 1988, *News and Notes, 1*(4). Reprinted by permission.

Prenatal (gestational) prevention takes many forms. Adequate nutritional intake is a must for pregnant women if the birth of infants with physical and mental defects is to be prevented. Malnutrition helps to cause premature births, low birth weight, and reduced mental functioning (Begab, 1974). This problem can be controlled. Through more efficient educational programs directed toward providing proper nutritional information and through technological advances like dietary supplements or nutritional meal systems delivered by mail (Beevy, 1978), the improper nutritional health of prospective mothers could be reduced drastically or (theoretically) eliminated completely.

Other preventive action is directed at eliminating or minimizing the effects of toxic substances and diseases that can damage the developing fetus. Chapter 4 covered the risks of various teratogens, for example, alcohol thoroughly, but it did not address the effects of medications taken during pregancy. Grossman and Tarjan (1987) point out that prescribed medications can have serious teratogenic or cytotoxic effects on the unborn child. Pregnant women who require certain drugs for regulatory reasons (e.g., epilepsy) are faced with a difficult decision. They should not take medications while pregnant and, if they must, they should keep them to a minimum during the first trimester. Grossman and Tarjan also warn that complications can arise from taking nonprescription drugs like aspirin, multivitamin preparations, or weight reduction agents.

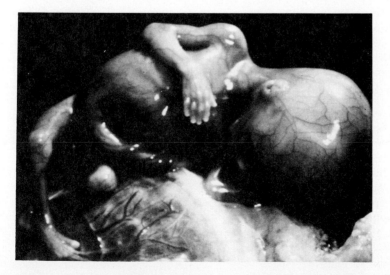

*Not too long ago, photographs of a fetus in utero were the stuff of science fiction. Perhaps surgery in utero to correct deformities will be possible—if not commonplace—in the near future.*

# AIDS AND MENTAL RETARDATION

The following information is part of an article that appeared in an issue of *News and Notes,* a quarterly newsletter of the American Association on Mental Retardation. It highlights the relationship of AIDS and mental retardation and the implications that relationship has for prevention and service delivery.

Although the impact of the AIDS epidemic has been felt widely throughout society, its significance to the provision of services to persons with mental retardation is an issue that has received little attention. But it likely that AIDS will alter the availability, content and financing of services for all persons with disabilities. In order to successfully meet these challenges, we must become educated about AIDS, and we must develop rational public policy that will serve the best interests of people with mental retardation and society at large.

The most important consideration in the provision of services to persons with mental retardation who are infected with HIV is related to transmission. Three routes of transmission remain the only ones demonstrated as clinically important. These are inoculation of blood by either transfusion or injection, sexual transmission, and perinatal transmission.

HIV infection in infants and children is a cause of mental retardation and disability. Central nervous system involvement occurs in 78% to 93% of children with symptomatic HIV infection. By August 1987, over 2,100 children in the United States were infected with AIDS or ARC. In the New York metropolitan area, HIV rivals Down syndrome as a cause of disability.

AIDS-related disabilities have placed a staggering burden on the service system in place to serve children with disabilities in New York. As the epidemic spread of HIV continues, this trend will be repeated throughout the nation. Thus, the need for additional early intervention programs, social services, and school-based programs is evident. However, HIV-infected children with disabilities must be served in the least restrictive environment. Recommendations that meet this goal have been developed by the American Academy of Pediatrics. The determination of whether a child with HIV should be allowed to attend school or day care should take into consideration the risk that the affected child in these settings might acquire infections (which are severe in immunocompromised children) and, conversely, the risk of possible HIV transmission to staff and other children.

The greatest difficulty presented in caring for persons with mental retardation who are infected with HIV lies in striking a balance between individuals' rights and the rights of the community at large. The use of ethical review committees has been proposed as a means of resolving this conflict. A multidisciplinary group representing medical, legal, ethical, administrative, staff, client, parent, and advocate perspectives could recommend policy and provide ethical consultation to parties involved in the care of clients. While the conduct of ethical review committees has potential difficulties, their benefit could be enormous.

The broad concerns and solutions discussed here are likely to have a profound impact on services for persons with mental retardation. While we are at the very beginning of the epidemic spread of HIV, we must develop policy that reflects our philosophical principles, current medical information, and the practical needs of serving people with disabilities. We must look past our individual fears and consider the reality of HIV transmission and the remote risk we undertake in providing services. Most importantly, we must exercise responsible leadership in deciding how we will meet these challenges.

From "AIDS and Mental Retardation" by T. Kastner, 1988, *News & Notes, 1*(4), pp. 2, 4. Reprinted by permission.

Prenatal techniques such as sonography, ultrasound, amniocentesis, and chorionic villus sampling (CVS) can effectively diagnose defects in a developing fetus. These techniques illustrate the innovations that are now available. It is possible to detect many (200 and 100, respectively) of the known genetic disorders through amniocentesis and CVS; however, this is far short of the 2,000 known genetic disorders. In all likelihood, technological advances will increase the number of conditions that can be identified prenatally. These techniques or others like them will probably also allow us to detect problems earlier and with minimum risk to the mother and fetus. This ability, in combination with the techniques described below, will greatly contribute to the prevention of mental retardation or the alleviation of its effects.

> This technology has significant ethical and sociopolitical implications as well.

If we have the instruments to detect prenatal problems today, then what options or techniques might we possibly have in the future? Currently, the typical options after detection are few—terminate the pregnancy or carry the fetus to term and deal with the defective infant. In the not-too-distant future is the possibility of embryonic medicine, where fetal surgery can be requested to redress certain deformities in utero. Pines (1973) describes another future possibility—prenatal programming of the developing brain.

Although the most highly developed of earthly creatures, *Homo sapiens* has the unenviable distinction of being the species with the longest period of vulnerability after birth. A neonate is quite helpless, and the probability of an infant's survival without assistance and protection is small. As we know, various birth traumas (such as anoxia and breech birth) can account for a number of conditions associated with mental retardation. Although traumatic birth episodes will always be with us, the frequency of these unfortunate events will decrease as medical techniques continue to be refined and developed.

With the continued sophistication of medical knowledge and service delivery, the science of screening newborns for metabolic deficiencies will continue to be perfected. Defects like PKU, hypoglycemia, galactosemia, and hypothyroidism, among others, can all be detected and treated early in an infant's life. What must be forestalled is the unacceptable paradox of researchers' developing the technology but not being able to apply it, for whatever (usually economic) reason.

As discussed in chapter 13, the issue of withholding treatment from severely handicapped infants has received and will continue to receive much attention. So far, the courts have supported parental sovereignty, but federal legislation may change this dramatically. The Critical Issues Subcommittee on Infant Concerns of The Association for Persons with Severe Handicaps (TASH, 1984) has issued recommendations:

1. Increase public and professional awareness of the issues pertaining to infanticide/euthanasia.

2. Support of legislation that prohibits the discrimination of medical treatment to infants who are also mentally retarded.
3. Support of federal, state, and local legislation and policies that increase services to families of infants who are severely handicapped.

As far as the prevention of mental retardation in the early childhood years is concerned, Smith and Smith (1978) emphasize the need to minimize environmental hazards, implement early stimulation projects, and reduce the incidence of accidents and child abuse. For instance, the evidence is mounting that nursing infants are at risk because breast milk can be contaminated by industrial chemicals (pesticides) that the mother has ingested (Elkington, 1985). Lead poisoning has not gone away either, as children are still being exposed to high levels of this toxic substance. Unacceptable lead levels are being found in such places as water catchment systems and drinking fountains in various areas of the country.

Systematic efforts to educate the public should be encouraged. The effectiveness of these programs must be evaluated, because the mere existence of educational programs does not by any means guarantee the acquisition of the needed information.

If technology and, more important, its application to the problems associated with mental retardation continue to blossom, then there is a real chance that the incidence of mental retardation due to biomedical causes *can* be reduced 50% by the year 2000. But this goal cannot be achieved without public support and encouragement.

*Psychosocial issues.*    Predictions about the psychosocial causes of retardation are more difficult to make because of the complexity of this concept. Socioeconomic status, poverty, race, environment, and culture have been related to retardation, but unfortunately, the questions they raise do not have simple solutions. It would be marvelous to eliminate poverty and to attenuate the problems faced by people in lower socioeconomic classes, but we must be realistic. Even though the PCMR's goal of reducing the incidence and prevalence of mental retardation to the lowest level possible in the next 10 years is admirable and even conceptually believable, we face many entrenched institutional obstacles. Let us consider a few of them.

First, regardless of our incontestable intention to eliminate poverty, this goal may be impossible. The perception of having eliminated poverty may indeed be achieved, but the reality of poverty will no doubt persist. In the 1976 Report to the President (PCMR, 1976a), the President's Committee cautioned that poverty should be viewed as a dual concept.

> The question of poverty is two-sided. *Absolute poverty* is officially measured in the United States as a fixed standard of real income based upon the prevailing cost of a minimum human diet. The percent of the population below this level has declined from 22.4 in 1959 to 11.9 in 1972. However, the proportionate distribution of incomes in American society has changed very little in that time,

with the lowest fifth of the population receiving a steady 4.5 to 5.5 percent of the aggregate income in each year in the United States from 1947 to 1972. This creates, the futurists suggest, a persistent condition of *relative poverty*. Projection of the continued decline of absolute poverty to near-zero could still leave the level of relative poverty unchanged. (pp. 42–43)(Emphasis added.)

Both dimensions of poverty pose continuing obstacles to the reduction of psychosocial causes of retardation in the future. Absolute poverty affects the ability of families to afford the necessities of life: housing, food, and adequate health care. Relative poverty affects one's status, often leading to "a chronic state of failure, dependency, defeat, hopelessness, helplessness, cultural impoverishment, under- and unemployment, and broken families" (Nanus, 1980, p. 75). Both kinds of poverty will continue to stand in the way of reducing psychosocial causes of retardation.

Many more persons are finding it more difficult to make it in today's world. A group of "new poor" is developing that has been described as "a much less homogeneous group that includes structurally unemployed persons, young people whose upward mobility opportunities have been closed off, the mentally ill, and the 'voluntary poor' " (*The Futurist,* 1986, p. 44). This group is best characterized as unemployed and homeless. They do not seem to use community resources to their advantage either through lack of knowledge or unwillingness. For those who have children, and their numbers are increasing, the conditions in which they live do not contribute to quality child-rearing. Whether some of these children are identified as mentally retarded some time during their school careers is secondary to the fact that many of them will display learning-related problems that school systems will have to deal with.

Our well established notions and attitudes toward the concept of cultural deprivation may need to be rethought. Frequently, little acknowledgment is given to the strengths of children who arrive daily at school from what is called a "deprived" environment. Barring the financial distinction between middle class and low socioeconomic status (SES), and the differences in educational opportunity that distinguish classes separated by income, there are few things intrinsically enriching about middle class culture that would, by contrast, render lower class environments "deprived." A child's use of nonstandard English, for example, need not spark the conclusion that the child's home life is substandard, for that language is a product of cultural factors not found in higher SES homes. The fact that most schools adhere to middle class mores and standards ensures that problems will arise if we insist that the student from a non-middle class background conform without question to this system. Ginsburg (1972) believes that children who are poor and who live in what we often refer to as "culturally deprived" environments actually have skills and strengths that are sufficient for adequate cognitive development, but that these skills and strengths are different from those of middle class children. The real tragedy may rest in the fact that "the language

# SOME THOUGHTS ABOUT HEALTH CARE

The following article which appeared in *The Futurist* in 1988, was based on data published by the Office of Technology Assessment, U.S. Congress. It highlights some of the critical issues facing the United States in providing adequate health care for those who lack financial resources.

### Investing in Children's Health

The high cost of poor health in infants and children suggests that even some expensive preventive strategies may be well worth their cost, according to a new report by the U.S. Congress Office of Technology Assessment.

For example, every low-birthweight birth averted by earlier or more-frequent prenatal care saves the U.S. health-care system $14,000–$30,000 in newborn hospitalization, rehospitalizations in the first year, and long-term health-care costs associated with low birthweight, OTA says. Nearly 7% of all U.S. newborns are low-birthweight babies (under 2,500 grams, or about 5 lbs., 8 oz.).

Low birthweight is one of the primary causes of infant mortality. Almost 40,000 babies (1% of all U.S. births) die in the first year of life each year. The United States ranks seventeenth among industrialized countries in infant mortality.

OTA identifies several other preventive strategies that the federal government might consider implementing to improve children's health:

☐ Encouraging the development of comprehensive school-based clinics for adolescents at high risk of unwanted pregnancy.
☐ Promoting effective newborn-screening programs. About 4,500 cases of detectable diseases causing death or mental retardation occur each year.
☐ Encouraging immunization and other preventive methods. Only 37% of U.S. infants were fully immunized against diphtheria, tetanus, and pertussis (whooping cough) in 1983.
☐ Encouraging the use of child safety restraints in automobiles.
☐ Encouraging the development of visiting-nurse programs in populations at high risk for low birthweight or child maltreatment.
☐ Improving poor children's access to physicians' care. From 1978 to 1984, the percentage of infants residing in poor families rose from 18% to 24%.

and intellectual skills that poor children do have are frequently ignored by the schools they attend" (Rappaport, 1977, p. 251)

None of what has been discussed above denies the importance of appropriate language development. Well designed early intervention programs that systematically develop language skills can help students do better in school. Preschool experiences seem to benefit all students. For this reason, many states are considering the implementation of publicly supported preschool classes for all students.

As standard of living improves, as more programs directed toward upgrading impoverished areas increase, as more efforts to provide early intervention to children at risk for school failure are established, and as our conception of cultural deprivation matures, opportunities to prevent cases of mental retardation due to psychosocial causes will undoubtedly increase. Generalized amelioration will occur only if there are *drastic* changes in our social structure, and such drastic changes are not likely.

P. L. 99-457 will also have an impact on prevention.

## TECHNOLOGICAL ADVANCES

Nowhere can we find more reason for optimism than in the application of technological advances to the area of mental retardation. Those of us in the field of special education may owe the Soviets more than we can imagine for launching Sputnik in the late 1950s, because this event sparked a technological renaissance that has been felt in every aspect of our lives. Many professional disciplines have joined together to influence divergent areas of special education. This multidisciplinary flavor is embodied in the interest in human exceptionalities shared by a great many physical and social scientists, engineers, and medical personnel. The engineering field, for instance, has contributed tremendous achievements that include prosthetic limbs, speech synthesizers, recording instruments, and computerized wheelchairs. The near future promises more biofeedback techniques, cosmetological devices, meals delivered through the mail, and a staggering array of computer-related services.

*New technologies.* Some examples of technological innovations that may have a positive impact on those who are mentally retarded are listed below.

☐ Interactive learning: Much education will take place at home through interactive technologies (interactive television, computers, videodiscs), thus reducing the need to go to a training setting.

☐ Computerized medical services: It will be possible to diagnose the prescribe treatment through telecommunication procedures.

☐ Electronic welfare machines: Machines like automated teller machines will be able to issue appropriate entitlements.

☐ Chemotherapy patches: Skin implants will be used to administer medicines at appropriate times; one pouch could hold a year's supply of medicine (Cain & Taber, 1987).

☐ Pharmacological intervention: New drugs will be available that can "heighten perception or increase learning speed" (Plog, 1980, p. 208).

☐ Assistive devices: Pocket-size telephones and beepers will be able, when connected to a transportation systems computer, to indicate when to get on or off a bus or subway (Plog, 1980).

These and other advances portend a positive future. This informational age, however, is not without its potential drawbacks. One is the possibility of isolation as telecommunications replace transportation as a requirement for work. As Linstone (1980) notes, "The substitution of communication for transportation might conceivably isolate the MR individual further rather than integrate him more fully into society" (p. 132). Another concern is the possible dehumanizing effects of a more technical, computerized society.

***Ethical concerns.***   The emerging technology appeals to us as a salve for many of the wounds of the day, but it also creates some ethical dilemmas.

> In science-based affairs, especially those of a biological kind like medicine, the hypothetical quickly becomes the actual. Future questions foreseen are suddenly present and pressing. The time lag is negligible between the theoretically possible and the clinically feasible. It is said that prophecy foreshortens time, that it treats what is to come as if it were a present fact. In this sense prophecy is a major part of biomedical ethics in these days. (Fletcher, 1974, p. xiv)

Obviously, one of the significant correlates to advancing technology is the ethical overlay with which we must concern ourselves. As Linstone (1977) states, "It has become increasingly apparent in the last several years that science and technology can no longer be considered 'neutral' " (p. 18). Issues like abortion, brain research, the withholding of treatment, the administration of controversial treatments (e.g., psychosurgery, chemotherapy), the use of aversive procedures (e.g., electroshock), euthanasia, organ transplantation from anencephalic infants, and experimentation on aborted fetuses can all be classified as "indeterminable issues" (Begelman, 1978). The rightness or wrongness of most of these is not readily apparent, and no consensus has been reached. Yet all these issues cause strong personal or professional sentiment. For instance, the use of an aversive device for treating serious behavior problems (the Self-Injurious Behavior Inhibiting System [SIBIS]) has precipitated strong professional resistance. Many professional groups in the field of mental retardation have testified against the use of this self-activating electroshock device for the following reasons: unknown long-term effects, safety considerations, its effectiveness in general, un-planned consequences, and the indignity of it (AAMR, 1988).

See chapter 13 for a discusion of individual rights

Whether or not these ethical issues are amenable to a single philosophical or legal solution, they must be taken seriously. We know all too well that the most vulnerable are invariably the least powerful to control what happens to them. Consequently, it is incumbent on us to ensure that some form of protection is provided for those who are mentally retarded through legal safeguards and standards of ethical practice. Without such protections, technology and science, no matter how beneficial, could go beyond their bounds.

## SERVICES

In recent times, services for individuals with mental retardation have had the guiding principle that *all* such persons are entitled to the same rights and privileges as those who are not retarded. Related to this is the notion that this group can learn and benefit from the services they receive. Whether most individuals are getting appropriate services is difficult to determine. Many are; others are not. Three overriding questions must be addressed in any future context: (*a*) Will persons with mental retardation receive necessary services? (*b*) How will they be delivered? (*c*) What will be the quality of these services?

*Infancy and early childhood.*   For children with retardation who are identified in infancy or early childhood, the enactment of P.L. 99-457 has a significant impact. These amendments to the Education for All Handicapped Children Act set the tone for service delivery to this group for the near future. Certain requirements, such as the individual family service plan (IFSP), should ensure that needed services are delivered to youngsters and their families in a more timely fashion. The concept and principles of transition must be applied to programs at this level. For instance, planning for the transition from infant programs to preschool programs will be necessary.

For many infants with severe complications, additional services will be provided as states respond to the incentives for serving this population. This is good news for the parents of these children, who have seen services come and go in the past according to the state of the economy. More parent support groups will also be established. These groups give parents opportunities to talk openly with each other about common problems and feelings.

Most children who are mildly retarded are not identified until they reach school age. Therefore, many students identified as at risk for being classified mentally retarded are served in early intervention programs. There are strong indications that these early efforts have positive outcomes on later performance (Lazar & Darlington, 1982; Rogers-Warren & Poulson, 1984). Although these programs seem to be effective, we do not know exactly which characteristics of them are responsible for the gains.

*School age.*   Services to students who are mentally retarded are shaped to some extent by trends in general education. Some dimensions of general education, extant or suggested, include:

- [ ] A "back to basics" movement
- [ ] An "excellence in education" movement
- [ ] A need to develop technologically literate students
- [ ] Fewer federal dollars
- [ ] More attention to the average student
- [ ] Concern for the alarming number of students who do not finish high school
- [ ] Competency testing requirements
- [ ] Concern for the individual needs of students. Cetron (1988) suggests that individual education programs will be developed for all students
- [ ] Extending the school day and the school year
- [ ] Reducing the size of classes

Many of these trends, one could argue, will have more of an effect on students with milder forms of retardation; but most will affect students with more severe involvement as well.

Students with severe and profound mental retardation will continue to receive services in self-contained settings for the foreseeable future. The field has made great strides in developing methodologies (e.g., community-based instruction) and curricula for this group. Concern for chronologically age-appropriate programming and the development of functional skills is extremely important. The *educability* of these individuals, however, remains a matter for controversy. Professionals have discussed whether some severely handicapped individuals have the right to an education or can even benefit from it (Kauffman & Krouse, 1981; Noonan, Brown, Mulligan, & Rettig, 1982). Debate over this issue is likely to persist, especially in times of limited financial resources.

In some noteworthy programs students with severe and profound retardation are integrated into the flow of their neighborhood schools on a frequent basis. Other programs that work to establish relationships between this group and students who are not retarded have also enjoyed much success.

The transition process is critical for students with severe or profound retardation, as their need for services is likely to last beyond the age of 21. Schools and adult service providers must link up early so that services are not interrupted. One group that is at a particular disadvantage in trying to locate appropriate services is those with severe and multiple handicaps. Adult service providers, especially those in the private sector, do not have the financial resources to meet the needs of this group. As a result, families are left without any real choices.

The situation is somewhat different for students with mild or moderate retardation. One factor that affects much of what we do with this group is the changes in it that have been noticed in recent years. If the observations of some (MacMillan & Borthwick, 1980; Polloway, Epstein, Patton, Cullinan, & Luebke, 1986) are correct, and students with mild retardation are now lower functioning than their predecessors of 10 years ago, then we may need to reexamine how best to serve this group.

Questions as to whether this "new" group of students with mild retardation can be mainstreamed (Polloway, 1984), can be merged with other compensatory education students (Leinhardt, Bickel, & Pallay, 1982; Reschly, 1987), or can be taught effectively in noncategorical settings become relevant. Additional questions come up about those students who are no longer classified as mildly mentally retarded.

Attention to adult outcomes and the lifelong needs of students who are mentally retarded must influence program planning. All areas of transition—employment and training, home and family, recreation and leisure, community participation, personal development, and health care (cf. Figure

*Programs like the Special Olympics help students who are retarded feel important and learn skills they can use in interacting with others.*

10.3)—must be addressed in the curricula of these students. And it will become even more important to examine which jobs in the future will be suited to those with retardation, particularly jobs in the service sector (Nanus, 1980).

Vocational training needs to be reevaluated. As the sophistication of the workplace increases, schools are no longer adequate to provide the training students need to operate the equipment that industry and business want them to learn to use. As Cain and Taber (1987) have indicated, the equipment that schools use to train students is usually obsolete by the time it is in place. A new partnership with business and industry is needed, and all parties will benefit. Students will learn how to use the latest technology, and businesses will ultimately get employees capable of using their equipment. The supported employment model will continue to be effective in this type of arrangement.

*Adulthood.* The complexities of everyday living necessitate that all of us look for help from time to time. This holds for those who are mentally retarded, too. It is essential that these individuals know how to use community resources for their own benefit. Another reality of today's society is that we must all be lifelong learners. Most people change jobs numerous times during their working careers, and such changes typically require some form of retraining. Adults who are retarded need to have access to services that assist them in the "passages" of adulthood as well. Cain and Taber (1987) state that rapid technological changes "will require that successful employees of the future be flexible, lifelong learners and that they be receptive to continuous change" (p. 64).

*Quality of services.*    Services, whether to children or to adults, do not alone ensure effective or high quality results. To guarantee the best return on our efforts we must strive for improvement in a number of areas. Hobbs's (1975) comments remain apropos.

> Services for all kinds of children remain a tangled thicket of conceptual confusions, competing authorities, contrary purposes, and professional rivalries, leading to the fragmentation of services and the lack of sustained attention to the needs of individual children and their families. (p. 282)

What seems to be needed is better coordination of services, answers to certain curricular questions (such as what should be taught and how it should be taught), evaluation on many fronts (teaching per se, materials, and methods), and improvements in the training of personnel. National authorities have examined the quality of education in general. If the quality of services is to be improved, then all professionals who interact with individuals who are mentally retarded must be prepared properly. For teachers, this means that teacher-training programs must be sensitive to the ever-changing demands placed upon both teacher and student. It also means that the typical inservice model must be drastically revised so as to provide the necessary information in the most efficacious manner. Competence must be demonstrated not only by teachers but also by community mental health workers, social workers, law enforcement personnel, juvenile officers, lawyers, judges, physicians, and anyone who can have a significant impact on the lives of individuals who are retarded.

## FAMILY SUPPORT

Family support means more than providing services to families (Turnbull, 1988). To have a member of the family who is mentally retarded taxes individuals within the family as well as the family as a unit. Families need certain services, but they also will benefit from the understanding and encouragement that others can provide.

It is critical for those of us in the field of mental retardation who work with families to realize that the family unit has changed. For example, the two-parent, intact family is becoming less common, and those who think that we will return to the days when it was the rule are misleading themselves. We are also forewarned to be sensitive to specific family values, attitudes, and unique situations. We must avoid judging families by our value systems, which may be different but not necessarily any more moral.

To assist many children who are mentally retarded we must understand that they are always part of some system. Typically, this system is the family—in whatever form it takes. A look at early intervention projects indicates that most definitely give attention to the inclusion of at least one parent. If we are to improve services to families in the future, then most assuredly we will have to involve the whole family and provide a number of services. Among these are counseling, respite care, informational resources, and active involvement of parents and families in the programming for their child with retardation. Hobbs (1975) refers to this active involvement aspect as "a new partnership among public agencies, professional people, and parents to achieve an optimal balance of shared, long-term responsibility for exceptional children" (p. 279).

Keniston and the Carnegie Council on Children (1977) have translated this need for services into family policy statements that remain appropriate today. Keniston and the Council use the term *public advocates* to mean those individuals whose efforts are directed toward improving conditions for children. Their policy statement offers goals that we should strive toward. The skeleton of this family policy is given below.

1. Public advocates should support jobs for parents and a decent living for all families.
2. Public advocates should support more flexible working conditions.
3. Public advocates should support an integrated network of family services.
4. Public advocates should support proper health care for children.
5. Public advocates should support improved legal protection for children outside their families. (pp. 216–220)

## AN AGENDA FOR THE FUTURE

### RESEARCH DIRECTIONS

Presaging future change, as we are attempting to do here, can be intriguing business. But we must be cautious, because we want to refrain from promising more than we can deliver; we must avoid grandiose claims like those made by many pioneers in this field in the first half of the 19th century—claims that later worked to the detriment of people with retardation.

Simply stated, there is and will continue to be a distinct need for continued research with, about, and for those who are mentally retarded in many areas, among them training and education, community living, and prevention. More important, we need new knowledge, developed by creative thinkers using both existing theories and new paradigms. Research, both basic and applied, should be encouraged, and systematic evaluation of its effectiveness and value should be undertaken. As Hobbs (1975) has pointed out, major policy decisions in the field of special education have historically been made without any verification. This is not a warning that should inhibit creative thinkers, but one that should spur them on.

One study that has attempted to identify the major research issues in the area of mild mental retardation provides some indication of issues that will

TABLE 15.4   Current Research Issues in Mild Retardation

| Issues |
| --- |
| Vocational and career education of students with mild retardation |
| Post-school adjustment of adults with mild retardation |
| Long-term effects of treatment programs |
| Implications of declassification for former EMR pupils |
| Generalization of intervention effects across settings |
| Early intervention |
| Assessment and training of cognitive skills |
| Programming for adolescents with mild retardation |
| Determining the least restrictive environment |
| Screening and identification of mildly handicapped pupils |
| Preparing and certifying teachers of students with mild retardation |
| Cross-categorical (or non-categorical) programming |
| Characteristics of "new EMRs" vs. the traditional EMR population |
| Assessment and training of social skills |
| Psychosocial causes of retardation |
| Management of classroom behavior problems |
| Assessment of adaptive behavior in students with mild retardation |
| Parent involvement |
| Intelligence testing of minority children |
| Effects of labeling |
| Genetic determinants of intelligence/retardation |

From "Current Research Issues in Mild Mental Retardation: A survey of the Field" by E. A. Polloway and M. H. Epstein, 1985, *Education and Training of the Mentally Retarded, 20,* p. 173. Reprinted by permission.

probably receive varying degrees of professional attention in the years ahead (Polloway & Epstein, 1985). These issues are presented in descending order of identified importance in Table 15.4.

As can be seen from examining Table 15.4, general concern centers on issues that pertain to programming, intervention efforts, and outcomes. The issues identified in the Polloway and Epstein study are relevant to a more capable group of individuals with mental retardation. For those who are less capable, important topics also include concern for programming and intervention. Key areas of adult living (employment, living arrangements, mobility, income maintenance, health coverage, personal development, and community involvement) discussed in chapter 11 are critical as well.

## FINAL THOUGHTS

We hope that the future will be characterized by improved conditions for all those who are handicapped. There is good reason to believe that influences such as advocacy groups, interest groups, and most important, social attitudes, will continue to shape the quantity and quality of programs and services for those who are mentally disabled.

Blatt (1987) has given us much to think about in his many writings. In his last major publication, *The Conquest of Mental Retardation,* he provided some thoughts that can help guide us as we prepare for the future.

> We will conquer mental retardation not only by better science, but by a better way of life. . . . Increasingly specialized knowledge about mental retardation will, in itself, do relatively little to ameliorate the problems faced by mentally retarded people. . . . In order to understand and respond to the voices of mentally retarded people, we must understand ourselves, our society, our institutions (in the broader sense), our values and our traditions. (p. 11)

We can influence the future in many ways by what we do or, at the very least, try to do today. We can no longer remain passive observers, but must become active participants in the problems and needs of persons who are mentally retarded. Our attention should focus not only on individuals with retardation but also on the public, because the key to the future rests there. Without positive public sentiment toward those who are mentally retarded, which must be nurtured by what happens today and reflected in financial support for our efforts, the outlook for this group is not favorable. Our highest priorities should be social acceptance of people who are mentally retarded, active participation on the behalf of all advocates, and the continued search for new knowledge.

# GLOSSARY

**Acquisition.** The initial development of a skill or chunk of knowledge.

**Adaptive behavior.** "Degree and efficiency with which the individual meets the standards of personal independence and social responsibility expected of his age and cultural group" (Grossman, 1983, p. 1).

**Advocacy.** The representation of the rights and interests of oneself or others in an effort to bring about change that will eliminate barriers to meeting identified needs.

**Amniocentesis.** Analysis of amniotic fluid during second trimester of pregnancy to allow for biochemical analysis of fetal cells; can indicate presence of genetic and chromosomal disorders and tell sex of fetus.

**Anoxia.** Lack of oxygen severe enough to cause tissue damage; can cause permanent brain damage and retardation.

**Antecedents.** Conditions or events that precede learning.

**Aptitute test.** Test, often standardized and norm-referenced, of an individual's relative abilities in a variety of fields.

**Assessment.** Collecting information on an individual for the purpose of making decisions about that person.

**At risk.** In danger of substantial developmental delay because of medical, biological, or environ- mental factors if early intervention services are not provided.

**Autosomes.** 22 matched pairs of chromosomes (44 out of normally present 46). *See* Sex chromosomes.

**Career education.** Education that prepares the individual for all the roles he or she will assume as an adult, including the roles of worker, citizen, and family member.

**Cerebral palsy.** Any neuromuscular disability resulting from damage to the brain at birth or during early years.

**Child-find.** Often the first step in the process of identifying children in need of services; generally involves a public awareness campaign.

**Chromosomes.** Threadlike bodies containing genes that occupy specific loci.

**Clinical judgment.** Judgment based on experience rather than measurement. Its use in determination of retardation puts burden of diagnosis on the individual examiner.

**Cognitive-developmental theory.** Proposed by Piaget. Suggests that each individual progresses through stages of development where specific cognitive skills are acquired through interaction with and adaptation to the environment and perception of that environment. Includes four ordered stages of development.

**Comprehensive workshop.** A sheltered workshop that includes transitional and extended services.

**Concrete operational stage.** Third stage in Piaget's cognitive-developmental theory, during which the child learns to classify and to solve concrete problems; lasts approximately from age 7 to age 11 in children who are not retarded.

**Consequences.** Something produced by a cause or set of conditions. If made contingent, consequences can facilitate learning.

**Construct validity.** The extent to which a test measures the factors that comprise the ability or skill the test purports to measure.

**Continuous reinforcement.** One-to-one correspondence between response and reinforcing consequence; best used to teach new responses.

**Criterion-referenced testing.** Measures a child's skill in terms of preestablished level of mastery in a given content area.

**Cultural-familial retardation.** General category for causes of cases of mental retardation where no organic defects are present.

**Deinstitutionalization.** Movement to decentralize large public institutions and move residents into smaller local centers and family settings, so as to provide the most natural and least restrictive environment in which handicapped persons can live and maximize their potential.

**Deletion.** In genetics, process where a portion of original genetic material is absent from a specific chromosomal pair.

**Development centers.** Sites for training in self-maintenance. These centers are exclusively nonvocational.

**Developmental delay.** A significant delay in one or more of the following areas of development: cognitive, speech/language, physical/motor, vision, hearing, psychosocial, and self-help skills.

**Developmental model.** Model suggesting that cognitive development of individuals who are retarded generally follows same sequence as that of individuals who are not, but at a slower rate.

**Developmental period.** "Time between conception and the 18th birthday" (Grossman, 1983, p. 11).

**Deviation IQ.** In contrast to ratio IQ concept, assumes IQ is normally distributed; distributes IQ on normal curve with 100 as average and a standard deviation that is the same for every age level.

**Difference/deficit model.** Model suggesting that cognitive development of individuals who are retarded is qualitatively different from that of individuals who are not retarded and therefore requires different teaching strategies.

**Dizygotic.** Describes twins who developed from two separate fertilized eggs.

**Dominant inheritance.** Inheritance in which an individual gene has control or can mask the other gene in the pair.

**Down syndrome.** A chromosomal anomaly that accounts for the largest percentage of cases of moderate and severe retardation. Generally accompanied by clinical manifestations like epicanthic folds, large tongue, broad flat bridge of nose, and poor muscle tone.

**Ecological inventory.** A process that involves the setting of educational goals on the basis of careful observations of the performance of a person who is not handicapped in real-world settings.

**Educationally subnormal.** Intellectually inadequate and in need of special academically oriented education.

**Etiology.** Cause or causes of a given condition.

**Executive control.** "The process one consciously goes through in order to analyze a problem, anticipate outcomes of various actions, decide how the problem should be solved and monitor progress toward the solution" (Campione, Brown, & Ferrara, 1982).

**Expectancy.** Anticipation of the result of a task or situation based on experiences in previous similar situations.

**Expectancy for failure.** Lower aspirations and goals in an effort to avoid additional failure; set by individuals who have accumulated failure experiences.

**Expressivity.** Capacity of a gene to affect the phenotype of an organism.

**Extended workshop.** A sheltered workshop that provides long-term employment for workers who cannot secure competitive employment in the community because of their handicap.

**Fading.** An antecedent approach used in teaching. The student responds to a cue or prompt that is gradually faded away.

**Feedback.** Information given to learner (or system) following a specific response.

**Formal operational stage.** Fourth stage in Piaget's cognitive-developmental theory, during which the child learns to think abstractly and reason by logic; begins around age 11 in children who are not retarded.

**Functional retardation.** Retardation maintained or worsened by institutional residents' living in stressful conditions; often includes engaging in self-stimulation.

**Gene.** Basic biological unit influencing the inheritance of traits.

**Genetics.** Study of heredity and variation.

**Genotype.** An inherited characteristic delineating a range in which a human trait develops.

**Grand mal.** The most severe type of epileptic seizure, in which the individual has violent convulsions, loses consciousness, and becomes rigid.

**Grouping of material.** Clustering information prior to presentation to facilitate memory and recall.

**Grouping of students.** Arranging students in the environment in such a way as to make it possible to work in the most effective, efficient manner.

**Handicapism.** "A set of assumptions and practices that promote differential and unequal treatment of people because of apparent or assumed physical, mental, or behavioral differences" (Bogdan & Biklen, 1977, p. 59).

**Heritability.** The proportion of total trait variance that is directly due to genetic, measurable factors.

**Heterozygous.** Describes pairs of genes carrying different traits.

**Homozygous.** Describes pairs of genes carrying the same trait.

**Hydrocephalus.** A disorder resulting from blockage of cerebrospinal fluid.

**Imitation.** Process of acquiring behavior through observation; can be both intentional and unintentional.

**Incidence.** The number of new cases of a condition identified within a population over a specific period of time.

**Incidental learning.** Learning that takes place outside a formal, structured learning environment.

**Individualized education program (IEP).** A document required by federal law detailing the year's plan for every child who is handicapped.

**Innate.** Inherent; used of abnormal chromosome arrangements present from conception but most often not the product of hereditary exchange.

**Input organization.** Organization and storage of information so it can be recalled when needed.

**Intelligence.** Ability to adapt, achieve, solve problems, interpret incoming stimuli to modify behavior, accumulate knowledge, or respond to items on an intelligence test; cannot be measured directly.

**Intelligence quotient (IQ).** Mental age divided by chronological age and multiplied by 100; gives an index of intellectual performance relative to others in the same age group.

**Interest inventory.** Test, usually not standardized or norm-referenced, of an individual's expressed interest in a variety of fields; may be in checklist or other informal format.

**Interindividual.** Said of comparison of one individual to other individuals.

**Intermittent reinforcement.** Reinforcement delivered after some, but not all, occasions of a behavior; best used to teach a student to maintain an acquired response.

**Intraindividual.** Said when comparing strengths and weaknesses of one individual.

**Itinerant teacher.** Special educator who provides the regular education teacher with consultation and some instructional services on a limited basis and gives support to the regular education teacher, who has the major responsibility for the child's educational program.

**Judgment-based assessment.** Appraisal according to a scale or checklist constructed by the examiner in order" to measure abilities not typically identified by standardized instruments.

**Karyotypes.** Graphic chromosomal pictures.

**Learned helplessness.** A pattern of submissiveness that develops in individuals when they discover that their actions are of no consequence and that outcomes are beyond their control.

**Learning.** Process whereby practice or experience results in a change in behavior not due to maturation, growth, or aging; cannot be directly measured or observed.

**Locus of control.** Where one perceives consequences of one's own behavior to originate. Can be either *internal* (resulting from one's own behavior) or *external* (resulting from outside forces).

**Long-term memory.** Ability to retrieve information from storage after a few days to months.

**Maintenance.** Ability needed to retain skills or knowledge over time.

**Mastery learning.** Technique of presenting material to a student at whatever rate the student can learn it satisfactorily.

**Mediation.** A verbal learning process whereby an individual connects a stimulus and a response.

**Meiosis.** Division and pairing of gametes to form the genetic foundation for an embryo.

**Memory.** Ability to retrieve stored information.

**Mental age.** A measure of intellectual level (as performance on a mental measurement test) recorded independently of chronological age.

**Mental retardation.** "Significantly subaverage general intellectual functioning resulting in or associated with concurrent impairments in adaptive behavior and manifested during the developmental period" (Grossman, 1983, p. 11).

**Metacognition.** *See* Executive Control.

**Mildly retarded.** Small deviation below the normal range of intelligence and adaptive behavior. Individuals who are mildly retarded can usually benefit from academic instruction and are often referred to as "educable" mentally retarded.

**Modeling.** An approach to teaching where the teacher demonstrates part or all of the behavior to

be learned and the student repeats the action immediately.

**Moderately retarded.** Functioning below mildly retarded. Individuals with this condition are usually identified at birth or shortly thereafter. Referred to as "trainable" mentally retarded. Program for these persons places emphasis on self-help and basic survival skills, along with appropriate academic and vocational training.

**Monozygotic.** Describes twins who developed from the split of a single fertilized egg.

**Mosaicism.** Uneven division of cells in mitosis, resulting in unequal or extra chromosomes.

**Myelomeningocele.** Condition characterized by a saclike mass on the spinal cord containing membrane tissue of the central nervous system.

**Nondisjunction.** Failure of one pair of chromosomes to split correctly, resulting in a trisomy. Produces such conditions as Down syndrome (Trisomy 21).

**Observational learning.** Learning from watching demonstrations by others.

**Ombudsman.** One whose role is to protect the rights of individuals seeking services from government agencies.

**Operant conditioning.** Systematic arrangement of environmental events and consequences so as to result in changes in behavior.

**Outerdirectedness.** Looking to others for guidance or cues in developing appropriate responses in demand situations.

**Penetrance.** Proportion of individuals within a particular population who possess a given gene and exhibit its genetic trait.

**Performance.** Observable behavior; can be basis for determining whether learning has occurred.

**Petit mal.** Epileptic seizure in which the individual loses consciousness, usually for less than half a minute; may occur very frequently in some children.

**Phenotype.** Trait that develops as a result of interaction between the inherited trait (genotype) and the environment.

**Phenylketonuria (PKU).** An inherited metabolic disease that can cause severe retardation; can now be detected at birth. Its detrimental effects can be prevented by a special diet.

**P.L. 94-142.** The Education for All Handicapped Children Act of 1975. This law provides free appropriate public education in the least restrictive environment to all children aged 3–21 who are handicapped.

**P.L. 99-457.** Law extending the rights and privileges afforded children who are handicapped under P.L. 94-142 to children between birth and 5 years.

**Polygenetic inheritance.** Inheritance in which more than one gene pair affects the appearance of a particular trait.

**Predictive validity.** Extent to which test performance predicts some other behavior.

**Preoperational stage.** Second stage in Piaget's cognitive-developmental theory, during which the child begins to use symbols and to imitate actions of others; lasts from approximately age 2 to age 7 in children without retardation.

**Prevalence.** Total number of cases of a disorder existing within a population at a particular place or at a particular time.

**Profoundly retarded.** Functioning at the lowest level of retardation and demonstrating retarded development in all areas, along with little communication or interaction with the environment. People who are profoundly retarded are heavily dependent on others to meet their basic physical needs.

**Prompts.** Stimuli presented together with a task in order to increase probability of eliciting a correct response.

**Prostheses.** Devices used to reduce or eliminate a specific handicap (e.g., artificial limbs, glasses, hearing aids).

**Pseudo-speciation.** The placing of certain human beings in a separate species on the basis of group characteristics such as race or handicap.

**Psychometric.** Describes a test that purports to measure intelligence or mental ability.

**Ratio IQ.** Index of a child's test performance relative to others in the same age group. Absolute

difference between MA and CA has a diminishing influence on IQ as the child gets older.

**Recessive inheritance.** Inherited traits that do not express themselves when paired with dominant genes and are influential only when matched with another identical recessive gene.

**Regular class program.** In special education, system where the student is in the regular education program but receives support through modification of regular and special education materials.

**Regular education initiative.** A proposal advanced by the federal government that recommends fundamental changes in the ways in which students with mild learning handicaps are educated.

**Reliability.** Extent to which a test yields the same or similar results upon repeated administrations.

**Resource room.** In special education, a secondary classroom where children in regular education classrooms receive extra help for areas of greatest need.

**Response chaining.** A technique whereby an activity is task analyzed and each unit taught in sequential fashion.

**Screening.** Processes used routinely with children to help find strengths and weaknesses and to identify individuals in need of more complete diagnostic study.

**Selective attention.** Focusing on particular dimensions of a learning task.

**Self-contained special class.** Special separate class for children who are handicapped; generally used when it is felt that the individual will not benefit from any regular education class instruction or activities.

**Sensorimotor stage.** First stage in Piaget's cognitive-developmental theory, during which the child makes purely physical responses to the environment; lasts from birth to approximately age 2 in children who are not retarded.

**Severely retarded.** Functioning at a level between moderately and profoundly retarded. Persons in this category show a high incidence of other handicaps, though they can generally communicate and can interact with the environment to some extent. People who are severely retarded generally do not benefit from academic training, but can learn self-help and communication skills.

**Sex chromosomes.** The pair of chromosomes that determines the sex of an individual. *See* Autosomes.

**Shaping.** Use of positive reinforcement for gradual improvement in behavior.

**Sheltered workshop.** A structured environment where individuals can learn work habits, receive training, and find salaried employment either within the workshop or in the community.

**Short-term memory.** Ability to retrieve information from storage for a period between a few seconds and a few hours.

**Social learning theory.** Theory that suggests that individuals interacting with the environment will exhibit either approach or avoidance behavior, depending on the expectancy of and value attached to the reinforcement or goals.

**Special day school.** Special school for students who are more severely disabled and who cannot function in the regular school environment.

**Special residential school.** Generally considered the most restrictive educational placement; usually considered only for students who are most severely handicapped and require 24-hour care.

**Standard deviation.** Unit used to measure the amount by which a particular score varies from the mean with respect to all the scores in a norm sample.

**Standard error of measurement.** A reliability measure; indicates the amount by which a subject's actual score is likely to differ from his true score (i.e., the score he or she would get if the test had no margin of error).

**Standardized test.** Any test, usually norm-referenced, that has been given to a large number of subjects and for which standard procedures for administration, scoring, and interpretation are published; standard procedures must be followed for results to be valid.

**Subaverage intellectual functioning.** "An IQ of 70 or below on standardized measures of intelligence. This upper limit is intended as a guideline; it could be extended through 75 or more, depending on the reliability of the test used" (Grossman, 1983, p. 11).

**Supported employment.** A model in which ongoing assistance is given persons with severe disabilities in order to facilitate employment and job retention.

**Syndrome.** A group of characteristics associated with a specific clinical disorder.

**Systematic instruction.** A well defined, replicable teaching process.

**Task analysis.** Breakdown of a large skill into its behavioral components.

**Teratogens.** Substances that can negatively affect pre- and postnatal development.

**Threshold variable.** Minimum requisite level of environmental stimulation required for normal development; not yet defined adequately (see Jensen, 1973).

**Toxemia.** Condition resulting from toxic substances in the blood; in pregnant women, can result in problems in the fetus.

**Toxoplasmosis.** A condition of poisonous blood.

**Transfer.** Ability to apply previously acquired knowledge to new tasks or problems.

**Transition.** A carefully planned process that helps a student achieve employment upon graduation.

**Transition programs.** Programs designed to identify appropriate intervention and provide training to facilitate the transition from school to life after school.

**Transitional workshop.** A sheltered workshop that concentrates on development of vocational skills so that the workers can eventually gain employment in the community.

**Translocation.** Exchange of a fragment of chromosomal material with incorrect chromosomal group. Can result in Down syndrome.

**Unitization.** Attempt to improve large institutions by breaking them into generally self-sufficient "units" with specific goals, responsibilities, and permanent staffing.

**Validity.** Extent to which a test measures what it purports to measure.

**Vocational education.** Education that prepares the individual for a specific trade or job or group of trades or jobs.

**Work activity centers.** Places that provide some work training but also train presumed prerequisites to work like grooming, home living, socialization, and academics.

**Work-study programs.** Programs developed to maximize a student's potential future employment through a combination of on-the-job experience and classroom instruction.

# REFERENCES

Abramowicz, H. K., & Richardson, S. (1975). Epidemiology of severe mental retardation in children: Community studies. *American Journal of Mental Deficiency, 80,* 18–39.

Abramson, P., Gravink, M., Abramson, L., & Sommers, D. (1977). Early diagnosis and intervention of retardation: A survey of parental reactions concerning the quality of services rendered. *Mental Retardation, 15*(3), 28–31.

Abroms, K. K., & Bennett, J. W. (1980). Current genetic and demographic findings in Down's syndrome: How are they presented in college textbooks on exceptionality? *Mental Retardation, 18,* 101–107.

Adams, G. L. (1984). *Normative adaptive behavior checklist.* Columbus, OH: Merrill.

Adelman, M. W. (1987). *Families in peril: An agenda for social change.* Cambridge: Harvard University Press.

Adelson, M. (1980). Mental retardation: Toward a different kind of future. In S. C. Plog & M. B. Santamour (Ed.), *The year 2000 and mental retardation* (pp.155–177). New York: Plenum Press.

Adubato, A., Adams, M. K., & Budd, S. (1981). Teaching a parent to train a spouse in child management techniques. *Journal of Applied Behavior Analysis, 14,* 193–205.

Algozzine, B., & Ysseldyke, J. E. (1981). Special education services for normal children: Better safe than sorry? *Exceptional Children, 48,* 238–243.

Allen, K. A. (1978). Early intervention for young severely and profoundly handicapped children: The preschool imperative. *AAESPH Review, 3,* 30–41.

Al-Mateen, M., Philippart, M., & Shields, W. D. (1986). Rett syndrome: A commonly overlooked progressive encephalopathy in girls. *American Journal of Diseases of Children, 140,* 761–765.

Altman, R., & Talkington, L. W. (1971). Modeling: An alternative behavior modification approach for retardates. *Mental Retardation, 9*(3), 20–23.

Amante, D., Van Houten, V. W., Grieve, J. H., Bader, C. A., & Margules, J. H. (1977). Neuropsychological deficit, ethnicity, and socioeconomic status. *Journal of Consulting & Clinical Psychology, 45,* 524–535.

Amara R. (1988). Health care tomorrow. *The Futurist, 22*(6), 16–20.

American Association on Mental Deficiency. (1975). *Position papers of the AAMD.* Washington, DC: Author.

American Association on Mental Retardation. (1988). *News and notes,* 1 (4).

American Educational Research Association, American Psychological Association, & National Council on Measurement in Education. (1985). *Standards for educational and psychological testing.* Washington, DC: American Psychological Association.

American Psychiatric Association. (1980). *Diagnostic and statistical manual of mental disorders.* (3rd ed.). Washington, DC: Author.

American Psychiatric Association. (1987). *Diagnostic and statistical manual of mental disorders* (3rd ed., rev.). Washington, DC: Author.

Anastasi, A. (1972). Four hypotheses with a dearth of data: Response to Lehrke's "A theory of X-linkage of major intellectual traits." *American Journal of Mental Deficiency, 76,* 620–622.

Anastasi, A. (1982). *Psychological testing.* (5th ed.). New York: Macmillan.

Anastasi, A. (1988). *Psychological testing* (6th ed.). New York: Macmillan.

Anderson, K. A. (1971). The "shopping" behavior of parents of mentally retarded children: The professional person's role. *Mental Retardation, 9*(4), 3–5.

Anderson, L., Dancis, J., & Alpert, M. (1978). Behavioral contingencies and self-mutilation in Lesch-Nyhan disease. *Journal of Consulting & Clinical Psychology, 46,* 529–536.

Angney, A., & Hanley, E. M. (1979). A parent-implemented shaping procedure to develop independent walking of a Down's syndrome child: A case study. *Education & Treatment of Children, 2,* 311–315.

Apffel, J. A., Kelleher, J., Lilly, M. S., & Richardson, R. (1975). Developmental reading for moderately retarded children. *Education & Training of the Mentally Retarded, 10,* 229–235.

Apgar, V. (1953). A proposal for a new method of evaluation of the newborn infant. *Current Researches in Anesthesia and Analgesia, 32,* 260–264.

*Armstrong v. Kline,* 476 F. Supp. 583 (1979).

Arthur, G. (1950). The Arthur Adaptation of the Leiter International Performance Scale. Chicago: C. H. Stoelting.

Azrin, N. H., & Foxx, R. M. (1971). A rapid method of toilet training the institutionalized retarded. *Journal of Applied Behavior Analysis, 4,* 89–99.

Baer, D. (1981). The nature of intervention research. In R. Schiefelbusch & D. Bricker (Eds.), *Early language: Acquisition and intervention.* Baltimore: University Park Press.

Bailey, D., Jr., & Wolery, M. (1984). *Teaching infants and preschoolers with handicaps.* Columbus, OH: Merrill.

Baines, R. A. (1980). Unequal protection for the retarded? *Amicus, 4,* 128–132.

Bajema, C. J. (1971). The genetic implications of population control. *Bio-Science, 21,* 71–75.

Baker, A. M. (1979). Cognitive functioning of psychotic children: A reappraisal. *Exceptional Children, 45,* 344–348.

Baker, B. L., Seltzer, G. B., & Seltzer, M. M. (1977). *As close as possible: Community residences for retarded adults.* Boston: Little, Brown.

Balkany, T. J., Downs, M. P., Jafek, B. W., & Krajicek, H. J. (1979). Hearing loss in Down's syndrome: A treatable handicap more common than generally recognized. *Clinical Pediatrics, 18,* 116–118.

Balla, D. A. (1976). Relationship of institution size to quality of care: A review of the literature. *American Journal of Mental Deficiency, 81,* 117–124.

Balla, D. A., & Zigler, E. (1979). Personality development in retarded persons. In N. R. Ellis (Ed.), *Handbook of mental deficiency: Psychological theory and research* (2nd ed., pp. 154–168). Hillsdale, NJ: Lawrence Erlbaum Associates.

Ballard, J. (1976). Active federal education laws for exceptional persons. In F. J. Weintraub, A. Abeson, J. Ballard, & M. LaVor (Eds.), *Public policy and the education of exceptional children.* Reston, VA: Council for Exceptional Children.

Ballard, J., Ramirez, B., & Zantal-Weiner, K. (1987). *Public law 94-142, section 504, and public law 99-457: Understanding what they are and are not.* Reston, VA: Council for Exceptional Children.

Baltes, P. B., & Brim, O. G., Jr. (1979). *Life-span development and behavior* (Vol. 2). New York: Academic Press.

Balthazar, E. E. (1971). *Balthazar scales of adaptive behavior, part one: Handbook for the professional supervisor.* Champaign, IL: Research Press.

Balthazar, E. E. (1973). *Balthazar scales of adaptive behavior, part two: Scales of social adaptation.* Palo Alto, CA: Consulting Psychologists Press.

Balthazar, E. E., & Stevens, H. A. (1975). *The emotionally disturbed, mentally retarded: A historical and contemporary perspective.* Englewood Cliffs, NJ: Prentice-Hall.

Bandura, A. (1969). *Principles of behavior modification.* New York: Holt, Rinehart, & Winston.

Barlow, C. F. (1978). *Mental retardation and related disorders.* Philadelphia: F. A. Davis.

Barnett, W. S. (1988). The economics of preschool special education under public law 99-457. *Topics in Early Childhood Special Education, 8,* 12–13.

Baroff, G. S. (1974). *Mental retardation: Nature, cause, and management.* New York: John Wiley.

Baroff, G. S., & Tate, B. G. (1967). Training the mentally retarded in the production of complex production: A demonstration of work potential. *Exceptional Children, 33,* 405–408.

Barton, E. S., Guess, D., Garcia, G., & Baer, D. (1970). Improvement on retardates' mealtime behaviors by time-out procedures using multiple baseline techniques. *Journal of Applied Behavior Analysis, 33,* 77–84.

Bateman, B. (1986). Equal protection for the handicapped. *Special Education Today* 14.

Baumeister, A. A., & Forehand, R. (1972). Effects of contingent shock and verbal command on body rocking of retardates. *Journal of Clinical Psychology, 28,* 586–587.

Baumeister, A. A., & Hamlett, C. L. (1986). A national survey of state-sponsored programs to prevent fetal alcohol syndrome. *Mental Retardation, 24,* 169–173.

Baumeister, A. A., & Muma, J. (1975). On defining mental retardation. *Journal of Special Education, 9,* 293–306.

Bayley, N. (1969). *Manual for the Bayley scales of infant development.* New York: Psychological Corporation.

Beasley, C. R. (1982). Effects of a jogging program on cardiovascular fitness and work performance of mentally retarded adults. *American Journal of Mental Deficiency, 86,* 609–613.

Beck, E. (1979, September). Brave new world of intelligence testing. *Psychology Today,* 27–41.

Beck, J. (1972). Spina bifida and hydrocephalus. In V. Apgar & J. Beck, *Is my baby all right?* New York: Simon & Schuster.

Becker, R. L. (1975). *Reading free vocational interest inventory.* Washington, DC: American Association on Mental Deficiency.

Becker, W. C. (1977). Teaching reading and language to the disadvantaged—What have we learned from field research? *Harvard Educational Review, 47,* 518–543.

Becker, W. C., & Carnine, D. W. (1980). Direct instruction: An effective approach to educational intervention with the disadvantaged and low performers. In B. B. Lahey & A. E. Kazdin (Eds.), *Advances in Clinical Child Psychology* (Vol. 3, pp. 429–469). New York: Plenum.

Becker, W. C., Engelmann, S., & Thomas, D. R. (1971). *Teaching: A course in applied psychology.* Chicago: Science Research Associates.

Beckman, P. J. (1983). Influence of selected child characteristics on stress in families of handicapped infants. *American Journal of Mental Deficiency, 88,* 150–156.

Beckman-Brindley, S., & Snell, M. E. (1984). *Family perspectives on parent participation in educational and behavioral programs.* Unpublished manuscript, University of Virginia.

Beevy, J. (1978, October). *Applications of biomedical and related technologies to instructional issues in the education of the severely and profoundly handicapped student.* Paper presented at the Fifth Annual Conference of the Severely/Profoundly Handicapped, Baltimore.

Begab, M. J. (1969). Casework for the mentally retarded—Casework with parents. In W. Wolfensberger & R. A. Kurtz (Eds.), *Management of the family of the mentally retarded.* New York: Follett.

Begab, M. J. (1973). The major dilemma of mental retardation: Shall we prevent it? Some social implications of research in mental retardation. *American Journal of Mental Deficiency, 78,* 519–529.

Begab, M. J. (1981). Issues in the prevention of psychosocial retardation. In M. J. Begab, H. C. Haywood, & H. L. Garber (Eds.), *Psychosocial Influences in Retarded Performance: Issues and Theories in Development* (pp. 3–28). Baltimore: University Park Press.

Begelman, D. A. (1978). Ethical issues for the developmentally disabled. In M. S. Berkler, G. H. Bible, S. M. Boles, D. E. Deitz, & A. C. Repp (Eds.), *Current trends for the developmentally Disabled.* Baltimore: University Park Press.

Beier, D. C. (1964). Behavioral disturbances in the mentally retarded. In H. A. Stevens & R. Heber (Eds.), *Mental retardation: A review of research.* Chicago: University of Chicago Press.

Bellak, L., & Bellak, S. S. (1974). *Children's apperception test.* Larchmont, N.Y.: C.P.S.

Bellamy, G. T., & Horner, R. H. (1987). Beyond high school: Residential and employment options after graduation. In M. E. Snell (Ed.), *Systematic instruction of persons with severe handicaps* (3rd ed., pp. 491–520). Columbus, OH: Merrill.

Bellamy, G. T., Horner, R. H., & Inman, D. P. (1979). *Vocational habilitation of severely retarded adults—A direct service technology.* Baltimore: University Park Press.

Bellamy, G. T., Rhodes, L. E., Mank, D. M., & Albin, J. M. (1988). *Supported employment: A community implementation guide.* Baltimore: Paul H. Brookes.

Bellamy, G. T., Sowers, J., & Bourbeau, P. E. (1983). Work and work-related services: Postschool options. In M. E. Snell (Ed.), *Systematic instruction of the moderately and severely handicapped* (2nd ed., pp. 300–334). Columbus, OH: Merrill.

Bellamy, T. (1985). Severe disability in adulthood. *Newsletter of The Association for Persons with Severe Handicaps, 11,* 6.

Belmont, J. M. (1966). Long-term memory in mental retardation. *International Review of Research in Mental Retardation, 1.*

Belmont, J. M. (1971). Medical-behavioral research in mental retardation. *International Review of Research in Mental Retardation, 5.*

Belmont, J. M., & Butterfield, E. C. (1971). Learning strategies as determinants of memory deficiencies. *Cognitive Psychology, 2,* 411–420.

Belmont, J. M., & Butterfield, E. C. (1977). The instructional approach to developmental cognitive research. In R. V. Kail & J. W. Hagen (Eds.), *Perspectives on the development of memory and cognition.* Hillsdale, NJ: Lawrence Erlbaum.

Bender, B., Fry, E., Pennington, B., Puck, M., Salonblatt, J., & Robinson, S. (1983). Speech and language development in 41 children with sex chromosome anomalies. *Pediatrics, 71,* 262–266.

Bennett, W. J. (1986). *What works: Research about teaching and learning.* Washington, DC: U.S. Government Printing Office.

Benton, A. L. (1964). Psychological evaluation and differential diagnosis. In H. A. Stevens & R. Heber (Eds.), *Mental retardation: A review of research.* Chicago: University of Chicago Press.

Bereiter, C., & Engelmann, S. (1966). *Teaching disadvantaged children in the preschool.* Englewood Cliffs, NJ: Prentice-Hall.

Berg, C., & Emanuel, I. (1987). Relationship of prenatal care to the prevention of mental retardation and other problems of pregnancy outcome. In *Developmental handicaps: Prevention and treatment* (pp. 45–70).

Berger, M., & Foster, M. (1982). A family systems perspective on working with families of young handicapped children. *Journal of the Division of Early Childhood, 1*(1), 17–23.

Bernstein, B. A. (1961). Social class and linguistic development: A theory of social learning. In H. A. Halsey, J. Floud, & C. A. Anderson (Eds.),

*Education, economy, and society.* New York: Free Press.

Bernstein, B. A. (1970). Sociolinguistic approaches to socialization: With some reference to educability. In F. Williams (Ed.), *Language and poverty* (pp. 25–61). Chicago: Markham.

Bienenstok, T., & Coxe, W. (1956). *Census of severely retarded children in New York state.* Albany: Interdepartmental Health Resources Board.

Bijou, S. W. (1983). The prevention of mild and moderate retarded development. In F. J. Menolascino, R. Neman, & J. A. Stark (Eds.), *Curative aspects of mental retardation: Biomedical and behavioral advances* (pp. 223–241). Baltimore: Paul H. Brookes.

Biklen, D. (1977a). Myths, mistreatment, and pitfalls: Mental retardation and criminal justice. *Mental Retardation, 15*(4), 51–57.

Biklen, D. (1977b). The politics of the institution. In B. Blatt, D. Biklen, & R. Bogdan (Eds.), *An alternative textbook in special education.* Denver: Love Publishing.

Binet, A., & Simon, T. (1961). The development of intelligence in children. Training School Bulletin, No. 11, 1961. (Reprinted in J. J. Jenkins & D. G. Paterson [Eds.], *Studies in individual differences.* New York: Prentice-Hall. Originally published 1916).

Bishop, J. E. (1982, January 29). Gene defect linked to retarded males: May solve mysteries. *Wall Street Journal.*

Blacher, J. (1984). Sequential stages of parental adjustment to the birth of a child with handicaps: Facts or artifact? *American Journal of Mental Deficiency, 2,* 55–68.

Blackhurst, A. E., & Berdine, W. H. (1981). *An introduction to special education.* Boston: Little, Brown.

Blackhurst, A. E., Doty, L., Geiger, W. L., Lauritzen, P., Lloyd, S., & Smith, P. D. (1987). *National directory of special education personnel preparation programs.* Washington, DC: National Information Center for Children and Youth with Handicaps.

Blackman, H. P. (1989). Special education place-ment: Is it what you know or where you live? *Exceptional Children, 55,* 459–462.

Blatt, B. (1987). *The conquest of mental retardation.* Austin: PRO-ED.

Blatt, B., & Kaplan, F. (1966). *Christmas in purgatory.* Boston: Allyn & Bacon.

Bleck, E. E., & Nagel, D. A. (Eds.). (1975). *Physically handicapped children: A medical atlas for teachers.* New York: Grune & Stratton.

Bleecker, S. E. (1987). Rethinking how we work: The office of the future. *The Futurist, 21*(4), 15–19.

Blunden, S. (1988). Programmatic features of quality services. In M. P. Janicki, M. W. Krauss, & M. M. Seltzer (Eds.), *Community residences for persons with developmental disabilities: Here to stay* (pp. 117–122). Baltimore: Paul H. Brookes.

*Board of Education of the Hendrick Hudson Central School District v. Rowley,* 458 U.S. 176 (1982).

Board for Rights of the Disabled (BRD). (1987). *1987–1989 report on developmental disabilities.* Richmond, VA: Author.

Bogdan, R. (1980). What does it mean when a person says, "I am not retarded"? *Education & Training of the Mentally Retarded, 15*(1), 74–79.

Boggs, E. M. (1988). The changing role of the federal government. In M. D. Powers (Ed.), *Expanding systems of service delivery for persons with developmental disabilities* (pp. 289–316). Baltimore: Paul H. Brookes.

Borkowski, J. G., Peck, V. A., & Damberg, P. R. (1983). Attention, memory, and cognition. In J. L. Matson & J. A. Mulich (Eds.), *Handbook of mental retardation* (pp. 479–497). New York: Pergamon.

Bourestrom, N. C. (1973). *Relocation report no. 3: Preparation for relocation.* Ann Arbor: Institute of Gerontology, University of Michigan and Wayne State University.

Bowe, F. (1978). *Handicapping America: Barriers to disabled people.* New York: Harper & Row.

Bower, A. C. (1978). Learning. In J. P. Das & D. Baine (Eds.), *Mental retardation for special educators.* Springfield, IL: Charles C Thomas.

Boyd, R. D. (1979). Systematic parent training through a home based model. *Exceptional Children, 45,* 647–648.

Bracken, B. A. (1987). Limitations of preschool instruments and standards for minimal levels of technical adequacy. *Journal of Psychoeducational Assessment, 4,* 313–326.

Braddock, D., Hemp, R., & Fujiura, G. (1987). National study of public spending for mental retardation and developmental disabilities. *American Journal of Mental Deficiency, 92,* 121–133.

Brady, P. M., Manni, J. L., & Winikur, D. W. (1983). Implications of ethnic disproportion in programs for the educable mentally retarded. *Journal of Special Education, 17,* 295–302.

Branlinger, E. (1985). Mildly mentally retarded secondary students' information about and attitudes toward sexuality and sex education. *Education & Training of the Mentally Retarded, 20,* 99–108.

Branlinger, E. (1988). Teachers' perception of the sexuality of their secondary students with mild mental retardation. *Education & Training in Mental Retardation, 23,* 24–37.

Brantley, D. (1988). *Understanding mental retardation: A guide for social workers.* Springfield, IL: Charles C Thomas.

Bregman, S. (1984). Assertiveness training for mentally retarded adults. *Mental Retardation, 22,* 12–16.

Bricker, D. D. (1978). A rationale for the integration of handicapped and nonhandicapped preschool children. In M. J. Guaralnick (Ed.), *Early intervention and the integration of handicapped and nonhandicapped children.* Baltimore: University Park Press.

Bricker, D. D. (1986). An analysis of early intervention programs: Attendant issues and future directions. In R. J. Morris & B. Blatt (Eds.), *Special education: Research and trends* (pp. 28–65). New York: Pergamon.

Bricker, D. D., & Dow, M. G. (1980). Early intervention with the young severely handicapped child. *Journal of The Association for the Severely Handicapped, 5,* 130–142.

Bricker, W. A., & Bricker, D. D. (1976). The infant, toddler, and preschool research and intervention project. In T. D. Tjossein (Ed.), *Intervention strategies for high risk infants and young children.* Baltimore: University Park Press.

Brinker, R. P., & Thorpe, M. E. (1984). Integration of severely handicapped students and the proportion of IEP objectives achieved. *Exceptional Children, 51,* 168–175.

Bristol, M., & Gallagher, J. J. (1982). A family focus for intervention. In C. Ramsey & P. Trohanis (Eds.), *Finding and educating the high risk and handicapped infant* (pp. 137–161). Baltimore: University Park Press.

Brolin, D. E. (1978). *Life-centered career education: A competency-based approach.* Reston, VA: Council for Exceptional Children.

Brolin, D. E. (1982). *Vocational preparation of persons with handicaps.* (2nd ed.). Columbus, OH: Merrill.

Brolin, D. E. (1986). *Life-centered career education: A competency-based approach* (rev. ed.). Reston, VA: Council for Exceptional Children.

Brolin, D. E., & D'Alonzo, B. J. (1979). Critical issues in career education for the handicapped student. *Exceptional Children, 45,* 246–253.

Brolin, D. E., Durand, R., Kromer, K., & Muller, P. (1975). Postschool adjustment of educable retarded students. *Education & Training of the Mentally Retarded, 10,* 144–149.

Brolin, D. E., & Kokaska, C. J. (1979). *Career education for handicapped children and youth.* Columbus, OH: Merrill.

Brolin, J. C., & Brolin, D. E. (1979). Vocational education for special students. In D. Cullinan & M. Epstein (Eds.), *Special education for adolescents: Issues and perspectives.* Columbus, OH: Merrill.

Bronfenbrenner, U. (1974). *A report on longitudinal evaluations of preschool programs: Vol. 2. Is early intervention effective?* Washington, DC: Department of Health, Education and Welfare Publication No. (OHD) 76-30025.

Bronfenbrenner, U. (1977). Toward an experimental ecology of human development. *American Psychologist, 32,* 513–531.

Bronicki, G. J., & Turnbull, A. P. (1987). Family-professional interactions. In M. E. Snell (Ed.), *Systematic instruction of persons with severe handicaps* (3rd ed.). Columbus, OH: Merrill.

Brooks, D. N., Wooley, H., & Kanjilal, G. C. (1972). Hearing loss and middle ear disorders in patients with Down's syndrome. *Journal of Mental Deficiency Research, 16,* 21–29.

Brooks, P. H., & McCauley, C. (1984). Cognitive research in mental retardation. *American Journal of Mental Deficiency, 88,* 479–486.

Browder, D. P., & Sullivan-Fleig, G. (1987). Involving parents in the educational process. In G. A. Robinson & E. A. Polloway (Eds.), *Best practices in Mental disabilities (Vol. 1).* Des Moines: Iowa Department of Education.

*Brown v. Board of Education of Topeka, Kansas,* 347 U.S. 483 (1954).

Brown, A. L. (1974). The role of strategic behavior in retardate memory. *International Review of Research in Mental Retardation, 7.*

Brown, A. L., & Campione, J. C. (1984). Three faces of transfer: Implications for early competence, individual differences, and instruction. In M. E. Lamb, A. L. Brown, & B. Rogoff (Eds.), *Advances in developmental psychology* (Vol. 3, pp. 143–192). Hillsdale, NJ: Lawrence Erlbaum.

Brown, A. L., Campione, J. C., & Murphy, M. D. (1974). Keeping track of changing variables: Long-term retention of a trained rehearsal strategy by retarded adolescents. *American Journal of Mental Deficiency, 78,* 453–466.

Brown, B. S., & Courtless, T. F. (1967). *The mentally retarded offender.* Washington, DC: President's Commission on Law Enforcement and Administration of Justice.

Brown, L. F., Branston, M. B., Hamre-Nietupski, S., Johnson, F., Wilcox, B., & Gruenewald, L. (1979). A rationale for comprehensive longitudinal interactions between severely handicapped students and nonhandicapped students and other citizens. *AAESPH Review, 4,* 3–14.

Brown, L. F., Branston, M. B., Hamre-Nietupski, S. M., Pumpian, I., Certo, N., & Gruenewald, L. (1979). A strategy for developing chronological-age-appropriate and functional curricular content for severely handicapped adolescents and young adults. *Journal of Special Education, 13,* 81–90.

Brown, L. F., Branston-McLean, M. B., Baumgart, D., Vincent, L., Falvey, M., & Schroder, J. (1979). Using the characteristics of current and subsequent least restrictive environments in the development of curricular content for severely handicapped students. *Journal of The Association for the Severely Handicapped, 4,* 407–424.

Brown, L. F., Nietupski, J., & Hamre-Nietupski, S. (1976). The criterion of ultimate functioning and public school services for severely handicapped students. In M. A. Thomas (Ed.), *Hey don't forget about me: Education's investment in the severely, profoundly, and multiply handicapped.* (pp. 2–15). Reston, VA: Council for Exceptional Children.

Brown, L. F., Nisbet, J., Ford, A., Sweet, M., Shiraga, B., York, R., & Loomis, R. (1983). The critical need for nonschool instruction in educational programs for severely handicapped students. *Journal of The Association for Persons with Severe Handicaps, 8,* 71–77.

Brown, L. F., Wright, E., & Hitchings, W. (1978). Guidelines for procuring work contracts for sheltered workshop clients. *Career Development for Exceptional Individuals, 1*(2), 88–96.

Brueckner, L. J., & Bond, G. L. (1955). *The diagnosis and treatment of learning difficulties.* Englewood Cliffs, NJ: Prentice-Hall.

Bruininks, R. H. (1978). *Bruininks-Oseretsky test of motor proficiency.* Circle Pines, MN: American Guidance Service.

Bruininks, R. H., Woodcock, R. W., Weatherman, R. F., & Hill, B. K. (1984). *Scales of independent behavior.* Allen, TX: DLM Teaching Resources.

*Buck v. Bell,* 274 U.S. 200 (1927).

Bull, M., & LaVecchio, F. (1978). Behavior therapy for a child with Lesch-Nyhan syndrome. *Developmental Medicine & Child Neurology, 20,* 368–375.

Bunker, M. C., Lambdin, M. A., Lynch, H. T., Mickey, G. H., Roderick, T. H., Van Pelt, J. C., & Fosnot, H. (1972, April 30). Will my baby be normal? *Patient Care.*

Burke, P. J., McLaughlin, M. J., & Valdivieso, C. H. (1988). Preparing professionals to educate handicapped infants and young children: Some policy considerations. *Topics in Early Childhood Special Education, 8*(1), 73–80.

Burks, H. F. (1983). *Burks' behavior rating scales: Preschool and kindergarten edition.* Los Angeles: Western Psychological Services.

*Burnham v. Dept. of Public Health,* 349 F. Supp. 1335 (N.D. Ga. 1972), rev'd, 503 f.sd 1319 (5th Cir. 1974).

Burt, C. (1966). The genetic determination of differences in intelligence. *British Journal of Psychology, 57,* 137–153.

Bush, W. J., & Waugh, K. W. (1982). *Diagnosing learning problems* (3rd ed.). Columbus, OH: Merrill.

Bzoch, K., & League, R. (1971). *Receptive-expressive emergent language scale.* Austin: PRO-ED.

Cain, E. J., & Taber, F. M. (1987). *Educating disabled people for the 21st century.* Boston: College Hill.

Cain, L. F., Levine, S., & Elzey, F. F. (1963). *Manual for the Cain-Levine Social Competency Scale.* Palo Alto, CA: Consulting Psychologists Press.

Caldwell, B. (1970). The rationale for early intervention. *Exceptional Children, 36,* 717–727.

Campbell, P. H. (1987a). Physical management and handling procedures with students with movement dysfunction. In M. E. Snell (Ed.), *Systematic instruction of persons with severe handicaps.* (3rd ed. pp. 174–187). Columbus, OH: Merrill..

Campbell, P. H. (1987b). Programming for students with dysfunction in posture and movement. In M. E. Snell (Ed.), *Systematic instruction of persons with severe handicaps.* (3rd ed., pp. 188–213). Columbus, OH: Merrill.

Campione, J. C., Brown, A. L., & Ferrara, R. A. (1982). Mental retardation and intelligence. In R. J. Sternberg (Ed.), *Handbook of human intelligence.* New York: Cambridge University Press.

Cancro, R. (Ed.). (1971). *Intelligence: Genetic and environmental influences.* New York: Grune & Stratton.

Capobianco, R. J., & Jacoby, H. B. (1966). The Fairfax plan: A high school program for mildly retarded youth. *Mental Retardation, 4*(3), 15–20.

Carlson, E. (1984). *Human genetics.* Lexington, MA: D.C. Heath.

Carney, I. H. (1987). Working with families. In F. P. Orelove & R. Sobsey (Eds.), *Multiple disabilities: A transdisciplinary approach.* Baltimore: Paul H. Brookes.

Carr, J. (1970). Mongolism: Telling the parents. *Developmental Medicine & Child Neurology, 12,* 213–221.

Carr, J. (1974). The effect of the severely subnormal on their families. In A. A. Clarke & A. D. B. Clarke (Eds.), *Mental deficiency: The changing outlook* (3rd ed.). New York: Free Press.

Carter, J. L. (1975). Intelligence and reading achievement of EMR in three educational settings. *Mental Retardation, 13*(5), 26–27.

Carter, J. L. (1987). Changing the look of mental retardation. *Psychology Today, 21*(9), 45.

Cassel, T. Z. (1976). A social-ecological model of adaptive functioning: A contextual developmental perspective. In N. A. Carlson (Ed.), *Final report. The contexts of life: A social-ecological model of adaptive behavior and functioning.* East Lansing, MI: Institute for Family and Child Study, Michigan State University.

Cassidy, V. M., & Stanton, J. E. (1959). *An investigation of factors involved in the educational placement of mentally retarded children: A study of differences between children in special and regular classes in Ohio.* (Cooperative Research Project No. 043). Columbus: Ohio State University.

Castellani, P. J. (1987). *The political economy of developmental disabilities.* Baltimore: Paul H. Brookes.

Casto, G., & Mastropieri, M. A. (1986). The efficacy of early intervention programs for handicapped children: A meta-analysis. *Exceptional Children, 52,* 417–424.

Cattell, J. M. (1963). Theory of crystallized intelligence: A critical experiment. *Journal of Educational Psychology, 54,* 1–22.

Cattell, R. B. (1947). *The measurement of intelligence of infants and young children.* New York: Psychological Corporation.

Cattell, R. B. (1950). Culture Fair Intelligence Test: Scale 1. Champaign, IL: Institute for Personality and Ability Testing.

Cegelka, P. T. (1979). Career education. In D. Cullinan & M. H. Epstein (Eds.), *Special education for adolescents: Issues and perspectives.* Columbus, OH: Merrill.

Cegelka, P. T., & Prehm, H. J. (1982). *Mental retardation: From categories to people.* Columbus, OH: Merrill.

Certo, N., Haring, N. G., & York, R. (1984). *Public school integration of severely handicapped students.* Baltimore: Paul H. Brookes.

Cetron, M. J. (1988). Class of 2000: The good news and the bad news. *The Futurist, 22*(6), 9–15.

Chan, K. S., & Rueda, R. (1979). Poverty and culture in education: Separate but equal. *Exceptional Children, 45,* 422–428.

Chaney, R. H., & Eyman, R. K. (1982). Etiology of mental retardation: Clinical vs. neuroanatomic diagnosis. *Mental Retardation, 20,* 123–132.

Cheseldine, S., & McConkey, R. (1979). Parental speech to young Down's syndrome children: An intervention study. *American Journal of Mental Deficiency, 83,* 612–620.

Chinn, P. C., Drew, C. J., & Logan, D. R. (1979). *Mental retardation: A life cycle approach* (2nd ed.). St. Louis: C. V. Mosby.

Cicirelli, V. G. (1969). *The impact of Head Start: An evaluation of the effects of Head Start on children's cognitive and affective development* (Vol. 1). Springfield, VA: Clearinghouse.

A citizen advocate (1978). Personal communication.

Clark, G. M. (1979). *Career education for the handicapped child in the elementary classroom.* Denver: Love Publishing.

Clark, G. M., & Knowlton, H. E. (1987). From school to adult living: A forum on issues and trends. *Exceptional Children, 53,* 546–554.

Clark, K. E., & Campbell, D. P. (1966). *Minnesota vocational interest inventory.* New York: Psychological Corporation.

Clarke, A. D. B., & Clarke, A. A. (1977). Projects for prevention and amelioration of mental retardation: A guest editorial. *American Journal of Mental Deficiency, 81,* 523–533.

Clarke, J. T. R., Gates, R. D., Hogan, S. E., Barrett, M., & MacDonald, G. W. (1987). Neuropsychological studies on adolescents with phenylketonuria returned to phenylalanine-restricted diets. *American Journal of Mental Retardation, 92,* 255–262.

Clausen, J. A. (1967). Mental deficiency: Development of a concept. *American Journal of Mental Deficiency, 71,* 727–745.

Clausen, J. A. (1972a). The continuing problem of defining mental deficiency. *Journal of Special Education, 6,* 97–106.

Clausen, J. A. (1972b). Quo vadis, AAMD? *Journal of Special Education, 6,* 51–60.

*Cleburne Living Center, Inc. v. City of Cleburne, Texas,* 735 F. 2d 832 (5th Cir. 1984).

Cleland, C. C., & Swartz, J. D. (1972). *Exceptionalities through the life span: An introduction.* New York: Macmillan.

Cleveland, D., & Miller, N. (1977). Attitudes and life commitments of older siblings of mentally retarded adults: An exploratory study. *Mental Retardation, 15*(3), 38–41.

Close, D. W., Sowers, J., Halpern, A. S., & Bourbeau, P. E. (1985). Programming for the transition to independent living for mildly retarded persons. In K. C. Lakin & R. H. Bruininks (Eds.), *Strategies for achieving community integration of developmentally disabled citizens* (pp. 161–176). Baltimore: Paul H. Brookes.

Clunies-Ross, G. G. (1979). Accelerating the development of Down's syndrome infants and young children. *Journal of Special Education, 13,* 169–177.

Coates, J. F. (1978). Population and education: How demographic trends will shape the U.S. *The Futurist, 12*(1), 35–42.

Cochran, W. E., Sran, P. K., & Varano, G. A. (1977). The relocation syndrome in mentally retarded individuals. *Mental Retardation, 15*(2), 169–177.

Coffman, T. L., & Harris, M. C. (1980). Transition shock and adjustments of mentally retarded persons. *Mental Retardation, 18*(3), 28–32.

Cohen, J. S. (1972). Vocational rehabilitation of the mentally retarded: The sheltered workshop. In J. H. Rothstein (Ed.), *Mental retardation: Readings and resources* (2nd ed.). New York: Holt, Rinehart, & Winston.

Cohen, L. (1981). Ethical issues in withholding care from severely handicapped infants. *Journal of The Association for the Severely Handicapped, 6*(3), 65–67.

Cohen, S. A. (1971). Dyspedagogia as a cause of reading retardation. In B. Bateman (Ed.), *Learning disorders* (Vol. 4). Seattle: Special Child Publications.

Coleman, L. J. (1977). An examination of seven techniques for evaluating the comprehensibility of instructional materials and recommendations for their use. *Education & Training of the Mentally Retarded, 12,* 339–344.

Coleman, R. W., & Provence, S. (1957). Environmental retardation (hospitalism) in infants living in families. *Pediatrics, 19,* 285–292.

Colletti, G., & Harris, S. L. (1977). Behavior modification in the home: Siblings as behavior modifiers, parents as observers. *Journal of Abnormal Child Psychology, 5,* 21–30.

Commission on Minority Participation in Education and American Life. (1988). *One-third of a nation.* Washington, DC: American Council on Education.

Committee on Education and Labor, U.S. House of Representatives. (1986). *Education of the Handicapped Act Amendments of 1986, Report 99-860, 99th Congress, 2nd Session.* Washington, DC: U.S. Government Printing Office.

*Community training and employment program* (COMTEP). (n.d.). Honolulu: Hawaii Association for Retarded Citizens.

Conley, R. W. (1973). *The economics of mental retardation.* Baltimore: John Hopkins University Press.

Conley, R. W., Noble, J. H., & Elder, J. K. (1986). Problems with the service system. In W. E. Kiernan & J. A. Stark (Eds.), *Pathways to*
*employment for adults with developmental disabilities* (pp. 67–84). Baltimore: Paul H. Brookes.

Connolly, A. (1978). Intelligence levels in Down's syndrome children. *American Journal of Mental Deficiency, 83,* 193–196.

Cook, P., Dahl, P., & Gale, M. (1977). *Vocational training and placement of the severely handicapped: Vocational opportunities.* Palo Alto, CA: American Institute for Research in the Behavioral Sciences.

Cooke, N. L., Heron, T. E., Heward, W. L., & Test, D. W. (1982). Integrating a Down's syndrome child in a classwide peer tutoring system: A case report. *Mental Retardation, 20,* 22–25.

Cordes, C. (1984). Will Larry P. face the supreme test? *Monitor, 15*(4), 1, 26–27.

Coulter, D. L. (1988a). Beyond Baby Doe: Does infant transplantation justify euthanasia? *Journal of the Association for Persons with Severe Handicaps, 13,* 71–75.

Coulter, D. L. (1988b). The neurology of mental retardation. In F. J. Menolascino & J. A. Stark (Eds.), *Preventive and curative intervention in mental retardation* (pp. 113–152). Baltimore: Paul H. Brookes.

Coulter, W. A., & Morrow, H. W. (Eds.). (1978). *Adaptive behavior: Concepts and measurements.* New York: Grune & Stratton.

Craig, E. M., & McCarver, R. B. (1984). Community adjustment. *International Review of Research in Mental Retardation, 12,* 95–122.

Crain, E. J. (1980). Socioeconomic status of educable mentally retarded graduates of special education. *Education & Training of the Mentally Retarded, 15,* 90–94.

Cravioto, J., DeLicardie, E. R., & Birch, H. G. (1966). Nutrition, growth, and neuro-integrative development: An experimental and ecological study. *Pediatrics, 38*(Suppl. 2), 319.

Crnic, K. A., Friedrich, W. N., & Greenberg, M. T. (1983). Adaptation of families with mentally retarded children: A model of stress, coping, and family ecology. *American Journal of Mental Deficiency, 88,* 125–138.

Crnic, L. S. (1984). Nutrition and mental development. *American Journal of Mental Deficiency, 88,* 526–533.

Crocker, A. C. (1981). The involvement of siblings of children with handicaps. In A. Milunsky (Ed.), *Coping with crises and handicaps.* New York: Plenum.

Cromwell, R. L. (1963). A social learning approach to mental retardation. In N. R. Ellis (Ed.), *Handbook of mental deficiency.* New York: McGraw-Hill.

Cronbach, L. J. (1969). Heredity, environment, and educational policy. *Harvard Educational Review, 39,* 338–347.

Cronin, M. E. (1988). Adult performance outcomes/ life skills. In G. Robinson, J. R. Patton, E. A. Polloway, & L. R. Sargent (Eds.). *Best practices in mental disabilities* (Vol. 2). Des Moines: Iowa Department of Education, Bureau of Special Education.

de la Cruz, F. (1985). Fragile X syndrome. *American Journal of Mental Deficiency, 90,* 119–123.

Cullari, S. (1984). Everybody is talking about the new institution. *Mental Retardation, 22,* 28–29.

Culleton, B. J. (1975). Amniocentesis: HEW backs test for prenatal diagnosis of disease. *Science, 190,* 537–540.

Cummings, T. S. (1976). The impact of the child's deficiency on the father: A study of fathers of mentally retarded and of chronically ill children. *American Journal of Orthopsychiatry, 46,* 246–255.

Cummings, T. S., Bayley, H., & Rie, H. (1966). Effects of the child's deficiency on the mother: A study of mothers of mentally retarded, chronically ill and neurotic children. *American Journal of Orthopsychiatry, 36,* 595–608.

Daker, M. G., Chidiac, P., Fear, C. N., & Berry, A. C. (1981, April). Fragile X in a normal male: A cautionary tale. *The Lancet,* 780.

Dalton, J., & Epstein, H. (1963). Counseling parents of mentally retarded children. *Social Casework, 44,* 523–530.

Danielson, L. C., & Bellamy, G. T. (1989). State variation in placement of children with handicaps in segregated environments. *Exceptional Children, 55,* 448–455.

Dator, J. (1988). The futures of care and "normal" behavior: Implications for those who are mentally retarded. *Education & Training in Mental Retardation, 23,* 248–252.

Davis, M. R. (1981). *A discussion of phenylketonuria and a comparison of behavioral characteristics.* Unpublished manuscript, Lynchburg College, Lynchburg, VA.

Delaney, E. A., & Hopkins, T. F. (1987). *The examiner's handbook: An expanded guide for Fourth Edition users.* Chicago: Riverside.

Delaney, S., & Hayden, A. (1977). Fetal alcohol syndrome: A review. *AAESPH Review, 2,* 164–168.

Denkowski, G. C., Denkowski, K. M., & Mabli, T. (1983). A fifty state survey of the current status of residential treatment programs for mentally retarded offenders. *Mental Retardation, 21,* 197–203.

Dennis, W. (1960). Causes of retardation among institutional children: Iran. *Journal of Genetic Psychology, 96,* 47–59.

Dennis, W., & Najaran, P. (1957). Infant development under environmental handicap. *Psychological Monographs, 71*(7).

Denny, M. (1980). Reducing self-stimulatory behavior of mentally retarded persons by alternative positive practice. *American Journal of Mental Deficiency, 84,* 610–615.

DeSilva, B. (1980, March 24). Retarded persons create a problem in criminal justice. *Washington Post,* pp. A6–A7.

DeVellis, R. F. (1977). Learned helplessness in institutions. *Mental Retardation, 15*(5), 10–13.

*Diana v. State Board of Education,* C-70-37 R.F.P. (N.D. California, Jan. 7, 1970, and June 18, 1972).

Dickerson, M., Hamilton, J., Huber, R., & Segal, R. (1974). *The aged mentally retarded: The invisible client—A challenge to the community.* Paper presented at the annual meeting of the American Association on Mental Deficiency, Toronto.

Dillon, R. F., & Stevenson-Hicks, R. (1983). Competence vs. performance and recent approaches to cognitive assessment. *Psychology in the Schools, 20,* 142–145.

*DISTAR Reading* (1971). Chicago: Science Research Associates.

Dix, D. (1976) Memorial to the Legislature of Massachusetts, 1843. (Reprinted in M. Rosen, G. R. Clark, & M. S. Kivitz [Eds.], *The history of mental retardation; Collected papers.* [Vol. 1]), Baltimore: University Park Press.

Dobzhansky, T. (1955). *Evolution, genetics, and man.* New York: John Wiley.

Dobzhansky, T. (1973). *Genetic diversity and human equality.* New York: Basic Books.

Doll, E. A. (1941). The essentials of an inclusive concept of mental deficiency. *American Journal of Mental Deficiency, 46,* 214–229.

Doll, E. A. (1953). *Measurement of social competence: A manual for the Vineland Social Maturity Scale.* Circle Pines, MN: American Guidance Service.

Doll, E. A. (1962). Historical survey of research and management of mental retardation in the United States. In E. P. Trapp & P. Hinestein (Eds.), *Readings on the exceptional child.* New York: Appleton-Century-Crofts.

Doll, E. A. (1965). *Vineland Social Maturity Scale: Condensed manual of directions* (1965 ed.). Circle Pines, MN: American Guidance Service.

Drew, C. J., & Espeseth, V. K. (1969). Transfer of training in the mentally retarded: A review. *Exceptional Children, 35,* 129–132.

Drew, C. J., Hardman, M. L., & Bluhm, H. P. (Eds.). (1977). *Mental retardation: Social and educational perspectives.* St. Louis: C.V. Mosby.

Drillien, C. M., & Wilkinson, E. M. (1964). Mongolism: When should parents be told? *British Medical Journal, 2,* 1306–1307.

Duff, R. S., & Campbell, A. G. M. (1973). Moral and ethical dilemmas in the special-care nursery. *The New England Journal of Medicine, 289,* 890–894. Reprinted in R. F. Weir (Ed.), *Ethical issues in death and dying.* New York: Columbia Press.

Dugdale, R. L. (1877). *The Jukes, a study in crime, pauperism, disease and heredity.* New York: Putnam.

Duker, P. (1975). Behavior control of self-biting in a Lesch-Nyhan patient. *Journal of Mental Deficiency Research, 19,* 11–19.

Duncan, C. P. (1975). Review of the science and politics of IQ. *American Journal of Psychology, 88,* 505–532.

Dunn, L. M. (Ed.). (1963). *Exceptional children in the schools.* New York: Holt, Rinehart, & Winston.

Dunn, L. M. (1968). Special education for the mildly retarded—Is much of it justifiable? *Exceptional Children, 35,* 5–22.

Dunn, L. M. (1973a). Children with mild general learning disabilities. In L. M. Dunn (Ed.), *Exceptional children in the schools: Special education in transition* (2nd ed., pp. 126–133). New York: Holt, Rinehart, & Winston.

Dunn, L. M. (Ed.). (1973b). *Exceptional children in the schools: Special education in transition* (2nd ed.). New York: Holt, Rinehart, & Winston.

Dunn, L. M., & Dunn, L. M. (1981). *Peabody picture vocabulary test—Revised.* Circle Pines, MN: American Guidance Service.

Dunn, L. M., & Markwardt, F. C. (1970). *Peabody individual achievement test.* Circle Pines, MN: American Guidance Service.

Dunst, C. J. (1986). Overview of the efficacy of early intervention programs. In B. Bickman & D. L. Weatherford (Eds.), *Evaluating early intervention programs for severely handicapped children and their families* (pp. 167–192). Austin, TX: PRO-ED.

Dunst, C. J., Trivette, C. M., & Cross, A. F. (1986). Roles and support networks of mothers of handicapped children. In R. R. Fewell & P. F. Vadasy (Eds.), *Families of handicapped children* (pp. 167–192). Austin, TX: PRO-ED.

Ebron, R., & Ebron, H. (1967). Measurement of attitudes toward the retarded and an application with educators. *American Journal of Mental Deficiency, 72,* 100–107.

Edelman, M. W. (1987). *Families in peril: An agenda for social change.* Cambridge: Harvard University Press.

Edgerton, R. B. (1967). *The cloak of competence: Stigma in the lives of mentally retarded.* Berkeley: University of California Press.

Edgerton, R. B. (1975). Issues relating to the quality of life among mentally retarded persons. In M. J. Begab & S. A. Richardson (Eds.), *The mentally retarded and society: A social science perspective.* Baltimore: University Park Press.

Edgerton, R. B. (1980). The study of community adaptation: Toward an understanding of lives in process. In E. D. Schulman, *Focus on the retarded adult: Programs and services.* St. Louis: C.V. Mosby.

Edgerton, R. B. (1984). Anthropology and mental retardation: Reseach approaches and opportunities. *Culture, Medicine, & Psychiatry, 8,* 25–48.

Edgerton, R. B., & Bercovici, S. M. (1976). The cloak of competence: Years later. *American Journal of Mental Deficiency, 80,* 485–497.

Edgerton, R. B., Bollinger, M., & Herr, B. (1984). The cloak of competence: After two decades. *American Journal of Mental Deficiency, 88,* 345–351.

Edmister, P., & Ekstrand, R. E. (1987). Preschool programming: Legal and educational issues. *Exceptional Children, 54,* 130–136.

Education Commission of the States. (1988). *Drawing in the family: Family involvement in the schools (PI88-2).* Denver: ECS Distribution Center.

Edwards, A. J., & Scannel, D. P. (1968). *Educational psychology: The teaching-learning process.* New York: International Textbook.

Elkind, D. (1981). *The hurried child.* Reading, MA: Addison-Wesley.

Elkington, J. (1985). *The poisoned womb.* New York: Viking Penguin.

Eller, P., Jordan, H., Parish, A., & Elder, P. (1979). Professional qualification: Mother. In R. York & E. Edgar (Eds.), *Teaching the severely handicapped* (Vol. 4). Seattle: AAESPH.

Ellis, N. R. (1963). The stimulus trace and behavioral inadequacy. In N. R. Ellis (Ed.), *Handbook of mental deficiency.* New York: McGraw-Hill.

Ellis, N. R. (1969). A behavioral research strategy in mental retardation: Defense and critique. *American Journal of Mental Deficiency, 73,* 557–566.

Ellis, N. R. (1970). Memory processes in retardates and normals. *International Review of Research in Mental Retardation, 4.*

Ellis, N. R., Balla, D., Estes, O., Warren, S. A., Meyers, C. E., Hollis, J., Isaacson, R. L., Palk, B. E., & Siegel, P. S. (1981). Common sense in the habilitation of mentally retarded persons: A reply to Menolascino and McGee. *Mental Retardation, 19,* 221–225.

Emde, R. N., & Brown, C. (1978). Adaptation to the birth of a Down's syndrome infant. *Journal of the American Academy of Child Psychiatry, 17,* 299–323.

Engel, E. (1977). One hundred years of cytogenetic studies in health and disease. *American Journal of Mental Deficiency, 82,* 109–117.

Engelmann, S. (1970). The effectiveness of direct verbal instruction on IQ performance and achievement in reading and arithmetic. In J. Hellmuth (Ed.), *The disadvantaged child* (Vol. 3). New York: Bruner/Mazel.

Engelmann, S. (1977). Sequencing cognitive and academic tasks. In R. D. Kneedler & S. G. Traver (Eds.), *Changing perspectives in special education.* Columbus, OH: Merrill.

Ensher, G. L., Blatt, B., & Winschel, J. F. (1977). Head Start for the handicapped: Congressional mandate audit. *Exceptional Children, 43,* 202–210.

Epstein, C. J. (1988). New approaches to the study of Down syndrome. In F. J. Menolascino & J. A. Stark (Eds.), *Preventive and curative intervention in mental retardation* (pp. 35–60). Baltimore: Paul H. Brookes.

Epstein, M. H., Cullinan, D., & Polloway, E. A. (1986). Patterns of maladjustment among mentally retarded children and youth. *American Journal of Mental Deficiency, 91,* 127–134.

Epstein, M. H., Polloway, E. A., Patton, J. R., & Foley, R. (1989). Mild retardation: Student characteristics and services. *Education & Training of the Mentally Retarded.*

Erickson, E. H. (1968). *Identity, youth and crisis.* New York: Norton.

Erickson, M. (1974). Talking with fathers of young children with Down's Syndrome. *Children Today, 3,* 22–25.

Estes, W. K. (1970). *Learning theory and mental development.* New York: Academic Press.

Eyman, R. K., Borthwick, S. A., & Tarjan, G. (1984). Current trends and changes in institutions for the mentally retarded. *International Review of Research in Mental Retardation, 12,* 178–195.

Eyman, R. K., Dingman, H., & Sabagh, G. (1966). Association of characteristics of retarded patients and their families with speed of institutionalization. *American Journal of Mental Deficiency, 71,* 93–99.

Eyman, R., Grossman, H., Tarjan, G., & Miller, C. (1987). *Life expectancy and mental retardation: A longitudinal study in a state residential facility.* Washington, DC: American Association on Mental Deficiency.

Eyman, R. K., & Miller, C. A. (1978). Introduction: A demographic overview of severe and profound mental retardation. In C. E. Meyers (Ed.), Quality of life in severely and profoundly mentally retarded people: Research foundations for improvement. *Monographs of the American Association on Mental Deficiency, 3,* ix–xii.

Eyman, R. K., O'Connor, G., Tarjan, G., & Justice, R. S. (1972). Factors determining residential placement of mentally retarded children. *American Journal of Mental Deficiency, 76,* 692–698.

Fallen, N. H., & Umansky, W. (1985). *Young children with special needs* (2nd ed.). Columbus, OH: Merrill.

Falvey, M. A. (1986). *Community-based curriculum: Instructional strategies for students with severe handicaps.* Baltimore: Paul H. Brookes.

Farber, B. (1959). Effects of a severely mentally retarded child on family integration. *Monograph of the Society for Research in Child Development, 24*(2, Whole No. 71).

Farber, B. (1963). Interactions with retarded siblings and life goals of children. *Marriage and Family Living, 25,* 96–98.

Farber, B. (1968). *Mental retardation: Its social context and social consequences.* Boston: Houghton Mifflin.

Farber, B. (1970). Notes on sociological knowledge about families with mentally retarded children. In M. Schreiber (Ed.), *Social work and mental retardation.* New York: John Day.

Farber, B. (1972). Effects of a severely retarded child on the family. In E. P. Trapp & P. Himelstein (Eds.), *Readings on the exceptional child.* (pp. 225–245). New York: Appleton- Century-Crofts.

Farber, B. (1975). Family adaptations to severely mentally retarded children. In M. Begab & S. A. Richardson (Eds.), *The mentally retarded and society: A social science perspective.* Baltimore: University Park Press.

Fernald, D. C. (1976). The Lesch-Nyhan syndrome, cerebral palsy, mental retardation and self-mutilation. *Journal of Pediatric Psychology, 1*(3), 51–55.

Feuerstein, R. (1979). Ontogeny of learning in man. In M. A. B. Brazier (Ed.), *Brain mechanisms in memory and learning: From the single neuron to man* (pp. 361–372). New York: Raven.

Feuerstein, R., Miller, R., Hoffman, M. B., Rand, Y., Mintzker, Y., & Mogens, R. J. (1981). Cognitive modifiability in adolescence: Cognitive structure and the effects of intervention. *Journal of Special Education, 15*(2), 269–287.

Fewell, R. R. (1986). A handicapped child in the family. In R. R. Fewell & P. F. Vadasy (Eds.), *Families of handicapped children* (pp. 3–34). Austin: PRO-ED.

Fewell, R. R., & Kelly, J. F. (1983). Curriculum for young handicapped children. In S. G. Garwood (Ed.), *Educating handicapped children* (pp. 407–433). Rockville, MD: Aspen.

Fewell, R. R., & Vadasy, P. F. (1986). *Families of handicapped children: Needs and supports across the life span.* Austin: PRO-ED.

Filler, J. W., Jr. (1976). Modifying maternal teaching style: Effects of task arrangement on the match-to-sample performance of retarded preschool-age children. *American Journal of Mental Deficiency, 80,* 602–612.

Fink, W., & Sandall, S. (1980). A comparison of one-to-one and small group instructional strategies on a word identification task by developmentally disabled preschoolers. *Mental Retardation, 18*(1), 34–35.

Fishler, K., Azen, C. G., Henderson, R., Friedman, E. G., & Koch, R. (1987). Psychoeducational findings among children treated for phenylketonuria. *American Journal of Mental Retardation, 92,* 65–73.

Fletcher, J. (1974). *The ethics of genetic control: Ending reproductive roulette.* Garden City, NY: Anchor.

Fletcher, J. (1975). The "right" to live and the "right" to die. In M. Kohl (Ed.), *Beneficent euthanasia.* Buffalo, NY: Prometheus.

Flynn, C., & Harbin, G. (1987). Evaluating interagency coordination efforts using a multidimensional, interactional, developmental paradigm. *Remedial & Special Education, 8*(3), 35–44.

Folio, M. R., & Fewell, R. R. (1983). *Peabody developmental motor scales and activity cards.* Allen, TX: DLM Teaching Resources.

Folkman, S., Schaefer, C., & Lazarus, R. S. (1979). Cognitive processes as mediators of stress and coping. In V. Hamilton & D. W. Warburton (Eds.), *Human stress and cognition.* New York: John Wiley.

Folling, A. (1934). Über Ausscheidung von Phenylbrenzträubensäure in den Harn als Stoffwechselanomalie in Verbindung mit Imbezilität. *Zeitschrift für physiologisch Chemie, 227,* 169–176.

Ford, A., & Miranda, P. (1984). Community instruction: A natural cues and corrections decision model. *Journal of The Association for Persons with Severe Handicaps, 9,* 79–88.

Forness, S. R. (1985). Effects of public policy at the state level: California's impact on MR, LD, and ED categories. *Remedial & Special Education, 6*(3), 36–43.

Forness, S. R., & Polloway, E. A. (1987). Physical and psychiatric diagnosis of pupils with mild mental retardation currently being referred for related services. *Education & Training of the Mentally Retarded, 22,* 221–228.

Forrest, M. (Ed.). (1987). *More integration/education.* Downsville: G. Alan Roeher Institute.

Fowle, C. M. (1968). The effect of the severely mentally retarded child on his family. *American Journal of Mental Deficiency, 73,* 468–473.

Fowler, S. A. (1988). Transition planning. *Teaching Exceptional Children, 20*(4), 62–63.

Fox, R. A., & Rosen, D. L. (1977). A parent administered token program for dietary regulation of phenylketonuria. *Journal of Behavior Therapy and Experimental Psychiatry, 8,* 441–443.

Foxx, R. M. (1982). *Decreasing behaviors of severely retarded and autistic persons.* Champaign, IL: Research Press.

Fraenkel, W. A. (1961). *The mentally retarded and their vocational rehabilitation: A resource handbook.* Arlington: TX: National Association for Retarded Children.

Frankenberger, W. (1984). A survey of state guidelines for identification of mental retardation. *Mental Retardation, 22*(1), 17–20.

Frankenburg, W. K. (1972). *Screening and assessment of young children at developmental risks.* Department of Health, Education, and Welfare Publication No. [05]73–91). Washington, DC: U.S. Government Printing Office.

Frankenburg, W. K., & Dodds, J. B. (1967). The Denver Developmental Screening Test. *Journal of Pediatrics, 71,* 181–191.

Fraser, F. C. (1977). Genetic counseling. In A. S. Baer (Ed.), *Heredity and society: Readings in social genetics* (2nd ed.). New York: Macmillan.

Fredericks, B. (1987, June). Back to the future: Integration revisited. *The Association for Persons with Severe Handicaps Newsletter,* p. 1.

Fredericks, H. D. B., Baldwin, V., Moore, W., Templeman, T. P., & Anderson, R. (1980). The Teaching Research data-based classroom model. *Journal of The Association for the Severely Handicapped, 5,* 211–223.

Fredericks, H. D. B., Riggs, C., Furey, T., Grove, D., Moore, W., McDonnel, J., Jordan, E., Hansen, W., Baldwin, V., & Wadlow, M. (1976). *The Teaching Research curriculum for moderately and severely handicapped.* Springfield, IL: Charles C Thomas.

Friedrich, W. N., & Friedrich, W. L. (1981). Psychosocial assets of parents of handicapped and nonhandicapped children. *American Journal of Mental Deficiency, 85,* 551–553.

Fuchs, L. S., & Fuchs, D. (in press). Curriculum based assessment. In C. R. Reynolds & R. R. Kamphaus (Eds.), *Handbook of psychological and educational assessment of children: Vol. 1. Intelligence and achievement.* New York: Guilford.

Fullan, M., & Loubser, J. J. (1972). Education and adaptive capacity. *Sociology of Education, 45,* 271–287.

Furlong, M. J., & LeDrew, L. (1985). IQ = 68 = mildly retarded? Factors influencing multidisciplinary team recommendations on children with FS IQs between 63 and 75. *Psychology in the Schools, 22,* 5–9.

*The Futurist.* (1986). The new poor: Jobless and homeless in the United States. *20*(2), 44.

Gage, N. L. (1972). IQ heritability, race differences, and educational research. *Phi Delta Kappan, 53,* 308–312.

Gallagher, J. J., Beckman, P. J., & Cross, A. H. (1983). Families of handicapped children: Sources of stress and its amelioration. *Exceptional Children, 50,* 10–19.

Gallup Organization Report for the President's Committee on Mental Retardation. (1976). Public attitudes regarding mental retardation. In R. Nathan (Ed.), *Mental retardation: Century of decision.* Washington, DC: President's Committee on Mental Retardation.

Gamble, C. J. (1951). The prevention of mental deficiency by sterilization, 1949. *American Journal of Mental Deficiency, 56,* 192–197.

Garber, H. L. (1988). *The Milwaukee project: Preventing mental retardation in children at risk.* Washington, DC: American Association on Mental Retardation.

Garber, H. L., & Heber, R. F. (1973). *The Milwaukee Project: Early intervention as a technique to prevent mental retardation.* Technical paper, University of Connecticut, Storrs, CT.

Garber, H. L., & Heber, R. F. (1981). The efficacy of early intervention with family rehabilitation. In M. J. Begab, H. C. Haywood, & H. L. Garber (Eds.), *Psychosocial influences in retarded performance: Strategies for improving competence* (Vol. 2, pp. 71–87). Baltimore: University Park Press.

Garber, H. L., & McInerney, M. (1982). Sociobehavioral factors in mental retardation. In P. T. Cegelka & H. J. Prehm, *Mental retardation: From categories to people.* Columbus, OH: Merrill.

Gardner, J. F., & Chapman, M. S. (1985). *Staff development in mental retardation services: A practical handbook.* Baltimore: Paul H. Brookes.

Garwood, S. J., Fewell, R. R., & Neisworth, J. T. (1988). Public Law 94-142: You can get there from here! *Topics in Early Childhood Special Education, 8,*(1), 1–11.

Gath, A. (1973). The school age siblings of mongol children. *British Journal of Psychiatry, 123,* 161–167.

Gearheart, B. R. (1980). *Special education for the 80's.* St. Louis: C.V. Mosby.

Geiger, W., Brownsmith, K., & Forgnone, C. (1978). Differential importance of skills for TMR students perceived by teachers. *Education & Training of the Mentally Retarded, 13,* 259–264.

Geik, I., Gilkerson, L., & Sponseller, D. B. (1982). An early intervention training model. *Journal of the Division for Early Childhood, 5,* 42–52.

Gelof, M. (1963). Comparison of systems of classification relating degree of retardation to measured intelligence. *American Journal of Mental Deficiency, 68,* 297–317.

*Georgia Association for Retarded Citizens v. McDaniel,* 740 F.2d 902 (11th Cir. 1984).

German, M. L., & Maisto, A. T. (1982). The relationship of a perceived family support system to the institutional placement of mentally retarded children. *Education & Training of the Mentally Retarded, 17,* 17–23.

Gertsen, R., Crowell, F., & Bellamy, T. (1986). Spillover effects: Impact of vocational training on the lives of severely retarded clients. *American Journal of Mental Deficiency, 19,* 501–506.

Gifford, J. L., Rusch, F. R., Martin, J. E., & White, D. M. (1984). Autonomy and adaptability: A proposed technology for maintaining work behavior. *International Review of Research in Mental Retardation, 12,* 285–318.

Gilhool, T. K. (1976). The right to community services. In M. Kindred, J. Cohen, D. Penrod, & T. Shaffer (Eds.), *The mentally retarded citizen and the law.* New York: Free Press.

Ginsburg, H. (1972). *The myth of the deprived child: Poor children's intellect and education.* Englewood Cliffs, NJ: Prentice-Hall.

Ginzberg, E., & Bray, D. W. (1953). *The uneducated.* New York: Columbia University Press.

Glass, G. V. (1983). Effectiveness of special education. *Policy Studies Review, 2,* (Special No. 1), 65–78.

Goddard, J. J. (1912). *The Kallikak family.* New York: Macmillan.

Goffman, E. (1961). *Stygma: Notes on the management of spoiled identity.* Englewood Cliffs, NJ: Prentice-Hall.

Gold, M. W. (1973). Research on the vocational habilitation of the retarded: The present, the future. *International Review of Research in Mental Retardation, 6.*

Gold, M. W. (1976). Task analysis of a complex assembly task by the retarded blind. *Exceptional Children, 43,* 78–84.

Gold, M. W. (1980). An alternative definition of mental retardation. In M. W. Gold (Ed.), *"Did I say that?" Articles and commentary on the Try Another Way System.* Champaign, IL: Research Press.

Golden, M., & Berns, B. (1976). Social class and infant intelligence. In M. Lewis (Ed.), *Origins of intelligence.* New York: Plenum.

Goldman, J. J. (1988). Prader-Willi syndrome in two institutionalized older adults. *Mental Retardation, 26,* 97–102.

Goodman, L. V. (1976). Bill of rights for the handicapped. *American Education, 12*(6), 6–8.

Goodman, N., & Tizard, J. (1962). Prevalence of imbecility and idiocy among children. *British Medical Journal, 1,* 216–219.

Gordon, L. V. (1967). *Gordon occupational checklist.* New York: Harcourt Brace Jovanovich.

Gottesman, I. (1963). Genetic aspects of intelligent behavior. In N. R. Ellis (Ed.), *Handbook of mental deficiency.* New York: McGraw-Hill.

Gottlieb, J. (1975). Public, peer, and professional attitudes toward mentally retarded persons. In M. J. Begab & S. A. Richardson (Eds.), *The mentally retarded in society: A social science perspective.* Baltimore: University Park Press.

Gottlieb, J. (1981). Mainstreaming: Fulfilling the promise? *American Journal of Mental Deficiency, 86,* 115–126.

Gottlieb, J., & Leyser, Y. (1981). Facilitating the social mainstreaming of retarded children. *Exceptional Education Quarterly, 1*(4), 57–69.

Gould, J. (1981). *The mismeasure of man.* New York: W. W. Norton.

Graham, F. K., Ernhart, C. B., Thurston, D., & Craft, M. (1962). Development three years after perinatal anoxia and other potentially damaging experiences. *Psychological Monographs, 76* (Whole No. 522).

Graham, M., & Scott, K. G. (1988). The impact of definitions of higher risk on services to infants and toddlers. *Topics in Early Childhood Special Education, 8*(3), 23–38.

Gray, G. (1975). Educational service delivery. In W. J. Cegelka (Ed.), *Educating the 24-hour retarded child.* Symposium conducted at the National Training Meeting on Education of the Severely and Profoundly Retarded. Arlington, TX: National Association for Retarded Citizens.

Gray, S. W., & Klaus, R. A. (1965). An experimental preschool program for culturally deprived children. *Child Development, 36,* 887–898.

Gray, S. W., & Klaus, R. A. (1968). The early training project for disadvantaged children: A report after five years. *Monographs for the Society for Research in Child Development, 33*(No. 4).

Great Lakes Area Regional Resource Center. (1986). "Medically fragile" handicapped children: A policy research paper. Columbus: Ohio State University.

Gresham, F. M. (1982). Misguided mainstreaming: The case for social skills training with handicapped children. *Exceptional Children, 48,* 422–433.

Griffiths, D. E. (1959). *Administrative theory.* Englewood Cliffs, NJ: Prentice-Hall.

Grossman, F. K. (1972). *Brothers and sisters of retarded children: An exploratory study.* Syracuse, NY: Syracuse University Press.

Grossman, H. J. (Ed.) (1973). *Manual on terminology and classification in mental retardation.* Washington, DC: American Association on Mental Deficiency.

Grossman, H. J. (Ed.) (1977). *Manual on terminology and classification in mental retardation.* Washington, DC: American Association on Mental Deficiency.

Grossman, H. J. (1983). *Classification in mental retardation.* Washington, DC: American Association on Mental Deficiency.

Grossman, H. J., & Tarjan, G. (1987). *AMA handbook on mental retardation.* Chicago: Division of Clinical Science, American Medical Association.

Gruber, B., Reeser, R., & Reid, D. H. (1979). Providing a less restrictive environment for profoundly retarded persons by teaching independent walking skills. *Journal of Applied Behavior Analysis, 12,* 285–297.

Gruenewald, L., Schroeder, J., & Yoder, D. (1982). Considerations for curriculum development and implementation. In B. Campbell & V. Baldwin (Eds.), *Severely handicapped/hearing impaired students* (pp. 163–180). Baltimore: Paul H. Brookes.

Guess, D., Horner, R. D., Utley, B., Holvoet, J., Maxon, D., Tucker, D., & Warren, S. (1978). A functional curriculum sequencing model for teaching the severely handicapped. *AAESPH Review, 3,* 202–215.

Gunzburg, H. C. (1958). Psychological assessment in mental deficiency. In A. A. Clarke & A. D. B. Clarke (Eds.), *Mental deficiency—The changing outlook.* London: Methuen.

Guralnick, M. J. (1981). The efficacy of integrating handicapped children in early education settings: Research implications. *Topics in Early Childhood Special Education, 1*(1), 51–71.

Guskey, T. R. (1980). Individualizing within the group-centered classroom: The Mastery Learning Model. *Teacher Education & Special Education, 3*(4), 47–54.

Guskin, S. L. (1977). Paradigms for research on attitudes toward the mentally retarded. In P. Mittler (Ed.), *Research to practice in mental retardation.* Baltimore: University Park Press.

Guttmacher, M., & Weihofen, H. (1952). *Psychiatry and the law.* New York: Norton.

Haggard, H. W., & Jellinek, E. M. (1942). *Alcohol explained.* Garden City, NY: Doubleday.

Hains, A. H., Fowler, S. A., & Chandler, L. K. (in press). Planning school transitions: Family and professional collaboration. *Journal of the Division for Early Childhood.*

*Halderman v. Pennhurst State School and Hospital,* 446 F. Supp. 1295 (E.D. Pa. 1977), aff'd in part, remanded in part. Nos. 84-1490, 78-1564, 78-1602 (3rd Cir. Dec. 13, 1979).

Hall, R. V., & Hall, M. C. (1980). *How to use systematic attention and approval (social reinforcement).* Lawrence, KS: H & H Enterprises.

Hallahan, D. P., & Kauffman, J. M. (1976). *Introduction to learning disabilities: A psychobehavioral approach.* Englewood Cliffs, NJ: Prentice-Hall.

Halle, J. W., Silverman, N. A., & Regan, L. (1983). The effects of a data-based exercise program on physical fitness of retarded children. *Education & Training of the Mentally Retarded, 18*(3), 221–225.

Halpern, A. S., & Benz, M. R. (1987). A statewide examination of secondary special education for students with mild disabilities: Implications for high school curriculum. *Exceptional Children, 54,* 122–129.

Halpren, R. (1987, September). Major social and demographic trends affecting young families: Implications for early childhood care and education. *Young Children,* pp. 34–40.

Hamilton, D. L., & Bishop, G. D. (1976). Attitudinal and behavioral effects of initial integration of white suburban neighborhoods. *Journal of Social Issues, 32,* 47–67.

Hamilton, D. L., & Segal, R. M. (Eds.). (1975).

*Proceedings of a consultation-conference on the gerontological aspects of mental retardation.* Ann Arbor: University of Michigan.

Haney, J. I. (1988). Toward successful community residential placements for individuals with mental retardation. In L. W. Heal, J. I. Haney, & A. R. Novak Amado (Eds.), *Integration of developmentally disabled individuals into the community* (2nd ed., pp. 125–168). Baltimore: Paul H. Brookes.

Hansen, J. C., Stevic, R. R., & Warner, R. W. (1972). *Counseling: Theory and process.* Boston: Allyn & Bacon.

Hanson, H. (1978). Decline of Down's syndrome after abortion reform in New York state. *American Journal of Mental Deficiency, 83,* 185–188.

Hanson, M. J. (1984). *Atypical infant development.* Baltimore: University Park Press.

Hanson, M. J., & Schwarz, R. H. (1978). Results of a longitudinal intervention program for Down's syndrome infants and their families. *Education & Training of the Mentally Retarded, 13,* 403–407.

Harbin, G. L. (1988). Implementation of P.L. 99-457: State technical assistance needs. *Topics in Early Childhood Special Education, 8*(1), 24–36.

Haring, N. G. (Ed.). (1977). *Developing effective individualized education programs for severely handicapped children and youth.* Washington, DC: Department of Health, Education, and Welfare.

Haring, N. G., & McCormick, L. (1986). *Exceptional children and youth* (4th ed.). Columbus, OH: Merrill.

Harth, R. (1977). Attitudes and mental retardation: Review of the literature. In C. J. Drew, M. L. Hardman, & H. P. Bluhm (Eds.), *Mental retardation: Social and educational perspectives.* St. Louis: C.V. Mosby.

Hasazi, S. B., Gordon, L. R., & Roe, C. A. (1985). Factors associated with employment status of handicapped youth exiting high school from 1979 to 1983. *Exceptional Children, 51,* 455–469.

Hashem, N., Ebrahim, A., & Nour, A. (1970). Classical and atypical phenylketonuria among Egyptians: Study of 10 families. *American Journal of Mental Deficiency, 75,* 329–335.

Haskins, J. S., & Stifle, J. M. (1978). *He will lift up his head: A report to the developmental disabilities office on the situation of handicapped Navajos and the implications thereof for all native Americans.* Washington, DC: Office of Human Development (DHEW).

Hauber, F. A., Rotegard, L. L., & Bruininks, R. H. (1985). Characteristics of residential services for older/elderly mentally retarded persons. In M. P. Janicki & H. M. Wisniewski (Eds.), *Aging and developmental disabilities: Issues and approaches* (pp. 327–350). Baltimore: Paul H. Brookes.

*The Hawaii Transition Project.* (1987). Honolulu: University of Hawaii, Department of Special Education.

Hawkes, N. (1979). Tracing Burt's descent into scientific fraud. *Science, 205,* 673–675.

Hawkridge, D., Chalupsky, A., & Roberts, A. (1968). *A study of selected programs for the education of disadvantaged children.* Palo Alto, CA: American Institute for Research in the Behavior Sciences.

Hayden, A. H., & McGinness, G. D. (1977). Bases for early intervention. In E. Sontag, J. Smith, & N. Certo (Eds.), *Educational programming for the severely and profoundly handicapped.* Reston, VA: Council for Exceptional Children.

Hayden, A. H., & Pious, C. G. (1979). The case for early intervention. In R. York & E. Edgar (Eds.), *Teaching the severely handicapped* (Vol. 4). Seattle: AAESPH.

Haywood, H. C. (1979). What happened to mild and moderate mental retardation? *American Journal of Mental Deficiency, 83,* 429–439.

Heal, L. W., Sigelman, C. K., & Switzky, H. N. (1978). Research on community residential alternatives for the mentally retarded. *International Review of Research in Mental Retardation, 9,* 209–249.

Healy, A., Keesee, P. D., & Smith, B. S. (1985). Early services for children with special needs: Transactions for family support. Iowa City: University of Iowa, Division of Developmental Disabilities.

Hearnshaw, L. S. (1979). *Cyril Burt, psychologist.* Ithaca, NY: Cornell University.

Heber, R. F. (1959). A manual on terminology and classification in mental retardation. *Monograph Supplement American Journal of Mental Deficiency, 62.*

Heber, R. F. (1961). A manual on terminology and classification in mental retardation (rev. ed.). *Monograph Supplement American Journal of Mental Deficiency, 64.*

Heber, R. F. (1964). Personality. In H. A. Stevens & R. F. Heber (Eds.), *Mental retardation: A review of research.* Chicago: University of Chicago Press.

Heber, R. F., & Deyer, R. B. (1970). Research on education and habilitation of the mentally retarded. In H. C. Haywood (Ed.), *Sociocultural aspects of mental retardation.* New York: Appleton-Century-Crofts.

Heber, R. F., & Garber, H. (1967). The Milwaukee project: A study of the use of family intervention to prevent cultural-familial mental retardation. In B. Z. Friendlender (Ed.), *The exceptional infant: Assessment and intervention.* New York: Bruner/Mazel.

Heber, R. F., & Garber, H. (1971). An experiment in prevention of cultural-familial mental retardation. In D. A. Primrose (Ed.), *Proceedings of the Second Congress of the International Association for the Scientific Study of Mental Deficiency.* Warsaw: Polish Medical Publishers.

Heller, T. (1984). Issues in adjustment of mentally retarded individuals to residential relocation. *International Review of Mental Retardation, 12,* 123–145.

Henderson, N. D. (1982). Human behavior genetics. In M. R. Rosenzweig & L. W. Porter (Eds.), *Annual Review of Psychology, 33,* 403–440.

Henderson, R. A., & Vitello, S. J. (1988). Litigation related to community integration. In L. W. Heal, J. I. Haney, & A. R. Novak Amado (Eds.), *Integration of developmentally disabled individuals into the community* (2nd ed., pp. 272–282). Baltimore: Paul H. Brookes.

Hentoff, N. (1977). *Does anybody give a damn?* New York: Knopf.

Herr, E. L. (1977). *The emerging history of career education: A summary view.* Washington, DC: National Advisory Council on Career Education.

Herr, S. S. (1984). The Phillip Becker case resolved: A chance for habilitation. *Mental Retardation, 22*(1), 35–39.

Herrnstein, R. (1979, September). I.Q. *The Atlantic Monthly, 228,* 43–65.

Herrnstein, R. J. (1982, August). IQ Testing and the media. *The Atlantic Monthly, 250,* 68–74.

Hess, R. D., & Shipman, V. C. (1965). Early experience and the socialization of cognitive modes in children. *Child Development, 36,* 869–886.

Heward, W. L., Dardig, J., & Rossett, A. (1979). *Working with parents of handicapped children.* Columbus, OH: Merrill.

Heward, W. L., & Orlansky, M. D. (1988). *Exceptional children.* Columbus. OH: Merrill.

Hewett, F. M., & Forness, S. (1977). *Education of exceptional learners* (2nd ed.). Boston: Allyn & Bacon.

Hill, B. K., & Lakin, K. C. (1986). Classification of residential facilities for individuals with mental retardation. *Mental Retardation, 24,* 107–115.

Hill, B. K., Lakin, K. C., Bruininks, R. H. (1988). Characteristics of residential facilities. In L. W. Heal, J. I. Haney, & A. R. Novak Amado (Eds.), *Integration of developmentally disabled individuals into the community* (2nd ed., pp. 89–124). Baltimore: Paul H. Brookes.

Hill, M., Hill, J. W., Wehman, P., & Banks, D. (1985). An analysis of monetary and nonmonetary outcomes associated with competitive employment of mentally retarded persons. In P. Wehman & J. W. Hill (Eds.), *Competitive employment for persons with mental retardation* (pp. 110–133). Richmond, VA: Virginia Commonwealth University, Rehabilitation, Research, and Training Center.

Hilliard, L. T., & Kirman, B. H. (1965). *Mental deficiency* (2nd ed.). London: Churchill.

Hiskey, M. (1966). *Hiskey-Nebraska test of learning aptitude.* Lincoln, NE: Union College Press.

Hobbs, N. (1975). *The futures of children*. San Francisco: Jossey-Bass.

*Hobson v. Hansen,* 269 F. Supp. 401 (D.D.C. 1967, *aff'd sub norm*).

Hodgkinson, H. L. (1985). *All one system: Demographics of education, kindergarten through graduate school*. Washington: Institute for Educational Leadership.

Hoefnagel, D., Andrew, E. D., Mireault, N. G., & Berndt, W. O. (1965). Hereditary choreathetosis, self-mutilation, and hyperuricemia in young males. *New England Journal of Medicine, 273,* 130–135.

Hollinger, C., & Jones, R. (1970). Community attitudes toward slow learners and mental retardates: What's in a name? *Mental Retardation, 8*(1), 1–23.

Holmes, C. S. (1982). Self monitoring reactivity and a severe feeding problem. *Journal of Clinical Child Psychology, 11,* 66–71.

Holroyd, J., & MacArthur, D. (1976). Mental retardation and stress on the parents: A contrast between Down's syndrome and childhood autism. *American Journal of Mental Deficiency, 80*(4), 431–436.

Hopkins, G. A. (1982). A comparison of cytogenetic groups of children with Down's syndrome on verbal and nonverbal measures. *Exceptional People Quarterly, 1,* 329–342.

Hopkins, T. F. (1988). The fourth edition of the Stanford-Binet: Alfred Binet would be proud . . . *Measurement and Evaluation in Counseling and Development, 21,* 40–42.

Houston, J. (1987, April). Panel initiates planning. In *A vision for the future* (p. 6). Montgomery, AL: AL SDOE.

Howard, E. (1971, November 21). Innisfree village to be a haven. *The Daily Progress*.

Howe, S. G. (1972). *On the causes of idiocy: Being the supplement to a report by S. G. Howe and other commissioners appointed by the Governor of Massachusetts to inquire into the conditions of the idiots of the Commonwealth dated February 25, 1848. With an appendix*. New York: Arno. (Originally published 1848).

Howell, K. W., & Morehead, M. K. (1987). *Curriculum-based evaluation for special and remedial education: A handbook for deciding what to teach*. Columbus, OH: Merrill.

Hoyt, K. B. (1982). Career education beginning of the end? Or a new beginning? *Career Development for Exceptional Individuals, 5,* 3–13.

Hresko, W. P., & Brown, L. (1984). *Test of early socioemotional development*. Austin: PRO-ED.

Hresko, W. P., Reid, D. K., & Hammill, D. D. (1981). *Test of early language development*. Austin: PRO-ED.

Huberty, T. J., Koller, J. R., & Ten Brink, T. D. (1980). Adaptive behavior in the definition of mental retardation. *Exceptional Children, 46,* 256–261.

Hull, J. T., & Thompson, J. C. (1980). Predicting adaptive functioning of mentally retarded persons in community settings. *American Journal of Mental Deficiency, 85*(3), 253–261.

Humphrey, G., & Humphrey, M. (Eds. & Trans.). (1962). *Wild boy of Aveyron*. New York: Appleton-Century-Crofts.

Hungerford, R. H., DeProspo, C. J., & Rosenzweig, L. E. (1948). The non-academic pupil. In *Philosophy of occupational education*. New York: Association of New York City Teachers of Special Education.

Hunt, J. McV. (1961). *Intelligence and experience*. New York: Ronald Press.

Hunt, J. McV. (1969). *The challenge of incompetence and poverty*. Urbana: University of Illinois Press.

Hunt, J. McV. (1988). Foreword. In H. L. Garber, *The Milwaukee Project: Preventing mental retardation in children at risk* (p. iv). Washington, DC: American Association on Mental Health.

Hunter, J., & Bellamy, G. T. (1977). Cable harness construction for severely retarded adults: A demonstration of training techniques. *AAESPH Review, 1*(7), 2–13.

Hurwitz, N. (1975, May). Communications networks and the urban poor. *Equal Opportunity Review*, pp. 1–5.

Hutt, M. L. (1947). A clinical study of "consecutive" and "adaptive" testing with the revised Stanford-Binet. *Journal of Consulting Psychology, 11,* 93–103.

Hutt, M. L., & Gibby, R. G. (1979). *The mentally retarded child: Development, training and education.* (4th ed.). Boston: Allyn & Bacon.

*In re Cavitt,* 1457 N.W. 2d. 171 (1967).

*In re Phillip B.,* 92 Cal. App. 3rd 796 (May 8, 1979).

Ingalls, R. P. (1978). *Mental retardation: The changing outlook.* New York: John Wiley.

Ingle, D. J. (1967). Editorial: The need to study biological differences among racial groups: Moral issues. *Perspectives in Biology & Medicine, 10,* 497–499.

Inhelder, B. (1968). *The diagnosis of reasoning in the mentally retarded.* New York: John Day.

Innisfree Village. (n.d.) Brochure. Crozet, Virginia.

Intagliata, J. C., & Willer, B. S. (1982). Reinstitutionalization of mentally retarded persons successfully placed into family-care and group homes. *American Journal of Mental Deficiency, 87,* 34–39.

Intagliata, J. C., Willer, B. S., & Cooley, F. B. (1979). Cost comparison of institutional and community-based alternatives for mentally retarded persons. *Mental Retardation, 14,* 154–156.

International League of Societies for the Mentally Handicapped. (1969). In R. H. Finch, *MR 69: Toward progress: The story of a decade. Report of the President's Committee on Mental Retardation.* Washington, DC: U.S. Government Printing Office.

*Irving Independent School District v. Tatro,* 104 S. Ct. 3371 (1984).

Is there a cure for mental retardation? (1980). *ARC News, 29*(3).

Itard, J. M. G. (1962). *Wild boy of Aveyron.* (G. Humphrey & M. Humphrey, Eds. and Trans.). New York: Appleton-Century-Crofts. (Original work published 1801).

*Jackson v. Indiana,* 406 U.S. 715 (1972).

Jacobson, J. W., Sutton, M. S., & Janicki, M. P. (1985). Demography and characteristics of aging and aged mentally retarded persons. In M. P. Janicki & H. M. Wisniewski (Eds.), *Aging and developmental disabilities: Issues and approaches* (pp. 115–142). Baltimore: Paul H. Brookes.

Jaffe, J. (1966). Attitudes of adolescents toward the mentally retarded. *American Journal of Mental Deficiency, 70,* 907–912.

Janicki, M. P., & Jacobson, J. W. (1986). Generational trends in sensory, physical, and behavioral abilities among older mentally retarded persons. *American Journal of Mental Deficiency, 90,* 490–500.

Janicki, M. P., & Jacobson, J. W. (1984). *Health and support services for mentally retarded elders living in foster care and group homes.* Symposium conducted at the 37th Annual Scientific Meeting of the Gerentological Society of America, San Antonio, TX.

Janicki, M. P., & MacEachron, A. E. (1984). Residential, health, and social service needs of elderly developmentally disabled persons. *The Gerontologist, 24,* 128–1376.

Janicki, M. P., Mayeda, T., & Epple, W. A. (1983). Availability of group homes for persons with mental retardation in the United States. *Mental Retardation, 21,* 45–51.

Janicki, M. P., Otis, J. P., Puccio, P. S., Rettig, J. H., & Jacobson, J. W. (1985). Service needs among older developmentally disabled persons. In M. P. Janicki & H. M. Wisniewski (Eds.), *Aging and developmental disabilities: Issues and approaches* (pp. 289–304). Baltimore: Paul H. Brookes.

Jaquish, C., & Stella, M. A. (1986). Helping special needs students move from elementary to secondary school. *Counterpoint, 7*(1), 1.

Jastak, J., MacPhee, H., & Whiteman, M. (1963). *Mental retardation: Its nature and incidence.* Newark: University of Delaware Press.

Jencks, C. (1972). Inequality: A reassessment of the effect of family and schooling in America. New York: Basic Books.

Jenkins, J. R., Speltz, M. L., & Odom, S. L. (1985). Integrating normal and handicapped preschoolers: Effects on child development and social interaction. *Exceptional Children, 52,* 7–18.

Jensen, A. R. (1950). The clinical management of the mentally retarded child and the parents. *American Journal of Psychiatry, 106,* 830–833.

Jensen, A. R. (1966). Verbal mediation and educational potential. *Psychology in the Schools, 3,* 99–109.

Jensen, A. R. (1969). How much can we boost IQ and scholastic achievement? *Harvard Educational Review, 39,* 1–123.

Jensen, A. R. (1973). *Educability and group differences.* New York: Harper & Row.

Jensen, A. R. (1980). *Bias in mental testing.* New York: Free Press.

Jensen, A. R. (1981). *Straight talk about mental tests.* New York: Free Press.

Johnson, C. F., Koch, R., Peterson, R. M., & Friedman, E. G. (1978). Congenital and neurological abnormalities in infants with phenylketonuria. *American Journal of Mental Deficiency, 82,* 375–379.

Johnson, D. R., Bruininks, R. H., & Thurlow, M. L. (1987). Meeting the challenge of transition service planning through improved interagency cooperation. *Exceptional Children, 53,* 522–530.

Johnson, G. O. (1959). Here and there the Onondaga census—Fact or artifact. *Exceptional Children, 25,* 226–231.

Johnson, L. J., & Beauchamp, K. D. (1987). Preschool assessment measures: What are the teachers using? *Journal of the Division for Early Childhood, 12,* 70–76.

Johnson, R. A. (1976). Renewal of school placement systems for the handicapped. In F. Weintraub, A. Abeson, J. Ballard, & M. LaVor (Eds.), *Public policy and the education of exceptional children* (pp. 47–61). Reston, VA: Council for Exceptional Children.

Johnson, T. E., Chandler, L. K., Kerns, G. M., & Fowler, S. A. (1986). What are parents saying about school transitions? *Journal of the Division for Early Childhood, 11,* 10–17.

Johnson, W. R. (1962). Special education for mentally handicapped—A paradox. *Exceptional Children, 19,* 62–69.

Johnson, W. R. (1971). Keynote address given at Planned Parenthood Center of Seattle, December 2–3, 1971. Unpublished manuscript.

Jones, K. L., Smith, D. W., & Hansen, J. W. (1976). The fetal alcohol syndrome: Clinical delineation. *Annals of the New York Academy of Science, 23,* 130–137.

Jones, K. L., Smith, D. W., Ulleland, C. N., & Streissguth, A. P. (1973, June 9). Pattern of malformation in offspring of chronic alcoholic mothers. *The Lancet, 1*(7815), 1267–1271.

Jones, P. R. (1981). *A practical guide to federal special education law: Understanding and implementing PL 94-142.* New York: Holt, Rinehart, & Winston.

Jordan, T. E. (1976). *The mentally retarded* (4th ed.). Columbus, OH: Merrill.

Juel-Nielsen, N. (1965). Individual and environment: A psychiatric-psychological investigation of monozygotic twins reared apart. *Acta Psychiatra et Neurologica Scandinaviae* (Monograph Suppl. No. 183).

Kagan, J. (1970). On class differences and early development. In V. Denenberg (Ed.), *Education of the infant and young child.* New York: Academic Press.

Kahn, H., & Bruce-Briggs, B. (1972). *Things to come: Thinking about the seventies and eighties.* New York: Macmillan.

Kakalik, J. S., Furry, W. S., Thomas, M. A., & Carney, M. F. (1981). *The cost of special education* (Rep. No. N1792-ED). Santa Monica, CA: Rand Corporation.

Kamin, L. J. (1974). *The science and politics of IQ.* Potomac, MD: Lawrence Erlbaum Associates.

Kanner, L. A. (1964). *A history of the care and study of the mentally retarded.* Springfield, IL: Charles C Thomas.

Kantner, H. M. (1969). *The identification of elements which contribute to occupational success and failure of adults classified as educable mentally retarded.* Unpublished doctoral dissertation, Arizona State University.

Karan, O., Wehman, P., Renzaglia, A., & Schuta, R. (1976). *Habilitation practices with the severely developmentally disabled.* Madison: University of Wisconsin, Waisman Center on Mental Retardation & Human Development.

Karnes, M. B. (1986). Future directions in early childhood education for exceptional children.

In J. J. Gallagher & B. B. Weiner (Eds.), *Alternative futures in special education* (pp. 42–64). Reston, VA: Council for Exceptional Children.

Karnes, M. B., Hodgins, A., & Teska, J. A. (1968). An evaluation of two preschool programs for disadvantaged children: A traditional and a highly structured experimental school. *Exceptional Children, 34,* 667–676.

Karnes, M. B., & Zehrbach, R. P. (1977). Alternative models for delivering services to young handicapped children. In J. B. Jordan, A. H. Hayden, M. B. Karnes, & M. M. Wood (Eds.), *Early childhood education for exceptional children.* Reston, VA: Council for Exceptional Children.

Kastner, L. S., Reppucci, N. D., & Pezzoli, J. J. (1979). Assessing community attitudes toward mentally retarded persons. *American Journal of Mental Deficiency, 84,* 137–144.

Kastner, T. (1988). AIDS and mental retardation. *American Association on Mental Retardation News & Notes, 1*(4), 2, 4.

Katz, E. (Ed.). (1972). *Mental health services for the mentally retarded.* Springfield, IL: Charles C Thomas.

Katz, S., & Yekutiel, E. (1974). Leisure time problems of mentally retarded graduates of training programs. *Mental Retardation, 12*(3), 54–57.

Kauffman, J. M. (1980). Where special education for disturbed children is going: A personal view. *Exceptional Children, 46,* 522–527.

Kauffman, J. M. (1987). Research in special education: A commentary. *Remedial & Special Education, 8*(6), 57–62.

Kauffman, J. M. (1989). *Characteristics of behavior disorders of children and youth.* (4th ed.). Columbus, OH: Merrill.

Kauffman, J. M., & Krouse, J. (1981). The cult of educability: Searching for the substance of things hoped for, the evidence of things not seen. *Analysis & Intervention in Developmental Disabilities, 1,* 53–60.

Kauffman, J. M., & Payne, J. S. (1975). *Mental retardation: Introduction and personal perspectives.* Columbus, OH: Merrill.

Kaufman, A. S., & Kaufman, N. L. (1983). *Kaufman assessment battery for children (K-ABC), interpretive manual.* Circle Pines, MN: American Guidance Service.

Kaufman, M. J., & Morra, L. G. (1978). The least restrictive environment: A major philosophical change. In E. L. Meyen (Ed.), *Exceptional children and youth: An introduction.* Denver: Love Publishing.

Kearsley, R. (1979, September). Quoted in B. Rice, Brave new world of intelligence testing. *Psychology Today,* pp. 27–41.

Keirn, W. C. (1971). Shopping parents: Patient problems or professional problem? *Mental Retardation, 9*(4), 6–7.

Keller, O. J., & Alper, B. S. (1970). Halfway houses: Community centered corrections and treatment. Lexington, MA: D.C. Heath.

Kelly, J. A., Wildman, R. G., & Berler, E. S. (1980). Small group behavioral training to improve the job interview skills repertoire of mildly retarded students. *Journal of Applied Behavior Analysis, 13,* 461–471.

Kemp, D. R. (1983). Assessing human rights committees: A mechanism for protecting the rights of institutionalized mentally retarded persons. *Mental Retardation, 21,* 13–16.

Keniston, K., & the Carnegie Council on Children. (1977). *All our children: The American family under pressure.* New York: Carnegie Corporation.

Kennedy, M. M., & Danielson, L. C. (1978). Where are unserved handicapped children? *Education & Training of the Mentally Retarded, 13,* 408–413.

Kenowitz, L., Zweibel, S., & Edgar, E. (1978). Determining the least restrictive educational opportunity for the severely and profoundly handicapped. In N. G. Haring & D. D. Bricker (Eds.), *Teaching the Severely Handicapped* (Vol. 3). Seattle: AAESPH.

Keogh, B. K. (1988). Perspectives on the Regular Education Initiative. *Learning Disabilities Focus, 4*(1), 3–5.

Keogh, B. K., & Daley, S. E. (1983). Early identification: One component of comprehensive services for at-risk children. *Topics in Early Childhood Special Education, 3*(3), 7–16.

Kerachsky, S., & Thornton, C. (1987). Findings from the STETS transitional employment demonstration. *Exceptional Children, 53,* 512–521.

Key, W. E. (1915). *Feeble-minded citizens in Pennsylvania.* Philadelphia: Public Charities Association of Pennsylvania.

Kidd, J. W. (1977). Comments from the executive director: The definitional dilemma. *Education & Training of the Mentally Retarded, 12,* 303–304.

Kidd, J. W. (1979). An open letter to the Committee on Terminology and Classification of AAMD from the Committee on Definition and Terminology of CEC-MR. *Education & Training of the Mentally Retarded, 14,* 74–76.

Kidd, J. W. (1983). The 1983 AAMD definition and classification of mental retardation: The apparent impact of the CEC-MR position. *Education & Training of the Mentally Retarded, 18,* 243–244.

King, F. (1975). Treatment of the mentally retarded character in modern American fiction. *Bulletin of Bibliography, 32*(3), 106–114, 131.

Kirk, S. A. (1958). *Early education of the mentally retarded: An experimental study.* Urbana: University of Illinois Press.

Kirk, S. A. (1962). *Educating exceptional children.* Boston: Houghton Mifflin.

Kirk, S. A. (1964). Research on the education of the mentally retarded. In H. A. Stevens & R. F. Heber (Eds.), *Mental retardation: A review of research.* Chicago: University of Chicago Press.

Kirk, S. A., & Gallagher, J. J. (1979). *Educating Exceptional Children* (3rd ed.). Boston: Houghton Mifflin.

Klein & Sheehan. (1987). Staff development: A key issue in meeting the needs of young handicapped children in day care settings. *Topics in Early Childhood Special Education, 7*(1), 13–27.

Kleinberg, J., & Galligan, B. (1983). Effects of deinstitutionalization on adaptive behavior of mentally retarded adults. *American Journal of Mental Deficiency, 88*(1), 21–27.

Kneedler, R. D., Hallahan, D. P., & Kauffman, J. M. (1984). *Special education for today.* Englewood Cliffs, NJ: Prentice-Hall.

Knowles, M. (1978). *The adult learner: A neglected species* (2nd ed.). Houston: Gulf.

Koch, R., Friedman, E. C., Azen, C., Wenz, E., Parton, P., Ledue, X., & Fishler, K. (1988). Inborn errors of metabolism and the prevention of mental retardation. In F. J. Menolascino & J. A. Stark (Eds.), *Preventive and curative intervention in mental retardation* (pp. 61–90). Baltimore: Paul H. Brookes.

Koegel, R. L. (1986). Social support and individual adaptation: A diachronic perspective. In L. L. Langness & H. G. Levine (Eds.), *Culture and retardation: Life histories of mildly mentally retarded persons in American society.* Boston: D. Reidel.

Koegel, R. L., Glahn, T. J., & Nieminen, G. S. (1978). Generalization of parent training results. *Journal of Applied Behavior Analysis, 11,* 95–109.

Kohlenberg, R. J. (1970). The punishment of persistent vomiting: A case study. *Journal of Applied Behavior Analysis, 3,* 95–109.

Kokaska, C. J. (1968). The occupational status of the educable mentally retarded: A review of follow-up studies. *Journal of Special Education, 2,* 369–377.

Kolstoe, O. P. (1961). An examination of some characteristics which discriminate between employed and not-employed mentally retarded males. *American Journal of Mental Deficiency, 66,* 472–482.

Kolstoe, O. P. (1972). *Mental retardation: An educational viewpoint.* New York: Holt, Rinehart, & Winston.

Kolstoe, O. P. (1975). Secondary programs. In J. M. Kauffman & J. S. Payne (Eds.), *Mental retardation: Introduction and personal perspectives.* Columbus, OH: Merrill.

Kolstoe, O. P. (1976). *Teaching educable mentally retarded children* (2nd ed.). New York: Holt, Rinehart, & Winston.

Kolstoe, O. P. (1981). Career education for the handicapped: Opportunities for the '80s. *Career*

*Development for Exceptional Individuals, 4,* 3–13.

Kolstoe, O. P., & Frey, R. M. (1965). *A high school work study program for mentally subnormal students.* Carbondale: Southern Illinois University Press.

Konig, K. (1966). The care and education of handicapped children. In C. Pietzner (Ed.), *Aspects of curative education.* Aberdeen, Scotland: Aberdeen University Press.

Krech, D., Rosenzweig, M. R., & Bennett, E. L. (1956). Dimensions of discrimination and level of cholinesterase activity in the cerebral cortex of the rat. *Journal of Comparative & Physiological Psychology, 49,* 261–268.

Kruger, R. (1980). Occupational information systems and their use in rehabilitation. *Rehabilitation Literature, 41,* 229–234.

Kugel, R. B. (1967). Familial mental retardation: Fact or fancy? In J. Hellmuth (Ed.), *The disadvantaged child* (Vol. 1). New York: Bruner/Mazel.

Kugel, R. B., & Parsons, M. H. (1967). *Children of deprivation: Changing the course of familial retardation.* Washington, DC: Children's Bureau.

Kugel, R. B., & Wolfensberger, W. (Eds.). (1969). *Changing patterns in residential services for the mentally retarded.* Washington, DC: U.S. Government Printing Office.

Kuhn, T. S. (1970). *The structure of scientific revolutions* (2nd ed.), Chicago: University of Chicago Press.

Kunzelmann, H. P., & Koenig, C. H. (1980). *REFER: Rapid exam for early referral.* Columbus, OH: Merrill.

Kurtz, D. P., Neisworth, J. T., & Laub, K. W. (1977). Issues concerning the early identification of handicapped children. *Journal of School Psychology, 15,* 136–140.

Kurtz, P. D. (1978). Family approaches. In J. T. Neisworth & R. M. Smith (Eds.), *Retardation: Issues, assessment, and intervention.* New York: McGraw-Hill.

Kurtz, R. A. (1977). *Social aspects of mental retardation.* Lexington, MA: Lexington Books.

LaBov, W. (1970). The logic of nonstandard English. In F. Williams (Ed.), *Language and poverty.* Chicago: Markham.

Lakin, K. C. (1983). Research-based knowledge and professional practices in special education for emotionally disturbed students. *Behavioral Disorders, 8,* 128–137.

Lakin, K. C., & Bruininks, R. H. (1985). Challenges to advocates of social integration of developmentally disabled persons. In K. C. Lakin & R. H. Bruininks, *Strategies for achieving community integration of developmentally disabled citizens* (pp. 313–330). Baltimore: Paul H. Brookes.

Lakin, K. C., Bruininks, R. H., Hill, R. K., & Hauber, F. A. (1982). Turnover of direct-care staff in a national sample of residential facilities for mentally retarded persons. *American Journal of Mental Deficiency, 87,* 64–72.

Lakin, K. C., Hill, B. K., & Bruininks, R. H. (1988). Trends and issues in the growth of community residential services. In M. P. Janicki, M. W. Krauss, & M. M. Seltzer (Eds.), *Community residences for persons with developmental disabilities: Here to stay* (pp. 25–43). Baltimore: Paul H. Brookes.

Lakin, K. C., Hill, B. K., Bruininks, R. H., & White, C. C. (1986). Residential options and future implications. In W. E. Kiernan & J. A. Stark (Eds.), *Pathways to employment for adults with developmental disabilities* (pp. 207–228). Baltimore: Paul H. Brookes.

Lambert, N. M., & Nicoll, R. C. (1976). Dimensions of adaptive behavior of retarded and nonretarded public school children. *American Journal of Mental Deficiency, 81,* 135–146.

Lambert, N. M., & Windmiller, M. B. (1981). *AAMD adaptive behavior scale—School edition.* Monterey, CA: Publishers Test Service.

Lambert, N. M., Windmiller, M. B., & Cole, L. J. (1975). *AAMD adaptive behavior scale, public school version.* Washington, DC: American Association on Mental Deficiency.

Lambie, D. Z., & Weikart, D. P. (1970). Ypsilanti Carnegie infant education project. In J. Hellmuth (Ed.), *The disadvantaged child* (Vol. 3). New York: Bruner/Mazel.

Landesman, S. (1988). Preventing "institutionalism" in the community. In M. P. Janicki, M. W. Krauss, & M. M. Seltzer (Eds.), *Community residences for persons with developmental disabilities: Here to stay* (pp. 105–116). Baltimore: Paul H. Brookes.

Landesmann-Dwyer, S. (1978). Behavioral changes in nonambulatory, profoundly mentally retarded individuals. In C. E. Meyers (Ed.), *Quality of life in severely and profoundly retarded people: Research foundations for improvement*. Washington, DC: American Association on Mental Deficiency.

Langness, L. L., & Levine, H. G. (Eds.). (1986). *Culture and retardation: Life histories of mildly mentally retarded persons in American society*. Boston: D. Reidel.

LaQuey, A. (1981). *Adult performance level adaptation and modification project*. Austin, TX: Educational Service Center, Region XIII.

*Larry P. v. Riles,* C-71-2270 (RFP, District Court for Northern California 1972).

Latib, A., Conroy, J., & Hess, C. M. (1984). Family attitudes toward deinstitutionalization. *International Review of Research in Mental Retardation, 12,* 67–95.

Laub, K. W., & Kurtz, D. P. (1978). Early identification. In J. Neisworth & R. M. Smith (Eds.), *Retardation: Issues, assessment and intervention*. New York: McGraw-Hill.

LaVor, M. L. (1976). Federal legislation for exceptional persons: A history. In F. J. Weintraub, A. Abeson, J. Ballard, & M. LaVor (Eds.), *Public policy and the education of exceptional children*. Reston, VA: Council for Exceptional Children.

LaVor, M. L. (1977). Federal legislation for exceptional children: Implications and a view of the field. In R. D. Kneedler & S. G. Tarver (Eds.), *Changing perspectives in special education*. Columbus, OH: Merrill.

LaVor, M. L., & Harvey, J. (1976). Head Start, Economic Opportunity, Community Partner-ship Act of 1974. *Exceptional Children, 42,* 227–230.

Lawrence, E. A., & Winschel, J. F. (1975). Locus of control: Implications for special education. *Exceptional Children, 41,* 483–490.

Lawry, G. (1972). Matching students with gaps: A real challenge. In *Vocational evaluation and curriculum modification*. Des Moines: Department of Public Instruction.

Lazar, I., & Darlington, R. (1982). Lasting effects of early education: A report from the consortium for longitudinal studies. *Monographs of the Society for Research in Child Development, 47.*

Leahy, R., Balla, D., & Zigler, E. (1987). Role taking, self image, and imitation in retarded and non-retarded individuals. *American Journal of Mental Deficiency, 86,* 372–379.

Lee, V. E., Brooks-Gunn, J., & Schnur, E. (1988). Does Head Start work? A 1-year follow-up comparison of disadvantaged children attending Head Start, no preschool, and other preschool programs. *Developmental Psychology, 24,* 210–222.

Lehr, D. M., & Brown, F. (1984). Perspectives on the severely handicapped. In E. L. Meyen (Ed.), *Mental retardation: Topics of today and issues of tomorrow*. Reston, VA: Council on Exceptional Children.

Lehrke, R. (1972a). A theory of X-linkage of major intellectual traits. *American Journal of Mental Deficiency, 76,* 611–619.

Lehrke, R. (1972b). Response to Dr. Anastasi and to the Drs. Nance and Engel. *American Journal of Mental Deficiency, 76,* 626–631.

Leinhardt, G., Bickel, W., & Pallay, A. (1982). Unlabeled but still entitled: Toward more effective remediation. *Teachers College Record, 84,* 391–422.

Lejeune, J., Gautier, M., & Turpin, R. (1959). Etudes des chromosomes somatiques de neuf enfants mongoliers. Paris, C. R. *Académie de Science, 248,* 1721–1722.

Leland, H. W. (1972). Mental retardation and adaptive behavior. *Journal of Special Education, 6,* 71–80.

Leland, H. W. (1973). Adaptive behavior and mentally retarded behavior. In R. K. Eyman, C. E. Meyers, & G. Tarjan (Eds.), Sociobehavioral studies in mental retardation. Monographs of the American Association on Mental Deficiency (No. 1), 91–99.

Leland, H. W. (1978). Theoretical considerations of adaptive behavior. In W. A. Coulter & H. W. Morrow (Eds.), *Adaptive behavior: Concepts and measurements*. New York: Grune & Stratton.

Lemkau, P., Tietze, C., & Cooper, M. (1962). Third paper: Mental hygiene problems in an urban district. *Mental Hygiene, 26,* 275–288.

Lemperle, G. (1985). Plastic surgery. In D. Lane & B. Stratford (Eds.), *Current approaches to Down's syndrome* (pp. 131–145). Sydney: Holt, Rinehart, & Winston.

Lemperle, G., & Rada, D. (1980). Facial plastic surgery in children with Down's syndrome. *Plastic & Reconstructive Surgery, 66,* 337–342.

Lenihan, J. (1976–1977). Disabled Americans: A history. *Performance, 27*(5, 6, 7), 1–72.

Lerner, J. W. (1981). *Learning disabilities: Theories, diagnosis and teaching strategies.* (3rd ed.). Boston: Houghton Mifflin.

Lesch, M., & Nyhan, W. L. (1964). A familial disorder of uric acid metabolism and central nervous system function. *American Journal of Medicine, 36,* 561–570.

Levitan, S. A., & Taggart, R. (1977). *Jobs for the disabled.* Washington, DC: Johns Hopkins University Press.

Levy, E., & McLeod, W. (1977). The effects of environmental design on adolescents in an institution. *Mental Retardation, 15*(2), 28–32.

Lewis, E. O. (1929). *Report of the mental deficiency committee* (Part 4). London: H. M. Stationery Office.

Lewis, J. F., & Mercer, J. R. (1978). The system of multicultural pluralistic assessment: SOMPA. In W. A. Coulter & H. W. Morrow (Eds.), *Adaptive Behavior: Concepts and measurements.* New York: Grune & Stratton.

Lewontin, R. C., Rose, S., & Kamin, L. J. (1984). *Not in our genes.* New York: Pantheon Books.

Libby, J. D., Polloway, E. A., & Smith, J. D. (1983). Lesch-Nyhan syndrome: A review. *Education & Training of the Mentally Retarded, 18,* 226–231.

Lillie, D. (1975, April). *Identification and screening.* Paper presented at the Infant Education Conference, San Antonio.

Lilly, M. S. (1986). The relationships between general and special eduation: A new face on an old issue. *Counterpoint, 10.*

Lindsley, O. R. (1964). Direct measurement and prosthesis of retarded behavior. *Journal of Education, 147,* 62–81.

Lindsley, O. R. (1966). An experiment with parents handling behavior at home. *Johnstone Bulletin, 9,* 27–36.

Linstone, H. A. (1977). *The postindustrial society and mental retardation.* Paper presented for the President's Committee on Mental Retardation.

Linstone, H. A. (1980). The postindustrial society and mental retardation. In S. C. Plog & M. B. Santamour (Eds.), *Strategies for achieving community integration of developmentally disabled citizens* (pp. 123–154). New York: Plenum.

Litton, F. W. (1978). *Education of trainable mentally retarded: Curriculum, methods, materials.* St. Louis: C.V. Mosby.

Lloyd, J. W., Crowley, E. P., Kohler, F. W., & Strain, P. S. (1988). Redefining the applied research agenda: Cooperative learning preferral, teacher consultation, and peer-mediated interventions. *Journal of Learning Disabilities, 21,* 43–52.

Lovett, D. L., & Harris, M. B. (1987). Important skills for adults with mental retardation: The client's point of view. *Mental Retardation, 25,* 351–356.

Lubin, R. A., Schwartz, A. A, Zigman, W. B., & Janicki, M. P. (1982). Community acceptance of residential programs for developmentally disabled persons. *Applied Research in Mental Retardation, 3,* 191–200.

Luiselli, J. K. (1978). Treatment of an autistic child's fear of riding a school bus through exposure and reinforcement. *Journal of Behavior Therapy & Experimental Psychiatry, 9,* 169–172.

Lund, K. A., & Bos, C. S. (1981). Orchestrating the preschool classroom: The early schedule. *Teaching Exceptional Children, 14,* 121–125.

Lyssky, D. K., & Gartner, A. (1987). Capable of achievement and worthy of respect: Education for handicapped students as if they were full-fledged human beings. *Exceptional Children, 54*(1), 69–74.

MacAndrews, C., & Edgerton, R. (1964). The everyday life of institutionalized "idiots." *Human Organism, 23,* 312–318.

Macarov, D. (1985). Overcoming unemployment: Some radical proposals. *The Futurist, 19*(2), 19–24.

MacArthur, C. A., Jr., Hagerty, G., & Taymans, J. (1982). Personnel preparation: A catalyst in career education for the handicapped. *Exceptional Education Quarterly, 3*(3), 1–8.

MacMillan, D. L. (1977). *Mental retardation in school and society.* Boston: Little, Brown.

MacMillan, D. L. (1982). *Mental retardation in school and society* (2nd ed.). Boston: Little, Brown.

MacMillan, D. L. (1988). "New" EMRs. In G. A. Robinson, J. R. Patton, E. A. Polloway, & L. R. Sargent (Eds.), *Best practices in mental disabilities* (Vol. 2). Des Moines: Iowa Department of Education.

MacMillan, D. L., & Borthwick, S. (1980). The new educable mentally retarded population: Can they be mainstreamed? *Mental Retardation, 18,* 155–158.

MacMillan, D. L., Jones, R. L., & Aloia, G. F. (1974). The mentally retarded label: A theoretical analysis and review of research. *American Journal of Mental Deficiency, 79,* 241–261.

MacMillan, D. L., Meyers, C. E., & Morrison, G. M. (1980). System-identification of mildly mentally retarded children: Implications for interpreting and conducting research. *American Journal of Mental Deficiency, 85*(2), 108–115.

Mallory, B. M. (1977). The ombudsman in a residential institution: A description of the role and suggested training areas. *Mental Retardation, 15*(5), 14–17.

Maloney, M. P., & Ward, M. P. (1978). *Mental retardation and modern society.* New York: Oxford University Press.

Mandell, C. J., & Gold, V. (1984). *Teaching handicapped students.* St. Paul, MN: West.

Mank, D. M., Rhodes, L. E., & Bellamy, C. T. (1986). Four supported employment alternatives. In W. E. Kiernan & J. A. Stark (Eds.), *Pathways to employment for adults with developmental disabilities* (pp. 139–154). Baltimore: Paul H. Brookes.

Manni, J. L., Winikur, D. W., & Keller, M. (1980). *The status of minority group representation in special education programs in the state of New Jersey.* Trenton: New Jersey State Department of Education. (ERIC Document Reproduction Service No. ED 203 575).

Marchetti, A. G. (1987). *Wyatt* v. *Stickney:* A consent decree. *Research in Developmental Disabilities, 8,* 249–259.

Marks, H. E., & Wade, R. (1981). A device for reducing object destruction among institutionalized mentally retarded persons. *Mental Retardation, 19,* 181–182.

Marland, S. P. (1971). Career education now. *The Education Digest, 36,* 9–11.

Marland, S. P. (1972). Career education: Every student headed for a goal. *American Vocational Journal, 47*(3), 34–36.

Marlowe, M., Errera, J., & Jacobs, J. (1983). Increased lead and cadmium disorders among mentally retarded children and children with borderline intelligence. *American Journal of Mental Deficiency, 87,* 477–483.

Marsh, R. L., Friel, C. M., & Eissler, V. (1975). The adult MR in the criminal justice system. *Mental Retardation, 13*(2), 21–25.

Martin, E. W. (1972). Individualism and behaviorism as future trends in educating handicapped children. *Exceptional Children, 38,* 517–525.

Martin, G., & Pear, J. (1983). *Behavior modification: What it is and how to do it.* Englewood Cliffs, NJ: Prentice-Hall.

Martinson, R. A. (1973). Children with superior cognitive abilities. In L. M. Dunn (Ed.), *Exceptional children in the schools* (2nd ed.). New York: Harper & Row.

Masland, R., Sarason, S., & Gladwin, T. (1958). *Mental subnormality.* New York: Basic Books.

Maslow, A. H. (1954). *Motivation and personality.* New York: Harper & Row.

Massie, W. (1962). Sheltered workshops: A 1962 portrait. *Journal of Rehabilitation, 28*(5), 17–20.

*Matthews v. Campbell,* Civil Action No. 78-0879-R (E.D. Va. July 16, 1979).

Matthews, W. S., Barabas, G., Cusack, E., & Ferrari, M. (1986). Social quotients of children with phenylketonuria before and after discontinuation of dietary therapy. *American Journal of Mental Deficiency, 91,* 92–94.

Maurer, S., Teas, S., & Bates, P. (1980). *Project A.M.E.S.* Des Moines: Iowa Department of Public Instruction.

May, D. C. (1988). Plastic surgery for children with Down syndrome: Normalization or extremism? *Mental Retardation, 26,* 17–19.

Mayo, L. W. (1962). *A proposed program for national action to combat mental retardation.* Report to the President's Committee on Mental Retardation. Washington, DC: U.S. Government Printing Office.

Mazzullo, M. (1977, April). *The mandate: to identify children with handicapping conditions.* (ERIC Document Reproduction Service No. ED 139-225).

McAfee, J. K., & Gural, M. (1988). Individuals with mental retardation and the criminal justice system: The view from the states' attorneys general. *Mental Retardation, 26,* 5–12.

McAfee, J. K., & Sheeler, M. C. (1987). Accomodation of adults who are mentally retarded in community colleges: A national study. *Education & Training in Mental Retardation, 22,* 262–267.

McBride, J. W., & Forgnone, C. (1985). Emphasis of instruction provided LD, EH, and EMR students in categorized and cross-categorical programming. *Journal of Research & Development in Education, 18*(4), 50–54.

McCarney, S. B., Leigh, J. E., & Cornbleet, J. A. (1983). *Behavior evaluation scale.* Columbus, MO: Educational Services.

McCarthy, M. M. (1983). The Pennhurst and Rowley decisions: Issues and implications. *Exceptional Children, 49,* 517–522.

McCarver, R. B., & Craig, E. M. (1974). Placement of the retarded in the community: Prognosis and outcome. *International Review of Research in Mental Retardation, 7.*

McDaniels, G. (1977). Successful programs for young handicapped children. *Educational Horizons, 56*(1), 26–27, 30–33.

McHale, J. (1980). Mental retardation and the future: A conceptual approach. In S. C. Plog & M. B. Santamour (Eds.), *The year 2000 and mental retardation* (pp. 19–70). New York: Plenum.

McKinney, J. D., & Hocutt, A. M. (1988). Policy issues in the evaluation of the Regular Education Initiative. *Learning Disabilities Focus, 4*(1), 15–23.

McKusick, V. A. (1982). *Mendelian inheritance in man: Catalogs of autosomal dominant, autosomal recessive, and X-linked phenotypes.* Baltimore: Johns Hopkins University Press.

McLaren, J., & Bryson, S. E. (1987). Review of recent epidemiological studies of mental retardation: Prevalence, associated disorders, and etiology. *American Journal of Mental Retardation, 92,* 243–254.

McLaughlin, M. J., Smith-Davis, J., & Burke, P. J. (1986). *Personnel to educate the handicapped in America: A status report.* College Park: University of Maryland, Institute for the Study of Exceptional Children and Youth.

McLoughlin, J. A., & Lewis, R. (1981). *Assessing special students.* Columbus, OH: Merrill.

McLoughlin, J. A., & Lewis, R. (1986). *Assessing special students* (2nd ed.). Columbus, OH: Merrill.

McNeil, M. C., Polloway, E. A., & J. D. Smith. (1984). Feral and isolated children: Historical review and analysis. *Education and Training of the Mentally Retarded, 19,* 70–79

Mecham, M. J., & Jones, J. D. (1978). *Utah test of language development—Revised.* Salt Lake City: Communication Research Associates.

Menolascino, F. J. (1974). The mentally retarded offender. *Mental Retardation, 12*(1), 7–11.

Menolascino, F. J., & Egger, M. L. (1978). *Medical dimensions of mental retardation.* Lincoln: University of Nebraska Press.

Menolascino, F. J., & McGee, J. J. (1981). The new institutions: Last ditch arguments. *Mental Retardation, 19,* 215–220.

Menolascino, F. J., & Stark, J. A. (1988). *Preventive and curative intervention in mental retardation.* Baltimore: Paul H. Brookes.

Mercer, C. D. (1983). *Students with learning disabilities* (2nd ed.). Columbus, OH: Merrill.

Mercer, C. D. (1987). *Students with learning disabilities* (3rd ed.). Columbus, OH: Merrill.

Mercer, C. D., & Mercer, A. R. (1985). *Teaching students with learning problems* (2nd ed.). Columbus, OH: Merrill.

Mercer, C. D., & Mercer, A. R. (1989). *Teaching students with learning disabilities* (3rd ed.). Columbus, OH: Merrill.

Mercer, C. D., & Payne, J. S. (1975a). Biological and environmental causes. In J. M. Kauffman & J. S. Payne (Eds.), *Mental retardation: Introduction and personal perspectives* (pp. 50–74). Columbus, OH: Merrill.

Mercer, C. D., & Payne, J. S. (1975b). Learning theories and their implications. In J. M. Kauffman & J. S. Payne (Eds.), *Mental retardation: Introduction and personal perspectives.* Columbus, OH: Merrill.

Mercer, C. D., & Snell, M. E. (1977). *Learning theory research in mental retardation: Implications for teaching.* Columbus, OH: Merrill.

Mercer, J. R. (1973a). *Labeling the mentally retarded.* Berkeley: University of California Press.

Mercer, J. R. (1973b). The myth of 3% prevalence. In R. K. Eyman, C. E. Meyers, & G. Tarjan (Eds.). Sociobehavioral studies in mental retardation. *Monographs of the American Association on Mental Deficiency* (No. 1).

Mercer, J. R. (1977). *System of multicultural pluralistic assessment: Technical manual.* New York: Psychological Corporation.

Mercer, J. R., & Lewis, J. F. (1977a). *System of multicultural pluralistic assessment: Parent interview manual.* New York: Psychological Corporation.

Mercer, J. R., & Lewis, J. F. (1977b). *System of multicultural pluralistic assessment: Student assessment manual.* New York: Psychological Corporation.

Mesibov, G. B. (1976). Mentally retarded people: 200 years in America. *Journal of Clinical Child Psychology, 5*(3), 25–29.

Meyen, E. L. (1978). *Exceptional children and youth: An introduction.* Denver: Love Publishing.

Meyer, D. J. (1986). Fathers of handicapped children. In R. R. Fewell & P. F. Vadasy (Eds.), *Families of handicapped children.* Austin: PRO-ED.

Meyer, L. H., & Putnam, J. (1988). Social integration. In V. Van Hasselt, P. Strain, & M. Hersen (Eds.), *Handbook of developmental and physical disabilities.* New York: Pergamon.

Meyers, C. E., & MacMillan, D. L. (1976). Utilization of learning principles in retardation. In R. Koch & J. Dobson (Eds.), *The mentally retarded child and his family: A multidisciplinary handbook* (2nd ed.). New York: Bruner/Mazel.

Meyers, R. (1980). *Like normal people.* New York: McGraw-Hill.

Miller, S. J., & Sloane, H. N. (1976). The generalization effects of parent training across stimulus settings. *Journal of Applied Behavior Analysis, 9,* 355–370.

*Mills v. Board of Education of District of Columbia,* 348 F. Supp. 866 (D.D.C. 1972).

Mithaug, D. E. (1979). A comparison of procedures to increase responding in three severely retarded, noncompliant young adults. *AAESPH Review, 4*(1), 66–80.

Mithaug, D. E., Horiuchi, C. N., & Fanning, P. N. (1985). A report on the Colorado statewide follow-up survey of special education students. *Exceptional Children, 51,* 397–404.

Mithaug, D. E., Martin, J. E., & Agran, M. (1987). Adaptability instruction: The goal of transitional programming. *Exceptional Children, 53,* 500–505.

Mosier, H. D., Grossman, H. J., & Dingman, H. F. (1962). Secondary sex development in mentally deficient individuals. *Child Development, 33,* 273–286.

Mosier, H. D., Grossman, H. J., & Dingman, H. F. (1965). Physical growth in mental defectives. *Pediatrics, 36,* 465–519.

Munro, J. D., Duncan, H. G., & Seymour, L. M. (1983). Effect of frontline staff turnover on the behavior of institutionalized mentally retarded adults. *American Journal of Mental Deficiency, 88,* 328–332.

Naisbitt, J. (1984). *Megatrends: Ten new directions transforming our lives.* New York: Warner.

Nance, W. E., & Engel, E. (1972). One X and four hypotheses: Response to Lehrke's "A theory of X-linkage of major intellectual traits." *American Journal of Mental Deficiency, 76,* 623–625.

Nanus, B. (1980). Living and working in the year 2000: Some implications for mental retardation policy. In S. C. Plog & M. B. Santamour (Eds.), *Strategies for achieving community integration of developmentally disabled citizens* (pp. 71–96). New York: Plenum.

Nardella, M. T., Sulzbacher, S. I., & Worthington-Roberts, B. S. (1983). Activity levels of persons with Prader-Willi syndrome. *American Journal of Mental Deficiency, 87,* 498–505.

National Advisory Committee on the Handicapped. (1976). *Annual Report.* Washington, DC: U.S. Office of Education.

National Association for Retarded Children (NARC). (1971). *Policy statements on the education of mentally retarded children.* Arlington, TX: Author.

National Association of School Psychologists (1983). *Specialty guidelines for the delivery of services by school psychologists.* Washington, DC: Author.

National Association of Sheltered Workshops and Homebound Programs. Publications Committee. (1961). *Planning a workshop: A growing responsibility.* Washington, DC: Author.

National Association of State Directors of Special Education. (1977). *Child find data: A report of feedback information.* Washington, DC: Author. (ERIC Document Reproduction Service No. ED 149 552).

National Association of Superintendents of Public Residential Facilities for the Mentally Retarded (1974). *Contemporary issues in residential programming.* Washington, DC: President's Committee on Mental Retardation.

Neisworth, J. T., & Bagnato, S. J. (1988). Developmental retardation. In V. B. Van Hasselt & M. Hersen (Eds.), *Psychological evaluation of the developmentally and physically disabled.* New York: Plenum.

Neisworth, J. T., Jones, R. T., & Smith, R. M. (1978). Body behavior problems: A conceptualization. *Education & Training of the Mentally Retarded, 13,* 265–271.

Neisworth, J. T., & Smith, R. M. (1975). *Modifying retarded behavior.* Boston: Houghton Mifflin.

Neisworth, J. T., & Smith, R. M. (1978). *Retardation: Issues, assessment and intervention.* New York: McGraw-Hill.

Nelson, C. M. (1977). Alternative education for the mildly and moderately handicapped. In R. D. Kneedler & S. G. Tarver (Eds.), *Changing perspectives in special education.* Columbus, OH: Merrill.

Nevin, A., & Thousand, J. (1988). Avoiding/limiting special education referrals: Changes and challenges. In M. C. Wang, M. C. Reynolds, & H. Wahlberg (Eds.), *Handbook of special education: Research and practice.* Oxford: Pergamon.

*New York Association for Retarded Children v. Rockefeller,* 357 F. Supp. 752 (E.D. N.Y. 1973). Final consent judgment entered, Civil Nos. 72C 356, 72C 357 (E.D. N. Y. entered May 5, 1975).

Newman, H. H., Freeman, F. N., & Holzinger, K. J. (1937). *Twins: A study of heredity and environment.* Chicago: University of Chicago Press.

Nietupski, J. A., & Hamre-Nietupski, S. M. (1979). Teaching auxiliary communication skills to severely handicapped students. *AAESPH Review. 4*(2), 107–123.

Nietupski, J. A., & Hamre-Nietupski, S. M. (1987). An ecological approach to curriculum development. In L. Goetz, D. Guess, & K. Stremel-Campbell (Eds.), *Innovative program design for individuals with dual sensory impairments.* Baltimore: Paul H. Brookes.

Nietupski, J. A., Hamre-Nietupski, S. M., Schuetz, G., & Ockwood, L. (1980). The delivery of communication therapy services to severely handicapped students: A plan for change. *Journal of The Association for the Severely Handicapped, 6*(1), 13–23.

Nihira, K. (1969). Factorial dimensions of adaptive behavior in adult retardates. *American Journal of Mental Deficiency, 73,* 868–878.

Nihira, K. (1976). Dimensions of adaptive behavior in institutionalized mentally retarded children and adults. *American Journal of Mental Deficiency, 81,* 215–226.

Nihira, K., Foster, R., Shellhaas, M., & Leland, H. (1969). *Adaptive behavior scales: Manual.* Washington, DC: American Association on Mental Deficiency.

Nihira, K., Foster, R., Shellhaas, M., & Leland, H. (1974). *AAMD adaptive behavior scale* (rev. ed.). Washington, DC: American Association on Mental Deficiency.

Nihira, K., Meyers, E., & Mink, I. T. (1983). Reciprocal relationship between home environment and development of TMR adolescents. *American Journal of Mental Deficiency, 88,* 139–149.

Nirje, B. (1969). The normalization principle and its human management implications. In R. B. Kugel & W. Wolfensberger (Eds.), *Changing patterns in residential services for the mentally retarded.* Washington, DC: U.S. Government Printing Office.

Nolley, D., & Nolley, B. (1984). Microcomputer data analysis at the clinical mental retardation site. *Mental Retardation, 22,* 85–89.

Noonan, M. J., Brown, F., Mulligan, M., & Rettig, M. A. (1982). Educability of severely handicapped persons: Both sides of the issue. *TASH Journal, 7,* 3–12.

Novak Amado, A. R. (1988). A perspective on the present and notes for new directions. In L. W. Heal, J. I. Haney, & A. R. Novak Amado (Eds.), *Integration of developmentally disabled individuals into the community* (2nd ed., pp. 299–306). Baltimore: Paul H. Brookes.

Nyhan, W. L. (1976). Behavior in the Lesch-Nyhan syndrome. *Journal of Autism & Childhood Schizophrenia, 6,* 235–252.

Nyhan, W. L., Johnson, H. G., Kaufman, I. A., & Jones, K. (1980). Serotonergic approaches to the modification of behavior in the Lesch-Nyhan syndrome. *Applied Behavior in Mental Retardation, 1,* 25–40.

Oberman, C. E. (1965). *A history of vocational rehabilitation in America.* Minneapolis: T. S. Denison.

O'Connell, J. C. (1986). Managing small group instruction in an integrated preschool setting. *Teaching Exceptional Children, 18,* 166–171.

*O'Connor v. Donaldson,* 493 F. 2d 507 (5th Cir. 1974), vacated and remanded on the issue of immunity, 95 S. Ct. 258b (1975).

O'Connor, N. (1966). The prevalence of mental defect. In A. A. Clarke & A. D. B. Clarke (Eds.), *Mental deficiency: The changing outlook.* New York: Free Press.

O'Connor, N. (1975). Imbecility and color blindness. *American Journal of Mental Deficiency, 62,* 83–87.

Office of Special Education and Rehabilitative Services. (1988). *Summary of existing legislation affecting persons with disabilities.* Washington, DC: U.S. Department of Education.

Ogden, C. K. (1934). *The system of basic English.* New York: Harcourt Brace Jovanovich.

Olbrisch, R. R. (1982). Plastic surgical management of children with Down's syndrome: Indications and results. *British Journal of Plastic Surgery, 35,* 195–200.

Olshansky, S. (1962). Chronic sorrow: A response to having a mentally defective child. *Social Casework, 43,* 190–193.

Olshansky, S. (1966). Parent responses to a mentally defective child. *Mental Retardation, 4*(4), 21–23.

O'Neill, C., & Bellamy, G. T. (1978). Evaluation of a procedure for teaching saw chain assembly to a severely retarded woman. *Mental Retardation, 16,* 37–41.

Orelove, F. P., & Sobsey, R. (1984). *Educating individuals with multiple disabilities.* Baltimore: Paul H. Brookes.

Orelove, F. P., & Sobsey, R. (1987). *Multiple disabilities: A transdisciplinary approach.* Baltimore: Paul H. Brookes.

Osgood, C., Gorsuch, L., & McGrew, B. (1966). *Survey of mental retardation services in the Kansas City metropolitan area.* Kansas City, MO: Institute for Community Studies.

Otto, P. L., Sulzbacher, S. I., & Worthington-Roberts, B. S. (1982). Sucrose-induced behavior changes of persons with Prader-Willi syndrome. *American Journal of Mental Deficiency, 86,* 335–341.

Overmier, J. B., & Seligman, M. E. P. (1967). Effects of inescapable shock upon subsequent escape and avoidance learning. *Journal of Comparative & Physiological Psychology, 63,* 22–33.

Page, E. G. (1972). Miracle in Milwaukee: Raising the IQ. *Educational Researcher, 15,* 8–16.

Page, E. G., & Grandon, G. M. (1981). Massive intervention and child intelligence: The Milwaukee Project in critical perspective. *Journal of Special Education, 15,* 239–256.

Paige, D. M. (1975). Nutritional deficiency and school performance. In R. A. Haslam & P. J. Valletutti (Eds.), *Medical problems in the classroom.* Baltimore: University Park Press.

Parker, R. M. (1983). *Occupational aptitude survey and interest schedule.* Austin: PRO-ED.

Parsons, C. L., Iacone, T. A., & Rozner, L. (1987). Effect of tongue reduction on articulation in children with Down's syndrome. *American Journal of Mental Deficiency, 91,* 328–332.

Pasamanick, B. (1959). Influence of sociocultural variables upon organic factors in mental retardation. *American Journal of Mental Deficiency, 64,* 316–320.

*PASE* (Parents in Action on Special Education) *v. Hannon,* U.S. District Court, N.D. Ill., No. 74 (3586) (July 1980).

Patrick, J. L., & Reschly, D. L. (1982). Relationship of state educational criteria and demographic variables to school-system prevalence of mental retardation. *American Journal of Mental Deficiency, 86,* 351–360.

Patterson, D. (1987). The causes of Down syndrome. *Scientific American, 52.*

Patton, J. R., & Browder, D. P. (1988). Transitions into the future. In B. Ludlow, R. Luckasson, & A. Turnbull (Eds.), *Transitions to adult life for persons with mental retardation: Principles and practices.* (pp. 293–311). Baltimore: Paul H. Brookes.

Patton, J. R., & Payne, J. S. (1986). Mild mental retardation. In N. G. Haring & L. McCormick (Eds.), *Exceptional children and youth* (4th ed., pp. 233–269). Columbus, OH: Merrill.

Patton, J. R., Payne, J. S., Kauffman, J. M., Brown, G. B., & Payne, R. A. (1987). *Exceptional children in focus* (4th ed.). Columbus, OH: Merrill.

Patton, J. R., & Polloway, E.A. (in press). Mild mental retardation. In N. G. Haring and L. P. McCormick (Eds.), *Exceptional children and youth* (5th ed.). Columbus, OH: Merrill.

Patton, J. R., & Polloway, E. A. (1982). The learning disabled: The adult years. *Topics in Learning & Learning Disabilities, 2*(3), 79–88.

Payne, J. S. (1962). *A prevalence survey of severely mentally retarded in Wyandotte County, Kansas.* Unpublished master's thesis, University of Kansas, Lawrence, KS.

Payne, J. S. (1971). Prevalence survey of severely mentally retarded in Wyandotte County, Kansas. *Training School Bulletin, 67,* 220–227.

Payne, J. S., & Chaffin, J. D. (1968). Developing employer relations in a work-study program for the educable mentally retarded. *Education & Training of the Mentally Retarded, 3.*

Payne, J. S., Kauffman, J. M., Patton, J. R., Brown, G. B., & DeMott, R. M. (1979). *Exceptional children in focus* (2nd ed.). Columbus, OH: Merrill.

Payne, J. S., & Mercer, C. D. (1974). Head Start. In S. E. Goodman (Ed.), *Handbook on contemporary education.* Princeton, NJ: Bowker.

Payne, J. S., Mercer, C. D., & Epstein, M. H. (1974). *Education and rehabilitation techniques.* New York: Behavioral.

Payne, J. S., Miller, A. K., Hazlett, R. L., & Mercer, C. D. (1984). *Rehabilitation techniques: Vocational adjustment for the handicapped.* New York: Human Science.

Payne, J. S., Polloway, E. A., Smith, J. E., & Payne, R. A. (1977). *Strategies for teaching the mentally retarded.* Columbus, OH: Merrill.

*Pennsylvania Association for Retarded Children*

(PARC) *v. Commonwealth of Pennsylvania,* Civil Action No. 71-42, 3- Judge Court (E.D. Pa., 1971).

Penrose, L. S. (1963). *The biology of mental deficiency.* London: Sidgwick & Jackson.

Penorse, L. S. (1966). *The biology of mental defect* (2nd rev. ed.). New York: Grune & Stratton.

Perkins, S. A. (1977). Malnutrition and mental development. *Exceptional Children, 43,* 214–219.

Perske, R. (1972). The dignity of risk and the mentally retarded. *Mental Retardation, 10*(1), 24–27.

Peters, J. M., Templeman, T. P., & Brostrom, G. (1987). The school and community partnership: Planning transition for students with severe handicaps. *Exceptional Children, 53,* 531–536.

Peterson, N. L. (1986). *Early intervention for handicapped and at-risk children: An introduction to early childhood special education.* Denver: Love Publishing.

Petzy, V. (1979). A model for employer commitment to job development. *Career Development for Exceptional Individuals, 2*(2), 80–89.

Phelps, L. A., & Lutz, R. J. (1977). *Career exploration and preparation for the special needs learner.* Boston: Allyn & Bacon.

Piaget, J. (1969). *The theory of stages in cognitive develoment.* New York: McGraw-Hill.

Pietzner, C. (1966). In C. Pietzner (Ed.), *Aspects of curative education.* Aberdeen, Scotland: Aberdeen University Press.

Pines, M. (1966). *Revolution in learning.* New York: Harper & Row.

Pines, M. (1973). *The brain changers: Scientists and the new mind control.* New York: Signet.

Pines, M. (1979, September). A head start in the nursery. *Psychology Today,* 56–68.

Plog, S. C. (1980). The year 2000 and mental retardation: An interpretation and critique. In S. C. Plog & M. B. Santamour (Eds.), *Strategies for achieving community integration of developmentally disabled citizens* (pp. 201–226). New York: Plenum.

Polloway, E. A. (1984). The integration of mildly retarded students in the schools: A historical review. *Remedial & Special Education, 5*(4), 18–28.

Polloway, E. A. (1987). Early age transition services for mildly mentally retarded individuals. In R. Ianacone & R. Stodden (Eds.), *Transitional issues and directions for individuals who are mentally retarded* (pp. 11–24). Reston, VA: Council for Exceptional Children.

Polloway, E. A., & Epstein, M. H. (1985). Current research issues in mild mental retardation: A survey of the field. *Education & Training of the Mentally Retarded, 20,* 171–174.

Polloway, E. A., Epstein, M. H., & Cullinan, D. (1985). Prevalence of behavior problems among educable mentally retarded students. *Education & Training of the Mentally Retarded, 20,* 3–13.

Polloway, E. A., Epstein, M. H., Patton, J. R., Cullinan, D., & Luebke, J. (1986). Demographic, social, and behavioral characteristics of students with educable mental retardation. *Education & Training of the Mentally Retarded, 21,* 27–34.

Polloway, E. A., Epstein, M. H., Polloway, C. H., Patton, J. R, & Ball, D. W. (1986). Corrective reading program: An analysis of effectiveness with learning disabled and mentally retarded students. *Remedial & Special Education, 7*(4), 41–47.

Polloway, E. A., Patton, J. R., Payne, J. S., & Payne, R. A. (1989). *Strategies for teaching learners with special needs* (4th ed.). Columbus, OH: Merrill.

Polloway, E. A., & Payne, J. S. (1975). Comparison of the AAMD Heber and Grossman manuals on terminology and classification in mental retardation. *Mental Retardation, 13,* (3), 12–14.

Polloway, E. A., Payne, J. S., Patton, J. R., & Payne, R. A. (1985). *Strategies for teaching retarded and special needs learners.* Columbus, OH: Merrill.

Polloway, E. A., & Smith, J. D. (1983). Changes in mild mental retardation: Population, programs, and perspectives. *Exceptional Children, 50,* 149–159.

Polloway, E. A., & Smith, J. D. (1984). The right to life: A survey of attitudes among the staff of a residential facility for mentally retarded persons. In J. D. Smith & E. A. Polloway (Eds.), *Special education in transition.* (pp. 83–88).

Lynchburg, VA: Vahnity Press/Lynchburg College.

Polloway, E. A., & Smith, J. D. (1987). Current status of the mild mental retardation construct: Identification, placement, and programs. In M. C. Wang, M. C. Reynolds, & H. J. Wahlberg (Eds.), *The handbook of special education: Research and practice* (pp. 1–22). Oxford: Pergamon.

Porteus, S. T. (1933). *The Porteus maze test.* New York: Psychological Corporation.

Potts, W. E., Schroer, R. J., & Taylor, H. A. (1984). *Counseling aids for geneticists.* Greenwood, SC: Greenwood Genetic Center.

Powell, T. H., Aiken, J. M., & Smylie, M. A. (1982). Treatment of involuntary euthanasia for severely handicapped newborns: Issues of philosophy and public policy. *Journal for The Association for the Severely Handicapped, 7*(4), 3–10.

Powell, T. H., & Ogle, P. A. (1985). *Brothers and sisters—A special part of exceptional families.* Baltimore: Paul H. Brookes.

President's Committee on Mental Retardation (PCMR). (1970). *The six-hour retarded child.* Washington, DC: U.S. Government Printing Office.

President's Committee on Mental Retardation (PCMR). (1974, April). Gallup poll shows attitudes on MR improving. *President's Committee on Mental Retardation Message.* Washington, DC: U.S. Printing Office.

President's Committee on Mental Retardation (PCMR). (1976a). *Mental retardation: Century of decision.* Washington, DC: U.S. Government Printing Office.

President's Committee on Mental Retardation (PCMR). (1976b). *Mental retardation: The known and the unknown.* Washington, DC: U.S. Government Printing Office.

President's Committee on Mental Retardation (PCMR). (1977). *Mental retardation: Past and present.* Washington, DC: U. S. Government Printing Office.

President's Committee on Mental Retardation (PCMR). (1978, March). Washington, DC: PCMR Newsclipping Service.

Prout, H. T., & Sheldon, K. L. (1984). Classifying mental retardation in vocational rehabilitation: A study of diagnostic practices and their adherence to accepted guidelines. *Rehabilitation Counseling Bulletin, 28,* 125–131.

Pueschel, S. M., Hays, R. M., & Mendoza, T. (1983). Familial X-linked mental retardation syndrome associated with minor congenital anomalies, macro-orchidism, and fragile-X chromosome. *American Journal of Mental Deficiency, 87,* 372–376.

Pulliam, J. D. (1968). *History of education in America.* Columbus, OH: Merrill.

Raech, H. (1966). A parent discusses initial counseling. *Mental Retardation, 4*(2), 25–26.

Ramey, C. T., Bryant, D. M., Sparling, J. J., & Wasik, B. H. (1985). Project CARE: A comparison of two early intervention strategies to prevent retarded development. *Topics in Early Childhood Special Education, 5*(2), 12–25.

Ramey, C. T., & Campbell, F. A. (1984). Preventive education for high-risk children: Cognitive consequences of the Carolina Abecedarian Project. *American Journal of Mental Deficiency, 88,* 515–523.

Ramey, C. T., & Haskins, R. (1981). The causes and treatment of school failure: Insights from the Carolina Abecedarian Project. In M. J. Begab, H. C. Haywood, & H. L. Garber (Eds.), *Psychosocial influences in retarded performance: Strategies for improving competence* (Vol. 2, pp. 89–112). Baltimore: University Park Press.

Rappaport, J. (1977). *Community psychology: Values, research, and action.* New York: Holt, Rinehart, & Winston.

Raven, I. C. (1958). *Standard progressive matrices, sets A, B, C, D, and E.* London: H.K. Lewis & Co.

Raynes, N. V., Bumstead, D. C., & Pratt, M. W. (1974). Unitization: Its effect on residential care practices. *Mental Retardation, 12*(4), 120–124.

Reed, E. W., & Reed, S. C. (1965). *Mental retardation: A family study.* Philadelphia: W. B. Saunders.

Reger, R., & Koppman, N. (1971). The child-oriented resource room. *Exceptional Children, 37,* 460–462.

Reitan, R. M., & Davison, L. A. (Eds.). (1974). *Clinical neuropsychology: Current status and applications.* Washington, DC: N.H. Winston & Sons.

Repp, A. C. (1983). *Teaching the mentally retarded.* Englewood Cliffs, NJ: Prentice-Hall.

Repp, A. C., & Deitz, D. (1979). Reinforcement-based reductive procedures: Training and monitoring performance of institutional staff. *Mental Retardation, 17,* 221–226.

Reschly, D. J. (1982). Assessing mild retardation: The influence of adaptive behavior, sociocultural status, and prospects for nonbiased assessment. In C. R. Reynolds & T. B. Gutkin (Eds.), *A handbook for school psychology.* New York: John Wiley.

Reschly, D. J. (1984). Beyond IQ test bias: The national academy panel's analysis of minority EMR overrepresentation. *Education Researcher, 13*(3), 15–19.

Reschly, D. J. (1987). Learning characteristics of mildly handicapped students: Implications for classification, placement, and programming. In M. C. Wang, M. C. Reynolds, & H. J. Wahlberg (Eds.), *The handbook of special education: Research and practice* (Vol. 1, pp. 35–58). Oxford: Pergamon.

Reschly, D. J. (1988a). Assessment issues, placement litigation, and the future of mild mental retardation classification and programming. *Education & Training in Mental Retardation, 23,* 285–301.

Reschly, D. J. (1988b). Incorporating adaptive behavior deficits into instructional programs. In G. A. Robinson, J. R. Patton, E. A. Polloway, & L. R. Sargent (Eds.), *Best practices in mental disabilities* (Vol. 2). Des Moines: Iowa Department of Education.

Resnick, O. (1988). Nutrition, neurotransmitter regulation and developmental pharmacology. In F. J. Menolascino & J. A. Stark (Eds.), *Preventive and curative intervention in mental retardation* (pp. 161–176). Baltimore: Paul H. Brookes.

Restak, R. (1975, September). Genetic counseling for defective parents: The danger of knowing too much. *Psychology Today,* pp. 21–23, 92–93.

Reynolds C. R. (1987). Playing IQ roulette with the Stanford-Binet, 4th edition. *Measurement & Evaluation in Counseling and Development, 20,* 139–141.

Reynolds, C. R. (1988). Sympathy not sense: The appeal of the Stanford-Binet fourth edition. *Measurement & Evaluation in Counseling and Development, 21,* 45.

Reynolds, C. R., & Clark, J. H. (1983). Assessment of cognitive abilities. In K. D. Paget & B. A. Bracken (Eds.), *The psychoeductional assessment of preschool children* (pp. 163–189). Orlando, FL: Grune & Stratton.

Reynolds, M. C. Wang, M. C., & Wahlberg, H. J. (1987). The necessary restructuring of special and regular education. *Exceptional Children, 53,* 391–398.

Rheingold, H. L. (1956). The modification of social responsiveness in institutional babies. *Monograph of the Society for Research in Child Development, 21* (No. 2).

Rheingold, H. L., & Bayley, N. (1959). Later effects of an experimental modification of mothering. *Child Development, 31,* 565–575.

Ribble, M. A. (1944). Infantile experience in relation to personality development. In J. McV. Hunt (Ed.), *Personality and the behavior disorders.* New York: Ronald.

Rich, D. (1985). *The forgotten factor in school success: The family.* Washington, DC: Home and School Institute.

Richards, B. W., Sylvester, R. E., & Brooker, C. (1981). Fragile X-linked mental retardation: The Martin-Bell syndrome. *Journal of Mental Deficiency Research, 25,* 253–258.

Richardson, S. A. (1981). Family characteristics associated with mild mental retardation. In M. J. Begab, H. C. Haywood, & H. L. Garber (Eds.), *Psychosocial influences in retarded performance: Strategies for improving competence.* (Vol. 2. pp. 29–32). Baltimore: University Park Press.

Rights Policy Reaffirmed. (1978, December). *The Daily Progress,* p. 1.

Rivera, G. (1972). *Willowbrook.* New York: Random House.

Roberts, M. (1986). Three mothers. In R. R. Fewell & P. F. Vadasy (Eds.), *Families of handicapped children* (pp. 193–220). Austin: PRO-ED.

Roberts, R. W. (1965). *Vocational and practical arts education: History, development, and principles* (2nd ed.). New York: Harper & Row.

Robertson, J. F. (1977). Grandmotherhood: A study of role conceptions. *Journal of Marriage & the Family, 39,* 165–174.

Robinault, I. P., & Denhoff, E. (1973). The multiple dysfunctions called cerebral palsy. In A. B. Cobb (Ed.), *Medical and psychological aspects of disability.* Springfield, IL: Charles C Thomas.

Robinson, H. B., & Robinson, N. M. (1970). Mental retardation. In P. H. Mussen (Ed.), *Carmichael's manual of child psychology* (3rd ed, (Vol. 2). New York: John Wiley.

Robinson, N. K., & Robinson, H. B. (1976). *The mentally retarded child* (2nd ed.). New York: McGraw-Hill.

Rogers, C. R. (1951). *Client-centered therapy: Its current practice, implications, and theory.* Boston: Houghton Mifflin.

Rogers, R. C., & Simensen, R. J. (1987). Fragile X syndrome: A common etiology of mental retardation. *American Journal of Mental Deficiency, 91,* 445–449.

Rogers-Warren, A. K., & Poulson, C. L. (1984). Perspectives on early childhood education. In E. L. Meyen (Ed.), *Mental retardation: Topics of today—Issues of tomorrow* (pp.67–68). Washington, DC: Council for Exceptional Children.

Roistacher, R. C., Holstrom, E. I., Cantril, A. H., & Chase, J. T. (1982). *Toward a comprehensive data system on the demographic and epidemiological characteristics of the handicapped population: Final report.* National Institute of Handicapped Research. (ERIC Document Reproduction Service No. ED 182 465).

Roos, P. (1975). Parents and families of the mentally retarded. In J. M. Kauffman & J. S. Payne (Eds.), *Mental retardation: Introduction and personal perspectives.* Columbus, OH: Merrill.

Rosen, L. (1955). Selected aspects in the development of the mother's understanding of her mentally retarded child. *American Journal of Mental Deficiency, 59,* 522–528.

Rosen, M. (1970). Conditioning appropriate heterosexual behavior in mentally and socially handicapped populations. *Training School Bulletin, 66,* 172–177.

Rosen, M. (1972, October). Psychosexual adjustment of the mentally handicapped. In M. S. Bass (Ed.), *Sexual rights and responsibilities of the mentally retarded.* Proceedings of the conference of the American Association on Mental Deficiency, Region IX, Newark, Delaware.

Rosen, M., Clark, G. R., & Kivitz, M. S. (1977). *Habilitation of the handicapped: New dimensions in programs for the developmentally disabled.* Baltimore: University Park Press.

Ross, A. O. (1976). *Psychological aspects of learning disabilities and reading disorders.* New York: McGraw-Hill.

Rotegard, L. L., Bruininks, R. H., & Krantz, G. C. (1984). State operated residential facilities for people with mental retardation: July 1, 1978–June 30, 1982. *Mental Retardation, 22,* 69–74.

Rotter, J. B. (1954). *Social learning and clinical psychology.* Englewood Cliffs, NJ: Prentice-Hall.

Rowe, P. (1984). Opportunity for the Retarded, Inc. says "Nuts" to counting bolts. *Human Development News,* pp. 2–3.

Rubin, R. A., Krus, P., & Balow, B. (1973). Factors in special class placement. *Exceptional Children, 39,* 525–532.

Rusch, F. R. (1979). Toward the validation of social/vocational class placement. *Mental Retardation, 17,* 143–145.

Rusch, F. R. (1983). Competitive vocational training. In M. E. Snell (Ed.) *Systematic instruction of the moderately and severely handicapped* (2nd ed., pp. 503–525). Columbus, OH: Merrill.

Rusch, F. R., & Mithaug, D. E. (1985). Competitive employment education: A systems-analytic approach to transitional programming for the student with severe handicaps. In K. C. Lakin & R. H. Bruininks (Eds.), *Strategies for achieving community integration of developmentally dis-*

*abled citizens* (pp. 177–192). Baltimore: Paul H. Brookes.

Rusch, F. R., Martin, J. E., & White, D. M. (1985). Competitive employment: Teaching mentally retarded employees to maintain their work behavior. *Education & Training of the Mentally Retarded, 20,* 182–189.

Russell, A. T., & Forness, S. R. (1985). Behavioral disturbance in mentally retarded children in TMR and EMR classrooms. *American Journal of Mental Deficiency, 89,* 338–344.

Russell, A. T., & Tanguay, P. E. (1981). Mental illness and mental retardation: Cause or coincidence? *American Journal of Mental Deficiency, 85,* 570–574.

Rutter, M. (1988). Biological basis of autism: Implications for intervention. In F. J. Menolascino & J. A. Stark (Eds.), *Preventive and curative intervention in mental retardation* (pp. 265–294). Baltimore: Paul H. Brookes.

Ryan, W. (1976), *Blaming the victim* (rev. ed.). New York: Vintage.

Rychlak, J. F. (1981). *Introduction to personality and psychotherapy: A theory construction approach* (2nd ed.). Boston: Houghton Mifflin.

Rynders, J. E., Spiker, D., & Horrobin, J. M. (1978). Underestimating the educability of Down's syndrome children: Examination of methodological problems in recent literature. *American Journal of Mental Deficiency, 82,* 440–448.

Sabatino, D. A. (1971). An evaluation of resource rooms for children with learning disabilities. *Journal of Learning Disabilities., 4,* 84–93.

Safer, N., Burnette, J., & Hobbs, B. (1977). Exploration 1993: The effects of future trends on services to the handicapped. *Focus on Exceptional Children, 11*(3), 21–23.

Sagan, C. (1977). *The dragons of Eden: Speculations of the evolution of human intelligence.* New York: Ballantine.

Sailor, W., & Guess, D. (1983). *Severely handicapped students: An instructional design.* Boston: Houghton Mifflin.

Sailor, W., Halvorsen, A., Anderson, J., Goetz, L., Gee, K., Doering, K., & Hunt, P. (1986). Community intensive instruction. In R. Horner, L. Meyer, & H. D. B. Fredericks (Eds.), *Education of learners with severe handicaps: Exemplary service strategies* (pp. 251–288). Baltimore: Paul H. Brookes.

Sailor, W., & Mix, B. J. (1975). The TARC Assessment System. Lawrence, KS: H & H Enterprises.

Salend, S. J., & Ehrlich, E. (1983). Involving students in behavior modification programs. *Mental Retardation, 21,* 95–100.

Sali, J., & Amir, M. (1970). Personal factors influencing the retarded person's success at work: A report from Israel. *American Journal of Mental Deficiency, 76,* 42–47.

Salisbury, C. (1986). Parenthood and the need for respite care. In C. Salisbury & J. Intagliata (Eds.), *Respite care: Support for persons with developmental disabilities and their families* (pp. 3–28. Baltimore: Paul H. Brookes.

Salvia, J., & Ysseldyke, J. E. (1981). *Assessment in special and remedial education.* Boston: Houghton Mifflin.

Salvia, J., & Ysseldyke, J. E. (1985). *Assessment in special and remedial education* (3rd ed.). Boston: Houghton Mifflin.

Salzburg, C. L., & Villani, T. V. (1983). Speech training by parents of Down syndrome toddlers: Generalization across settings and instructional contexts. *American Journal of Mental Deficiency, 87,* 403–413.

*San Antonio Independent School District v. Rodriguez,* 411 U.S. (1973).

Sandgrund, A., Gaines, R. W., & Green, A. H. (1974). Child abuse and mental retardation: A problem of cause and effect. *American Journal of Mental Deficiency, 79,* 327–330.

Sarason, S. B. (1974). *The psychological sense of community.* San Francisco: Jossey-Bass.

Sarason, S. B. (1985). *Psychology and mental retardation: Perspectives in change.* Austin: PRO-ED.

Sargent, L. R., & Fiddler, D. A. (1987). Extended school year programs: In support of the concept. *Education & Training of the Mentally Retarded, 22,* 3–11.

Sattler, J. (1974). *Assessment of Children's Intelligence.* Philadelphia: W.B. Saunders.

Sattler, J. (1982). *Assessment of children's intelligence and special abilities* (2nd ed.). Boston: Allyn & Bacon.

Scarr, S., & Carter-Saltzman, L. (1982). Genetics and intelligence. In R. J. Sternberg (Ed.), *Handbook of human intelligence* (pp. 798–896). Cambridge: Cambridge University Press.

Scarr-Salapatek, S. (1971a). Race, social class and IQ. *Science, 174,* 1285–1295.

Scarr-Salapatek, S. (1971b). Unknowns in the IQ equation. *Science, 174,* 1223–1228.

Schakel, J. A. (1987, June). Preschool practices, problems, & issues: A summary of the results of the Preschool Interest Group Questionnaire. *Preschool Interests,* p. 3.

Schalock, R. L., & Lilley, M. A. (1986). Placement from community based mental retardation programs: How well do clients do after 8–10 years? *American Journal of Mental Deficiency, 90,* 669–676.

Scheerenberger, R. C. (1976a). *Current trends and status of public residential services for the mentally retarded, 1974.* Madison, WI: National Association of Superintendents of Public Residential Facilities for the Mentally Retarded.

Scheerenberger, R. C. (1976b). *Deinstitutionalization and institutional reform.* Springfield, IL: Charles C Thomas.

Scheerenberger, R. C. (1977). A study of public residential facilities, 1976. *Mental Retardation, 15*(5), 58.

Scheerenberger, R. C. (1979). *Public residential services for the mentally retarded.* Madison, WI: National Association of Superintendents of Public Residential Facilities for the Mentally Retarded.

Scheerenberger, R. C. (1982). Public residential services, 1981: Status and trends. *Mental Retardation, 20,* 210–215.

Scheiderman, G., Lowden, J. A., & Rae-Grant, Q. (1978). Tay-Sachs and related storage diseases: Family planning. *Mental Retardation, 16,* 13–15.

Schiefelbusch, R. (1972). Language disabilities of cognitively involved children. In Irwin & M. Marge (Eds.), *Principles of childhood language disabilities.* Englewood Cliffs, NJ: Prentice-Hall.

Schloss, P. J., Smith, M. A., & Kiehl, W. (1986). Rec club: A community centered approach to recreational development for adults with mild to moderate retardation. *Education and Training of the Mentally Retarded,* 282–288.

Schreibman, L., O'Neill, R. E., & Koegel, R. L. (1983). Behavioral training for siblings of autistic children. *Journal of Applied Behavior Analysis, 16,* 129–138.

Schulman, E. D. (1980). *Focus on the retarded adult: Programs and services.* St. Louis: C.V. Mosby.

Schultz, F. R. (1983). Phenylketonuria and other metabolic diseases. In J. A. Blackman (Ed.), *Medical aspects of developmental disabilities in children birth to three,* Iowa City: University of Iowa Press.

Schultz, R., Wehman, P., Renzaglia, A., & Karan, O. (1978). Efficacy of contingent social disapproval on inappropriate verbalizations of two severely retarded males. *Behavior Therapy, 9,* 657–662.

Schumaker, J. B., & Deshler, D. D. (1988). Implementing the Regular Education Initiative in secondary schools: A different ball game. *Journal of Learning Disabilities, 21,* 36–42.

Schuta, R. P., Jostes, K. F., Rusch, F. R., & Lamson, D. S. (1980). Acquisition, transfer, and social validation of two skills in a competitive employment setting. *Education & Training of the Mentally Retarded, 15,* 306–311.

Schutz, R. P. (1988). New directions and strategies in habilitation services: Toward meaningful employment outcomes. In L. W. Heal, J. I. Haney, & A. R. Novak Amado (Eds.), *Integration of developmentally disabled individuals into the community* (2nd ed., pp. 193–210). Baltimore: Paul H. Brookes.

Schweinhart, L. J., Berreuta-Clement, J. R., Barrett, W. S., Epstein, A. S., & Weikart, D. P. (1985). Effects of the Perry preschool programs on youths through age 19: A summary. *Topics in Early Childhood Special Education, 5*(2), 26–35.

Scientific seer: Rudolf Steiner. (1969). *MD, the Medical News Magazine, 13,* 245–250.

Seat, P. D., & Broen, W. E. (1977). *Personality inventory for children.* Los Angeles: Western Psychological Services.

Seguin, E. O. (1846). *Traitement moral, hygiène et éducation des idiots et des autres enfants arrières. Paris: Baillier.*

Seligman, M. E. P. (1975). *Helplessness: On depression, development, and death.* San Francisco: Freeman.

Sells, C. J., & Bennett, F. C. (1977). Prevention of mental retardation: The role of medicine. *American Journal of Mental Deficiency, 82,* 117–129.

Sells, C. J., & Paeth, S. (1987). Health and safety in day-care. *Topics in Early Childhood Special Education, 7*(1), 61–72.

Seltzer, M. M. (1984). Correlates of community opposition to community residences for mentally retarded persons. *American Journal of Mental Deficiency, 89*(1), 1–8.

Seltzer, M. M., & Krauss, M. (1987). *Aging and mental retardation: Extending the continuum.* Washington, DC: American Association on Mental Retardation.

Seltzer, M. M., & Seltzer, G. (1978). *Context for competence: A study of retarded adults living and working in the community.* Cambridge, MA: Educational Projects.

Semmel, M., & Dickson, S. (1966). Cognitive reactions of college students to disability labels. *Exceptional Children, 32,* 443–450.

Shearer, M. S., & Shearer, D. E. (1972). The Portage Project: A model for early childhood education. *Exceptional Children, 39,* 210–217.

Shevin, M. (1982). The use of food and drink in classroom management programs for severely handicapped children. *Journal of The Association for the Severely Handicapped, 7,* 40–46.

Shields, J. (1962). *Monozygotic twins.* London: Oxford University Press.

Shipe, D., Neisman, L. E., Chung, C.-Y., Darnell, A., & Kelley, S. (1968). The relationship between cytogenetic constitution, physical stigmata, and intelligence in Down's syndrome. *American Journal of Mental Deficiency, 72,* 789–797.

Shockley, W. B. (1974, November 5). *The moral obligation to diagnose the American Negro tragedy on the basis of statistical evidence.* Paper presented at the University of Virginia.

Shuey, A. M. (1966). *Testing of Negro intelligence* (2nd ed.). New York: Social Science.

Shushan, R. D. (1974). *Assessment and reduction of deficits in the physical appearance of mentally retarded people.* Unpublished doctoral dissertation, University of California at Los Angeles.

Silverstein, A. B. (1971). Deviation social quotients for the Vineland Social Maturity Scale. *American Journal of Mental Deficiency, 76,* 348–351.

Simeonsson, R. J., Huntington, G. A., & Parse, S. A. (1980). Assessment of children with severe handicaps: Multiple problems—Multivariate goals. *Journal of The Association for the Severely Handicapped, 5*(1), 55–72.

Simons, R. (1987). *After the tears.* San Diego: Harcourt Brace Jovanovich.

Singh, N. N. (1980). The effects of facial screening on infant self-injury. *Journal of Behavior Therapy & Experimental Psychiatry, 11,* 131–134.

Skeels, H. M. (1942). A study of the effects of differential stimulation on mentally retarded children: A follow-up report. *American Journal of Mental Deficiency, 46,* 340–350.

Skeels, H. M. (1966). Adult status of children with contrasting early life experiences. *Monographs of the Society for Research in Child Development, 31* (No. 3).

Skeels, H. M., & Dye, H. B. (1939). A study of the effects of differential stimulation on mentally retarded children. *Convention Proceedings American Association on Mental Deficiency, 44,* 114–136.

Skrtic, T. (1986). The crisis in special education knowledge: A perspective. *Focus on Exceptional Children, 17*(7), 1–16.

Sloan, W., & Birch, J. W. (1955). A rationale for degrees of retardation. *American Journal of Mental Deficiency, 60,* 258–264.

Slosson. R. L. (1971). *Slosson intelligence test.* East Aurora, NY: Slosson Educational Publications.

Smith, A. L., Piersel, W. C., Filbeck. R. W., & Gross, E. J. (1983). The elimination of mealtime food stealing and scavenging behavior in an institutionalized severely mentally retarded adult. *Mental Retardation, 21,* 255–259.

Smith, B. J. (1986). *A comparative analysis of selected federal programs serving young children.* Chapel Hill, NC: START.

Smith, B. J., & Strain, P. S. (1984). The argument for early intervention (Factsheet). *ERIC Digest.* Reston, VA: Council for Exceptional Children.

Smith, B. J., & Strain, P. S. (1988). Early childhood special education in the next decade: Implementing and expanding P.L. 99-457. *Topics in Early Childhood Special Education, 8*(1), 34–47.

Smith, B. J., Vincent, L., Toole, A., Garland, C., Dunst, C., McCarten, K., Williamson, G., Jesien, G., McLean, M., Zeitlin, S., Karnes, M. B., McCollum, J., Monahan, R., & Odom, S. (1987, March). *Position statements and recommendations relating to PL 99-457 and other federal and state early childhood policies.* Reston, VA: Council for Exceptional Children.

Smith, D. D., & Smith, J. O. (1978). Trends. In M. E. Snell (Ed.), *Systematic instruction of the moderately and severely handicapped.* Columbus, OH: Merrill.

Smith, D. W., Jones, K. L., & Hansen, J. W. (1976). Perspectives on the cause and frequency of the fetal alcohol syndrome. *Annals of the New York Academy of Science, 23,* 138–139.

Smith, D. W., & Wells, M. E. (1983). Use of a microcomputer to assist staff in documenting resident progress. *Mental Retardation, 21,* 111–115.

Smith, D. W., & Wilson, A. A. (1973). *The child with Down's syndrome (mongolism).* Philadelphia: W.B. Saunders.

Smith, J. D., (1981). Down's syndrome, amniocentesis and abortion: Prevention or elimination? *Mental Retardation, 19,* 8–11.

Smith, J. D. (1984). Pediatric euthanasia, handicapped infants, and special education: A challenge to our advocacy. *Exceptional Children, 51.*

Smith, J. D. (1985). *Minds made feeble: the myth and legacy of the Kallikaks.* Rockville, MD: Aspen Systems.

Smith, J. D. (1987). *The other voices: Profiles of women in the history of special education.* Seattle: Special Child.

Smith, J. D. (1988a). *Psychological profiles of conjoined twins: Heredity, environment and identity.* New York: Praeger.

Smith, J. D. (September, 1988b). CEC-MR position statement on the right of children with mental retardation to life sustaining medical care and treatment. *CEC-MReport.*

Smith, J. D. (1989). On the right of children with mental retardation to life sustaining medical care and treatment: A position statement. *Education & Training in Mental Retardation, 24,* 3–6.

Smith, J. D. (1989). *The sterilization of Carrie Buck.* New York: New Horizons.

Smith, J. D., & Polloway, E. A. (1983). Changes in mild mental retardation: Population, programs and perspectives. *Exceptional Children, 50,* 149–159.

Smith, J. E., & Payne, J. S. (1980). *Teaching exceptional adolescents.* Columbus, OH: Merrill.

Smith, J. O., & Arkans, J. R. (1974). Now more than ever: A case for the special class. *Exceptional Children, 40,* 497–502.

Smith, M. A., & Schloss, P. J. (1988). Teaching to transition. In P. J. Schloss, C. A. Hughes, & M. A. Smith (Eds.), *Community integration for persons with mental retardation* (pp. 1–16). Boston: College Hill.

Smith, R. M. (1968). *Clinical teaching: Methods of instruction for the retarded.* New York: McGraw-Hill.

Smith, R. M. (1969). Fundamentals of informal educational assessment. In R. M. Smith (Ed.), *Teacher diagnosis of educational difficulties.* Columbus, OH: Merrill.

Smith, R. M. (1974). *Clinical teaching: Methods of instruction for the retarded* (2nd ed.). New York: McGraw-Hill.

Smith, R. M., & Neisworth, J. T. (1975). *The exceptional child: A functional approach.* New York: McGraw-Hill.

Smith, R. M., Neisworth, J. T., & Greer, J. C. (1978). Classification and individuality. In J. T. Neisworth & R. M. Smith (Eds.), *Retardation: Issues, assessment and intervention.* New York: McGraw-Hill.

*Smuck v. Hobson,* 408 F. 2d 175 (D.C. Cir 1969).

Snell, M. E. (1983). Functional reading. In M. E. Snell (Ed.), *Systematic instruction of the moderately and severely handicapped* (2nd ed., pp. 324–385). Columbus, OH: Merrill.

Snell, M. E. (Ed.). (1987). *Systematic instruction of persons with severe handicaps* (3rd ed.). Columbus, OH: Merrill.

Snell, M. E., & Beckman-Brindley, S. (1984). Family involvement in intervention with children having severe handicaps.

Snell, M. E., & Renzaglia, A. M. (1986). Moderate, severe, and profound handicaps. In N. G. Haring & L. McCormick (Eds.), *Exceptional children and youth* (4th ed., pp. 271–310). Columbus, OH: Merrill.

Snyderman, M., Rothman, S. (1987). Survey of expert opinion on intelligence and apitude testing. *American Psychologist, 42,* 137–144.

Sobsey, R., & Bieniek, B. (1983). A family approach to functional sign language. *Behavior Modification, 7,* 488–502.

Soeffing, M. (1975). Abused children are exceptional children. *Exceptional Children, 42,* 126–133.

Solnit, A. J., & Stark, M. H. (1961). Mourning and the birth of a defective child. *Psychoanalytic Study of the Child, 16,* 523–537.

Sontag, E., Burke, P., & York, R. (1973). Considerations for serving the severely handicapped in the public schools. *Education & Training of the Mentally Retarded, 8*(2), 20–26.

*Souder v. Brennan,* Civil Action No. 482–73 (D.D.C., filed March 13, 1973).

Sparrow, S. S., Balla, D. A., & Cicchetti, D. V. (1984). *Vineland adaptive behavior scales.* Circle Pines, MN: American Guidance Service.

Spicker, H. H. (1971). Intellectual development through early childhood education. *Exceptional Children, 37,* 629–640.

Spitz, H. H. (1966). The role of input organization in the learning and memory of mental retardates. *International Review of Research in Mental Retardation, 2.*

Spitz, H. H. (1973). Consolidating facts into the schematized learning and memory of mental retardates. *International Review of Research in Mental Retardation, 6.*

Spitz, H. H. (1979). Beyond field theory in the study of mental deficiency. In N. R. Ellis (Ed.), *Handbook of mental deficiency: Psychological theory and research* (2nd ed.). Hillsdale, NJ: Lawrence Erlbaum Associates.

Spitz, R. A. (1945). Hospitalism: An inquiry into the genesis of psychiatric conditions in early childhood. *Psychoanalytic Study of the Child, 1,* 53–74.

Spitz, R. A. (1946a). A follow-up report. *Psychoanalytic Study of the Child, 2,* 113—117.

Spitz, R. A. (1946b). Anaclitic depression. *Psychoanalytic Study of the Child, 2,* 313–342.

Spooner, F., & Spooner, D. (1984). A review of chaining techniques: Implications for future research and practice. *Education & Training of the Mentally Retarded, 10,* 114–124.

Spradlin, J. E. (1968). Environmental factors and the language development of retarded children. In S. Rosenberg & J. H. Koplin (Eds.), *Developments in applied psycholinguistic research.* New York: MacMillan.

Spreat, S., Telles, J. L., Conroy, J. W., Feinstein, C., & Colombatto, J. J. (1987). Attitudes toward deinstitutionalization: National survey of families of institutionalized persons with mental retardation. *Mental Retardation, 25,* 267–274.

Springer, N. S., & Fricke, N. L. (1975). Nutrition and drug therapy for persons with developmental disabilities. *American Journal of Mental Deficiency, 80,* 317–322.

Spruill, J. (1988). Review of the Stanford-Binet Intelligence Scale: Fourth Edition. *Test Critiques, 6,* 114–127.

Staats, A. W. (1975). *Social behaviorism.* Homewood, IL: Dorsey.

Staats, A. W., & Burns, G. L. (1981). Intelligence and child development: What intelligence is and how it is learned and functions. *Genetic Psychology Monographs, 104,* 237–301.

Stainback, W., & Stainback, S. (1983). A review of research on the educability of profoundly retarded persons. *Education & Training of the Mentally Retarded, 18*(2), 90–100.

Stainback, W., & Stainback, S. (1984). A rationale for the merger of special and regular education. *Exceptional Children, 51,* 102–111.

Stark, J. A. (1983). The search for cures in mental retardation. In F. J. Menolascino, R. Neman, & J. A. Stark (Eds.), *Curative aspects of mental retardation: Biomedical and behavioral advances* (pp. 1–6). Baltimore: Paul H. Brooks.

Stark, J. A., Menolascino, F. J., & Goldsbury, T. L. (1988). An updated search for the prevention of mental retardation. In F. J. Menolascino & J. A. Stark (Eds.), *Preventive and curative intervention in mental retardation* (pp. 3–25). Baltimore: Paul H. Brookes.

Stebbins, L. B., St. Pierre, R. G., Proper, E. C., Anderson, R. B., & Cerva, T. R. (1977). *Education as experimentation: A planned variation model* (Vol. 4–A). Cambridge, MA: Abt Associates.

Stein, Z., & Susser, M. (1975). Public health and mental retardation: New Power and new problems. In M. Begab & S. A. Richardson (Eds.), *The mentally retarded and society: A social science perspective.* Baltimore: University Park Press.

Steinmiller, G., & Retish, P. (1980). The employer's role in the transition from school to work. *Career Development for Exceptional Individuals, 3*(2), 87–91.

Stephens, T. M. (1978). *Social skills in the classroom.* Columbus, OH: Cedars.

Stephens, T. M., Hartman, A. C., & Lucas, V. H. (1978). *Teaching children basic skills: A curriculum handbook.* Columbus, OH: Merrill.

Stephens, W. E. (1966). Category usage of normal and subnormal children on three types of categories. *American Journal of Mental Deficiency, 71,* 266–273.

Stephens, W. E. (1972). Equivalence formation by retarded and nonretarded children at different mental ages. *American Journal of Mental Deficiency, 77,* 311–313.

Stern, W. (1912). The psychological methods of testing intelligence. In G. M. Wipple (Ed.), *Education & Psychological Monographs* (No. 13).

Sternat, J., Messina, R., Nietupski, J. A., Lyon, S., & Brown, L. (1977). Occupational and physical therapy services for severely handicapped students: Toward a naturalized public school service delivery model. In E. Sontag, J. Smith, & N. Certo (Eds.), *Educational programming for the severely and profoundly handicapped.* Reston, VA: Council for Exceptional Children.

Sternberg, R. J., & Spear, L. C. (1985). A triarchic theory of mental retardation. *International Review of Research in Mental Retardation, 13,* 301–326.

Stodden, R. A., & Boone, R. (1987). Assessing transition services for handicapped youth: A cooperative interagency approach. *Exceptional Children, 53,* 537–545.

Stodden, R. A., & Browder, P. M. (1986). Community based competitive employment preparation of developmentally disabled persons: A program description and evaluation. *Education & Training of the Mentally Retarded, 21,* 43–53.

Stokes, T. F., & Baer, D. M. (1977). An implicit technology of generalization. *Journal of Applied Behavior Analysis, 10,* 349–367.

Stone, R., & Newcomer, R. (1985). Health and social services policy and the disabled who have become old. In M. P. Janicki & H. M. Wisniewski (Eds.), *Aging and developmental disabilities: Issues and approaches* (pp. 27–40). Baltimore: Paul H. Brookes.

Stoops, E., Rafferty, M., Johnson, R. E. (1981). *Handbook of educational administration: A guide for the practitioner* (2nd ed.). Boston: Allyn & Bacon.

Strain, P. S., & Cardisco, L. K. (1983). Child characteristics and outcomes related to mainstreaming. In J. Anderson & T. Black (Eds.), *Issues in preschool mainstreaming* (pp. 47–64). Chapel Hill, NC: TADS.

Strain, P. S., Guralnick, M. J., & Walker, H. M. (1986). *Children's social behavior: Assessment, development, and modification.* New York: Academic.

Strain, P. S., & Smith, B. J. (1986). A counter-interpretation of early intervention effects: A response to Casto and Mastropieri. *Exceptional Children, 53,* 260–265.

Strauch, J. D. (1970). Social contact as a variable in the expressed attitudes of normal adolescents toward EMR pupils. *Exceptional Children, 36,* 495–500.

Stremel-Campbell, K., Cantreel, D., & Halle, J. (1977). Manual signing as a language system and as a speech initiator for the non-verbal severely handicapped student. In E. Sontag, J. Smith, & N. Certo (Eds.), *Educational programming for the severely and profoundly handicapped.* Reston, VA: Council for Exceptional Children.

Strichart, S. S., & Gottlieb, J. (1983). Characteristics of mild mental retardation. In T. L. Miller & E. E. Davis (Eds.), *The mildly handicapped student* (pp. 37–65). New York: Grune & Stratton.

Strickland, S. P. (1971). Can slum children learn? *American Education, 7*(6), 3–7.

Strully, J. (1986, November). *Our children and the regular education classroom: Why settle for anything less than the best?* Paper presented at the convention of The Association for Persons With Severe Handicaps, San Francisco.

Strully, J. (1987, October). *All children can learn together: No more segregation of any kind.* Paper presented at the convention of the Iowa Chapter of The Association for Persons with Severe Handicaps, Ames, IA.

*Stump v. Spartman,* 98 S. Ct. 1099 (1978).

Suran, B. G., & Rizzo, J. V. (1983). *Special children: An integrative approach* (2nd ed.). Dallas: Scott, Foresman.

Sutton, M. S. (1983). *Treatment issues of the elderly institutionalized developmentally disabled individual.* Paper presented at the Annual Convention of the American Psychological Association, Anaheim, CA.

Szymanski, L. S. (1980). Psychiatric diagnosis of retarded persons. In L. S. Szymanski & P. E. Tanguay (Eds.), *Emotional disorders of mentally retarded persons: Assessment, treatment, and consultation* (p. 61–83). Baltimore: University Park Press.

Talkington, L. W. (1971). Outreach: Delivery of services to rural communities. *Mental Retardation, 9*(5), 27–29.

Tallman, I. (1965). Spousal role differentiation and the socialization of severely retarded children. *Journal of Marriage & the Family, 27,* 37–42.

Tarjan, G. (1964, April 9–11). The next decade: Expectations from the biological sciences. *Mental retardation: A handbook for the primary physician* (Report of the American Medical Association) (pp. 123–133).

Tarjan, G., Wright, S. W., Eyman, R. K., & Keeran, D. V. (1973). Natural history of mental retardation: Some aspects of epidemiology. *American Journal of Mental Deficiency, 77,* 369–379.

Tarpley, H. D., & Schroeder, S. R. (1979). Comparison of DRO and DRI on rate of suppression of self-injurious behavior. *American Journal of Mental Deficiency, 84,* 188–194.

Taylor, S. J., & Biklen, D. (1979). *Understanding the law: An advocate's guide to the law and developmental disabilities.* Syracuse, NY: Syracuse University and the Mental Health Law Project.

Taylor, S., & Bogdan, R. (1977). A phenomenological approach to "mental retardation." In B. Blatt, D. Biklen, & R. Bogdan (Eds.), *An alternative textbook in special education: People, schools, and other institutions.* Denver: Love Publishing.

Taylor, S. J., McCord, W., & Stanford, J. S. (1981). Medicaid dollars and community homes: The community ICF/MR controversy. *TASH Journal, 7,* 59–64.

Terman, L. M. (1921). Intelligence and its measurement: A symposium. *Journal of Educational Psychology, 12,* 127–133.

Terman, L. M., & Merrill, M. A. (1960). The Stanford-Binet intelligence scale (2nd rev.). Boston: Houghton-Mifflin.

Terman, L. M., & Merrill, M. A. (1973). *The Stanford-Binet intelligence scale* (3rd rev.). Boston: Houghton Mifflin.

Tew, B. J., Lawrence, K. M., Payne, H., & Rawnsley, K. (1977). Marital stability following the birth of a child with spina bifida. *British Journal of Psychiatry, 131,* 79–82.

The Association for Persons with Severe Handicaps (TASH). (1984). *Legal, economic, psychological, and moral considerations on the practice of withholding medical treatment from infants with congenital defects* (Monograph No. 1). Seattle: Author.

Thompson, T., & Grabowski, J. (1972). *Behavior modification of the mentally retarded.* New York: Oxford University Press.

Thompson, W. R., & Grusec, J. (1970). Studies of early experience. In P. H. Mussen (Ed.), *Carmichael's manual of child psychology* (Vol. 1). New York: John Wiley.

Thompson, W. R., & Heron, W. (1954). The effects of restrictive early experiences in the problem-solving capacity of dogs. *Canadian Journal of Psychology, 8,* 17–31.

Thorndike, R. L., & Hagen, E. P. (1969). Measurement and evaluation in psychology and education (3rd ed.). New York: John Wiley.

Thorndike, R. L., Hagen, E. P., & Sattler, J. M. (1968a). *Guide for administering and scoring the fourth edition: Stanford-Binet Intelligence Scale.* Chicago: Riverside.

Thorndike, R. L., Hagen, E. P., & Sattler, J. M. (1968b). *Technical manual: Intelligence scale, fourth edition.* Chicago: Riverside.

*Time.* (1970, October 26), pp. 77–79.

Townsend, C., & Mattson, R. (1981). The interaction of law and special education: Observing the emperor's new clothes. *Analysis & Intervention in Developmental Disabilities, 1,* 75–89.

Tredgold, A. F. (1937). *A textbook of mental deficiency.* Baltimore: Wood.

Tucker, S. M. (1978). *Fetal monitoring and fetal assessment in high-risk pregnancy.* St. Louis: C.V. Mosby.

Turkington, C. (1987). Special talents. *Psychology Today, 20,* 42–46.

Turnbull, A. P. (1982). Preschool mainstreaming: A policy and implementation analysis. *Educational Evaluation & Policy Analysis, 4*(3), 281–291.

Turnbull, A. P. (1985). Moving from being a professional to being a parent: A startling experience. In A. P. Turnbull & H. R. Turnbull (Eds.), *Parents speak out.* (2nd ed.). Columbus, OH: Merrill.

Turnbull, A. P. (1988). The challenge of providing comprehensive support to families. *Education & Training in Mental Retardation, 23,* 261–272.

Turnbull, A. P., Brotherson, M. J., Bronicki, G. J., Benson, H. A., Houghton, J., Roeder-Gordon, C., & Summers, J. A. (1985). *How to plan for my child's adult future: A three-part process to future planning.* Lawrence, KS: Future Planning Project, University Affiliated Facility, Bureau of Child Research.

Turnbull, A. P., Summers, J. A., & Brotherson, M. J. (1986). Family life cycle: Theoretical and empirical implications and future directions for families with mentally retarded members. In J. J. Gallagher & P. M. Vietze (Eds.), *Families of handicapped persons* (pp. 45–65). Baltimore: Paul H. Brookes.

Turnbull, A. P., & Turnbull, H. R. (Eds.). (1978). *Parents speak out.* Columbus, OH: Merrill.

Turnbull, A. P., & Turnbull, H. R. (1985). *Parents speak out: Then & now.* (2nd ed.). Columbus, OH. Charles E. Merrill.

Turnbull, H. R. (1975). *Legal aspects of the developmentally disabled.* Topeka, KS: National Organization on Legal Problems of Education.

Turnbull, H. R. (1980, April 18). *Legal issues and challenges in special education.* Address given at Spring Special Education Forum, University of Virginia, Charlottesville.

Turnbull, H. R. (1983). Fundamental rights, Section 504 and Baby Doe. *Mental Retardation, 21,* 218–221.

Turnbull, H. R. (1986). *Free appropriate public education: The law and children with disabilities.* Denver: Love Publishing.

Turnbull, H. R. (1988). Ideological, political, and

legal practices in the community-living movement. In M. P. Janicki, M. W. Krauss, & M. M. Seltzer (Eds.), *Community residences for persons with developmental disabilities: Here to stay* (pp. 15–24). Baltimore: Paul H. Brookes.

Turner, R. (1976). *Project: Zero reject. A system for locating and planning for unserved handicapped children.* (ERIC Document Reproduction Service No. ED 144 312).

Turnure, J., & Zigler, E. (1964). Outer-directedness in the problem solving of normal and retarded children. *Journal of Abnormal & Social Psychology, 69,* 427–436.

Ullman, L. P., & Krasner, L. (1969). *A psychological approach to abnormal behavior.* Englewood Cliffs, NJ: Prentice-Hall.

Ulrich, D. A. (1985). *Test of gross motor development.* Austin: PRO-ED.

Umbreit, J., & Ostrow, L. S. (1980). The fetal alcohol syndrome. *Mental Retardation, 18,* 109–111.

United States Bureau of the Census, (1985). *Current population reports: Household and family characteristics, March 1984* (Series P-20, No. 398). Washington, DC: U.S. Government Printing Office.

United States Department of Education. (1988). *Tenth annual report to Congress on the implementation of the Education of the Handicapped Act.* Washington, DC: Division of Innovation and Development, Office of Special Education Programs.

United States Department of Labor. (1970). *Manual for the USES nonreading aptitude test battery.* Washington, DC: U.S. Government Printing Office.

United States House of Representatives. (1986). *House Report 99-860.* Washington, DC: U.S. Government Printing Office.

United States Office of Education/Bureau for the Education of the Handicapped. (1974). *Request for proposal 74-10: Programs for severely handicapped children and youth.* Washington, DC: Author.

*United States v. University Hospital, State University of New York at Stonybrook,* 729 F.2d 144 (2d Cir. 1984).

Utley, C. A., Lowitzer, A. C., Baumeister, A. A. (1987). A comparison of the AAMD's definition, eligibility criteria, and classification schemes with state departments of education guidelines. *Education & Training in Mental Retardation, 22,* 35–43.

Vadasy, P. F. (1986). Single mothers: A social phenomenon and population in need. In R. R. Fewell & P. F. Vadasy (Eds.), *Families of handicapped children.* Austin: PRO-ED.

Van Etten, C., & Van Etten, G. (1976). The measurement of pupil progress and selecting instructional materials. *Journal of Learning Disabilities, 9,* 4.

Van Etten, G., Arkell, C., & Van Etten, C. (1980). *The severely and profoundly handicapped: Programs, methods, and materials.* St. Louis: C.V. Mosby.

Vincent, L., Davis, J., Brown, P., Broome, K., Miller, J., & Gruenewald, L. (1983). *Parent inventory of child development in nonschool environments.* Madison, WI: Madison Metropolitan School District Early Childhood Program, Active Decision Making by Parents Grant.

Virginia State Department of Education, Division of Special Education. (1977). *Summary of the Education for All Handicapped Children Act of 1975, Public Law 94-142.* Richmond: Author.

Vitello, S. J. (1976). The institutionalization and deinstitutionalization of the mentally retarded in the United Sates. In L. Mann & D. A. Sabatino (Eds.), *The third review of special education.* New York: Grune & Stratton.

Voeltz, L. M. (1982). Effects of structured interactions with severely handicapped peers on children's attitudes. *American Journal of Mental Deficiency, 86*(4), 380–390.

Vogelsberg, R. T. (1986). Vermont's employment training programs. In F. R. Rusch (Ed.), *Competitive employment: Service delivery models, methods, and issues* (pp. 35–50). Baltimore: Paul H. Brookes.

Vogelsberg, R. T., & Schutz, R. P. (1988). Establishing community employment programs for persons with severe disabilities: Systems designs and resolutions. In M. D. Powers (Ed.), *Expanding systems of service delivery for persons with developmental disabilities* (pp. 127–148). Baltimore: Paul H. Brookes.

Waisbren, S. E. (1980). Parents' reactions after the birth of a developmentally disabled child. *American Journal of Mental Deficiency, 84,* 245–251.

Wald, P. M. (1976). Personal and civil rights of mentally retarded citizens. In M. Kindred, J. Cohen, D. Penrod, & T. Shaffer (Eds.), *The mentally retarded citizen and the law.* New York: Free Press.

Walker, H. M. (1983). *Walker problem behavior identification checklist.* Los Angeles: Western Psychological Services.

Walker, J. E., & Shea, T. M. (1980). *Behavior modification: A practical approach for educators.* St. Louis: C.V. Mosby.

Walker, N. W. (1987). The Stanford-Binet, 4th edition: Haste does seem to make waste. *Measurement & Evaluation in Counseling & Development, 20,* 135–138.

Walker, N. W. (1988). Response to Hopkins: Emotional loyalty does not a good rejoinder make. *Measurement & Evaluation in Counseling & Development, 21,* 43–44.

Wallace, G., & Kauffman, J. M. (1978). *Teaching children with learning problems* (2nd ed.). Columbus, OH: Merrill.

Wallace, G., & Larsen, S. C. (1978). *Educational assessment of learning problems: Testing for teaching.* Boston: Allyn & Bacon.

Wallace, J., Burger, D., Neal, H. C., Van Breno, M., & Davis, D. E. (1976). Aversive conditioning use in public facilities for the mentally retarded. *Mental Retardation, 14*(2), 17–19.

Waller, J. H. (1971). Achievement and social mobility: Relationships among IQ score, education, and occupation in two generations. *Social Biology, 19,* 252–259.

Wallin, J. W. (1955). *Education of mentally handicapped children.* New York: Harper & Row.

Walls, R. T., Warner, T. J., Bacon, A., & Zane, T. (1977). Behavior checklists. In J. D. Cone and A. B. Hawkins (Eds.), *Behavioral assessment: New*

*directions in clinical psychology.* New York: Bruner/Mazel.

Walmsley, S. A. (1978). A life and death issue. *Mental Retardation, 16,* 387–389.

Wang, M. C., Reynolds, M. C., & Wahlberg, H. J. (1986). Rethinking special education. *Educational Leadership, 44*(1), 26–31.

Wannarachue, N., Ruyalcaba, R., & Kelley. (1975). Hypogonadism in Prader-Willi syndrome. *American Journal of Mental Deficiency, 79,* 592–603.

Watson, J. B. (1930). *Behaviorism* (rev. ed.). Chicago: University of Chicago Press.

Watson, J. S., & Ramey, C. I. (1972). Reactions to response-contingent stimulation in early infancy. *Merrill-Palmer Quarterly, 18,* 219–229.

Wechsler, D. (1939). *The measurement of adult intelligence.* Baltimore: Williams & Wilkins.

Wechsler, D. (1944). *The measurement of adult intelligence* (3rd ed.). Baltimore: Waverly.

Wechsler, D. (1967). *Wechsler preschool and primary scale of intelligence: Manual.* San Antonio: Psychological Corporation.

Wechsler, D. (1974). *Wechsler intelligence scale for children: Manual* (revision of 1949 ed.). San Antonio : Psychological Corporation.

Wechsler, D. (1981). *Manual for Wechsler adult intelligence scale—revised.* San Antonio Psychological Corporation.

Weger, J., Tschantz, G., & Walters, M. (1986). *Reliability of preschool diagnosis.* Program presented at the annual meeting of the National Association of School Psychologists, Hollywood, FL.

Wehman, P. (1974). Instructional strategies for improving toy play skills of severely handicapped children. *AAESPH Review, 1,* 125–135.

Wehman, P., Hill, J. W., & Koehler, F. (1979). Helping severely handicapped persons enter competitive employment. *AAESPH Review, 4,* 274–290.

Wehman, P., & Kregel, J. (1985). A supported work approach to competitive employment of individuals with moderate and severe handicaps. *Journal of The Association for Persons with Severe Handicaps, 10*(1), 3–11.

Wehman, P., Kregel, J., & Barcus, J. M. (1985). From school to work: A vocational transition model for handicapped students. *Exceptional Children, 52,* 25–37.

Wehman, P., Kregel, J., & Seyfarth, J. (1985). Transition from school to work for individuals with severe handicaps: A follow-up study. *Journal of The Association for Persons with Severe Handicaps, 10,* 132–136.

Wehman, P., Wood, W., Everson, J. M., Goodwyn, R., & Conley, S. (1988). *Vocational education for multihandicapped youth with cerebral palsy.* Baltimore: Paul H. Brookes.

Weikart, D. P., & Lambie, D. Z. (1970). Early enrichment in infants. In V. Denenberg (Ed.), *Education of the infant and young child.* New York: Academic.

Weikart, D., et al. (1984). *Changed lives: The effects of the Perry preschool program on youths through age 19.* Ypsilanti, MI: Highscope Educational Research Foundation.

Wells, C. E. (1973). Will vocational education survive? *Phi Delta Kappan, 54,* 369–80.

*Welsch v. Likins,* 375 F. Supp. 487 (D. Minn. 1974).

Westling, D. L. (1986). *Introduction to mental retardation.* Englewood Cliffs, NJ: Prentice-Hall.

White, B. L. (1975). *The first three years.* Englewood Cliffs, NJ: Prentice-Hall.

White, K. R., & Casto, G. (1984). *An integrative review of early intervention efficacy studies with at-risk children: Implications for the handicapped.* Logan: Early Intervention Research Institute, Utah State University.

White, O. R., Edgar, E., & Haring, N. G. (1978). *Uniform performance assessment system.* Seattle: Experimental Education Unit, Child Development and Mental Retardation Center, University of Washington.

White, O. R., & Haring, N. G. (1978). Evaluating educational programs serving the severely and profoundly handicapped. In N. G. Haring & D. Bricker (Eds.), *Teaching the severely handicapped* (Vol. 3). Seattle: American Association for the Education of the Severely/Profoundly Handicapped.

Whitehead, C. W. (1986). The sheltered workshop dilemma: Reform or replacement *Remedial & Special Education, 7*(6), 18–24.

Whitman, T. L., Borkowski, J. G., Schellenbach, C. J., & Nath, P. S. (1987). Predicting and understanding developmental delay of adolescent mothers: A multidimensional approach. *American Journal of Mental Deficiency, 92,* 40–56.

Wiener, D., Anderson, R. J. & Nietupski, J. A. (1982). Impact of community-based residential facilities for mentally retarded adults on surround property values using realtor analysis methods. *Education & Training of the Mentally Retarded, 17*(4), 278–282.

Wilbur, H. (1976). *Eulogy to Edouard Seguin. Remarks made at Seguin's funeral, Clamécy, France, 1880.* (Reprinted in M. Rosen, G. R. Clark, & M. S. Kivitz [Eds.], *The history of mental retardation: Collected papers* [Vol. 1]). Baltimore: University Park Press.

Will, M. C. (1984). *OSERS programming for the transition of youth with disabilities: Bridges from school to working life.* Washington, DC: Office of Special Education and Rehabilitative Services (OSERS), U.S. Department of Education.

Will, M. C. (1986). Educating children with learning problems: A shared responsibility. *Exceptional Children, 52,* 411–415.

Willer, B., & Intagliata, J. (1981). Social-environmental factors as predictors of adjustment of deinstitutionalized mentally retarded adults. *American Journal of Mental Deficiency, 86*(3), 252–259.

Williams, H. M. (1963). *Education of the severely retarded child.* Washington, DC: U.S. Government Printing Office.

Williams, W., Brown, L., & Certo, N. (1975). Components of instructional programs for severely handicapped students. In L. Brown, T. Crowner, W. Williams, & R. York (Eds.), *Madison's alternative for zero exclusion: A book of readings* (Vol. 5). Madison, WI: Madison Public Schools.

Wilson, G. T. (1974). *Community recreation programming for handicapped children.* Arlington, VA: National Recreation and Park Association.

Wilton, K. M., & Irvine, J. (1983). Nutritional intakes of socioculturally mentally retarded children vs. children of low and average socioeconomic status. *American Journal of Mental Deficiency, 88*(1), 79–85.

Winick, M. (1969). Malnutrition and brain development. *Journal of Pediatrics, 74,* 667.

Wolery, M. R. (1978). Self-stimulatory behavior as a basis for devising reinforcers. *AAESPH Review, 3*(1), 23–29.

Wolf, M. M. (1978). Social validity: The case for subjective measurement or how applied behavior analysis is finding its heart. *Journal of Applied Behavior Analysis, 11*(2), 203–214.

Wolfensberger, W. (1967). Counseling parents of the retarded. In A. A. Baumeister (Ed.), *Mental retardation: Appraisal, education, and rehabilitation.* Chicago: Aldine.

Wolfensberger, W. (1969). A new approach to decision-making in human management services. In R. B. Kugel & W. Wolfensberger (Eds.), *Changing patterns in residential services for the mentally retarded.* Washington, DC: President's Committee on Mental Retardation.

Wolfensberger, W. (1972). *The principle of normalization in human services.* Toronto: National Institute on Mental Retardation.

Wolfensberger, W. (1975). *The origin and nature of our institutional models.* Syracuse, NY: Human Policy.

Wolfensberger, W. (1983). Social role valorization: A proposed new term for the principle of normalization. *Mental Retardation, 21,* 234–239.

Wolfensberger, W. (1985). An overview of social role valorization and some reflections on elderly mentally retarded persons. In M. P. Janicki & H. M. Wisniewski (Eds.), *Expanding systems of service delivery for persons with developmental disabilities* (pp. 127–148). Baltimore: Paul H. Brookes.

Wolpert, J. (1978). *Group homes for the mentally retarded: An investigation of neighborhood property impacts.* Princeton, NJ: Princeton University Press.

Wolraich, M. L. (1983). Hydrocephalus. In J. A. Blackman (Ed.), *Medical aspects of developmen-*

*tal disabilities in children birth to three.* Iowa City: University of Iowa Press.

Woodward, W. M. (1963). The application of Piaget's theory to research in mental deficiency. In N. R. Ellis (Ed.), *Handbook of mental deficiency.* New York: McGraw-Hill.

Woodward, W. M. (1979). Piaget's theory and the study of mental retardation. In N. R. Ellis (Ed.), *Handbook of mental deficiency: Psychological theory and research* (2nd ed). Hillsdale, NJ: Lawrence Erlbaum.

World Health Organization (WHO) (1978). *International classification of diseases* (9th rev.) Washington, DC: Author.

Wright, L. (1973). Aversive conditioning of self-induced seizures. *Behavior Therapy, 4,* 712–713.

Wuerch, B. B., & Voeltz, L. M. (1981). *Ho'onanea program: A leisure curriculum component for severly handicapped children and youth.* Baltimore: Paul H Brookes.

Wuerch, B. B., & Voeltz, L. M. (1982). *Longitudinal leisure skills for severely handicapped learners.* Baltimore: Paul H. Brookes.

*Wyatt v. Aderholt,* 368 F. Supp. 1382, 1383 (M.D. Ala. 1974).

*Wyatt v. Hardin,* Civil Action No. 3195-N (M.D. Ala. Oct. 23, 1978).

*Wyatt v. Ireland,* Civil Action No. 3195-N (M.D. Ala. 1979).

*Wyatt v. Stickney,* 344 F. Supp. 387, 344 F. Supp. 373 (M.D. Ala. 1972), 334 F. Supp. 1341, 325 F. Supp. 781 (M.D. Ala. 1971), 772 aff'd sub nom. *Wyatt v. Aderholt,* 503 F.2d 1305 (5th Cir. 1974).

York, J., Long, E., Caldwell, N., Brown, L., Zanella Albright, K., Rogan, P., Shiraga, B., & Marks, J. (1985). Teamwork strategies for school and community instruction. In L. Brown, B. Shiraga, J. York, A. Udvari-Solner, K. Zanella Albright, P. Rogan, E. McCarthy, & R. Loomis (Eds.), *Educational programs for students with severe intellectual disabilities* (Vol. 15, pp. 229–276). Madison, WI: Madison Metropolitan School District.

*Youngberg v. Romeo,* 102 S. Ct. 2452 (1982).

Younie, W. J., & Rusalem, H. (1971). *The world of*

*rehabilitation: An atlas for special education.* New York: John Day.

Ysseldyke, J. E. (1978) Assessment of retardation. In J. T. Neisworth & R. M. Smith (Eds.), *Retardation: Issues, assessment and intervention.* New York: McGraw-Hill.

Zantal-Weiner, K. (1987). *Child abuse and the handicapped child.* Reston, VA: ERIC Clearinghouse on Handicapped and Gifted Children.

Zarfas, D. E., & Wolf, L. C. (1979). Maternal age patterns and the incidence of Down's syndrome. *American Journal of Mental Deficiency, 83,* 353–359.

Zeaman, D., & House, B. J. (1963). The role of attention in retardate discrimination learning. In N. R. Ellis (Ed.), *Handbook of mental deficiency.* New York: McGraw-Hill.

Zeaman, D., & House, B. J. (1979). A review of attention theory. In N. R. Ellis (Ed.), *Handbook of mental deficiency: Psychological theory and research* (2nd ed.). Hillsdale, NJ: Lawrence Erlbaum.

Zehrback, R. R. (1975). Determining a preschool handicapped population. *Exceptional Children, 42,* 76–83.

Zigler, E. (1966). Research on personality structure in the retardate. *International Review of Research in Mental Retardation, 1.*

Zigler, E. (1969). Development versus difference theories of mental retardation and problems of motivation. *American Journal of Mental Deficiency, 73,* 536–556.

Zigler, E. (1973). The retarded child as a whole person. In D. K. Routh (Ed.), *The experimental psychology of mental retardation.* Chicago: Aldine.

Zigler, E. (1978). National crisis in mental retardation research. *American Journal of Mental Deficiency, 83,* 1–8.

Zigler, E., & Balla, D. A. (1977). Impact of institutional experience on the behavior and development of retarded persons. *American Journal of Mental Deficiency, 82,* 1–11.

Zigler, E., & Balla, D. A. (1981). Issues in personality and motivation in mentally retarded persons. In M. J. Begab, H. C. Haywood, & H. L. Garber (Eds.), *Psychosocial influences in retarded performance: Issues and theories of development* (Vol. 1, pp. 197–218). Baltimore: University Park Press.

Zigler, E., Balla, D. A., & Hodapp, R. (1984). On the definition and classification of mental retardation. *American Journal of Mental Deficiency, 89,* 215–230.

Zigler, E., & Cascione, R. (1977). Head Start has little to do with mental retardation: Reply to Clarke and Clarke. *American Journal of Mental Deficiency, 82,* 246–249.

Zigler, E., & Seitz, V. (1982). Social policy and intelligence. In R. J. Sternberg (Ed.), *Handbook of human intelligence* (pp. 586–641). Cambridge: Cambridge University Press.

Zigman, W. S., Schupf, N., Lubin, R. A., & Silverman, W. P. (1987). Premature regression of adults with Down syndrome. *American Journal of Mental Retardation, 92,* 161–168.

Zimmerman, I. L., Steiner, V. G., & Pond, R. E. (1979). *Preschool language scale: Revised edition.* Columbus, OH: Merrill.

Zirpoli, T. (1986). Child abuse and children with handicaps. *Remedial & Special Education, 7*(2), 39–48.

Zucker, S. H., & Polloway, E. A. (1987). Issues in identification and assessment in mental retardation. *Education & Training in Mental Retardation, 22,* 69–76.

Zwerling, I. (1954). Initial counseling of parents with mentally retarded children. *Journal of Pediatrics, 44,* 469–479.

# ABOUT THE AUTHORS

**James R. Patton** is Associate Professor of Special Education at the University of Hawaii at Manoa. He is experienced in teaching students with special needs at the elementary, secondary, and postsecondary levels. His research interests include curriculum development, lifelong learning, instructional methodology, and teaching science. Currently he is developing integrated curricula for elementary-aged students and functional curricula for secondary-aged students. Jim earned his M.Ed. and Ed.D. from the University of Virginia.

**Mary Beirne-Smith** is an Assistant Professor of Special Education at the University of Alabama. Her previous experience includes regular and special education classroom teaching and special education public school administration. Her current interests center on academic interventions for students with mild learning handicaps, and teacher effectiveness. Mary received her B.S. from Longwood College and her M.Ed. and Ed.D. from the University of Virginia.

**James S. Payne** is Dean of the School of Education of the University of Mississippi. He earned, with honors, the Ed.D. in special education/mental retardation from the University of Kansas. To his teaching, he brings a wealth of information from his experiences in vocational counseling; hiring and training the retarded in restaurant and custodial services; planning a sheltered workshop; directing a Head Start preschool program; general managing an automobile dealership; and consulting attorneys in cases regarding the rights of the handicapped. Jim has been active at the national level with ARC-US since 1975 and has authored many articles and books.

**Diane M. Browder** is Assistant Professor of Education at Lehigh University, Bethlehem, Pennsylvania. She taught special education for two years in a rural elementary setting. Diane has consulted with residential programs, group homes, and adult treatment centers. Presently she is a consultant to programs serving the severely emotionally disturbed. She received a B.A. from Duke University in psychology in 1975, an M.Ed. in 1976, and a Ph.D. from the University of Virginia in special education with an emphasis on severe/profound disabilites in 1981.

**Richard F. Ittenbach** is a doctoral candidate in the School Psychology program at the University of Alabama and is currently on internship with the St. Cloud Community School System and the university-affiliated program division of the University of Minnesota. His previous experience includes teaching elementary and secondary science, undergraduate statistics, and a graduate course in psychoeducational assessment. Rick considers research design, assessment of mental and special abilities, and the study of personality his principal areas of research interest. He received his B.S. in biology from Butler University in 1980, his M.Ed. in counseling from Auburn University in 1984, and his Ed.D. in educational research from the University of Alabama in 1988.

Eric D. Jones   is an associate professor at Bowling Green State University. He has taught bilingual Navajo children with mild learning handicaps. He has also worked with persons with severe handicaps in both recreation and community employment settings. Currently he is conducting research on procedures for the instruction of persons with severe handicaps and on the acceptability of behavioral interventions. Eric received an A.B. in experimental psychology at Bucknell University, an M.A. in special education at the University of Northern Colorado, and an Ed.D. in special education and program evaluation from the University of Virginia.

John Nietpuski   is Associate Professor of Special Education at the University of Northern Iowa. He is a former teacher of students with moderate/severe mental retardation. He has recently worked on a project designed to develop supported employment programs. His research interests focus on integrating students into regular education, developing community-based training programs, recreation/leisure skill programming, and business orientation to job development. In 1985, he received the *Educator of the Year Award* from the Association for Retarded Citizens of the United States. John received his Ph.D. from the University of Wisconsin/Madison.

Edward A. Polloway   is Professor of Education and Human Development at Lynchburg College, Lynchburg, Virginia, where he currently serves as Associate Dean of the College as well. His previous experience includes teaching elementary and special education public school classes. He has published numerous books and journal articles, is past president of CEC-MR and currently serves on the Terminology and Classification Committee of the AAMR. He received his B.A. from Dickinson College and his M.Ed. and Ed.D. from the University of Virginia.

Greg A. Robinson   is the State Consultant for Mild and Moderate Disabilities in the Bureau of Special Education of the Iowa Department of Education. A doctoral candidate at Iowa State University, he has experience as a school psychologist and special education teacher. Greg has numerous publications and presentations in the field of mental retardation. His current interests include functional assessment and curriculum development. Greg received his B.S. in education from Northern Illinois University and his M.S. in school psychology from Illinois State University.

Carol H. Thomas   is Associate Professor and chair of the Department of Early Childhood and Special Education at the Texas Woman's University and is involved in the teacher training program from the undergraduate to the doctoral level. Previous professional experience includes several years' classroom teaching with exceptional children and school psychologist. She earned a B.A. in psychology and an M.S. in school psychology from Radford University, and an Ed.D. in special education from the University of Virginia. She has published in the areas of mental retardation, services to the handicapped, and bilingual special education.

# NAME INDEX

Abramson, L., 453
Abramson, P., 453
Abroms, K. K., 139
Adams, G. L., 286
Adams, M. K., 429, 430
Adelson, M., 537
Adubato, A., 429, 430
Agran, M., 343, 351
Aiken, J. M., 157
Albin, J. M., 386, 387
Algozzine, B., 315
Al-Mateen, M., 146
Aloia, G. F., 476
Alpert, M., 135
Amado, A. R., 536
Amara, R., 532
American Educational Research
    Association, 292
American Psychological Association,
    292
Amir, M., 390
Anastasi, A., 283
Anderson, I., 135
Anderson, J., 251
Anderson, K. A., 454
Anderson, R., 296
Anderson, R. B., 183, 190
Anderson, R. J., 397
Andrew, E. D., 135
Angney, A., 432
Apffel, J. A., 201
Apgar, V., 152
Arkell, C., 325
Arthur, G., 93
Association for Retarded Citizens of
    the United States, 400
Azen, C., 133, 135

Bacon, A., 323
Baer, D., 216, 480
Baer, D. M., 251
Bagnato, S. J., 282, 290
Bailey, D., Jr., 263, 264, 293
Bajema, C. J., 165
Baker, A. M., 146
Baker, B. L., 395
Baldwin, V., 296
Balkany, T. J., 219
Ball, D. W., 190
Balla, D. A., 62, 65, 106, 182, 204, 205,
    286, 514, 523
Ballard, J., 267
Balow, B., 312
Baltes, P. B., 430
Balthazar, E. E., 109, 110, 203, 205,
    334
Bandura, A., 213
Banks, D., 358
Barabas, G., 133
Barcus, J. M., 255
Barnett, W. S., 270
Baroff, G. S., 192
Barrett, M., 133
Barrett, W. S., 191
Bateman, B., 463, 468, 469
Bates, P., 244
Baumeister, A. A., 59, 60, 61, 129, 491,
    508
Baumgart, D., 246, 313
Bayley, N., 93
Beasley, C. R., 225
Beauchamp, K. D., 292
Beck, E., 95
Beck, J., 138
Becker, R. L., 368

Becker, W. C., 190, 335
Beckman, P. J., 244, 430, 449
Beckman-Brindley, S., 431
Beevy, J., 541
Begab, M. J., 182, 433, 538, 541
Begelman, D. A., 548
Beler, D. C., 147
Bellak, L., 284
Bellak, S. S., 284
Bellamy, G. T., 253, 359, 383, 386, 387
Bellamy, T., 236, 358
Belmont, J. M., 140, 213
Bender, B., 144
Benjamin, 264
Bennett, J. W., 139
Bennett, W. J., 243
Benson, H. A., 244
Benton, A. L., 146
Benz, M. R., 373
Bercovici, S. M., 378, 379
Berdine, W. H., 255
Bereiter, C., 185, 439
Berg, C., 134, 145, 174
Berger, M., 277
Berler, E. S., 321
Berndt, W. O., 135
Berns, B., 94
Berreuta-Clement, J. R., 191
Berry, A. C., 141
Bickel, W., 550
Bieniek, B., 432, 433
Bijou, S. W., 58
Biklen, D., 38, 421, 465, 508, 526
Binet, A., 83, 84
Birch, H. G., 136
Birch, J. W., 99, 101
Bishop, G. D., 405

# SUBJECT INDEX